Community Organizing and Community Building for Health and Welfare

Community Organizing and Community Building for Health and Welfare

Third Edition

MEREDITH MINKLER

RUTGERS UNIVERSITY PRESS

NEW BRUNSWICK, NEW JERSEY, AND LONDON

Second paperback printing, 2012

LIBRARY OF CONGRESS CATALOGING-IN-PUBLICATION DATA

Community organizing and community building for health and welfare / edited by
Meredith Minkler. — 3rd ed.
    p. cm.
Includes bibliographical references and index.
ISBN 978-0-8135-5299-6 (hardcover : alk. paper) — ISBN 978-0-8135-5300-9
(pbk. : alk. paper) — ISBN 978-0-8135-5314-6 (e-book)
    1. Health promotion.   2. Community health services—Citizen participation.
3. Community organization.   4. Community development.   I. Minkler, Meredith.
    RA427.8.C64   2012
    362.12—dc23

2011037604

A British Cataloging-in-Publication record for this book is available from the
British Library.

Visit our website: http://rutgerspress.rutgers.edu

Manufactured in the United States of America

In loving memory of Roy S. Minkler, an extraordinary
father and human being.
And with deep appreciation to my role models in
public health and social justice,
Angela Glover Blackwell, H. Jack Geiger,
Joyce Lashof, Donald H. Minkler, and S. Leonard Syme

CONTENTS

PART SIX
Using the Arts and the Internet as Tools for Community Organizing and Community Building

PART SEVEN
Building, Maintaining, and Evaluating Effective Coalitions and Community Organizing Efforts

ILLUSTRATIONS

Figures

Tables

Boxes

ACKNOWLEDGMENTS

A wise friend once told me, "If you want to get something done, ask someone who's overcommitted." I owe a large debt to the many overcommitted individuals who made the time to help write this book. Ranging in discipline from public health education, social work, medicine, and community psychology to law, urban and regional planning, and political and social science, they were invited because of their demonstrated commitment to health and social equity. But they also were selected because of their gifts in telling their stories and sharing the theory, methods, tools, and perspectives that are so central to community organizing and community building practice. Each writes from the heart, and their combination of passion and professionalism has contributed greatly to the final product. Although all the authors gave selflessly, I am particularly indebted to my friend and colleague Cheryl Hyde, who helped me envision a new book that would expand its lens to more broadly address social work macro practice, as well as the *isms* and the centrality of critical self-reflection on power and privilege in our work. Her gifts as a scholar and practitioner are evident in her several written contributions, and in less visible ways throughout the new volume.

I am also deeply grateful to the team at Rutgers University, and particularly to my editor, Peter Mickulas, who believed in this project from the beginning, and to Larissa Klein, Suzanne Kellam, Romaine Perin, and Bryce Schimanski, who helped make this final edition a reality.

Many colleagues, practitioners, and community activists have shared with my fellow authors and me case studies and examples, ethical dilemmas faced in practice, and new ways of conceptualizing key aspects of community organizing and community building. Although too numerous to mention here by name, their contributions are cited throughout the book, and they are deserving of special thanks and recognition.

Like many of my coauthors, I have been blessed in the choice of a profession that places a strong emphasis on the centrality of empowerment and social justice for health and well-being. Numerous public health leaders and social justice activists have inspired me in their unstinting efforts to promote health and social equity, but several in particular—Angela Glover Blackwell, Joyce Lashof, Pam Tau Lee, Shaw San Liu, Henrik Blum, H. Jack Geiger, Gary Grant, Donald Minkler, Naeema Mahammad, S. Leonard Syme, Dorothy Nyswander, Victor

Sidel, Arnold Perkins, and Steve Wing—have been special role models, to whom I am deeply grateful.

My colleagues at the School of Public Health have been a tremendous source of support and encouragement, and I wish to acknowledge especially those current and former colleagues in community health education and health and social behavior who have contributed to my own thinking in the areas of community organizing, community building, and health disparities: Ray Catalano, Darlene Francis, Denise Herd, Leonard Duhl, Seth Holmes, Rachel Morello-Frosch, Amani Nuru Jeter, Emily Ozer, Cheri Pies, William Satariano, S. Leonard Syme, William Vega, and Lawrence Wallack. The school's staff, and particularly Ghada Haddad and Teresa Liu, have also been wonderful sources of support and encouragement.

I also owe a great debt to my colleagues at PolicyLink, and especially Angela Glover Blackwell, Judith Bell, Victor Rubin, and Mildred Thompson, whose commitment to "lifting up what works"™ and using the lessons of community building on the ground to help inform and shape healthy public policy, is a source of tremendous inspiration.

Like its predecessors, this third edition owes its existence to my current and former gradate students at the University of California, Berkeley, and I owe them immense gratitude for teaching me far more about community organizing, community building, and cultural humility than I could ever have hoped to teach them. Although too numerous to name, my doctoral students in particular have influenced my thinking and expanded my horizons, while also becoming treasured friends and colleagues, and working with them, as well as my MPH students, has been a blessing and an honor.

My other best teachers have been people on the front lines, and I wish to acknowledge especially some of my early and more recent teachers—restaurant workers in Chinatown and members and staff of the Chinese Progressive Association and the former Tenderloin Senior Organizing Project, Concerned Citizens of Tillery, the Gray Panthers, the former Youth Empowerment Strategies Project, the disability rights movement, and the staff and Youth Community Council members of CHAMACOS. Their leaders and members have deepened my understanding of what committed organizing and community building are all about, while reminding me of the importance of the Native American and disability movements' mantra, "Nothing about us without us."

I also owe great thanks to the scholars, former scholars, leadership, staff, and advisory board of the W. K. Kellogg Foundation's Community Health Scholars Program, from whom I also have learned a great deal about community-based participatory research and its deep roots in community building. Finally, and for more than a decade, I have had the privilege of learning from the masters—older activists honored through the California Senior Leaders Program and the California Senior Leaders Alliance they helped create. With their motto, "Don't think outside the box—think outside the warehouse,"—the Senior Leaders have brought wisdom and lifelong modeling of effective community building and organizing, and I am grateful to them; to our project's current and former directors, Lisa Romero, Marty Martinson, Julia Caplan, and Analilia P. Garcia, and Associate Director Meena G. Nair; and to the California Wellness Foundation and the Atlantic Philanthropies for their belief in and support of this work.

The third edition of this book came to fruition thanks in part to the stimulation and support of my family and friends. My parents were lifelong supporters and role models, providing encouragement and love beyond measure, even as their days grew more difficult. A school principal and believer in celebrating black history long before it was popular, my late father, Roy Minkler, was my inspiration and shining star, and the greatest teacher I have ever known, both in the public schools and with his own five children. My mother, Frances Minkler, has shown in her ten-year struggle with Alzheimer's the same gifts of love, concern for others, and optimism that has characterized her entire life. My late uncle, Donald H. Minkler, was a tremendous role model and source of pride and love. His long and courageous battle with Alzheimer's, like his lifelong giving as a physician, teacher, and international family planning leader, touched many lives. My siblings, Donna, Jason, Chris, and Joan, and my large extended family have, each in his or her own way, contributed to this project, as have close friends, including Frederick Marais, Marty Martinson, Rena Pasick, Kathleen Roe, Rusty Springer, Lawrence Wallack, Nina Wallerstein, and others too numerous to mention.

The sheer mechanics of a project like this one can be overwhelming, and I owe a special debt to my dear friend and right arm, Patricia Wakimoto, without whose caring and commitment, organization skills, and unfailing sense of humor this project never could have been completed, much less done ahead of schedule. Ghada Haddad, Jamie Elmasu, Amanda Wong, Meena Nair, Rebecca Braun, Analilia P. Garcia, Jya Plavin, and Laura Spautz also made real contributions and I am deeply grateful to them, and to Angela Ni, whose brilliant mind and wonderful global health contributions never cease to amaze and inspire me.

Although I did the lion's share of the work on this book in the wee hours to avoid cutting into family and work time, any project of this type takes a toll. I am very am grateful to my husband, Jerry Peters, for his love, support, patience, and outstanding dinners night after night, and to our son, Jason, for his love, sense of humor, resilience, and the many ways in which he keeps me grounded. Marquis Parks also has brought love, thoughtfulness, and his thousand-kilowatt smile into our home, and I am deeply grateful. Together with my parents and siblings, they have been a constant reminder that real "family values" are embedded, in large part, in the support and love that families, however they are defined, give to and receive from their members.

Community Organizing and
Community Building for
Health and Welfare

PART ONE

Introduction

Public health leader Bill Foege is fond of telling the story of a man who goes into a store and doesn't steal anything, but changes all the price tags. As Foege suggests, we are living in a time when the price tags are being radically changed around. In the United States, money for education, early childhood programs, and supportive services for the most vulnerable is being radically cut back, while unemployment remains high and big business reaps substantial monetary gain. These threads are among many that form the tapestry within which public health professionals, social workers, community psychologists, and other social change professionals now find themselves working. The troubled global economy and the almost unprecedented gaps between rich and poor, continued wars in the Middle East, the global AIDS epidemic, massive federal deficits, and the weakening of the "social fabric" also are among these problematic threads.

Yet at the same time the context in which we work includes increasing societal diversity; unprecedented possibilities in communication and interaction presented by the Internet and social media (see chapters 15, 16, and 21); and breathtaking scientific breakthroughs, enabling us to address a plethora of health and medical conditions at increasing speed.

From a public health perspective, narrowing, but still pervasive, health disparities are deeply troubling. And while the health care reform bill signed into law in 2010 is rightfully lauded for its accent on prevention, it is criticized on the left for not going far enough (see chapter 21) and from the right as an example of more "big government" intrusion.

Within this complex contextual tapestry, where does grassroots community building and community organizing fit in? And for those of us in fields like public health, social work, and urban and regional planning, will this aspect of our work even bear mention in the challenging years ahead?

The two opening chapters of this book argue that community building and community organizing have never been more important and that public health professionals, social workers, and other social change professionals have a critical role to play in such work. Juxtaposed against the backdrop of today's troubled economy and complex health and social challenges, chapter one highlights the growing emphasis on concepts like community partnerships, community empowerment, capacity building, and individual and community empowerment. While acknowledging that the reality of the accent on community and community participation has not begun to match the rhetoric (DeFilippis et al. 2010; Raphael 2008), it points to such trends as the growth in community-based organizations, a global health cities and communities movement, and the increasing use of tools such as coalitions; Facebook and other social media venues; media advocacy; and partnerships between communities, academics, and health departments in the fight against some of our most intractable health and social problems. Chapter 1 highlights as well the significance of the election of Barack Obama as not only the first African American president, but also the first community organizer to lead the country, and someone one whose assent was due in substantial part to his campaign's effective use of both traditional and online organizing (Dreier 2008).

Chapter 1 suggests that health educators, social workers, and other social change professionals can usefully adapt and apply community organizing and community building in their efforts to work with communities to combat HIV/AIDS, domestic violence, asthma, homelessness, and a host of other health and social problems. But the chapter also makes a case for what it calls a "purer" approach to community organizing, in which communities are helped to mobilize around the issues that they—not we as outsiders—identify and wish to collectively address. The role of the outside organizer in this latter approach is seen as one of helping to create the conditions in which community groups can determine their own health and social agenda and act effectively to help bring about the changes they wish to see.

Chapter 1 also introduces the concept of community building, which in recent years has achieved increasing currency in fields like health education, social work, community psychology, and urban planning (see, for example, Blackwell and Colmenar 2000; Corburn 2009; Diers 2006; chapter 20 and appendix 1). As described in more detail in chapter 5, however, an alternative perspective on community building views it not as a "strategic framework" or approach to fixing problems, but rather as an orientation to community practice, accenting building the capacities of complex and multidimensional communities, of which we as organizers and other practitioners are a part (see chapter 5).

The three major purposes of this book are highlighted in chapter 1. These are the following: pulling together recent thinking in community organizing and community building theory and practice; using theory-driven case studies to illustrate the concepts, principles, and methods explored; and raising and engaging the reader in reflecting on many of the tough questions and ethical challenges that often are inherent in community practice.

This first chapter also introduces Jacqueline Mondros and Scott Wilson's (1994, 14–15) notion of health educators, social workers, and other social change professionals as "conscious contrarians": sharing a particular worldview or set of beliefs and values, a power analysis that rejects dominant ways of thinking about power and its distribution, and a "deliberate career choice" that reflects the other two. To this I add two other characteristics—the Native American Heyoehkahs' tradition of "doing things differently" and challenging traditional ways of thinking and, finally, a determination to openly confronting racism, while committing oneself to continuing self-reflection and to what Melanie Tervalon and Jane Murray-Garcia (1998) term "cultural humility." Although the reader may identify other dimensions of "conscious contrarianism" that inform his or her professional practice and ways of being, these five are offered as a beginning place for thinking about our roles in community building and organizing for health.

Chapter 1 concludes with an overview of the various chapters and appendixes that constitute this book, illustrating in the process some of the central themes or threads (such as concerns with empowerment, community capacity building, and cultural humility) that run throughout. It is hoped that together, these offerings will provide the reader with an understanding of the theoretical base, ethical challenges, and practical tools needed for engagement in this work, and with a new or renewed appreciation of community organizing and community building as potent approaches for improving the public's health and social well-being.

The first part of this book would not be complete without prominent mention of the organizing philosophy of the man who, at this writing, occupies the most powerful office in the land and whose campaign for the presidency has been described by many as a strong, contemporary example of community organizing writ large (Dreier 2008; Hyatt 2008). President Obama's classic piece "Why Organize? Problems and Promise in the Inner City" was originally published in 1988 as he reflected on his work as a young organizer in Chicago's South Side. And although some of the language and key players have changed (e.g., with the emergence and dramatic growth of Occupy Wall Street and the replacement of the Moral Majority with the Tea Party movement), his message for organizers rings as true today as it did over twenty years ago. Obama has often commented that his experiences as a community organizer were the best preparation he had for the presidency. And as he tells his stories of his work with the Gamaliel Foundation (discussed in chapter 4) and all he's learned from "ordinary folks" who come together to make change, a wonderfully uplifting view of what organizing can be unfolds. In Obama's words, "organizing teaches, as nothing else does, the beauty and strength of everyday people" (1998, 4) and how working collaboratively with "everyday people" can help us build healthy and strong communities.

REFERENCES

Blackwell, A. G., and R. A. Colmenar. 2000. "Community Building: From Local Wisdom to Public Policy." *Public Health Reports* 115, nos. 2 and 3:161–166.

Corburn, J. 2009. "Toward the Healthy City: People, Places, and the Politics of Urban Planning." Cambridge, Mass.: MIT Press.

DeFilippis, J., R. Fisher, and E. Shragge. 2010. *Contesting Community: The Limits and Potential of Local Organizing*. New Brunswick, N.J.: Rutgers University Press.

Diers, J. 2006. *Neighborhood Power: Building Community the Seattle Way*. Seattle: University of Washington Press.

Dreier, P. 2008. "Will Obama Inspire a New Generation of Organizers?" *Dissent*, June 25. http://www.dissentmagazine.org/online.php?id=109.

Hyatt, S. 2008. "The Obama Victory, Asset-Based Development, and the Re-politicization of Community Organizing." *North American Dialogue* 11, no. 2:17–26.

Mondros, J. B., and S. M. Wilson. 1994. *Organizing for Power and Empowerment*. New York: Columbia University Press.

Obama, B. 1988. "Why Organize? Problems and Promise in the Inner City." *Illinois Issues* (Sangamon State University [now the University of Illinois at Springfield]), August/September.

Raphael, D. 2008. "Grasping at Straws: A Recent History of Health Promotion in Canada." *Critical Public Health* 18, no. 4:483–495.

Tervalon, M., and J. Murray-Garcia. 1998. "Cultural Humility vs. Cultural Competence: A Critical Distinction in Defining Physician Training Outcomes in Medical Education." *Journal of Health Care for the Poor and Underserved* 9, no. 2:117–125.

1

Introduction to Community Organizing and Community Building

MEREDITH MINKLER

When former New York City mayor and presidential candidate Rudy Giuliani asked disparagingly during the 2008 primary campaign, "What's a community organizer?" he did more than unleash a rash of soon forgotten letters to the editor and blogs. National organizations, including the Society for Public Health Education and the National Association of Social Workers, adopted position papers reaffirming the centrality of community organizing in their craft. And both presidential candidate Barack Obama's eloquent articulation of the importance of community building and organizing and the success of a well-orchestrated real-world and online organizing campaign in his assent to the presidency brought much renewed attention to the field and its methods (Daniels 2011; Dreier 2008; Hyatt 2008; Wolff 2010).

But the reality of a former community organizer in the White House is just one of several factors that have transformed the landscape of community building and community organizing in the early twenty-first century. By December 2010, just three countries had populations bigger than Facebook, with its close to 600 million members (Stengel 2010), and large numbers of communities and community-based organizations were expanding their reach and visibility through YouTube, Twitter, and other "new media" channels. With cell phones doubling as cameras and video recorders, and once expensive technologies now in the hands of countless Americans, even in low-income neighborhoods, the power of such approaches for helping to build healthy communities has never been greater (see chapters 15 and 16). Yet community organizing on the Internet is no more immune from racism, xenophobia, and other destructive forces than is organizing in the virtual world, and the relative anonymity the Internet provides may indeed allow such uses to flourish (Daniels 2009).

The use of new and more traditional organizing approaches, including coalition building and the creation of effective partnerships, is being seen in the fights for (and against) health care reform, immigrant rights, gay marriage, restricted soda sales in schools, and a multitude of programs, practices, and policies that could strengthen and improve—or set back—the public's health and well-being. As this book goes to press, the mass protest movement Occupy Wall Street, with its motto "We are the 99 percent," has engaged millions of people from New York and Washington, D.C., to Oakland, California, and in small towns and large urban centers across the land. Giving voice to "populist demands for jobs, fair taxes and corporate oversight" (Scherer 2011), the Occupy movement has brought together participants and supporters spanning a wide range of social classes, racial/ethnic groups and ages. Despite occasional property damage by fringe elements in a few locations, by October 2011, over half of Americans polled (54 percent) had a favorable image of the Occupy movement, compared with just a third for the Tea Party movement (Scherer 2011).

Rapidly changing demographics in the United States, with more than half the nation projected to be composed of people of color well before midcentury, also has underscored the centrality of community building and organizing approaches that emphasize cultural sensitivity and humility (Tervalon and Murray-Garcia 1998). A theme that will resurface many times in this book, cultural humility is the notion that while we can't be competent in another's culture, we can engage in self-reflection, learning our own biases, being open to others' cultures, and committing ourselves to authentic partnership and redressing power imbalances (Tervalon and Murray-Garcia 1998; Chávez et al. 2008). Further, and particularly in the difficult economic times that followed the Great Recession, which began in late 2007, the need for, on the one hand, identifying and building on community assets and strengths (Kretzmann and McKnight 1993; see chapter 10) and, on the other, realizing that low-resource communities in particular cannot be expected to thrive without substantial external resources, opportunities, and support (DeFilippis et al. 2010; Hyatt 2008; see chapter 6) has rarely been greater.

This book is designed for professionals and students in fields, such as health education, social work, community psychology, and urban and regional planning, that lie at the interface of health, broadly defined, and social systems and communities. The book's diverse contributors share a belief that community organizing and community building must occupy a central place in health education, health promotion, and related fields in the twenty-first century. With Lawrence Wallack and his colleagues (1993, 5), we argue that "contemporary public health is as much about facilitating a process whereby communities use their voice to define and make their health concerns known as it is about providing prevention and treatment." As professionals concerned with helping communities have their voices heard and their strengths realized and nurtured, health educators and their allies in fields such as health planning and social welfare have a critical role to play.

Playing this role and doing so effectively has seldom been more necessary—or more challenging. On the positive side, the importance of broadening our gaze beyond the individual to the community and broader systems levels is increasingly accepted. Prestigious bodies such as the Institute of Medicine (Gebbie et al.

2003), the National Institutes of Health (McCloskey et al. 2011), and the World Health Organization (2008) have emphasized community collaboration and empowerment as essential tools in the fight to improve health and eliminate health disparities. *Community empowerment, community participation*, and *community partnerships* similarly are among a litany of terms used with increasing frequency by government agencies, philanthropic organizations, and policymakers alike. Although the reality of the accent on community has never matched the rhetoric (DeFilippis et al. 2010; Robertson and Minkler 1994), clear movement in this direction is evident on a number of fronts. In the United States, a plethora of new community-based organizations and coalitions have sprung up in the past three decades, and through these, local communities have mobilized to fight environmental racism, food insecurity, and "obesogenic" built environments; HIV/AIDS; the targeting of youth and communities of color by the tobacco and alcohol industries; and cutbacks in basic social services for people with disabilities and other vulnerable groups. On a global scale, the twenty-five-year-old Healthy Cities Movement counts among its members approximately one thousand official community projects (www.healthycities.org), with estimates reaching fifteen thousand worldwide (Evelynne deLeeuw, personal communication, April 18, 2011). These projects are using intersectoral cooperation and high-level public participation to assess their health and mobilize their resources to create healthy cities and communities (Corburn 2009; see chapter 9). The recent celebration of the twenty-fifth anniversary of Healthy Cities, and the highlighting of community empowerment as a continued "fundamental approach" in health promotion (Fawcett et al. 2010), provide examples of the continued centrality of community participation in the field.

The concepts of *empowerment* and *community participation*, defined as the "twin pillars" of the new health promotion movement (Robertson and Minkler 1994), also are reflected in the World Health Organization's landmark Ottawa Charter (WHO 1986). In it, *health promotion* famously was defined as "a process of enabling people to increase control over and to improve their health" (1). Health promotion further was described as focusing on "achieving equity in health . . . and ensuring equal opportunities and resources to enable all people to achieve their fullest health potential" (1–2).

Although bold early efforts to live up to this vision were observed in cities like Toronto, Ontario (see chapter 6), "a market-dominated approach to public policy" (Raphael 2008b, 484) has been among the factors leading to health promotion being reduced to a focus primarily on "the holy trinity of tobacco use, diet, and physical activity" (Nettleton 1997, 319). Whether in Canada, the United States, or other postindustrial nations, an uphill battle is fought when "individual responsibility for health" and welfare is not accompanied by an equally important accent on increasing individual and community "response-ability" in part through healthy environments and healthy public policies (Minkler 1994). As PolicyLink points out, "One number may determine how healthy you are and how long you live. It is not your weight, cholesterol count, or any of those numbers doctors track in patients. It is your address" (Bell and Lee 2011, 16). Neighborhoods and broader environments and policies that fail to nurture residents and their communities, physically, socially and emotionally or spiritually, are a major contributor to many of the problems faced in early twenty-first-century America.

Troubling forces also lie in the fact that economic inequalities have reached levels not seen since 1928, with 23 percent of income in 2007 concentrated in the hands of the top 1 percent, and half of all income going to the top 10 percent of the population (Saez 2009; Reich 2010). Economist Lester Thurow's question of almost two decades ago, "How far can inequality rise before the system cracks?" (1996, 2) has taken on even greater urgency in the first two decades of the twenty-first century.

The health and social implications of these continuing inequities, as well as inequities along racial/ethnic lines, remain profound. As public health leader H. Jack Geiger points out, "One of the most persistent facts of life—and death—in the United States is that African Americans, Native Americans, Hispanics, and members of many Asian sub groups live sicker, die younger, and more often experience inferior health care, in comparison to those of the white majority" (2006, 261). The role of racism and differential treatment based on race or ethnicity is increasingly recognized as a major public health problem. A landmark Institute of Medicine meta-analysis of over one hundred studies of health care among insured Americans, for example, revealed stark disparities, with people of color significantly less likely to receive appropriate treatment for heart disease, HIV/AIDS, and a host of other conditions, even in cases where comparable insurance coverage was in place (Smedley et al. 2002).

Important steps forward were taken with the articulation of a federal commitment to "eliminating health disparities" (USDHHS 1998) and with the recommitment to this goal as a central focus of Healthy People 2010 and 2020, the nation's blueprint for achieving health and health equity (USDHHS 2011). Passage and signing by President Obama of historic, if far from perfect, health care reform legislation in 2010, discussed in more detail in chapter 21, marked a further important step in this direction. But a decade after the September 11, 2001, terrorist attacks on the World Trade Center and the Pentagon, continuing costly wars in the Middle East, coupled with a major recession, have deflected attention from more serious efforts to confront head on the ending of racial and ethnic inequalities in health. Individual and institutionalized racism and the undercurrent of racial and ethnic tensions in our society are sadly alive and well, and as scholar and commentator Harris-Perry (2011) has pointed out, optimistic talk of a new "post-racial society" in the wake of Obama's victory was wishful thinking at best. Indeed, the profound and continuing racial/ethnic health and social inequities in our society are constant reminders that the "problem of the color line" articulated by W.E.B. Du Bois over one hundred years ago remains very much a part of our reality.

To the problems posed by continuing tensions and inequities around race, class, gender, and sexual orientation, Harvard's Robert Putnam (2000) has added the loss of social capital—such "features of social life" as norms of reciprocity, social networks, and trust. He offers a stark picture of an America where television "privatizes our leisure time" and supplants our connections with communities. Putnam's analysis has been justifiably criticized as overly simplistic (Diers 2006; Hawe and Shiell 2000; Wallerstein 2002; see also chapter 3), and he and others have been careful to argue that "social capital is not an alternative to providing greater financial resources and public services to poor communities (Saegert et al. 2001, 2; Putnam 2000; Kawachi et al. 2008). Still others argue that online connections are contributing to both on- and offline community engagement (see chapter 15), albeit in new forms and levels of intensity. Yet the heart of Putnam's message still resonates with many who feel increasingly disconnected and disenfranchised in a land where ever more sophisticated technology and an impoverished sense of individual and community embeddedness often lie side by side.

Finally, as this book goes to press, a conservative political climate, and a historic deficit and prolonged recession, are enabling even mainstream politicians in the United States to advocate openly for cutbacks in government commitments to health care and entitlements for the poor and other vulnerable groups. And while HIV/AIDS, violence, asthma, teen pregnancy, depression, and a host of other preventable and treatable problems continue to affect large numbers of Americans and their families, public health—and, we would add, social welfare—remain "the poor relation of medicine" (Hemenway 2010, 1657), funded at levels that can't begin to match the need. Within such a climate, where is the place for community organizing and community building in our professional practice?

The third edition of this book is premised on the belief that such approaches have never been more relevant or necessary. Like the first two volumes, it advocates for the adaptation and use of community organizing principles and methods in response to a whole host of public health and social issues, such as substance abuse, homelessness, HIV/AIDS, and childhood obesity. But it also advocates for a "purer" approach to community organizing, defined as a process through which communities are helped to identify common problems or goals, mobilize resources, and in other ways develop and implement strategies for reaching the goals they collectively have set (chapter 3). In this latter process, the professional's role is one of helping to create the conditions in which community groups, rather than outside experts, can determine and set the health agenda and then act effectively to help transform their lives and the life of their community (see chapters 7 and 8). In the words of Kathleen M. Roe, health education leader and former president of the Society for Public Health Education, "effective community organizing requires a sharp analysis of power and politics, a keen sense of time and place, and an abiding hope for what is possible. It requires the ability to listen, to find common ground, and to inspire others with words, actions, and courage. It also requires the ability to understand complex problems, mobilize resources, and achieve things that matter."

This third edition focuses on both community organizing and community building. As suggested in chapter 5, community building is an orientation to practice focused on community, rather than a strategic framework or approach, and on building capacities, not fixing problems. Further, it conceptualizes community as "an inclusive, multidimensional, and dynamic system" of which the practitioner is a part. Many other conceptualizations of community building have gained currency in fields such as urban and regional planning (Corburn 2009) and community economic development and also are discussed and illustrated later in this book (see chapter 20 and appendix 2). For the most part, however, it is with the perspective on community building as a capacity-building orientation to practice that this book resonates most closely.

Increased attention to community building, and not merely community organizing around health issues, is well justified from a public health perspective. The "fraying social fabric" and feelings of lack of embeddedness in families and communities represent a public health as well as a social hazard; the lack of a sense of connection to others has long been associated with heart disease, depression, risky health behaviors, and a variety of other adverse health outcomes (Berkman 2000; James et al. 2001; Kawachi et al. 2008). Professionals who draw upon their resources to support community building and who "engage community members in new relationships and new ways of thinking about health promotion" (Roe and Thomas 2002, 122) and health and social equity can make a real contribution to improving the public's health and welfare.

Social Change Professionals as "Conscious Contrarians"

Close to two decades ago, Jacqueline Mondros and Scott Wilson (1994, 14–15) described community organizers as conscious contrarians. They delineated three components of conscious contrarianism: a particular worldview or set of beliefs and values about people and society, a power analysis that rejects the dominant ways of thinking about power and how power is distributed, and a deliberate selection of work (community organizing) that is consistent with the other two. Health educators, social workers, and other social change professionals may be described as conscious contrarians along these three dimensions, but I would add a fourth and fifth as well. Borrowed from the old Native American tradition of the Heyoehkahs, or "sacred clowns," and the more recent concept of "Positive Deviance" (Pascale et al. 2010), the fourth dimension involves our role in "doing things differently" and thus challenging traditional ways of thinking (Tilleras 1988; Pascale et al. 2010). Finally, the fifth dimension involves the increasing willingness of community organizers to openly confront issues of racism and other -isms, and to demonstrate cultural humility (Tervalon and Murray-Garcia 1998) as they engage with others in our increasingly diverse society and world.

Worldview

Like professional organizers, health educators, social workers, and other social change professionals engaged in community organizing and community building tend to share a worldview characterized by "a strong sense of what is just in and for the world" (Mondros and Wilson 1994, 15). Concerns with justice, fairness, the application of democratic principles, and a sense of collective responsibility thus can be seen to characterize the worldview reflected in such fields as public health (Wallack and Lawrence 2005), community psychology, and social welfare (Reisch 2010). Indeed, as Beauchamp (1976) argued over thirty-five years ago, social justice is the very foundation of public health and is an ethic that contrasts sharply with the dominant American worldview, characterized by a market-justice orientation emphasizing individual responsibility. As Robertson (1999), Wallack and Lawrence (2005), and others further suggest, "The language of public health is indeed "a moral discourse that links health promotion to the pursuit of the common good" (Robertson 1999, 118). The major role that individuals can play in improving their health through smoking cessation, diet and exercise, and other lifestyle modifications has, of course, been well demonstrated (McGinnis and Foege 1993; USDHHS 2011). And health educators and other professionals often play an important role in helping to create programs through which individuals can be enabled to change unhealthy habits and in other ways improve their own and their families' health status and well-being. But without discounting the importance of such work, the worldview of professionals in fields like public health and social work recognizes its limitations. This alternative worldview sees health and well-being as intimately tied to social and environmental conditions and suggests that the *primary* focus of intervention be at the community and policy levels rather than at the level of the individual (Cohen et al. 2010; Gebbie et al. 2003; Navarro and Muntaner 2006; Wallack and Lawrence 2005). With the World Health Organization's Commission on Social Determinants of Health, they recognize that strengthening health equity means focusing on "the 'causes of the causes'—the fundamental structures of social hierarchy and the socially determined conditions these create in which people grow, live, work, and age" (Marmot 2007, 1153).

The dimension of the social change practitioner's worldview that sees health and social problems as deeply grounded in a broader social context is very much in keeping with a power analysis that departs from mainstream ways of thinking about how and why societal resources are allocated as they are. But another critical dimension deserves mention as well, and that involves the embracing of diversity and multiculturalism not as a problem or obstacle to be dealt with but as a rich resource and opportunity to be seized. In a nation such as the United States, where politicians can make political hay through their promotion of border patrols, and a clamping down on the rights of immigrants and of lesbian, gay, bisexual, and transgender (LGBT) people, there is increasing need for professionals who can emphasize the many ways in which society benefits from its growing heterogeneity. The "respect for diversity" that health education leader Dorothy Nyswander (1967) laid out over forty-five years ago as a central criterion against which to measure her professional work has only increased in significance in the intervening decades as we move quickly toward our oxymoron status as a "majority-minority" nation. The value of inclusion rather than exclusion and the embracing of diversity as a means of enriching the social fabric are central to the worldview of practitioners in community health education and social work and the other social change professionals who engage in what Angela Blackwell and her colleagues (2002) call "searching for the uncommon common ground."

Power Analysis

Closely intertwined with the worldview just described is a power analysis that differs sharply from the dominant ideology. As Mondros and Wilson have pointed out, "Mainstream definitions of who benefits in society and why are questioned along class, racial, ethnic, gender and other lines" (1994, 15).

While typically not articulated as such, the power analysis of social change professionals often is rooted in political economy. This theoretical framework accepts Max Weber's (1978) classic definition of power as the probability that an individual or a group will have its will win out despite the resistance of others. A power analysis rooted in political economy argues that resources are allocated not on the basis of relative merit or efficiency but on the basis of power (Bryant et al. 2010; Lukes 2005; Minkler et al. 1994–1995). The unequal distribution of wealth, health, and life chances in a society is seen in this analysis as heavily determined by the interaction of political, economic, and sociocultural factors (Navarro and Muntaner 2004; Hofrichter 2003). The dynamics of race/ethnicity, class, and gender and the role of broad social influences in determining how health and social problems get defined and treated or ignored are among the central issues with which political economy is concerned, and each has a great deal to say about the nature of power in society.

As suggested in subsequent chapters, feminist perspectives on community organizing and community practice (Hyde 2008; see chapter 12) together with community building (Diers 2006; Himmelman 2001; Kretzmann and McKnight 1993; Wolff 2010) and perspectives accenting cross-cultural practice (Gutiérrez et al., in press) often contain an alternative power analysis that stresses "power with" and "power to" (French 1986) rather than more traditional and hierarchical notions of "power over."

Although the contributors to this book offer a number of perspectives on power, their power analyses have in common a rejection of the dominant notion that power accrues to individuals and groups on the basis of merit. Further, and whether visualized primarily in terms of power over or power to and power with, the role of factors such as race, class, gender, and sexual orientation in influencing power and access to societal resources is a critical component of the power analysis of contributors to this volume. For theorists and activists like Canada's

Dennis Raphael (2008a, 16) an important part of our worldview may also involve looking beyond the "social determinants of health" so popular in today's public health lexicon to ask as well, *What are the political and economic determinants of the social determinants of health?"*

Of equal importance as that of the authors' power analyses, however, are their conceptualizations of empowerment. As discussed in chapter 3, empowerment is "a social-action process that promotes participation of people, organizations, and communities toward the goals of increased individual and community control, political efficacy, improved quality of community life, and social justice" (Wallerstein 2002, 73). Yet as also discussed in subsequent chapters, a cautionary attitude toward the rhetoric of empowerment is important as well. For particularly in times of fiscal retrenchment, the language of individual and community empowerment and self-reliance frequently is being invoked by conservative policymakers to justify cutbacks in entitlement programs and health and social services. Indeed, as Ronald Labonte points out, "Divorced of its historical contingency, empowerment is more a sop than a challenge to the status quo" (quoted in Bernstein et al. 1994, 287). While embracing authentic notions of empowerment, then, part of the worldview of health educators and other social change professionals involves a rejection of the argument that individual and community empowerment can take the place of a broader societal-level commitment to creating the conditions in which people and communities can be healthy. Further, a commitment to genuine empowerment stresses the impor- tance of not only *distributive justice* (or fair allocation of resources and hazards) but also *procedural justice*, through which marginalized groups get "a seat at the table—and stay at the table, having a real voice in decision making affecting their lives" (Minkler 2010, S184).

Deliberate Career Choice

The third component of Mondros and Wilson's (1994, 16) conscious contrarianism involves the deliberate seeking out of jobs "that at least appear to contain the possibility to promote change." As suggested previously, the promotion of change that organizers embrace is most heavily concentrated on the community and broader institutional and societal levels.

Fields such as public health, social work, and community psychology bring little fame, glory, or money to those who select them. In Dan Callahan's words, disease prevention and health promotion "still remain the step-children of the American health care system: accepted but not well fed, praised but not always allowed in the living room, beloved unless they start making real financial demands" (1995, 2). Within this context, the goal of facilitating empowerment can be particularly hard to live up to when funding is not only grossly inadequate but also often categorical in nature, requiring that we focus on a disease or health or social problem that may be of little concern to people in their neighborhoods. Yet the increasing emphasis being placed by funders, health and government agencies and departments, and policymakers on strategies such as community participation, partnerships, and coalition building offers unique opportunities to help broaden still further the scope of our professional contributions to improving the public's health and well-being. In the United States, the work many communities are now doing to fight the environmental and policy-related causes of asthma, food insecurity, transportation inequities, and other health and social problems (see chapter 20) offer fertile grounds for an increased emphasis on community building as a vital part of our professional roles. In short, and particularly at this critical juncture in our history, the choice of a career in fields such as public health, social work, and urban and community planning can offer real opportunities for helping to create the conditions in which healthier communities and societies can emerge. As Barbara Kingsolver reminds us in her novel *Animal Dreams*, "The very least you can do with your life is to figure out what to hope for. And the most you can do is to live inside that hope. Not admire it from a distance but live right in it, under its roof" (1990). In choosing a career that accents community organizing and community building, we are in a very real sense choosing to live inside the hope we share for a healthier society and a healthier world.

Doing Things Differently, or "The Power of Positive Deviance"

A fourth dimension of conscious contrarianism may be found in what Pascale and colleagues (2010) call "the power or positive deviance," and in the related and earlier Native American tradition of the Heyoehkahs—those individuals in the tribe who challenged people's thinking and shook them up. As Perry Tilleras explains, the function of the sacred clowns, who were also known as *contrarians*, "was to keep people from getting stuck in rigid ways of thinking and living" (1988, viii). And so these tribal members, who were often gay, "lived backward," walking and dancing backward and doing everything contrary to the norm. Tilleras describes the gay community's early response to HIV/AIDS as in keeping with the Heyoehkah tradition: "When the normal response was to react with fear and panic, there were people dancing backwards, responding with love and confidence. . . . When the normal reaction to a diagnosis was isolation, the Heyoehkahs dragged us into community" (1988, viii).

In their more recent rendering of this approach, Pascale and colleagues describe "the power of Positive Deviance" as grounded in the notion that every community contains groups or individuals whose unusual ways of thinking and doing things allow them to come up with better solutions to problems than do their similarly resourced peers. Positive Deviance identifies and builds on local assets and is genuinely community driven in helping communities find effective strategies and formulate plans of action to promote the adoption and dissemination of their new approaches (2010).

For organizers, community health educators, social workers, community psychologists, and other social change professionals, Positive Deviance and the Heyoehkah tradition of doing things differently is a familiar one. Whereas traditional medicine looks for pathogens and other agents of disease causation, we look for the strengths on which people and communities can build in achieving and maintaining health. And whereas in business and many other professions "getting ahead" means pushing one's self and one's achievements, the good community organizer, health educator, or social worker typically remains in the background so that achievements and victories are seen as being of and by people and communities rather than of and by outside professionals.

Confronting Racism and Embracing Cultural Humility

To the preceding list may be added a fifth and final dimension of conscious contrarianism, namely, actively confronting and attempting to address racism (and other -isms) in our personal and professional lives, and in our society. As Makani Themba points out, racism in America is like "the gorilla in the living room. It's running through the place making noises, and everyone is sitting politely trying to ignore it" (1999, 157). Ironically, the tendency to avoid dealing openly with racism has persisted even in the wake of Healthy People 2020's again naming the elimination of health disparities as one of its overarching goals (USDHHS 2011). Indeed, and with a few important exceptions (e.g., substantial dialogue in the aftermath of Hurricane Katrina); regular, mandatory dialogues and trainings on the -isms in some local health departments (see chapter 8); the Open Society initiative of the Society for Public Health Education (www .sophe.org); and the 2011 National Conference on Research on Discrimination and Health supported by the National Institutes of Health and other federal agencies, the important new emphasis in public health practice and research on eliminating health disparities has not been accompanied by serious confrontation with the issues of race and racism that are so intimately interconnected with these disparities.

For conscious contrarians in fields like public health and social work, the need to "talk the walk" for racial justice (Cutting and Temba-Nixon 2006) is a paramount commitment. Race matters in our continued need to commit ourselves to the elimination of health disparities, and it matters in the way we approach our work. In the latter regard, as Tervalon and Murray-Garcia point out, it matters that we approach our work not with the goal of achieving "cultural competence" (a discrete end point), but rather with "cultural humility," which, as noted above, is defined as involving a "lifelong commitment to self-evaluation and self-critique," to redress power imbalances and "develop and maintain mutually respectful and dynamic partnerships with communities" (1998, 118; see chapters 7 and 8). For professionals who are also Caucasian and working with communities of color, the vital need for recognizing and confronting the many sources of "white privilege" or "invisible systems conferring dominance" on the basis of one's skin color (McIntosh 1989) is especially critical. Yet as Cheryl Hyde (appendix 3) points out, community practice professionals, regardless of skin color, need to pay far greater attention to reflecting on "who we are" as individuals and on how the multiple dimensions of our own cultural realities (e.g., race/ethnicity, class, sexual orientation, religion) influence our ways of being and relating in community.

In these and other ways, health educators, social workers, community psychologists, and other social change professionals are indeed contrarians. As such, they play a role that is highly consistent with the philosophy and methods of community organizing and community building.

Purposes and Organization of the Book

Although the third edition of this book expands on its predecessors in several important ways, as described below, it shares with them the same three purposes. First, it attempts to put together in one place much of the critical recent thinking in community organizing and community building theory and practice. These contributions address both long-valued aspects of organizing, such as issue selection and participation, and newer approaches to "healthy community assessment" (chapter 9), coalition community action (chapter 17), online community building and organizing (chapter 15), and media advocacy (chapter 22) that have played transformative roles in organizing over the past two decades. The inclusion of an in-depth comparison of traditional Alinsky-brand (1972) social action organizing with Freirian (1973) community building and organizing (chapter 4); a stronger accent on race/ethnicity, including the special challenges and strengths involved in organizing with and by immigrant communities (chapter 12–14) and a critical reflection on dealing with our own *-isms* (appendix 3); the role of social media and new methods such as "videovoice" (Catalani et al. 2011; see chapters 15 and 16), and the expanded focus on the use of community organizing as a potent approach to influencing policy in health care reform and other areas (chapters 20 and 21) are among the additions to this third edition.

Second, the book attempts to demonstrate, through a series of case studies, the concrete application of many of the concepts and methods discussed in real-world organizing and community building settings. Most of these case studies demonstrate the adaptation and use of community organizing and community building strategies by health educators and other social change professionals as part of their efforts to address such problems as cancer, obesity, and health care reform. In other case examples, however, the health educator, social worker, or other social change professional engages in a purer approach to organizing, creating the conditions in which communities can identify and address their own health and social issues, as when immigrant restaurant workers in chapter 14 are helped to create a low-wage-worker bill of rights. The frequent use of such analytical case studies and illustrations is designed to help bridge the still sizable gap between theory and practice in community organizing and community building.

A third and final purpose of the book is to make explicit the kinds of hard questions and ethical challenges that should be reflected upon continually by those of us who engage in community organizing or community building as part of our professional practice. Questions regarding the appropriate role of people in positions of privilege vis-à-vis community empowerment; the problem of conflicting priorities between one's agency or funder and the community; competing visions of "the community"; potential unanticipated consequences of an organizing intervention; issues of working across boundaries in terms of race, class, or other dividing lines; and questions of how to develop empowering, rather than disempowering, approaches to community health assessment and the evaluation of community health initiatives are among the types of questions with which we grapple. By raising these questions rather than providing pat answers, the book attempts to foster an approach to community organizing and community building that is, above all, self-critical, reflective, and respectful of the diverse communities with which health professionals are engaged.

Before providing a chapter-by-chapter overview of what this third edition includes, however, I must state up front what it does not contain. First, the book does not provide a step-by-step approach to community organizing or community building, which may be found elsewhere (cf. Bobo et al. 2010; Sen 2003; Staples 2004; Homan 2011). Second, this volume is not intended as a comprehensive casebook, and consequently it cannot begin to do justice to the myriad exciting community organizing and community building efforts taking place among and with different racial/ethnic communities in both urban and rural areas or in communities based on shared interests locally or internationally. Third, this volume does not attempt to cover the substantial literature on social movements for health and social justice, which themselves are the topic of a number of comprehensive volumes (cf. Della Porta and Diani 2006; Brown et al. 2012) Finally, this book is focused primarily on community organizing and community building efforts in the United States and, to a lesser extent, in Canada. Although globalization is a frequent backdrop for the perspectives offered, and while we hope that many of the principles and case studies will have relevance beyond the borders of North America, space limitations, and the importance of adequately taking context into account, precluded a broader geographic focus. Given these limitations, it is hoped that this book enables the reader to think critically about community organizing and community building for health and welfare, asking hard questions and exploring their relevance in practice settings.

The next three chapters together provide several conceptual frameworks and approaches within which community organizing and community building for health can be understood. We begin with an early piece by President Barack Obama, in which he eloquently asks—and answers—the bedrock question "Why organize?" Although originally published in 1988 when a young Obama reflected on his work as an organizer in Chicago's South Side, the piece provides a compelling introduction to the thinking of one of the most important figures of our time. Further, and while some of the players have changed (with Occupy Wall Street bringing class back into the national discourse and with the Moral Majority of the 1990s giving way to the Tea Party, an example noted earlier), the lessons of this chapter about core principles and approaches in community organizing practice have stood the test of time.

In chapter 3, Meredith Minkler and Nina Wallerstein then provide an expanded theoretical and historical introduction to community organizing and community building and highlighting several key themes (e.g., power and empowerment, community capacity, and participation) to set the stage for their more detailed examination in later chapters. The popular concept of social capital also is introduced and critically examined in this chapter. In chapter 4, Marty Martinson and Celina Su then provide an in-depth comparison of the philosophy and methods of two giants in the field—Saul D. Alinsky and Paulo Freire. With the former known as the "father of social action organizing" and the latter as one of the most influential adult educators of modern times, whose methods subsequently were adapted and used by community organizers, Alinsky (1972) and Freire (1973) provide different yet seminal contributions to much of the more recent thinking and work in the field.

Cheryl Walter and Cheryl Hyde end this section by shifting our focus from community *organizing* to *community* in all its complexity, and of which we as practitioners are a part. As noted above, the authors propose a way of framing community practice that focused more on capacity building than on solving specific problems, and their conceptualization is consonant with a number of important skills for social change professionals and is offered here as a means of challenging us to reflect more critically on our roles in community.

In part 2, we turn our attention to the challenging and often difficult role of health educators, social workers, and other social change professionals as community organizers. Canadian scholar and activist Ronald Labonte begins in chapter 6 by questioning some of the prevailing wisdom about community and raising a number of cautions for health workers who engage in community development or community organizing toward the goal of building authentic partnerships. Stressing the difference between *community-based* and true *community development/community organizing* approaches, he provides a number of criteria to be met if authentic partnerships between health agencies and communities are to be realized.

Several of the hard questions and issues raised by Labonte are examined in greater detail in chapter 7, as Meredith Minkler, Cheri Pies, and Cheryl Hyde provide theoretical perspectives and case examples that shed light on the ethical and practical challenges frequently faced by health educators, social workers, community psychologists, and other professionals in their roles as community organizers and capacity builders. Problems such as conflicting priorities, the potential for negative unanticipated consequences, and role of the *-isms* and phobias (racism, sexism, homophobia, etc.) in our work are explored. Questions are posed throughout for practitioners and social change professionals to ask themselves in an effort to make more explicit the difficult ethical terrain in which we operate.

We conclude this part with a more detailed look, by Galen Ellis and Sheryl Walton, at how genuine partnerships can be built between health departments and communities when capacity building and cultural humility are seriously addressed. Through three case studies applying a successful model that works on internal (health department) change and not merely changing "the community," chapter 8 shares promising practices that build on issues raised in the preceding chapters in this part.

Two of the most important—and neglected—aspects of the health or social change professional's role as organizer involves his or her involvement in the processes of community assessment and issue selection. Chapters 9 and 10 are based on the premise that assessments need to stress community strengths and assets rather than merely needs or perceived problems and that such assessments should truly be "of, by, and for" the community. In chapter 9, Trevor Hancock and Meredith Minkler introduce this perspective and challenge the reader to think not in terms of a *community health assessment* but rather of a broader, *healthy community assessment*, using a range of tools to broaden the lens through which we view such processes. In chapter 10, this approach is translated into practice in the form of John McKnight and John Kretzmann's classic piece, "Mapping Community Capacity." The reader is provided with a simple, yet effective, tool that can help communities—and the professionals who work with them—find and map the building blocks or strengths and assets that can in turn be called upon in the building of healthier communities.

We conclude this part by turning our attention to the related area of issue selection with communities. In chapter 11, Lee Staples lays out the criteria for a "good issue," as well as the factors to be considered in "cutting" the issue as part of a strategic analysis. Frequently drawing on case examples, he helps illuminate the many ways in which outside professionals can help ensure that the issue selected comes from the community and is cut in ways that help the community achieve its goals.

A major theme running through much of this book involves the role of community organizing and community building in and across diverse groups. In chapter 12, Lorraine Gutiérrez and Edith Lewis describe their approach to organizing with women of color through the application of an empowerment framework stressing principles of education, participation, and capacity building. Arguing that existing models of community organizing fail to adequately address the strengths, needs, and concerns of women of color, they present a feminist perspective on organizing that specifically addresses problems and issues for organizing by and with this population.

In chapter 13, Laura Linnan and her colleagues offer a unique approach to health education and community building to address health disparities, using as a base African American beauty salons and barbershops. The historical significance of these cultural sites of meaning—which were among the first African American–owned and –run businesses and important community meeting places—is provided as a critical backdrop to two exemplary case studies of their contemporary use in addressing health problems while building on community strengths. Although the examples are not community organizing in the traditional sense, this chapter demonstrates the utility and importance of respecting, and partnering with, valued cultural institutions in the fight against health disparities.

We conclude part 5 with a case study that demonstrates how popular education, community organizing, and community-based participatory research (CBPR) can be a potent mix for helping a low-income immigrant community address some of its deepest concerns. Charlotte Chang and her colleagues describe popular education and CBPR as approaches intimately interconnected with community organizing in an action-oriented study of and by Chinatown restaurant workers to address occupational health and safety. The engagement of all partners throughout this process is emphasized, as are the action outcomes of the work and the use of participatory evaluation throughout.

Although community building and organizing often conjure up images of community meetings and door-to-door canvassing, many exciting new approaches to this work have come into play in recent years. In part 6, we consider the powerful and rapidly growing role of the Internet and social media in community organizing and community building, as well as the role of the arts in "real world" as well as virtual applications toward these ends. In chapter 15, Nickie Bazell Satariano and Amanda Wong provide a provocative look at the power of the Internet for community assessment, building, and organizing. Drawing on a diversity of Internet venues, approaches, and case study applications, they illustrates how the Internet and web-based social media have dramatically improved access to information and organizing tools, enabled the formation of new communities, and provided powerful new approaches to social change. Yet they also remind us that such tools are effective only when embedded in a broader and carefully designed strategy that includes "real world" engagement as well as cyberactivism. The existence of a shrinking but still important digital divide, resulting in unequal access to the Internet, also is discussed.

In chapter 16, Marian McDonald and her colleagues then explore the usefulness of a wide variety of art forms for community organizing around health and social issues. The theoretical bases for using the arts in organizing are explored, and examples, including the AIDS Memorial Quilt and the Clothesline Project, the latter tackling violence against women and children, are used to illustrate the promise of such approaches. The chapter highlights photovoice, an increasingly popular approach to social change using cameras and dialogue (Wang and Burris 1997). It then explores the newer and related approach, videovoice (Catalani et al. 2011) and illustrates its use in post-Katrina New Orleans for community building, assessment, and policy advocacy.

Building and maintaining effective coalitions has increasingly been recognized as vital components of much effective community organizing and community building. In chapter 17, Frances Butterfoss and Michelle C. Kegler offer their coalition model for community action, a theoretical model that emerged in large part from practice in the field. After briefly introducing the benefits and challenges of coalitions, the chapter provides a set of constructs and "practice-proven propositions" for understanding coalition development, maintenance, and effective functioning. The various stages of coalitions and the tasks associated with each are described, with attention to such key issues as coalition context, leadership and staffing, and dealing with conflict. The authors further emphasize the need for careful documentation of both short-term successes and longer-term impacts, toward the end of improving practice.

In chapter 18, Adam Becker and his colleagues then illustrate this theoretical approach in action through their in-depth look at a community coalition in a largely Puerto Rican Chicago neighborhood and its efforts to fight childhood obesity within a broad social ecological and organizing framework. Following a brief look at this major public health problem, the authors describe the formation and evolution of this community-wide coalition, whose activities included the formation of a walking club and a producemobile, as well as rooftop gardens at schools and the allocation of local parkland for urban gardening. Challenges such as fluid coalition membership are discussed, as are the ways in which this case study both supported and deviated from various practice-based theory propositions in the coalition community action model.

A central dilemma faced by professionals as organizers is how to facilitate the evaluation of community organizing and community building efforts in ways that do not disempower communities in the process. In chapter 19, Chris Coombe describes how the process of evaluation can be used as a capacity-building tool in organizing, as well as a source of knowledge for project improvement through a systematic and collaborative approach known as participatory or empowerment evaluation (Fawcett et al. 2003). Limitations of traditional approaches to evaluation are discussed, the theoretical underpinnings of participatory evaluation described, and an eight-step process offered for applying this approach in the messy and complex world of community organizing and coalition building.

In the final part of this volume, we turn our attention to affecting policy through community organizing and community building. In chapter 20, Angela Glover Blackwell and her colleagues offer an overview of the policymaking process and roles for advocates in that process and then use two case studies to illustrate how community organizing helped bring about changes in local, regional, and state policy. The cases, involving, first, a community-academic partnership to improve community reintegration for incarcerated persons in Harlem, New York and, second, the role of faith-based organizations, ISAIAH and its partners, in improving equity in public transportation in Minneapolis, Minnesota, help make the case for approaches to policymaking that include community engagement and a "health in all policies" perspective throughout the work.

We then turn, in Chapter 21, first to Jacquie Anderson and Michael Miller's critical examination of how community organizing approaches were used to help bring about the historic Patient Protection and Affordable Care Act of 2010. Emphasizing the "systems of advocacy" involved in this work, and discussing the challenges faced as well as the contributors to ultimate passage, Anderson and Miller offer the perspectives of a key organizational leader—Community Catalyst— and its partners in helping pass this landmark legislation. For many, however, the limitations of a health care reform effort that does not include universal coverage have stoked efforts on the state level to achieve more progressive approaches to health care reform. This chapter concludes, therefore, with organizer and activist Andrew McGuire's discussion of current efforts in the nation's largest state to provide universal coverage through a "Medicare for All" (single payer) system. With a special focus on the CaliforniaOneCare campaign, and the critical role of community organizing and coalition building, including both grassroots and "netroots" organizing efforts, this fascinating state-level effort is illuminated.

In many of the preceding chapters, the power of the mass media in influencing the form and outcomes of organizing campaigns has been illustrated. We conclude this part, however, with Lori Dorfman and Priscilla Gonzalez's more detailed look at media advocacy, or the strategic use of mass media to promote policy initiatives (Wallack et al. 1993). The potent role of media advocacy in enabling community groups and advocates to reframe local and national problems such as the obesity epidemic and change the ways in which they are presented and viewed is highlighted, as is its role as a critical tool for building healthier communities through advocacy for healthy public policy.

The volume ends with eleven appendixes designed to provide the reader with concrete tools and applications that correspond to a number of the chapter themes and issues raised. Ranging from an action-oriented community assessment technique to the use of digital technology in community mapping, to a thoughtful reflection by a leading social work scholar and activist on the need for exploring and dealing with one's own cultural identity in order to more effectively work in communities, the appendixes are designed to help social change professionals put into practice some of the messages central to community organizing and community building.

Although this book is written primarily for students and practitioners in fields such as community health education, social work, community psychology, and urban and regional planning, we hope it will be of interest as well to a wide range of social justice activists concerned with the many hard questions and realities that surround community building and organizing in the early twenty-first century. As in the first edition, the contributors to this volume have attempted to write provocatively and critically, challenging the reader—and each other—to ask hard questions and to rethink some of our most basic assumptions. We ask you, the reader, to join us in this process of critical questioning and dialogue as you seek to apply theory to practice, and practice to the rethinking of theory, toward the end of helping build health and social equity and more caring and humane communities and societies.

REFERENCES

Alinsky, S. D. 1972. *Rules For Radicals: A Practical Primer for Realistic Radicals.* New York: Random House.

Beauchamp, D. 1976. "Public Health as Social Justice." *Inquiry* 12:3–14.

Bell, J., and M. M. Lee. 2011. *Why Place and Race Matter: Impacting Health through a Focus on Race and Place.* Oakland, Calif.: PolicyLink.

Berkman, L. F. 2000. "Social Integration, Social Networks, and Health." In *Encyclopedia of Health and Behavior,* edited by Norman B. Anderson 2:754–759. Thousand Oaks, Calif.: Sage.

Bernstein, E., N. Wallerstein, R. Braithwaite, et al. 1994. "Empowerment Forum: A Dialogue between Guest Editorial Board Members. *Health Education Quarterly* 21, no. 3:281–294.

Blackwell, A. G., S. Kwoh, and M. Pastor. 2002. *Searching for the Uncommon Ground: New Dimensions on Race in America.* New York: Norton.

Bobo, K., J. Kendall, and S. Max. 2010. *Organizing for Social Change.* 4th ed. Santa Ana, Calif.: Forum Press.

Brown, P., R. Morello-Frosch, and S. Zavestoski. 2012. *Contested Illnesses: Citizens, Science, and Health Social Movements.* Berkeley and Los Angeles: University of California Press.

Bryant, T., D. Raphael, and M. Rioux. 2010. *Staying Alive: Critical Perspectives on Health, Illness, and Health Care.* 2nd ed. Toronto: Canadian Scholars' Press.

Catalani, C., L. Campbell, S. Herbst, B. Springgate, B. Butler, and M. Minkler. 2012. "Videovoice: Community Assessment in Post-Katrina New Orleans." *Health Promotion Practice* 13, no. 1:18–28.

Callahan, D. 1995. "Issues in Health Promotion and Disease Prevention." Unpublished report, Hastings Center, Hastings-on-Hudson, N.Y.

Chávez, V., B. Duran, Q. E. Bakcr, M. M. Avila, and N. Wallerstein. 2008. "The Dance of Race and Privilege in Community-Based Participatory Research." In *Community-Based Participatory Research for Health: From Processes to Outcomes,* edited by M. Minkler and N. Wallerstein, 91–103. 2nd ed. San Francisco: Jossey-Bass.

Cohen, L., V. Chávez, and S. Chehimi. 2010. *Prevention Is Primary: Strategies for Community Well-Being.* 2nd ed. San Francisco: Jossey-Bass.

Corburn, J. 2009. *Toward the Healthy City: People, Places, and the Politics of Urban Planning.* Cambridge, Mass.: MIT Press.

Cutting, H., and M. Themba-Nixon. 2006. *Talking the Walk: A Communications Guide for Racial Justice.* Oakland, Calif.: AK Press.

Daniels, J. 2009. *Cyber Racism: White Supremacy Online and the New Attack on Civil Rights.* Lanham, Md.: Rowman and Littlefield.

———. 2011. "Case Study: Web 2.0, Health Care Policy, and Community Health Activism." In *Policy and Politics for Nurses and Other Advocates,* edited by D. M. Nickitas, D. J. Middaugh, and N. Aries, 277–285. Boston: Jones and Bartlett.

DeFilippis, J., R. Fisher, and E. Shragge. 2010. *Contesting Community: The Limits and Potential of Local Organizing.* New Brunswick, N.J.: Rutgers University Press.

Della Porta, D., and M. Diani. 2006. *Social Movements: An Introduction.* Malden, Mass.: Blackwell.

Diers, J. 2006. *Neighborhood Power: Building Community the Seattle Way.* Seattle: University of Washington Press.

Dreier, P. 2008. "Will Obama Inspire a New Generation of Organizers?" *Dissent,* June 25. http://www.dissentmagazine.org/online.php?id=109.

Fawcett, S., P. Abeykoon, M. Arora, M. Dobe, L. Galloway-Gilliam, L. Liburd, and D. Munodawafa. 2010. "Constructing an Action Agenda for Community Empowerment at the 7th Global Conference on Health Promotion in Nairobi." *Global Health Promotion* 17, no. 4:52–56.

Fawcett, S. B., R. I. Boothroyd, J. A. Schultz, V. T. Francisco, V. Carson, and R. Bremby. 2003. "Building Capacity for Participatory Evaluation within Community Initiatives." *Journal of Prevention and Intervention in the Community* 26, no. 2:21–36.

Freire, P. 1973. *Education for Critical Consciousness*. New York: Seabury Press.

French, M. 1986. *Beyond Power: On Women, Men, and Morals*. London: Abacus.

Gebbie, K., L. Rosenstock, and L. M. Hernandez. 2003. *Who Will Keep the Public Healthy? Educating Public Health Professionals for the 21st Century*. Washington, D.C.: Institute of Medicine.

Geiger, H. J. 2006. "Health Disparities: What Do We Know? What Do We Need to Know? What Should We Do?" In *Gender, Race, Class, and Health: Intersectoral Approaches*, edited by A. J. Schulz and L. Mullings, 261–288. San Francisco: Jossey-Bass.

Gutiérrez, L., A. Dessel, E. Lewis, and M. Spencer. In press. "Promoting Multicultural Communication and Collaboration: Dialogue, Mediation, Consensus Building, and Intergroup Empowerment." In *Handbook of Community Practice*, edited by M. O. Weil. 2nd ed. New York: Sage.

Harris-Perry, M. 2011. *Sister Citizen: Shame, Stereotypes, and the Black Woman in America*. New Haven, Conn.: Yale University Press.

Hawe, P., and A. Shiell. 2000. "Social Capital and Health Promotion: A Review." *Social Science and Medicine* 51:71–885.

Hemenway, D. 2010. "Why We Don't Spend Enough on Public Health." *New England Journal of Medicine* 362, no. 18:1657–1658.

Himmelman, A. 2001. "On Coalitions and the Transformation of Power Relations: Collaborative Betterment and Collaborative Empowerment." *American Journal of Community Psychology* 29, no. 2:277–284.

Hofrichter, R. 2003. "The Politics of Health Inequities." In *Health and Social Justice: Politics, Ideology, and Inequality in the Distribution of Disease*, edited by R. Hofrichter, 1–56. San Francisco: Jossey-Bass.

Homan, M. S. 2011. *Promoting Community Change: Making It Happen in the Real World*. 5th ed. Pacific Grove, Calif.: Brooks/Cole.

Hyatt, S. 2008. "The Obama Victory, Asset-Based Development, and the Re-politicization of Community Organizing." *North American Dialogue* 11, no. 2:17–26.

Hyde, Cheryl A. 2008. "Feminist Social Work Practice." In *Encyclopedia of Social Work*, edited by T. Mizrahi and L. Davis, 216–221. 20th ed. New York: Oxford University Press.

James, S. A., A. Schulz, and J. van Olphen. 2001. "Social Capital, Poverty, and Community Health: An Exploration of Linkages." In *Social Capital and Poor Communities*, edited by S. Saegert, J. P. Thompson, and M. R. Warren, 165–199. New York: Russell Sage Foundation.

Kawachi, I., S. V. Subramanian, and D. Kim. 2008. *Social Capital and Health*. New York: Springer Science and Business Media.

Kingsolver, B. 1990. *Animal Dreams*. New York: Perennial Books.

Kretzmann, J. P., and J. L. McKnight. 1993. *Building Communities from Inside Out: A Path toward Finding and Mobilizing a Community's Assets*. Evanston Ill.: Center for Urban Affairs and Policy Research.

Lukes, S. 2005. *Power: A Radical View*. 2nd ed. Basingstoke, U.K.: Palgrave Macmillan.

Marmot, M. 2007. "Achieving Health Equity: From Root Causes to Fair Outcomes." *Lancet 370*, no. 9593:1153–1163. Published on behalf of the Commission on Social Determinants of Health.

McCloskey, D. D., M. A. McDonald, J. Cook, S. Heurtin-Roberts, S. Updegrove, D. Sampson, et al. 2011. "Community Engagement: Definitions and Organizing Concepts from the Literature." In *Principles of Community Engagement*, by Clinical and Translational Science

Awards Consortium Community Engagement Key Function Committee Task Force on Principles of Community Engagement. 2nd ed. NIH Publication No. 11–7782. Washington, D.C.: National Institutes of Health.

McGinnis, J. M., and W. H. Foege. 1993. "Actual Causes of Death in the United States." *Journal of the American Medical Association* 270:2207–2212.

McIntosh, P. 1989. "White Privilege: Unpacking the Invisible Knapsack." *Peace and Freedom*, July/August, 10–12.

Miller, M. 2009. *A Community Organizer's Tale: People and Power in San Francisco.* Berkeley: Calif.: Heyday Books.

Minkler, M. 1994. "Challenges for Health Promotion in the 1990's: Social Inequities, Empowerment, Negative Consequences, and the Public Good." *American Journal of Health Promotion* 8, no. 6:403–413.

———. 2010. "Linking Science and Policy through Community-Based Participatory Research to Eliminate Health Disparities." Supplement, *American Journal of Public Health* 100, no. 1:S81–S87.

Minkler, M., S. P. Wallace, and M. MacDonald. 1994–1995. "The Political Economy of Health: A Useful Theoretical Tool for Health Education Practice." *International Quarterly of Community Health Education* 15, no. 2:111–125.

Mondros, J. B., and S. M. Wilson. 1994. *Organizing for Power and Empowerment.* New York: Columbia University Press.

Navarro, V., and C. Muntaner. 2006. *Political and Economic Determinants of Population Health and Well-Being.* Amityville, N.Y.: Baywood.

Nettleton, S. 1997. "Surveillance, Health Promotion, and the Formation of a Risk Identity." In *Debates and Dilemmas in Promoting Health*, edited by M. Sidell, L. Jones, J. Katz, and A. Peberdy, 314–324. Buckingham, U.K.: Open University Press.

Nyswander, D. 1967. "The Open Society: Its Implications for Health Educators." *Health Education Monographs* 1, no. 1:3–13.

Pascale, R., J. Sternin, and M. Sternin. 2010. *The Power of Positive Deviance: How Unlikely Innovators Solve the World's Toughest Problems.* Boston: Harvard Business Press.

Putnam, R. 2000. *Bowling Alone: The Collapse and Revival of American Community.* New York: Simon and Schuster.

Raphael, D. 2008a. "Getting Serious About the Social Determinants of Health: New Directions for Public Health Workers." *Promotion and Education.* 15 no. 3:15–20.

———. 2008b. "Grasping at Straws: A Recent History of Health Promotion in Canada." *Critical Public Health* 18, no. 4:483–495.

Reich, R. 2010. *Aftershock: The Next Economy and America's Future.* New York: Alfred A Knopf.

Reisch, M. 2010. "Defining Social Justice in a Socially Unjust World." In *Educating for Social Justice: Transformative Experiential Learning*, edited by J. M. Bierkenmaier, A. Cruce, J. Curley, E. Burkemper, R. J. Wilson, and J. J.Stretch, 11–28. Chicago: Lyceum Books.

Robertson, A. 1999. "Health Promotion and the Common Good: Theoretical Considerations." *Critical Public Health.* 9 no. 2: 117–133.

Robertson, A., and M. Minkler. 1994. "The New Health Promotion Movement: A Critical Examination." *Health Education Quarterly* 21, no. 3:295–312.

Roe, K. M., and S. Thomas. 2002. "REACH 2010: Engaging the Circle of Research and Practice to Eliminate Health Disparities: An Interview with Imani Ma'at." *Health Promotion Practice* 3, no. 2:120–124.

Saegert, S. J., J. P. Thompson, and M. R. Warren. 2001. *Social Capital and Poor Communities.* New York: Russell Sage Foundation.

Saez, E. 2009. *Striking It Richer: The Evolution of Top Incomes in the United States.* Berkeley: University of California, Berkeley, Department of Economics.

Scherer, R. 2011. "Taking It to the Streets." *Time* 178, no. 16, 20–24.

Sen, R. 2003. *Stir It Up: Lessons in Community Organizing and Advocacy.* San Francisco: Jossey-Bass.

Staples, L. 2004. *Roots to Power: A Manual for Grassroots Organizing.* 2nd ed. Westport, Conn.: Praeger.

Smedley, B. D., A. Y. Stith, and A. R. Nelson. 2002. *Unequal Treatment: Confronting Racial and Ethnic Disparities in Health Care.* Washington, D.C.: Institute of Medicine, National Academy Press.

Stengel, R. 2010. "Only Connect: Mark Zuckerberg and Facebook Are Changing How We Interact—and What We Know about Each Other. *Time,* December 15. http://www.time .com/time/specials/packages/article/0,28804,2036683_2037181_2037179,00.html

Tervalon, M., and J. Murray-Garcia. 1998. "Cultural Humility vs. Cultural Competence: A Critical Distinction in Defining Physician Training Outcomes in Medical Education." *Journal of Health Care for the Poor and Underserved* 9, no. 2:117–125.

Themba, M. N. 1999. *Making Policy, Making Change: How Communities Are Taking Law into Their Own Hands.* Oakland, Calif.: Chardon Press.

Thurow, L. 1996. *The Future of Capitalism.* New York: William Morrow.

Tilleras, P. 1988. *The Color of Light: Meditations for All of Us Living with AIDS.* San Francisco: Harper and Row.

U.S. Department of Health and Human Services (USDHHS). 1998. *Call to Action: Eliminating Racial and Ethnic Disparities in Health.* Washington, D.C.: U.S. Department of Health and Human Services and Grantmakers in Health.

———. 2011. *Healthy People 2020.* Brochure. www.healthypeople.gov.

Wallack, L., L. Dorfman, D. Jernigan, and M. Themba. 1993. *Media Advocacy and Public Health: Power for Prevention.* Newbury Park, Calif.: Sage.

Wallack, L., and R. Lawrence. 2005. "Talking about Public Health: Developing America's 'Second Language.'" *American Journal of Public Health* 95, no. 4:567–570.

Wallerstein, N. 2002. "Empowerment to Reduce Health Disparities." *Scandinavian Journal of Public Health* 30, no. S59:72–77.

Wang, C. C., and M. Burris. 1997. "Photovoice: Concept, Methodology, and Use for Participatory Needs Assessment. *Health Education and Behavior* 24:369–387.

Weber, Max. 1978. *Economy and Society: An Outline of Interpretive Sociology.* Edited by G. Roth and C. Wittich. New York: Bedminister Press.

Wolff, T. 2010. *The Power of Collaborative Solutions: Six Principles and Effective Tools for Building Healthy Communities.* San Francisco: Jossey-Bass.

World Health Organization (WHO). 1986. "Ottawa Charter for Health Promotion." *Canadian Journal of Public Health* 77, no. 6:425–430.

World Health Organization, Commission on Social Determinants of Health. 2008. *Closing the Gap in a Generation: Health Equity through Action on the Social Determinants of Health.* Geneva: World Health Organization. http://www.who.int/social_determinants/ thecommission/en/.

2

Why Organize?

Problems and Promise in the Inner City

BARACK OBAMA

Over the past five years, I've often had a difficult time explaining my profession to folks. Typical is a remark a public school administrative aide made to me one bleak January morning, while I waited to deliver some flyers to a group of confused and angry parents who had discovered the presence of asbestos in their school.

"Listen, Obama," she began. "You're a bright young man, Obama. You went to college, didn't you?"

I nodded.

"I just cannot understand why a bright young man like you would go to college, get that degree and become a community organizer."

"Why's that?"

"Cause the pay is low, the hours is long, and don't nobody appreciate you." She shook her head in puzzlement as she wandered back to attend to her duties.

I've thought back on that conversation more than once during the time I've organized with the Developing Communities Project, based in Chicago's far south side. Unfortunately, the answers that come to mind haven't been as simple as her question. Probably the shortest one is this: It needs to be done, and not enough folks are doing it.

The debate as to how black and other dispossessed people can forward their lot in America is not new. From W.E.B. DuBois to Booker T. Washington to Marcus Garvey to Malcolm X to Martin Luther King Jr., this internal debate has raged between integration and nationalism, between accommodation and militancy, between sit-down strikes and boardroom negotiations. The lines between these strategies have never been simply drawn, and the most successful black leadership has recognized the need to bridge these seemingly divergent approaches. During the early years of the Civil Rights movement, many of these issues became submerged in the face of the clear oppression of segregation. The debate was no longer whether to protest, but how militant must that protest be to win full citizenship for blacks.

Twenty years later, the tensions between strategies have reemerged, in part due to the recognition that for all the accomplishments of the 1960s, the majority of blacks continue to suffer from second-class citizenship. Related to this are the failure—real, perceived and fabricated—of the Great Society programs initiated by Lyndon Johnson. Facing these realities, at least three major strands of earlier movements are apparent.

First, and most publicized, has been the surge of political empowerment around the country. Harold Washington and Jesse Jackson are but two striking examples of how the energy and passion of the Civil Rights movement have been channeled into bids for more traditional political power. Second, there has been a resurgence in attempts to foster economic development in the black community, whether through local entrepreneurial efforts, increased hiring of black contractors and corporate managers, or Buy Black campaigns. Third, and perhaps least publicized, has been grass-roots community organizing, which builds on indigenous leadership and direct action.

Proponents of electoral politics and economic development strategies can point to substantial accomplishments in the past 10 years. An increase in the number of black public officials offers at least the hope that government will be more responsive to inner-city constituents. Economic development programs can provide structural improvements and jobs to blighted communities.

In my view, however, neither approach offers lasting hope of real change for the inner city unless undergirded by a systematic approach to community organization. This is because the issues of the inner city are more complex and deeply rooted than ever before. Blatant discrimination has been replaced by institutional racism; problems like teen pregnancy, gang involvement and drug abuse cannot be solved by money alone. At the same time, as Professor William Julius Wilson of the University of Chicago has pointed out, the inner city's economy and its government support have declined, and middle-class blacks are leaving the neighborhoods they once helped to sustain.

Neither electoral politics nor a strategy of economic self-help and internal development can by themselves respond to these new challenges. The election of Harold Washington in Chicago or of Richard Hatcher in Gary were not enough to bring jobs to inner-city neighborhoods or cut a 50 percent drop-out rate in the schools, although they did achieve an important symbolic effect. In fact, much-needed black achievement in prominent city positions has put us in the awkward position of administering underfunded systems neither equipped nor eager to address the needs of the urban poor and being forced to compromise their interests to more powerful demands from other sectors.

Self-help strategies show similar limitations. Although both laudable and necessary, they too often ignore the fact that without a stable community, a well-educated population, an adequate infrastructure and an informed and employed market, neither new nor well-established companies will be willing to base themselves in the inner city and still compete in the international marketplace. Moreover, such approaches can and have become thinly veiled excuses for cutting back on social programs, which are anathema to a conservative agenda. In theory, community organizing provides a way to merge various strategies for neighborhood empowerment. Organizing begins with the premise that (1) the problems facing inner-city communities do not result from a lack of effective solutions, but from a lack of power to implement these solutions; (2) that the only way for communities to build long-term power is by organizing people and money around a common vision; and (3) that a viable organization can only be achieved if a broadly based indigenous leadership—and not one or two charismatic leaders—can knit together the diverse interests of their local institutions.

This means bringing together churches, block clubs, parent groups and any other institutions in a given community to pay dues, hire organizers, conduct research, develop leadership, hold rallies and education campaigns, and begin drawing up plans on a whole range of issues—jobs, education, crime, etc. Once such a vehicle is formed, it holds the power to make politicians, agencies and corporations more responsive to community needs. Equally important, it enables people to break their crippling isolation from each other, to reshape their mutual values and expectations and rediscover the possibilities of acting collaboratively—the prerequisites of any successful self-help initiative.

By using this approach, the Developing Communities Project and other organizations in Chicago's inner city have achieved some impressive results. Schools have been made more accountable; job training programs have been established; housing has been renovated and built; city services have been provided; parks have been refurbished; and crime and drug problems have been curtailed. Additionally, plain folk have been able to access the levers of power, and a sophisticated pool of local civic leadership has been developed.

But organizing the black community faces enormous problems as well. One problem is the not entirely undeserved skepticism organizers face in many communities. To a large degree, Chicago was the birthplace of community organizing, and the urban landscape is littered with the skeletons of previous efforts. Many of the best-intentioned members of the community have bitter memories of such failures and are reluctant to muster up renewed faith in the process.

A related problem involves the aforementioned exodus from the inner city of financial resources, institutions, role models and jobs. Even in areas that have not been completely devastated, most households now stay afloat with two incomes. Traditionally, community organizing has drawn support from women, who due to tradition and social discrimination had the time and the inclination to participate in what remains an essentially voluntary activity. Today the majority of women in the black community work full time, many are the sole parent, and all have to split themselves between work, raising children, running a household and maintaining some semblance of a personal life—all of which makes voluntary activities lower on the priority list. Additionally, the slow exodus of the black middle class into the suburbs means that people shop in one neighborhood, work in another, send their child to a school across town and go to church someplace other than the place where they live. Such geographical dispersion creates real problems in building a sense of investment and common purpose in any particular neighborhood.

Finally, community organizations and organizers are hampered by their own dogmas about the style and substance of organizing. Most still practice what Professor John McKnight of Northwestern University calls a "consumer advocacy" approach, with a focus on wrestling services and resources from the outside powers that be. Few are thinking of harnessing the internal productive capacities, both in terms of money and people, that already exist in communities.

Our thinking about media and public relations is equally stunted when compared to the high-powered direct mail and video approaches successfully used by conservative organizations like the Moral Majority. Most importantly, low salaries, the lack of quality training and ill-defined possibilities for advancement discourage the most talented young blacks from viewing organizing as a legitimate career option. As long as our best and brightest youth see more opportunity in climbing the corporate ladder than in building the communities from which they came, organizing will remain decidedly handicapped.

None of these problems is insurmountable. In Chicago, the Developing Communities Project and other community organizations have pooled resources to form cooperative think tanks like the Gamaliel Foundation. These provide both a formal setting where experienced organizers can rework old models to fit new realities and a healthy environment for the recruitment and training of new organizers. At the same time the leadership vacuum and disillusionment following the death of Harold Washington have made both the media and people in the neighborhoods more responsive to the new approaches community organizing can provide. Nowhere is the promise of organizing more apparent than in the traditional black churches. Possessing tremendous financial resources, membership and—most importantly—values and biblical traditions that call for empowerment and liberation, the black church is clearly a slumbering giant in the political and economic landscape of cities like Chicago. A fierce independence among black pastors and a preference for more traditional approaches to social involvement (supporting candidates for office, providing shelters for the homeless) have prevented the black church from bringing its full weight to bear on the political, social and economic arenas of the city.

Over the past few years, however, more and more young and forward-thinking pastors have begun to look at community organizations such as the Developing Communities Project in the far south side and GREAT in the Grand Boulevard area as a powerful tool for living the social gospel, one which can educate and empower entire congregations and not just serve as a platform for a few prophetic leaders. Should a mere 50 prominent black churches, out of the thousands that exist in cities like Chicago, decide to collaborate with a trained organizing staff, enormous positive changes could be wrought in the education, housing, employment and spirit of inner-city black communities, changes that would send powerful ripples throughout the city.

In the meantime, organizers will continue to build on local successes, learn from their numerous failures and recruit and train their small but growing core of leadership—mothers on welfare, postal workers, CTA drivers and school teachers, all of whom have a vision and memories of what communities can be. In fact, the answer to the original question—why organize?—resides in these people. In helping a group of housewives sit across the negotiating table with the mayor of America's third largest city and hold their own, or a retired steelworker stand before a TV camera and give voice to the dreams he has for his grandchild's future, one discovers the most significant and satisfying contribution organizing can make.

In return, organizing teaches as nothing else does the beauty and strength of everyday people. Through the songs of the church and the talk on the stoops, through the hundreds of individual stories of coming up from the South and finding any job that would pay, of raising families on threadbare budgets, of losing some children to drugs and watching others earn degrees and land jobs their parents could never aspire to—it is through these stories and songs of dashed hopes and powers of endurance, of ugliness and strife, subtlety and laughter, that organizers can shape a sense of community not only for others, but for themselves.

ACKNOWLEDGMENTS

"Why Organize? Problems and Promise in the Inner City" was first published in the August/September 1988 *Illinois Issues* (published by then–Sangamon State University, now the University of Illinois at Springfield). Reprinted with permission of the publisher.

PART TWO

Contextual Frameworks
and Approaches

O ver twenty years ago, political scientist Richard Couto (1990) pointed out that "because Americans have so little sense of community, we pay a great deal of attention to it." He suggested that "our rose-tainted view of community and the processes we describe as empowerment, community development, and community organizing" have led to considerable conceptual confusion. That confusion in turn has enabled both political liberals and conservatives to claim these concepts and to use the term grass roots "as if it were herbal medicine for current public problems and to renew American social health" (144).

The past two decades have seen increased attention to community, spurred in part by Robert Putman's (2000) lamenting of the disappearance of "civic America" with the erosion of "social capital," or mutual trust, social networks, and norms of reciprocity anchoring people within communities.

The contributors to this part attempt to move us beyond the prevailing confusion by offering conceptual frameworks and models within which community, community organizing, and community building can be better understood. Although additional perspectives on these concepts are offered throughout the book, this initial section seeks to lay a foundation for their subsequent exploration.

In chapter 3, Meredith Minkler and Nina Wallerstein offer initial definitions of *community organizing* and *community building* and underscore the centrality of the notion of empowerment to both of these processes. Introducing a theme that appears throughout much of the book, they suggest that real community organizing must begin with a group or community's identification of its issues and goals, rather than with the goals or concerns of a health department, social service organization, or outside organizer or funder.

Following a brief historical overview, Minkler and Wallerstein introduce the best-known typology of community organizing and intervention, developed by Jack Rothman (2008) and evolving into its current form to emphasize three primary modes: community capacity development, social planning and policy, and social advocacy. Alternative and complementary models also are explored, including collaborative empowerment, community building, and both feminist organizing and organizing with and by people of color (Hyde 2005; Gutierrez and Lewis, chapter 12).

The heart of this chapter is the discussion of several key concepts in community organizing and community building central to effecting change on the community level. Empowerment and critical consciousness, community capacity and social capital, the principles of participation and "starting where the people are," and issue selection are each examined briefly, as is the often neglected area of measurement and evaluation in community building and organizing. Although this chapter covers a wide terrain, it necessarily does so "once over lightly," as a prelude to the more in-depth discussion of many of the issues and topics raised in subsequent chapters.

The next two chapters in this part each look in more detail at several of the major approaches to community organizing and community building practice introduced in chapter 3. Marty Martinson and Celina Su begin in chapter 4 by introducing the philosophy and approach of two of the individuals whose contributions to our thinking and practice in these areas have been among the most profound: Saul David Alinsky (1972), the "father" of social action organizing, and adult educator Paulo Freire (1973, 1994), whose "education for critical consciousness" has been seminal for many in the way we think about community practice and transformative change processes. Martinson and Su begin by situating the thinking and actions of these key figures in their personal biographies and go on to lay out Alinsky's vision and approach using vivid case examples to illuminate its classic and more contemporary applications. In so doing, they also point up the continued substantive role the Alinsky approach plays in both local organizing and the development of broader social movements in the early years of the twenty-first century.

With a few notable exceptions (see Su 2009) textbooks on community organizing seldom give more than passing mention to Freire's approach and its potential and actual applications in community building and community organizing. Chapter 4 highlights several concrete applications of Freire's pedagogy and its application in addressing community concerns regarding education in the Bronx, New York, and an innovative social action program with adolescents in Albuquerque, New Mexico. In each of these case studies, an emphasis on equality and mutual respect between group members and facilitators, and the use of problem-posing dialogue and "action based on critical reflection," Freire's approach takes traditional community organizing in important new directions. It further complements and extends the approaches to community building described by McKnight and Kretzmann (chapter 10) Walter and Hyde (chapter 5), and others whose work is highlighted in this text.

Although a number of promising applications of the Freirian approach now can be found in health education, social work, education, community psychology and related fields (Carroll and Minkler 2000; Foster-Fishman et al. 2005; Wallerstein et al. 2005; Wilson et al. 2007), Martinson and Su focus on three examples that well illuminate the contrasts between Alinsky and Freire-inspired community organizing, as well as the different and shared challenges they may involve.

We conclude this part with new thinking about community building practice by social work theorists and activists Cheryl Walter and Cheryl Hyde. Whereas many popular writings on community organizing and other forms of community practice offer "strategic frameworks" to guide our actions (cf. Homan 2011; Rothman 2007, 2008; Staples 2004 and chapter 11), chapter 5 offers instead an orientation to practice, and to community, that sees the latter as a dynamic and complex system of which we as practitioners are a part. It views our role not as solving discrete problems, but rather as building community capacities. Walter and Hyde also explore in more depth the notion of community itself, highlighting seminal work by Ronald Warren (1978) and others, and showing how contemporary scholarship on social capital builds on and extends these early conceptualizations. Finally, chapter 5 helps us dig deeper into the meaning and complexity of community building practice using the example of a largely white, middle-class feminist health center and the self-reflection and subsequent changes its staff must put into place to better connect with the broader and more diverse geographic and cultural community of which it also is a part.

The approach to community building offered by Walter and Hyde differs from that of many in its emphasis on the professional as part of community rather than an outsider. As noted in chapter 1, it also differs in important ways from the more macro approach to community building captured in the principles laid out by Angela Glover Blackwell and Ray Colmenar in appendix 1. Yet the skills for community building practice that Walter and Hyde elaborate, including awareness of the dynamic quality of community and an accent on consciousness, have great relevance for health educators, social workers, community psychologists, urban planners, and other social change professionals who work on the community level. Their conceptualization of community building presents an important new way of thinking about our roles in community and both complements and challenges more traditional approaches offered elsewhere in this volume.

REFERENCES

Alinsky, S.D. 1972. *Rules for Radicals: A Pragmatic Primer for Realistic Radicals*. New York: Vintage Books.

Carroll, J., and M. Minkler. 2000. "Freire's Message for Social Workers: Looking Back, Looking Ahead." *Journal of Community Practice* 8, no. 1:21-36.

Couto, R. A. 1990. "Promoting Health at the Grass Roots." *Health Affairs* 9, no. 2:144-151.

Foster-Fishman, P., B. Nowell, Z. Deacon, M. A. Nievar, and P. McCann. 2005. "Using Methods That Matter: The Impact of Reflection, Dialogue, and Voice." *American Journal of Community Psychology* 36, nos. 3/4:275-291.

Freire, P. 1973. *Education for Critical Consciousness*. New York: Seabury Press.

———. 1994. *Pedagogy of Hope*. New York: Continuum.

Homan, M. 2011. *Promoting Community Change: Making It Happen in The Real World*. 5th ed. Pacific Grove, Calif.: Brooks/Cole.

Hyde, C. A. 2005. "Feminist Community Practice." In *Handbook on Community Practice*, edited by M. Weil, 360-371. Newbury Park: Sage.

Rothman, J. 2007. "Multi Modes of Intervention at the Macro Level." *Journal of Community Practice* 15, no. 4:11-40.

———. 2008. "Multi Modes of Community Intervention." *Strategies of Community Intervention*, edited by J. Rothman, J. L. Erlich, and J. E. Tropman, 141-170. 7th ed. Peosta, Iowa: Eddie Bowers.

Staples, L. 2004. *Roots to Power*. 2nd ed. Westport, Conn.: Praeger.

Su, C. 2009. *Streetwise for Book Smarts: Grassroots Organizing and Education Reform in the Bronx*. Ithaca, N.Y.: Cornell University Press.

Wallerstein, N., V. Sanchez, and L. Velarde. 2005. "Freirian Praxis in Health Education and Community Organizing: A Case Study of an Adolescent Prevention Program." In *Community Organizing and Community Building for Health*, edited by M. Minkler, 218-236. 2nd ed. New Brunswick, N.J.: Rutgers University Press.

Warren, R. L. 1978. *The Community in America*. Chicago: Rand McNally.

Wilson, N., M. Minkler, S. Dasho, N. Wallerstein, and A. Martin. 2007. "Getting to Social Action: The Youth Empowerment Strategies (YES!) Project." *Health Promotion Practice* 14, no. 1:201-217.

3

Improving Health through Community Organization and Community Building

Perspectives from Health Education and Social Work

MEREDITH MINKLER
NINA WALLERSTEIN

Although health education and social work professionals have developed and adapted numerous approaches and change strategies in recent years, the principles and methods loosely referred to as community organizing remain a central method of practice. We define community organizing as the process by which community groups are helped to identify common problems or change targets, mobilize resources, and develop and implement strategies to reach their collective goals. The newer and related concept of community building is viewed here not so much as a "strategic framework" as an *orientation to community* through which people who identify as members engage together in building community capacity rather than "fixing problems" through the application of specific and externally driven strategies (see chapter 5).[1]

Implicit in both these definitions is the concept of empowerment, classically defined by Rappaport (1984) as an enabling process through which individuals or communities take control over their lives and environments. Indeed, we argue that without empowerment that enhances community competence or problem-solving ability, community organizing is not taking place.

Strict definitions of *community organization* suggest that the needs or problems should be identified by groups within the community, and not by an outside organization or change agent. Thus, while a public health or social work professional may help mobilize a community around HIV/AIDS prevention or access to mental health services, he or she can't be said to be doing community organizing in the pure sense unless the community itself has identified this as a key area for organizing (see chapter 7).

Community organization is important in fields like health education and social work partially because it reflects one of their fundamental principles, that of "starting where the people are" (Nyswander 1956). The public health professional, social worker, or urban and regional planner who begins with the community's felt needs will more likely be successful in the change process, and in fostering true community ownership of programs and actions. Community organizing also is important in light of evidence that social participation itself can be significant in improving perceived control, empowerment, individual coping capacity, health behaviors, and health status (Marmot 2009; Kegler et al. 2009; Wallerstein 2006). Finally, the heavy accent being placed on community partnerships, coalitions, and community-based health initiatives by government agencies, philanthropic organizations, and nongovernmental organizations (NGOs) both in North America and globally (Corburn 2009; Diers 2006; Fawcett et al. 2010; USDHHS 2011) suggests the need for further refining theory, methods, and measurement techniques.

Following a brief historical grounding, the chapter covers concepts of community, community organization and community building models, and several key theories and topical areas in these fields, each of which will be explored more deeply in later chapters.

Community Organization and Community Building in Historical Perspective

The term *community organization* was coined by American social workers in the late 1800s in reference to their efforts to coordinate services for newly arrived immigrants and the poor. Yet as Garvin and Cox (2001) pointed out, although community organization is often seen as the offspring of the settlement house movement, several important milestones should by rights be included in any history. Prominent are (1) African American efforts in the post-Reconstruction period to salvage newly won rights that were rapidly slipping away; (2) the Populist movement, which began as an agrarian revolution and became a multisectoral coalition and a major political force; and (3) the labor movement of the 1930s and 1940s, which taught the value of forming coalitions around issues, the importance of full-time professional organizers, and the use of conflict as a means of bringing about change (Garvin and Cox 2001).

Within the field of social work, early approaches to community organization stressed collaboration and consensus as communities were helped to self-identify and to increase their problem-solving ability (DeFilippis et al. 2010; Garvin and Cox 2001). By the 1950s, however, a new brand of community organization was gaining popularity that stressed confrontation and conflict strategies for social change. Most closely identified with Saul Alinsky (1969, 1972), social action organizing emphasized redressing power imbalances by creating dissatisfaction with the status quo among the disenfranchised, building community-wide identification, and helping members devise winnable goals and nonviolent conflict strategies as a means to bring about change (Miller 2009; Rothman 2008; see chapter 4).

From the late 1950s on, strategies and tactics of community organization were increasingly applied to broader social change objectives, through the civil rights movement, followed by the women's movement, LGBT (lesbian, gay, bisexual, and transgender) organizing, disability rights work, and antiwar organizing and more recently efforts to achieve marriage equality, the rights of immigrants, and environmental and climate justice, to name but a few. As discussed in chapter 1, however, co-optation of Alinsky and other sources of social action–organizing strategies have facilitated causes that may be antithetical to the public's health and well-being (Daniels 2009; Vogel 2010). Widespread use of the Internet also has increased dramatically, with groups across the political spectrum going online to build community and identify and organize supporters on a mass scale (Vogel 2010; see chapter 15). Additionally, and while originating as a philosophy and approach to adult literacy for transformative social change, the popular education approach developed by Brazilian adult educator Paulo Freire in the early 1970s quickly gained traction both in low-resource countries and in the United States and other advanced industrialized nations as a potent new method in community organizing in social work, health education, literacy, and other areas (Carroll and Minkler 2000; Su 2009; Wallerstein and Auerbach 2004; see chapter 4).

In the health field, a major emphasis on community participation began in the 1970s and led to the World Health Organization's adoption in 1986 of a new approach to health promotion that stressed increasing people's control over the determinants of their health, high-level public participation, and intersectoral cooperation (WHO 1986). Reflecting this new approach, the global Healthy Cities movement promotes sustainable environments and processes through which governmental organizations and NGOs create healthy public policies, achieve high-level participation in community-driven projects, and, ultimately, reduce inequities between groups (Corburn 2009; O'Neill and Simard 2006).

Alongside these developments, an appreciation for *community building* has grown, conceptualized as an orientation that emphasizes community assets and shared identity, whether or not task-oriented organizing takes place (see chapter 5 and appendix 1; Chávez et al. 2010; Rothman 2007, 2008). Community building is reflected in efforts such as the National Black Women's Health Imperative (formerly the Black Women's Health Project) (www.blackwomenshealth.org), an organization that for close to three decades has emphasized "harnessing the collective power of black women" by bringing individuals and organizations together around a common agenda. Using advocacy, leadership training, and education of black women and girls through local efforts, including multicity Walking for Wellness events, a Leadership Development Institute, policy briefings, and other activities, the organization also melds community building with community organizing methods to improve black women's health. Such community building projects are strength based and borrow, from feminist organizing, an accent on the integration, through dialogue, of personal and political experiences (Frisby et al. 2009; Hyde 2005).

Finally, a growing interest in community-based participatory research in health, social work, urban planning, and related fields has brought community organizing principles into the domain of research, challenging more traditional "outside expert"–driven approaches to "equitably" engage community partners throughout the research process, build local capacity, and "balance research and action" (Israel et al. 2008; Cargo and Mercer 2008; Minkler 2005a; Minkler and Wallerstein 2008; Wing et al. 2008).

The Concept of Community

Integral to a discussion of community organization and community building is an examination of the concept of *community*. While typically thought of in geographic terms, communities may also be based on shared interests or characteristics such as race/ethnicity, sexual orientation, or occupation (Fellin 2001; Rothman 2007, 2008). Historically, communities have been defined as (1) *functional spatial units* meeting basic needs for sustenance; (2) *units of patterned social interaction*; or (3) symbolic units of collective identity (Hunter 1975). Eng and Parker (1994) added a fourth definition, in which community is a social unit where people come together politically to make change.

Two sets of theories are relevant to understanding the concept of community. The first, the *ecological system perspective*, is particularly useful in the study of autonomous geographic communities, focusing as it does on population characteristics, such as size, density and heterogeneity, the physical environment, the social organization of the community, and the technological forces affecting it. In contrast, the *social systems perspective*, classically articulated by Warren (1963) focuses primarily on formal and informal organizations that operate dynamically within a given community, exploring the interactions of community subsystems (economic, political, etc.) both horizontally within the community and vertically, as they relate to other systems of power (Fellin 2001; DeFilippis et al., 2010).

Clearly, a person's perspective on community influences his or her view of the appropriate domains and functions of the community organization process. Community development specialists (for example, agricultural extension workers and Peace Corps volunteers) have focused on *geographic communities*. In contrast, proponents of a broader social action approach (Alinsky 1972; Miller 2009; Sen 2003), have encouraged organizing around *issues* such as public housing and unemployment, in recognition of the tremendous impact of those larger socioeconomic issues on local communities. Finally, as Chávez and colleagues (2010) and others (Bankhead and Erlich 2008; Gutiérrez and Lewis, chapter 12, this volume) have suggested, an appreciation of the history of particular societal oppressions and modes of survival within communities of color should be a major consideration. In African American communities, for example, West (1993) has argued that market exploitation led to a shattering of religious and civic organizations that had historically buffered these communities from hopelessness and nihilism. He called for community change through re-creating a sense of agency and political resistance based on "subversive memory—the best of one's past without romantic nostalgia" (19). Likewise, in American Indian communities today, there is a burgeoning cultural renewal movement that embraces organizing and healing from intergenerational historical traumas that were wrought by the dominant society (Walters and Simoni 2002; Walters et al. 2011). A view of community that incorporates such a perspective would support building on preexisting social networks and strengths, emphasizing self-determination and empowerment (see chapter 12). The different models of community organization and community building described in this and subsequent chapters and appendixes illustrate how alternative assumptions about the nature and meaning of community heavily shape our conceptualization and practice.

Models of Community Organization

While community organizing frequently is treated as though it were a single model of practice, several different typologies have been developed. The best known was developed by renowned social work and community organization theorist Jack Rothman (2001) and consists of three distinct but overlapping models of practice. The language and sophistication of these concepts, originally described as *locality development*, *social planning*, and *social action*, have recently been broadened (Rothman 2007, 2008). *Community capacity development* stresses consensus and cooperation as an organizing approach and building group identity and problem-solving ability as key goals. This revised nomenclature avoids a narrower geographic focus implied by *locality development* and strongly incorporates the community building notion. *Social planning and policy* stresses the use of data and rational-empirical problem solving, while also making room for new approaches, including participatory planning and policy development, in keeping with the spirit of true community organizing than the earlier term *social planning*. Finally, the third category, *social advocacy*, like its predecessor, *social action*, emphasizes the use of pressure tactics, including confrontation, to help bring about concrete changes to redress power imbalances, and is more in keeping with social change tactics and strategies used in the early twenty-first century (Rothman 2007, 2008). As discussed in subsequent chapters, these include both neighborhood actions and far larger efforts, often aided by Internet organizing, to foster national and even global change efforts, like refugee relief and climate change, or actions involving in which identity based on race/ethnicity or sexual orientation (e.g., legalizing gay marriage).

Rothman originally presented the models as three ideal types, but with some mixing among them. There might be a given form of mixing at the outset and then different combinations as conditions change over time. Rothman's later work elaborated and detailed the mixed forms, highlighting a *predominant mode* and two other *composite modes*, one or both of which can be included in a piece of action (e.g., community capacity development that combines with social advocacy to stress identity activism) (Rothman 2007, 2008). Feminist community organizing, for example, may combine the goals and assumptions of social advocacy organizing with methods that often are consistent with community capacity development (Hyde 2005, 2008; Rothman 2007). Similarly, the Healthy Heartlands Initiative, across five midwestern states, combines faith-based community capacity development, planning and policy (or "setting the table with technical experts"), and social advocacy toward legislators and other key players to promote racial and health equity (Ayers 2010; see also chapter 20).

Alternative models of community capacity development also have been proposed, including Gardner's (1991) classic approach to building community, Himmelman's (2001) "collaborative empowerment," Wolff's (2010) approach to building healthy communities through collaborative engagement, and Walter and Hyde's community building approach (see chapter 5). These models can be seen partially as descendants of the community development model in their emphases on self-help and collaboration, yet they extend beyond community development, which is often externally driven and may implicitly accept the status quo. They take their parentage, rather, from community-driven development, where community concerns lead the organizing in a process that creates healthy and more equal power relations (Hyde 2005, 2008; see also chapter 6). (See figure 3.1).

These community building models emphasize community strengths, not as yearning for the good old days but as a diversity of groups and systems that identify and nurture shared values and goals. Himmelman's (2001) "collaborative empowerment model" and Wolff's (2010) principles for building healthy communities, for example, include many of the steps from traditional organizing (e.g., clarifying a community's purpose and vision and building a community's power base), but put their heaviest accent on enabling communities to play the lead, so that real empowerment, rather than merely "community betterment," is achieved. McKnight's (1995) notion of "regenerating community" (161) has at its heart enabling people to recognize and contribute their "gifts," which represent the building blocks or assets of a community enabling it to care for its members.

Along similar lines, Walter and Hyde's (chapter 5) community building approach describes community building practice as a way of orienting one's self in community that places "community, not the community or the community organizer . . . at the center of practice" and theory. Their approach is rooted in an understanding of community as "an inclusive, multidimensional, and dynamic system, of which we, as practitioners, are a part." As noted above, this approach stresses building capacity over outside expert–driven problem solving.

While placing a similarly strong emphasis on identifying and promoting community strengths, a macroconceptualization of community building also emphasizes regional economic development and federal and state policy-level reinvestment in local communities as critical (Blackwell and Colmenar 2000; Pastor et al. 2009; see appendix 1).

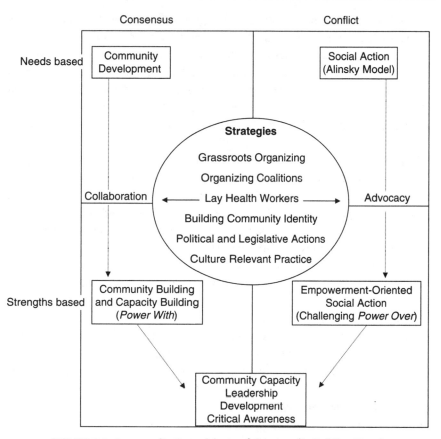

FIGURE 3.1 Community Organizing and Community Building Typology

Lying midway between the older community organizing models and newer conceptualizations of community building are models incorporating elements of each, such as "feminist organizing" (Hyde 2005, 2008). As Hyde (2005) and others point out, feminist organizing need not address "quintessentially feminist issues" such as gender-based violence or pay equity; rather, "it is the empowering aspects of such endeavors that render them feminist" (361). In Stall and Stoeker's view (2005) in a "women-centered" model, "power begins in the private sphere of social relationships" but once again, the goal of their organizing approach is empowerment, or "the cultivation of individual and collective skills and resources for social and political action" (203).

As noted in Chapter 1 and discussed in more detail in Chapter 8, there is an increasing accent on "cultural humility" in community organizing and community building. Described by Tervalon and Garcia (1998), not as an end point but as an openness to others' cultures and an ability to listen to our own internal dialogue, this concept is well captured in the organizing and strength-based work of organizations like the Prevention Institute, based in Oakland, California (Chávez et al. 2010). Finally, the coalition-building model and related collaborative approaches are alternately defined as examples of community organization practice or as strategies used across models. Coalitions and regional collaboratives are increasingly popular in diverse areas of health, social work, and urban and regional planning, including asthma management and prevention; homelessness, violence, and obesity prevention; and health-focused land use planning (see Lamb et al. 2011; Zakocs and Edwards 2006; Butterfoss 2007; see chapters 17, 18, and 20).

In sum, several models of community organizing and community building have surfaced within the past two decades to complement earlier organizing approaches. In figure 3.1, we integrate new perspectives and older models, presenting a typology that incorporates both needs- and strengths-based approaches. Along the needs-based axis, "community development," as primarily a consensus model, is contrasted with Alinsky's "social action" conflict-based model. The newer strengths-based models contrast a community building capacity approach with a more task-focused social action approach. When we look at primary strategies, we see that consensus approaches, whether needs based or strengths based, primarily use collaboration strategies, whereas conflict approaches use advocacy strategies and ally building to support advocacy efforts. Several concepts span these two strengths-based approaches, such as community competence, leadership development, and the multiple perspectives on gaining power. Again, as with the Rothman model, many organizing efforts use a combination of these strategies at different times throughout the life of an organizing campaign and community building process.

Concepts in Community Organization and Community Building Practice

While no single unified model of community organization or community building exists, several key concepts are central to these efforts: empowerment and critical consciousness, community capacity, issue selection, and the evaluation and measurement issues, presented below and summarized in table 3.1.

Empowerment and Critical Consciousness

While the term *empowerment* has been justifiably criticized as a "catchall phrase" in social science (Rappaport 1984), it represents a central tenet of community organization and community building practice. Within public health, empowerment or community empowerment have been variously defined, from communities achieving equity (Marmot et al. 2008) or having the capacity to identify problems and solutions (Goodman et al. 1999) to participatory self-competence in the political life of the community (Wandersman and Florin 2000) to the "expansion of assets and capabilities of people to participate in, negotiate with, influence, control, and hold accountable institutions that affect their lives" (Narayan 2002, xviii).

TABLE 3.1.

Key Concepts in Community Organizing and Community Building

Concept	Definition	Application
Empowerment	Social action process for people to gain mastery over their lives and the lives of their communities	Community members assume greater power or expand their power from within to create desired changes
Critical consciousness	A consciousness based on reflection and action in making change	Engage people in dialogue that links root causes and community actions
Community capacity	Community characteristics affecting its ability to identify, mobilize, and address problems	Community members participate actively in the life of their community through leadership, social networks, and access to power
Issue selection	Identifying winnable and specific targets of change that unify and build community strength	Identify issues through community participation; decide targets as part of a larger strategy
Participation and relevance	Community organizing should "start where the people are" and engage community members as equals	Community members create their own agenda based on felt needs, shared power, and awareness of resources

In these definitions, empowerment is an action-oriented concept with a focus on removing barriers and transforming power relations between communities, institutions, and public agencies. It assumes that community cultural strengths and assets can be strengthened. The dialogue process of Paulo Freire (1970), with its accent on critical consciousness, or action based on critical reflection through dialogue, is central, as is the understanding that empowerment is exercised in multiple domains, from personal through political and collective action (Laverack 2004; Narayan 2002; Su 2009; Wallerstein 2006).

Bearing this in mind, a broader definition is most useful—one that considers empowerment a social action process by which individuals, communities, and organizations gain mastery over their lives in the context of changing their social and political environment to improve equity and quality of life (Wallerstein 1992, 2006).

As a theory and methodology, community empowerment is multilayered, representing both processes and outcomes of change for individuals, the organizations of which they are a part, and the community social structure itself (Zimmerman 2000). "Psychological empowerment" includes people's perceived control in their lives, their critical awareness of their social context, and their political efficacy and participation in change (Peterson et al. 2006). Empowerment challenges the perceived or real "powerlessness" that comes from the injuries of poverty, chronic stressors, lack of control, and insufficient resources to meet demands, or what Syme (2004) has termed lack of "control over destiny."

Organizational empowerment incorporates both *processes* of organizations (e.g., whether they are acting to influence societal change) and *outcomes*, such as their effectiveness in gaining new resources (Hughey et al. 2008). At the community level, community empowerment outcomes can include increased sense of community; more civic engagement; and actual changes in policies, transformed conditions, or increased resources that may reduce inequities (Wallerstein 2006). As communities become empowered and better able to engage in collective problem solving, key health and social indicators may reflect this with rates of alcoholism, divorce, suicide, and other social problems beginning to decline. Moreover, the empowered community that effectively works for change can bring about changes in some of the very problems that contributed to its ill health in the first place (Minkler 2005b).

Community Capacity, Social Capital, and Social Networks

Closely related to the concept of empowerment is the notion of *community capacity*, defined as "the characteristics of communities that affect their ability to identify, mobilize, and address social and public health problems" (Goodman et al. 1999, 259). Community capacity has been articulated as having multiple dimensions: active participation, leadership, rich support networks, skills and resources, critical reflection, sense of community, understanding of history, articulation of values, and access to power (Goodman et al. 1999, Goodman 2009; Lempa et al. 2008). As McCloskey and her colleagues (2011) point out, "When carried out with context in mind, capacity building is an integral part of community engagement efforts, necessary for challenging power imbalances and effectively addressing problems" (15).

Definitions of *community capacity* have drawn from related concepts, such as *community competence* and *social capital*. *Community competence* originally was defined by community psychologist Cottrell (1983) as "the various component parts of the community being able to collaborate effectively on identifying the problems and needs of the community; to achieve a working consensus on goals and priorities; to agree on ways and means to implement the agreed upon goals; to collaborate effectively in the required actions."

From its origins in political science (Putnam 2000; Skocpol 2003), social capital has been embraced in public health, social welfare, and planning, as the features of social organization that facilitate coordination and cooperation for mutual benefit. Within epidemiology, social capital has been correlated with poor health status (Kawachi et al. 2008) and has been operationalized as a horizontal relationship between community members, with variables of trust, reciprocity, and civic engagement as well as a vertical linking relationship with external communities and people in positions of power (Kawachi et al., 2008; Cockerham 2007; Szreter and Woolcock 2004). While an important descriptor of community well-being, social capital itself is *not* a strategy, and requires community organizing and capacity-building approaches in order to strengthen social capital outcomes.

Social networks, or the relationships in which people are embedded, and the social support they give and receive through these networks, are important to consider within the context of community capacity building (Berkman 2000; Fowler and Christakis 2008). Social network–mapping techniques, for example, may be employed to help identify natural helpers or leaders within a community, help these natural leaders in turn identify their own networks, identify high-risk groups within the community, and involve network members in undertaking their own community assessment and actions necessary to strengthen networks within the community (Amsden and VanWynsberghe 2005; Eng et al. 2009; McKnight and Kretzmann 1992; see chapters 9 and 10). Finally, leadership development represents a key aspect of fostering community capacity. In particular, development of leaders able to stimulate people to be self-reflective, to think critically and across differences, identifying problems and potential solutions outside their comfort zones, is critical (Jones et al. 2010; Brown and Mazza 2005; Lasker and Guidry 2009).

As Gutiérrez and Lewis (chapter 12) suggest, an emphasis on leadership development may be especially important in communities of color where "a unidirectional outreach approach" often treats such communities as "targets of change rather than active participants and collaborators." Further, and in the diverse communities in which many of us live, work and play, and age, leadership requires "reclaiming courage," embodied in the "strong early voices" that often are silenced in polite adult society (Browne and Mazza 2005, 62–63).

Lay health worker strategies have been key for promoting community empowerment, capacity, community competence, social capital, and community leadership, especially if they emphasize transformations in the lay health workers themselves, changes in clinical and community practices, instead of only their impact on clients (Eng et al. 2009; Nemcek and Sabatier 2003).

Issue Selection, Participation, and Relevance

One of the most important steps in community organization practice involves effective differentiation between *problems*, or things that are troubling, and *issues* the community feels strongly about (Miller 2009). As Alinsky (1972), Miller (2009), and Staples (2004) suggest, a good issue must be winnable, be simple and specific, unite members of the group, and involve them in a meaningful way in achieving problem resolution. It should affect many people and build up the community or organization (giving leadership experience, increased visibility, etc.). Last, it should be part of a larger plan or strategy (see chapters 4 and 11).

Community groups can use a variety of methods to obtain data for issue selection, including analysis of available secondary data; and face-to-face processes, such as focus groups, door-to-door surveys, town halls, and others, which assess felt needs, increase sense of participation, and ensure relevance to the community (see chapter 11). The DataCenter in Oakland, California, has promoted trainings to democratize research and extend the type of information residents can collect to better understand their communities, from available secondary data to perceptions of spiritual/cultural relevance (http://www.datacenter.org/). Each of these methods, whether in virtual communities or online, are useful, however, only to the extent that they enable the discovery of the real issues of concern to the community.

Community organizers also have adopted strategies from organizational development in creating strategic action plans to prioritize issues by available resources, appropriate timelines, and barriers to reaching goals (VeneKlasen and Miller 2002). Politically minded organizers have included an analysis of the power brokers, allies, and resisters in choosing an issue that may be feasible to win (Themba 1999; Ritas et al. 2008; see chapter 20).

Thoughtfully undertaken, and with a strong accent on participation and relevance, issue selection processes can contribute to community empowerment and serve as a positive force for social change. They further can build community research capacity along with leadership development, critical for building strong and sustainable organizations and coalitions (Lasker and Guidry 2009; Weiss 2003; Wolff 2010; www.datacenter.org). Visual technologies, such as photovoice (Wang and Burris 1997) and the newer related videovoice approach (Catalani et al. 2012; chapter 16), combine issue selection with a positive emphasis on community strengths and assets to educate and stimulate change (see chapter 16); these too are proving increasingly popular for issue selection and subsequent analysis and action.

As noted in chapter 1, a major new contributor to community organizing and community building in the early twenty-first century involves the power of the Internet for data collection, issue selection, assessing allies and opposition, and numerous other facets of the work (Lee 2011; Fawcett et al. 2003a). As discussed in chapter 15, in addition to providing seemingly limitless access to data about public health issues and concerns, the Internet can provide a plethora of tools for assessing communities and their needs and strengths and engaging in many other key stages of community building and advocacy. The Community Tool Box (http://ctb.ku.edu/), for example, offers thousands of pages on topics that include assessing community needs and resources, creating and maintaining coalitions, influencing policy development, and evaluating and sustaining the work. Through hands-on tools and case studies, the site both supports online organizers and provides assistance with community building and advocacy in the real world offline.

The particular value of the Internet for community assessment and subsequent organizing and community building in and with groups that may be geographically dispersed or otherwise marginalized or hard to reach should be underscored (see chapter 15). Residents of rural areas; people with disabilities; family caregivers; lesbian, gay, bisexual, or transgender (LGBT) youth; and Native Americans in hundreds of different tribes (Jones et al. 2008) who nevertheless share some critical issues are among the communities for whom online organizing or community building, with opportunities to share success stories, concerns, and emerging best practices, may be particularly well suited; and these sites are growing (see, for example, http://www.messageinabox.tacticaltech .org/bloggingcasestudies).

Finally, and as discussed in chapter 15, websites and resources for professionals in health promotion and related fields (e.g., Community Campus Partnerships for Health [www.ccph/info.org]) provide a wealth of resources and tools for collaborative assessment and issue selection, as well as subsequent stages in community organizing and community building.

Measurement and Evaluation Issues

A challenge for many community organizing and community building efforts has been the difficulty of adequately addressing evaluation processes and outcomes, partially due to funding constraints, lack of knowledge about how to build meaningful evaluation into organizing efforts, and difficulty determining appropriate outcomes. The continually evolving nature of community organizing and related community-based initiatives, complex and dynamic contexts, and the fact that these projects often seek change on multiple levels further make many traditional evaluative approaches ill suited to such organizing endeavors (Connell et al. 1995; Fetterman and Wandersman 2005; Springett and Wallerstein 2008; see chapter 19). Finally, the focus of many standard evaluation approaches on long-term change in health and social indicators may miss the shorter-term system-level impacts with which community organizing is heavily concerned, such as improvements in organizational collaboration, community capacity, and healthier public policies or environmental conditions (Fawcett et al. 2003a; Springett and Wallerstein 2008).

With some notable exceptions (cf. Alliance for Social Justice 2010; Minkler 2005a), the lack of formal evaluations of most community organizing efforts, coupled with the fact that many who are engaged in these projects lack the time and resources needed to write up and publish their results, have made it difficult to amass a literature of "successful" and "unsuccessful" organizing efforts, and the hallmarks of each, critical parts of building evidence for the field. Although many characteristics of successful community collaborations have been identified— such as shared vision, strong leadership, skills in building alliances across differences, and a focus on process and not merely task achievement (Butterfoss 2007; Chavez et al. 2010; Lasker and Guidry 2009; Wolff 2010; Zakocs and Edwards 2006)—much remains to be examined and assessed. Careful evaluation and documentation of both successful and unsuccessful community organizing projects must be a vital part of this new database.

A growing number of new tools and resources exist for professionals inter-ested in evaluating community organizing, coalitions, and related efforts. Key among them are Foster and Louie's (2010) summary of tools for measuring community organizing, the Public Health Agency of Canada's *Community Capacity Building Tool* (Maclellan-Wright et al. 2007); Butterfoss and Kegler's community coalition action model (Butterfoss 2007; see chapter 17) and Wolff's *The Power of Collaborative Solutions* (2010) (see also Granner and Sharpe 2004; Mattessich et al. 2001; Mizrahi and Rosenthal 2008; Zakocs and Edwards 2006; appendix 5).

Similarly, both newer and time-tested approaches to understanding and measuring community empowerment and multilevel perceived control (Israel et al. 1994 and appendix 10; Narayan 2002; Wallerstein 2006; Zimmerman 2000); community capacity and competence (Eng and Parker 1994; MacLellan-Wright et al. 2007); and civic engagement and social capital (Kawachi et al. 2008) are increasingly being used in efforts to better assess these critical aspects of community organizing and related work.

Despite advances in measurement for capturing these kinds of changes, how-ever, there are limits to any tool or set of scales. Self-report measures of individu-als cannot capture the full organizational and community-level processes over time. Qualitative approaches are needed to enhance understanding of the context; dynamics of change; and outcomes such as transformed conditions, new policies, participation, and political voice.

Equally important to the development of validated scales may be the process by which communities develop their own sets of capacity and empowerment indicators. Sample indicators of capacity and sustainability for communities or partnerships may be found in both classic early pieces (e.g., Connell et al. 1995; Norris 1997; Maltrud et al. 1997; Wallerstein et al. 2002) and newer metrics focusing on changes in community processes, such as grassroots participation, and in short-term systems-level outcomes, such as the development of new programs and capacity, as a result of the organizing or initiative experience (cf. Brown and Mazza 2005; Israel et al. 2005; Maclellan-Wright et al. 2007; Wolff 2010). The Pan American Health Organization's (2005) participatory evaluation handbook for healthy municipalities, which contains both a participatory cycle of gathering evidence and recommendations on multilevel indicators and outcomes, also is helpful in this regard. As noted above, it is these middle-level outcomes, rather than long-term changes in self-rated health and other health or social indicators, that are often most important in documenting changes in community capacity and empowerment.

Another major contribution to the literature in this area may be found in the domain of empowerment evaluation (Fetterman, 1996; Fetterman and Wandersman 2005), defined as "an interactive and iterative process by which the community, in collaboration with the support team, identifies its own health issues, decides how to address them, monitors progress toward its goals and uses the information to adapt and sustain the initiative" (Fawcett et al. 1996, 169).

Fawcett and his colleagues (1997, 2001, 2003b) have helped tailor empowerment evaluation methods more directly to the evaluation of community coalitions for health and related organizing efforts. Their Community Tool Box website (http://ctb.ku.edu/) discussed above, is being widely used to foster more rigorous and empowering approaches to such evaluation.

Finally, the development of new participatory evaluation approaches for community-based participatory research in programs addressing cancer disparities (Scarinci et al. 2009), health and safety among immigrant workers (see chapter 14), youth engagement (Foster-Fishman et al. 2005), guidelines for measuring partnership effectiveness (Israel et al. 2005; Mercer et al. 2008), and models for exploring the pathways from process to outcomes in this work (Wallerstein et al. 2008) may provide important perspectives and tools for those wishing to undertake participatory evaluation of community organizing and community building efforts.

The availability of new theoretical contributions and practical tools that lend themselves to evaluation of community organizing unfortunately does not solve the problem of insufficient funding and/or commitment to carrying out high-quality evaluative research. Yet the increased attention of both foundation and government funders to evaluation and measurement issues in community organizing and community-based initiatives is encouraging. If translated into increased funding, this increased attention, together with the availability of new measurement tools and processes, should help spur major advances in the evaluation and documentation of community organizing and community building.

Summary

The continued pivotal role of community organization in health education and social work practice reflects both this approach's time-tested efficacy and its fit with the most fundamental principles of these fields. Community organization thus stresses strengths-based approaches; the principle of relevance, or starting where the people are; the principle of participatory issue selection and choice of actions; and the importance of creating environments in which individuals and communities can become empowered as they increase their community capacity or problem-solving ability.

Similarly, newer conceptualizations of community building stress many of the same principles, within an overall approach that focuses on community growth and change from the inside, through increased group identification; discovery, nurturing, and mapping of community assets; and creation of "critical consciousness," all toward the end of building stronger and more caring communities. Finally, new tools and approaches, including the power of the Internet for facilitating community organizing and community building, have greatly increased the reach of these methods over the past decade.

Whether engaged in "pure" community-driven organizing around issues the community identifies or borrowing skills from community organizing and community building practice, professionals in fields like public health, social work, and planning can challenge themselves to examine their own dynamic of power, with their professional colleagues and community members, to understand the complexities of working in partnership toward the goals of community ownership and empowerment (Wallerstein 1999; see appendix 3). In sum, both community organizing and community building practice bring essential strategies in a wide variety of community and organizational settings and may hold particular relevance in the changing sociopolitical climate of the twenty-first century.

ACKNOWLEDGMENTS

The authors are grateful to colleagues Cheryl A. Hyde and Jack Rothman for their helpful insights and comments on an earlier draft of this chapter. Portions of this chapter are based on M. Minkler, N. Wallerstein, and N. Wilson, "Improving Health through Community Organizing and Community Building," in *Health Behavior and Health Education: Theory, Research, and Practice*, edited by K. Glantz, F. M. Lewis, and B. K. Rinker (San Francisco: Jossey-Bass, 2007). © 2007 by Jossey-Bass. This material is used by permission of John Wiley and Sons, Inc.

NOTE

1. The term *community building* is increasingly being used in fields such as urban planning but in a broader sense. Although placing a similarly strong emphasis on identifying and promoting community strengths and capacity, for example, this more macro conceptualization also emphasizes regional economic development and federal- and state-policy-level reinvestment in local communities (Blackwell and Colmenar 2000; see appendix 1).

REFERENCES

Alinsky, S. D. 1969. *Reveille for Radicals*. Chicago: University of Chicago Press.
———. 1972. *Rules for Radicals: A Practical Primer for Realistic Radicals*. New York: Random House.
Alliance for Social Justice. 2010. "Resources for Evaluating Community Organizing." http://www
    .afj.org/for-nonprofits-foundations/reco/.
Amsden, J., and R. VanWynsberghe. 2005. "Community Mapping as a Research Tool with
    Youth." *Action Research* 3, no. 4:357–81.
Ayers, J. 2010. "Healthy Heartland: A Community-Driven Plan for Building a Healthy America."
    Unpublished report, ISAIAH, Minneapolis, Minn.
Bankhead, T., and J. Erlich. 2008. "Practitioner Competency in Communities of Color."
    In *Strategies of Community Intervention*, edited by J. Rothman, J. L. Erlich, and J. E. Tropman.
    Peosta, Iowa: Eddie Bowers.
Berkman, L. F. 2000. "Social Integration, Social Networks, and Health." In *Encyclopedia of
    Health and Behavior*, edited by N. B. Anderson, 754–759. Thousand Oaks, Calif.: Sage.
Blackwell, A. G., and R. Colmenar. 2000. "Community Building: From Local Wisdom to Public
    Policy." *Public Health Reports* 113, nos. 2 and 3:167–173.

Brown, C. R., and G. J. Mazza. 2005. *Leading Diverse Communities: A How-To Guide for Moving from Healing into Action*. San Francisco: Jossey-Bass.

Butterfoss, F. 2007. *Coalitions and Partnerships in Community Health*. San Francisco: Jossey-Bass.

Cargo, M., and S. L. Mercer. 2008. "The Value and Challenges of Participatory Research: Strengthening Its Practice." *Annual Review of Public Health* 2, no. 9:325–350.

Carroll, J., and M. Minkler. 2000. "Freire's Message for Social Workers: Looking Back and Looking Ahead." *Journal of Community Practice* 8, no. 1:21–36.

Catalani, C., L. Campbell, S. Herbst, B. Springgate, B. Butler, and M. Minkler. 2012. "Videovoice: Community Assessment in Post-Katrina New Orleans." *Health Promotion Practice* 13, no. 1:18–28.

Chávez, V. M., N. Minkler, N. Wallerstein, and M. Spencer. 2010. "Community Organizing for Health and Social Justice." In *Prevention Is Primary: Strategies for Community Well-Being*, edited by V. Chávez, L. Cohen, and S. Chehimi, 87–112. 2nd ed. San Francisco: Jossey-Bass.

Cockerham, W. 2007. *Social Causes of Health and Disease*. Cambridge, U.K.: Polity Press.

Community Tool Box Online Documentation System. http://ctb.ku.edu/en/services/ods.aspx.

Connell, J. P., A. C. Kubisch, L. B. Schorr, and C. H. Weiss, eds. 1995. *New Approaches to Evaluating Community Initiatives: Concepts, Methods, and Contexts*. Washington, D.C.: Aspen Institute.

Corburn, J. 2009. *Toward the Healthy City: People, Places, and the Politics of Urban Planning*. Cambridge, Mass.: MIT Press.

Cottrell, L. S., Jr. 1983. "The Competent Community." In *New Perspectives on the American Community*, edited by R. Warren and L. Lyon, 401–412. Homewood, Ill.: Dorsey Press.

Daniels, J. 2009. *Cyber Racism: White Supremacy Online and the New Attack on Civil Rights*. Lanham, Md.: Rowman and Littlefield.

DeFilippis, J., R. Fisher, and E. Shragge. 2010. *Contesting Community: The Limits and Potential of Local Organizing*. New Brunswick, N.J.: Rutgers University Press.

Diers, J. 2006. *Neighborhood Power: Building Community the Seattle Way*. Seattle: University of Seattle Press.

Eng, E., and E. Parker. 1994. "Measuring Community Competence in the Mississippi Delta: The Interface between Program Evaluation and Empowerment." *Health Education Quarterly* 21, no. 2:199–220.

Eng, E., S. Rhodes, and E. Parker. 2009. "Natural Helper Models to Enhance a Community's Health and Competence." In *Emerging Theories in Health Promotion Practice and Research*, edited by R. DiClemente, R. A. Crosby, and M. C. Kegler, 303–330. 2nd ed. San Francisco: Jossey-Bass.

Fawcett, S., P. Abeykoon, M. Arora, M. Dobe, L. Galloway-Gilliam, L. Liburd, and D. Munodawafa. 2010. "Constructing an Action Agenda for Community Empowerment at the 7th Global Conference on Health Promotion in Nairobi." *Global Health Promotion* 17, no. 4:52–56.

Fawcett, S., A. Paine-Andrews, V. T. Francisco, J. Schultz, K. P. Richter, J. Berkeley-Patton, and J. L. Fisher. 2001. "Evaluating Community Initiatives for Health and Development." In *Evaluation in Health Promotion Approaches*, edited by I. Rootman, D. McQueen, L. Potvin, J. Springett, and E. Ziglio, 241–270. European Series, no. 92. Copenhagen: World Health Organization.

Fawcett, S. B., R. I. Boothroyd, J. A. Schultz, V. T. Francisco, V. Carson, and R. Bremby. 2003. "Building Capacity for Participatory Evaluation within Community Initiatives." *Journal of Prevention and Intervention in the Community* 26, no. 2:21–36.

Fawcett, S. B., R. K. Lewis, A. Paine-Andrews, V. T. Francisco, K. P. Richter, E. L. Williams, and B. Copple. 1997. "Evaluating Community Coalitions for Prevention of Substance Abuse: The Case of Project Freedom." *Health Education and Behavior* 24, no.6:812–828.

Fawcett, S. B., A. Paine-Andrews, V. Francisco, J. Schultz, K. P. Richter, R. K. Lewis, K. J. Harris, et al. 1996. "Empowering Community Health Initiatives through Evaluation." In *Empowerment Evaluation*, edited by D. Fetterman, S. Kaftarian, and A. Wanderman, 161–187. Thousand Oaks, Calif.: Sage.

Fawcett S. B., J. A. Schultz, V. L. Carson, V. A. Renault, and V. T. Francisco. 2003. "Using Internet-Based Tools to Build Capacity for Community-Based Participatory Research and Other Efforts to Promote Community Health and Development." In *Community-Based Participatory Research*, edited by M. Minkler and N. Wallerstein, 155–178. San Francisco: Jossey-Bass.

Fellin, P. 2001. "Understanding American Communities." In *Strategies of Community Intervention*, edited by J. Rothman, J. Erlich, and J. Tropman, 118–133. 5th ed. Itasca, Ill.: F. E. Peacock.

Fetterman, D. M. 1996. "Empowerment Evaluation: An Introduction to Theory and Practice." In *Empowerment Evaluation: Knowledge and Tools for Self-Assessment and Accountability*, edited by D. M. Fetterman, S. J. Kaftarian, and A. Wandersman, 3–46. Thousand Oaks, Calif.: Sage.

Fetterman, D., and A. Wandersman, eds. 2005. *Empowerment Evaluation*. Thousand Oaks, Calif.: Sage.

Foster, C. C. and J. Louie. 2010. "Grassroots Action and Learning for Social Change: Evaluating Community Organizing." Center for Evaluation Innovation. http://www.innonet.org/client_docs/File/center_pubs/evaluating_community_organizing.pdf.

Foster-Fishman, P., B. Nowell, Z. Decon, M. A. Neivar, and P. McCann. 2005. "Using Methods That Matter: Reflection, Dialogue, and Voice." *American Journal of Community Psychology* 36, no. 3–4:275–291.

Fowler, J., and N. A. Christakis. 2008. "Dynamic Spread of Happiness in a Large Social Network: Longitudinal Analysis over 20 Years in the Framingham Heart Study." *British Medical Journal* 337:a2338.

Freire, P. 1970. *Pedagogy of the Oppressed*. New York: Seabury Press.

Frisby, W., P. Maguire, and C. Reid. 2009. "The F Word Has Everything To Do with It: How Feminist Theories Inform Action Research." *Action Research* 7, no. 1:13–29.

Gardner, J. 1991. *Building Community*. Washington, D.C.: Independent Sector Leadership Studies Program.

Garvin, C. D., and F. M. Cox. 2001. "A History of Community Organizing since the Civil War with Special Reference to Oppressed Communities." *Strategies of Community Intervention*, 65–100. 6th ed. Itasca, Ill.: Peacock.

Goodman, R. M. 2009. "A Construct for Building the Capacity of Community-Based Initiatives in Racial and Ethnic Communities: A Qualitative Cross-Case Analysis." *Journal of Public Health Management and Practice* 15, no. 2: E1–8.

Goodman, R. M, M. Speers, K. McLeroy, S. Fawcett, M. Kegler, E. Parker., S. R. Smith, T. D. Sterling, and N. Wallerstein. 1999. "Identifying and Defining the Dimensions of Community Capacity to Provide a Basis for Measurement." *Health Education and Behavior* 25, no. 3:258–278.

Granner, M. L., and P. A. Sharpe. 2004. "Evaluating Community Coalition Characteristics and Functioning: A Summary of Measurement Tools." *Health Education Research* 19, no. 5:514–532.

Himmelman, A. 2001. "On Coalitions and the Transformation of Power Relations: Collaborative Betterment and Collaborative Empowerment." *American Journal of Community Psychology* 29, no. 2:277–84.

Hughey, J., N. A. Peterson, J. B. Lowe, and F. Oprescu. 2008. "Empowerment and Sense of Community: Clarifying Their Relationship in Community Organizations." *Health Education Behavior* 35, no. 5:651–663.

Hunter, A. 1975. "The Loss of Community: An Empirical Test through Replication." *American Sociology Review* 40, no. 5:537–552.

Hyde, C. A. 2005. "Feminist Community Practice." In *Handbook of Community Practice*, edited by M. Weil, 360–371. Thousand Oaks, Calif.: Sage.

———. 2008. "Feminist Social Work Practice." In *Encyclopedia of Social Work*, edited by T. Mizrahi, L. Davis, and M. Weil, 216–221. 20th ed. New York: Oxford University Press.

Israel, B., B. Checkoway, A. Schulz, and M. Zimmerman. 1994. "Health Education and Community Empowerment: Conceptualizing and Measuring Perceptions of Individual, Organizational, and Community Control." *Health Education Quarterly* 21, no. 2:149–170.

Israel, B., P. M. Lantz, R. J. McGranaghan, D. L. Kerr, and J. R. Guzman. 2005. "Detroit Community-Academic Urban Research Center: In-Depth Semistructured Interview Protocol for Board Evaluation, 1996–2002." In *Methods in Community-Based Participatory Research*, edited by B. Israel, E. Eng, A. J. Schulz, and E. A. Parker, 425–433. San Francisco: Jossey-Bass.

Israel, B. A., A. J. Schulz, E. A. Parker, A. B. Becker, A. J. Allen, and J. R. Guzman. 2008. "Critical Issues in Developing and Following Community-Based Participatory Research Principles." In *Community-Based Participatory Research for Health: From Process to Outcomes*, edited by M. Minkler and N. Wallerstein, 47–62. 2nd ed. San Francisco: Jossey-Bass.

Jones, M., S. Frazier, C. Percy, J. L. Stowell, K. Maltrud, and N. Wallerstein. 2008. In *Community-Based Participatory Research for Health: From Process to Outcomes*, edited by M. Minkler and N. Wallerstein, 171–180. 2nd ed. San Francisco: Jossey-Bass.

Jones, M., R. Rae, S. Frazier, K. Malthus, F. Varela, C. Percy, and N. Wallerstein. 2010. "Healthy Native Communities Fellowship: Advancing Leadership for Community Changes in Health." *Indian Health Service Provider*, December, 279–284.

Kawachi, I., S. V. Subramanian, and D. Kim. 2008. *Social Capital and Health*. New York: Springer Science and Business Media.

Kegler, M. C., J. E. Painter, J. M. Twiss, R. E. Aronson, and B. Norton. 2009. "Evaluation Findings on Community Participation in the California Healthy Cities and Communities Program." *Health Promotion International* 24, no. 4:300–310.

Lamb, A. K., B. A. Ervice, M.N.A. Lorenzen, B. Prentice, and S. White. 2011. "Reducing Asthma Disparities by Addressing Environmental Inequities: A Case Study of Regional Asthma Management and Prevention's Advocacy Efforts." Supplement, *Community Health* 34, no. 1:S54–S62.

Lasker, R. D., and J. A. Guidry. 2009. *Engaging the Community in Decision Making: Case Studies Tracking Participation, Voice and Influence*. Jefferson, N.C.: McFarland.

Laverack, G. 2004. *Health Promotion Practice, Power, and Empowerment*. Thousand Oaks, Calif.: Sage.

Lee, T. 2011. *Mobilizing Communities in a Connected Age: A Portfolio Assessment of Advocacy Organizations*. San Francisco: ZeroDivide.

Lempa, M., R. M. Goodman, J. Rice, and A. B. Becker. 2008. "Development of Scales Measuring the Capacity of Community-Based Initiatives." *Health Education and Behavior* 35:298–315.

Maclellan-Wright, M. F., D. Anderson, S. Barber, N. Smith, B. Cantin, et al. 2007. "The Development of Measures of Community Capacity Building for Community-Based Funding Programs in Canada." *Health Promotion International* 22, no. 4:299–306.

Malthus, K., M. Polacsek, and N. Wallerstein. 1997. *Participatory Evaluation Workbook for Community Initiatives*. Albuquerque: University of New Mexico, Masters in Public Health Program.

Marmot, M. 2009. "Harveian Oration: Health in an Unequal World." *Lancet* 368:2081–2094.

Marmot, M., S. Friel, R. Bell, T. A. Houweling, and S. Taylor. 2008. "Closing the Gap in a Generation: Health Equity through Action on the Social Determinants of Health." *Lancet* 372, no. 9650:1661–1669.

Mattessich, P. W., M. Murray-Close, B. R. Monsey, and Wilder Research Center. 2001. *Collaboration: What Makes It Work.* 2nd ed. Saint Paul, Minn.: Amherst H. Wilder Foundation.

McCloskey, D. D., M. A. McDonald, J. Cook, S. Heurtin-Roberts, S. Updegrove, D. Sampson, et al. 2011. "Community Engagement: Definitions and Organizing Concepts from the Literature." In *Principles of Community Engagement,* by Clinical and Translational Science Awards Consortium Community Engagement Key Function Committee Task Force on Principles of Community Engagement. 2nd ed. NIH Publication No. 11–7782. Washington, D.C.: National Institutes of Health.

McKnight, J. 1995. "Regenerating Community." In *The Careless Society and Its Counterfeits,* 161–172. New York: Basic Books.

McKnight, J. L., and J. P. Kretzmann. 1992. *Mapping Community Capacity.* Evanston, Ill.: Center for Urban Affairs and Policy Research, Northwestern University.

Mercer, S. L., L. W. Green, M. Cargo, M.A. Potter, M. Daniel, R. S. Olds, and E. Reed-Gross. 2008. "Reliability-Tested Guidelines for Assessing Participatory Research Projects." In *Community-Based Participatory Research for Health: From Process to Outcomes,* edited by M. Minkler and N. Wallerstein, 407–418. 2nd ed. San Francisco: Jossey-Bass.

Miller, M. 2009. *A Community Organizer's Tale: People and Power in San Francisco.* Berkeley, Calif.: Heyday Books.

Minkler, M. 2005a. "Community-Based Research Partnerships: Challenges and Opportunities." *Journal of Urban Health* 82, no. 2S:3–12.

———. 2005b. "Community Organizing among the Elderly Poor in San Francisco's Tenderloin District." In *Community Organizing and Community Building for Health,* edited by M. Minkler, 272–288. New Brunswick, N.J.: Rutgers University Press.

Minkler, M., and N. Wallerstein. 2008. "Introduction to CBPR: New Issues and Emphases." In *Community-Based Participatory Research: From Process to Outcomes,* edited by M. Minkler and N. Wallerstein, 5–19. 2nd ed. San Francisco: Jossey-Bass.

Mizrahi, T., and B. B. Rosenthal. 2008. "Complexities of Coalition Building: Leaders' Successes, Strategies, Struggles and Solutions." In *Strategies of Community Intervention,* edited by J. Rothman, J. L. Erlich, and J. E. Tropman, 471–490. 7th ed. Peosta, Iowa: Eddie Bowers.

Narayan, D. 2002. *Empowerment and Poverty Reduction: A Sourcebook.* Washington, D.C.: World Bank.http://books.google.com/books?hl=en&lr=&id=MkDiPZO6ZXoC&oi=fnd&pg=PR11&dq=deepa+narayan&ots=rd_R_Y3kbX&sig=R69RhTJQD6YVXh5j2YKbbqeCuaY#v=onepage&q&f=false.

Nemcek, M. A., and R. Sabatier. 2003. "State of Evaluation: Community Health Workers." *Public Health Nursing* 20, no. 4:260–70.

Norris, T. 1997. *The Community Indicators Handbook: Redefining Progress.* Denver, Colo.: Tyler Norris Associates.

Nyswander, D. B. 1956. "Education for Health: Some Principles and Their Application." *Health Education Monographs* 14:65–70.

O'Neill, M., and P. Simard. 2006. "Choosing Indicators to Evaluate Healthy Cities Projects: A Political Task?" *Health Promotion International* 21, no. 2:145–152.

Pan American Health Organization. 2005. *Participatory Evaluation of Healthy Municipalities: A Practical Resource Kit for Action.* Washington, D.C.: Pan American Health Organization.

Pastor, M., C. Brenner, and M. Matsuoka. 2009. *This Could Be the Start of Something Big: How Social Movements for Regional Equity Are Reshaping Metropolitan America.* Syracuse, N.Y.: Cornell University.

Peterson, N. A., J. B. Lowe, J. Hughey, R. J. Reid, M. A. Zimmerman, and P. W. Speer. 2006. "Measuring The Intrapersonal Component of Psychological Empowerment: Confirmatory Factor Analysis of the Sociopolitical Control Scale." *American Journal of Community Psychology* 38, no. 3–4:287–97.

Putnam, R. D. 2000. *Bowling Alone: The Collapse and Revival of American Community*. New York: Simon and Schuster.

Rappaport, J. 1984. "Studies in Empowerment: Introduction to the Issue." *Prevention in Human Services* 3, no. 2/3:1–7.

Ritas, C., M. Minkler, A. Ni, and H. Halpin. 2008. "Using CBPR to Promote Policy Change: Exercises and Online Resources." In *Community-Based Participatory Research: From Process to Outcomes*, edited by M. Minkler and N. Wallerstein, 453–458. 2nd ed. San Francisco: Jossey-Bass.

Rothman, J. 2001. "Approaches to Community Intervention." In *Strategies of Community Intervention*, edited by J. Rothman, J. L. Erlich, and J. E. Tropman, 27–64. 6th ed. Itasaca, Ill.: FE Peacock.

———. 2007. "Multi Modes of Intervention at the Macro Level." *Journal of Community Practice* 15, no. 4:11–40.

———. 2008. "Multi Modes of Community Intervention." In *Strategies of Community Intervention*, edited by J. Rothman, J. L. Erlich, and J. E. Tropman, 141–170. 7th ed. Peosta, Iowa: Eddie Bowers.

Scarinci, I. C., et al. 2009. "Planning and Implementation of a Participatory Evaluation Strategy: A Viable Approach in the Evaluation of Community-Based Participatory Research Programs Addressing Cancer Disparities." *Evaluation and Program Planning*, 32, no. 3:221–228.

Sen, R. 2003. *Stir It Up: Lessons in Community Organizing and Advocacy*. San Francisco: Jossey-Bass.

Skocpol, T. 2003. *Diminished Democracy: From Membership to Management in American Civic Life*. Norman: University of Oklahoma Press.

Springett, J., and N. Wallerstein. 2008. "Issues in Participatory Evaluation." In *Community-Based Participatory Research for Health*, edited by M. Minkler and N. Wallerstein, 199–215. 2nd ed. San Francisco: Jossey-Bass.

Stall, S., and R. Stoeker. 2005. "Toward a Gender Analysis of Community Organizing Models: Liminality and the Intersection of Spheres." In *Community Organizing and Community Building For Health*, edited by M. Minkler, 296–217. 2nd ed. New Brunswick, N.J.: Rutgers University Press.

Staples, L. 2004. *Roots to Power: A Manual for Grassroots Organizing*. 2nd ed. Westport, Conn.: Praeger.

Su, C. 2009. *Streetwise for Book Smarts: Grassroots Organizing and Education Reform in the Bronx*. Ithaca, N.Y.: Cornell University Press.

Syme, S. L. 2004. "Social Determinants of Health: The Community as an Empowered Partner." *Preventing Chronic Disease* 1, no. 1:1–8.

Szreter, S., and M. Woolcock. 2004. "Health by Association? Social Capital, Social Theory, and the Political Economy of Public Health." *International Journal of Epidemiology* 33, no. 4:650–667.

Tervalon, M., and J. Garcia. 1998. "Cultural Humility versus Cultural Competence: A Critical Distinction in Defining Physician Training Outcomes in Multicultural Education." *Journal of Health Care for the Poor and Underserved* 9, no. 2:117–25.

Themba, M. 1999. Making Policy Making Change: How Communities are Taking Law into Their Own Hands. Oakland, CA.: Chardon Press.

U.S. Department of Health and Human Services (USDHHS). 2011. "Healthy People 2020." www.healthypeople.gov.

VeneKlasen, L., and V. Miller. 2002. *A New Weave of Power, People, and Politics*. Oklahoma City, OK: World Neighbors.

Vogel, K. 2010. "Right Loves to Hate, Imitate Alinsky." Politico. http://dyn.politico.com/printstory.cfm?uuid=7D78B2CE-18FE-70B2-A889E10B1C707BA6.

Wallerstein, N. 1992. "Powerlessness, Empowerment, and Health: Implications for Health Promotion Programs." *American Journal of Health Promotion* 6:197–205.

———. 1999. "Power between Evaluator and Community: Research Relationships within New Mexico's Healthier Communities." *Social Science and Medicine* 49:39–53.

———. 2006. "Evidence of Effectiveness of Empowerment Interventions to Reduce Health Disparities and Social Exclusion." *Health Evidence Network*, World Health Organization, http://www.euro.who.int/HEN/Syntheses/empowerment/20060119_10

Wallerstein, N., and E. Auerbach. 2004. *Problem-Posing at Work: English for Action.* 2nd ed. Edmonton, Alberta, Canada: Grass Roots Press.

Wallerstein, N., J. Oetzel, B. Duran, G. Trafoya, L. Belone, and E. Rae. 2008. "What Predicts Outcomes in CBPR?" In *Community-Based Participatory Research: From Process to Outcomes*, edited by M. Minkler and N. Wallerstein, 371–392. 2nd ed. San Francisco: Jossey-Bass.

Wallerstein, N., M. Polacsek, and K. Malthus. 2002. "Participatory Evaluation Model for Coalitions: A Systems Indicator Approach from New Mexico." *Journal of Health Promotion Practice* 3, no. 3:361–373.

Walters, K. L., R. E. Beltran, D. Huh, and T. Evans-Campbell. In press. "Dis-placement and Dis-ease: Land, Place, and Health among American Indians and Alaska Natives." In *Communities, Neighborhood, and Health: Expanding the Boundaries*, edited by L. M. Burton, S. P. Kemp, M. C. Leung, S. A. Matthews, and D. T. Takeuch. New York: Springer.

Walters, K. L., and J. M. Simoni. 2002. "Reconceptualizing Native Women's Health: An 'Indigenist' Stress-Coping Model." *American Journal of Public Health* 92, no. 4:520–524.

Wandersman, A., and P. Florin. 2000. "Citizen Participation and Community Organizations." In *Handbook of Community Psychology*, edited by J. Rappaport and E. Seidman, 247–272. Dordrecht, Netherlands: Kluwer Academic.

Wang, C., and M. A. Burris. 1997. "Photovoice: Concept, Methodology, and Use for Participatory Assessment." *Health Education and Behavior* 24, no. 3:369–387.

Warren, R. 1963. *The Community in America.* Chicago: Rand McNally.

West, C. 1993. *Race Matters.* Boston: Beacon Press.

Wing, S., R. A. Horton, N. Muhammad, G. R. Grant, M. Tajik, and K. Thu. 2008. "Integrating Epidemiology, Education, and Organizing for Environmental Justice: Community Health Effects of Industrial Hog Operations." *American Journal of Public Health* 98, no. 8:1390–7.

Wolff, T. 2010. *The Power of Collaborative Solutions: Six Principles and Effective Tools for Building Healthy Communities.* San Francisco: Jossey-Bass.

World Health Organization (WHO). 1986. *Ottawa Charter for Health Promotion.* Copenhagen: World Health Organization.

Zakocs, R., and E. Edwards. 2006. "What Explains Community Coalition Effectiveness? A Review of the Literature." *American Journal of Preventive Medicine* 30, no. 4:351–361.

Zimmerman, M. 2000. "Empowerment Theory: Psychological, Organizational, and Community Levels of Analysis." In *Handbook of Community Psychology*, edited by E. S. Julian Rappaport, 43–63. New York: Kluwer Academic/Plenum.

4

Contrasting Organizing Approaches

The "Alinsky Tradition" and Freirian Organizing Approaches

MARTY MARTINSON

CELINA SU

Community organizing efforts across the country and the globe reflect a range of models with different philosophies and strategies for systematically bringing people together to bring about social change. This chapter explores two such models of community organizing—the "Alinsky tradition" and Freirian approaches. Here, we examine the key components of each model, contrast the basic assumptions and strategies embedded in each, and identify the ways in which these models might complement or learn from each other. Community organizing in practice, of course, rarely reflects an ideal model in its pure form, as each effort requires strategies and tactics that are specific to the given situation (Rothman 2008; Sen 2003). Nevertheless, the influence of the ideas and practices of Saul D. Alinsky and Paulo Freire over the past several decades have been significant and thereby warrant more detailed examination.

Saul Alinsky (1909–1972)

Born into a middle-class Jewish immigrant household in Chicago, Alinsky worked as an early labor organizer with the Congress of Industrial Organizations (CIO) and emerged in the 1930s as a formidable community organizer when he worked with the Back of the Yards neighborhood in Chicago. There, he built an "organization of organizations" that brought together churches, labor, and service organizations to successfully fight for expanded social services, education, and other community needs in the meatpacking and stockyards section of Chicago. As community organizer Mike Miller (2009) notes, Alinsky "borrowed from the tough approach of the industrial union movement, grafted its strategy and tactics onto the poor, working-class communities that surrounded the great industrial stockyards of the Midwest, and found in local traditions and values the ideas that supported organizing" (10). Alinsky's efforts succeeded in achieving his goal of using "people power" to counter the "money power" of the Chicago political machine and to gain seats at the decision-making tables (Miller 2009).

After the successes of the Back of the Yards Neighborhood Council (BYNC), Alinsky founded the Industrial Areas Foundation in the 1940s to expand the BYNC model to other parts of the country. Alinsky employed and promoted a conflict-oriented and pragmatic style of organizing. As he pronounced, "The first step in community organizing is community disorganization," achieved by identifying the controversial issues upon which people feel most compelled to act (Alinsky 1971, 116–7). While Alinsky himself said that there is no such thing as a step-by-step "prescription" for organizing, as each effort requires situation-specific tactics, the ideas and strategies he described in his books *Reveille for Radicals* (1946) and *Rules for Radicals* (1971) suggest that there are general principles to be followed in an Alinsky tradition of community organizing.

The Alinsky Tradition of Community Organizing

According to Alinsky, the organizer's role is that of an outsider who agitates, listens to the concerns of the people, and then mobilizes them to act on those concerns. In order to do this, the organizer needs to establish legitimacy in the community—or, as he phrased it, "get a license to operate" (1971, 98). The organizer gets this license by demonstrating "credentials of competency" (101) through prior successes and by agitating within the community so that people will voice their concerns and invite the organizer in to help. In Alinsky's words, the organizer must "agitate to the point of conflict," "rub raw the resentments of the people of the community," and "fan the latent hostilities of many of the people to the point of overt expression" (1971, 116–117). The organizer then helps people move from this generalized discontent to focusing on specific issues around which they can organize campaigns and create change. Overall, the organizer must persuade the people that they *can* do something about those issues *if* they mobilize to create a mass-based organization. Again, quoting Alinsky (1971): "As long as you feel powerless and unable to do anything about it, all you have is a bad scene. . . . The organizer makes it clear that organization will give them the power, the ability, the strength, the force to be able to do something about these particular problems. It is then that a bad scene begins to break up into specific issues, because now the people can do something about it. What the organizer does is convert the plight into a problem. . . . The organization is born out of the issues and the issues are born out of the organization" (119–120).

The issues to be addressed through the community organization must be selected appropriately. Alinsky noted that a "good issue" is one that is simple, specific, and winnable (1971; Miller 2009; Staples 2004; see chapter 11). This stands in contrast to other strategies that may integrate broader ideological issues into organizing, such as antiracism or antiviolence campaigns (Sen 2003; Su 2009). For Alinsky, rather than taking on such ideological issues, it is essential to choose specific battles that can be won rather quickly in order to give the community a sense of confidence and achievement.

Related to this focus on a specific, winnable issue, Alinsky also asserted the importance of choosing a campaign target—a specific individual or organization that has the power to make decisions and therefore make change (Sen 2003). In Alinsky's (1971) words, "Pick the target, freeze it, personalize it, and polarize it" (130). For example, when organizing with the low-income African American community in Rochester, New York, Alinsky identified Eastman Kodak, the antilabor industrial giant of Rochester, as being largely responsible for the economic plight of the community. After picking this target, he "froze" it with the provocative comment to the media that "the only thing Eastman Kodak has done on the race issue in America has been to introduce color film" (137). Alinsky then personalized and polarized this target by deliberately expressing confusion over the identity of one of the directors of Eastman Kodak. W. Allen Wallis had a history of discriminating against African Americans in his position as president of the local university. When the media asked Alinsky about Wallis, the former's response was, "Wallis? Which one are you talking about—Wallace of Alabama, or Wallis of Rochester— but I guess there isn't any difference" (137). At the time, Alabama governor George Wallace was a strong segregationist; in 1963 he had famously stood in the doorway of the University of Alabama to stop two black students from entering. Therefore, Alinsky's quip struck a nerve and was widely quoted.

Alinsky was well known for his controversial approach to "the ethics of means and ends," which he detailed in *Rules for Radicals* (1971, 26). His list of ten rules pertaining to these ethics is summed up well in rule number ten, which states, "You do what you can with what you have and clothe it with moral garments." In general, he believed that the ends can justify the means, depending on whose side you are on, how passionate you feel about the issue, or how close you are to defeat.

Importantly, Alinsky believed that no action should be taken until the "mass power base" had been built, for without that base, the organizer "has nothing with which to confront anything" (Alinsky 1971, 113). Therefore, the initial focus of Alinsky organizing efforts is to build the organization through recruitment of huge numbers of people. Once these numbers are obtained, the organizer then helps the people identify specific, concrete actions using that "people power" and concurrently assesses the power base of the opposition (Alinsky 1971).

Overall, as Minkler (2005) described, Alinsky-tradition organizing "emphasize[s] redressing power imbalances by creating dissatisfaction with the status quo among the disenfranchised, building community-wide identification, and helping members devise winnable goals and nonviolent conflict strategies as a means to bring about change" (28). In the end, this kind of social action organizing serves to shift power from being concentrated among elite power brokers to being shared with previously marginalized communities, which, through their organizing into a mass power base, gain access to the decision-making table. The power structure is changed in terms of which individuals or groups hold power and how much power they hold. In the following passage, Alinsky (1971) dramatically illustrates how community organizing moves individuals from a place of invisibility and voicelessness to that of visibility and influence:

> A man is living in a slum tenement. He doesn't know anybody and nobody knows him. He doesn't care for anyone because no one cares for him. On the corner newsstand are newspapers with pictures of people like Mayor Daley and other people from a different world—a world that he doesn't know, a world that doesn't know that he is even alive. When the organizer approaches him part of what begins to be communicated is that through the organization and its power he will get his birth certificate for life, that he will become known, that things will change from the drabness of a life where all that changes is the calendar. This same man, in a demonstration at City Hall, might find himself confronting the mayor and saying, "Mr. Mayor, we have had it up to here and we are not going to take it any more." Television cameramen put their microphones in front of him and ask, "What is your name, sir?" "John Smith." Nobody ever asked him what his name was before. . . . Nobody ever asked him what he thought about anything before. Suddenly he's alive! (121)

Present-Day Examples of Alinsky-Tradition Organizing

While Alinsky's specific ideas and strategies have been critiqued, debated, and revised over the years, there are several powerful community organizations—including the Alinsky-founded Industrial Areas Foundation (IAF)—which continue to help constituents build broad-based coalitions. By 2010, this strategy of building "organizations of organizations" had grown into a vast network of over sixty IAF affiliates across the United States and in Canada, Germany, and the United Kingdom, training leaders in over forty organizations and representing over a thousand institutions and a million families (www.industrialareasfoundation .org). In Alinsky style, these coalitions are formed through both shared values and self-interest in a "scratch my back and I'll scratch yours" exchange (Miller 2009, 12). After Alinsky's death in 1972, some of his associates, such as his successor Ed Chambers at IAF, modified the Alinsky approach to create more sustainable structures while maintaining most of the key components of the Alinsky tradition (Kleidman 2004). Yet the IAF remained heavily focused on power, describing itself as "non ideological, strictly nonpartisan but proudly, and persistently, political" (www.industrialareasfoundation.org). Other notable examples of Alinsky-tradition "organization of organizations" are PICO (formerly the Pacific Institute for Community Organizing); the Direct Action Training and Research Center (DART); and the Gamaliel Foundation, discussed here and in chapter 2.

Gamaliel describes itself as "a grassroots network of non-partisan, faith-based organizations . . . that organizes to empower ordinary people to effectively participate in the political, environmental, social and economic decisions affecting their lives" (http://www.gamaliel.org). Gamaliel's "general standards of organizers" directly reflect Alinsky's rules for community organizers, including building an organizational base through recruitment of dues-paying members and organizations, being committed to the self-interest of the community organization, developing local leaders, remaining in the background as an organizer and leaving it to local leaders to serve as spokespeople for local organizations, and helping communities identify specific and winnable issues (http://www.gamaliel.org/AboutUs/Careers/GeneralStandards.aspx; see also chapter 2).

In the Alinsky tradition, the main strategy of Gamaliel's organizers is to build broad and powerful faith-based community organizations and train local leaders in low-income communities. One of the more than sixty community organizations affiliated with Gamaliel is Minnesota's ISAIAH, a coalition of congregations that have mobilized to address issues of racial and economic justice (see chapter 20). In the Alinsky tradition that strives to bring together diverse groups to "struggle together to realize their common interests" and "[build] relationships that cut across historic lines of antagonism" (Miller 2009, 12), ISAIAH has taken on the challenge to "build all the bridges necessary to craft one organization out of the interests of new immigrants and old ones; city-dwellers and suburbanites; activists and people for whom acting in the public arena is new" (www.isaiah-mn.org).

Outcomes of ISAIAH's successful organizing efforts include their leveraging of $68 million in state funds to clean up three thousand acres of toxic "brownfields" in Minneapolis and St. Paul, Minnesota (Kleidman 2004); securing a dedicated state funding stream for public transportation; obtaining land and funding for affordable senior housing; working with coalition partners to restore $1.5 million in funding for battered women's shelters and services; and successfully advocating for increased funding from the state for public education (www.isaiah-mn.org; see chapter 20). ISAIAH's specific organizing tactics reflect the Alinsky tradition in their use of confrontational strategies and mass protest efforts. One such tactic involves their use of media-capturing stunts such as their "Honest Abes" truth-telling campaign to protest the inequity of transportation access. In this 2008 effort, a dozen ISAIAH leaders, wearing beards and stovetop hats, greeted legislators as the latter entered a House transportation hearing. A similarly Alinsky-style tactic involved their organization of a mass demonstration in front of the headquarters of UnitedHealth—the largest private health insurance company in the United States. At the ISAIAH rally, a local reverend delivered a sermon declaring, "If they [UnitedHealth] win, the people who you care about, the people standing here, the people who you want to have health care will lose. . . . It is not okay to profit on other people's despair." Meanwhile, protestors carried signs with photos of people who had died or were ill because they were denied or could not afford health insurance. Other ISAIAH members blocked entry into the building until they were arrested (http://www.isaiah-mn.org).

Critiques of the Alinsky Approach

The original Alinsky organizing model has been substantially criticized over the years, in part because of its insistence on organizations' maintaining a non-ideological stance. The model's failure to adequately build local capacity and leadership, and the limitations of its focus on local targets in an increasingly multinational world with powerful corporate capital that crosses local and national borders, also have been critiqued (Delgado 1986; DeFilippis et al. 2010; Stall and Stoecker 2005).

Critics have also focused on the approach's resistance to directly confronting issues of race and racism (Chavez et al. 2010; Delgado 1986). Community organizing trainer and activist Rinku Sen (2003) describes the antiracist critique as being centered on three key concerns: the predominance of white staff and formal leaders in community organizations, the hesitation among many organizations to take on issues of racism, and the inflexibility of the rules and tactics of organizing that do not always fit the values and experiences of communities of color. Sen (2003) and Stall and Stoecker (2005) also underscore the feminist or gender-based critique of the Alinsky tradition, with key concerns including the emphasis on "public sphere" interventions, the lack of work/life balance for organizers, the use of narrow self-interest as a primary motivation, and the reliance on conflict and confrontational tactics.

Many organizations in the Alinsky tradition have adapted their practices to address such concerns. Gamaliel, for example, has developed a multiracial leadership and included a component of political education in its training of leaders (Kleidman 2004). And such traditional Alinsky organizations as the IAF and PICO are much more attentive today to community capacity-building (Sen 2003; Miller 2009).

Yet rather than adapt a modified and modernized Alinsky-type model, many other community organizations have developed alternative approaches to frame their organizing efforts in ways that better match their philosophical and cultural values. The "woman-centered organizing" model described by Stall and Stoecker (2005) and the model for organizing with women of color described by Lorraine Gutierrez and Edith Lewis (see chapter 12) are illustrative. We turn now to an approach that has become increasingly recognized across geographic, gender, and cultural lines as a significantly different approach to Alinsky's community organizing—Paulo Freire's (1972) model of liberation, or popular, education for critical consciousness and structural transformation and its use in community organizing and community building.

Paulo Freire (1921–1997)

Paulo Freire grew up in northwest Brazil in a middle-class family that then endured hunger and poverty during the Great Depression. Although Freire was trained as a lawyer, his passion was adult education. After working as a teacher, he began to study and critique the Brazilian education system for its perpetuation of the oppression, exploitation, and powerlessness of poor people. Freire challenged the traditional "banking system" of education, in which teachers "deposit" information into students' heads, waiting for the students to uncritically absorb their knowledge (Freire 1972). The danger of this sort of banking education, according to Freire, was that it kept learners from attaining a "critical consciousness" regarding sources of oppression and inequity; it thereby kept people from becoming agents of social change in their lives and their communities.

Freire promoted an alternative model of education that supports human liberation and makes people the subjects of their own learning (Chavez et al. 2010; Freire 1972; Wallerstein et al. 2005). He argued that in order to build a stronger democracy, education must be rooted in the lived experiences of the people who are learning and in the development of critical consciousness. Rather than the teacher simply treating students as "empty vessels" in a manner that promotes passivity and perpetuates the status quo, the responsibility of the teacher in liberation education is to support social justice and social change by facilitating a process whereby marginalized people can come to realize the sources of their oppression as an essential step in mobilizing to change it. Freire reflected on his own role as an educator working with poor farmers: "I cannot remain neutral. . . . I must intervene in teaching peasants that their hunger is socially constructed, and work with them to help identify those responsible for this social construction, which is, in my view, a crime against humanity" (Freire and Macedo 1995, 391).

Popular Education and Liberation Education

At the heart of Freire's approach is popular education, which, as Bernard (2002) notes, "begins with people's own experiences. It gives them the tools to analyze their situation and take action to transform themselves and their conditions" (7). Although we focus here on Freire's use of popular, or liberation, education, it should be pointed out that the approach itself preceded him. As noted in chapter 14, for example, the Highlander Center, which Myles Horton founded in Appalachian Tennessee in the early 1930s, has used popular education and literacy since its inception as a means of promoting civic participation and social action organizing (Horton 1998; Horton and Freire 1990). In their classic book, *We Make the Road by Walking* (1990), Horton and Freire indeed reflect on their mutual commitment to this approach and on how their own paths intersected and complemented one another's as fellow travelers.

While Freire's work is grounded in popular education, he himself tended to use the term *liberation* (or *liberatory*) *education* more frequently, and therefore we use the term *liberation education* in this chapter. Freire first employed his liberation education ideas in the early 1960s in a pilot literacy program with three hundred sugarcane sharecroppers. The success of that program led to his development of broader literacy campaigns for the poor in Brazil through which people learned to read while they also learned to "'read' the political and social situation in which they lived" in order to transform it (Carroll and Minkler 2000, 23–24) . When President João Goulart's government was overthrown in 1964 by a coup d'état, Freire was imprisoned and then forced into exile in Chile, during which time he further developed his ideas about education and human liberation from oppression (Freire 2000). This approach to education, which he and others have shared throughout the world, has come to be known by many names, including *popular education, critical pedagogy, empowerment education, liberatory practice,* and, as we refer to it here, *liberation education* (Chávez et al. 2010; hooks 1994; Su 2009; Wallerstein et al. 2005).

Freire described the key principles and strategies of liberation education in a number of writings, including *Pedagogy of the Oppressed* (1972). A Freirian approach to liberation education involves a facilitated social action process in which groups come together in "culture circles" to listen to each other, engage in dialogue about the struggles in their lives and the social and historical roots of those struggles, envision and employ collective actions to create change, and reflect upon those actions as they develop further actions for change (Wallerstein and Bernstein 1988). Thus, the act of learning is not divorced from the social, economic, and political conditions of their everyday lives. Rather than emphasizing right or wrong answers, teachers act as facilitators in helping students (or "learner-teachers") think through issues and put forward their own analyses. This methodology of listening-dialogue-action-reflection represents a participatory model of learning that promotes the development of *conscientization,* or critical consciousness that leads to action. As such, the process is transformative for both the individual and the community (Freire 1972; Chávez et al. 2010).

The initial listening process allows group members to hear from each other and identify key issues of common concern. Together, they then engage in dialogue in a manner that allows them to employ critical thinking around the issues they have identified. This facilitated process, in Freirian tradition, often uses codes or triggers—visual, audio, or other forms of representation of the concerns raised by the participants—as catalysts for the dialogue (see appendix 9). As Wallerstein and her colleagues (2005) describe, "A good trigger is a creation from the listening process that captures the emotional meaning of key problematic issues and the social context of these issues in participants' lives yet does not present solutions" (224). One early example of such a trigger was an unlabeled bottle of medicine, received by a low-income elder in a crowded San Francisco clinic. Facilitators used this bottle to engage this man, and his fellow single-room-occupancy hotel residents, in a dialogue about their experiences with health care and the root problem of a two-tiered medical care system (Minkler and Cox 1980).

In New Mexico, youth in the Adolescent Social Action Program created and used videos and fotonovelas as triggers to engage other youth and community members in dialogues regarding the high rates of substance abuse among Native American, Latino, and low-income white communities (Wallerstein et al. 2005). Using the trigger as a prompt, the facilitator engages participants by asking questions about how the problems they have identified affect their daily lives, what the broader social and structural issues that perpetuate the problem might be, and what actions they might take to address the problem and thereby transform their reality. The S-H-O-W-E-D model (Shaffer 1983) has been used as a problem-posing guide to encourage this kind of critical thinking and thereby raise critical consciousness. Wallerstein and her colleagues (2005) describe the following sample questions represented by this acronym:

> What do you *SEE*, or how do we name this problem?
>
> What's really *HAPPENING* to the individual/people represented here?
>
> How does this story relate to *OUR* lives, and how do we feel about it?
>
> *WHY* does this happen? Why has this person experienced these problems as an individual or a family member? Why do we face these problems on a community or societal level?
>
> How might we become *EMPOWERED* now that we better understand the collective nature of the problem?
>
> What can we *DO* about these problems? (224)

Liberation education has, at its core, the Freirian concept of *praxis*—the fusion of theory (or reflection) and action that people engage in to create personal and community change (Blackburn 2000; Freire 1994; Wallerstein and Bernstein 1988). As Blackburn (2000) notes, praxis both feeds and results from the process of critical consciousness. Freire believed that social change can happen only through the development of critical consciousness, because people must understand the root causes of their daily life conditions before they can work toward addressing and transforming those root causes. As Soler-Gallart and Brizuela describe in their introduction to Freire's (2000) book *Cultural Action for Freedom* (published posthumously), Freire believed that "the only road to humanization of both the oppressed and the oppressors is through transformation of the structures that dehumanize them. This requires their commitment to understanding the denounced reality and to a theory of action that supports the announced transformation" (2).

Liberation Education as a Community Organizing Approach

As theories of action for structural transformation, liberation education and critical pedagogy have long been adopted by people outside the field of education—including community organizers and public health activists—as essential strategies for mobilizing communities to work for social change. As Sen (2003) notes, community organizations have embraced a number of key components of liberation education to inform their organizing approaches. These premises include the following: people learn better when learning is connected to their day-to-day lives; people "have the seeds of knowledge within themselves" that can be discovered and nurtured in the right environment; and traditional teacher-student hierarchies must be abolished to create shared power with all participants being teacher-learners in an environment of liberation education (105). According to Sen, when community organizers use popular-education approaches, and particularly in leadership development, there is "greater engagement of participants in the material [skills of organizing], more opportunities to build community among members, and more opportunities to raise participants' confidence by stressing internal knowledge" (105). In addition to these benefits for the organizing and leadership development processes, using the methods of liberation education may also advance two critical dimensions in changing the reality of people's lives and moving toward social justice as they "democratize the learning process and produce new knowledge for all involved" (Sen 2003, 106).

One example of a Freirian approach to community organizing for health is the Adolescent Social Action Program (ASAP). Initiated in 1982 and continuing its work for over two decades, ASAP was a youth-centered, intergenerational prevention program with the goal of reducing morbidity and mortality from substance abuse and related problems among youth living in high-risk environments (Wallerstein et al. 2005). Implementing a Freirian model of empowerment education, ASAP was both a health education and a community organizing effort. Beginning with listening sessions, the youth visited hospitals and local jails to hear the stories of people whose lives were affected by substance abuse. In subsequent facilitated dialogues, the youth shared stories of how substance abuse and related issues affected their own lives, identified broader environmental forces that contributed to the problem, and developed ideas for how to respond individually and collectively. Through these processes, the community organizing aspect of the project emerged as increasing student interest led to youth organizing across local schools to increase visibility and critical consciousness about substance abuse and other community concerns. This, in turn, spurred youth involvement in state policy, developing and advocating for local policy changes related to tobacco use, and engaging in other social action projects. Through their engagement with the statewide YouthLink project, for example, some ASAP youth helped introduce bills in the state legislature to secure more appropriate sentencing and counseling for young people arrested for driving while intoxicated, improved resources for homeless youth, and so forth (Wallerstein 2002). As Wallerstein and her colleagues (2005) described, the empowerment education approach was an essential strategy for moving students from individual to collective action: "Empathy with each other and critical analysis of social forces in a safe group context created a bridge between one-dimensional behavioral change and group efforts for social change. The youths were encouraged to engage in dialogue about their own lives and their relationships to their communities to develop an awareness of school and neighborhood resources in order to build socially responsible behaviors. Active participation was a key tenet of ASAP" (222).

Although we focus in this chapter primarily on examples from the fields of health and education, Freire felt a special kinship with social workers and, particularly in his later years, made a special effort to direct many of his ideas to this group (Freire 1990; Carroll and Minkler 2000). Freire (1990) thus wrote of his desire to sharpen still further in his social work students, colleagues, and friends the qualities of "activism," "permanent critical curiosity," tolerance," and "patient impatience" with and in the world. He considered these qualities central to social work practice (7–8). Yeich (1996) and other social workers subsequently have used his approach in their work with the homeless, persons with mental illness, and other vulnerable populations (Carroll and Minkler 2000).

Comparing Alinskyite and Freirian Approaches

A book by one of this chapter's authors, *Streetwise for Book Smarts* (Su 2009), compares the practical application of Alinskyite and Freirian approaches to community organizing. The book's four case study organizations were all working to address school violence and local school reform, had similar levels of resources with which to organize, and had similar core constituencies—primarily poor and near poor communities of color (Latino, African American, and African) who lived in the Bronx, New York, and whose children attended local schools. Despite these similarities, the organizations used very different strategies that emerged from different cultural practices within each organization: "It was not just what they did but *how* they did it that mattered" (Su 2009, 3). The differences in the *what* and the *how* of their organizing efforts were explained in large part by their adherence to either an "Alinskyite tool kit" or a "Freirian tool kit."

The two case studies whose organizational cultures and practices reflected the Alinsky approach were the Bronx chapter of the Association of Community Organizations for Reform Now (ACORN) and the Northwest Bronx Clergy and Community Coalition (NWBCCC). The two case studies that employed the Freirian tool kit were Sistas and Brothas United—a student activist group that was associated with NWBCCC but that used a organizing model different from that of their umbrella organization—and Mothers on the Move.

An organizational culture includes not just articulated values but also normative practices, such as "how organizers talk to and relate to leaders and members, how meetings are conducted, and how decisions about campaigns are made" (Su 2009,11). Among the four groups, the Alinskyite and Freirian approaches differed in three key areas: (1) the emphasis of organizational activities, (2) their approaches to organizational versus personal development, and (3) the nature of leadership development and of the organizer-leader relationship (see table 4.1). This following is a summary of these key areas of difference.

TABLE 4.1.

Comparing the Alinsky and Freirian Approaches

Key Area of Difference	Alinskyite Approach	Freirian Approach
Emphasis of organizational activities	Recruitment and campaigns	Emotional and cultural exchange
Focus of development	Organizational development	Individual development
Organizer-leader relationship	Organizer as teacher-guide	Organizer as partner

Reprinted from C. Su, *Streetwise for Book Smarts: Grassroots Organizing and Education Reform in the Bronx* (Ithaca, N.Y.: Cornell University Press, 2009) by permission of the author and publisher.

Alinsky Tool Kit: ACORN Bronx and Northwest Bronx Clergy and Community Coalition

Emphasis of Organizational Activities: Recruitment and Campaigns

The organizational activities of ACORN Bronx and NWBCCC predominantly focused on recruitment of members and issue campaigns. As previously noted, recruiting large numbers of people to build a power base is a critical component of organizing efforts using an Alinsky approach. The ACORN Bronx organizers' work schedules exemplified this. Working from 11:00 A.M. to 10:00 P.M. on weekdays and half a day on Saturdays, organizers spent four to five hours each day doing door-knocking outreach to recruit members and another three hours in the evenings calling existing or lapsed members to encourage them to renew their memberships and attend meetings. The occasional ACORN Bronx member-ship meetings were focused on specific campaigns and allowed members to "quickly learn about the organization's work and about the roles they could play in assisting the organization to grow and secure campaign wins" (Su 2009, 56). NWBCCC also held mostly campaign-related activities, and they integrated recruitment efforts into these activities. The impact of each issue campaign on the entire *organization* was kept front and center, with "strength in unity" as a key theme. In Alinsky fashion, organizers in both groups were sure to tie these broad-reaching campaigns to the shared self-interests of the membership.

The benefits of these Alinsky-type approaches could be seen in their success-ful use of mass mobilization for and against policy proposals. For example, NWBCCC garnered six thousand extra classroom seats in the South Bronx schools by successfully lobbying the city during its capital plan decision-making process, which occurs only once every five years. Meanwhile, ACORN Bronx helped to mobilize opposition to a citywide referendum that would have allowed Edison Schools, a for-profit school management firm, to take over a few underperforming schools. Statewide, ACORN's New York chapters used their impressive legion of organizers and members to join the teachers' union and ensure high voter turnout at the referendum, and they ultimately defeated the pro-Edison votes by a four-to-one margin.

Emphasis on Organizational Development

By organizing activities that were predominantly geared toward recruitment and current campaigns, ACORN Bronx and NWBCCC demonstrated an Alinsky-type emphasis on organizational development over personal development. ACORN enhanced its capacity as a broad-based organization by generating revenue through membership dues. These dues helped strengthen the organization by holding organizers accountable to the members. As one ACORN organizer described, "It's coming out of your pocket. You're paying my salary [so that] in essence, I need to bust my ass for you" (Su 2009, 59). ACORN Bronx also built the organization by involving members and leaders in campaigns that extended beyond the Bronx and supported citywide or national issues. This helped to strengthen the larger city-, state-, and national-level ACORN organization and create massive scale in its broader campaigns.

NWBCCC also emphasized organizational development as it employed new dues systems and bylaws during the study's fieldwork period. Unlike ACORN, however, it used its large membership base to engage in a variety of activities driven by neighborhood offices rather than by broader citywide or national agendas. In the end, NWBCCC was adept at balancing organizational development with individual interests, while maintaining its focus on the organization as a whole.

Nature of Leadership Development: Organizer as Teacher-Guide

In terms of leadership development, both ACORN Bronx and NWBCCC positioned the organizer as a *teacher-guide* to the local leaders. This leadership development approach sees the organizer imparting information, tools, and strategies to the local leaders, with the former holding the key to accessing power and the latter learning from the organizer how to gain access to that power (Sen 2003). Alinsky (1971) saw this as an important distinction: "The leader goes on to build power to fulfill his desires, to hold and wield the power for purposes both social and personal. . . . The organizer finds his goal in creation of power for others to use" (80). NWBCCC took more time to provide local leaders with in-depth training in how to obtain access to that power than did ACORN Bronx, but the role of organizer as teacher-guide to the leaders was consistent for both organizations (Su 2009).

Struggles Faced by This Organizational Culture

Some of ACORN Bronx's and NWBCCC's struggles reflect common challenges of the Alinsky tradition. To different degrees, the emphasis on recruitment and

organizational growth occurred at the expense of in-depth membership participation and leadership development. This, in turn, contributed to high turnover
rates in both staff and membership. A more substantive sort of tension arose with
the pragmatic, nonideological Alinsky-tradition of organizational development
and issue selection. When some local leaders wanted to take on political issues
such as police brutality and racial profiling, they were discouraged from doing so
because the issues were deemed too controversial or divisive. As noted earlier,
this nonideological stance often includes maintaining a "color-blind" approach to
issues of race/ethnicity that is frequently critiqued as a weakness in the Alinsky
model and that, in many cases, has been modified by some newer organizations
using the Alinsky tradition (Sen 2003; Su 2009).

Freire Tool Kit: Sistas and Brothas United
and Mothers on the Move

Emphasis of Organizational Activities: Emotional and Cultural Exchange

In contrast to the Alinsky-type focus on campaigns and recruitment, the Freirian
approach was generally more holistic and less pragmatic, with activities like soul
food events, fiction book clubs, hip-hop workshops, "sister-bonding" and rap
sessions, ball games, and tutoring and yoga. The following description of a typical
day in the office of Sistas and Brothas United (SBU) suggests a very different
approach to organizing from that demonstrated by the Alinskyite model:

> Every day, dozens of teenagers showed up to discuss local education
> politics, conduct orientation sessions without the supervision of organizers,
> carry out research, chair meetings, and strategize campaigns. . . . One girl
> sat alone. . . . "Leila," another girl asked, "[w]hat's up?" Leila quickly slid a
> composition book across the main table and said, "Last page." The other
> girl quickly opened the composition book and read a poem to herself. She
> then nodded, walked over, and gave Leila a hug. The scene evoked images
> of support groups, therapy sessions, or conflict resolution meetings. It did
> not conform to traditional notions of community organizing in the United
> States. Yet these participants were empowering themselves in a way that
> belied traditional notions of service organizations too. (Su 2009, 76–77)

While many of the activities at SBU and Mothers on the Move (MOM) did not
appear to be directly related to campaigns or recruitment, a closer look at their
use of Freirian approaches revealed that many of the socializing, consciousness-
raising, and political education activities served as foundational components
of their community organizing strategies. In addition to providing informal
opportunities for the development of relationships and trust between members,
these activities allowed participants to engage in dialogue about the issues that
concerned them and to identify the root causes of those issues. As previously

described, Freire emphasized the importance of engaging in critical reflection and dialogue *before* deciding on a course of action. He noted in *Pedagogy of the Oppressed* (1972) that without critical reflection, social change cannot occur, because "the context of the situation, that is, oppression, remains unchanged. . . . To surmount the system of oppression, [people] must first critically recognize its causes, so that through transforming action they can create a new situation" (31–32). This kind of critical reflection and dialogue was integrated into SBU's and MOM's organizational activities.

Emphasis on Individual Development

Dovetailing with this wide range of activities, an emphasis on individual development alongside organizational campaigns was evident in the Freirian organizations. Organizers often blurred the line between "traditional" community organizing and social services. MOM, for instance, developed out of a literacy class for Latina mothers astounded by news reports on Bronx schools. MOM's organizers then continued their attention to individual development with the use of the Social Justice Organizing Training Matrix, which included ten categories, each with a skills list, including both the predictable ones, for example, "relational organizing" and public relations, and also such atypical skills as "body practice (the integration of healthy living practices in personal life through diet, exercise, and recreation) . . . and leadership for family, work, and life" (Su 2009, 97).

Similarly, SBU paid careful attention to individual development through peer tutoring, spoken word workshops, and informal socializing. One organizer described this essential component of developing emerging leaders when he noted, "I spend quality time hanging out with leaders. . . . We talk about how they're doing in schools. We get into family business, get them to the right resources, and get them to advocate for themselves. Building them as individuals is as important as campaign work. . . . We need to build the skills and inner confidence so that they can maintain a certain level of conversation amongst themselves" (87).

Through these opportunities for individual development, leaders and members of SBU and MOM experienced personal transformation that often led them to a greater commitment to the work of the organization and, notably, to each other.

Nature of Leadership Development: Organizer as Partner

In keeping with Freire's notions of a liberatory, rather than banking, mode of pedagogy, organizers at MOM and SBU also worked hard to engage member-leaders as partners. Leaders repeatedly stated that friendship and solidarity, not just overlapping self-interests per se, underlay their decision to join the organizations. One SBU leader noted, "We were friends already; it was a connection we already had. . . . If it had been a regular . . . organizer, it would have been, 'Oh, another routine thing, you got to listen to older people do this, and say that'" (Su 2009, 89).

Rather than building interchangeable leaders, organizers encouraged individual members to pursue tailored interests and build expertise in the policy issues, research methods, or organizing activities they found most compelling. Thus, meetings at SBU and MOM were more likely than those at the Alinsky-type organizations to include leaders' taking turns in reporting back findings from research, or presenting ideas for an ongoing campaign, to the larger group. They were also more likely to insist upon active consensus at meetings, whereby each attendee explicitly approved or questioned an agenda item before votes were taken. Ultimately, organizers hoped to engage in dialogue, which Freire (1972) stated is essential to "generating critical thinking" (81).

Struggles Faced by This Organizational Culture

Partly because the Freire-inspired model of organizing is most participatory and focused on building both trust and relationships, it is also quite a bit more labor intensive. With less emphasis on large numbers, and more on individual transformation and building deep, sustainable foundations of support based on relationships, Freirian groups struggle to achieve the large scale of Alinskyite groups. These organizations further emphasize the importance of looking at root causes, not just winnable issues, making it that much more difficult to capture the "clincher" of a decisive campaign victory. Indeed, as Schutz (2007) has argued, Freirian approaches do not always help marginalized constituencies move beyond social critique and build concrete political power. Still, one MOM organizer insisted that "we have a moral imperative—that we as organizers of color also deeply feel—to take on . . . nonwinnable issues if that is where the people are at and what they are feeling!" (Su 2009, 102). Ideally, this sort of deep-seated commitment helps to build sustainable, meaningful participation and lifetime activists for social change overall, not just for the specific campaigns or organizations.

Implications for Policymaking

The Alinsky- and Freire-inspired organizational cultures yielded different political strategies for policy reform. Overall, the Alinsky-type groups aimed to "pursue strategies that help constituents to win referenda of existing policy proposals or elections, engage in confrontational strategies, and build broad-based coalitions in the name of 'color-blind' equality," in which race and ethnicity are not explicitly addressed (Su 2009, 3). In contrast, the Freirian-style SBU and MOM primarily worked to construct and implement *new* policy proposals (rather than support existing ones), engaged in mostly *collaborative* strategies (rather than confrontational ones), and addressed issues of race and ethnicity *directly and adeptly* (rather than taking a "color-blind" approach).

Further, while the Freirian groups emphasized means as much as ends, and deliberately blurred the two, the Alinsky groups' strategies followed Alinsky's quip that "the end justifies almost any means" (1971, 29). While Freire insisted that critical dialogue be interwoven throughout the organizing and policymaking processes, Alinsky called for "policy after power" (104), so that actions are not taken until the mass organization had been mobilized. As Alinsky noted, "change comes from power and power comes from the organization" (113). Overall, the impression, when looking at these different policymaking strategies in terms of the case studies, is that "the Alinskyite groups ultimately tried to help their constituents obtain a larger slice of the social, political, and economic pie while the Freirian ones tried to make the school system a whole new kind of bigger, better pie altogether" (Su 2009, 3).

Conclusion: Learning from Both Models

While the Alinsky tradition and Freirian approaches to community organizing differ in their philosophies, strategies, and end goals, each offers a useful and relevant framework for creating social and structural change to improve the public's health and welfare and advance social justice. For example, Alinsky-type groups play an important role in helping to mobilize popular support for specific legislative bills, like the historic health care reform bill signed into law in 2010. In contrast, a Freirian model may be more promising in helping urban communities address complex, seemingly intractable problems like geographical concentrations of respiratory illness, where no single problem source or "target" exists (González et al. 2007).

Much can be learned from the respective strengths and limitations of each of these models in terms of how they might complement each other to create a stronger model overall. None of the case study organizations in Su's study perfectly fit Alinsky or Freirian archetypes. Nor should they. Freirian groups can learn to achieve greater scale and clinch campaign wins from Alinsky-type groups, while Alinskyites can help to prevent organizer and member-leader burnout, sustain policy formulation strategies, and tackle seemingly (but not inherently) divisive issues by learning from Freirian groups. As Sen (2003) has noted:

> There is a danger of moving too far into political education without grounding in an action plan. Some feminists and racial justice organizers, for example, have reacted to Alinskyist limitations by creating programs that are heavy on leadership training and political education but light on campaigns and action. I can understand the temptation. Providing extensive developmental programs for twenty people we can count on is much easier than constantly recruiting and politically orienting new people so they too can confront the power structure. Likewise, it is often easier to simply recruit those new people over and over again than to deal with the contradictions residing in the ideas of our members. The beauty of innovation in organizing emerges from the marriage of the two: political education creates the reflection and growth opportunities that motivate action, and action provides the expression of newly clarified values. (182)

Using a combination of Alinsky-type and Freirian approaches, community organizing efforts that are aimed at improving the well-being of our communities and environment can attain the "people power" necessary to gain influence in the policymaking process while also facilitating transformative experiences through which people gain a greater sense of control over their lives through a social action process focused on critical consciousness and praxis.

ACKNOWLEDGMENTS

Portions of this chapter were adapted from Celina Su, *Streetwise for Book Smarts: Grassroots Organizing and Education Reform in the Bronx*. Copyright 2009. Used by permission of the publisher, Cornell University Press.

REFERENCES

Alinsky, S. D. 1946. *Reveille for Radicals*. Chicago: University of Chicago Press.
———. 1971. *Rules for Radicals: A Pragmatic Primer for Realistic Radicals*. New York: Vintage Books.
Bernard, E. 2002. "Popular Education: Training Rebels with a Cause." In *Teaching for Change: Popular Education and the Labor Movement*, edited by L. Delp, M. Outman-Kramer, S. J. Schurman, and K. Wong, 6–8. Los Angeles: UCLA Center for Labor Research and Education.
Blackburn, J. 2000. "Understanding Paulo Freire: Reflections on the Origins, Concepts, and Possible Pitfalls of His Educational Approach." *Community Development Journal* 35, no. 1:3–15.
Carroll, J., and Minkler, M. 2000. "Freire's Message for Social Workers: Looking Back and Looking Ahead." *Journal of Community Practice* 8:21–36.
Chávez, V., M. Minkler, N. Wallerstein, and M. S. Spencer. 2010. "Community Organizing for Health and Social Justice." In *Prevention Is Primary*, edited by L. Cohen, S. Chehimi, and V. Chávez, 87–112. 2nd ed. San Francisco: Jossey-Bass.
DeFilippis, J., R. Fisher, and E. Shragge. 2010. *Contesting Community: The Limits and Potential of Local Organizing*. New Brunswick, N.J.: Rutgers University Press.
Delgado, G. 1986. *Organizing the Movement: The Roots and Growth of ACORN*. Philadelphia: Temple University Press.
Freire, P. 1972. *Pedagogy of the Oppressed*. Translated by Myra Bergman Ramos. New York: Herder and Herder.
———. 1990. "A Critical Understanding of Social Work." Translated by Marilyn Moch. *Journal of Progressive Human Services* 1, no. 1:3–9.
———. 1994. *Pedagogy of Hope*. New York: Continuum.
———. 2000. *Cultural Action for Freedom*. Harvard Educational Review Monograph Series, no. 1. Rev. ed. Cambridge: Harvard Educational Review.
Freire, P., and D. P. Macedo. 1995. "A Dialogue: Culture, Language, and Race." *Harvard Educational Review* 65:377–402.
González, E. R., R. P. Lejano, G. Vidales, R. F. Conner, et al. 2007. "Participatory Action Research for Environmental Health: Encountering Freire in the Urban Barrio." *Journal of Urban Affairs* 29:77–100.
hooks, b. 1994. *Teaching to Transgress: Education as the Practice of Freedom*. New York: Routledge.
Horton, M. 1998. *The Long Haul: An Autobiography*. Garden City, N.Y.: Doubleday.
Horton, M., and P. Freire. 1990. *We Make the Road by Walking: Conversations on Education and Social Change*. Philadelphia: Temple University Press.

Kleidman, R. 2004. "Community Organizing and Regionalism." *City and Community* 3:430–21.

Miller, M. 2009. *A Community Organizer's Tale: People and Power in San Francisco.* Berkeley: Calif.: Heyday Books.

Minkler, M. 2005. "Community Organizing with the Elderly Poor in San Francisco's Tenderloin District." In *Community Organizing and Community Building for Health*, edited by M. Minkler. 2nd ed., 272–287. New Brunswick, N.J.: Rutgers University Press.

Minkler, M., and K. Cox. 1980. "Creating Critical Consciousness in Health: Applications of Freire's Philosophy and Methods in the Health Care Setting." *International Journal of Health Services* 10:311–322.

Rothman, J. 2008. "Multi Modes of Community Intervention." In *Strategies of Community Intervention*, edited by J. Rothman, J. L. Erlich, and J. E. Tropman, 141–170. 7th ed. Peosta, Iowa: Eddie Bowers.

Schutz, A. 2007. "Education Scholars Have Much to Learn about Social Action: An Essay Review." *Education Review* 10, no. 3. http://edrev.asu.edu/essays/v10n3index.html.

Sen, R. 2003. *Stir It Up: Lessons in Community Organizing and Advocacy.* San Francisco: Jossey-Bass.

Shaffer, R. 1983. *Beyond the Dispensary.* Nairobi, Kenya: Amref.

Stall, S., R. Stoecker. 2005. "Toward a Gender Analysis of Community Organizing Models: Liminality and the Intersection of Spheres." In *Community Organizing and Community Building for Health*, edited by M. Minkler, 196–217. 2nd ed. New Brunswick, N.J.: Rutgers University Press.

Staples, L. 2004. *Roots to Power: A Manual for Grassroots Organizing.* 2nd ed. Westport, Conn.: Praeger.

Su, C. 2009. *Streetwise for Book Smarts: Grassroots Organizing and Education Reform in the Bronx.* Ithaca, N.Y.: Cornell University Press.

Wallerstein, N. 2002. "Empowerment to Reduce Health Disparities." Supplement, *Scandinavian Journal of Public Health* 30, no. 59:72–77.

Wallerstein, N., and E. Bernstein. 1988. "Empowerment Education: Freire's Ideas Adapted to Health Education." *Health Education Quarterly* 15:379–394.

Wallerstein, N., V. Sanchez, and L. Velarde. 2005. "Freirian Praxis in Health Education and Community Organizing: A Case Study of an Adolescent Prevention Program." In *Community Organizing and Community Building for Health*, edited by M. Minkler, 218–236. 2nd ed. New Brunswick, N.J.: Rutgers University Press.

Yeich, S. 1996. "Grassroots Organizing with Homeless People: A Participatory Approach." *Journal of Social Issues* 52:111–121.

5

Community Building Practice

An Expanded Conceptual Framework

CHERYL L. WALTER
CHERYL A. HYDE

Note from Cheryl A. Hyde: In the original version of this chapter, Walter (1997) argued that community needed to be understood as more than simply a geographic unit. She persuasively made the case that community be understood as a dynamic, multidimensional entity and that relationships were a critical element in community practice, including the relationship between the practitioner and other community members. In both this and her subsequent work, Walter essentially anticipated key developments in the community building literature. The current version of this chapter, rewritten by Walter and Hyde, incorporates this newer scholarship that affirms the original insights made by Walter over fifteen years ago.

HOW WE CONCEPTUALIZE community powerfully influences what we see and what we do in community practice. We draw upon theories of community, and models of community practice rooted in those theories, to orient ourselves, to assess what is going on, and to help us make decisions concerning what to do, why, and how.

Community practice often is defined and categorized primarily according to various *strategies and methods of practice*. For example, in their overview of community practice, Weil and Gamble (2005, 128) identify eight different models distinguished by strategic preferences. In his classic, and now revised, work, Jack Rothman (2007, 28) presents a community intervention framework with these key approaches: planning and policy, community capacity development, and social advocacy. He then suggests that these approaches can be blended, though his is nonetheless a framework that essentially privileges the "strategic engine" of a given model (see chapter 3). This, and similar, approaches to community practice (for example, see Homan 2011; Sen 2003; Staples 2004) operate from the assumption that strategies, when appropriately matched with the situation, will rectify the challenge or problem. The community, then, serves as the arena in which strategies and tactics are identified and used by the practitioner.

In contrast, the community practice orientation that we present in this chapter differs in three important ways. First, the focus is on community, and not a strategic framework. Rather than being wedded to a specific strategic repertoire, the practitioner is flexible in his or her use of strategies and tactics; the situation, including, importantly, the community partner or group, guides strategic selection rather than a strategic framework being imposed from outside. Second, community is understood as an inclusive, multidimensional, and dynamic system, of which we, as practitioners, are a part. This complexity encompasses the beliefs and actions of individuals, groups, and organizations and extends to connections beyond the community's boundaries. Third, community practice is about building capacities, not fixing problems. This necessitates recognition of the strengths of individuals, groups and organizations (see chapter 10), and attendant relationships and networks.

A *community building practice orientation* seeks to engage with the multiple dimensions of community, recognizing the range of perspectives and relationships that exist and integrating diverse strategies and methods of practice. The goal is to build the capacity of the entire system, and all its participants, to operate as community. In deeply and broadly engaging with the relational dynamics of practice, this approach shares common ground with the community psychology and social capital literature (Block 2008; Chaskin et al. 2001; Figueira-McDonough 2001; Putnam 2000; Putnam and Feldstein 2003; Pyles 2009; Reed 2005; M. R. Warren 2001; Wuthnow 1998).

Understanding Community

Before delineating the key elements and dimensions of community building practice, we need to consider how community is defined. In practice, we generally are taught to conceive of the community as being a neighborhood of people with whom we work; the people within a city or county dealing with a particular issue or problem to which our organization provides services; or people with a shared racial, ethnic, gender, or sexual orientation identity. As classically defined by Ronald Warren (1963), "the community," in this sense, is a boundaried social or demographic unit involving a neighborhood or people who share a common issue or interest with which practitioners interact to bring about change. Another way of stating this is that a community can be defined by shared space or area, common ties, or social interaction (Hardcastle and Powers 2004, 91). Typically, though, the community is understood in the geographic sense with relationships and identity based on sense of place, which in the United States, with the continued high level of neighborhood segregation, tends to tie closely to other sources of community identification, such as race and ethnicity (Bell and Lee 2011). Rubin and Rubin (2007) broaden the more place-based definition of community by noting that there are nongeographic entities called "communities of interest" (i.e., professional associations, social movement participation, and political affiliations). For example, during the 1960s, the Student Nonviolent Coordinating Committee, a broad civil rights organization and network, was known as "the beloved community." Today, the gay or LGBT (lesbian, gay, bisexual, transgender) community and the well-organized disability rights community remain important sources of affiliation and collective identity.

Recognizing these "communities of interest" has been an important part of a significant shift over the past decade in how we conceptualize community and community practice. The approach presented here reflects this shift, as we emphasize the importance of changing focus from *the community* as a social/demographic entity or unit with which we interact, to *community* as a multidimensional/dynamic whole, or system, of which we are a part. To develop an understanding of community, then, we need to articulate, visualize, and examine the unique qualities exhibited by each of these dimensions and how they in turn come together to make up the complex and dynamic "system" of community.

Within this framework, we need to be vigilant about our role as community practitioners, the organization we work with and its agenda, and the objectives of the sources that fund our work. By not explicitly acknowledging the multiple constituencies and interests that are engaged with and exist within the community, as an integral part of the community, we run the risk of oversimplifying issues, of seeing and attempting to address problems only at the community level, and of being self-serving and society serving, as opposed to community serving, with our interventions (Rivera and Erlich 1995; Pyles 2009). Although the imperative "Start where the people are" is familiar to most health educators and other social change practitioners, we need to be mindful of the risks that can sabotage that focus, such as being driven by funding, which can fundamentally alter our priorities and the ways we interact with the community (see chapter 7).

Whether defined by geographic or "nonplace" parameters, community can be understood as a social system composed of various interlocking local subsystems: production-distribution-consumption, socialization, social control, social participation, and mutual support (R. L. Warren 1963). A community needs these subsystems to function effectively, although as Hardcastle and Powers (2004) note, institutions and organizations external to the community may fulfill these functions. In addition to understanding what each of these subsystems provides for a community, Warren argues that they also interact with one another, creating an interdependency among the subsystems.

Long before contemporary discussions of social capital, R. L. Warren (1963) also had stated that the health of a community could be assessed by analyzing two dimensions: (1) vertical patterns of integration, which are the connections with institutions and organizations beyond the community; and (2) horizontal patterns of integration, or the relationships between social, economic, political, and cultural entities within the community. Figueira-McDonough (2001) expanded on this framework by differentiating between primary and secondary networks on the horizontal dimension and also noting the importance of tracking the relative mobility of community members as an indicator of area health and well-being. Community can be described as dynamic and emergent in that it is continually being created and re-created, its parameters and relationships taking shape and changing shape, through the actions and interactions of people and organizations.

Proponents of social capital theories also often use Warren's work as a foundation for their discussions on bridging and bonding social capital. As discussed briefly in chapter 3, social capital is the value that comes from connections within and between social networks—the building of trust, collective norms and reciprocating relationships. Three types of social capital exist: *bonding*—strengthening existing relationships; *bridging*—building new relationships; and *linking*—fostering linkages between community members and community organizations (Figueira-McDonough 2001; Putnam 2000; Skocpol 2003). Social capital is the communal "glue" necessary for community capacity building and collective action, and an important contributor to individual and community health and well-being (Kawachi et al. 2008).

Understanding patterns of integration is important in our work as community building practitioners, since they express the relative strength of reciprocity, dependency, and participation among and between internal and external units (Hardcastle and Powers 2004). For example, a community with high vertical integration and low horizontal integration relies heavily on noncommunity resources to meet the needs of its members; such communities are often referred to as "client neighborhoods" because of this dependency (see chapter 10). In contrast, a community that exhibits high horizontal but low vertical integration, sometimes referred to as a *parochial community*, probably has a strong sense of communal identity but may not be able to get needed resources, found outside the community, that are necessary for functioning. Understanding this helps provide an important context for practice as well as the foundation for understanding the multidimensional nature of community.

Explicit in the orientation to community that we propose is that people develop and negotiate relationships, and that these processes shape, and are shaped by, the capacities of the community and its economic, political, cultural, and civic subsystems. Thus, an integral part of any community building effort is facilitating these relationships that then serve as the backbone for healthy community functioning. It is therefore puzzling that many (perhaps even most) accounts of community building either ignore or only minimally address this relational aspect of practice. There are, of course, exceptions. In *The Other Side of Organizing* (1982), Steve Burghardt effectively argues for placing the "personal," including relationships, at the center of practice. Advocates of feminist approaches to organizing often underscore the centrality of emotional bonds in practice (Gutiérrez and Lewis 1994; Hyde 2005; Weil et al. 1998; see chapter 12). And Loretta Pyles (2009) offers an extended discussion on negotiating the emotional and relational terrains that come with organizing. This means that we need to understand what motivates people to engage in and remain committed to community work—what are their values, aspirations, and expectations? While inevitably messier than frameworks that are strategy driven, approaches that place relationships at the heart of any effort also tend to be more authentic. Yet while noting that networks and linkages are central to community functioning, most approaches focus on the importance of leaders, organizations, and opportunities (see, for example, Chaskin et al. 2001; Staples 2004; see chapter 11). The community building practitioner needs to be aware of and engaged in the relationships that are built between people as well as with the organizational units of which they are a part.

By virtue of involvement in relationships with one another, every organization and every person at every level within both the horizontal and vertical dimensions is potentially a part of community. The people and organizations included in this conceptualization of community represent multiple stakeholders with diverse interests, those referred to as the community in all their diversity, as well as those formerly considered to be outside the community but who, in actuality, have critical roles in its health and well-being. These organizations include those for which we as practitioners work, the funders of our work and the providers of services for the community. Using this broader lens, even regulatory institutions may be seen as part of community, as when a state Environmental Protection Agency (EPA) requires that a toxic polluter in a largely low-income community of color change its practices to ensure that local residents are not harmed or when a state agency closes down an organization, such as a medical clinic, because of various code violations and consumer complaints. Those residing in the neighborhood or those closest to the issue in terms of experience may be seen as being local or intimately involved. Those farther removed who influence the issue or locality because they control resources are more remote. But all may be integral to community.

Such an orientation has special relevance for the increasing numbers of us who, by virtue of our race, gender, class, or sexual orientation, consciously identify as part of the community in which we are working. But even those not so identified can benefit from this broader reconceptualization of community because it enlarges what we take into account when orienting ourselves in practice and thereby reveals additional avenues for practice activity.

Once we broaden our conceptualization of community and allow it to become *how we orient ourselves in community practice*, we are more likely to understand our own influence (as practitioner) on a given initiative. That those of us engaged in community occupy a variety of positions in relation to the issue or locality around which community is defined suggests that we will often have different interests, experiences, levels of power, and perspectives. These differences are reflected in our consciousness, manifested in the identities and values we hold; the language we use to name and label; and the themes of the "stories" we tell regarding ourselves and our roles, each other, and how we are related.

The inclusion of consciousness in our conceptualization of community is fundamental to this shift from *the* community to community. In the view of the community as a functional unit, consciousness has no central role, which may lead us in practice to overlook its impact. For example, beliefs around whether people who are poor "deserve" assistance have a direct impact on what kind of social and health policies and services are implemented, on what barriers to access to these services are erected, and on how people who are recipients and providers of those services feel. If we view community as a multidimensional system, consciousness becomes one of the important dimensions to consider in community practice. Consciousness, as Freire (1973) argued so eloquently, is the mesh that joins us in community, the full spectrum of perceptions, cultural constructs, and frameworks through which interaction with one another and our environment is filtered and shared. In our actions, this consciousness and these relationships are played out and emerge as the substance of what community is.

Finally, community has to do not just with engagement in relationship but, ultimately, with the quality of the relationship. Calling something community does not necessarily make it so. There can be greater or lesser degrees of "communityness." As Philip Selznick (1992) aptly points out, simply because community is often found in common residence, for example, does not make common residence an essential or defining feature of community. This is increasingly clear in an era in which many of us do not even know the names of our closest neighbors. And, as we have all likely experienced, the word *community* is often used even where little true community can be found. An organization, for example, can create token "community involvement" to satisfy a funding mandate or may use precious community resources without ever actually intending to share power or seriously consider community recommendations (for a fuller discussion of this problem and its implications, see chapter 7).

Selznick (1992) further suggests that "a group is a community to the extent that it encompasses a broad range of activities and interests, and to the extent that participation implicates whole persons rather than segmental interests or activities. Thus understood, community can be treated as a variable aspect of group experience" (358) Selznick goes on to argue that "a framework of shared beliefs, interests, and commitments unites a set of varied groups and activities. Some are central, others peripheral, but all are connected by bonds that establish a common faith or fate, a personal identity, a sense of belonging, and a supportive structure of activities and relationships. The more pathways are provided for participation in diverse ways and touching multiple interests . . . the richer is the experience of community" (358–359). Similarly, John Gardner (1991) argued over twenty years ago that the essential ingredients of community included shared vision, sense of purpose and values, wholeness incorporating diversity, caring, trust, teamwork, respect and recognition, communication, participation, affirmation, investment, and links beyond the community.

Conceptualizing community in this way enables us to see ourselves and each other as part of a dynamic system that is continually being created and re-created and that affects and is affected by our consciousness and actions. Everything within the dimensions is related, influenced by and influencing all the dimensions, and coming together to make a complex and inextricable whole. This is one of the qualities that make community a system.

Community Building Practice

The shift to a new way of conceptualizing community has important implications for community practice. First, it places *community*, not *the community* and not *the community organizer*, at the center of practice. Rather than being the social unit with which practitioners interact as various strategies are employed, community becomes the milieu in which we as community practitioners interact with people and organizations and of which we are an integral part. With community at the center, a broad and inclusive continuum of community participants and stake-holders is encompassed in a way that extends to each power and recognition of their contribution to building and shaping community. This means that regardless of the context or level we occupy—whether as a person facing an issue, a resident in a neighborhood, a volunteer, a professional providing services, an administrator, a student, or a high-level official—we can be practicing community.

Second, thinking of community as multidimensional, involving people and organizations at many levels, consciousness, actions, and context, allows us to model greater complexity. By perceiving community as a complex whole, we develop our ability to perceive and work with the actual complexity that exists. This enables us to take more information and relationships into account when orienting ourselves in practice; and it suggests many possible levels and areas with which to engage and in which to work. Further, by highlighting the interrelatedness of the dimensions, it shows us how we might have an impact on multiple dimensions simultaneously with our efforts.

Third, if we perceive community not as an existing unit that needs to be organized differently but as a dynamic and emergent whole embodying varying degrees of communityness that is continually being built or created, then the building of community will be one of the central concerns and activities of community practice. Community is created or built, or not, with each of our actions; with our consciousness concerning ourselves, others, and the issues; and with our relationships, whatever the task. As Michael Fabricant and Robert Fisher (2002, 6) suggest, it attends heavily to process as "the basis upon which relationships are built." Within this vision of community building, "process and content are inseparable" (Senge 1995, 52). Congruence between what we do and how we do it, a joining of ends and means, is essential if we aim to foster communication, participation, diversity, identity, a shared vision, and the other elements and ingredients of community. Opportunities for building and practicing community are continually available, whether in communicative/expressive events or functional activities, such as meetings, document writing, telephone calls, theater productions, picnics and parties, marches/rallies, program operations, legislation, policy implementation, or budgeting.

Fourth, community practice then becomes less an intervention or coming between and more an interchange, where each of us is changed through coming together. Learning to engage with one another with respect and trust, developing partnerships, and attending to our consciousness and actions call upon us as whole persons. This, in turn, necessitates that we be open to learning and change within ourselves and not just trying to create change outside ourselves in the community or in institutions (see chapter 8 and appendix 3). This change can involve conflict, emotion, identity crises, and ethical dilemmas; and it may require that we confront racism, classism, sexism, handicappism, "professionalism," and homophobia in ourselves, in others, and in institutions as we struggle for "wholeness incorporating diversity."

The essence of a community building orientation to practice is in how we conceptualize and relate to community. It is not an approach that employs a particular strategy for intervening in the community. Rather, it is a practice orientation that begins from perceiving community as a multidimensional, dynamic, and emergent whole of which we are a part. This whole includes people, organizations, consciousness, actions, and context; and it can exhibit greater or lesser degrees of communityness. The practice orientation proposed here seeks to build community through fostering the ingredients of community and engaging with the multiple dimensions of community both as an approach to doing things and as a desired outcome. What unites this work is that it is grounded in constructing community through building trust, building relationships, building ways of working together, and building understanding. Community building is a way of doing things, attending to all these dimensions to involve everyone, to develop us as people, to build shared visions and goals, and to take action together.

Community Building: A Case Example

The following case example illustrates what can happen when practitioners shift their orientation from strategy specific to one of building community. Since its inception in the mid-1980s, members of what we will call the Feminist Health Center (located in a southwestern urban area) were committed to a highly politicized self-help model for women's health. Through health clinics, educational workshops, and political programs, staff and volunteers promoted a radical feminist perspective that called for women having full and complete control of all aspects of their health and well-being. This political framework extended to the governance of the organization. Members adhered to a collectivist model in which everyone participated in decisions and operations of the center. The center's external connections primarily were with other women's self-help health centers across the United States.

The organization's ideology, and especially its governance strategy, necessitated a high degree of commitment and involvement. Despite a radical rhetoric that supported disenfranchised people and communities in the United States and third world countries, however, the center's membership was overwhelming white women with access to other sources of income. Women who availed themselves of the center's services also fit these demographics. In effect, the center operated as a small, tightly integrated club with high demands in terms of member participation and little connection to the dynamics of its immediate geographic community.

This exclusivity would be challenged, however, by two factors. First, members began to question the effectiveness of their governance strategy, specifically the time requirements and overall efficiency of the collectivist process. With an economic and political climate increasingly hostile to women's reproductive rights and social services, the women began to consider whether other ways of operating, even if they diverged somewhat from a radical ideology, would be a better path to survival. The economic and political climate also significantly shaped the second factor, in that this region was targeted by increasingly anti-immigrant actions. Specifically, the Immigration and Naturalization Service (INS) began to do "sweeps" of the area, picking up any individual who might be in the country illegally. This meant that members of the local Latino community, who mostly were migrant farmworkers, were targets of raids and other deportation measures. Fear and suspicion soon became commonplace within the community.

Even though the Feminist Health Center (FHC) was not well networked locally, its members were not completely isolated from what was occurring in the larger geographic community. Members decided to join a fledgling coalition that offered sanctuary and assistance to immigrants. Whenever the INS was spotted, a phone tree was activated that warned coalition members that a raid or other action was imminent. Community organizations, including the FHC, would then provide space where immigrants could hide during INS sweeps. Sometimes entire families would seek assistance during these actions.

Interesting dynamics emerged during these times when Latino families sought refuge at the FHC. As center members began to interact with the immigrants, they soon recognized that even the most basic health care was needed by these individuals and their families. FHC members wrestled with the implications of opening up the center to people who could not participate as fully as traditional members did and to including men and children as part of their client base. As substantial as these changes would be, FHC members began to realize the benefits of this emerging sense of community. In other words, through the relationship and community building that occurred during emergency times, the FHC was able to see a new version of itself that was firmly planted in community.

From this starting point, the FHC transformed into a community-based wellness center that offers educational health programs and medical services to women, men, and children. The center has partnered with the county health board to promote culturally sensitive nutrition programs and with the local school district to facilitate adult literacy programs among its adult clients. Both the board and the staff expanded to include male practitioners; overall, the membership was greatly diversified. Offerings and literature now are bilingual. And while no longer run as a collective, the center does encourage participation from staff, volunteers, and community members. For example, its board of directors has designated community and patient positions, which have authentic (rather than token) participation in governance. A number of staff, including several physician assistants and patient advocates, are Latinas from the immigrant community.

This brief account doesn't capture the angst of this transformation process. A number of the center's original members left—upset that the women-centered, collectivist model was being abandoned. Those who remained spoke poignantly of the challenges involved in this dramatic change, but also underscored that once they had engaged with the Latino community they could not turn back. In other words, the relationships and actual experience of communityness took precedent over operative strategies. Now, the FHC is fully embedded in its broader geographic community and specifically has developed an authentic partnership with the immigrant community. In turn, "the community" has embraced the FHC as a critical actor in health care, specifically, and community capacity building in general.

Skills and Principles for Community Building Practice

Since how we do what we do is essential to the building of community, it is critical that we develop translatable skills and principles for fostering community, participation, and creativity in the planning and conducting of activities and events. These skills and principles for building community must be relevant for use in a broad range of situations, with a broad range of people, and at many levels. They should also lend themselves to being taught to others through modeling and opportunity for practice. A preliminary list of skills for building community includes management of interconnectedness, communication, process awareness, process commentary, creative planning, and personhood:

- Management of interconnectedness involves systems thinking, direction, coordination, facilitation, appreciation, and affirmation.
- Communication through the medium of speech, writing, music, art, film, or movement, coupled with the willingness and ability to listen, see, and understand, and to ask questions, serves to make human experience accessible and thus human community possible.
- Process awareness involves awareness of the dynamic quality of community and the ability to attend to the here and now on multiple levels and in multiple dimensions simultaneously.

- Process commentary involves the ability to articulate process and to bring the discussion of what's going on into the here and now.
- Creative planning involves the reconciliation and unification of multiple visions, where possible, toward the design of programs and the use of resources.
- Personhood involves clarity, strength, commitment, vision, integrity, flexibility, the willingness to take leadership, trust and respect, responsibility, follow-through, the ability to exchange positive energy, and the willingness to change.

These are skills that can be developed and employed by all of us in every aspect of community practice, whether as health educators, social workers, volunteers, consumers, or administrators; whether working with peers, clients, constituents, managers, coalitions, state or county workers, legislators, or students.

Along with skills for building community, there are "operating principles for building community" that can be used to guide our practice (Brown et al. 1996, 525–529). These principles include the following:

- Focus on real work.
- Keep it simple.
- Act.
- "Build from good, expect better, make great."
- Seek what unifies.
- Do it when people are ready.
- Design spaces where community can happen.
- Find and cultivate informal leaders.
- Learn how to host good gatherings.
- Acknowledge people's contributions.
- Involve the whole person.
- Celebrate.

Practicing these skills and principles is a lifelong process, both professional and personal. Ultimately, it is about the kind of community we want to be a part of. These are things we already do, whether consciously or not, whether well or not. Practicing them consciously while seeking to build community is community building practice.

REFERENCES

Bell, J., and M. M. Lee 2011. *Place and Race Matter: Impacting Health through a Focus on Race and Place.* Oakland, Calif.: PolicyLink.

Block, P. 2008. *Community: The Structure of Belonging.* San Francisco: Berrett-Koehler.

Brown, J., B. Smith, and D. Isaacs. 1996. "Operating Principles for Building Community." In *The Fifth Discipline Fieldbook: Strategies and Tools for Building a Learning Organization,* ed. P. M. Senge, A. Kleiner, C. Roberts, R. B. Ross, and B. J. Smith, 525–529. New York: Currency Doubleday.

Burghardt, S. 1982. *The Other Side of Organizing: Personal Dilemmas and Political Demands.* Rochester, Vt.: Schenkman Books.

Chaskin, R., P. Brown, S. Venkatesh, and A. Vidal. 2001. *Building Community Capacity.* New York: Aldine de Gruyter.

Fabricant, M., and R. Fisher. 2002. "Agency-Based Community Building in Low Income Neighborhoods: A Praxis Framework." *Journal of Community Practice* 10, no. 2:1–22.

Figueira-McDonough, J. 2001. *Community Analysis and Praxis: Toward a Grounded Civil Society.* Philadelphia: Brunner-Routledge.

Freire, P. 1973. *Education for Critical Consciousness.* New York: Seabury Press.

Gardner, J. W. 1991. *Building Community.* Washington, D.C.: Independent Sector Leadership Studies Program.

Gutiérrez, L., and E. Lewis. 1994. "Community Organizing with Women of Color: A Feminist Approach." *Journal of Community Practice* 1, no. 2:23–44.

Hardcastle, D. and P. Powers. 2004. *Community Practice: Theories and Skills for Social Workers.* 2nd ed. New York: Oxford University Press.

Homan, M. 2011. *Promoting Community Change: Making It Happen in the Real World.* 5th ed. Pacific Grove, Calif.: Brooks/Cole.

Hyde, C. A. 2005. "Feminist Community Practice." In *Handbook on Community Practice,* edited by M. Weil, 360–371. Newbury Park: Sage.

Kawachi, I, S. V. Subramanian, and D. Kim. 2008. *Social Capital and Health.* New York: Springer Science and Business Media.

Putnam, R. 2000. *Bowling Alone: The Collapse and Revival of American Community.* New York: Simon and Schuster.

Putnam, R., and L. Feldstein. 2003. *Better Together: Restoring the American Community.* New York: Simon and Schuster.

Pyles, L. 2009. *Progressive Community Organizing: A Critical Approach for a Globalizing World.* New York: Routledge.

Rothman, J. 2007. Multi Modes of Intervention on the Macro Level. *Journal of Community Practice* 15, no. 4:11–40.

Rubin, H., and I. Rubin. 2007. *Community Organizing and Development.* 4th ed. Boston: Allyn and Bacon.

Rivera, F. G., and J. L. Erlich. 1995. "Introduction: Prospects and Challenges." In *Community Organizing in a Diverse Society,* edited by F. G. Rivera and J. L. Erlich. Boston: Allyn and Bacon.

Selznick, P. 1992. *The Moral Commonwealth: Social Theory and the Promise of Community.* Berkeley and Los Angeles: University of California Press.

Sen, R. 2003. *Stir It Up: Lessons in Community Organizing and Advocacy.* San Francisco: Jossey-Bass.

Senge, P. M. 1995. Creating Quality Communities. In *Community Building: Renewing Spirit and Learning in Business,* edited by K. Godzdz, 49–55. San Francisco: New Leaders Press.

Skocpol, T. 2003. *Diminished Democracy: From Membership to Management in American Civic Life.* Norman: University of Oklahoma Press.

Staples, L. 2004. *Roots to Power: A Manual for Grassroots Organizing.* 2nd ed. Westport, Conn.: Praeger.

Walter, C. L. 1997. "Community Building Practice: A Conceptual Framework." In *Community Building and Community Organizing for Health,* edited by Meredith Minkler, 68–83. New Brunswick, N.J.: Rutgers University Press.

Warren, M. R. 2001. *Dry Bones Rattling: Community Building to Revitalize American Democracy.* Princeton, N.J.: Princeton University Press.

Warren, R. L. 1963. *The Community in America.* Chicago: Rand McNally.

Weil, M., and D. Gamble. 2005. "Evolution, Models and the Changing Context of Community Practice." In *The Handbook of Community Practice*, edited by M. Weil, 117–150. Thousand Oaks, Calif.: Sage.

Weil, M., D. Gamble, and E. Williams. 1998. Women, Communities, and Development. In *The Role of Gender in Practice Knowledge: Claiming Half the Human Experience*, edited by J. Figueira-McDonough, F. E. Netting, and A. Nichols-Casebolt, 241–286. New York: Garland Press.

Wuthnow, R. 1998. *Loose Connections: Joining Together in America's Fragmented Communities.* Cambridge, Mass.: Harvard University Press.

PART THREE

Building Effective Partnerships and Anticipating and Addressing Ethical Challenges

One of the most important parts of the professional's role in community organizing and other aspects of community practice involves building and maintaining effective partnerships that enable working with, not on, communities. Yet as DeFilippis and colleagues (2010) point out, the very notion of community is—and should be—contested, particularly in light of its increasing co-optation by the state in ways that support the current political economy—"and those who benefit from it most" (3).

This part begins with just such a critique, as Canadian scholar and activist Ronald Labonte looks more deeply at some of the assumptions that underlie our notions of community and our related approaches to community development (or organizing) work. Drawing on both his extensive work as a health promotion consultant nationally and internationally, and his in-depth study of the Toronto health department, Labonte begins by asking professionals to free themselves from their often uncritical and romanticized notions of community. In a similar vein, he reminds us that community involvement and decentralized decision making, although wonderful concepts in theory, may translate into tokenism, both sapping a community's limited energy and inadvertently supporting government cutbacks (see also Bryant et al. 2010).

Labonte then applies this attitude of critical rethinking to the whole domain of community development (which, he reminds us, has roughly the same meaning in Canada as *community organizing* does in the United States). Central to this discussion is the distinction he draws between *community-based* efforts and true *community development* work. In the former, Labonte suggests, health professionals or their agencies define and name the problem, develop strategies for dealing with it, and involve community members to varying degrees in the problem-solving process. In contrast, community development or organizing supports community groups as they identify problems or issues and plan strategies for confronting them. Building on these and related distinctions, Labonte suggests that community development approaches are far more conducive to the building of authentic partnerships. The latter require, among other things, that "all partners [establish] their own power and legitimacy" and that community workers support community group partners, whether or not the latter buy into the concerns and mandates of the professional or the agency.

In chapter 7, Meredith Minkler, Cheri Pies, and Cheryl Hyde revisit many of the issues and challenges raised in chapters 5 and 6, focusing special attention on the ethical dimensions of these issues. Six areas are explored: the problem of conflicting priorities; the difficulties involved in eliciting genuine rather than token community participation; cross-cultural misunderstanding and problems of real and perceived racism in organizing; the dilemmas posed by funding sources; the sometimes problematic, unanticipated consequences of our organizing efforts; and questions of whose common good is being addressed by the organizing effort.

Drawing on both theoretical literature and relevant case studies, the authors highlight the ethical challenges raised in each of these areas and pose hard questions for the professional as organizer regarding his or her assumptions, appropriate roles, and potential courses of action. Several tools are provided, such as the DARE criteria for measuring empowerment—Who determines the goals of the project? Who acts to achieve the goals? Who receives the benefits? Who evaluates the project? (Rubin and Rubin 2007)—and the "publicity test of ethics" for helping communities decide whether to accept money from a controversial source. The real purpose of the chapter, however, is to raise questions, rather than answer them. A key message of the chapter—and indeed of this whole section of the book—is that careful questioning of our assumptions and values and careful exploration of the ethical dimensions of our work must be preliminary and ongoing aspects of our professional practice.

This message is well illustrated in chapter 8, as Galen Ellis and Sheryl Walton share case studies of lessons in cultural humility and the need for broader systems change as three local health departments attempt to partner with their local communities in ambitious community building and -organizing projects. Using a strengths-based approach, and acknowledging from the outset numerous opportunities for cultural misunderstandings and miscommunications, the authors offer a deeply personal and nuanced account of the genesis and evolution of the Healthy Neighborhoods Project in West Contra Costa County, California, and its successful replication in the neighboring city of Berkeley, and finally in the Sobrante Park neighborhood of East Oakland. The particular challenges posed by community distrust of health departments and universities, cultural misunderstanding on multiple levels, clashes between community and bureaucratic needs and ways of doing things, and professional discomfort over true sharing of power and control with community residents are among the difficult issues with which this chapter grapples. The particular difficulties faced by one of the authors as an "outsider within" also are candidly shared, as are the accomplishments of these three inspiring projects and the lessons learned on all sides about such collaborative community building and -organizing efforts. Particularly impressive, moreover, is how lessons learned in the early Healthy Neighborhoods Project are proactively addressed in its replications. Particularly noteworthy, for example, is the fact that the large Alameda County Department of Health Services required all its employees to attend monthly meetings on racism and other -isms, and on the changes needed within the health department itself if community change was to be realized (Iton 2006). This genuine display of cultural humility in turn contributed to the success of the Sobrante Park healthy neighborhoods project. Further, the capacity of the key health department staff consultant to the Sobrante Park project (Walton) for building alliances across differences, and bringing together the Latino and African American communities in this neighborhood, is an exciting testament to what can be accomplished in such communities.

The term *professional* has been defined as "one who knows very, very well very, very little." Although professionals in fields such as community health education, social work, community psychology, and health planning often pride themselves on being generalists rather than narrow technocrats, the humility implied in that definition is important, particularly in relation to our work with communities. For the more we appreciate the fact that we know "very well, very little" about communities, their needs, and their resources (at least in relation to how much communities tend to know), the more likely we are to engage in practice that is empowering and respectful of the communities with which we are engaged. At the conclusion of this part, it is hoped that readers will be more comfortable with the need to privilege community knowledge and insights, in part by active listening (Chávez et al. 2010), and in part by the kind of self refection and humility that fosters active listening and engagement in the first place.

REFERENCES

Bryant, T., D. Raphael, and M. Rioux. 2010. *Staying Alive: Critical Perspectives on Health, Illness, and Health Care*. 2nd ed. Toronto: Canadian Scholars' Press.

Chávez, V., M. Minkler, N. Wallerstein, and M. Spencer. 2010. "Community Organizing for Health and Social Justice." In *Prevention Is Primary: Strategies for Community Well-Being*, edited by V. Chávez, L. Cohen, and S. Chehimi, 87–112. 2nd ed. San Francisco, Calif.: Jossey-Bass.

DeFilippis, J., R. Fisher, and E. Shragge. 2010. *Contesting Community: The Limits and Potential of Local Organizing*. New Brunswick, N.J.: Rutgers University Press.

Iton, T. 2006. "Tackling the Root Causes of Health Disparities through Community Capacity Building." In *Tackling Health Inequities through Public Health Practice: A Handbook for Action*, edited by R. Hofrichter, 115–136. Washington D.C.: National Association of County and City Health Officials.

Rubin, H., and I. Rubin. 2007. *Community Organizing and Development*. 4th ed. New York: Macmillan.

6

Community, Community Development, and the Forming of Authentic Partnerships

Some Critical Reflections

RONALD LABONTE

It is hard to be critical of community when one spends most of the day working in the stuffy cubicles of a government building or in the isolated cubbyhole offices of universities. Community represents something more positive and affirming than the bureaucratic rigidities or academic competitiveness of one's daily working experience. It is difficult to question community's importance when the only positive comments about frontline workers' efforts come from small groups gathered in church basements or cluttered storefront agency meeting rooms. Yet questioning and critiquing the notion of community are precisely what I propose to do in this chapter. My concern is that an uncritical adoption of community rhetoric can, paradoxically, work against empowerment ideals that lie at the heart of many health practitioners' intent.

Let me clarify the meaning of a few key terms before proceeding. Several concepts bearing a *community* label are now common in the health sector, notably as in *community organization*, *community mobilization*, and *community development*. Different people use different terms to mean the same thing. In Canada, for example, *community development* is often used to describe what in the United States is called *community organizing*. For purposes of my argument, *community organizing* refers to efforts to create a new group or organization, often with the assistance of an outsider, such as a health promoter (Rothman 2008). *Community mobilization* describes attempts to draw together a number of such groups or organizations into concerted actions around a specific topic, issue, or event. *Community development* (or *community organizing* in the United States) incorporates both but describes a particular practice in which both practitioner and agency are committed to broad changes in the structure of power relations in society through the support they give community groups (Labonte 1996; Miller 2009).

This chapter examines the continued conceptual confusion that surrounds the term *community* and offers five cautions about its uncritical invocation in health and social practice. Drawing in part on insights gained through my in-depth study of the Toronto Department of Public Health in the 1990s (Labonte 1996) and through more recent observations, I argue that, even though the concept of *community development* continues some of this confusion, the practice of community development has considerable potential for fostering self-reliance and the creation of authentic partnerships with communities. The chapter concludes by presenting nine characteristics of authentic partnerships that health educators and other social change professionals are encouraged to strive for in our practice.

The Contested Meaning of Community

Numerous historical developments have contributed to the conceptual prominence of community in health work. Although a detailed discussion is beyond the scope of this chapter, these factors include rising health care costs, the declining effectiveness and efficiency of medical treatment, and a growing appreciation of the role of individual and community factors in disease causation and prevention (Lalonde 1974; Cockerham 2006; Fawcett et al. 2011).

As noted in earlier chapters, the centrality of community and the importance of community organizing for health were reflected in such influential documents as the Ottawa Charter for Health Promotion (World Health Organization 1986), which regarded "the empowerment of communities, their ownership and control of their own endeavors and destinies," as the heart of the "new" health promotion. Many commentators view community as the venue for, if not the very definition of, the new health promotion practice (Robertson and Minkler 1994; Fawcett et al. 2011), a view commonly expressed by practitioners themselves (Diers 2004). But there is little agreement on what community means. As Walter and Hyde suggest in chapter 5, a general weakness of professional/institutional discourses on community has been the largely atheoretical and uncritical way in which the term has entered common usage.

Initially in the health field, *community* was simply a reflexive adjective. In Canada, hospitals became community health centers, nurses became community health workers, state health departments became community health departments, and health promotion and health education programs became community-based efforts. In the syntax of everyday language, community ceased being a subject, a group of people acting with their own intent, and became an object (community as a "target" for health programs) or an adjective to the real subjects, which remained health institutions, which had become, by linguistic sleight of hand, community modified. The problem was not that community-enamored practitioners and their agencies did not know their grammar well. The problem was the way in which community became objectified as fact and posited as a solution to all health problems rather than treated as a definitional conundrum whose development is inherently problematic.

When community is defined at all, it is usually in the static vocabulary of data, creating categories based on identity (the poor community, the women's community, a particular ethnocultural community), geography (the neighborhood, the small town, a particular housing project), or issue (the environmental community, the heart health community, the social justice community). Often, community is simply assumed to be those persons using the services of an institution and living within administratively drawn catchment boundaries (the hospital community, the school community, the university community).

Community has all these elements—identity, geography, issue, even institutional relations—but it is also more. *Community* derives from the Latin *communitas*, meaning "common or shared," and the *ty* suffix, meaning "to have the quality of." Sharing is not some demographic datum; it is the dynamic act of people being together. Community is, in effect, organization. There is no "poor community" outside of poor persons coming together to share their experience and act upon transforming it. There is no "women's community" outside of two or more women sharing their reality, empowering themselves to act more effectively upon it. As the Toronto Department of Public Health (1994b) defined community almost two decades ago, it "is a group of individuals with a common interest, and an identity of themselves as a group. We all belong to multiple communities at any given time. The essence of being a community is that there is something that is 'shared.' We cannot really say that a community exists until a group with a shared identity exists" (n.p.). Even recognition of the active, organizational nature of community, however, does not fully clarify the term.

Romanticization

Community, as implied in the landmark Ottawa Charter (Epp 1986) and some more recent documents, can do no wrong (see DeFilippis et al. 2010). The building of stronger communities, for example, is often regarded as an elemental strategy for strengthening community health. Although it is important to accept community self-determination in principle, it is also vital to recognize that what communities do for their own health may be inimical to a broader public health. Nazi Germany was a classic example of a strong community. So, too, are many right-wing fringe groups, such as the Ku Klux Klan or other white supremacist militia organizations. Similarly, one could define as a community lobbyists against stricter pollution controls, and people who work together to block supportive housing for persons with mental disabilities. Neighborhoods, towns, cities, and states are filled with myriad communities, as often in conflict with one another as seeking consensus and understanding. Under conditions of conflict, which community should be supported, and why? Without the question being linked to a political theory of social organization and change and an analysis of social power relations, it cannot be answered, and the notion of community becomes somewhat fatuous. Worse, it becomes romanticized in a way that can obscure very real and important power inequities between different communities that may subtly imperil the health and well-being of less powerful groups, for example, the community of urban land developers versus the community of the homeless.

Bureaucratization

Whose interests are most served by increasing community involvement in health? What is it exactly that health workers are asking communities to become involved in? Apart from concerns over tokenism (participation without authority), community involvement in health programs may not always "strengthen" the community. Health professionals may bureaucratize thriving community initiatives if they are insensitive to the fact that a community organizing or community development approach to issues is intrinsically unmanageable by conventional planning standards, which rigidly specify goals, objectives, and outcomes before action can begin (Labonte 1993). Even when health agencies engender new initiatives, they may unintentionally sap the political vitality of community group leaders. One health educator was able to extract "permission" from her senior managers to involve local activists on a housing and health committee, but after a year little progress had been made (Labonte 1993). She had been involving community activists in her bureaucratic process of committee meetings, reports, and senior management approvals rather than assisting the activists in directly lobbying decision makers and collaborating with them in a partnership for social change. This effectively, if unintentionally, silenced the political voice of some of the strongest community leaders.

Antiprofessionalism

Just as health authorities can risk elitism in their desire to demonstrate health promotion "leadership," community groups and some of their health worker supporters can undermine effective collaborations through a festering antiprofessionalism. Professional is not the antithesis of community. Indeed, the Latin root of the word *professional* means "to profess" or "to vow," a reference to the medieval practice of surrendering personal gain to the larger community of a religious order or workers' guild. It is true that health professionals, like others in the "poverty industry," can increase the victimization of people living in socially disadvantaged conditions through their attitudes and exercise of power over their "clients." But to imply, as some have, that most past public health practice has been wrong or that, as John McKnight (1987) has argued, "resources empower; services do not" denigrates the community of health workers. It reinforces a we/they polarity and ignores the formative role that respectfully delivered, useful, and usable services have often played in developing new community organizations and overcoming the isolation of society's most marginalized or oppressed (Hyatt 2008; Labonte 1993).

Many health professionals are also community activists, and all persons, employed or otherwise, are members of many different communities. If professionals respect the leadership prerogative of community groups, or if, as Walter and Hyde suggest in chapter 5, they see themselves as part of the community, there is no reason for them to be self-deprecatory or to disparage the value of their own "professional" efforts. Indeed, community groups supported by health workers not infrequently cite the professional status, legitimacy, and influence such workers bring to the relationship, which community groups use to enhance their own social change efforts (see chapter 5). The process of policy change, for example, can be likened to a nutcracker (Labonte 1993). One arm is the data-rich reports, policy documents, charters, and frameworks produced by health professionals primarily for internal consumption and bureaucratic legitimacy. The other arm, exerting the greatest force, is community group pressure on politicians, "cracking" the issue against the more conservative arm of professional validation. Both arms are necessary, if different in their strategic placement and use in creating healthy social change.

Decentralization

The decentralization of decision making over public programs, another oft-cited tenet of community organization or community development, allows for programs unique to community groups and their perceived needs. But the concept must be tempered with the recognition that most economic and social policy is national and transnational in nature. Local decision making can be only within narrow parameters at best and is unlikely to include substantial control over economic resources (DeFilippis et al. 2010). As a policy analyst with the Worldwatch Institute noted two decades ago, small may be beautiful, but it may also be insignificant (Durning 1989). This is not to argue the intractable nature of the health-damaging aspects of our present social structure. Just as apathy can become a barrier to the organizing efforts of less powerful groups, cynicism (an apathy of the better-off with bigger vocabularies) can undermine the efforts of health workers to support such organizing efforts. Nonetheless, practitioners must append a strong advocacy component for macrolevel policy changes at senior government levels to their drive for decentralized decision making. Otherwise, they may subtly "privatize" by rendering strictly local the choices available to people and mystifying the actual exercise of political power by national and transnational economic elites.

The rhetoric of decentralized local control may also inadvertently support growing social inequities by failing to defend social programs against fiscal restraint or regressive tax reform by more senior government levels. Indeed, part of the appeal of community, especially to neoliberals and neoconservatives, is that it can readily justify dramatic social service cutbacks in the name of increasing community control (Hyatt 2008; DeFilippis et al. 2010). It is instructive that, in Canada at least, decentralized community decision making in health care became a fact only as public funding for health care began shrinking, hospitals began to close, and thousands of health care workers began to lose their jobs (Bryant et al. 2010).

Self-Help

The promotion of self-help and mutual aid groups parallels the call for decentralized decision making. Professional coordination of self-help networks is sometimes advanced as a means of "humanizing" the welfare system and of coping with program cutbacks driven by neoliberal economic policies. The first rationale is sound; the second accepts the reprivatization of social policy, better known as charity. That self-help groups can be empowering and health enhancing is undeniable. But there is typically no recognition in government policies on health promotion and community development that self-help primarily taps the volunteer energies of women, society's "traditional" care providers. Will government support and professional coordination of self-help simply increase voluntarism at the economic expense of women? Moreover, the type of self-help usually being promoted is what is sometimes called "defensive"—groups of people with a common problem or disease providing peer support.

There is also a history of "offensive" self-help, those groups concerned with meso- and macrolevel social change strategies. These groups are less likely to receive government or other outside support, because they are regarded as being too political, self-interested, or advocacy oriented. Yet unless the right of groups to lobby for changes in government policy is recognized and supported in health promotion funding policy (though this again raises the dilemma of which groups advocating for which issues), the self-help ethos restricts to a personal level problems that have both personal and political dimensions.

Community Development: Assumptions, Cautions, and Potential

Many of the cautions just raised cut to the quick of community development as a specific health practice. (I remind American readers again that my use of this term includes much of what they may associate with community organization.) There is no theory of community development, any more than there is a singular theory of or approach to health promotion. Rather, the term describes a range of practices within the many other sectors in which it has existed historically, such as international development, literacy, economic development, housing, and social work/social services.

Community development involves assumptions about the nature of society; social change; and the relationship among community developers, state agencies, and community groups. These assumptions are sometimes made explicit in community development and community organization literature and models (e.g., Rothman 2008). But they are rarely explicitly present in government or other health agency policy statements on community development and often remain unexplored among practitioners themselves (Labonte 1996). One succinct and representative statement of these assumptions was that of the Toronto Department of Public Health (1994b), which defined community development as "the process of supporting community groups in identifying their health issues, planning and acting upon their strategies for social action/social change, and gaining increased self-reliance and decision-making power as a result of their activities" (n.p.). There are five important components to this definition.

Community development describes a relationship between outside institutions and community groups. First, the "doer" of community development in the health field typically is a health department or nonprofit health agency or organization. This may strike some readers as patronizing. Do not communities develop themselves? Yes, but when they do, they engage in what Walter and Hyde (chapter 5) term *community building*; rarely (if ever) do they describe it as *community development*. The latter term historically refers to the actions of institutions in relation to lay people, whether conceived of as interest groups or as persons living within some geographic space. When practitioners recognize themselves as the subjects of community development, they are forced to ask, "What do we intend by these relations?" Ideally, the answer should be to nurture relations with and among institutions and community groups that are more equitable in their power sharing. As health workers with the Toronto Department of Public Health (1994a) noted close to twenty years ago, "The goal of community development . . . is really trying to establish a more equitable power relationship between institutions and community groups" (n.p.). This requires that practitioners acknowledge the initial differences in power (status, authority, resources, legitimacy) that exist among themselves, their agency, and community groups. If practitioners presume without questioning that they are "equals" with community groups, they risk making invisible the types of power that they do hold "over" groups, however, thereby increasing the risk of abusing that power or of failing to recognize the potential for making it available to groups for their own use (Wallerstein 1999; see chapter 7 and appendix 4). A helpful tool in this regard is the "ladder of community participation" developed by heath educators at the Contra Costa County Department of Health Services in California (Morgan and Lifshay 2006), and through which health professionals can better see the level of control they, and their community partners, actually possess in any given project or partnership (see appendix 4).

Community development is always a matter of choosing some groups over others. Second, accepting a professional interest in community development compels practitioners to ask, "Which groups we're actually interested in, and why?" Wallack and Lawrence (2005) argue that health promotion implies an advocacy framework that supports those whose living conditions provide them with less material forms of power, such as income, authority over resources, or political legitimacy. One of the difficulties encountered in practice is that the choices made by health workers and their agencies are rarely made explicit or include only those groups that might agree to mobilize around particular health issues, such as heart health or anti-tobacco advocacy. This renders choice a matter of personal preference or institutional convenience.

There is an ethical concern in the first instance: public agencies should be publicly accountable. Favoritism in choice should be informed by an explicit analysis of the social determinants of health and theories of social change and power relations, not simply by ideologies kept from organizational or public view and debate. There are both an ethical and a political concern in the second instance. An early study of a Canadian health department found that social assistance recipients with the greatest health, organizational, and empowerment needs represented only 17 percent of practitioners' caseloads (Browne et al. 1995). Most health workers' time was spent with reasonably well-functioning and well-resourced middle-class individuals and groups, a finding common to many other local health departments (Labonte 1996). To the extent that community development is a public resource that can help to effect a redistribution in material resources (DeFilippis et al. 2010), a high ratio of middle-class clients or groups represents an upward redistribution of resources that contradicts the social justice rhetoric of documents such as the Ottawa Charter.

Community development involves "making private troubles public issues." Third, community development work is not support group work. We can distinguish a "support group" from a "community group" on the basis of whether its members primarily look inward to their immediate psychosocial needs or primarily look outward to the socioenvironmental context that creates those needs in the first place. To paraphrase C. Wright Mills (1956), community groups transform the private troubles of support groups into public issues for policy remediation. Support group work, or defensive self-help, is central to what many public health nurses, educators, and social workers and some community organizers do. It is fundamentally important work and necessary to community development, for without the support of a group, many historically marginalized people will lack the confidence to look outward to the harder-to-change sociopolitical conditions that created their marginality in the first place.

But whereas support group work concerns the creation of healthy (equitable) power relations within groups, community development concerns the creation of healthy (equitable) power relations among community groups and institutions, or offensive self-help. The reason for making this distinction is twofold. It prevents *community development* (or *organizing*) from becoming a term so large in practice that it no longer serves any useful conceptual purpose (DeFilippis et al. 2010), a critique often, and aptly, made of health promotion (Robertson and Minkler 1994). It also requires that health professionals and their agencies grapple with power relations at a higher level of social organization, and not restrict themselves to the necessary but insufficient work of support group development.

Community development is not simply bringing institutional programs into "community" settings. Fourth, we can distinguish between community-based and community development approaches to our work. The distinction lies in who sets the agenda and who names the issue or problem (see table 6.1). In the community-based approach, the agency finds existing individuals or groups and links up its programs with them. It is an important approach to public health, but it is not community development, which attempts to support community groups in resolving concerns as group members define them (Morgan and Lifshay 2006; see appendix 4). Of course, as already noted, not all groups or group concerns will or should be supported. Community development requires making choices that,

TABLE 6.1.

Community-Based and Community Development Programming

Community-Based Programming	*Community Development Programming*
The process in which health professionals or health agencies define the health problem, develop strategies to remedy the problem, involve local community members and groups to assist in solving the problem, and work to transfer major responsibility for an ongoing program to local community members and groups.	The process of organizing or supporting community groups in their identification of important concerns and issues and their ability to plan and implement strategies to mitigate their concerns and resolve their issues.
Example: Nobody's Perfect or heart health programs	*Example:* Healthy Communities projects
Characteristics	*Characteristics*
▪ The problem name is given. ▪ There are defined program time lines. ▪ Changes in specific behaviors or knowledge levels are the desired outcome. ▪ Decision-making power rests principally with the institution.	▪ The problem name starts with that of the community group, and then is negotiated strategically— that is, to a problem naming that advances the shared interests of the group and the institution. ▪ Work is longer term, requiring many hours. ▪ A general increase in the group's capacities is the desired outcome. ▪ Power relations are constantly negotiated.

in turn, require explicit analyses of social power relations and agency/staff commitments to shifting these relations toward greater equity. But much community organizing and community mobilizing work in health concerns itself primarily with specific diseases, lifestyle behaviors, and those public policies that influence their risks (Alvaro et al. 2011; Labonte 1993; Labonte and Robertson 1996; Raphael 2010). These issues may not always be of concern to poorer groups or localities. To the extent that institutional support and financial resources for community work are streamed through these "set agendas," the more political empowerment work of groups or localities can actually be undermined (see chapter 7).

Community development, however, can emerge from a community-based program, just as community-based programs sometimes arise in the context of a larger community development effort (Labonte and Robertson 1996; Bell and Standish 2005). In the first instance, the practice issue becomes one of health workers and their agencies accepting as legitimate and finding ways to support action on more structurally defined health problems (e.g., unemployment, violence, food insecurity, or environmental racism) that participants in community-based programs (e.g., asthma prevention) might raise as concerns. In the second instance, the practice issue becomes one of health workers and their agencies negotiating the content and timing of community-based programs with local citizens so that they fit within the context of other political mobilizations within localities.

Community development promotes self-reliance, not self-sufficiency. Fifth, in defining community development as a process of creating more equitable relationships among groups and institutions, we can bury the myth of community self-sufficiency. According to that myth, the community group is able to mobilize or provide its own resources and the skills to enable it to function autonomously from others. This is often assumed to be the goal of community development or a measure of maximum community participation (Bjaras et al. 1991). However, the health sector's rhetorical acceptance of such terms as *partnerships* and *intersectoralism* should lead practitioners and their agencies to foster equitable and effective interdependencies rather than to promote the autonomy of localities. Self-reliance, as a contrasting concept, means that "the community group is able to negotiate the terms of its interdependence with external professionals, organizations and institutions" (Toronto Department of Public Health 1994b, n.p.). The goal of community development is not self-sufficiency; it is the ability of the group to negotiate its own terms of relationship with those institutions (agencies) that support it.

Community Development and the Creation of Effective and Authentic Partnerships

An equitably negotiated arrangement among different groups is often referred to by the shorthand notion of *partnership*. Whether practitioners and their agencies rally behind the ideas of community organization, community mobilization, or community development, they are essentially entering a partnership with a variety of different groups or organizations.

Effective Partnerships and Conflict

Community development may strive for inclusivity in community building, for agreement among as broad a collection of community groups as possible. The reality, however, is that powerless groups usually seek to shift skewed social relations by limiting the power that other groups have over them. Powerless individuals often create their identity as a community group only in opposition to or conflict with groups that are more powerful than themselves. This dynamic has been at the base of the confrontational approach to community organizing favored by Saul Alinsky and his adherents (Alinsky 1971; Miller 2009; see chapter 4) and has been used successfully to create communities from the seemingly intractable conditions of isolation and apathy (Labonte 1993; Miller 2009; Su 2009; chapter 4). More generally, research in social identity theory finds that group identities often require conflictual forms of "who's in/who's out" boundary setting (Abrams and Hogg 1990), and a large body of sociological theory argues that intergroup conflict is the norm rather than the exception and provides the necessary "fuel" for social change.

Even Barbara Gray (1989), whose work on collaboration theory is seminal to an understanding of partnerships, acknowledges that collaboration usually requires a period when less powerful groups establish their legitimacy through conflictual relations with more powerful groups. But conflict may also be necessary during collaboration. One reason that environmental groups now participate in collaborative policy bodies with industry and government is that they have demonstrated they are able, through direct conflictual actions, to prevent unilateral decisions by the other parties. Those environmental groups that participate in collaboration generally no longer engage in direct action. But if all environmental groups ceased conflict relations with industry or government, what would prevent a return to unilateral decision making by either of the two more powerful stakeholders?

The Striving for Collaboration

That intergroup conflict is healthy and perhaps essential to social change should not lead health workers to shun the necessity of uniting diverse, conflicting groups at some higher level of community. Community-as-ideal, the moral resonance of the word, is what gives it power and appeal (Lyon 1989), even if this ideal must be approached with an analytical caution about how it can be used for anticommunity right-wing political agendas (DeFilippis et al. 2010). Nonetheless, as Gardner (1991) classically remarked, pluralism without commitment to the common good is pluralism gone berserk. Pragmatically, the community born in conflict or struggle rarely survives the eventual peace "unless those involved create the institutional arrangements and non-crisis bonding experiences that carry them through the year-in-year-out tests of community functioning" (14).

Gray (1989) provides a comprehensive partnership model for promoting those functions, which she describes as "collaboration." Successful intergroup collaboration, which she defines as "a mutual search for information and solutions," has five features that characterize the process-as-outcome. First, recognition of stakeholder interdependence is enhanced. Second, differences are dealt with constructively. Third, joint ownership of decisions is developed. Fourth, stakeholders assume collective responsibility for "managing the problem domain" through formal and informal agreements. Fifth, the process is accepted as continually emergent.

There are several steps in effective collaboration, the first and most important being problem setting. This requires a "common definition of the problem," a "commitment to collaborate," and "identification of the stakeholders." This stage subsumes a prenegotiation stage, the goal of which is to arrive at a common definition of problem and intent broad enough to get stakeholders to the table. This differentiates collaboration from the usual form of government or other health agency consultation, in which the issue and desired outcome are already defined.

Effective collaboration requires the efforts of persons Gray labels "midwives," the community developers of organizations-as-communities. These midwives (functionally distant from all the stakeholders) work with the stakeholders before the former come to the table, seeking to find the "superordinate goal" that Muzafir Sherif (1966) years ago argued was the basis for initiating any reduction in intergroup conflict. This goal must be "compelling for the groups involved, but . . . unattainable by [any] one group, singly; hence it is not identical with 'common goal.' . . . [It must also] supersede all other goals each group may have" (88).

Whatever the superordinate goal is that initiates intergroup collaboration and conflict resolution, the conditions for authentic collaboration allow a sharper delineation of the differences among consultation, involvement, and participation (collaboration). Briefly, consultation involves the seeking of information from citizens, but with no ongoing dialogue. Involvement does involve dialogue, but such dialogue is typically controlled by the government or outside agency. Citizen involvement tends to be advisory only, around a problem or issue that the government or outside agency has predetermined or named. There is no agreement on power sharing. In contrast, true participation involves negotiated relationships with citizens, who are treated as constituencies and take part in "naming the problem" or selecting the issue. All affected groups participate, and resources are made available to enable the full participation of less powerful groups (Arnstein 1969; Labonte 1993; Morgan and Lifshay 2006; see appendix 4).

What makes for the effective and authentic partnerships that community development creates? Building on the forgoing and drawing on Panet-Raymond's (1992) insights gleaned from attempts to forge relations between community health and social service centers and neighborhood volunteer centers in Quebec, we might say that partnerships exist only when

1. All partners have established their own power and legitimacy. This often requires a period of conflict and some enduring strain between powerful and powerless groups. The provision of resources to these groups is one facet of community development work, provided such resources remain in the autonomous control of the groups.
2. All partners have well-defined mission statements. They have a clear sense of their purpose and organizational goals.
3. All partners respect one another's organizational autonomy by finding a visionary goal that is larger than any one of their independent goals. This requires extensive midwifing work to set the shared agenda. The achievement of this shared agenda is another facet of community development work.
4. Community group partners are well rooted in the locality. They have a constituency to which they are accountable.
5. Institutional partners have a commitment to partnership approaches in work with community groups.
6. Clear objectives and expectations of the partners are developed. The partners create a commitment among themselves to jointly "manage the problem domain."
7. Written agreements are made that clarify objectives, responsibilities, means, and norms. Regular evaluation allows adjustments to these agreements.
8. Community workers have clear mandates to support community group partners without attempting to get them to "buy into" the institutional partner's mandate and goal. This distinguishes community development from community-based approaches to work.
9. All partners strive for and nurture the human qualities of open-mindedness, patience, respect, and sensitivity to the experiences of persons in all partnering organizations.

Conclusion

Community is a potent idea, but its reality is the more modest process of people organizing themselves, or being organized, into identity-forging, issue-solving groups. The multiplicity of people's group (community) experiences requires health practitioners and their agencies to specify clearly whom they mean when they invoke the term. Romantic notions of community are more likely to support neoliberal political agendas, the dismantling of social welfare programs, and the upward redistribution of wealth and power than they are to empower localities in any significant way. As health practitioners attempt to organize people or to support community groups, they must be wary of "colonizing" these groups with institutional, often disease-based ways of defining health issues. Moreover, they must locate their choice of issues and groups to support within some analytical framework of society and social change. This framework needs to take account of the many forms of power that partly constitute the relationship among institutions, health professionals, and community groups, for the essence of community development (community organizing) is the transformation of these power relations such that there is more equity within and between institutions and groups.

At base, community development opposes those inequalities between people that are created by people and their economic and political practices. For as French philosopher Raymond Aron once commented, "When inequalities become too great, the idea of community becomes impossible."

ACKNOWLEDGMENTS

Portions of this chapter are based on "Community Empowerment: The Need for Political Analysis," *Canadian Journal of Public Health* 80, no. 2 (1989): 87–88 and "Community Development and Partnerships," *Canadian Journal of Public Health* 84, no. 4 (1993): 237–240. Adapted and reprinted by permission of the Canadian Public Health Association.

REFERENCES

Abrams, D., and M. Hogg, eds. 1990. *Social Identity Theory: Constructive and Critical Advances.* New York: Springer-Verlag.

Alinsky, S. 1971. *Rules for Radicals: A Practical Primer for Realistic Radicals.* New York: Random House.

Alvaro, C., L. A. Jackson, S. Kirk, et al. 2011. "Moving Canadian Governmental Policies beyond a Focus on Individual Lifestyle: Some Insights from Complexity and Critical Theories." *Health Promotion International* 26, no. 1:91–99.

Arnstein, S. 1969. "A Ladder of Citizen Participation." *American Institute of Planners* 35, no. 4:216–224.

Bell, J. and M. Standish. 2005. "Communities and Health Policy: A Pathway for Change." *Health Affairs* 24, no. 2:339–342.

Bjaras, G., B.J.A. Haglund, and S. Rifkin. 1991. "A New Approach to Community Participation Assessment." *Health Promotion International* 6, no. 3:199–206.

Browne, G., C. Roberts, J. Byrne, C. Byrne, et al. 1995. "Public Health Nursing Clientele Shared with Social Assistance: Proportions, Characteristics, and Policy Implications." *Canadian Journal of Public Health* 86, no. 3:155–161.

Bryant, T., D. Raphael, and M. Rioux. 2010. *Staying Alive: Critical Perspectives on Health, Illness, and Health Care.* 2nd ed. Toronto: Canadian Scholars' Press.

Cockerham, W. C. 2006. *Social Causes of Health and Disease.* Cambridge, U.K.: Polity.

DeFilippis, J., R. Fisher, and E. Shragge. 2010. *Contesting Community: The Limits and Potential of Local Organizing.* New Brunswick, N.J.: Rutgers University Press.

Diers, J. 2004. *Neighborhood Power: Building Community the Seattle Way.* Seattle: University of Washington Press.

Durning, A. 1989. "Mobilizing at the Grassroots." In *State of the World 1989,* ed. L. Brown et al. New York: Norton.

Epp, J. 1986. *Achieving Health for All: A Framework for Health Promotion.* Ottawa: Health and Welfare Canada.

Fawcett, S., P. Abeykoon, M. Arora, M. Dobe, et al. 2011. "Constructing an Action Agenda for Community Empowerment at the 7th Global Conference on Health Promotion in Nairobi." *Global Health Promotion* 17, no. 4:53–56.

Gardner, J. 1991. *Building Communities.* Washington, D.C.: Independent Sector Leadership Studies Program.

Gray, B. 1989. *Collaborating: Finding Common Ground for Multiparty Problems.* San Francisco: Jossey-Bass.

Hyatt, S. 2008. "The Obama Victory, Asset-Based Development, and the Re-politicization of Community Organizing." *North American Dialogue* 11, no. 2:17–26.

Labonte, R. 1993. *Health Promotion and Empowerment: Practice Frameworks.* Toronto: Centre for Health Promotion/Participation.

———. 1996. *Community Development in the Public Health Sector: The Possibilities of an Empowering Relationship between State and Civil Society.* Ph.D. diss., York University, Ontario.

Labonte, R., and A. Robertson. 1996. "Health Promotion Research and Practice: The Case for the Constructivist Paradigm." *Health Education Quarterly* 23, no. 4:431–447.

Lalonde, M. 1974. *A New Perspective on the Health of Canadians.* Ottawa: Health and Welfare Canada.

Lyon, L. 1989. *The Community in Urban Society.* Toronto: Lexington Books.

McKnight, J. 1987. "Comments at Prevention Congress III." Waterloo, Ontario.

Miller, M. 2009. *A Community Organizer's Tale: People and Power in San Francisco.* Berkeley, Calif.: Heyday Books.

Mills, C. W. 1956. *The Power Elites.* New York: Oxford University Press.

Minkler, M. 1994. "Challenges for Health Promotion in the 1990's: Social Inequities, Empowerment, Negative Consequences, and the Public Good." *American Journal of Health Promotion* 8, no. 6:403–413.

Morgan, M. A., and J. Lifshay. 2006. *Community Engagement in Public Health.* Martinez, Calif.: Contra Costa Department of Health Services, Public Health Division. http://www .barhii.org/resources/downloads/community_engagement.pdf.

Panet-Raymond, J. 1992. "Partnership: Myth or Reality?" *Community Development Journal* 27, no. 2:156–165.

Raphael, D. 2010. "Setting the Stage: Why Quality of Life? Why Health Promotion?" In *Health Promotion and Quality of Life in Canada: Essential Readings,* edited by D. Raphael. Toronto: Canadian Scholars' Press.

Robertson, A., and M. Minkler. 1994. "New Health Promotion Movement: A Critical Perspective." *Health Education Quarterly* 21, no. 3:295–312.

Rothman, J. 2008. "Multi Modes of Community Intervention." In *Strategies of Community Intervention,* edited by J. Rothman, J. L. Erlich, and J. E. Tropman, 141–170. 7th ed. Peosta, Iowa: Eddie Bowers.

Sherif, M. 1966. *Group Conflict and Cooperation.* London: Routledge and Kegan Paul.

Su, C. 2009. *Streetwise for Book Smarts: Grassroots Organizing and Education Reform in the Bronx.* Ithaca, N.Y.: Cornell University Press.

Toronto Department of Public Health. 1994a. "Making Choices." Toronto Department of Public Health, Toronto.

———. 1994b. "Making Communities." Toronto Department of Public Health, Toronto.

Wallack, L., and R. Lawrence. 2005. "Talking about Public Health: Developing America's Second Language." *American Journal of Public Health* 94, no. 4:567–570.

Wallerstein, N. 1999. "Power between Evaluator and Community: Research Relationships within New Mexico's Healthier Communities." *Social Science and Medicine* 49:39–53.

World Health Organization. 1986. *Ottawa Charter for Health Promotion.* Copenhagen: WHO Europe.

7

Ethical Issues in Community Organizing and Capacity Building

MEREDITH MINKLER
CHERI PIES
CHERYL A. HYDE

Fields such as public health and social work may be described as "an inescapably moral enterprise[s]," concerned as they are with determining what we as societies and communities ought to do to pursue the public's health and well-being (Petrini 2010; Dunn 1983). These, and related social change professions are governed by codes of ethics (for example, see National Association of Social Workers (2008) and the Coalition of National Health Education Organizations (2010) that serve as primarily prescriptive guidelines for appropriate conduct. Central to these codes are core values—social justice, empowerment, participation, wellness, self-determination, dignity, and respect.

Ethical dilemmas arise when these values come into conflict while solutions are sought to a given problem or an intervention is implemented (Harrington and Dolgoff 2008). Recognizing and resolving these dilemmas is an essential skill for practitioners, including community organizers, health educators, and capacity builders. And while there are numerous frameworks for ethical decision making, this process boils down to three essential elements: the means, the circumstances, and the ends being sought (Childress 2007). In this chapter, we present some common ethical dilemmas in community practice.

Community organizer Saul Alinsky asserted that "the ends justify the means," essentially putting a higher value on what is accomplished than on how it is accomplished (Alinsky 1972; see also chapter 4). This approach, however, presents ethical questions and also risks downplaying core values. With respect to the means, we argue that community determination and participation are critical. The active involvement of people, beginning with what they define as the needs and goals, results in communal ownership of the initiative, the development of competencies, and reduced vulnerability to outside manipulation. Because community involvement and capacity building are primary objectives, this "means" also distinguishes true community organizing from other approaches, such as consultation and outside expert–driven planning. The significant emphasis in organizing on fostering community determination may at first suggest that the health or social work professional as organizer does not need to engage in extensive ethical reflection; after all, many of the processes in which he or she is already involved make increased freedom of choice for the community a central goal. Yet despite these lofty goals and guiding principles, the practice of community organization is, in reality, one of the most ethically problematic arenas in which health educators, social workers, urban planners, and other practitioners function.

A primary reason why community organization is fraught with ethical challenges has to do with the *circumstances* that inform the effort. Circumstances are essentially the political, economic, cultural, and social contexts of an organizing campaign or intervention. These circumstances can include the reasons that community mobilization is necessary in the first place. They also can refer to obstacles with which a community must contend in order to be successful. It is possible (even probable) that circumstances will conflict with one another, thus generating ethical conflicts. Social factors, such as strong community networks, that might support an organizing effort can be undermined by economic realities that result in competition for scarce resources. For example, two community-based organizations representing communities of color with shared interests (e.g., environmental justice or violence prevention) may find themselves in competition for the same source of funding. It is incumbent upon the practitioner to, first, be able to identify circumstances relevant to the community organizing campaign or initiative and, second, work with community members so that they develop analytical skills in understanding and responding to relevant circumstances.

All too often we find ourselves searching for answers to the ethical challenges we face in the hopes that by doing so, we can move ahead with plans and programs designed to help achieve an initiative's goals. But a resolution of these dilemmas may be less important than a continuing commitment to the process of articulating them, as well as the values and assumptions that inform our practice. In the interest of real community participation and empowerment, how do we facilitate dialogue rather than direct it? How do we tease apart our own agenda from that of the community? And what happens when there are multiple, and often conflicting, community agendas? These are just a few of the questions we face, and whether and how we think about them will have critical implications for our work.

This chapter explores six areas in which health educators, social workers, and other practitioners frequently experience tough ethical dilemmas in relation to the community organizing and community building aspects of their roles. These areas are (1) the eliciting of real, rather than symbolic, participation; (2) the challenges of conflicting priorities; (3) the dilemmas posed by funding sources and regulatory organizations; (4) the perils of cultural conflict, including challenging the -*isms* (racism, sexism, etc.); (5) the unanticipated consequences of organizing; and (6) the matter of whose "common good" is being addressed through the organizing effort. Case examples are used to illustrate factors that contribute to, as well as possible resolution strategies for, community ethical dilemmas.

Community Participation: Real or Symbolic?

Community participation has historically has been recognized as a central value in public health, social work, education, urban and regional planning, and other areas that emphasize, in part, organizing and capacity building (Corburn 2009; Green and Kreuter 1990; Reisch 2010a; Wallerstein 2006). In the 1970s, calls for "maximum feasible participation" coincided with the birth of the neighborhood health center movement (DeBuono et al. 2007). As noted in chapter 3, community or public participation, together with the concept of empowerment, emerged as the "defining feature" of both the health promotion movement (Robertson and Minkler 1994) and community capacity-building efforts in fields including public health, social work, community psychology, and urban and regional planning (Wallerstein 2006; Corburn 2009; Reisch 2010a, 2010b). Within such arenas, as McCloskey and her colleagues (2011, 13) note, "meaningful community participation extends beyond physical involvement to include generation of ideas, contribution to decision making, and sharing of responsibility."

Despite the increased rhetoric of participation, however, acting on calls for high-level community involvement has proved difficult indeed. As Gail Siler-Wells (1989) pointed out more than two decades ago, "Behind the euphemisms of participation and empowerment lay the realities of power, control and ownership" (142). And even as we attempt to blur hierarchical distinctions by talking in the health field, for example, about health care "providers" and "consumers" and calling for partnerships between health professionals and communities, these power imbalances remain (Minkler 1994).

In an early attempt to bring clarity to these issues of control and ownership, health planner Sherry Arnstein (1969) developed a "ladder of participation." The bottom rungs of the ladder were two forms of "nonparticipation"—therapy and manipulation. In the middle were several "degrees of tokenism"—placation, consultation, and informing—through which community members were heard and might have a voice but did not necessarily have their input heeded. Finally, the top rungs of the ladder were three degrees of "citizen power"—partnership, delegated power, and true citizen power. More recently, Morgan and Lifshay (2006; see also appendix 4) developed a "ladder of community participation" specifically related to local health departments and the communities they serve. Although acknowledging that in some circumstances, such as a sudden epidemic or other health emergency, the health department must "call the shots" on its own, the authors note that even in such circumstances, outcomes are more likely to be effective if these top-down directives are built on a high degree of authentic prior partnership and trust between the health department and the community (see appendix 4).

Yet authentic community participation and determination is easier said than done, and this gap between ideal and real is where ethical dilemmas reside. Although much contemporary practice in fields like health promotion uses the rhetoric of high-level community participation, it in fact tends to operate at the lower rungs of the participation ladder, as professionals "attempt to get people in the community to take ownership of a professionally defined health agenda" (Roberston and Minkler 1994). As R. Labonte (1990) cautioned over forty years ago, such an approach "raises the specter of using community resources primarily as free or cheaper forms of service delivery in which community participation is tokenistic at best and co-opted at worst" (7).

In other instances, the community's input may be sought and then discounted, further reinforcing unequal power relationships between practitioners and communities. The experience of some community advisory boards provides a good case in point. When taken seriously by professionals, community advisory boards (CABS) or committees can make a real difference in the ways in which health educators and other practitioners approach community-based programs and initiatives. As true partners in decision making, such boards can provide valuable input on community needs and strengths, the likely effectiveness of alternative organizing strategies, and the cultural nuances and sensitivities that need to be respected and addressed.

Increasingly, however, CABS are established in response to a funding mandate or similar inducement rather than out of a sincere concern for eliciting and acting on community input. In such instances, community boards often perceive that they are expected to serve as rubber-stamp mechanisms for decisions that the health professionals have already made.

Finally, even programs committed to community participation through advisory boards and the like may occasionally find themselves ignoring input that conflicts with predetermined projects and plans—sometimes at considerable cost. An unfortunate example of this occurred in what is in many respects a national model for effective health promotion on multiple levels—the California Tobacco Control Program (CTCP). We use this example to underscore that even the best programs can slip into paternalistic ways of doing things on occasion, with negative results.

The CTCP was created when a successful ballot initiative in 1992 put a twenty-five-cent tax on cigarettes and allocated a quarter of the money generated to anti-tobacco health education and advocacy. The program has been extremely successful and has been largely credited with the fact that the state's decline in cigarette smoking during the 1990s was three times the national average (California Tobacco Control Program 2010).

Part of the CTPC's early activity involved supporting groups such as the African American Tobacco Control Education Network (AATCEN), which addressed the heavy targeting of cigarette advertising to people of color and helped to mount a culturally sensitive counter advertising campaign. When professionals at the

CTCP first designed a proposed billboard aimed at the African American community, they showed it to the AATCEN's Advisory Group for its feedback. The billboard depicted a young African American man smoking a cigarette under the caption "Eric Jones just put a contract out on his family for $2.65. Secondhand smoke kills." Advisory Group members perceived the proposed ad as extremely racist, and they strongly urged that it not be used. Rather than heed the group's concerns, however, the CTCP did run the ad and received the same kind of negative reaction from community members.

The story behind that billboard is a sad and poignant reminder that it is not enough to "talk the talk" of community competence and community participation. We must indeed be willing to "walk the walk"—in this case, letting an advisory board composed of African American community members teach the rest of us how to avoid further stigmatizing of their community in the name of health promotion (Minkler 1994).

It is easy to see how only paying lip service to the concept of community participation can lead to a healthy suspicion on the part of communities and community groups regarding the agenda of the community organizer. Without a strong commitment to real community participation, we risk undermining our future efforts and dissipating the often fragile trust that communities invest in us. The credibility of the community organizer can be easily undermined when community group members sense that their participation is only symbolic, thus leading the community to question the commitment of the organizer and others to the community's real issues. Recognition of the importance of self-determination for communities, coupled with commitment to the concept of true partnership, must serve as guiding principles for ensuring meaningful community participation.

A useful tool in applying these guiding principles is offered by community organizers Herbert Rubin and Irene Rubin (1992, 77) in the form of the "DARE" criteria of empowerment:

Who Determines the goals of the project?

Who Acts to achieve them?

Who Receives the benefits of the actions?

Who Evaluates the actions?

The more often we can answer these questions by responding, "The community," the more likely our partnerships and community organizing efforts are to be contributing to real community empowerment and high-level participation.

Conflicting Priorities

For health educators, social workers, and other professionals who find themselves simultaneously responsible to a health or social service agency employer, to the communities being served by that agency, and to the funding sources supporting the particular project or program, a frequent dilemma faced is one of conflicting priorities. This is particularly so when the practitioner is charged with facilitating consumer participation in the agency and acting as an advocate for the community. From an agency perspective, for example, our role may be seen as helping people choose from a narrow range of options that fit within the organization or funder's predetermined goals. When agency agendas fail to correspond to the needs and desires of the community, the health educator or social worker faces difficult ethical dilemmas involving the degree to which she or he will feel comfortable complying with agency expectations and directives.

Two ethical precepts that lie at the heart of community organizing and community building—self-determination and justice—are helpful for thinking about and addressing such dilemmas. Both reflect an inherent faith in people's ability to accurately assess their strengths and needs and their right to act upon these insights in setting goals and determining strategies for achieving them.

In the language of health education and social work, these ethical precepts are reflected in Dorothy Nyswander's (1956) early admonition to "start where the people are." Yet this may be easier said then done. When an HIV/AIDS prevention program has as its goal the promotion of safer sex, in part through mobilization of a community around the prevention of HIV and other sexually transmitted infections, and when the community in question is more concerned about drug abuse or violence, should the health professional put on the back burner, for the time being, the agency's formal agenda and truly start where the people are? Within the bounds of certain limiting conditions to be discussed later, our response to this question is affirmative, since in choosing to start where the people are, the practitioner asserts a commitment to the principles of self-determination and liberty and the rights of individuals and communities to affirm and act on their own values.

Yet there is a practical rationale for starting where the people are as well. When this ethical principle has been followed, when trust in the community has been demonstrated, and when the immediate concerns of people have received primary attention, the organizer's original concerns frequently then are seen by the community's members as having relevance for their lives. Through careful listening, and the asking of thoughtful, probing questions, the organizer may learn how the issue she or he is concerned about is perceived by the local community, what the community's primary issues are, and whether bridges or links can be found between these seemingly disparate agendas.

An early experience of the Asian Pacific Environmental Network (APEN), based in Richmond, California, is illustrative. APEN (www.APEN.org) wanted to organize the local Laotian refugee community around the high levels of toxins to which it was being exposed through the estimated 350 industrial facilities in their county, including a large Chevron Oil refinery. Contamination of the fish on which many refugees were dependent for their livelihood, as well as the ground in which they grew crops, were among the topics around which APEN hoped to organize (APEN 2002). Upon meeting and dialoging with the refugees, however, APEN staff learned that this community had far more pressing concerns, such as how to grow better vegetables to support their families. APEN's organizing agenda was consequently put aside while the organizers addressed the community's concerns, including the provision of tips on vegetable gardening. This show of genuine attention to the community's agenda increased APEN's credibility among the refugees, who then became interested in what APEN had to share about toxic exposures. Several refugees began mapping toxic waste sites in their community and in other ways setting the stage for organizing around environmental hazards in their neighborhood. The Laotian Organizing Project (LOP) began slowly in 1995 under the APEN umbrella, often taking "baby steps," such as getting residents to each bring five neighbors or friends to a meeting (Buckley and Walters 2005). After a major refinery spill in 1999, followed by two additional leaks, LOP began a campaign to demand that the county department of health services and the board of supervisors establish a multilanguage phone alert system so that Laotians and others with little or no English proficiency would get timely information on how to "shelter in place," and so on, when such problems occurred (Sze 2004). Their success in getting this system adopted by the county, their effective monitoring, and their subsequent work in environmental justice attracted national attention (Buckley and Walters 2005). Yet had the APEN organizers not initially been willing to begin with the refugees' priority—growing better crops—this impressive work on a shared organizing agenda would likely not have come to fruition.

Although we have focused thus far on the problem of conflicting priorities between "the community" and a practitioner's agency, tensions around conflicting priorities may also surface when there are multiple communities or community factions with different and often competing agendas. A community committed to AIDS prevention, for example, may be deeply torn over an effort to organize around getting a needle exchange program. A mixed-use residential community near the proposed site of a new "big box" store, such as Wal-Mart or Home Depot, may be divided between those residents wishing to organize against this perceived threat to local businesses and certain increase in traffic, and those who see the store as a source of needed employment. The social worker or other professional's efforts to organize in situations like this may generate more conflict and confrontation than consensus among community members (see chapter 11). In such instances, the importance of questioning whether to intervene, and if so on what level and with what ethical precepts, takes on added importance.

Dilemmas Posed by Funding Sources, Rules, and Regulations

Restrictions imposed on community-based organizations by funders and other key stakeholders are among the most frequently mentioned sources of ethical conflict (Hyde 2010). Practitioners report that the type of, and access to, programs and activities can be severely limited by the rules of a resource provider or state regulatory agency. Organizers and other community-based practitioners must continually assess whether to engage in compliance at the risk of accessibility and innovation.

Particularly in times of several economic constraints, the realities of funding availability, and the nature and source of funding for organizing projects can severely limit the extent to which the principle of starting where the people are can be put into practice. Declining availability of both government and foundation funding, for example, sometimes has resulted in community-based organizations' and community coalitions' considering or accepting financial support from sources they may not previously have countenanced—sources that sometimes have invisible strings attached. Where a funding source may pose a direct real or perceived conflict of interest for an organization, such problems may intensify.

One of the best-known examples of this dilemma arose over twenty years ago when Mothers Against Drunk Driving (MADD) first accepted a sizable donation from Anheuser-Busch, the nation's largest beer manufacturer. Widely identified as "one of the most successful public health grassroots citizen advocacy organizations in the United States in the past century" (Fell and Voas 2006, 195), MADD is credited with substantially contributing to the dramatic drop in in alcohol-related traffic fatalities from thirty thousand at the time of its founding (1980) to under seventeen thousand in 2004 (Fell and Voas 2006). Yet when the organization accepted the beer company's $180,000 donation (making Anheuser-Busch its second-largest contributor), MADD's increasingly close affiliation with the alcohol industry was widely viewed as having compromised the organization's ability to take a strong stand on the liquor industry's role in the nation's alcohol problem (Marshall and Oleson 1994). In defense of MADD, Dejong and Russell (1995) pointed up the organization's leadership role in pushing for a national minimum drinking age and other policy changes opposed by the alcohol industry. Yet as these analysts also point out, MADD did not significantly strengthen its position on alcohol advertising until some years later—after it had cut its ties to an industry that, it belatedly concluded, "was truly not interested in solving problems due to the misuse of alcohol," despite its propaganda to the contrary (234).

Even when money comes without apparent strings, conflicts between an agency or group's values and those of a potential financial sponsor may raise difficult ethical questions. AIDS prevention organizations around the country, for example, have been offered substantial financial support from alcohol and tobacco companies to help underwrite AIDS walks, media campaigns, and other events. For health professionals aware of the harmful effects of tobacco and heavy drinking, and of the elevated rates of substance abuse in many marginalized communities, accepting such donations may seem morally and ethically untenable. Yet the community-based organizations or groups with which they work may either feel no conflict or agree with Saul Alinsky (1972) that in organizing, the ends (in this case, getting support for a needed community event or campaign) justify the means.

To help avoid situations like these, some public health and social work professionals have begun working with "alternative sponsorship projects," which link health and social programs and organizing efforts with alternative corporate or other sources of financial assistance, in the process dealing a public relations blow to alcohol and tobacco companies. Still other organizers have helped community coalitions and programs to decide whether to accept funding from a controversial source by applying what has been called the "the publicity test of ethics." This simple test involves having a group ask itself whether its reputation or integrity would be damaged if the source of funding for a particular project became known.

Such strategies are important, but in a time of major fiscal retrenchment in health and social services and declining support for a whole host of worthy organizing endeavors, they do not begin to solve the problem of severe funding constraints. When the need is great, where should the line be drawn? And when community participation and empowerment are a value, who draws the line? In meetings with community members about a financial offer of assistance from a source that may pose ethical implications, practitioners not infrequently are confronted with the reaction "We need the money—go for it!" Are we truly promoting community participation and empowerment if we disregard the community's desire to accept needed resources from a source we may consider problematic? Or will the community's long-run agenda be undermined if taking the money may at some point put constraints on decision making, priority setting, or program direction? If what we are after is promotion of the common good, how do we accomplish this in a climate of declining public funding and the concurrent pull of likely support from potentially problematic sources? These are but a few of the kinds of questions health educators and other social change professionals need to ask themselves in relation to the funding of programs and organizing efforts with which they are associated.

Where government or philanthropic funding has been received for a public health or social welfare project accenting community participation, additional funding-related dilemmas also may arise. The community's priorities may shift over time, for example, or members' interest may wane before project completion. Does the health or social work professional in this instance urge the community group to continue working on what is now a low priority in order to fulfill a funding mandate? Does she or he propose returning the remaining money to the funders? Or does she or he approach the funding source about accepting the community's change in direction and continuing to provide overall project support, despite the group's failure to complete the efforts originally emphasized?

This challenge was faced by the Tenderloin Senior Organizing Project (TSOP) a nonprofit that for sixteen years fostered community building and organizing among low-income elderly residents of single-room-occupancy hotels in San Francisco (Minkler 2005). TSOP was committed to "starting where the people are" and addressed only those issues (e.g., violence prevention and improved healthy food access) identified by the residents themselves, while also working to increase individual and community capacity and empowerment. In one instance, the mostly female residents of several TSOP hotels wanted to begin a multipronged nutrition program, including creating on-site minimarkets, a "no-cook cookbook" for residents who were not allowed to cook in their rooms, and participation in a food bank. The TSOP nutrition project, funded by a three-year grant from a local foundation, worked well in the first eighteen months, but after that, residents' interest began to wane as they became excited about other priorities. After talking with the residents, project staff approached the foundation about renegotiating the terms of the original grant. They thus were able to establish a new funding agreement, through which TSOP residents would complete those aspects of the project in which they remained interested (e.g., the cookbook), while scaling back on others, and continuing to engage in the leadership and capacity building aspects of the work that went beyond any particular content area (Minkler 2005).

Writing grants that emphasize community capacity-building outcomes and processes as a key part of the project being undertaken, and working with funders if shifts in the areas of concern to participants do arise, are important (albeit not foolproof) means of helping ensure continuity of funding while still honoring community priorities. As Paul Tough (2008) has pointed out with respect to the internationally acclaimed Harlem Children's Zone in New York (www.hcz.org), processes need to be put in place with funders and other supporters that foster better alignment with potentially changing community priorities, as long as more bedrock concerns with community capacity building, leadership, and participation are maintained.

Still another set of ethical challenges may arise for community organizers working with nonprofit organizations in the United States that have tax-exempt 501(c)3 (nonprofit) status, and therefore are limited in the amount of lobbying activity in which they may engage.[1] Briefly, *lobbying* refers to direct or indirect (administrative support) activities that influence legislative efforts (i.e., bills, resolutions, and acts) by Congress, a state legislature, local council, or similar governing body. Educational activities intended to inform, but not advocate for a given side, are not considered lobbying efforts. Although nonprofits can legally engage in a certain amount of lobbying, some funders become uncomfortable when *any* advocacy on behalf of a particular legislative measure is undertaken by a 501(c)3 organization they support.

A recent example may be found in the California Senior Leaders Alliance (CSLA), a grassroots organizations of diverse older volunteer organizers and activists that grew out of a foundation-funded program honoring and training outstanding older volunteers in the state (www.calseniorleaders.org). After seven years of successful operation, the parent program ran into difficulty when its members (most of whom are from underserved communities) wanted to move from educating the public and policymakers about new legislation benefiting low-income elders to actually advocating for a particular bill in the state capitol. Although the group's funder was sympathetic, it did not feel it could support such activity, and when a newspaper cover story highlighted the work of the senior leaders at the state capitol as "advocates" for a particular bill, the group had to cease such work until alternative funding could be found. By raising individual donations for unrestricted use, and seeking an additional grant from a second foundation that *was* willing and able to support such advocacy more directly, the CSLA was able to maintain its original funding while moving, with its new funding base, into advocacy arenas not previously sanctioned. For professionals working with either a 501(c)3 or a 501(c)4 agency (which permits somewhat greater, albeit still limited degrees of freedom with respect to lobbying), it is critical to know and respect the constraints posed by particular funding sources, and to work with community groups on better understanding what is and is not permitted by particular funders and other agency affiliations.

Cultural Conflicts and the *-Isms*

It is not uncommon for professionals engaged in community organizing and capacity building to be culturally different from community members or constituent groups. Further, communities themselves are increasingly diverse. Consequently, opportunities for cultural misunderstandings and for real or perceived racism, sexism, homophobia, or other problems between the practitioner and the community, and within communities, are unfortunately plentiful. It is essential that the practitioner be willing to deal openly with cross-cultural misunderstandings by employing the critical organizing and capacity building skills of listening and dialoguing, participatory planning, and self-reflection (see chapters 4 and 8). Moreover, the practitioner must often juggle the cultural norms and values of a given community with broader ethical values grounded in egalitarianism or justice (DeFilippis et al. 2010; see chapter 6).

Many cultural misunderstandings result from well-intentioned, though either naive or incompetent, actions by the organizer that unfortunately can lead to mistrust or ill will. For example, an outside organizer who attempted to show cultural sensitivity by ordering "Asian food" for a community meeting whose attendees were largely Korean, Chinese, Thai, Laotian, and Filipino faced an angry reaction from some when the meal turned out to consist solely of Chinese cuisine. Although the matter may seem minor, some group members thought that the organizer's food choice reflected the larger society's disrespectful tendency to lump together all Asians (and Asian Pacific Islanders). In this instance, the organizer took the important step of acknowledging her mistake and asking the group to decide on the food for subsequent meetings. In response, some offered to contribute their own favorite dishes, while others identified good and inexpensive restaurants serving their native cuisine; the next meeting included a plethora of diverse ethnic treats. Since the four most important words in community organizing may well be *"refreshments will be served,"* taking care to involve communities in this way, and respecting community food preferences, is not an extraneous detail. Our handling of such situations can demonstrate cultural humility, if we approach them with a humble attitude characterized by acknowledgement of our own biases and ignorance, an openness to others' cultural reality, and a sincere desire to listen and to learn (Tervalon and Murray-Garcia 1998; Chávez et al. 2010; Reed et al., in press; see appendix 3).

The practitioner may also need to address intragroup cultural conflicts; communities rarely are free of the *-isms*. Discriminatory or culturally offensive statements and actions can emerge at any time in a community campaign, and the practitioner will need to exhibit dexterity in both respecting the community's opinions or customs while also creating a space for that community's education or development. For one of this chapter's authors (Hyde), a fairly routine community meeting was made difficult when the group's leader began to make homophobic comments. Not wanting to confront the leader publicly, the practitioner chose to have a private, one-on-one conversation with this individual after the meeting in order to explain how hurtful those comments were. Because these two women already had developed a solid working relationship, they were able to have an honest discussion and reach an agreement on how to proceed, which included the leader not offering her personal opinions that were so upsetting. Even though the practitioner lost an initial opportunity to address this with the group, the leader appreciated not being called out publicly in front of her members. Maintaining that relationship proved important in enabling the outside practitioner to return to the group at a later date for a workshop on how to deal with various *-isms*, including homophobic remarks. In this case, building trust was given priority over immediately addressing discriminatory comments, though they were examined within an educational (and safe) context.

With an increasingly contentious public political discourse, a practitioner may also need to assist a community or constituency group in dealing with hate speech directed their way. An organizer needs to be adept at guiding community members toward ethical practices (especially when the initial tendency might be to return vitriol with more of the same), while also acknowledging the hurtful experience. Practitioners who work with low-income people often contend with mean-spirited stereotypes (such as laziness, leeching off the system) directed toward that group; stereotypes that typically are laden with classist, racist, or sexist meaning. Helping a group developed an empowered and dignified sense of self is a tremendous gift to share with marginalized people.

Finally, and as discussed in chapter 8, dealing with cultural conflict and the *-isms* cannot be fully or effectively done in communities unless agency staff and practitioners are also willing and able to deal with their own *-isms*. In Alameda County, California, the former health department director required that the entire agency staff attend two- to three-hour monthly meetings dealing with racism and related issues. Internal changes in the health department and its staff's attitudes, beliefs, and behaviors were seen as equally important as fostering change in the neighborhoods served by the organization (Iton 2006; see chapter 8). Tools like McIntosh's (1989) classic "White Privilege" checklist, and Undoing Racism workshops, may be useful as well in helping professionals confront their own -*isms* and cultivate the cultural humility (Tervalon and Murray-Garcia 1998) necessary for effective and culturally sensitive practice (see also appendix 3). Such work is far from easy, however. As Wallerstein (1999, 49) points out, even practitioners like herself with long ties to a more marginalized community may be unaware of the "power of authority" represented by their own multiple power bases—and how failure to adequately own and address these may sabotage relationships. As this public health leader further notes, to facilitate true community empowerment and genuine partnerships, "we need to understand our personal biographies of race, education or social status, or gender and other identities" and how they in turn inform our community partnerships (49).

Unanticipated Consequences

The guiding principles of fostering self-determination and meaningful participation can go a long way toward helping to avoid many of the problems that can plague the community organizing process. Yet even when these principles are followed, organizing efforts may result in outcomes or by-products that were unanticipated and that may have negative consequences. Two examples are illustrative, one in the area of injury prevention campaigns and the second in the training of community health workers to enhance their skills in areas such as leadership and community organizing.

Many recent prevention and health promotion campaigns have done an excellent job of involving youth, people of color, LGBT (lesbian, gay, bisexual, and transgender) groups, and other traditionally neglected communities in the design and pretesting of programs and materials aimed at better reaching these populations. At the same time, however, health promotion and community organizing efforts often inadvertently reproduce and transmit problematic aspects of the dominant culture.

A poignant early example of this is found in the work of Caroline Wang (1992), who identifies the stigmatization of people with disabilities that is often communicated through well-meaning injury prevention campaigns. One in a series of billboards, for example, featured a teenager in a wheelchair with the caption "If you think fourth period English is endless, try sitting in a wheelchair for the rest of your life!" Another, with the caption "One for the road," showed a man on crutches with his leg partially amputated. As Wang points out, the implicit message in such ads is "Don't let this happen to you!" Although well intended, these messages reinforce already powerful negative prejudices in our society against people with disabilities. At a time when the disabled were organizing to assert their rights and break down negative societal stereotypes, such campaigns were particularly demoralizing. In the words of one person with a disability on viewing the injury prevention ads, "I feel like I should be preventing myself!" (Wang 1992).

In our attempts to avoid negative and unanticipated consequences like this one, the principle of high-level community involvement—and in this case, the reaching out to an overlooked community (people with disabilities)—can stand us in good stead. Such an approach is illustrated in the close coordination between two strong advocacy and organizing groups based in the San Francisco Bay Area— the World Institute on Disability (WID) and the Trauma Foundation. Although the latter's raison d'être is injury prevention, its president, Andrew McGuire, formerly served as chair of the board of WID, and he and other foundation staff have remained strong advocates for the recognition and treatment of disabled people as full participants in American society.

In some instances, of course, the very nature of the processes involved in community organizing can have negative unanticipated consequences. The train- ing of "health promoters" or community health workers in both low-resource and postindustrialized nations provides a case in point. From a health education and a community organizing standpoint, such activities makes eminent sense, for they typically identify and build on the strengths of natural helpers in a commu- nity and address issues of homophily (e.g., that people often learn best and prefer to receive services from people who are "like themselves" in terms of race, social class, etc.). Many excellent models for community health worker training, more- over, put a heavy accent on empowerment (Eng et al. 2009), often employing methods such as Paulo Freire's (1968, 1973) "education for critical consciousness" (see chapter 4).

Yet as Freire (1968) himself has cautioned, leadership training can alienate the community members who are involved, making them strangers in their own communities. Once they have been trained and, in a sense, "indoctrinated" into the culture of the public health or social welfare organization or department, community health workers may find it difficult to relate to or interact with their peers as they had previously. In one recent case, an environmental health coalition in a Latino community found that the impressive local women it hired and trained as *promotoras* (lay health workers and organizers) were being called *chismosas*, or "gossips," by older women in the community, and even sometimes by husbands suspicious of their wives' new roles (Minkler et al. 2010). Is it the train- ing they receive that gives them a new vocabulary and consequently a different way of addressing identified problems? Is it the fact that they feel some unstated pressure to "fit in" to the agency that hired them, where most people are profes- sionally trained and where the culture of the office environment is different from the culture of the community or neighborhood? Or is it that once someone who is identified as a community leader tries to mobilize a community around an issue— even one acknowledged as being of local importance—she or he is distrusted as being "on the other side"? How should we proceed when we are committed to involving indigenous community workers in the process of education and organizing, yet are aware that such efforts may serve to alienate these individuals from their communities and serve to limit their credibility in the community? In the case of the environmental health coalition highlighted above, the coalition head, a white male, began by going out for beer with the local men to dispel suspicion about their wives and partners' involvement as *promotoras*. Additional outreach to other community members, and the establishment of a tutoring and training program for children, not only dissipated initial suspicion of the *promotoras*, but also resulted in heavy community turnout at city council meetings and other venues, in turn contributing to the policy changes that were achieved (Minkler et al. 2010).

Still another unanticipated consequence of training community members as health workers, group leaders, and organizers is that they may use the skills they have acquired to manipulate other members of the community. However, numerous examples from North America and around the world of effective lay health worker programs and leadership training activities on the local level suggest that this strategy is, on balance, a critical one for improving health and welfare contributing to individual and community empowerment (Eng et al. 2009; Schulz et al. 2001; Wallerstein 2006). The task for health educators, social workers, and other professionals then remains one of determining how best to help participants acquire the tools they need for effective leadership and organizing, while at the same time communicating the responsibilities this new training imposes, as well as some of the difficulties and challenges they may need to anticipate.

Thoughts on the Common Good

Acknowledging and confronting the ethical dilemmas discussed above may help enhance community capacity building and ultimately greater empowerment of community groups. When we start where the people are, we make every attempt to be responsive to the needs, concerns, and agendas of a particular community, thereby affirming a commitment to self-determination and liberty, as well as promoting the rights of individuals to act on their own values. The question remains—Do we have an ultimate end in our efforts of promoting and preserving the common good of the communities with which we work? And if so, whose common good is being addressed, and who is determining what constitutes the common good? Finally, should we also be concerned with notions of common good that transcend local communities?

Alinsky (1972) long argued that a cardinal rule in effective community organizing is to appeal to self-interest: people will not organize unless they see what's in it for them. However, particularly in a country such as the United States, which is characterized by a heavy accent on rugged individualism, stressing only self-interest may feed into an already impoverished notion of the common good. As

Lester Thurow (1996) pointed out twenty-five years ago, the dominant American ideologies—capitalism and democracy—"have no 'common good,' no common goals toward which everyone is collectively working. Both stress the individual and not the group. . . . Neither imposes an obligation to worry about the welfare of the other. . . . In both, individual freedom dominates community obligations" (159).

In part because of the individual focus of these dominant ideologies, the very debate over public or common good in the United States has been badly constrained. In Larry Churchill's (1987) words, our notions of justice are based on "a moral heritage in which answers to the question 'what is good?' and 'what is right?' are lodged definitively in a powerful image of the individual as the only meaningful level of moral analysis" (21). Churchill went on to argue that "a more realistic sense of community is one in which there are shared perceptions of the value of individual lives and a social commitment to protect them all equitably" (101).

The lack of a more genuine sense of community and of a well-developed notion of the common good may be particularly troubling for health educators, social workers, and other social change professionals for whom a strong sense of social justice often lies at the base of their personal and professional values (see chapter 1). As suggested earlier, moreover, although an appeal to self-interest may be pragmatic in helping to mobilize a community for the achievement of its self-interested goals, there are dangers in this limited approach. Key among these is the fact that a local community group may fail to see or reflect on the connection between its goals and concerns and the broader need for social justice in a democratic society (DeFilippis et al. 2010; Labonte 2009; see chapter 6). Consequently, even though a focus on self-interest may be necessary from an organizing perspective, we would argue that it is too narrow to be sufficient.

We would, however, advocate against an overly simplistic utilitarian notion of the common good that focuses solely on achieving the greatest good for the greatest number. For the latter may not truly reflect the ends that those engaged in community organizing are attempting to realize. Instead, we may want to look toward a definition of common or collective good that both speaks to local organizing efforts and includes a broader vision of society.

The beginning of the twenty-first century has been a time of renewed moral reflection in fields like public health and social work. In a seminal contribution, Wallack and Lawrence (2005) note that although values consonant with public health and social work, such as "equity, compassion and social responsibility," have historically played a key role in organizing around social problems, "most Americans do not articulate these values nearly as easily as they use the language of individualism" (568). As these theorists go on to note, developing what Robert Bellah and his colleagues (1996) call "America's second language'—"the language of interconnection, is critical because once the moral focus is broadened, the definition of and response to public health problems"—and we would add, to problems in social work, education and other arenas—can grow as well (570).

Practitioners who engage in organizing and other community-based work must engage in this discussion, reflection, and debate both to understand the issues and to bring their perspectives to a dialogue that will be critical to the future of communities, community organizing, and community participation. Through such discussions, we can help demonstrate how community organizing can serve as a bridge to thinking more deeply about the collective good not only of this or that community but also of the broader society.

Conclusion

Throughout this chapter, we have been asking hard questions that go to the core of our practice as community organizers. As health educators, social workers, and other social change professionals, we often operate on the implicit assumption that our interventions are ethically justifiable, since they are derived from community-identified needs. Yet the principles of starting where the people are and working closely with communities to translate their goals into reality, while critical to ethically sound practice, do not exempt us from the need to engage in frequent, thoughtful, ethical reflection. All too often, such reflection on the ethical issues in community organizing has been an afterthought, occurring as a result of unanticipated dilemmas and ethical issues. By making such reflection and dialogue instead an early and continuing part of our organizing efforts, we as professionals can enhance our ability to ensure that the actions we take in working with communities meet the criteria of ethically sound practice.

Although we have tried to address a number of specific ethical dilemmas in this chapter, many others cannot be anticipated, given the ever-changing contexts in which we work. We must commit ourselves to articulating the dilemmas we face in our practice as community organizers, with special attention to recognizing the contradictions with which we must cope and understanding where our responsibilities lie.

It is critical, moreover, for us to be able to identify and articulate not only the ethical dilemmas we face but also the underlying values that drive our work. How do we communicate the importance of the values of community participation and empowerment when we find ourselves in ethically challenging situations? When conflicting priorities present us with the task of meeting different needs and different (and sometimes conflicting) agendas, how do we make explicit the values that can help ensure that we do "the right thing"? When our agencies or funders propose what is really only symbolic or lip service community participation and capacity building, how do we formulate effective values-based arguments to reinforce the importance of not only bringing community members to the table but also hearing their concerns and ensuring that their input is heavily reflected in the final product? Finally, what role can we play in helping community groups reflect on their own values as a means of grappling with difficult dilemmas over issue selection or whether to accept funding from a potentially ethically problematic source? And what role can we play in helping communities to explore the connections between their perceptions of their own common good and a broader vision of society?

Although we cannot anticipate the possible consequences of all our actions, we can anticipate that some consequences of our community organizing efforts will be different from what was expected. We must remind ourselves to expect the unexpected and to recognize that in the process we are likely to find ourselves in ethically challenging situations that require discussion, dialogue, and difficult choices.

NOTE

1. According to the Internal Revenue Service, nonprofit organizations may select one of two methods to determine excessive lobbying activity: (1) the Substantial Part Test, in which disproportionate organizational activities (direct and indirect) concern lobbying or (2) the Expenditure Test, in which the organization (depending on size) cannot exceed $1 million dollars direct (i.e., staff time lobbying) and indirect (i.e., secretarial support) expenditures (http://www.irs.gov/charities/index.html). It is the responsibility of the organization to maintain necessary records that demonstrate that the lobbying activities remain within appropriate limits (for more information, see http://www .irs.gov/charities/article/0,,id=163392,00.html).

REFERENCES

Alinsky, S. D. 1972. *Rules for Radicals: A Practical Primer for Realistic Radicals.* New York: Random House.

Asian Pacific Environmental Network (APEN). 2002. "From Refugee Camps to Toxic Hot Spots: About the Laotian Community in Richmond, CA." www.apen@apen4ej.org.

Arnstein, S. 1969. "A Ladder of Citizen Participation." *Journal of American Institute of Planners* 35, no. 4:216–224.

Bellah, R. N., R. Madsen, W. M. Sullivan, A. Swidler, and S. M. Tipton. 1996. *Habits of the Heart.* 2nd ed. Berkeley and Los Angeles: University of California Press.

Buckley, T., and J. Walters. 2005. "Developing Leadership and Political Capacity among Laotian Refugees: Healing a Culture, Building a Community; Laotian Organizing Project." Evans Center for Public Affairs, University of Washington. http://hallway.evans .washington.edu/cases/details/developing.leadership.and.political.capacity.

California Tobacco Control Program, California Department of Public Health. 2010. "Two Decades of the California Tobacco Control Program: California Tobacco Survey, 1990–2008." http://www.cdph.ca.gov/.

Chávez, V., M. Minkler, N. Wallerstein, and M. S. Spencer. 2010. "Community Organizing for Health and Social Justice." In *Prevention Is Primary: Strategies for Community Well-Being,* edited by L. Cohen, C. Chávez, and S. Chehimi, 87–112. 2nd ed. San Francisco: Jossey-Bass.

Childress, J. F. 2007. "Methods in Bioethics." In *The Oxford Handbook of Bioethics,* edited by B. Steinbock, 15–45. New York: Oxford University Press.

Churchill, L. 1987. *Rationing Health Care in America: Perceptions and Principles of Justice.* South Bend, Ind.: University of Notre Dame Press.

Coalition of National Health Education Organizations. 2010. "Code of Ethics." http://www .cnheo.org/.

Corburn, J. 2009. *Toward the Healthy City: People, Places, and the Politics of Urban Planning.* Cambridge, Mass.: MIT Press.

DeBuono, B., A. R. Gonzalez, and S. Rosenbaum. 2007. *Moments in Leadership: Case Studies in Public Health Policy and Practice.* New York: Pfizer.

DeFilippis, J., R. Fisher, and E. Shragge. 2010. *Contesting Community: The Limits and Potential of Local Organizing.* New Brunswick, N.J.: Rutgers University Press.

Dejong, W., and A. Russell. 1995. "MADD's Position on Alcohol Advertising: A Response to Marshal and Oleson." *Journal of Public Health Policy* 16, no. 2:231–238.

Dunn, W. 1983. *Values, Ethics, and the Practice of Policy Analysis.* Lexington, Mass.: Lexington Books.

Eng, E., S. Rhodes, and E. Parker. 2009. "Natural Helper Models to Enhance a Community's Health and Competence." In *Emerging Theories in Health Promotion Practice and Research*, edited by R. DiClemente, R. A. Crosby, and M. C. Kegler, 303–330. 2nd ed. San Francisco: Jossey-Bass.

Fell, J. C., and R. B. Voas. 2006. "Mothers against Drunk Driving (MADD): The First 25 Years." *Traffic Injury Prevention* 7, no. 3:195–212.

Freire, P. 1968. *Pedagogy of the Oppressed.* New York: Seabury Press.

———. 1973. *Education for Critical Consciousness.* New York: Seabury Press.

Green, L. W., and M. Kreuter. 1990. "Health Promotion as a Public Health Strategy for the 1990's." *Annual Review of Public Health* 11:319–334.

Harrington, D., and R. Dolgoff. 2008. "Hierarchies of Ethical Principles for Ethical Decision Making in Social Work." *Ethics and Social Welfare* 2, no. 2:183–196.

Hyde, C. 2010. "What's Ethics Got to Do with It? Using Evidence to Inform Management Practice." In *Evidence-Based Practice in Organization and Community Settings*, edited by M. Roberts-DeGennero and S. Fogel, 35–53. Chicago: Lyceum Press.

Iton, T. 2006. "Tackling the Root Causes of Health Disparities through Community Capacity Building." In *Tackling Health Inequities through Public Health Practice: A Handbook for Action*, edited by R. Hofrichter, 115–136. Washington D.C.: National Association of County and City Health Officials.

Labonte, R. 1990. "Empowerment: Notes on Professional and Community Dimensions." *Canadian Review of Social Policy* 26:1–12.

———. 2009. "Social Inclusion/Exclusion and Health: Dancing the Dialectic." In *Social Determinants of Health: Canadian Perspectives*, edited by D. Raphael, 269–279. 2nd ed. Toronto: Canadian Scholars' Press.

Marshall, M., and A. Oleson. 1994. "In the Pink: MADD and Public Health Policy in the 1990s." *Journal of Public Health Policy* 15, no. 1:54–68.

McCloskey, D. D., M. A. McDonald, J. Cook, S. Heurtin-Roberts, D. Updegrove, D. Sampson et al. 2011. "Community Engagement: Definitions and Organizing Concepts from the Literature." In *Principles of Community Engagement*, by Clinical and Translational Science Awards Consortium Community Engagement Key Function Committee Task Force on Principles of Community Engagement. 2nd ed. NIH Publication No. 11–7782. Washington D.C.: National Institutes of Health.

McIntosh, P. 1989. "White Privilege: Unpacking the Invisible Knapsack." *Peace and Freedom*, July/August, 10–12.

Minkler, M. 1994. "Challenges for Health Promotion in the 1990's: Social Inequities, Empowerment, Negative Consequences, and the Public Good." *American Journal of Health Promotion* 8, no. 6:403–413.

———. 2005. "Community Organizing among the Elderly Poor in San Francisco's Tenderloin District." In *Community Organizing and Community Building for Health*, edited by M. Minkler, 272–288. New Brunswick, N.J.: Rutgers University Press.

Minkler, M., A. P. Garicia, J. Williams, T. LoPresti, and J. Lilly. 2010. "Sí, Se Puede: Using Participatory Research to Promote Environmental Justice in a Latino Community in San Diego, CA." *Journal of Urban Health* 87, no. 5:796–812.

Morgan, M. A., and J. Lifshay. 2006. *Community Engagement in Public Health*. Martinez, Calif.: Contra Costa Department of Health Services, Public Health Division. http://www.barhii.org/resources/downloads/community_engagement.pdf.

National Association of Social Workers. 2008. "Code of Ethics." http://www.naswdc.org/pubs/code/code.asp.

Nyswander, D. 1956. "Education for Health: Some Principles and Their Application." *California Health* 14 (November): 65–70.

Petrini, C. 2010. Ethics-Based Public Health Policy? *American Journal of Public Health* 911, no. 2:197.

Reed, B. G., P. A. Newman, Z. Suarez, and E. A. Lewis. In press. "Interpersonal Practice beyond Diversity and towards Social Justice: The Importance of Critical Consciousness." In *Social Work Practice*, edited by B. Seabury, B. Seabury, and C. Garvin. 2nd ed. New York: Sage.

Reisch, M. 2010a. "Defining Social Justice in a Socially Unjust World," In *Educating for Social Justice: Transformative Experiential Learning*, edited by J. M. Bierkenmaier, A. Cruce, J. Curley, E. Burkemper, R. J. Wilson, and J. J. Stretch, 11–28 Chicago: Lyceum Books.

———. 2010b. "Teaching about Social Justice through a Multi-media Format." In *Educating for Social Justice: Transformative Experiential Learning*, edited by J. M. Bierkenmaier, A. Cruce, J. Curley, E. Burkemper, R. J. Wilson, and J. J. Stretch, 127–148. Chicago: Lyceum Books.

Robertson, A., and M. Minkler. 1994. "New Health Promotion Movement: A Critical Examination." *Health Education Quarterly* 21, no. 3:295–312.

Rubin, H., and I. Rubin. 1992. *Community Organizing and Development*. 2nd ed. New York: Macmillan.

Schulz, A. J., B. A. Israel, E. A. Parker, M. Lockett, Y. Hill, and R. Wills. 2001. "The East Side Village Health Worker Partnership: Integrating Research with Action to Reduce Health Disparities." *Public Health Reports*. 116 no. 6:548–557.

Siler-Wells, G. L. 1989. "Challenges of the Gordian Knot: Community Health in Canada." In *International Symposium on Community Participation and Empowerment Strategies in Health Promotion*. Bielefeld, Germany: Center for Interdisciplinary Studies, University of Bielefeld.

Sze, J. 2004. "Asian American Activism for Environmental Justice." *Peace Review* 16, no. 2: 149–156.

Tervalon, M., and Murray-Garcia, J. 1998. "Cultural Humility vs. Cultural Competence: A Critical Distinction in Defining Physician Training Outcomes in Medical Education." *Journal of Health Care for the Poor and Underserved* 9, no. 2:117–125.

Thurow, L. 1996. *The Future of Capitalism*. New York: William Morrow.

Tough, P. 2008. *Whatever It Takes: Geoffrey Canada's Quest to Change Harlem and America*. New York: Houghton Mifflin.

Wallack, L., and R. Lawrence. 2005. "Talking about Public Health: Developing America's 'Second Language.'" *American Journal of Public Health* 95, no. 4:567–570.

Wallerstein, N. 1999. "Power between Evaluator and Community: Research Relationships within New Mexico's Healthier Communities." *Social Science and Medicine* 1999, no. 49: 39–53.

———. 2006. "The Effectiveness of Empowerment Strategies to Improve Health." Health Evidence Network. Copenhagen: World Health Organization. http://www.euro.who.int/HEN/Syntheses/empowerment/20060119_10.

Wang, C. 1992. "Culture, Meaning, and Disability: Injury Prevention Campaigns in the Production of Stigma." *Social Science and Medicine* 3, no. 5:1093–1102.

8

Building Partnerships between Local Health Departments and Communities

Case Studies in Capacity Building and Cultural Humility

GALEN ELLIS

SHERYL WALTON

The path toward effective partnerships between local health departments and communities is fraught with obstacles and sometimes seemingly insurmountable challenges. It is a journey that requires great perseverance, flexibility, humility, and caring. Success is heavily dependent on the ability of organizations and individual staff to commit themselves to deeply examining their own personal and professional beliefs, behaviors, and assumptions about culture and relationships. There also is a critical need to document and disseminate findings about the outcomes of such efforts, particularly in the wake of the growing emphasis on evidence-based practice and "practice-based evidence" (Green 2006).

This chapter describes and critically analyzes the Healthy Neighborhoods Project in Contra Costa County, California, and its subsequent replication in neighboring health departments and communities. We begin by reviewing the background and context in which this model was developed, using as a conceptual framework McKnight and Kretzmann's (1990) asset-based community development (ABCD) model (see chapter 10), Lasker and her colleagues' (2001) concept of *partnerships synergy*, and Tervalon and Murray-Garcia's (1998) concept of *cultural humility*. Following the case study presentations, we then draw on experiences from each of these partnerships to highlight lessons learned and promising practices.

Conceptual Framework

Let's put aside our preconceived notions of each other and instead each of us—the residents, the community agencies, and the health department—come to the table and offer up our varied gifts that we can pool to transform our community.

—Joyce White, resident activist, city of Richmond

The statement above well captures the philosophical base and value orientation of the Healthy Neighborhoods Project. Joyce's remark also nicely reflects the grounding of the project in McKnight and Kretzmann's (1990) ABCD model. As discussed in chapter 10, these theorists propose moving away from the "deficit mentality" at the base of much human services work to instead identify and build on individual and community assets. Whereas the traditional needs-oriented assessment approach teaches people to see themselves with special problems to be addressed by outsiders, the ABCD approach encourages community members to recognize, actively develop, and mobilize their own assets.

The HNP also well reflects Lasker and her colleagues' (2001) notion of "partnership synergy." Building on definitions of *synergy* as "the power to combine the perspectives, resources, and skills of a group of people and organizations," Lasker and her colleagues (2001) suggest that "the synergy that partners seek to achieve through collaboration is more than a mere exchange of resources. By combining the individual perspectives, resources, and skills of the partners, the group creates something new and valuable together—something that is greater than the sum of its parts" (184).

Lasker and her colleagues further argue that increased creativity, comprehensive thinking, practicality, and transformative potential are unique advantages of collaboration. Without using the term, resident activist Joyce White clearly was describing the power of partnership synergy in her statement about pooling gifts to "transform our community."

A final component of the Healthy Neighborhoods Project's conceptual framework lies in the concept of cultural humility. As noted in chapters 1 and 3, Tervalon and Murray-Garcia (1998) originally used this term primarily in reference to race and ethnicity, noting that although we can never become truly competent in another's culture, we can engage openly, acknowledging the limitations of our understanding and seeking to broaden that understanding. Building on this approach, we describe cultural humility as the ability to listen both to persons from other cultures and to our own internal dialogue. When we do that, we discover how easily we discount another's truth when it passes through our own cultural lens.

But cultural humility also includes understanding and addressing the impacts of professional cultures, which tend to be highly influenced by white, western, patriarchal belief systems, as these help shape interactions between health departments and local communities. As suggested in this and other chapters, sharing power can be an important outcome of having and demonstrating cultural humility in such contexts.

Linking the concepts of cultural humility, ABCD and partnership synergy provides an overarching hypothesis that partnerships will be improved and longer-term health and social outcomes more easily achieved in low-income communities of color when (1) residents are engaged in and driving community development; (2) critical public health capacities of government staff are increased, particularly with respect to cultural humility; and (3) public agencies and their staffs undergo cultural and systems change. Each of these dimensions, along with the asset-building and partnership synergy models described above, are illustrated in the case studies that follow.

The Healthy Neighborhoods Project and Its Evolution

Launching the Healthy Neighborhoods Project in the Community

West Contra Costa County is composed primarily of people of color and includes many deep pockets of poverty. In 1994, the Healthy Neighborhoods Project began as a pilot project in Pittsburg, California, and was soon replicated in five additional neighborhoods. In each of them, the health department had been frustrated by attempts to engage communities in public health projects. The department's attempts to mobilize the community around tobacco control in the early 1990s, in the wake of several tobacco control policy victories and an influx of cigarette tax dollars, was emblematic of the frustrations experienced (Ellis et al. 1996). A long history of failed efforts and mistrust between the department, the nearby University of California, Berkeley (which often used this community for its own research purposes), and community-based organizations made dialogue with grassroots local leaders difficult at best, particularly since the tobacco control initiative did not address a real community-identified need (Ellis et al. 1996; Syme 2004).

To illustrate this, imagine a community fraught with economic stress and gang violence. Enter the professional health educator (making a good salary with benefits) with her antismoking program. She understands that community involvement is critical to public health and seeks the buy-in from key leaders. What she may not understand, whether she is new to the department or not, is the following:

- It is likely that the community leaders she is approaching are already tapped for other categorical programs the health department has rolled out into the community. Furthermore, the local university has probably sought to involve them in community surveys and other research efforts.
- Every community needs assessment, every research study, and nearly every intervention has focused on community deficits and thereby directly or indirectly reinforced the view that these neighborhoods are cesspools of problems, undermining community self-esteem.
- In many communities, an influx of resources for one health program or another seldom has resulted in outcomes that residents could tangibly see or feel. Instead, many residents have concluded that the primary benefits of such programs are salaries for outside professionals and publications for faculty members.
- There may be a select group of community-based organizations (CBOs) that have well-established relationships with the health departments and are

eager to accept contracts and other resources to partner on a health program. However, as suggested in chapter 5, these CBOs don't always have a good track record of engaging residents on the grassroots level, may represent particular interest groups rather than the larger community, or both.

After several years of good intentions being met with anger, mistrust, or at best, passive indulgence, Contra Costa Health Department staff did two things. First, and despite having their time paid for by categorical dollars for tobacco control, they spent long hours in the community, with the blessing of the public health director, supporting local efforts to address two areas that *were* of great concern to residents: substance abuse and gang violence. Second, they decided to broaden outreach beyond the traditional CBOs and ask residents in the community, who were respected by their neighbors, how to proceed. And this is how the conversation with Joyce in her kitchen came about.

In collaboration with community leaders and leadership in the health department, one of the authors (Ellis) who was then a program manager with the health department, launched the Healthy Neighborhoods Project, using the ABCD approach (chapter 10) to help residents identify and build on their assets by stimulating community involvement and developing and implementing a resident-driven action plan to address local issues and concerns.

At the heart of the Healthy Neighborhoods Project were the hiring and training of a project coordinator, 6 resident community organizers, and 120 neighborhood health advocates (NHAs) who made up neighborhood action teams in each participating neighborhood. Local teams were recruited by the project coordinator and organizers. The criteria for participation included living in the neighborhood, reflecting the diversity of the community, having a sincere interest in improving the neighborhood, and being willing to commit oneself to participating for one year. All team members participated in two to three days of initial training in areas that included community organizing, asset mapping, participatory evaluation, and team building. An initial training activity, which introduced them to the model of capacity building, also inventoried their own strengths and skills, which later were mobilized in their neighborhoods.

The community organizers and NHAs also participated in biweekly in-service sessions throughout the year on topics such as recruitment; meeting facilitation; public speaking; and media advocacy, or the strategic use of media to frame issues from a community or health perspective (see chapter 22). Hands-on technical assistance also was provided by the project coordinator (coauthor Walton), who worked closely with each neighborhood team on a weekly basis and assisted individual organizers and advocates with personal and professional skill development. With the assistance of health education staff, residents conducted community asset mapping and planned and facilitated community forums. Similarly, a health department evaluator helped the NHAs design a community assessment instrument, which they then used to conduct door-to-door surveys with approximately five hundred residents to learn, among other things, what people liked about their neighborhood and what they'd like to see changed. Following the survey, health advocates were again trained to help in data analysis and interpretation, and their analysis later was described by the evaluator as demonstrating a sophisticated understanding of their community (in Minkler 2000).

In keeping with the Healthy Neighborhoods Project's accent on cultural humility, and consistent with a growing body of evidence that resident participation, control, and increased social capital can have substantial health and social benefits (Cockerham 2007; Kawachi et al. 2008; Wallerstein 2006), service providers and local elected officials also received some training to enable them to make a critical paradigm shift. Since even the best-meaning providers and professional staff can inadvertently create dependency by relating to community members as recipients of services (McKnight and Kretzmann 1995), the staff, along with elected officials and other policymakers thus were taught how to avoid jargon, and how to step back and allow residents to voice their opinions in their own time and on their own terms. At resident training sessions and community meetings, for example, providers and elected leaders were asked to observe and be available as resources, but to refrain from advocating or voting when decisions were being made.

Challenges and Dilemmas

The grounding of the Healthy Neighborhoods Project (HNP) in an asset-based and culturally humble approach, and its inclusion of staff as well as resident training, proved an effective model for synergistic partnership, and one that helped generate a number of impressive outcomes as outlined below. At the same time, however, many obstacles and challenges were faced at each stage of the process which had to be carefully addressed.

When the HNP was first being conceived, for example, a key community member walked out of a planning meeting angry and in tears. Later it was discovered that all the good intentions of the staff in gaining input from residents and plotting them on flip charts felt more to her like outsiders trying to control the process. HNP staff had to find the humility to hear her truth, despite the strong belief on their part that they were facilitating a participatory process. The tendency is to defend and blame; the essential capacity is to suspend beliefs long enough to hear and accept the truth of another.

Particular difficulties also sometimes arose for staff of color who not infrequently found themselves in the position of the "outsider within." For although the socialization process in professions crosses racial and ethnic lines, many professionals of color feel as though they live in two worlds (Chávez et al. 2008). From a capacities point of view, they are bicultural. Yet from a personal point of view, meeting their professional demands, while effectively translating and brokering for the community, can be extremely stressful. In the HNP, staff of color also sometimes expressed the feeling that they were doing twice the work of fellow staff members who were not culturally identified with the community, and who therefore did not occupy these dual roles.

Regardless of one's race or ethnicity, the process of authentic community building can be painful and sometimes frightening to staff who are used to the predictability of the dominant professional culture. Health department staff who are comfortable with that aspect of their professional role as someone who values "caring for" and "providing service," for instance, may not as easily accept the necessity in community building of being engaged fully, authentically, and truthfully with community members. Not to reveal our pain, our limitations, our mistakes, and our own process of opening and evolving itself is a barrier to the kinds of connections that must be made to build community. As Vanier (1989) pointed out over twenty years ago, "In all of us and in every community, there is the fear of challenge; and the danger of covering up tensions and the things that are not going well, or at least refusing to look at them and to confront them" (135).

Challenges Internal to the Health Department

While the HNP was unfolding in the community, a parallel process was taking place inside the walls of the health department, which similarly involved confronting and addressing challenges. An initial challenge, for example, involved facilitating the new notion of "braided funding streams" through which categorical money from tobacco, maternal child health, and other areas was combined to support the new project. This process itself sometimes led to turf issues, which were exacerbated when tobacco prevention staff developed a project to which no identifiable health issue were attached. Since the HNP supported neighborhood priorities whatever they were, personnel in other health department arenas often were concerned that HNP staff might be moving in on their territory.

Additionally, some public health staff questioned the HNP philosophy, believing that health departments are most effective in addressing large county-wide policy issues through work with agencies and institutions. Others felt it was more appropriate for government to obtain large grants and subcontract to CBOs to work directly with residents, rather than working on the grassroots level themselves. In other parts of the health department, direct service staff had trouble abandoning the problem-solving focus of categorical programs and sought to evolve the role of neighborhood teams into outreach workers to promote predefined health goals.

The HNP staff, recognizing the importance of having other relevant health department programs "on board" before the project commenced, convened several meetings in hopes of addressing staff concerns. Although some remained skeptical, the project eventually went forward with strong support from the department's director, who recognized that strong and authentic resident involvement was essential to creating a healthy community.

Along with the larger challenges of securing systems change in the acceptance of a project like the HNP by health department personnel were numerous bureaucratic obstacles that had to be overcome if the project was to succeed. For example, paying wages to nontraditional employees such as community organizers may present a significant hurdle if those employees do not fit existing job classifications. Similarly, "kitchen-table organizing" wouldn't live up to its name without food. Yet many expenses essential to the project's success, such as for food, child care, translation, gifts or incentives, and stipends or resident travel, may be disallowed by public agencies and traditional funders. HNP staff had to learn to plan in advance for rigidities in the organizational structure that could become stumbling blocks. Alternative mechanisms such as finding a fiscal agent to handle petty cash funds or special bank accounts for discretionary expenses were established during the early days of the HNP to help overcome such obstacles. But community residents also had to be prepared for the numerous frustrations that result from dealing with a large bureaucracy.

Organizational culture and systems change also were needed with respect to "normal working hours." Since residents typically were more available to meet during the early evenings, weekends, and some holidays, flex hours and incentives, for example, allowing some health department staff to work from noon to 9:00 P.M., were important accommodations. In part as a result of such flexibility within the department, a solid resident team consistently would appear for meetings with staff, and when residents were eventually invited during work hours to attend quarterly meetings with health department programs, they often would make arrangements to attend.

Ironically, the very success of the HNP led to particularly difficult challenges as the project reached maturity. A goal of the HNP, for example, was to provide county jobs for residents. Many members of the strong cadre of community organizers and NHAs trained through the project could have been major assets to the county health department in regular, paid staff capacities. However, the civil service system requirements for such jobs, which often included college degrees, tended to be above the qualifications of even the most exceptional and best-trained resident team members. As will be suggested later, substantial cultural and system change are necessary within public agency bureaucracies to help overcome such obstacles.

Project Accomplishments and Continued Challenges

Despite the many challenges and dilemmas faced, residents involved in Contra Costa's HNP have successfully applied their skills to advocate for neighborhood services and environmental modifications to improve health and quality of life in each neighborhood. These accomplishments have included advocating for and bringing about changes on multiple levels and in many diverse areas, including

- installation of speed bumps;
- removal of a tobacco billboard targeting youth;

- successful competition for a one-hundred-thousand-dollar grant for job skills training;
- creation of a mural capturing residents' vision of what a healthy community should look like and painted by forty youth under the direction of a local artist;
- successful advocating for additional evening and weekend bus service, increased police patrols, and improved street lighting and trash pickup;
- successful obtaining of funding for youth sports programs; and
- establishment of computer classes.

As residents experienced success in achieving immediate community priorities, they also began to participate in larger health department initiatives that would improve their neighborhoods. Residents thus served on a regional Partnership for Health advisory board, and an environmental health advisory board. Other residents worked with the health department to develop new community health indicators that better reflected the concerns of local residents. Resident advocates were key to both obtaining funds to build the Center for Health in North Richmond, and implementing a Bucket Brigade, in which residents in a community where oil refineries proliferate, were trained to trap air samples in order to identify and report toxic chemical releases (El-Askari et al. 1998; Minkler 2000).

On another level, an important accomplishment of this project was its success in helping to change attitudes within the health department itself about the value of a cross-disciplinary, strengths-based project like this one. Support for the HNP in the health department became widespread, as members of the different HNP neighborhoods teams became more visible in local government and planning bodies, expressing their personal and community visions for their neighborhoods. Experienced HNP participants also actively shared their perspectives in health department planning processes, such as the development of the county's Chronic Disease Prevention Plan. Finally, a subsequent HNP's director drew on the lessons of the HNP in her role as a trainer with a Centers for Disease Control and Prevention–funded after-school empowerment program, Youth Empowerment Strategies (YES!), in six local elementary and middle schools (Wilson et al. 2007).

Although these accomplishments represent important and tangible outcomes of the HNP, a continuing challenge involved evaluating the impacts of the HNP on individual-level health and well-being. Using Israel et al.'s (1994) scale for measuring perceived control (see also appendix 10), the project evaluator revealed significant increases in participating residents' perceptions concerning their ability to influence their lives, their community's control over decisions affecting it, and so forth. At the same time, as he noted, the plethora of health interventions operating in the county simultaneously, including close to a dozen different prenatal programs, made it impossible to detect with any certainty the actual impacts of the HNP in particular health domains. Finally, even in an area where significant health behavior changes did appear to result from the project (e.g., a significantly higher participation rate in a new child health insurance program in areas where the NHAs were active), cuts in funding for the database established to track such changes made further follow-up impossible. Since a major goal of projects such as the HNP is to build individual and community capacity toward the ultimate end of helping to eliminate health disparities, difficulties presented in the area of project evaluation remain a major challenge.

Adapting and Replicating the Model

In 1999 and 2004, respectively, and building on the lessons of the HNP in East and West Contra Costa County, the Berkeley City Public Health Department and the Alameda County Public Health Department began to lay the groundwork for similar projects in Berkeley and two neighborhoods in Oakland. Like Contra Costa, Berkeley and Oakland are ethnically and culturally diverse, with great disparities in wealth and health status between the predominantly white population living in the hills and the disproportionately African American, Latino, and other racial/ethnic group populations living in the flatlands (Iton 2006). Also like Contra Costa, both Berkeley and Oakland have a wealth of assets, including their diversity; Berkeley's role as home to one of the world's top universities; and in both cities, a long tradition of social activism, high-level civic engagement, and progressive public health departments. The hiring, in both cities, of one of the founders of the HNP helped create an environment in which a replication projects could be mounted.

Community Building and Cultural Humility in Berkeley, California

As Saul Alinsky (1972) and other organizers (see chapters 4 and 11) point out, a key to successful organizing often rests with timing and the presence of a catalytic event that increases receptivity to change. In Berkeley, such an event took place with the release and wide publicizing of the 1999 *City of Berkeley Health Status Report* (Namkung and Ducos 1999), which uncovered and analyzed the city's racial/ethnic health disparities. The twenty-year gap in life expectancy between the mostly white men living in the hills and the mostly African American men in the flatlands grabbed headlines, as did the finding that Berkeley had larger racial and ethnic health disparities than any of the surrounding Bay Area regions (Namkung and Ducos 1999).

Two prominent local policymakers used the occasion of the report's release to call a town hall meeting on the topic of health disparities in the city. Approximately 220 South and West Berkeley residents, policymakers, health care providers, and others participated in this lively meeting. Residents of many different racial and ethnic groups from the flatland neighborhoods and elsewhere voiced the strong conviction at this meeting that they themselves needed to do something about the disparities problem, including organizing, collecting their own data, and working to address racism. Serving at the time as a consultant to the health department, one of the authors (Walton) recognized the HNP model as an ideal fit and began by providing technical assistance to health department staff in areas such as principles of capacity building and expansion of diverse cultural and language services prior to working on the development of community teams. Subsequently hired as director of community capacity building, Walton was well positioned to help the HNP model become a reality.

The town hall meeting provided an excellent starting place for this process, and a cross section of sixty meeting participants, most of them residents, voluntarily chose to meet monthly, and two active resident-driven community action teams (CATs) were formed in South and West Berkeley. With technical assistance from Walton and funding from the city and federal governments, the CATs went through an intensive training and other steps (e.g., the creation of a community survey instrument) similar to those of the original HNP, but modified to focus more heavily on social and economic determinants of health. As part of their work, the Berkeley CATs also organized a well-attended racial and ethnic community health summit, which provided residents, policymakers, and others opportunities for education, small-group work, and encouragement to speak openly about racism, politics, and other root causes of the racial and ethnic health disparities in their community. Aware that racism is experienced by residents beyond their local borders (as when they shopped for groceries or went to banks or health care facilities in neighboring cities), the CATs expanded their invitation list beyond the city limits. This regional approach in turn helped them network with other collaboratives, concerned about these same issues, without losing sight of local assets and concerns.

Members of the CATs also made a difference, in part through their active involvement with the city's Neighborhood Services Initiative, which promotes dialogue with community residents and businesses to improve city services.

The CATs conducted door-to-door surveys using these interaction opportunities to offer immediate referrals and subsequent follow-up for residents who needed health and other city services. CAT members also worked with Berkeley youth programs to recruit and train hard-to-reach young people, to involve them in action planning around health disparities and foster their participation in an assortment of youth-guided leadership and capacity-building activities. As one indication of the perceived value of the work of the CATs, the city of Berkeley health status reports began including the work and results of the CATs in their documentation (Namkung et al. 2003).

Like the original HNP, the Berkeley project developed innovate ways of addressing logistical and practical challenges. For example, a respected community clinic began providing free health and dental coverage for the CAT organizers until they were full-time employees covered by city benefits. This organization also served as a fiscal agent for the CATs so that they could respond to funding opportunities on short notice and provide stipends for the intensive participation of some residents.

The Berkeley replication project faced numerous challenges, among them the fact that if CAT members were hired as staff they had to follow city policy and could no longer contact their local council members, or lead a media advocacy campaign, without permission from the city manager's office. Despite such obstacles, the project was highly effective in meeting its goals and objectives, aided by the fact that the leadership of the Public Health Division increasingly mirrored the diversity of the city it serves. This diversity helped provide a safe environment in which staff could not only confront and strategize around issues or race and racism as they arose, but also meet monthly at staff meetings and retreats to discuss topics such as the different forms of racism (Jones 2000), cultural humility (Tervalon and Murray-Garcia 1998), and unequal health and medical treatment by race/ethnicity (Smedley et al. 2002) and use them in grappling with the challenges faced. In the words of a health department leader who was integral to these efforts, "It takes incredible courage, trust, faith, social consciousness, and commitment from the leadership of all levels of the health department, as well as undying willpower, to prevent [issues of racism and its consequences] from getting isolated and buried."

The Sobrante Park Project: A City-County Neighborhood Initiative

Building on the original HNP and the Berkeley replication, and borrowing in part too from the more generic Mobilizing for Action through Planning and Partnerships model (Iton 2006), an adaptation of the HNP began in Oakland in 2004. The Alameda County Public Health Department (ACPHD) began by hiring the HNP's cofounder (Walton) and identifying two communities—West Oakland and Sobrante Park, in East Oakland—on which to focus. The Sobrante Park project, described here, involved a small, low-income, largely African American and Latino neighborhood of approximately three thousand residents, 46 percent of whom where under age twenty-four. The neighborhood had a high crime rate and a single entry point, adjacent to a badly blighted park and liquor store in which drug use and other crime took place.

The ACPHD's work in Sobrante Park was premised on creating a seamless partnership between the county public health department and the City of Oakland Human Services Department and building a strong city-county neighborhood initiative that would support true, community-driven public health. Its goals were to support and improve "four key protective/resilience factors: (1) positive adult-youth relationships, (2) meaningful opportunities for community participation, (3) high career/employment opportunities for youth, and (4) improved race/ethnic inter-group relations" (Iton 2006, 128).

As in the original HNP, the Sobrante Park project began with a baseline door-to-door survey to identify resident concerns, but also strengths and things they liked about the neighborhood. Members of a core team of residents, representatives of local schools, faith-based groups, organizations, and staff were trained in conducting the survey, which was completed by 219 adults and an additional 100 youth initially, and repeated every three years by the ACPHD. Over seventy of the original survey participants indicated that they would like to be more involved in the neighborhood, and were separately invited to provide follow-up contact information.

A daylong community forum, in both Spanish and English, was held to share survey findings with the community, emphasize the neighborhood strengths identified, and develop priority action items. The more than ninety residents who attended articulated three interrelated goals: (1) improving the local park at the community's entrance to enable safe recreation for youth and safe entrance into the area, (2) reducing drug dealing and drug use, and (3) developing more activities for youth (Iton 2006). Resident Action Councils (RACs) then were developed to help address these and related concerns, with sixty members, two-thirds of them youth, participating in a sixteen-hour leadership training program covering topics including community organizing, asset mapping, media advocacy, regionalism, and undoing racism. An additional sixteen hours in disaster preparedness also was provided. At monthly meetings, RAC members then brainstormed ideas and helped develop and implement action plans, with technical assistance as needed from the health department and city staff. City staff provided a full-time community building specialist to work along with public health department staff.

Among the many successful developments that grew from such planning was Keeping It Real—a daylong youth event, planned and organized by multiethnic youth and supported by adult allies to deter crime. This event was subsequently held annually on the day that gangs previously had used to terrorize the community. Keeping It Real was one of a number of efforts funded by the Sobrante Park Healthy Eating, Active Living mini-grants program. Designed to build the capacity of residents, and primarily youth, the mini-grants program engaged young people in developing the grant application and criteria and recruiting, selecting, and funding grantees from Sobrante Park. In three years, over twenty-five thousand dollars in nutrition program funding was used to provide mini-grants of one hundred dollars to twenty-five hundred dollars each.

Although originally, subgroups of the RAC were created for and by the African American and predominately Spanish-speaking Latino residents, an overarching concern of the health department, as noted above, was with improving relationships between these two groups. Ironically, the tragedy of Hurricane Katrina in 2005 and its aftermath of a badly mismanaged "relief effort" proved an important catalyst for beginning this process. In a meeting shortly after the disaster, Walton asked the community two questions: "If a [Katrina] happened here, would the city respond to your needs immediately?" and "Would you need to be here for each other?" In response to the sudden realization of their interdependence, the two groups began meeting together, taking turns wearing simultaneous translation equipment and working on projects, such as mini-grants for youth and Time-Banking, which further enhanced their collaboration.

Through Dr. Edgar Cahn's TimeBanking method, developed in 1980, for example, member residents and organizations were able to exchange goods and services, "banking" onetime credit for each hour of service provided (e.g., tutoring a child for another resident, or changing someone's tire). The Sobrante Park TimeBank program resulted in "a multi-ethnic, cross generational network" (Iton 2006, 131) that further deepened growing trust and respect between groups. Begun in 2006, the community's TimeBank program has close to two hundred members at this writing and averages close to five hundred service hours each quarter.

Additional events, such as cooking classes featuring both soul food and Hispanic dishes and recipes, and the sharing of each other's racial/ethnic celebrations such as Posada (a Latino procession celebrating the birth of Christ) and Kwanzaa (a uniquely African American cultural celebration held the day after Christmas) continued to enhance collaboration and trust between the two groups. Together with park restoration and blight cleanup, youth training and employment opportunities, community health fairs in which more than four hundred residents participate, the opening of a school-based health clinic, and other dimensions of the work, Sobrante Park has proved a remarkable model of community building and organizing to address health disparities. It further has shone a spotlight on one community/health department's success in helping formerly separate racial/ethnic groups develop a genuine sense of shared community.

As in the original HNP and the Berkeley replication, however, critical to the success of the Sobrante Park project was the fact that it occurred in tandem with sincere community capacity building and change efforts *within the county public health department* and municipal agencies themselves. By meeting together biweekly for three hours, for example, the ACPHD and what is now the City of Oakland Neighborhood Services Division were able to cut red tape and develop creative solutions to better serve the needs of communities like Sobrante Park. Because the health department was unable to give stipends directly to residents, for example, it developed a relationship with a local fiscal agent, to whom it could subcontract for this purpose, enabling Sobrante Park residents to participate in leadership training and be compensated for their time.

The Alameda County Public Health Department also took the courageous step of requiring that all its hundreds of staff, including receptionists and the highest-level administrators, participate in monthly trainings in which they learned about cultural humility, community engagement, and capacity building and explored racism and other prejudicial attitudes and behaviors in a safe environment. Such internal capacity building, and particularly "working on its own -*isms*—and particularly racism—was critical to the department's success in effectively engaging with diverse communities and developing genuine and respectful partnerships.

Lessons Learned and Implications for Public Health Practice

This chapter began by suggesting that three key areas are critical to the development of effective community-health department partnerships and, over the long term, to improved health outcomes in low-income communities: resident-driven community development; increasing the community-based capacities of public health staff, particularly with respect to cultural humility; and cultural and systems change within public agencies. We now highlight several lessons from the original HNP and its replications in two neighboring areas to underscore the importance of each of these domains.

As noted earlier, the importance of an ongoing and steadfast commitment to high-level resident involvement in leadership, decision making, and control has been widely documented in the literature (see Lasker and Guidry 2009; Wallerstein 2006) and similarly was illustrated throughout the HNP and its replications in both Berkeley and Sobrante Park. However, the commitment to the process of sharing power must be unwavering, consistent, and authentic. Resident engagement relies on the strategic development of capacities, on the part of both community members and institutional players. Finally, successful partnerships are reliant on the full understanding and buy-in of agency chains of command in order to avoid the derailment of a process when turning over control becomes too risky.

Cultural Humility as a Critical Public Health Capacity

Over fifteen years ago, civic leader Calvin Freeman noted, "Our organizations will change only when we undergo personal and social change; when we recognize who we are, where we come from, and the baggage we carry with us; when we recognize that we are not culture neutral; when we find ways to confront the often uncomfortable subjects of race and racism in ways that lead to understanding and action; when we find new ways to communicate and listen effectively; and most importantly, when we find ways to increase our personal and professional power by sharing it with those we serve" (1996, 1).

The importance of involving local health department staff in community-based public health interventions, and in ensuring that the public health workforce is well trained in cultural sensitivity and participatory approaches to facilitate this work in today's diverse communities, has been well documented (Gebbie et al. 2003). In a study of more than four hundred local health departments, Parker and her colleagues (2003) indeed identified "communicating with minority populations," identifying community strengths as well as weaknesses, enhancing community input into problem identification and planning, and partnering with community groups and agencies as among twenty-seven core public health competencies.

Integral to the achievement of each of these is cultural humility, a quality that our experience with the original HNP and its replications suggest is perhaps the single most important for "partnership synergy" (Lasker et al. 2001) with low-income communities of color. To paraphrase Peled-Elhanan (2002), the commitment to and increasing skillfulness of the HNP staff in "being willing to hold back your ideologies, or your truth, or your personal and national narrative, and make room in yourself for the truth and the narrative of the other," was vital to project success.

Our experience underscores the centrality of culture in any change process. This may mean finding participatory and other processes that are more rooted in the cultures of the various communities involved. And it points up the importance as well of staff understanding of the importance of building culturally sensitive relationships before becoming immersed in collaborative planning and decision making.

Public Health Leadership and Systems Change

Engaging in a genuine partnership with communities requires giving up a degree of control over outcomes.

–Wendel Brunner, director, Contra Costa County Department of Public Health

A critical counterpart to the relationship-building and cultural-humility capacities of staff involved in resident partnership development is committed public health leadership, which in turn is vital to systems change. An important lesson of the HNP in Contra Costa County and its replications in Berkeley and Sobrante Park in fact involves the necessity of high-level leadership in the department committing to sharing power and to the kinds of internal systems changes that need to take place for projects like this to succeed.

The highly visible role of the Contra Costa County public health director, for example, including his leveraging of funds from categorical programs for the HNP, was critical to the ability of this project to materialize in the first place. The director's role also laid the groundwork for long-term, sustainable changes in how the department's community wellness and prevention programs are structured and managed, and it set an important precedent to which other departments throughout the state could turn. Similarly, monthly department-wide meetings to address issues like cultural humility and racism were critical to the success of the Alameda County Public Health Department in Sobrante Park.

Facilitating synergistic partnerships between health departments and communities means supporting nontraditional work hours for some health department staff, carving out funds for refreshments and child care, and in other ways accommodating local community needs. But it also may mean finding ways to address a civil service system whose rigid job classifications and requirements often preclude the hiring of local residents who have received training and shown immense promise in their work with projects like the HNP. The health departments in Contra Costa County, the city of Berkeley, and Alameda County each tackled the civil service system to open up job opportunities for residents, or to find ways to compensate them for their work. In the original HNP, the original community organizers, who were fully trained, were employed in full-time benefited positions, maintaining the same flexibility in hours, and encouraged and allowed to maintain their identity as residents.

Yet even when progress is made in hiring, significant job-related challenges remain. In Berkeley, as noted earlier, institutional culture and systems changes thus were needed on the municipal level such that resident/staff organizers would have the freedom to mount community organizing campaigns without being hamstrung by bureaucratic rules and regulations preventing or severely compromising such activity.

A final lesson from the HNP experience involves the critical need for planning for sustainability. Even prior to the Great Recession of 2008, cuts in funds for health departments have been such that the levels of support initially received for programs like the HNP often have made them difficult to sustain. Such realities highlight the importance of building strong relationships between health departments and other city and county offices so that the latter begin to view such projects as benefiting their own work, for example, as sources of trained residents who can be resources across multiple domains. At the same time, however, creative and diversified fund-raising plans must be developed to enable such programs to thrive even if government funding is reduced. Health department staff should pursue the growing number of foundations and other philanthropic organizations that now support comprehensive community-based health initiatives and that may be vital to the future of programs like these.

Conclusion

Local health departments committed to authentic, meaningful engagement with residents cannot be wary or hesitant about the commitment it takes to undertake such partnerships. As this chapter suggests, there are many perils on such a journey. From the personal process of cultural humility and acknowledgment of institutionalized racism, to the leadership commitment to sweeping systems changes, and the exposing of painful truths about the racial and ethnic health disparities that affect our neighborhoods, following this path requires courage. Yet as this chapter also demonstrated, the payoffs for doing so may be substantial for both communities and health departments themselves.

The Healthy Neighborhoods Project and its replications in Berkeley and Sobrante Park were used to illustrate how three different health departments attempted to engage meaningfully with local communities through community-driven efforts to help address locally identified problems. By identifying and building on community assets, and attending to issues of race, ethnicity, and racism both in the community and internally, and by recognizing and responding to the need for system change and responsive leadership, as well as high-level community participation, both case studies illustrate the challenges and the promise of partnership approaches to addressing complex health and social problems.

REFERENCES

Alinsky, S. D. 1972. *Rules for Radicals: A Practical Primer for Realistic Radicals.* New York: Vintage Books.

Chávez, V., B. Duran, Q. E. Baker, M. M. Avila, and N. Wallerstein. 2008. "The Dance of Race and Privilege in Community-Based Participatory Research." In *Community-Based Participatory Research for Health*, edited by M. Minkler and N. Wallerstein, 91–103. 2nd ed. San Francisco: Jossey-Bass.

Cockerham, W. 2007. *Social Causes of Health and Disease.* Cambridge, U.K.: Polity Press.

El-Askari, G. A., et al. 1998. "The Healthy Neighborhoods Project: A Local Health Department's Role in Catalyzing Community Development." *Health Education and Behavior* 25, no. 2:146–159.

Ellis, G. A., R. L. Hobart, and D. F. Reed. 1996. "Overcoming a Powerful Tobacco Lobby in Enacting Local Smoking Ordinances: The Contra Costa County Experience." *Journal of Public Health Policy* 17, no. 1:28–46.

Ellis, G. A., D. F. Reed, and H. Scheider. 1995. "Mobilizing a Low-Income African American Community around Tobacco Control: A Force Field Analysis." *Health Education Quarterly* 22, no. 4:443–457.

Freeman, C. 1996. "Building Multicultural Organizations." *Public Health Watch* (California Public Health Association–North).

Gebbie, K., L. Rosenstock, and L. M. Hernandez. 2003. *Who Will Keep the Public Healthy? Educating Public Health Professionals for the 21st Century.* Washington, D.C.: Institute of Medicine.

Green, L. W. 2006. "Public Health Asks of Systems Science: To Advance Our Evidence-Based Practice, Can You Help Us Get More Practice-Based Evidence?" *American Journal of Public Health* 96, no. 3:1–3.

Israel, B. A., B. N. Checkoway, A. J. Schulz, and M. A. Zimmerman. 1994. "Health Education and Community Empowerment: Conceptualizing and Measuring Perceptions of Individual, Organizational, and Community Control." *Health Education Quarterly* 21, no. 2:149–170.

Iton, T. 2006. "Tackling the Root Causes of Health Disparities through Community Capacity Building." In *Tackling Health Inequities through Public Health Practice: A Handbook for Action*, edited by R. Hofrichter, 115–136. Washington D.C.: National Association of County and City Health Officials.

Jones, C. P. 2000. "Levels of Racism: A Theoretic Framework and a Gardener's Tale." *American Journal of Public Health* 90, no. 8:1212–1215.

Kawachi, I., S. V. Subramanian, and D. Kim. 2008. *Social Capital and Health.* New York: Springer Science and Business Media.

Kretzmann, J. P., and J. L. McKnight. 1995. *Building Communities from the Inside Out: A Path toward Finding and Mobilizing a Community's Assets.* Evanston, Ill.: Center for Urban Affairs and Policy Research, Northwestern University.

Lasker, R. D., and J. A. Guidry. 2009. *Engaging the Community in Decision Making.* Jefferson, N.C.: McFarland.

Lasker, R. D., E. A. Weiss, and R. Miller. 2001. "Partnership Synergy: A Practical Framework for Studying and Strengthening the Collaborative Advantage." *Milbank Quarterly* 79, no. 2:179–205.

McKnight, J., and J. Kretzmann. 1990. *Mapping Community Capacity*. Evanston, Ill.: Center for Urban Affairs and Policy Research, Northwestern University.

Minkler, M. 2000. "Participatory Action Research and Healthy Communities." *Public Health Reports* 115, nos. 1 and 2:191–197.

Namkung, P., and J. Ducos. 1999. *City of Berkeley Health Status Report, 1999*. Berkeley, Calif.: City of Berkeley Department of Health and Human Services, Public Health Division.

Namkung, P., J. Ducos, V. Alexander, and K. Tehrani. 2003. *City of Berkeley Health Status Report, 2002: Low Birth Weight*. Berkeley, Calif.: City of Berkeley Department of Health and Human Services, Public Health Division.

Parker, E., L. H. Margolis, E. Eng, and C. Henriquez-Roldán. 2003. "Assessing the Capacity of Health Departments to Engage in Participatory, Community-Based Public Health. *American Journal of Public Health* 93, no. 3:472–476.

Peled-Elhanan, N. 2002. "Not Being Afraid of Another Person's Truth: We Have Betrayed Our Children." *Jerusalem Post*, November 28.

Smedley, B. D., A. Y. Stith, and A. R. Nelson. 2002. *Unequal Treatment: Confronting Racial and Ethnic Disparities in Health Care*. Washington, D.C.: Institute of Medicine, National Academy Press.

Syme, S. L. 2004. "Social Determinants of Health: The Community as an Empowered Partner." *Preventing Chronic Disease* 1, no. 1:1–8.

Tervalon, M., and J. Murray-Garcia. 1998. "Cultural Humility vs. Cultural Competence: A Critical Distinction in Defining Physician Training Outcomes in Medical Education." *Journal of Health Care for the Poor and Underserved* 9, no. 2:117–125.

Vanier, J. 1989. *Community and Growth*. New York: Paulist Press.

Wallerstein, N. 2006. "The Effectiveness of Empowerment Strategies to Improve Health." Health Evidence Network. Copenhagen: World Health Organization. http://www.euro.who.int/HEN/Syntheses/empowerment/20060119_10.

Wilson, N, M. Minkler, S. Dasho, et al. 2007. "Getting to Social Action: The Youth Empowerment Strategies (YES!) Project." *Health Promotion Practice* 14, no. 1:201–217.

PART FOUR

Community Assessment and Issue Selection

Fields such as public health, social work, and city and regional planning typically focus considerable attention on needs assessment and use a variety of methods to determine the problems and needs being experienced by the groups or communities involved. Increasingly, however, the importance of shifting our gaze from a narrowly conceived needs assessment to a broader community assessment has been realized. Reflecting this change in emphasis, the first two chapters in this part provide approaches to community assessment that go well beyond needs assessment as it is typically conceived and indeed reject the narrow needs assessment approach as rooted in a "deficit thinking" mentality that can harm, rather than enhance, our efforts at community organizing and community building for health.

Trevor Hancock and Meredith Minkler begin in chapter 9 by posing a series of questions that get to the heart of the whys and hows of community assessment for health. Drawing in part on the former's extensive experience as a key architect of the healthy cities movement worldwide, they indeed suggest that the very focus of such efforts should move from community health assessment to healthy community assessment if we are to pay adequate attention to the numerous factors affecting the health and well-being of communities. Arguing that community assessments are needed, not only for the information they provide for and about change, but also for empowerment, the authors make the case for assessment that is truly of, by, and for the community. Expanding on John McKnight's (1995) statement that "institutions learn from studies, communities learn from stories," they further point up the need for collecting both stories and more traditional "study" data as part of a comprehensive assessment process.

Hancock and Minkler use Sylvia Marti-Costa and Irma Serrano-Garcia's (1983) categorization of assessment techniques according to the degree of contact with community members that they entail as a framework within which to explore a number of assessment techniques and approaches. This chapter makes a strong case for the use of multiple methods, with an accent placed on those methods, such as the development and use of community or neighborhood indicators (Bauer 2003; Howell et al. 2003), that empower individuals and communities, in part through their active involvement in and ownership of the assessment process.

A critical part of the shift from a needs assessment to a community assessment focus involves appreciating that communities are not simply collections of needs or problems but vital entities possessing many strengths and assets. Chapter 10 presents a classic contribution to the community assessment literature, namely, John McKnight and John Kretzmann's approach to "mapping community capacity." Pointing out that the needs-focused approach to low-income communities has led to deficiency-oriented policies and programs, they propose instead a capacity-oriented model. The community mapping technique they provide looks first to "primary building blocks"–those assets such as people and their talents and associations– located in the neighborhood and largely under its control. In a spirit consistent with Cheryl Walter and Cheryl Hyde's (chapter 5) expanded notion of community, however, they also have us consider nonprofit organizations, local businesses, and the like that are located in the neighborhood and that, although largely controlled by outsiders, nevertheless may constitute important "secondary building blocks."

The sample neighborhood needs map and contrasting neighborhood assets map included in this chapter offer students and practitioners a graphic illustration of how changing our orientation from deficiencies to strengths can transform our perceptions of communities, as well as those communities' images of themselves. Although the chapter addresses itself to geographic communities, the approach it demonstrates clearly can be adapted for use in a workplace or common interest community as well.

Closely connected to community assessment is working with communities in ways that enable them, rather than outsiders, to determine the goals and issues around which they wish to mobilize. In chapter 11, Lee Staples, author of the classic organizing text *Roots to Power* (2004), draws our attention to this pivotal area as he explores the topic of selecting and "cutting" the issue. Echoing a theme that runs throughout much of the book, Staples argues that issues should indeed come from the members and potential members of a community. At the same time, he sees the outside professional as having a critical role to play in helping community groups become familiar with the criteria of good issues so that they can select foci for action that measure up against these important yardsticks for success. As he suggests, a good issue is one about which the community feels deeply. But it also is an issue that is winnable, serves to unite the community, provides opportunities for leadership development and broad-based member participation, and is consistent with the long-range goals and strategies of the organization (Miller 2009).

Staples also explores in detail the process organizers refer to as "cutting the issue," or deciding who gets what from whom and how and why they intend to get it. Using diverse examples from social work and health-related organizing efforts in the United States, he describes and illustrates the issue-cutting process and how it fits within the conduct of a broader strategic analysis. Four core concerns—appealing to diverse constituencies; testing alternative possible solutions and coming up with strong goals and objectives; selecting the right targets; and finding the "handles" (e.g., laws, regulatory processes, or broken campaign promises) that can used to open an opportunity for change—are discussed. The need for careful strategic analysis also is emphasized here, and illustrated elsewhere in this volume (see chapter 18 and appendix 7), as a critical part of the organizer's tool kit.

REFERENCES

Bauer, G. F. 2003. "Sample Community Health Indicators on the Neighborhood Level." In *Community-Based Participatory Research for Health*, edited by M. Minkler and N. Wallerstein. 438–445. San Francisco: Jossey-Bass.

Howell, E. M., K. Pettit, B. A. Ormond, and G. T. Kingsley. 2003. "Using the National Neighborhood Indicators Partnership to Improve Public Health." *Journal of Public Health Management and Practice* 9, no. 3:235–242.

Marti-Costa, S., and I. Serrano-Garcia. 1983. "Needs Assessment and Community Development: An Ideological Perspective." *Prevention in Human Services* 2, no. 4:75–88.

McKnight, J. 1995. *The Careless Society: Community and Its Counterfeits*. New York: Harper Collins.

Miller, M. 2009. *A Community Organizer's Tale: People and Power in San Francisco*. Berkeley, Calif.: Heyday Books.

Staples, L. 2004. *Roots to Power: A Manual for Grassroots Organizing*. Westport, Conn.: Praeger.

9

Community Health Assessment or Healthy Community Assessment

Whose Community? Whose Health? Whose Assessment?

TREVOR HANCOCK

MEREDITH MINKLER

$\mathbf{M}$any questions need to be asked concerning the performance of a community health assessment. In this chapter, we discuss a number of these questions and provide examples of assessment processes that we believe illustrate promising approaches. As our title implies, we believe that to be truly empowering and health promoting, assessment should be of the community, by the community, and for the community.

Why Assess?

In a seminal article written almost thirty years ago, Sylvia Marti-Costa and Irma Serrano-Garcia (1983) argued that, far from being neutral or objective, needs assessment is in reality an ideological process that can serve political purposes ranging from system maintenance and control to the promotion of social change and consciousness-raising. At one end of the ideological continuum are needs assessments designed to support and justify the status quo. Although they may include some efforts at "fine-tuning" the way the system functions, they do not question or wish to change the ideological commitments on which that system is based (Marti-Costa and Serrano-Garcia 1983). The health educator trying to increase attendance at agency-sponsored community health fairs, for example, might well conduct an assessment to determine whether the event's hours and location were problematic for local residents. But if the agency had already committed to health fairs as its modus operandi for community health outreach, the health educator would not be expected—or would not want—to determine residents' perceptions of whether the fairs really addressed their primary health needs.

In contrast, an assessment open to higher-level change would actively involve community residents not only in helping the agency or organization critically rethink its mission and activities but also becoming more skilled and empowered themselves in the process. The purposes of such an assessment, as Marti-Costa and Serrano-Garcia (1983) have suggested, would be to

- measure, describe, and understand community lifestyles;
- assess community resources to lessen external dependency;
- return needs assessment data to facilitate residents' decision making;
- provide skill training, leadership, and organizational skills;
- facilitate collective activities and group mobilization; and
- enable consciousness-raising.

The purposes of a "needs" assessment and the values and assumptions underlying this process, in short, heavily influence the choice of assessment techniques, the interventions proposed, the use of data obtained, and the perceptions of who owns the data in the first place.

Rationale behind Community Health Assessment

For professionals concerned with community organizing and community building for health and welfare, there are two reasons for the imperative placed on effective and comprehensive community health assessments: information is needed for change, and it is needed for empowerment.

Information for Change

The first kind of information has three purposes: to stimulate change or action, to monitor change or action, and to assess the impact of change (Hancock 1988; Hancock et al. 2000a, 2000b). Information that will stimulate change must carry "social and political punch." Such information includes hard data and stories that point up differences, particularly inequalities in health and the social and physical determinants of health among different groups and sectors in the community. Given the short-term basis of much social and political action, such data also must be sensitive to short-term change, focusing on inequalities where there is a reasonable chance of seeing some change in a comparatively brief period of time. Although it is critical to document differences in mortality rates for lung cancer or heart disease, for example, this needs to be balanced by information on people's perceived state of health, their social and physical living conditions, and their behaviors, all of which may be more likely to reflect changes in the short term following some policy or community action.

The change rationale for community assessment also involves the need for information about the processes of change or of action. As a result, such assessment must put a heavy accent on stories and observations that may help unearth, for example, potential precursors to change. These might include widespread community knowledge of a new project, the establishment of participatory mechanisms such as intersectoral committees, evidence of the development of new skills (e.g., in leadership and media advocacy), and indicators of political commitment to the project at the local level. Such intermediate-level activities may in turn lead to other actions (such as health-promoting policies) that will ultimately lead to better health.

Information that will assess the impact of change on health can function as a baseline of the individual and community dimensions of health. Here *health* is defined broadly to include physical, mental, and social well-being in both subjective and objective terms. Regular repetitions of the baseline measures via surveys and other instruments must be conducted to assess change.

Information for Empowerment

An entirely different, but equally important, reason for wanting information about health is that knowledge is power and as such a component of empowerment. As discussed in chapter 3, the process of empowerment is central to the World Health Organization's (WHO 1986) definition of health promotion. Individuals and communities can become truly empowered only if they have the knowledge required to assess their situation and to take action—backed by sufficient power—to make change happen. The most obvious way of defining and obtaining information is to ask the community itself for its definition of a good or healthy community. In so doing, the health promotion professional is helped to identify the most important components about which information must be collected. But by asking the community how to define health, assess progress, and measure change, he or she is also helping to further the *process* of cmpowerment.

If the community is to use information, whether hard data or stories, it must be physically, socially, and culturally accessible. Information should be presented via easily accessed Internet sites and local media, as well as in local community settings such as libraries, community centers, faith-based organizations, and schools. Reports need to be written simply, and in the dominant language of the community, even in postindustrial nations such as Canada and the United States. Fully 60 percent of Canadians aged sixteen and over, for example, have low health literacy (1 or 2 on a 5-point scale) and as such "lack the capacity to obtain, understand and act upon health information and services and to make appropriate health decisions on their own" (Canadian Council on Learning 2007) because they have a health literacy level of only 1 or 2 (on a 5-point scale). Dissemination of information in audio and video formats, including Facebook and other social media that the majority of the population now use, is also critical (see chapters 15 and 16).

Information from a healthy community assessment also can and should be used as the basis for study groups, work circles, and other adult and popular education strategies, including literacy training and English as a Second Language (ESL) courses. An early example of the latter took place in a Healthy Boston project in the linguistically diverse Allston-Brighton area. A communitywide assessment meeting, conducted in half a dozen languages and attended by over three hundred people, uncovered concerns about inadequate housing, HIV/AIDS, and other topics. An effort then was made to incorporate some of these issues into the neighborhood's ESL programs. By combining ESL with leadership training, advocacy training, and field internships for over forty residents, the project further helped create a cadre of individuals who could serve as "cultural liaisons" between their cultural community and health and social service agencies, as well as the larger city and neighborhood.

Knowing how well one's community functions, how much it cares about the well-being and quality of life of its citizens, and how choices that affect health are made—and by whom—enables people to more fully and actively participate in the life of the community (see Diers 2006).

Whose Community, Whose Health?

We have referred thus far to "the community." But as earlier chapters have suggested, the real question is, Which community are we referring to? Professionals working with geographic communities often focus on a particular neighborhood, and this is indeed the level with which people tend to identify. Yet since one of the intents of the healthy city/community process is to stimulate local government involvement in and commitment to improving the health of the community, the boundaries for assessment may also often be municipal boundaries. The first challenge, then, is to assess the healthy community process and situation both at the municipal level and at the level of the community or neighborhood.

A second challenge is to conceptualize health in a broad enough manner that we can look well beyond such traditional indicators as morbidity and mortality to embrace WHO's (1948) view of health as "a state of complete physical, mental and social well being, and not merely the absence of disease and infirmity." As discussed below, community members often have creative and meaningful ways of conceptualizing health for themselves. The challenge for the health professional is to pay more attention to how the members of the community define health and to incorporate their definitions for assessing the health of the community.

Needs or Capacities?

Professor and community builder John McKnight (Kretzmann and McKnight 1993; see chapter 10) describes the importance of the "associational life," or the informal and formal community-based organizations and networks that form the underpinnings of the community. This is similar to what Robert Putnam (2000) calls "civicness" or social solidarity. McKnight has been particularly concerned with having professionals change their focus from individual and community deficits that require services to assets and capacities that enable community building (see chapter 10).

The implications of such a 180-degree shift in how we view people and communities are profound. For they suggest that we should reevaluate the entire way in which we conceive of the role of professionals in the community—as enablers and facilitators rather than providers of services—and the purpose of those services. From the perspective of assessment of the community's health, McKnight's approach has two important implications. First, it underscores the importance of assessing capacity and not merely "needs," and second, it reminds us that the process of that assessment should itself contribute to the capacity of people and communities and to community health. Without discounting the importance of also recognizing and addressing the very real needs faced by communities, particularly in times of diminishing resources (Hyatt 2008; see chapter 1), McKnight's approach provides a useful corrective in ensuring that we don't in the process fail to engage communities themselves in identifying their assets, as well as the challenges they face. As Seattle-based community builder Jim Diers (2006) notes, "Communities have a knack for converting a problem into an asset, whether it is a graffiti-covered wall, a vacant lot, an abandoned building, a dead tree, garden waste, . . . or incessant rain" (171). Community gardens, of which an estimated eighteen thousand exist in the United States at this writing (American Community Gardens Association 2011), provide one such potent example. Community development, capacity building with respect to gardening and nutrition, economic development, intergenerational and intercultural action, improved nutrition, and the creation of green space are among the many benefits associated with these gardens (Ozer 2007; Twiss et al. 2003).

Community Health Assessment or Healthy Community Assessment?

To understand the difference between a community health assessment and a healthy community assessment, it is necessary to begin with a clear understanding of what is meant by the term *healthy community*. The most commonly accepted definition was developed by Hancock and Duhl for WHO in 1986 (24), and is used today by such bodies as the Centers for Disease Control and Prevention (2010): "A healthy [community] is one that is continually creating and improving those physical and social environments and expanding those community resources which enable people to mutually support each other in performing all the functions of life and in developing to their maximum potential." As this definition suggests, a healthy community is a process, not a status. Although low mortality and morbidity are important, a healthy community is not necessarily one that has the highest health status in a conventional sense, but one that is striving with every fiber of its being to be more healthy. Ideally, this would be reflected in a commitment at all levels from the political to the personal, across all sectors, and involving all stakeholders around the common focus of improving the health, well-being, and quality of life of the community and its members. The closer a community is to this ideal, the closer it is to being a healthy community.

Over twenty-five years ago, and based on a wide range of literature, Hancock and Duhl (1986) suggested the following eleven key elements of a healthy community, which have stood the test of time:

1. A clean, safe, high-quality environment (including housing quality)
2. An ecosystem that is stable now and sustainable in the long term
3. A strong, mutually supportive, and nonexploitative community
4. A high degree of public participation in and control over the decisions affecting one's life, health, and well-being
5. The meeting of basic needs (food, water, shelter, income, safety, work) for all the city's people
6. Access to a wide variety of experiences and resources, with the possibility of multiple contacts, interaction, and communication
7. A diverse, vital, and innovative city economy
8. Encouragement of connectedness with the past, with the cultural and biological heritage, and with other groups and individuals
9. A city form that is compatible with and enhances the preceding parameters and behaviors
10. An optimum level of appropriate public health and sick care services accessible to all
11. High health status (both high positive health status and low disease status)

Importantly, only one of these eleven refers directly to health status, which is the usual focus of a community health assessment.

A good place to begin a healthy community assessment is to consider the classical epidemiological elements of place, time, and person. Here, however, *place* refers to the geography and environment of the community, *time* refers to its history and development, and *person* refers to the demographic profile of the community. Much can be learned about a community's health by understanding these three elements. The community's geography will reveal some of the factors likely to affect health, such as climate, natural resources (especially water and food sources), natural hazards, air and water quality, and wind direction, all of which usually define where low-income populations will live (downwind, downstream, and downhill—or uphill if the hills are dangerous!). The community's history provides important information on the major economic, political, and social forces that have shaped the community's evolution and that explain many of the present circumstances that influence the health of the community. Finally, the community's present demography—such factors as age and gender distribution and racial/ethnic and socioeconomic characteristics—provides further information that enables us to anticipate some of the health-related issues facing the community.

Specific issues can be examined regarding each of the eleven components of a healthy community and others that are considered important by the community:

- Do people in the community have access to such basic prerequisites for health as food, shelter, education, clean water, clean and safe environments, and sustainable resources?
- What is the degree of equity (or inequity) in the community?
- How strong is civic or associational life?
- How do urban design and architecture affect health in this community?
- What is being done to improve health?
- How rich is the cultural life of the community, its artistic, creative, and innovative elements?
- What is the environmental quality of the community, what is its impact on regional and local ecosystems, and what is being done to minimize that impact?
- Does everyone have access to basic primary care?

Several illustrations are useful in demonstrating what such an approach to assessment might look like. The Women's Benchmarks indicators in Pittsburgh, Pennsylvania, for example, include a wide range of factors such as changes over time in the proportion of female-headed households, of elderly women living alone, and of women compared with men in higher education (Bangs et al. 2004). Similarly, early "sustainable Seattle" indicators included wild salmon runs through local streams, gallons of water consumed per capita, usage rates for libraries and community centers, and "provocative" indicators (items for which the quality and validity of the data may be in doubt but that make people think), such as the amount of beef versus vegetables eaten per capita. Finally, a community in Hawaii identified the presence of Manapua trucks—small fast-food trucks that visit local communities—as an indicator of declining community health for four reasons: they replace home cooking and family dining, the nutritional quality of the food they provide is poor, they make it easier for children to buy cigarettes, and they harm local businesses by undercutting them and taking money out of the community. As these examples suggest, communities can offer thoughtful indexes of local health status.

A healthy community assessment would also need to look at the processes under way in the community that are believed to be related to health and the extent to which health is taken into account or is a focus for action. On the level of the city or formally defined municipality, for example:

- Does the municipal council take health into account in its policy deliberations, explicitly developing healthy public policy?
- Is there a mechanism for health impact assessment?
- Do the local planning department and other government bodies understand the impacts of planning and design on health?

- Is the economic sector (e.g., the chamber of commerce, business improvement associations) part of the process?
- Do businesses understand the importance of health for their activities?
- Do they understand the importance of equitable access to the basic determinants of health for the entire population?
- Are neighborhood and resident groups involved? In what way?
- Are the environmental groups and organizations involved? The school boards? Faith-based organizations? The police? Local politicians at all levels of government?

Finally, a healthy community assessment would take the time to determine not only formal leadership at the local level but also those informal leaders who can be identified through such methods as reputational and decisional analysis. The former technique involves having knowledgeable community members formally or informally "nominate" residents who play a powerful role in community affairs. The latter technique has informants describe recent community decisions and the roles played by various key participants in actually bringing about those decisions. Among the questions that may be used to help identify informal leaders are the following:

- Whom do people in this neighborhood go to for help or advice?
- Whom do children go to?
- When the community has had a problem in the past, who has been involved in working to solve it?
- Who gets things done in the community?
- If I could only talk to three people in this community, who would they be? (Eng and Blanchard 1990–1991; Israel 1985; Minkler and Hancock 2008; Sharpe et al. 2000; see also appendix 2)

By studying the processes of community action and change on multiple levels and uncovering multiple players in these processes, the healthy community assessment greatly broadens its potential for subsequently involving these diverse stakeholders in building a healthier community.

We have argued so far that several categories of information for and about health are needed for assessment at the local level. These include the following (Hancock 1988):

- People's perceptions of the strengths and resources of their communities, as well as their individual and collective health and well-being
- Stories about the formal and informal processes of developing healthy cities and healthy communities
- Data and stories about the community's physical and social environment
- Data and stories about inequities in health and about the prerequisites necessary to address these inequities

- Health status data, at the neighborhood or small-area level, incorporating mortality and morbidity data
- Both subjective and objective assessments of physical, mental, and social well-being

This is a much broader approach than is usually thought of when professionals develop a community health status report, which is for the most part concerned with only the last of these categories. A healthy community assessment is much more than a community health assessment.

How Do We Assess?

Knowing what to assess is only part of the approach to healthy community assessment; we also need to determine how the process can contribute to the health of the community. This process question is vital, requiring that we consider carefully both the type of information that is collected and the degree of involvement with the community during the data-collection process.

The Type of Information Collected

As John McKnight is fond of pointing out, "Institutions learn from studies; communities learn from stories." Studies are usually data rich and, with the important exception of community-based participatory approaches to research noted below, tend to be carried out by academics and professionals working "on" rather than "with" communities. The data are analyzed to yield information, but the knowledge that is acquired is seldom returned to the community, and as a result there is little increase in wisdom. Stories, in contrast, represent the accumulated and almost folkloric wisdom of a community. Stories contain knowledge that can be adapted and applied by other communities. Further, if we accept that knowledge is power, the empowering potential of stories as a source of information about health becomes apparent.

Without discounting the importance of hard data and studies in robust community assessments, the value of combining such data with the lay knowledge of community members has been well demonstrated (Wang and Pies 2004). People can learn much about the health of their communities by listening to and telling stories, whether around the kitchen table, at community meetings, through the Internet or local media, or through events that celebrate successes or acknowledge loss. As discussed in chapter 16, community participation in the arts and literature also can be particularly potent means of gaining such insights (Catalani et al. 2012; McDonald et al. 2006–2007).

Stories can form the basis of studies, with qualitative ethnographic research often providing a more formal means of listening to and learning from stories. The work of Penelope Canan and her colleagues in Molokai is illustrative (Olsen et al. 1985). When these researchers asked villagers what they valued about their communities, one of the things they identified was "the slow pace of life."

When then asked how to measure pace of life, community members suggested counting the number of alarm clocks in each village: if the number of alarm clocks went up, the villagers were clearly losing their slow pace of life (Canan 1993). As this story illustrates, people know what is important to them, and they have the ability to identify innovative and meaningful measures that make sense in their own community. Ethnographic studies and other means of gathering and really listening to people's stories can provide critical information for an assessment of community health and well-being.

Of course, quantitative approaches and studies also have an important role to play in assessing communities and community health. Such approaches can provide documentation of health inequalities within and between communities, which are often starkly dramatized through studies of infant mortality rates and the like. Quantitative methods often have the advantages of perceived scientific rigor, large denominators, and forms of data analysis that make the findings readily accessible to policymakers and others who "need the numbers" to make a case for new legislation or other proposed actions. For quantitative studies to live up to their potential with regard to being an empowering community assessment, however, they must transfer information and knowledge to members of the community and, ideally, involve community members in the research process as well. This approach, which increasingly is termed *community-based participatory research* (CBPR) starts with a topic of concern to the community, "equitably" involves all partners throughout the research process, involves colearning and local capacity building, balances research and action, and it committed to sustainability over the long haul (Israel et al. 2005; Minkler and Wallerstein 2008).

A case study from a low-income, largely Latino community in Southern California is illustrative of how more empowering and participatory approaches to community research may be achieved. Once a vibrant heart of the Latino community in San Diego County, Old Town National City was turned into a "dumping ground for toxic polluters" as a result of legislation passed by an all-white city council in the 1960s (Environmental Health Coalition 2005). The small community quickly became home to a plethora of auto body and paint shops, which contributed to high asthma rates and other health and quality-of-life problems.

Partnering with academic researchers and other allies, the community's Environmental Health Coalition undertook a multifaced CBPR project to help uncover the "numbers and stories" that could help make the case for policy-level change. In addition to powerful in-house GIS (geographic information systems) data (used, for example in the creation of "visual footprints" showing the disproportionate burden of pollution borne by residents of Old Town National City when compared with three adjacent communities), the coalition staff hired neighborhood women as *promotoras de salud* (health promoters) who were trained in survey research methods, land use planning, community organizing, policy advocacy, and other areas. Six of the *promotoras* in turn designed and conducted a door-to-door community assessment, which uncovered high rates of childhood asthma, as well as overwhelming neighborhood interest in relocating polluting industries outside the town (Environmental Health Coalition 2005). These multimethod findings, together with disease burden data from academic partners at the University of Southern California and the *promotoras'* own stories, which they presented in testimony before the city council, played a substantial role in getting several policy victories. These included the passage of both a 2006 ordinance designed to phase out polluting industries, and a specific plan, in 2010, requiring that health impacts and community input be included in all further city decision making (Minkler et al. 2010).

In sum, a balance of studies and stories make up the information needed to assess communities and community health. How this information is collected, the purposes for which it is sought, and whether the findings are then returned to the community play a critical role in determining the empowering potential of the assessment process.

The Degree of Involvement with the Community

Numerous techniques and approaches can be employed to obtain the types of information needed, and a comprehensive listing is beyond the scope of this chapter. A helpful framework for thinking about these alternative methods is provided in Marti-Costa and Serrano-Garcia's (1983) suggestion that assessment techniques can be grouped into categories defined by the extent to which they involve contact between the outside professional and members of the community. Since contact with and high-level involvement of community residents in the assessment process are vital parts of community organizing and community building for health, special attention should be given to methods that foster community involvement and consciousness-raising as part of the assessment process. At the same time, as noted earlier, the utility of studies that produce hard data, including some that may involve no-contact or minimal-contact methods, should be appreciated.

NO-CONTACT METHODS. Demographic and social indicators, such as divorce and unemployment rates and morbidity and mortality statistics, are often the first types of data looked at by health professionals charged with conducting a community needs assessment. Presented in the form of rates and percentages, small-area analyses, or dynamic modeling, studies using such data often have the advantages of a large numerical base or a representative sample and an aura of "scientific objectivity." No-contact methods such as multivariate analysis can document such factors as the impacts of race and class on mortality rates in neighboring communities; as such, these methods can provide information that may be vital in demonstrating health inequalities in a format that legislators and advocacy groups can use in fighting for health resources.

However, use of such methods is based on the assumption that "the community needs and problems that appear in official statistics are representative of community problems" (Marti-Costa and Serrano-Garcia 1983, 81). That assumption, of course, is not always warranted. Statistics on mental health treatment, for example, may indicate a dramatic change in the types of mental illnesses in a given community when what it fact has changed are the service categories for which mental health agencies receive funding. Mental health professionals thus may simply be labeling what they see creatively in order to continue treating persons they believe to be in need.

In addition to statistical studies, no-contact methods often include a documents review, with pertinent "documents," including community newspapers or newsletters, written progress reports from health and social service departments or other agencies, and community bulletin boards (both virtual and online), whose contents may give a flavor for the kinds of issues and resources represented in a given community. Like the collection by outside professionals of health and other demographic and social indicator data, such methods, when used without community involvement, lack the potential to facilitate local empowerment or mobilization.

Increasingly, however, the term *no-contact methods* is becoming something of a misnomer. With mobile phones and other devices now more powerful than the huge corporate and university computers of the 1970s, for example, opportunities have vastly expanded for community members to be involved in the collection and use of data that were formerly within the exclusive purview of researchers and professionals. Resources like the Community Tool Box (http://ctb.ku.edu), which includes more than seven thousand pages of how-to information to assist communities and professionals in issue identification and a host of other areas, are among a wealth of new Internet-based systems that greatly enhance the ability of local communities to effectively study, mobilize around, and address shared concerns (see chapter 15). By helping community members become conversant with such tools and their applications in the assessment process, professionals can greatly expand the empowering potential of many so-called no-contact methods.

MINIMAL-CONTACT OBSERVATIONAL METHODS. A variety of observational methods may be useful for the health professional wishing to gain some initial impressionistic sense of the community with which he or she will be working. One such technique involves the initial use of a neighborhood "windshield tour" or walk-through. Using this approach, the health educator or other social change professional or community member walks or drives slowly through a neighborhood, ideally on different days of the week and at different times of the day, while being "on the lookout" for a whole variety of potentially useful indicators of community health and well-being. As described in appendix 2, observing the condition of houses and automobiles, the nature and degree of activity level, and social interaction between residents and the like can provide valuable impressionistic information, as can sitting in a neighborhood coffee shop or observing at a community forum or PTA meeting. Looking at the content of bulletins boards online or in community centers, libraries, faith-based organization buildings, and local stores or at the public notices posted online or stapled to utility poles also can provide valuable clues to local "hot" issues in the community (Eng and Blanchard 1990–1991; Minkler and Hancock 2008; Sharpe et al. 2000; see appendix 2).

As in the case of the no-contact methods, minimal-contact approaches increasingly are being used in ways that promote community involvement and hold the potential for facilitating empowerment. Health department sponsored efforts such as the Healthy Neighborhood Project described in chapter 8 (see also El-Askari et al. 1998), for example, train neighborhood residents to use walk-throughs, asset mapping, and other techniques, viewing their community through fresh eyes as they gather impressionistic data that then can be shared and compared with that of other members of the assessment team. Once again, if our goal in community assessment is not solely to stimulate, monitor, and assess the impact of change but also to further empowerment, exploiting opportunities for increased community contact and involvement is critical.

INTERACTIVE CONTACT METHODS. This category of methods includes techniques such as key-informant interviews, door-to-door surveys, and a variety of small-group methods for eliciting data and stories about a local community. Among these various techniques, three are particularly deserving of mention. The first of these, discussed in detail in chapter 4, is Paulo Freire's (1973) education for critical consciousness. Through the use of a problem-posing method, group members are asked questions that cause them to critically reflect on their lives and the life of their community. The "generative themes" that emerge from this process, and that capture the hopes and concerns of the people, frequently offer rich insights into their assessments of community and community health.

A second small-group method with particular utility in community assessment is Delbecq and his colleagues' (1975) nominal group process. A structured process designed to foster creativity, encourage conflicting opinions, and prevent domination by a few vocal individuals, the nominal group method is especially helpful in encouraging the participation of marginal group members.

The third approach, the focus group, holds perhaps the greatest current appeal among small-group methods used in community assessment. The focus group brings together, under the direction of a professional or trained moderator, a small group of community members who, in a confidential and nonthreatening discussion, address a series of questions concerning their feelings, in this case, about their community (Krueger and Casey 2000). Employed by health agencies, philanthropic foundations, community-based organizations, and local policymakers, focus groups have considerable potential for providing the stories and perceptions that can greatly enrich the overall community assessment. They further increasingly are being employed with community partners as cofacilitators and interpreters of findings, adding additional benefits to the process from both a data-collection and an empowerment perspective. A number of other contact methods lend themselves to use with either small or larger groups and two of these—photovoice (Wang and Pies 2004) and videovoice (Catalani et al. 2011), as well as community mapping and community asset mapping (Kretzmann and McKnight 1993)—are discussed respectively in chapters 16 and 10 (see also appendix 2). Another increasingly popular method, however, involves working collaboratively with communities to develop community health indicators (CHIs) that characterize a neighborhood or community as a whole, rather than simply the individuals or subgroups of which it is composed. As Patrick and Wickizer (1995) suggest, such indicators may be thought of as "a community analogue to health-risk appraisal for individuals" (72). The number, type, and visibility of no smoking signs in workplaces; the proportion of shelf space in small grocery stores devoted to produce compared with packaged foods and sodas, and the proportion of a community's children under age two with up-to-date immunizations are all examples of potent community health indicators.

A limited set of quantitative and qualitative measures that indicate the current health status of the community, CHIs can also suggest how the community's health status, broadly defined, is changing over time. Good community indicators should reflect both health determinants (such as environmental quality and social cohesion) and process dimensions (such as education and civil rights). Finally, to be relevant to both policymakers and the general public, community indicators should have several key qualities (Hancock et al. 2000a, 2000b):

- Face validity—they make sense to people.
- Theoretical and empirical validity—they measure an important health determinant or dimension.
- Social value—they measure things people care about.
- Valency—they are powerful and carry social and political punch.

Many of these considerations were demonstrated in a community indicators project in Oakland, where community, academic, and health department partners meet over several months and developed an initial list of ten categories of indicators, with more specific indicators under each (Bauer 2003). "Intension to stay in the neighborhood" thus was used as an indicator of "community attraction," while "street violence" appeared under "community health and safety." These indicators in turn were used as the basis of a community survey, in which residents were asked to indicate both their *level of concern* about each given item and their *level of interest in taking action*. Findings like the facts that almost three-quarters of residents assigned "high importance" to "street violence," and that over half reported "high interest in action" on this item (Bauer 2003) helped point the way for potential subsequent issue selection and community mobilization.

Also known as neighborhood health indicators, the local-level data collected through such efforts increasingly are being used in the development of healthy public policy. The National Neighborhood Indicators Partnership exemplifies such work, serving as an intermediary in a collaborative effort that uses relevant information from diverse cities in the United States to inform broader community building and policymaking (Howell et al. 2003).

A common theme throughout this chapter has involved the importance of asking—and having community members ask themselves—the kinds of questions that provoke meaningful discussion about community, health, and healthy communities. Whether in the context of focus groups or key informant interviews or as part of large town hall meetings or community dialogues, such questions might include the following:

- What do you like best about living in this community?
- What would you like to see changed?
- Is this a good place to raise children? (Why or why not?)
- Do people in the neighborhood socialize with one another often? Do you socialize with others here?
- If youth get into a fight in this community, are adult residents likely to intervene?
- How would you characterize the relationship between members of different racial or ethnic groups in the neighborhood?
- Who gets things done? (Eng and Blanchard 1990–91; Minkler and Hancock 2008; Israel 1985; Sharpe et al. 2000; see also appendix 2)

Questions like these often generate a wealth of initial data and stories about a community, and also may help in the identification of a core group of informal leaders who then may be brought together, engaged in a similar dialogue, and encouraged to be key participants in a community organizing or community building project (see appendix 2). The results of such data collection further may be presented either in narrative form or in charts and graphs that summarize key findings (Minkler and Hancock 2008; Sharpe et al. 2000). As suggested above, however, the richest and most honest answers may emerge when local residents themselves conduct the interviews and then help in analyzing or interpreting the results (see chapter 8).

Although contact methods by definition involve community residents, their potential for truly facilitating empowerment depends on the how these methods are employed. Focus groups and key informant interviews, for example, can be disempowering if they only seek information about community needs and problems and ignore or discount the participants' knowledge of their community's resources and assets. In contrast, a contribution to community capacity building may be made when questions are asked that encourage residents to reflect on and contribute to a broader understanding of community strengths. Question such as, What are the things you like best about your community? What makes this a good or healthy community in which to live? and How have people here come together in the past to make a decision or solve a problem? are among those that can help residents think positively about the strengths of their communities. Community asset mapping techniques, as described in the next chapter, similarly represent a powerful means for community members to work together in identifying the strengths and potential "building blocks" of their neighborhoods, and not merely its problems and deficiencies. By revealing an appreciation of the community by the outsider, and engaging informants in a process of thinking critically about the strengths and competencies of their community, such techniques and questions can make a real difference in the information obtained and in the community's willingness to be actively involved in the assessment process.

MULTIMETHOD ASSESSMENT. Clearly, no one method or approach to community assessment can capture the richness and complexity of communities and community health. A strong case should therefore be made for the use of multiple methods, or what researchers refer to as *triangulation.* Mobilizing for Action through Planning and Partnerships, or MAPP (http://www.naccho.org/tools.chm), is one such approach, and was developed by the National Association of County and City Health Officials, working collaboratively with the Centers for Disease Control and Prevention. Using this strategic planning tool, public health leaders help communities prioritize public health issues as well as resources for addressing them. Case vignettes, as well as a variety of user-friendly assessment techniques and resources, are available at the website for those wishing to apply this multimethod approach (Iton 2006).

Regardless of the scale on which a community assessment is conducted, it is likely to be most effective if it combines multiple methods, respects both stories and studies, and places its heaviest emphasis on eliciting high-level community participation throughout the assessment process.

Summary

This chapter has attempted to build on the ideological framework provided by Marti-Costa and Serrano-Garcia (1983), as well as more recent insights developed through the healthy cities movement, to propose an empowering approach to community assessment for health. Both stories and studies are vital if we are to stimulate, monitor, and assess the impact of change and at the same time facilitate the empowerment that comes with knowledge, specifically with the transfer of knowledge to communities. Likewise, no single assessment tool or technique is sufficient in and of itself to sensitively and accurately capture community or community health. That is better accomplished by multiple methods, especially those that serve to empower individuals and communities while making explicit the realities of the community, its resources, and its health.

REFERENCES

American Community Gardens Association. 2011. http://communitygarden.org/.

Bangs, B., S. Licthenwalter, S. Hughes, et al. 2004. *Women's Benchmarks Report*. Pittsburg: University of Pittsburg. www.ucsur.pitt.edu/files/frp/MSAWomensBenchmarks.pdf.

Bauer, G. 2003. "Sample Community Health Indicators at the Neighborhood Level." In *Community-Based Participatory Research for Health*, edited by M. Minkler and N. Wallerstein, 438–450. San Francisco: Jossey-Bass.

Canadian Council on Learning. 2007. *Health Literacy in Canada: Initial Results from the International Adult Literacy and Skills Survey*. Ottawa: Canadian Council on Learning.

Canan, P. 1993. Paper presented at Emory University/CDC workshop on quality-of-life indicators, Atlanta, Georgia.

Catalani, C., L. Campbell, S. Herbst, B. Springgate, B. Butler, and M. Minkler. 2012. "Videovoice: Community Assessment in Post-Katrina New Orleans." *Health Promotion Practice* 13, no. 1:18–28.

Centers for Disease Control and Prevention. 2010. "Healthy Places." http://www.cdc.gov/healthyplaces/about.htm.

Delbecq, A., A. H. Van de Ven, and D. H. Gustafson. 1975. *Group Techniques for Program Planning: A Guide to Nominal Group and Delphi Processes*. Glenview, Ill.: Scott, Foresman.

Diers, J. 2006. *Neighborhood Power: Building Community the Seattle Way*. Seattle: University of Washington Press.

El-Askari, G. J. Freestone, K. L. Irizarry, K. L. Kraut, et al. 1998. "The Healthy Neighborhoods Project: A Local Health Department's Role in Catalyzing Community Development." *Health Education and Behavior* 25, no. 2:146–159.

Eng, E., and L. Blanchard. 1990–1991. "Action-Oriented Community Diagnosis: A Health Education Tool. *International Journal of Community Health Education* 11, no. 2:93–110.

Environmental Health Coalition. 2005. *Reclaiming Old Town National City: A Community Survey*. National City, Calif.: Environmental Health Coalition.

Freire, P. 1973. *Education for Critical Consciousness*. New York: Seabury Press.

Hancock, T. 1988. "Information for Health at the Local Level." Paper presented at the Health in Towns Conference, WHO Europe and the Council of Europe, Vienna.

Hancock, T., and L. Duhl. 1986. *Healthy Cities: Promoting Health in the Urban Context*. Copenhagen: WHO Europe.

Hancock, T., R. Labonte, and R. Edwards. 2000a. "Indicators That Count! Measuring Population Health at the Community Level." Supplement, *Canadian Journal of Public Health* 90 no. 1: 22–26.

———. 2000b. *Indicators That Count: Population Health Indicators at the Community Level*. ParticipAction Report # HP-10–0207. Toronto: Centre for Health Promotion, University of Toronto.

Howell, E. M., K. Pettit, B. A. Ormond, G. T. Kingsley. 2003. "Using the National Neighborhood Indicators Partnership to Improve Public Health." *Journal of Public Health Management and Practice* 9, no. 3:235–242.

Hyatt, S. 2008. "The Obama Victory, Asset-Based Development, and the Re-politicization of Community Organizing." *North American Dialogue* 11, no. 2:17–26.

Israel, B. A. 1985. "Social Networks and Social Support: Implications for Natural Helper and Community Level Interventions. "*Health Education Quarterly* 12, no. 1:65–80.

Israel, B., E. Eng, A. J. Schulz, and E. A. Parker. 2005. *Methods in Community-Based Participatory Research for Health*. San Francisco: Jossey-Bass.

Iton, T. 2006. "Tackling the Root Causes of Health Disparities through Community Capacity Building." In *Tackling Health Inequities Through Public Health Practice: A Handbook for*

Action, edited by R. Hofrichter, 115–136. Washington D.C.: National Association of County and City Health Officials.

Kretzmann, J. P., and J. L. McKnight. 1993. *Building Communities from inside Out: A Path toward Finding and Mobilizing a Community's Assets*. Evanston Ill.: Center for Urban Affairs and Policy Research.

Krueger, R. A., and M. A. Casey. 2000. *Focus Groups: A Practical Guide for Applied Research*. 3rd ed. Newbury Park, Calif.: Sage.

Marti-Costa, S., and I. Serrano-Garcia. 1983. "Needs Assessment and Community Development: An Ideological Perspective." *Prevention in Human Services* 2, no. 2:75–88.

McDonald M., G. Antunez, and M. Gottemoeller. 2006–2007. "Using the Arts and Literature in Health Education." Silver Anniversary Series, *International Quarterly of Community Health Education* 27, no. 3:265–278.

Minkler, M., A. P. Garicia, J. Williams, T. LoPresti, and J. Lilly. 2010. "Sí, Se Puede: Using Participatory Research to Promote Environmental Justice in a Latino Community in San Diego, CA." *Journal of Urban Health* 87, no. 5:796–812.

Minkler, M., and T. Hancock. 2008. "Community-Driven Asset Identification and Issue Selection." In *Community-Based Participatory Research for Health*, edited by M. Minkler and N. Wallerstein, 153–167. 2nd ed. San Francisco: Jossey-Bass.

Minkler, M., and N. Wallerstein, eds. 2008. *Community-Based Participatory Research for Health*. San Francisco: Jossey-Bass.

Olsen, M., P. Canan, and M. Hennesey. 1985. "A Value-Based Community Assessment Process." *Social Methods and Research* 13, no. 3:325–361.

Ozer, E. 2007. "The Effects of School Gardens on Students and Schools: Conceptualization and Considerations for Maximizing Healthy Development." *Health Education and Behavior* 34, no. 6:846–863.

Patrick, D. L., and T. M. Wickizer. 1995. "Community and Health." In *Society and Health*, edited by B. C. Amick, S. Levine, Q. R. Tarlov, and D. C. Walsh, 46–92. New York: Oxford University Press.

Putnam, R. 2000. *Bowling Alone: The Collapse and Revival of American Community*. New York: Simon and Schuster.

Sharpe, P. A., M. L. Greany, P. R. Lee, S. W. Royce. 2000. "Assets-Oriented Community Assessment." *Public Health Reports, 2000* 113, nos. 2 and 3:205–211.

Twiss J., B. S. Dickinson, S. Duma, B. A. Kleinman, H. Paulsen, and L. Rilveria. 2003. "Community Gardens: Lessons Learned from California Healthy Cities and Communities." *American Journal of Public Health* 93, no. 9:1435–1438.

Wang, C. C., and C. A. Pies. 2004. "Family, Maternal, and Child Health through Photovoice." *Maternal and Child Health Journal* 8, no. 2:95–102.

World Health Organization (WHO). 1948. "Constitution of the World Health Organization." Adopted by the International Health Conference in New York, 1946, and entered into force April 7, 1948.

———. 1986. *Ottawa Charter for Health Promotion*. Copenhagen: WHO Europe.

10

Mapping Community Capacity

JOHN L. MCKNIGHT

JOHN P. KRETZMANN

No one can doubt that our older cities these days are deeply troubled places. At the root of the problem are the massive economic shifts that have marked the past two decades. Hundreds of thousands of industrial jobs have either disappeared or moved away from the central city and its neighborhoods. And while many downtown areas have experienced a "renaissance," the jobs created there are different from those that once sustained neighborhoods. Either these new jobs are highly professionalized, and require elaborate education and credentials for entry, or they are routine, low-paying service jobs without much of a future. If effect, these shifts in the economy, and particularly the removal of decent employment possibilities from low-income neighborhoods, have removed the bottom rung from the fabled American "ladder of opportunity." For many people in older city neighborhoods, new approaches to rebuilding their lives and communities, new openings toward opportunity, are a vital necessity.

Traditional Needs-Oriented Solutions

Given the desperate situation, it is no surprise that most Americans think about lower-income urban neighborhoods as problems. Such areas are noted for their deficiencies and needs. This view is accepted by most elected officials, who codify and program this perspective through deficiency-oriented policies and programs. Then, human service systems—often supported by foundations and universities— translate the programs into local activities that teach people the nature of their problems and the value of services as the answer to their problems. As a result, many low-income urban neighborhoods are now environments of service where behaviors are affected because residents come to believe that their well-being depends upon being a client. They see themselves as people with special needs to be met by outsiders. And gradually, they become mainly consumers of services with no incentive to be producers. Consumers of services focus vast amounts of creativity and intelligence on the survival-motivated challenge of outwitting the "system" or on finding ways—in the informal or even illegal economy—to bypass the system entirely.

There is nothing "natural" about this process. Indeed, it is the predictable course of events when deficiency- and needs-oriented programs come to dominate the lives of neighborhoods where low-income people reside.

The Capacity-Focused Alternative

The alternative is to develop policies and activities based on the capacities, skills, and assets of low-income people and their neighborhoods.

There are two reasons for this capacity-oriented emphasis. First, all the historic evidence indicates that significant community development takes place only when local community people are committed to investing themselves and their resources in the effort. This is why you can't develop communities from the top down, or from the outside in. You can, however, provide valuable outside assistance to communities that are actively developing their own assets.

The second reason for emphasizing the development of the internal assets of local urban neighborhoods is that there is very little prospect that large-scale industrial or service corporations will be locating in these neighborhoods. Nor is it likely that significant new inputs of federal money will be forthcoming soon. Therefore, it is increasingly futile to wait for significant help to arrive from outside the community. The hard truth is that development must start from within the community and, in most of our urban neighborhoods, there is no other choice.

Unfortunately, the dominance of the deficiency-oriented social service model has led many people in low-income neighborhoods to think in terms of local needs rather than assets. These needs are often identified, quantified, and mapped through conducting "needs surveys." The result is a map of the neighborhood's illiteracy, teenage pregnancy, criminal activity, drug use, and so on.

But in neighborhoods where there are effective community development efforts, there is also a map of the community's assets, capacities, and abilities. For it is clear that even the poorest city neighborhood is a place where individuals and organizations represent resources upon which to rebuild. The key to neighborhood regeneration is not only to build upon those resources that the community already controls but also to harness those that are not yet available for local development purposes.

The process of identifying capacities and assets, both individual and organizational, is the first step on the path toward community regeneration. Once this new "map" has replaced the one containing needs and deficiencies, the regenerating community can begin to assemble its assets and capacities into new combinations, new structures of opportunity, new sources of income and control, and new possibilities for production.

Mapping the Building Blocks for Regeneration

It is useful to begin by recognizing that not all community assets are equally available for community building purposes. Some are more accessible than others. The most easily accessible assets, or building blocks, are those that are located in the neighborhood and controlled by those who live there. The next most accessible are those assets that are located in the neighborhood but controlled elsewhere. The least accessible are those potential building blocks located outside the neighborhood and controlled by those outside the neighborhood.

Therefore, we will "map" community assets based upon the accessibility of assets to local people. We turn now to a more detailed discussion of each of these clusters of building blocks.

Primary Building Blocks—Assets and Capacities Located inside the Neighborhood, Largely under Neighborhood Control

This cluster of capacities includes those that are most readily available for neighborhood regeneration. They fall into two general categories: the assets and capacities of individuals and those of organizations or associations. The first step in capturing any of these resources is to assess them, which often involves making an inventory.

INDIVIDUAL CAPACITIES. Our greatest assets are our people. But people in low-income neighborhoods are seldom regarded as "assets." Instead, they are usually seen as needy and deficient, suited best for life as clients and recipients of services. Therefore, they are often subjected to systematic and repeated inventories of their deficiencies with a device called a "needs survey."

The starting point for any serious development effort is the opposite of an accounting of deficiencies. Instead, there must be an opportunity for individuals to use their own abilities to produce. Identifying the variety and richness of skills, talents, knowledge, and experience of people in low-income neighborhoods provides a base upon which to build new approaches and enterprises.

To assist in identifying the skills and abilities of individuals, an inventory of capacities can be developed—a simple survey designed to identify the multitude of abilities within each individual. Neighborhood residents have used the "capacity inventory" to identify the talents available to start new enterprises. For example, people have begun a new association of home health care providers and a catering business. Public housing residents in a number of cities have formed local corporations to take over the management of their developments. They immediately needed to identify the skills and abilities of neighbors in order to be effective. The capacity inventory provided the necessary information allowing people to become producers rather than problems.

PERSONAL INCOME. Another vital asset of individuals is their income. It is generally assumed that low-income neighborhoods are poor markets. However, some studies suggest that there is much more income per capita than is assumed. Nonetheless, it is often used in ways that do not support local economic development. Therefore, effective local development groups can inventory the income, savings, and expenditure patterns of their neighborhoods. This information is basic to understanding the neighborhood economy and developing new approaches to capturing local wealth for local development.

THE GIFTS OF LABELED PEOPLE. There is rich potential waiting to be identified and contributed by even the most marginalized individuals. Human service systems have labeled these people "retarded," "mentally ill," "disabled," "elderly," and so on. They are likely to become dependents of service systems, excluded from community life, and considered burdens rather than assets to community life.

In the past two decades, there has been a growing number of unique community efforts to incorporate "labeled" people into local organizations, enterprises, and community associations (O'Connell 1988a). Their gifts and abilities are identified and are introduced to groups that value these contributions. The results have been amazing demonstrations as the "underdeveloped" hospitality of neighborhood people has been rediscovered and gifts, contributions, and capacities of even the most disabled people are revealed.

INDIVIDUAL LOCAL BUSINESSES. The shops, stores, and businesses that survive in low-income neighborhoods—especially those smaller enterprises owned and operated by individual local residents—are often more than economic ventures. They are usually centers for community life as well. Any comprehensive approach to community regeneration will inventory these enterprises and incorporate the energies and resources of these entrepreneurs into neighborhood development processes. The experience and insight of these individual entrepreneurs might also be shared with local not-for-profit groups and with students.

HOME-BASED ENTERPRISES. It is fairly simple to inventory the shops, stores, and businesses in low-income neighborhoods. However, as neighborhoods become lower income, there is often an increase in informal and home-based enterprise. Local development groups have begun to make an effort to understand the nature of these individual entrepreneurs and their enterprises. After gathering information about them, development groups can identify the factors that initiated such enterprises and the additional capital or technical assistance that could increase their profits and the number of people they support.

Associational and Organizational Capacities

Beyond individual capacities are a wide range of local resident-controlled associations and organizations. What follows is an initial inventory.

CITIZENS' ASSOCIATIONS. In addition to businesses and enterprises, low-income communities have a variety of clubs and associations that do vital work in assuring productive neighborhoods. These groups might include service clubs, fraternal organizations, women's organizations, artistic groups, and athletic clubs (see appendix 2). They are the infrastructure of working neighborhoods. Those involved in the community building process can inventory the variety of these groups in their neighborhoods, the unique community activities they support, and their potential to take on a broader set of responsibilities (O'Connell 1988b). Then these groups can become a part of the local asset development process. Or they may affiliate in other ways (e.g., by creating a congress of neighborhood associations).

ASSOCIATIONS OF BUSINESSES. In many older neighborhoods, local business people are not organized. Where they are organized, they are not informed about effective joint partnerships in neighborhood economic development. Connecting local businesses with each other and expanding their vision of their self-interest in community development are a major effort of effective community building activities.

FINANCIAL INSTITUTIONS. Relatively few older neighborhoods have a community-oriented financial institution, such as a bank, savings institution, or credit union. But where they do exist, they are invaluable assets.

One ambitious and successful example of a locally controlled financial institution is the South Shore Bank in Chicago. The bank has been a continuing experiment in how to capture local savings and convert them to local residential and commercial development. A related effort in Bangladesh, called the Gameen Bank, is a successful experiment in very small capitalization for small community enterprises (Nanda 1999). Similar experiments are taking place in the United States and other countries involving credit unions and other entities (Schreiner and Woller 2003). All these inventions are new tools to capture local wealth for local development. Their presence or potential is a central resource for the future of a developing community.

CULTURAL ORGANIZATIONS. People in low-income neighborhoods are increasingly giving public expression to their rich cultural inheritance. Celebrating the history of the neighborhood, and the peoples who have gathered there, is central to forming a community identity and countering the negative images that originate outside the community. Neighborhood history fairs; celebrative block and neighborhood parties featuring the foods, music, dancing, and games of diverse peoples; cross-cultural discussions and classes; oral history projects; theatrical productions based on oral histories—all these hold great potential for building strong relationships among residents and for regaining definitional control of the community. In many neighborhoods, local artists are central to the creation of these expressions.

COMMUNICATIONS ORGANIZATIONS. Strong neighborhoods rely heavily on their capacity to exchange information and engage in discussions. Neighborhood newspapers, particularly those controlled by local residents, are invaluable public forums. So, too, are less comprehensive media such as newsletters, fliers, and even bulletin boards. In addition, both local access cable TV and local radio hold promise as vehicles relevant to community building.

FAITH-BASED ORGANIZATIONS. Finally, any list of organizational assets in communities would be woefully incomplete without the local expressions of faith-based life. Local parishes, congregations, and temples have involved themselves increasingly in the community building agenda, sometimes through community organizations or community development groups (Miller 2009), sometimes simply building on the strengths of their own members and networks. In fact, the ability of local faith-based institutions to call upon related external organizations for support and resources constitutes a very important asset (for more on the work of two such faith-based community organizations, the Gamaliel Foundation [http://www.gamaliel.org/] and ISAIAH [http://www.isaiah.org/], see chapters 2 and 20).

SUMMARY. In summary, then, the primary building blocks include those community assets that are most readily available for rebuilding the neighborhood. These involve both individual and organizational strengths. Our initial list includes the following:

Individual Assets	*Organizational Assets*
Skills, talents, and experience of residents	Associations of businesses
Individual businesses	Citizens' associations
Home-based enterprises	Cultural organizations
Personal income	Communications organizations
Gifts of labeled people	Faith-based organizations

Secondary Building Blocks: Assets Located within the Community but Largely Controlled by Outsiders

Although a good many individuals and associational capacities are already within the control of the people who live in the neighborhood, others, though physically a part of the community, are directed and controlled from outside. To capture these assets for community building purposes, neighborhood actors will not only conduct inventories but also construct strategies designed to enhance the regenerative uses of these assets. The examples that follow fall into three categories: private and nonprofit organizations, public institutions and services, and other physical resources.

PRIVATE AND NONPROFIT ORGANIZATIONS

Institutions of higher education. Private and public junior colleges, colleges, and universities remain in, or adjacent to, many older urban neighborhoods. However, they are often quite detached from the local community. Community building groups are creating new experiments with partnerships in community development between local institutions of higher education and other groups that that are mobilizing community capacities. Organizations such as Community-Campus Partnerships for Health (www.ccph/info) are among those encouraging such connections, and the increased emphasis on engaged scholarship and community-based participatory research also are noteworthy in this regard (Fitzgerald et al. 2011; see chapters 13 and 14).

Hospitals. Next to public schools, hospitals are the most prevalent major institution remaining in many older neighborhoods. They are a tremendous reserve of assets and resources to support initiatives in community enterprise. In many cases, hospitals, clinics and health maintenance organizations (HMOs) have created innovative local partnerships. Creative development groups are exploring the nature of the development assets controlled by their local hospitals, clinics, or HMOs.

Social service agencies. Although often dedicated to the delivery of individual service to their clients—an activity that does not necessarily contribute to community building—local social service agencies do have the potential to introduce capacity-oriented strategies to their programs. Many, in fact, have begun to see economic development and job creation as appropriate activities, while others have entered into networks and partnerships with community organizations and neighborhood development groups for community building purposes.

PUBLIC INSTITUTIONS AND SERVICES. Of the range of public institutions and services that exist in low-income communities, a few deserve to be highlighted for their community building potential.

Public schools. Big-city schools have often become so separate from local community initiatives that they are a liability rather than an asset. The Carnegie Commission on Public Education has said that the most significant educational failing of the local public school is its separation from the work and life of the community. Therefore, localities need to teach their schools how to improve their educational function by connecting themselves to community development efforts. As an integral part of community life, rather than an institution set apart, the local public school can begin to function as a set of economic and human resources aimed at regenerating the community (McKnight 1987).

Police. As with all other local institutions, the police need to participate in the neighborhood revitalization enterprise. Much of the hesitance about new investment of all kinds relates to issues of security. Therefore, local police officials should be asked to join the asset development team, acting as advisers and resources to development projects. In a number of instances, responsive police departments have joined with local community organizations and other groups to devise and carry out joint safety and anticrime strategies. The new accent on community policing in many low-income neighborhoods is an important example.

Fire departments. In both small towns and large cities, the local fire department boasts a tradition of consistent interaction with the community. Because of the sporadic nature of their important work, firefighters are often available for various activities in the neighborhood (although recent major cutbacks in firefighter staff have limited such availability). Retrieving and building upon that tradition are an important strategy for community building.

Libraries. Many older neighborhoods contain branches of the public library, often underfunded and underused. Considered not only as a repository for books and periodicals but also as the center of a neighborhood's flow of information, the library becomes a potentially critical participant in community regeneration. For example, neighborhoods that choose to enter into a community-planning process will need localized information on which to base their deliberations. The availability of library-based personal computers can enhance access to relevant databases. The library can also provide space for community meetings and initiate community history and cultural projects.

Parks. In many low-income communities, the local parks have fallen into disrepair and are often considered uninviting and even dangerous. But when local citizens organize themselves to reclaim these areas, parks can be restored not only physically but also functionally. As symbols of community accomplishment, they can become sources of pride and centers for important informal relationship building. Often, groups of existing associations will take joint responsibility for renewing and maintaining a local park (Diers 2006; Minkler et al. 2006).

PHYSICAL RESOURCES. Besides the private and public institutions in the neighborhood, numerous physical assets are available. In fact, many of the most visible "problems" of low-income neighborhoods, when looked at from an asset-centered perspective, become opportunities instead. A few examples follow.

Vacant land, vacant commercial and industrial structures, vacant housing. Most older urban neighborhoods are thought to be "blighted," with vacant lots, empty sites of old industry, and unused industrial and commercial buildings. However, in some U.S. cities, local groups have found creative and productive methods to regenerate the usefulness of both the land and the buildings (Diers 2006; see chapter 14). The community gardens movement, which today boosts some eighteen thousand gardens in the United States alone (American Community Gardens Association 2011), frequent begins with publicly owned vacant lots. Community members identify potential new uses, create tools to inventory and plan for local reuses, and organize the redevelopment process. Similarly, abandoned housing structures are often structurally sound enough to be candidates for locally controlled rehabilitation efforts.

Energy and waste resources. The costs of energy and waste collection are relentless resource drains in older neighborhoods. As their costs escalate, they demand a disproportionate and growing share of the limited income of poorer people. As a result, maintenance of housing is often forgone, and deterioration speeds up. However, in some neighborhoods, this "problem" has become an opportunity. New local enterprises are developing to reduce energy use and costs and to recycle waste for profit. These initiatives need to be identified, nurtured, and replicated.

SUMMARY. These secondary building blocks are private, public, and physical assets, which can be brought under community control and used for community building purposes. Our initial list includes the following:

Private and Nonprofit Organizations	*Public Institutions and Services*
Higher education institutions	Public schools
Hospitals, clinics, and HMOs	Police
Social service agencies	Libraries
	Fire departments
	Parks

Physical Resources

Vacant land, commercial and industrial structures, housing

Energy and waste resources

Potential Building Blocks: Resources Originating outside the Neighborhood, Controlled by Outsiders

In this final cluster are resource streams that originate outside the neighborhood, but that nonetheless might be captured for community building purposes.

There is a sense in which all local public expenditures are potential investments in development. However, in low-income neighborhoods they are usually expenditures for the maintenance of an impoverished neighborhood and for individuals in the absence of work. We need tools and models for converting public expenditures into local development investments. In addition to the public institutions cited above, two other public expenditures are critical.

WELFARE EXPENDITURES. In areas like Cook County, Illinois, large, albeit shrinking funds are expended annually by government for low-income programs for people whose income falls below the official poverty line. This substantial investment is distributed so that on a per capita basis, poor people receive well over half this money in the form of services rather than as actual income. This creates an impoverished family dependent on services. Creative community groups are developing new experiments whereby some of these welfare dollars are reinvested in enterprise development and independence.

PUBLIC CAPITAL-IMPROVEMENT EXPENDITURES. Most neighborhoods are the site of very substantial "infrastructure" investments. In downtown areas, these dollars leverage private investment. In neighborhoods, the same funds are usually applied only to maintenance functions. Effective community development groups are creating experiments to convert local capital improvement funds into development dollars.

PUBLIC INFORMATION. Wherever we have seen community innovation in local neighborhoods, the people there have had to gain access to information not normally available. What is the vacancy ratio in the worst buildings? How many teachers have skills that could help our development corporation? What time do the crimes that threaten our shopping center occur? How much property is off the tax roles? What does the city plan to invest in capital improvements? Unfortunately, most useful development planning data are collected for the use of "downtown" systems. But as neighborhoods become responsible for their future, information must be decoded and decentralized for local use.

Some neighborhoods have done pioneering work in developing methods to translate systems data into neighborhood information. This "neighborhood information" is an invaluable asset in the development process.

SUMMARY. These potential building blocks include major public assets, which ambitious neighborhoods might begin to divert to community building purposes. At the beginning, at least, these are the following:

Welfare expenditures

Public capital information expenditures

Public information

Two Community Maps

This chapter only begins to map the assets that exist in every neighborhood and town. It is a new map that can guide us toward community regeneration.

But there is another map, an old map of neighborhood deficiencies and problems. As we noted at the outset, it is a "needs-oriented" neighborhood map created by "needs surveys." This is a powerful map, teaching people in low-income neighborhoods how to think about themselves and the place where they live.

This map is initiated by groups with power and resources that ask neighborhood people to think of themselves in terms of deficiencies in order to gain access to the resources controlled by these groups. Among the groups that ask neighborhood people to inventory their problems, needs, and deficiencies are government agencies, foundations, universities, United Ways, and the mass media. Indeed, the institutions that produce this map not only teach people in low-income neighborhoods that their needs, problems, and deficiencies are valuable. They also teach people outside these neighborhoods that the most important thing about low-income people and their neighborhoods is their deficiencies, problems, and needs. In this way, low-income people, helping institutions, and the general public come to follow a map that shows that the most important part of low-income neighborhoods is the empty, deficient, needy part. An example of this neighborhood needs map is in figure 10.1.

It is true that this map of needs is accurate. But it is also true that it is only half the truth. It is like a map of the United States that shows only that portion east of the Mississippi River. The United States is also the portion west of the

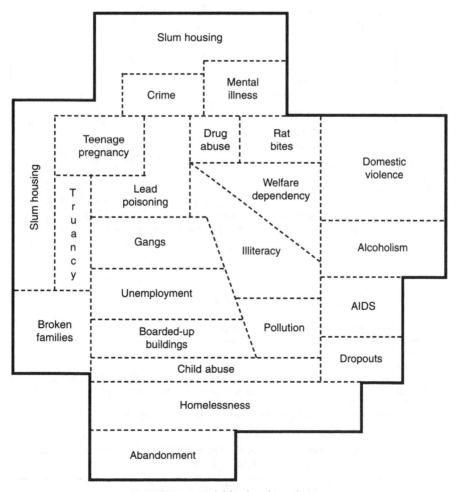

FIGURE 10.1 Neighborhood Needs Map

Mississippi River, and a map omitting the west is obviously inadequate in the most fundamental ways.

Similarly, every neighborhood has a map of riches, assets, and capacities. It is important to recognize that this is a map of the same territory as the neighborhood needs map. It is different because it shows a different part of the

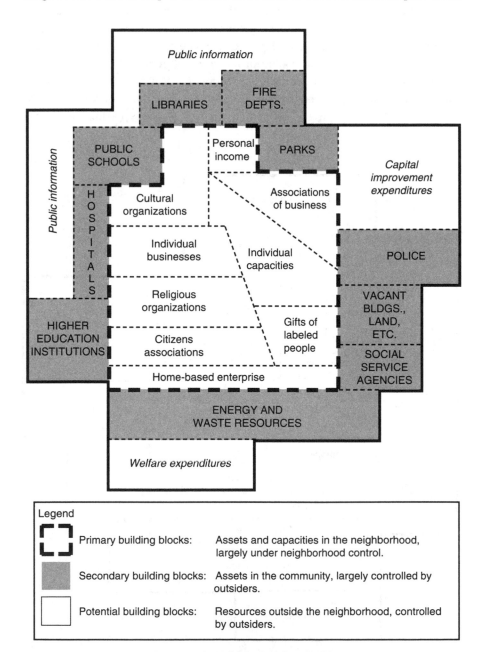

FIGURE 10.2 Neighborhood Assets Map

neighborhood. But the most significant difference about this capacity map is that it is the map a neighborhood must rely on if it is to find the power to regenerate itself.

Communities have never been built upon their deficiencies. Building community has always depended upon mobilizing the capacities and assets of a people and a place. That is why a map of neighborhood assets is necessary if local people are to find the way toward empowerment and renewal. An example of a neighborhood assets map is in figure 10.2.

Finally, it is important to remember that this assets map is very incomplete because it does not even begin to identify all of the assets of every community. As more and more neighborhood regeneration processes are created, residents will identify many more skills, capacities, riches, assets, potential, and gifts to place on the map.

Using the Capacities Map

Most of the assets listed above already exist in many low-income neighborhoods. They are waiting to be inventoried and turned toward the goal of rebuilding communities.

Different communities will approach this challenge with different strategies. Leaders in every community, however, will need to consider at least three questions that are central to the rebuilding task:

1. Which organizations can act most effectively as "asset development organizations" in our neighborhood?
2. What kinds of community-wide research, planning, and decision-making processes can most democratically and effectively advance this rebuilding process in our neighborhood?
3. Having inventoried and enlisted the participation of major assets inside the community, how might we build useful bridges to resources located outside the community?

Asset Development Organizations

To begin with, who might lead the community building process? Where might the necessary asset development organizations be found?

Two kinds of existing community associations are particularly well suited to the task of knitting together a neighborhood's various assets and capacities. The first, already central to the lives of many older city neighborhoods, is the multi-issue community organization, built along the "organization of organizations" model of the late Saul Alinsky (1972; Miller 2009). Community organizers already understand the importance of associational life to the well-being of the neighborhood and to the empowerment of the local residents. A number of these community organizations are beginning to incorporate a capacity-oriented approach to community building in their ongoing activities.

The second potential asset development organization is, of course, the community development corporation. Groups that are dedicated to community economic development have often worked hard to assemble the business assets available to the neighborhood. Many have championed strategies emphasizing local purchasing and hiring and have encouraged homegrown enterprise development. All these approaches can only be strengthened as the local development corporation broadens and deepens its knowledge of community capacity.

Together or separately, these two types of community-based organizations are well suited to the challenge of asset development. But in many communities, neither the multi-issue organizing group nor the development corporation may exist. In these settings, neighborhood leaders face the challenge of creating a new asset development organization. This new organization may be built on the strengths and interests of existing citizens associations and will challenge those associations to affiliate for these broader purposes.

The Community-Planning Process

Having identified or created the asset development organization, community leaders face the challenge of instituting a broad-based process of community planning and decision making. Capacity-oriented community planning will no doubt take many different forms. But all of them will have at least these characteristics in common:

1. The neighborhood planning process will aim to involve as many representatives of internally located and controlled assets as possible in the discussion and decisions. In fact, the map of neighborhood assets provides an initial list of potential participants in the planning effort.
2. The neighborhood planning process will incorporate some version of a community capacity inventory in its initial stages.
3. The neighborhood planning process will develop community building strategies that take full advantage of the interests and strengths of the participants and will aim toward building the power to define and control the future of the neighborhood.

Building Bridges to outside Resources

Finally, once the asset development organization has been identified and has begun to mobilize neighborhood stakeholders in a broad-based process of planning, participants will need to assemble the many additional resources needed to advance the community building process. This will involve constructing bridges to persons and organizations outside the neighborhood.

It is clear that no low-income neighborhood can "go it alone." Indeed, every neighborhood is connected to the outside society and economy. It is a mark of many low-income neighborhoods that they are uniquely dependent on outside and human service systems. What they need, however, is to develop their assets and become interdependent with mainstream people, groups, and economic activity.

Organizations leading developing communities often create unique bridges to the outside society. These are not to government alone. Instead, they bridge to banks, corporations, churches, other neighborhood advocacy groups, and so on (McKnight 1987). These bridged relationships in the nongovernmental sector are vital assets in opening new opportunities for local residents and enterprises.

The task of the asset development organization, then, involves both drawing the map and using it. It involves leading the community interests into capacity-oriented planning and creating the organizational power to enable that process to become the map of the neighborhood's future. The challenge facing the asset development organization, and all the participants in the neighborhood planning process, is both daunting and filled with promise. However, meeting this challenge to rebuild our neighborhoods from the inside out is crucial to the hopes and aspirations of city dwellers everywhere.

ACKNOWLEDGMENTS

Adapted from *Mapping Community Capacity* (Evanston, Ill.: Center for Urban Affairs and Policy Research, Northwestern University, 1988), by permission of the authors.

REFERENCES

Alinsky, S. D. 1972. *Rules for Radicals: A Practical Primer for Realistic Radicals*. New York: Random House.
American Community Gardens Association. 2011. http://communitygarden.org/.
Diers, J. 2006. *Neighborhood Power: Building Community the Seattle Way*. Seattle: University of Washington Press.
Fitzgerald, H., C. Burack, and S. Seifer, eds. 2011. *Handbook for Engaged Scholarship: Contemporary Landscapes, Future Directions*. Vol. 1, *Institutional Change*. East Lansing: Michigan State University.
McKnight, J. 1987. *The Future of Neighborhoods and the People Who Reside There: A Capacity-Oriented Strategy for Neighborhood Development*. Evanston, Ill.: Neighborhood Innovations Network, Center for Urban Affairs and Policy Research, Northwestern University.
Miller, M. 2009. *A Community Organizer's Tale: People and Power in San Francisco*. Berkeley, Calif.: Heyday Books.
Minkler, M., V. Brechwich Vásquez, J. Warner, H. Stuessey, and S. Facente. 2006. "Sowing the Seeds of Sustainable Change: A Community-University Research and Action Partnership in Indiana and Its Aftermath." *Health Promotion International* 21, no. 4: 293–300.
Nanda, P. 1999. "Women's Participation in Rural Credit Programmes in Bangladesh and Their Demand for Formal Health Care: Is There a Positive Impact?" *Health Economics* 8, no. 5:415–428.

O'Connell, M. 1988a. *Getting Connected: How to Find Out about Groups and Organizations in Your Neighborhood*. Evanston, Ill.: Neighborhood Innovations Network, Center for Urban Affairs and Policy Research, Northwestern University.

————. 1988b. *The Gift of Hospitality: Opening the Doors of Community to People with Disabilities*. Evanston, Ill.: Neighborhood Innovations Network, Center for Urban Affairs and Policy Research, Northwestern University.

Schreiner, M., and G. Woller. (2003) "Microenterprise Development Programs in the United States and in the Developing World." *World Development* 31, no. 9:1567–1580.

11

Selecting and "Cutting" the Issue

LEE STAPLES

Issue campaigns are both ends and means. Grassroots community organizations (GCOs) are formed as vehicles to address issues of concern. The process of taking collective action on those issues helps develop the group's capacity to accomplish future goals and objectives. A GCO's ability to deal successfully with any issue is a function of its level of organizational development. Organizations grow through experience and practice; issue campaigns are the very lifeblood of that process. Through them, new people are attracted, existing members remain active, and leadership abilities flourish. The importance of this interrelationship between organizational development and issue campaigns can't be overemphasized (Staples 2004).

Many years ago, Warren Haggstrom (1971) introduced the concept of "organizational mileage" as a means of assessing the degree of organizational development attained by a grassroots group. The best issue campaigns will develop organizational mileage while simultaneously appealing to the self-interests of community members. Therefore, when choosing an issue, a community organization must be concerned about not only *whether it can be won* but *how the campaign will develop the group.*

Issues to organize around can be found by talking with community members and trying out various themes. This kind of exploration can be done through organizational meetings, actions, events, door knocking, and house meetings. For health educators and social workers, focus groups or community forums also are popular methods for finding and testing issues and community-perceived needs. The role of the organizer is one of listening actively, asking questions, agitating, and facilitating the issue-cutting process (Miller 2009).

It may be tempting simply to discuss a possible issue among the top leadership, but this common mistake overlooks one key factor. These leaders may be so committed to the organization that they are no longer typical of rank-and-file members and, as such, may be very poor judges of which issue campaigns will appeal most widely and deeply to the membership. Within the organization, issues should be tested and selected with as much bottom-up participation as possible.

There are two key dimensions—depth and breadth. *Depth* refers to how intensely community members feel about an issue, while *breadth* relates to how widespread that concern is. The strongest issues will be felt deeply by a broad cross section of the community (Bobo et al. 2010; Sen 2003; Staples 2004). For instance, a proposal to close a popular community health clinic in a low-income urban neighborhood might be strongly opposed by virtually everyone living in the area. This issue would have both depth and breadth, thereby helping to ensure that large numbers of the affected constituency would participate in collective action to resist the closure.

In the same neighborhood, people living close to an abandoned house taken over by drug dealers would likely be deeply concerned. However, residents located ten blocks away might not even be aware of the existence of the problem. This potential issue would have depth but not a lot of breadth. A solid core of highly committed people could probably be recruited to take action, but the base from which to draw participants would be circumscribed. For GCOs, these are the second-best type of issue.

In the same geographic area, beautification of parks might be widely supported yet not on many people's top-ten list of concerns. Issues that have a broad, but also a bland, self-interest draw are the third most desirable. A lack of passion raises serious questions about community members' degree of potential involvement. Finally, if the appeal of an issue is neither broad nor deep (for example, in this hypothetical low-income neighborhood, a proposal to limit offshore oil drilling), forget about it.

While GCOs should embark on new campaigns only after considerable discussion and analysis, at times they have little choice but to respond to a particular issue. For instance, a neighborhood group would be expected to react quickly to a local industry accused of polluting a nearby river or the suspension of weekly trash pickup. Similarly, an immigrant-rights group hardly could overlook a legislative proposal to eliminate state health coverage for low-income, legally registered noncitizens. The positive aspect of such situations is that many people will be highly interested and ready to take action. The danger is that the organization may be forced to bite off more than it can chew. In instances such as these, the community group really can't afford to walk away if it wants to do the right thing while retaining its credibility. It's a time to fight the good fight—win, lose, or draw (Staples 2004).

Many organizations will also choose to be involved in more than one issue campaign at a time. This usually is desirable if the group already has a multi-issue focus and won't spread itself too thin in the process. Key factors to consider are resources, level of organizational development, and the demands of other campaigns. Timing is another significant factor (Alinsky 1972; Miller 2009; Sen 2003).

Several campaigns can be run simultaneously if some are relatively quick and others are more protracted. Each situation must be assessed individually within the context of the two primary goals: *winning basic issues of immediate concern to the members* and *furthering organizational development.*

The normal rules for decision making will vary according to the particular community group's structure. But, fundamentally, the process should be democratic and involve as many members as possible. A democratic process helps insure that a broad base of members begins to feel ownership of both the issue campaign and the developing strategy.

Additionally, all decisions about issues should be made on a *strategic* basis, using a well-thought-out approach to achieve a goal and specific objectives. Strategic thinking is systematic, logical, analytical, and highly focused on achieving desired ends. Formulating a successful strategy requires the ability to anticipate likely outcomes. Each action option will produce a reaction from the target system; strategic planning and analysis allow more accurate predictions about the probable results from each alternative (Barry 1997; see appendix 7). As organizations mature, their leaders and members become able to take on increasingly more complex issue campaigns with strategies that unfold in a series of steps, each predicated on the outcome of the last. Like chess masters, the best strategists will be able to think through the implications of most variables and then lay out the stages and timetable of the campaign through to their logical ending point.

Since organizational resources are limited and not every issue can be addressed, it is not sufficient to simply choose an issue and then develop a strategy. Rather, an issue should be chosen on the basis of a strategic analysis that determines in advance whether it can be won and if it will produce organizational mileage (Bobo et al. 2001; Sen 2003; Staples 2004).

Organizational Mileage Considerations

Organizational mileage can be assessed by examining ten factors: membership, leadership, staffing, structure, goal attainment, target systems influenced, strategy and tactics employed, finances, allies, and communications. Before making a decision to embark on a new issue campaign, it is helpful to address the following questions, all of which have implications for development across one or more of these ten dimensions. Although the complete answers may not be known until *after* the organization actually engages in a systematic postcampaign evaluation process, much can be determined and predicted ahead of time. This list isn't exhaustive but is illustrative of the kind of thinking needed to do a strategic analysis that maximizes the potential for organizational mileage:

- Is the issue consistent with the long- and middle-range goals of the organization?
- Will the issue be unifying or divisive?

- What is the group's capacity to undertake this issue campaign at the present time?
- Will the campaign help the organization grow?
- Will the campaign provide a good educational experience for leaders and members, developing their consciousness, independence, and skills?
- Will the group receive credit for a victory on the issue, improve its credibility, and increase its overall visibility?
- How will the campaign affect organizational resources?
- Will the campaign develop new allies or enemies?
- Will the campaign emphasize collective action, producing new strategies, tactics, or issues?
- Will the campaign produce a significant victory?

Consistency

Is the issue consistent with the long-range goals of the organization? How will this issue campaign fit in with the overall organizational vision and mission? Will it help move the group along that path or involve a detour or even a basic change in direction? For instance, a health access organization in a low-income neighborhood might be considering involvement in a campaign to fight cutbacks in bus service—an issue of concern to many members. While not dealing specifically with health in a narrow sense, the transportation issue might have a direct impact on many of the organization's low-income constituents.

Before making a decision on this issue, we need to consider the campaign's impact on future organizational directions. Will other health access issues be neglected while the transportation campaign is undertaken, or will this fight complement other organizational actions? Does this signal the start of a new multi-issue approach? Is this issue a "one-shot" effort or does it naturally lead to similar, but more ambitious, transportation campaigns? Is this issue aligned with the basic values of the group's members? Will this campaign build the power of the organization to represent the interests of low-income residents better than other issues? Beyond these questions, what *are* the long- and middle-range goals and how have they been determined?

Unity

Will the issue be unifying or divisive? Serious internal splits will weaken any grassroots organization, so it's critical to consider how a potentially divisive issue relates to the organization's ultimate goals (Alinsky 1972; Bobo et al. 2001; Miller 2009). One faction may contend that by taking a position, the GCO will virtually destroy itself, while others may argue that if a stand isn't taken, the group won't be worth saving, because "if you don't stand for something, you'll fall for anything." A clear understanding of one fundamental principle is essential: any issue campaign that weakens the organizational base jeopardizes the attainment of all other goals.

It may be possible to have both a broad organizational base and an almost perfect score on that "great ideological issues" chart in the sky. However, the group that bites the bullet on too many divisive issues may find itself with a pure ideological record but only a handful of self-righteous true believers. An organization needs to stand up for its principles and goals. But to develop real power and clout, it also needs a lot of people standing up in solidarity as members and activists.

An important safeguard is a *democratic decision-making process.* Both organizers and leaders need to avoid imposing their own ideological goals and visions on the rest of the organization. When controversial divisive issues arise, organizers and leaders need to come to grips with their own feelings and try to separate these from their roles within the group (Miller 2009; Sen 2003). When this isn't possible, it should be acknowledged honestly, and those whose positions run counter to the group's consensus should withdraw as much as possible from the issue or, in some cases, even leave the organization. Any good campaign on a significant issue will attract new people who agree with the group's position and action. But it will also flush out some members who didn't really understand or accept the basic aims of the organization to begin with. Such minor losses of membership are healthy and should be expected.

Oftentimes, a potentially divisive issue can turn out to be unifying if it's cut and framed in a positive way. A low-income community hard hit by epidemics of drug use and HIV/AIDS may be heavily divided over whether to mobilize in favor of a needle exchange program when the issue is cut in terms of condoning or not condoning the use of illicit drugs. But when a health professional can provide evidence that needle exchange programs reduce the spread of HIV without encouraging drug use, the issue can be cut instead in the positive terms of disease prevention.

Problems of divisiveness are often more complex for multi-issue organizations than for single-issue groups, since they usually have a more diverse multi-constituency base. Again, the interests of different community subgroups need to be weighed against the organization's long-term goals. Often, common ground can be found by identifying shared or similar interests and creatively reframing issues accordingly (Wolff 2010). It is important for the group's leadership to play an active role to prevent different factions from digging in their heels before fully exploring less divisive alternatives.

Grassroots community organizations also need to be aware of the potential for *external* divisions. A first step is determining whether other grassroots organizations are working on the same issue. Perhaps there will be opportunities for an alliance or formal coalition (Sen 2003). Competition on the same issue generally should be avoided, as "muscling in" aggressively on another group's issue can alienate community members, generate negative publicity, upset funders, turns off potential allies, or enable target systems to play one group off against the other. Only when the other group clearly "sells out the community," or takes a totally different approach on the issue, should this option even be considered.

Sometimes, opponents will be able to divide an organization from its potential allies. For example, tobacco companies have frequently provided funding for Cinco de Mayo parades and other cultural events in heavily Latino areas. In doing so, these companies may drive a wedge between community groups seeking much needed financial backing and public health professionals working to fight the increased targeting of people of color in cigarette advertising (see chapter 7). Questions of unity and divisiveness must be considered carefully before any issue is selected, since a mistake in this area can have profound and lasting impacts on the organization.

Capacity

What is the organization's capacity to undertake this issue at the present time? The two key variables are the level of organizational development and timing. Factors to consider include the number of people whom the group can mobilize; the quality and quantity of its leadership, staff, and volunteers; structural capacity to take on another issue; the level of agreement/disagreement from the target system; financial resources; the group's ability to work with existing or potential allies; and the effectiveness of its internal and external communications systems. There is potential for organizational *growth* in most issue campaigns, and a GCO frequently increases its mileage in the process of addressing a new issue. That said, the question still remains as to whether the capacity exists to take on *this particular issue at this moment*. If the requisite level of development hasn't been achieved, there is a very good chance that the organization won't be able to succeed. This is particularly true if the change effort is ambitious and serious resistance can be expected from the target system.

Even a well-developed group may have difficulties if the timing is wrong. For instance, the organization may be heavily involved in one or more other campaigns that drain its resources and limit its ability to focus enough attention on the new issue. External problems might include strained relations with important allies, upcoming state or municipal elections that require organizational work, attacks in the media from various opponents, or loss of a key funding source. Or there may be internal challenges, such as divisions between one or more organizational factions, a recent turnover in leadership or staff, a funding crisis, or an upcoming annual convention or membership renewal drive. An organization's willingness and ability to take on a new issue can vary dramatically over time, depending on what else is on its plate.

Research shows that occasionally, minimal social action can almost guarantee a victory if a variety of situational factors are in place. Such campaigns are called "fixed fights" or "cinch fights" (Alinsky 1972) and provide an opportunity for both a concrete success and the development of organizational mileage. Such fixed fights are especially valuable in the early stages of an organization's life, when there's a great need to win on an issue and establish a strong track record. Often, the greatest difficulty in such cases may be acting quickly and decisively enough to get credit and establish genuine credibility. Further, as in an early Alinsky campaign in which a community group was urged to "demand" that certain child welfare services be restored (Alinsky 1972), cinch fights can create ethical challenges if group members are not told in advance that victory would be theirs for the asking, and instead are led to believe that their own confrontational demands resulted in the win. Although in the Alinsky case a sense of empowerment followed the win, had group members found out that the organizers had withheld information (e.g., about the ease of getting services restored just by asking), they may have rightfully felt manipulated.

While a fixed fight can furnish a welcome and timely victory, the quest for such situations should be kept in perspective. Groups shouldn't fall into the trap of only hunting for sure things. The best campaigns stretches all facets of an organization, forcing it to extend itself fully as it challenges the status quo and pushes for social change. Creating a good mix of difficult issues with fixed fights is a strategic task requiring skillful analysis and a keen sense of timing.

Growth

Will the campaign help the organization grow? An organization's ultimate source of power is in large numbers of involved community members. The best campaigns will have depth and breadth of appeal on immediate, specific, and winnable issues (Alinsky 1972). Campaigns should lend themselves to the kind of systematic face-to-face recruitment that can be done through one-on-ones, door knocking, home visits, house meetings, networking (virtual or online), and presentations to community groups (Miller 2009). As the various phases of the campaign unfold, ample opportunity for direct participation by large numbers of people should be built into all organizational activities. This is accomplished most effectively through participatory collective action tactics (Alinsky 1972; Staples 2004). The recruitment and involvement of large numbers of people will provide much of the leverage necessary to win the issue campaign, while simultaneously expanding and building the membership base.

But a good campaign also should engage and develop new leaders, with leadership spread among many people rather than lodged in the hands of a few. This collective form of leadership depends on the infusion of new people who bring added skills and energy to the group (Brown et al. 2005). A good issue campaign should be able to attract additional leaders and involve them in important roles. In some cases, people who never before were active will participate, while in other instances, former "second-line" leaders will move into positions of increased responsibility and prominence. Most organizations periodically suffer the loss of some leaders, and the infusion of new leadership blood through issue campaigns can compensate for such attrition.

Some issues are particularly effective in expanding organizational membership and leadership because they appeal to more than one natural constituency. Environmental justice issues increasingly fall into this category, since they usually affect a very broad cross section of the community. An excellent example is provided by the Chelsea Collaborative Greenspace Committee's campaign to prevent a diesel-fueled electrical power plant from being constructed within one-quarter mile of a low-income city's elementary school complex (Bongiovani 2010). More than half of Chelsea residents are people of color, and upon learning about the proposed construction of the power plant, the collaborative's leadership immediately viewed the situation as a clear case of environmental racism and classism.

Outreach and recruitment methods included talking with parents who were picking up their children at school, speaking with teachers, educating youth, talking with those suffering from asthma and other illnesses, door knocking, presenting at other organizations' meetings, speaking at religious services, and talking with people on the streets. Hundreds of residents attended community meetings, and more than three hundred took part in an action where they chanted, carried signs, wore dust masks, played musical instruments, and carried a model of a mock power plant that emitted smoke. They called on the company's CEO to withdraw the proposal to site a power plant in Chelsea. When he continued to refuse, Greenspace activists reached out to a broad array of allies, including environmental and health organizations, elected officials, public health institutions, and energy experts.

A more militant protest took place at Boston University, where the CEO (a BU alumnus) was receiving an award for building clean energy wind generated plants in other (whiter) parts of the state. The ceremony was disrupted as angry Chelsea residents, including large numbers of young people, marched into the student union room where the ceremony was taking place. Activists passed out leaflets denouncing the CEO as an environmental hypocrite and a larger group dramatically unrolled a banner from the balcony demanding, "Chelsea Deserves Clean Air!"

Later, at its annual Earth Day celebration, using a classic Alinsky (1972) tactic, Greenspace gave the CEO a "Dirty Dozen Award" as one of the twelve-worst polluters in the state. Greenspace members continued to organize community meetings, hold demonstrations, testify at public hearings, work closely with their allies, and pressure government regulators to refuse to grant a permit for the construction. Finally, after approval had been delayed for more than eleven years, the company quietly withdrew its application to build the power plant in November 2007. This successful campaign dramatically enlarged the group's membership base and expanded the leadership core (Bongiovani 2010).

Education

Will the campaign provide a good educational experience for leaders and members, developing their consciousness, independence, and skills? As famed adult educator John Dewey (1946) pointed out, people learn best through action and experience. An issue campaign can provide an educational experience that dozens of consciousness-raising sessions, workshops, books, films, or seminars could never match. In a campaign, learning takes place within the context of actual life experience; there is a unique opportunity for the development of political awareness and analytical, strategic-planning abilities. Skills can be learned in a wide range of areas from action research to recruitment, meeting facilitation, campaign planning, to media and legislative advocacy. The development of these abilities and skills will lessen the group's dependence on organizers and other professionals (Sen 2003; Su 2009; Miller 2009).

Learning takes place in a four-step process that should involve as many people as possible: (1) analyzing situations and envisioning social change, (2) making plans accordingly, (3) carrying those plans into action, and (4) evaluating the results (Chavez 1990). There is often a tendency to concentrate on developing frontline leadership. But using campaign opportunities to educate the full membership, and particularly second-line leaders who may later move into top positions, should not be overlooked (Miller 2009; Su 2009; Staples 2004).

Obviously, while it is not always functional to have the entire membership involved in intricate strategic planning, people can be polled by the leadership on various options, and briefings before all actions can explain the strategic line of thinking to everyone. The more people feel part of the process of making organizational decisions and plans, the greater their sense of ownership and investment in the campaign. And to the extent that those campaigns achieve success, active participants will develop perceptions of increased self- and collective efficacy concerning specific organizing tasks (Pecukonis and Wenocur 1994) as well as a more generalized sense of "control over destiny" (Syme 2004), believing in their own ability to gain a greater measure of control over their life circumstances (see also appendix 10).

The evaluation of issue campaigns provides an excellent opportunity to develop greater political awareness, increased critical consciousness, and a more sophisticated analysis of how social systems work. For instance, and particularly in the aftermath of the Great Recession, a campaign to force a local bank to invest more home improvement and mortgage funds within the neighborhood naturally leads to an analysis of how banks operate and investment patterns work to the disadvantage of low-income people. Similarly, a campaign to clean up a hazardous waste site in a neighborhood of color logically moves to the subject of environmental racism, which in turn links to analysis and critique of the roles of both government and the private sector in perpetuating institutional racism.

The immediate campaign provides a specific context and experience within which these larger issues can be raised, especially through popular education

(Freire 1970, 1973; Su 2009; see chapters 4 and 14). Hopefully, this process will lead to new campaigns on the larger issues themselves, rather than simply intellectual dialogue. For instance, local campaigns by PICO (formerly the Pacific Institute for Community Organizing) to prevent foreclosures have linked to a national campaign to hold big banks more accountable for their policies and actions. Making changes in individual borrowers' loans has evolved into national efforts to eliminate predatory lending practices. Likewise, PICO's campaign Bring Health Reform Home has made the connection between policy change at the national level and concrete changes in local communities that help "break the cycle of poverty and create better life opportunities for lower-income families." As community members develop greater understanding of their local group's potential to bring about small but important changes in their lives, they become more committed to building a powerful organization capable of winning larger victories and achieving more systemic change. This has become a matter of greatly increased prominence in the aftermath of the Great Recession of 2008.

Credit

Will the group receive credit for a victory on the issue, improve its credibility, and increase its overall visibility? A community organization should be aggressive about taking credit where credit is due. First, an organization's ability to raise funds and secure additional resources may be linked to the credit it receives for its victories. Second, new members may be attracted by the organization's publicity and winning image. Third, the group may be able to establish greater respect and credibility as a result of receiving more credit.

An organization may receive *internal* credit within the community or *external* credit, typically secured through the press and electronic media. Most organizations are very conscious of the type of press and other media coverage they receive and go to some pains to secure it (see chapter 22). Unfortunately, it isn't always forthcoming. When it is not, the group still may receive proper credit "on the street" within its own community.

Sometimes the organization needs to help the process along at the local level. For example, imagine a community group that has successfully pressured city officials to improve trash collection in the neighborhood. The mayor orders the sanitation commissioner to correct the problems, only after being confronted by angry organization members. But the press fails to cover this action, and the news story erroneously credits the mayor for "taking bold, aggressive action to improve neighborhood conditions." Leaders and members could attempt to tell the real story through phone calls, via the group's newsletter, and by word of mouth. There also might be an effort to undertake media advocacy or, in this case, getting the media to reframe the story from the community's perspective (see chapter 22). Regardless, the group would be able to get some measure of credit within its own community. Since politicians often compete directly with grassroots organizations for credit on a number of issues, and since they often have greater ability to influence the media, variations on this scenario are unfortunately quite common.

A distinction also should be made between credit and credibility; the two frequently go together, but not necessarily. A group that has credibility will be taken seriously. In the example above, while the organization failed to receive external credit, it certainly increased its credibility with the mayor. Occasionally, things may work the other way. An organization may get credit for a victory when in fact it played a minor role. For instance, a piece of health legislation for which a GCO lobbied may have been passed by a legislative body simply as a bargaining chip in a power struggle played out between two state senators. The organization may claim and receive credit for its passage, but if the group plays this game too often—as it might be tempted to do—it may actually lose credibility among legislators who know the real story. There also is the added danger of leaders and members believing their own press when the stories aren't true. This can lead to overconfidence, confusion over the group's true source of power, and a drift away from collective action tactics.

Some leaders and members may be inclined to ask, "Who cares who gets the credit as long as we get a victory on our issue?" But to build organizational mileage, credit and visibility *are* important. Although success is difficult to predict, the best campaigns ideally have the potential for giving the organization increased visibility, credit, and credibility.

Resources

How will the campaign affect organizational resources? Obviously, the availability of organizational resources will affect the outcome of any issue campaign, as discussed above. But the reverse also is true. Campaigns, both successful and unsuccessful, often have a lasting impact on a group's resources. Clearly, internal and external visibility, credit, and credibility also have a direct bearing on fund-raising efforts. The organization that can attach to a funding proposal an impressive list of victories along with an array of good press web links and articles certainly improves its chances of receiving external funding. Private foundations or large individual contributors often have "favorite issues," such as health access, preventing youth violence, or environmental justice. While an organization should never "prostitute" itself by choosing issues simply to get funded, leaders and members should have a working knowledge of the fund-raising potential of their campaigns as they make decisions.

Of course, the effect of issue campaigns on external funding can cut both ways. For example, an organization that funds part of its staff through municipal training slots should be aware of the implications of taking on the mayor in a nasty fight. This is why grassroots community organizations should think long and hard before accepting any government funds. Similarly, a group funded by the United Way or an old-line conservative foundation shouldn't be surprised when a militant campaign for health care for the homeless leads to its funding being cut off. Organizations may choose to engage in those campaigns in spite of the risk. But the funding implications of campaigns should be considered and weighed carefully before any decisions are made. There may be sound organizational reasons for taking on a campaign that jeopardizes funding, but there's no excuse for not anticipating and preparing for the contingencies of such decisions beforehand.

Door-to-door and telephone canvassing for large numbers of small contributions falls somewhere between external and internal fund-raising. Many factors affect the canvassers' ability to raise money, including their enthusiasm, persistence, charm, and technical ability to deliver a good pitch. Nevertheless, organizational name recognition and issues that appeal to the donor's own self-interest are usually key ingredients for success. Issues appealing to the self-interest of the donor raise interesting questions, since contributions are often solicited from middle-class or upper-income people. Controversial campaigns organized around issues such as welfare rights, squatters' housing, or immigrant rights usually won't play as well in the suburbs as property tax reform or homeowners' insurance rates. Organizations need to be careful not to succumb to "mission drift" in an effort to appeal to potential donors whose self-interests aren't fully aligned with those of their core constituency.

Finally, internal fund-raising, through both membership dues and various grassroots events, can be affected by issue campaigns. Obviously, greater visibility, credit, and credibility will enhance a group's ability to raise funds in its own community. Certain issue campaigns generate more new members than others, and more people are ready to buy a raffle ticket, attend a fund-raising event, or make a donation when they care about the issues the organization is tackling. Internally divisive issues naturally will split an organization's grassroots funding base.

Beyond direct funding, other organizational resources will also be affected by any issue campaign. These range from supplies, such as computers, use of equipment, and technical expertise to—most important—the time of leaders, members, staff, and volunteers. Successful campaigns frequently attract future direct or in-kind donations of supplies and equipment, along with more volunteers. As organizer and advocate Hebert Chao Gunther likes to say, "More than anything else, Americans want to be on the winning side."

Just as leaders and members develop political and organizational skills through actual campaigns, staff members learn from direct experience. A good issue campaign should provide an opportunity to increase the knowledge and skills of new staff and challenge the abilities of veterans. Generally, success breeds success in organizing, with the best staffs developing in the most effective organizations. As with any other organizational resource, staff must be cultivated and nurtured carefully and used wisely.

After answering the question, Do we have the resources necessary to win? another question still remains: Is this the *best* use of our resources and what will be the *effect* on the rest of the organization? While the resources may exist to win on an issue, the organizational payoff may not be worth the sacrifices it entails. Choosing to work on a particular issue may mean not taking on several other issues, or becoming involved in an all-consuming effort that forces other issues and activities to be neglected. Thus, when examining potential issues, it isn't enough to simply analyze whether they're winnable; the overall impact on funding and other organizational resources should be considered as well.

Allies and Enemies

Will the campaign develop new allies or enemies? As an old labor union saying goes, "Make no permanent friends or enemies." These are wise words for both unions and GCOs, particularly when dealing with politicians. Allies and opponents frequently shift from issue to issue. Nevertheless, relationships may be established that have lasting effects, particularly between organizations. Issue campaigns provide a test under fire where feelings of either trust or distrust may be engendered. Organizations that work together formally in coalitions or more loosely as allies on an issue campaign have an opportunity to cooperate on specific actions, activities, and tasks. A relatively new and unknown grassroots group might derive concrete assistance, as well as a measure of needed legitimacy, from working with a large, established organization. Both positive and negative experiences are bound to have some carryover effect, setting the stage for future joint efforts. As Texas Industrial Areas Foundation lead organizer Ernesto Cortes Jr. (1993) pointed out, "Establishing and maintaining relationships with both adversaries and allies is a critical component of the capacity to survive the contradictions of politics. . . . If you cannot have a real conversation with your opponent, he or she will never become your ally" (5).

But sometimes an organization helps define itself and what it stands for through the ongoing opposition it tackles (Wallack et al. 1999; see chapter 22). This was well illustrated in the campaign organized against Hornell Brewing Company by United Indian Nations, the Circle of Strength/Healthy Nations Project, several local Native American health centers, and other local and national organizations concerned with the health of multicultural communities. The company had expropriated the name and image of a revered Native American spiritual leader, Crazy Horse, to sell forty-ounce malt liquor to young people, targeting inner-city communities. Denouncing the use of the Crazy Horse name as "insulting and degrading" to Native Americans, but unable to convince the brewing company to cease using this label, the groups formed the Campaign Against Cultural Exploitation, which organized a widely publicized boycott of both Crazy Horse malt liquor and the manufacturer's popular Arizona iced tea. As this example illustrates, community organizations establish much of their identity through the kinds of issues and targets they choose and the types of campaigns they wage. When community groups are making these decisions, it's important to look at the long-term organizational significance of the friends and enemies they choose.

Tactics

Will the campaign emphasize collective action, producing new strategies, tactics, or issues? The issues that produce the most organizational mileage will be those that provide the most opportunities for direct participation by large numbers of people. Campaigns that have a high level of community involvement enable organizational leaders and members to experience their own power through collective action. Some issues may offer possibilities for different types of engagement. In a classic example, ACORN (Association of Community Organizations for Reform Now), before its demise, waged a multistage, multilevel campaign against the predatory lending practices of Household Finance Realty Corporation in more than a dozen states. The overall plan to protect low-income neighborhoods from predatory loans included a wide variety of strategies and tactics, including massive outreach and membership recruitment, action research, creative direct action tactics, a corporate strategy, litigation, legislation, a regulatory strategy, legislation, and sophisticated and skillful media relations work. Ultimately, pressure on multiple state regulators and attorneys general secured a settlement from the company distributing $484 million to individual borrowers (an average of $2,000 per individual borrower), plus another $120 million allocated to a foreclosure prevention fund for Household borrowers. Thousands of borrowers were able to keep their homes, and a giant corporation was required to make changes that saved consumers hundreds of millions of dollars going forward. The campaign contributed to the drive for new legislation against predatory lending around the country and helped move state regulators to take unprecedented concerted action in this area.

In addition to producing new strategies or tactics, a good issue also may create opportunities for additional, related campaigns. Sometimes a logical progression can also be seen ahead of time. For instance, the primary value of a particular effort to establish a landlord-tenant commission is that it sets up future opportunities for direct action, establishing a new arena in which to resolve grievances against targeted landlords. In another case, a campaign may set the stage for escalation. For example, an attempt to ensure that patients with psychiatric disabilities in state hospitals have the right to shower in privacy may, in turn, progress to a larger campaign for a patients' bill of rights. In other words, success on one issue can lay the groundwork for future efforts. The potential for either spinning off or escalating campaigns can be an important factor in predicting how much organizational mileage any one issue might create.

Victory

Will the campaign produce a significant victory? There may be times when community groups are forced to take on an issue and "fight the good fight" even when prospects for success are dim. But organizations need victories in order to grow and flourish. The next section will focus on how to develop a winning strategy. Of course, in the vast majority of cases, issues shouldn't be chosen unless there's a real possibility for success, particularly when the group is newly formed.

What constitutes a "significant" victory? While external credit and credibility are important, the organization's members must decide whether a particular victory will make a substantial difference in their lives. Is the issue important and can it be resolved successfully? For example, can a community garden be established, a stop sign erected at a dangerous intersection, a closed neighborhood health center reopened, one hundred units of affordable housing built, community benefit guidelines instituted for all hospitals in the state? At another level, will the organization be strengthened in the process, increasing its power and the members' capacity to gain a greater measure of control over their lives in the future?

When considering questions of organizational mileage, it is important to make a further distinction between types of issues—*recruitment* and *maintenance*. Recruitment issues lend themselves to systematic outreach efforts that can attract large numbers of new participants and members. Examples are any issues that great numbers of people care about deeply, such as the high cost of prescription drugs for the elderly, the closing of a neighborhood school, summer jobs for youth, a large increase in utility bills, or the discovery of a hazardous waste dump near a low-income residential area. These issues can help build the organization by providing a steady influx of new activists and leaders.

Maintenance issues do little to build the organization numerically, but can provide mileage in other ways. These are issues that don't have a strong self-interest draw for many people, but still concern the organization's leadership and core group of activists. They often present opportunities to develop better social policy. Frequently, they take positions on a specific piece of legislation, such as an act increasing the interest penalty on overdue property taxes or a city ordinance to open housing authority meetings to the public. Maintenance issues can provide mileage by producing victories, establishing new allies, generating additional resources, developing enhanced political skills, and increasing visibility and credibility.

Organizational mileage is gained when maintenance campaigns are politicized and unite different neighborhoods. For example, vacant lots are a traditional neighborhood concern, and collective action to clean them up is a common focus for many groups. But these local efforts will produce more organizational mileage if neighborhood groups combine to advocate a city ordinance that charges landlords the cost of cleanups and places liens on their property for unpaid bills. Winning the ordinance creates new campaign opportunities by targeting individual landowners and demanding city enforcement. However, serious problems can arise when organizations stop recruiting and concentrate too heavily on maintenance issues that involve a only small core of activists.

Winning victories, empowering people, and bringing about change are what organizing is all about. Without good strategic thinking, none of this is possible.

Before organizers and community groups make an action plan, a preliminary phase of strategy development is critical. A central component of this strategic development consists of cutting and framing the Issue.

Cutting and Framing the Issue

To develop the basic outlines of an issue campaign, it is useful to ask, *who* wants to get what from whom and how will this be brought about? (Katz 1980). Answers to this four-part question help us identify the action group that seeks change, what goals and objectives they are pursuing, the target system whom they intend to activate or influence, and how they will employ handles to achieve their ends. The issue is *cut* and *framed* when these questions are answered. Additional factors to consider follow.

Action Group

The people *who* participate in an issue campaign will feel that it is in their own self-interest. Obviously, issues appeal differently to different constituencies. For instance, anti-tobacco organizing has been an issue of deep concern to many middle-class activists. But in a low-income neighborhood where issues of basic survival confront people daily, tobacco may have little immediacy compared with illicit drugs, AIDS, inadequate housing, unemployment, and violent crime. However, if the issue is cut properly, it may well attract both constituencies. For example, in some low-income neighborhoods, people of color, recognizing their self-interest in opposing the heavy targeting of their communities by tobacco advertisers, have mobilized around this issue (Ellis et al. 1995). Even in a low-income neighborhood with severe housing problems, an organizer might have little success recruiting people to a "housing" meeting, because of the problem's appearing to be too broad. Specific issues must be cut to appeal to particular constituencies: rent control to appeal to tenants, low-interest home improvement loans to homeowners, or a lead paint program to renters with young children.

The depth of an issue's appeal is partly a function of the emotional response it triggers. Frequently, defensive issues (e.g., "stop the cutbacks," "stop the highway") seem to arouse more passion than efforts to win a positive reform or program. Often, positive efforts are actually framed in negative terms. Thus a campaign to bring in more city services adopts the slogan "Save the Neighborhood," whereas a traffic light campaign is conducted under the banner "Stop Endangering our Kids." Like the proverbial straw that breaks the camel's back, such issues may be able to activate people who have never participated before. Often these are NIMBY (not in my back yard) issues that provoke a strong emotional response from community members who perceive that their interests are being threatened. Not surprisingly, spontaneous organizing efforts and single-issue mobilizations, or SIMs (Delgado 1997), have frequently grown out of defensive situations.

Of course, many campaigns to bring about positive change also generate plenty of emotion. Issues such as HIV/AIDS, a living wage, abortion, affordable housing, and immigrants' rights have moved into action many thousands of people on both the left and the right over the past few years. Furthermore, any group that seeks to empower people must move beyond defensive responses that simply "tame" the behavior of institutional decision makers, to proactive campaigns that transform power relationships (Miller 2009). But it is critical to frame these positive efforts in a manner that generates sufficient passion to motivate lots of people. Typically, the action group will combine both current and potential members recruited around the new issue, and successful resolution will be correlated with the number of people actively involved.

Goals and Objectives

Goals are broad statements about *what* people want done to solve a problem or to make a change, such as an end to human rights violations in psychiatric hospitals, removal of lead paint or asbestos from a local school, prevention of threatened cutbacks in medical care access for low-income people, or establishment of smoke-free workplaces. *Objectives* are specific outcomes that contribute to the achievement of goals and are time sensitive, such as adoption of a new mental health department policy on the use of forced restraints and seclusion in state psychiatric hospitals by Memorial Day; creation of parent site councils in all schools by the following academic year; passage of a graduated state income tax in the upcoming legislative session; traffic lights at five dangerous intersections within two months; or access to health care, education, and driver's licenses for immigrants within one year. The overall goals of an issue campaign should be clear and compelling and community members need to strongly support them. *Cutting* and *framing* the issue necessitates determining *what* specific objectives will move the group toward its ultimate goal. Objectives must be concrete and realistic.

Possible solutions to the problem at hand should be tested with a number of people as part of the issue-cutting and -framing process. It's important to start by finding out which options community members really want. This should be a true bottom-up process, not merely a ratification of the goals and objectives of leaders, organizers, planners, politicians, or various interested parties. Testing different alternatives helps people develop ownership of both the issue and the strategy to resolve it. This investment is essential for the campaign to be truly broad based and participatory. Community members will be motivated to invest time and energy only if they feel passionate about the issue's goals and objectives.

Once there's a general sense of the preferable solutions, the group must determine how realistic the various possibilities are. This is an area where *action research* plays a key role. Good research is essential in order to predict the potential for accomplishing particular objectives. As much as possible, the group's leaders should be involved in the research process. New information learned should be shared with the full action group. For example, as soon as it's discovered that the housing authority is sitting on an unspent sum of money provided by the Department of Housing and Urban Development to "solve the trash problems," public housing tenants who are unhappy with the dumpsters provided for trash collection should be informed. Similarly, where drastic cuts in federal funding or local tax revenues make a proposed solution totally unrealistic, there should be a discussion of these obstacles, rather than an avoidance of the subject. Formulating objectives is a dynamic process that continues to evolve as more information is gathered and various viable options are presented.

The specifics will continue to be shaped and refined as more factors are weighed and analyzed. At this point in time, as the issue first is cut and framed, it is sufficient to draw the broad outline of what is wanted. Again, it should be emphasized that *what* the objectives will be is a function of *who* the action group is, the target system *whom* they intend to activate or influence, and *how* they can use *handles* to achieve their ends.

Target System

To pursue its objectives, the action group attempts to influence a *target system*, which may be internal (e.g., motivating community members to participate) or external (e.g., pressuring institutional decision makers to do what they otherwise would not). There are a number of factors to consider when determining whom to target. The first is identifying someone who has the power to make concrete, specific decisions on the action group's objectives. It is impossible to fight a whole bureaucracy; individuals who can make the necessary decisions should be singled out as targets and not be allowed off the hook. It is critical that the right target be chosen in the first place. Understanding the target's self-interest helps the action group assess the degree of leverage that it can bring to bear. The group will have the ability to influence the target to the extent that it can have an effect on positive or negative self-interests, such as votes, customers, public image, career advancement, or retaining positions.

When choosing to target an institution, solid research is critical. It is important to understand the decision-making process thoroughly, and then to fix responsibility accurately with one or more key individuals who can meet the organization's requests/demands and who also will be accessible to pressure from the action group, such as the governor, a corporate CEO, the mayor, a commissioner, the city council, a hospital administrator, or the school committee. In doing so it is essential to ascertain the "chain of command" and also to distinguish between formal and informal decision-making processes, remembering that those who wield the most power may not always occupy the most visible positions. The action group may have to move first on those who are officially responsible to "smoke out" the powers-that-be. In other instances, the best strategy is to move directly on the hidden powers. In addition, the group may call for strict adherence to orthodox decision-making procedures, or it may push for creative changes in established practices.

There is nothing like a villain to energize a campaign. For instance, M-POWER (Massachusetts People/Patients Organized for Wellness, Empowerment and Rights) targeted the director of a large psychiatric hospital where patients were receiving poor care and where three deaths had occurred in one year. On Valentine's Day, the director was confronted by a large demonstration, during which M-POWER members passed out empty heart-shaped boxes that had contained chocolates, now containing cards asking him to "have a heart" and treat patients with dignity and proper care. Under continued pressure from this action group, the director soon resigned, and a new director took office and promised reform.

Sometimes a community organization has limited direct leverage vis-á-vis a particular target. In such instances, *indirect secondary targets* may be used. For example, a health care coalition might target a teaching hospital to pressure it to institute preventive programs for infant mortality, childhood obesity, adolescent smoking, and diabetes in the low-income neighborhood where it's located. If the hospital CEO were unresponsive to the action group, the group might target individual members of the facility's board. The members might be more vulnerable to negative publicity than the CEO might be, and they might even support the coalition's goals and objectives. Or they may remain neutral on the matter, especially if the publicity is bad for their business and individual reputations. While the CEO might not be responsive to the direct action of the community coalition, he or she most likely would pay attention to pressure from influential board members. Indirect secondary targets should be chosen for two criteria: (1) ability to influence the primary target and (2) vulnerability to pressure from the action group.

Handles

Just as you need a handle to open a door, you need a handle to grab hold of an organizing issue. *Handles* are points of leverage that an action group can use to influence or activate a target system. Handles could be *situations* that make a target more vulnerable to pressure from community members (e.g., upcoming elections, scandals, conflicts of interest, hazardous waste spills or other crises), *precedents* that set the stage for similar demands, *regulatory processes* that can be used to gain new information or to mobilize large numbers of people to attend public hearings and testify, or *incidents* such as a tragic traffic accident at a dangerous intersection where community residents have been trying to get a traffic light installed unsuccessfully. Handles provide a means for *how* change efforts move from the realm of hope to real accomplishments; they enable proponents of change to *overcome resistance or inertia*. The leverage of handles gets target systems moving in the right direction, making decisions and taking action in ways that are consistent with the action group's goals and objectives for social change. Handles can be either positive incentives (carrots) or negative sanctions (sticks).

All things being equal, carrots are preferable to sticks, since positive incentives make it more likely that the affected target system will really internalize changes with positive payoffs. Community development projects frequently use a wide variety of positive *internal* incentives to encourage people to get involved in a change effort. For instance, inducements such as food, music, awards, certificates of participation, tickets to an amusement park, or prizes might be handles to encourage youth to participate in a neighborhood cleanup. A community clinic might hold a health fair with similar attractions, as well as face painting for kids, a radio personality, and local entertainment.

Positive incentives also might be used to help frame issues in "win-win" terms for *external* target systems. Judy Meredith's "hero opportunity" concept is relevant here (Meredith and Dunham 2004). The idea is that individual decision makers can look good and gain a measure of credit by agreeing to help an action group meet its incentives. Thus, an elected official—especially one facing a strong challenger in an upcoming election—might act to meet a community group's request to open a new youth center or to sponsor an inclusionary zoning ordinance. While this phenomenon is inconsistent with the discussion above regarding the importance of community groups receiving credit for their accomplishments, there are times when the trade-off for support and ultimate success is worth the sacrifice.

Unfortunately, all things *aren't* equal, which is often why a grassroots community organization is formed in the first place. Under such circumstances, stronger forms of collective action are necessary, and handles are used to pressure targets to act in a particular manner or to modify or stop certain activities. Handles also can provide a reason for *why* the action group's position is justifiable, such as a broken promise, an existing law that hasn't been enforced, or a contradiction. Thus, the concept entails both a *tool* that an action group can use to maximize its power on an issue as well as a *rationale* that underscores the legitimacy of the campaign when the issue is framed.

For instance, a study or report releasing new information can place target systems on the defensive. The data could be produced by a third party or by the organization's own research. On January 22, 2004, ACORN released *Speaking the Language of Care: Language Barriers to Hospital Access in America's Cities*, a study documenting how non-English speakers were struggling to be understood at hospitals around the country. The research was gathered by Spanish-speaking ACORN members in seven states and Washington, D.C. Eighty-five hospitals were contacted to determine whether Spanish-speaking staff was available as required by federal law (this is also a handle). In 56 percent of cases, no Spanish-speaking staff could be found. The health care implications were obvious, and ACORN immediately began demanding meetings with hospital CEOs to ensure that adequate plans for translation services were put in place across the United States.

Bureaucratic regulations often allow great latitude in interpretation. At times, a strict interpretation may serve organizational interests, while frequently a broad definition may be more advantageous for the action group. Louis Lowy, a mentor and former colleague, often pointed out that bureaucrats operate in three arenas: what they *must* do to fulfill the basic requirements of their positions, what they *must not* do to exceed their authority, and what they *may* do at their discretion. Handles can be found in all three areas.

For example, since housing inspectors *must* enforce the state sanitary code, a tenants' group can use this handle to hold their feet to the fire, making sure that absentee slumlords are held properly accountable. Police officers, teachers, immigration officials, and public housing personnel *must not* abuse the very real power that they hold and, if they do so, a community group must be ready and able to use accountability handles to "tame" this misuse. Discretionary judgments made by those in authority can have profound impacts on whether community members get access to health care, housing, education, safety, social services, benefits, employment or training. The fact that these individuals *may* act in way that is consistent with the objectives of an action group provides a handle of possibility.

Similar to broken promises, *contradictions* present a clear case of a disconnection or gap between rhetoric and reality. When an action group frames its issues to publicize such gaps, it can usually operate from a stance of "moral superiority," enabling it to place the target in a defensive, if not indefensible, position. Generally, the media is quick to pick up on stories depicting contradictory behavior, strengthening the group's leverage in the process.

The Ride Advocacy Project (RAP) offers a good example. Boston Self Help, a disability rights group, initiated this campaign to improve conditions for users of the Ride, a special program by the Massachusetts Bay Area Transportation Authority (MBTA). The premise behind this service is both progressive and sensitive to the needs of disabled people. Special vans give door-to-door transportation to medical appointments, classes, and work for disabled and elderly people, who are unable to negotiate the physical rigors of riding MBTA buses and subway cars.

But there was a contradiction between the Ride's official description and its actual operations. A number of profit-making companies were contracted to provide the transportation. Regular users complained bitterly about calling to request service and being left to wait for several hours or never being picked up at all. Users also frequently encountered rude drivers, dirty vans, and long waits for return rides back home. This contradictory situation rallied a determined action group to pressure the MBTA to make the Ride live up to the service standards described in the MBTA's public relations materials.

In contrast to incidents, *events* (as defined here) are usually scheduled and fairly predictable. Using them allows for more forethought and planning. Events provide handles and excellent opportunities for direct action because they occur at a fixed time and place where an organization can go to frame an issue and gain access to and confront a target. Typical examples are a corporation's annual stockholder's meeting, a speech or visit by a public official, the dedication of a new building, a special public hearing, or a political fund-raising dinner. Such events frequently offer very good opportunities for media coverage.

In 2000, presidential candidates George W. Bush and Al Gore held three face-to-face debates. Health care costs had been a disputed topic during the campaign, and on the day of the Boston debate, Massachusetts Senior Action Council (MSAC) held a rally with more than six hundred people at the Pfizer drug company. The action was designed to draw attention to the obscene profits of the pharmaceutical industry and to push for a new national Medicare program for seniors and disabled people. Predictably, the rally was coupled with the debate as the lead story on the evening news, and both candidates were asked to address the high drug costs experienced by seniors. The debate served as a handle for MSAC to generate momentum for its campaign for health care reform.

I would submit that handles are the single most important variable in cutting and framing an issue. The examples offered above are illustrative rather than exhaustive. Handles are usually present in some form, although they may not be readily apparent. It is very often not a question of *whether* they exist, but rather *where* and *when* they can be found.

These four elements—action group, goals and objectives, target system, and handles—are interrelated, and should not be considered separately or sequentially. They define the basic outline of a potential issue and, when established, can be used to cut and frame the issue.

Issue Selection and Strategic Analysis: A Final Note

This chapter has focused on the criteria that community organizations should consider when selecting new issues. It also has examined the elements that constitute the process of cutting the issue—a vital part of strategic development. While a full discussion of strategic analysis is beyond the scope of this chapter (see Staples 2004), a few key points follow.

First, a SWOT analysis (Barry 1997) in which one lays out the internal strengths and weaknesses of the action group and the opportunities and threats in the external environment, provides an excellent tool for initial analysis. This approach enables proponents of a social change to make a rigorous assessment of the positive and negative factors that will directly affect chances for success (see appendix 7).

Second, a force field analysis (Lewin 1947; see appendix 7) is a valuable tool for assessing the level of agreement that exists between an action group and a target system, and the helping and hindering forces that will affect the change effort. Conducting a force field analysis helps inform the selection of appropriate strategies. Roland Warren's (1975) strategic guidelines for this purpose have stood the test of time. In these, he contended that three major types of change strategies should be used, depending upon the level of agreement between change proponents and target systems. *Collaborative strategies* are effective when there is broad agreement among all parties on the goals of the change effort. *Campaign strategies* can be used when there are differences among the parties that may be resolved through persuasion. Adversarial *contest strategies* should be employed when there are significant differences among the parties and little hope of achieving consensus through persuasive arguments.

Third, while the mechanics of a strategic analysis are quite simple, the depth of the analysis is what really counts. Assumptions should not be made quickly or superficially, and nothing should be taken for granted. Most important, the various factors should be viewed dynamically rather than statically. Action and change are the goals, and not just analysis of the status quo for the sake of analysis. Too often, when done by academicians, such studies lead to explanations and rationalizations for why no change is possible. Organizers and leaders must avoid such "analysis paralysis" and concentrate on how action can alter the various forces to achieve victory.

Finally, several other key factors should be part of any strategic analysis. These include *opposition, objective conditions, organizational capacity*, and *support*. An analysis of these four factors should answer several basic questions: Who is against you? What is beyond your control that affects chances for success (both positively and negatively)? What is your action group capable of doing? What is the possibility for assistance from allies or from joining a coalition? Whether it is done formally through a strategic analysis or more informally, analysis of these factors, in conjunction with the process of cutting the issue, should give a reasonably accurate picture of the level of organizational action and clout necessary to achieve success.

In sum, an organization must weigh multiple factors and consider many variables when choosing and cutting issues, in addition to developing effective strategies. But the group should be careful not to analyze and strategize to the point where no actual campaign can materialize. It is impossible to plan for or imagine every single possibility. There is a time to act!

ACKNOWLEDGMENTS

Adapted from "Analyze, Strategize, and Catalyze: Issues and Strategies," in *Roots to Power: A Manual of Grassroots Organizing*, by Lee Staples, 2nd ed. (Westport, Conn.: Praeger, 2004), 99–137. Copyright © 2004 by Praeger Publishers. Reproduced with permission of the publisher.

REFERENCES

Alinsky, S. D. 1972. *Rules for Radicals: A Practical Primer for Realistic Radicals.* New York: Random House.

Barry, B. W. 1997. *Strategic Planning Workbook for Nonprofit Organizations.* St. Paul, Minn.: Amherst H. Wilder Foundation.

Bobo, K., J. Kendall, and S. Max. 2010. *Organizing for Social Change.* 5th ed. Santa Ana, Calif.: Seven Locks Press.

Bongiovani, R. (2010). *Organizing for Environmental Justice in Chelsea.* Boston: Boston School of Social Work.

Brown, C. R., and G. J. Mazza. 2005. *Leading Diverse Communities.* San Francisco: Jossey-Bass.

Chavez, M. 1990. "Empowerment in Practice." *Networking Bulletin: Empowerment and Family Support* 1, no. 3:25.

Cortes, E., Jr. 1993. "No Permanent Friends, No Permanent Enemies." *Shelterforce*, January–February, 3.

Delgado, G. (1997). *Beyond the Politics of Place*. Oakland, Calif.: Applied Research Center.

Dewey, J. 1946. *The Public and Its Problems: An Essay in Political Inquiry*. Chicago: Gateway Books.

Ellis, G., D. F. Reed, and H. Scheider. 1995. "Mobilizing a Low-Income African-American Community around Tobacco Control: A Force Field Analysis." *Health Education Quarterly* 22, no. 4:443–457.

Freire, P. 1970. *Pedagogy of the Oppressed*. Translated by M. B. Ramos. New York: Seabury Press.

———. 1973. *Education for Critical Consciousness*. New York: Seabury Press.

Haggstrom, W. C. 1971. "The Theory of Social Work Method." Unpublished paper.

Katz, J. 1980. *Action Research*. Washington, D.C.: Institute for Social Justice.

Lewin, K. 1947. "Quasi-Stationary Social Equilibria and the Problem of Social Change." In *Readings in Social Psychology*, edited by T. M. Newcomb and E. L. Hartley, 340–44. New York: Holt, Rinehart and Winston.

Meredith, J. C., and C. Dunham. 2004. "Real Clout: Rules and Tools." In *Roots to Power*, by L. Staples, 234–253. 2nd ed. New York: Praeger.

Miller, M. 2009. *A Community Organizer's Tale: People and Power in San Francisco*. Berkeley, Calif.: Heyday Books.

Pecukonis, E. V., and S. Wenocur. 1994. "Perceptions of Self and Collective Efficacy in Community Organization Theory and Practice." *Journal of Community Practice* 1, no. 2:5–21.

Sen, R. 2003. *Stir It Up: Lessons in Community Organizing and Advocacy*. San Francisco: Jossey-Bass.

Staples, L. 2004. *Roots to Power*. 2nd ed. New York: Praeger.

Su, C. 2009. *Streetwise for Book Smarts: Grassroots Organizing and Education Reform in the Bronx*. Ithaca, N.Y.: Cornell University Press.

Syme, S. L. 2004. "Social Determinants of Health: The Community as an Empowered Partner." *Preventing Chronic Disease* 1, no. 1:1–8.

Wallack, L., K. Woodruff, L. Dorfman, and I. Diaz. 1999. *News for a Change: An Advocate's Guide to Working with the Media*. Thousand Oaks: Sage.

Warren, R. 1975. "Types of Purposive Social Change at the Community Level." In *Readings in Community Organization Practice*, edited by R. M. Kramer and H. S. Specht. 2nd ed., 134–149. Englewood Cliffs, N.J.: Prentice-Hall.

Wolff, T. 2010. *The Power of Collaborative Solutions: Six Principles and Effective Tools for Building Healthy Communities*. San Francisco: Jossey-Bass.

PART FIVE

Community Organizing and Community Building within and across Diverse Groups and Cultures

The past quarter century has witnessed a growing appreciation of the community organizing and community building efforts that are taking place among and with women; people of color; people with disabilities; lesbian, gay, bisexual and transgender people; and other diverse groups. For the most part, however, this wealth of experience has not been well represented in the literature. Furthermore, what literature does exist has suggested that traditional models of community organizing are often ill suited to work with marginalized groups, whose reality tends to differ markedly from that of the architects of many of these models (Gutiérrez et al., in press).

This part begins in chapter 12 with Lorraine Gutiérrez and Edith Lewis's thoughtful approach to organizing with women of color, which stresses the utility of feminist perspectives for developing a culture- and gender-relevant model of practice. The special accent placed on both the theory development and the lived experience of women of color in Gutiérrez and Lewis's model have led to its becoming a classic in the field, and this updated presentation of their work underscores its continued relevance.

Using as a framework interrelated principles of education, participation, and capacity building, the authors draw on the literature, and on a wealth of personal experience in social work, to develop an approach that acknowledges and confronts the combined effects of racism, classism, and sexism. Building in part on the early work of Felix Rivera and John Erlich (1995), Gutiérrez and Lewis's model sees varying roles for organizers, depending, in part, on their degree of oneness and identification with the community in question. Regardless of the role played, however, Gutiérrez and Lewis argue that a number of precepts are critical to effective organizing with women of color, among them learning actively, recognizing and embracing the conflict inherent in cross-cultural work, involving women of color early on in leadership roles, and in other ways contributing to community capacity.

The roles of history and culture in community practice with people of color is then developed by Laura Linnan and her colleagues in chapter 13, where they present an in-depth look at the historical and present-day significance of barbershops and beauty salons as cultural sites of meaning, community education, and organizing that extend well beyond their surface roles. When professor and social commentator Melissa Harris-Perry (2011) recently joked that she left Princeton for Tulane University so that she could get her hair done, she was speaking to much deeper issues than personal grooming. In that same vein, the comfort of entering an African-owned and -run beauty salon or barbershop in the life of black women and men has not been lost on health educators, who have recognized the critical role these venues could play in helping provide health education and further sense of community critical to the reduction of health disparities. From Project BEAUTY in central North Carolina to the HAIR project targeting the high rates of prostate cancer among African American men in Pittsburgh, we see in chapter 13 the application of community building and health education principles to two unique and successful efforts to address health disparities by "starting where the people are" and developing educational messages in and with community members in "places of strength, safety, rich cultural heritage, and social connections." In these case studies, shop owners and workers are key to efforts at reducing health disparities, serving as, for example, lay health advocates, while other forms of community engagement (e.g., through the BEAUTY project's use of an active community advisory board) also contributed to these highly effective interventions. Although not offering a traditional community organizing example, this chapter is included because for many professionals in fields like health education and social work, learning to call upon and use some of the lessons of more traditional community building and organizing can also help us engage a community around issues, such as prostate cancer screening and improving diet and fitness, critical to building healthier communities and reducing health disparities.

In the final chapter in this part, Charlotte Chang and her colleagues illustrate the potent combination of popular education, community organizing, and participatory research in work with an immigrant population–low-wage restaurant workers in San Francisco's Chinatown–to build individual and community capacity while studying and addressing some of the major problems facing this community. Like the preceding chapter, this one involves multiple partners–in this case, a community-based organization in the heart of Chinatown, the local health department, two major universities, and immigrant workers themselves. The chapter also shows the goodness-of-fit between community organizing and community-based participatory research (CBPR), as well as the grounding of such work in a "popular education" approach based in the lived experience of community members themselves and accenting individual and community empowerment and action based on critical reflection (Freire 1973, 1994; Su 2009; see chapter 4). Finally, the chapter illustrates the utility of an ecological and multimethod approach stressing worker training in organizing and research, data collection on multiple levels, and participatory evaluation as an approach to both collectively studying the project's processes and outcomes and helping improve its processes and dynamics along the way. But it also illustrates the commitment of popular education, CBPR, and community organizing to action for social change, in this case, using study findings to work for changes in programs, practices, and policies that could improve working conditions in this community and nationally, through a low-wage-worker bill of rights.

Chang and her colleagues talk openly about the challenges this work entailed, from conflicting community-academic time lines and power differentials to the labor-intensive nature of the work (see also Wing et al. 2008). But they stress above all the power of this approach as a force for change, grounded in the experience of workers and their growing ability to articulate their concerns in the corridors of power, as well as in strong and collaborative data collection for developing the evidence base that is increasingly important in using community organizing to best advantage as a force for change.

REFERENCES

Freire, P. 1973. *Education for Critical Consciousness.* New York: Seabury Press.
——. 1994. *Pedagogy of Hope.* New York: Continuum.

Gutiérrez, L., A. Dessel, E. Lewis, and M. Spencer. In press. "Promoting Multicultural Communication and Collaboration: Dialogue, Mediation, Consensus Building, and Intergroup Empowerment." In *Handbook of Community Practice*, edited by Marie O. Weil. 2nd ed. New York: Sage.

Harris-Perry, M. 2011. *Sister Citizen: Shame, Stereotypes, and the Black Woman in America*. New Haven, Conn.: Yale University Press.

Rivera, F., and J. Erlich, eds. 1995. *Community Organizing in a Diverse Society*. 2nd ed. Boston: Allyn and Bacon.

Su, C. 2009. *Streetwise for Book Smarts: Grassroots Organizing and Education Reform in the Bronx*. Ithaca, N.Y.: Cornell University Press.

Wing, S., R. A. Horton, N. Muhammad, G. R. Grant, M. Tajik, and K. Thu. 2008. "Integrating Epidemiology, Education, and Organizing for Environmental Justice: Community Health Effects of Industrial Hog Operations." *American Journal of Public Health* 98, no. 8:1390–1397.

12

Education, Participation, and Capacity Building in Community Organizing with Women of Color

LORRAINE M. GUTIÉRREZ

EDITH A. LEWIS

The field of community organizing has only recently begun to address the need for an approach to practice that respects and builds on the special challenges posed by our increasingly diverse society. Although much community organizing has taken place among women and communities of color, for example, surprisingly little attention has been paid to the ways in which race, gender, ethnicity, or social class will affect the organizing effort. This oversight has often prevented organizers from working effectively with women or communities of color (Few et al. 2003; Gutiérrez et al., in press, 2005; McGoldrick and Hardy 2008). By failing to recognize and take into account the many ways in which issues of oppression affect organizing work, organizers can perpetuate the objectification and exploitation of these groups (Abu-Lughod 2002). Organizers whose own racial or ethnic stereotypes distort their view of communities of color, for example, will be ineffective in building leadership or working in partnership (Abram et al. 2005; Few 2007; R. G. Jones 2010; Guadelupe and Lum 2005). In this way, community organizing efforts can perpetuate the very problems they were designed to solve.

This chapter begins by examining several recent contributions to our thinking about organizing with women of color, with special attention to the contributions of feminist perspectives on organizing. An empowerment framework stressing education, participation, and capacity building is then developed and used to explore different dimensions of effective community organizing with women of color. Examples of organizing both within and across racial/ethical groups are provided to illustrate many of the points made and offer lessons for social change professionals in their roles as organizers.

Multicultural Perspectives on Community Organizing

Much of the literature that does exist on multicultural organizing emphasizes the ways in which organizers can develop cultural competence for working in partnership with communities. In particular, this literature has stressed the ways in which organizers can use their own self-awareness to build bridges for work within communities. Organizers are encouraged to take the role of the learner in approaching a community and discovering its problems and strengths (Chávez et al. 2010; Guadelupe and Lum 2005; Gutiérrez et al. 2005).

Several scholars, most notably Felix Rivera and John Erlich (1998), have made critical contributions to organizing with communities of color by positing that the appropriate roles for the organizer are best determined by his or her relationship to the community (Midgley 2007; Prigoff 2000; Spencer et al. 2000; Yoshihama and Carr 2003). If the organizer is a member of the community, analysts argue, then the most intimate or primary contact is appropriate. Primary contact would involve immediate and personal grassroots work with the community. In contrast, an organizer who is of a similar ethnic or racial background but not of the community should instead be involved on the secondary level. This level would involve participation as a liaison between the community and the larger society (Dolphyne et al. 2001). The tertiary level of contact would be most appropriate for those who are not members of the group. They can provide valuable contributions to the community through consultation and the sharing of technical knowledge. For example, outside professionals interested in participating in community work with a local African American neighborhood could first establish relationships with key individuals in the community. The professional as organizer's responsibilities would be those defined by the community, no matter how insignificant these might seem on the surface. Efforts to learn the strengths of the community as they are exemplified in daily learning activities within the community would be a primary activity for the organizer. In this way, the organizer's willingness to use the ethno-conscious perspective of "noninterference" would be recognized in time by residents, and more opportunities for work with that community might be revealed (Barrios and Egan 2002; Lewis 2009).

Bradshaw and colleagues (1994) proposed that a "hybrid model" of organizing that integrates aspects of the Saul Alinsky (1972) approach to social action organizing with relevant perspectives from feminist organizing be used with communities of color. Flexibility, leadership identification and training, the appropriate use of both collaborative and confrontational tactics, and the role of the organizer as a learner and facilitator are among the characteristics of this hybrid model (Stall and Stoecker 2008. Of particular importance in this model are skills for developing cultural competence, which enables the outside organizer to better understand, respect, and learn from the community (Hyde 2004, 2008; P. Jones 2007). These skills involve (1) cultivating awareness of one's own understanding of the community, (2) finding ways to learn more about the local community through key informants, (3) working as partners to develop local leadership, and (4) focusing on ways to build cohesiveness within and between ethnic communities. As is by now clear, the most critical role of the organizer indeed is that of a learner who approaches the community to understand and facilitate change (Lewis and Gutiérrez 2003).

Contributions from Feminism

Much of the conceptual and practice-based literature on organizing with women has been written from a Western feminist perspective (Few et al. 2003; Hyde 2008; Lewis 2009). Feminist approaches can contribute to organizing with women of color through their emphasis on integrating personal and political issues through dialogue. Feminist organizing assumes that sexism is a significant force in the experiences of all women and one that lies at the root of many of the problems they face (Segal and Martinez 2008). Therefore, a major focus for organizing with women of color is to identify ways in which sexism, racism, and other forms of oppression are affecting their lives (Reed et al. 2010). Common methods for feminist organizing include the development of consciousness-raising groups, engagement in reflexive practice, creation of alternative services, and use of social action that incorporates street theater and other holistic methods (Lewis and Gutiérrez 2003; Hyde 2008; R. G. Jones 2010).

An important focus of feminist approaches is reflected in their concern with developing ways to work across differences. All women are thought to be a part of a "community" of women, as well as members of their own specific communities. Therefore, organizers need to work to bridge differences between women based on such factors as race, class, physical ability, and sexual orientation on the principle that diversity is strength (Wilson et al. 2010). The goal for feminist organizing has been most effective when carried out from a multicultural perspective (Lewis et al. 2001; Stall and Stoecker 2008).

Organizing with Women of Color

Very little literature has looked specifically at methods for organizing women of color. Yet as we have discussed in the majority of our collaborative writing, organizing by women within ethnic communities in the United States has a rich and diverse history. For example, the organization of black women's clubs in the United States a century ago by leaders such as Ida B. Wells Barnett was instrumental in developing nursing homes, day care centers, and orphanages within African American communities. These clubs also organized for social change, particularly on anti-lynching and anti-rape campaigns and in the foundation of organizations such as the National Urban League (Collins 2000; Taylor 2005; Stall and Stoecker 2008).

Women of color have always worked to improve conditions within their communities and in society in general and have been more likely than European-American middle-class women to see community activism as a natural outgrowth of their gender role (Lewis 2009; Rosado and Barreto 2002). During the mid- to late twentieth century, for example, women played important roles in the movement for equality and civil rights within ethnic minority communities (Lewis et al. 2001; Gutiérrez and Lewis 1999). Neighborhood violence, economic issues, and environmental concerns are but a few of the areas on which women of color in urban communities have organized (Taylor 2005; Rosado and Barreto 2002; Segal and Martinez 2007).

Effective community organizing efforts build upon these traditions. By looking at these historical and contemporary efforts, we can identify ways to draw upon their strengths and learn from and adapt the strategies that already exist. As noted earlier, the role of the organizer can and should vary according to her relationship to the community or the issue being addressed (Rivera and Erlich 1998). To determine the appropriate role, we must involve the community in defining the issues it wishes to address and the strategies it feels will be most effective and culturally appropriate in attempting to achieve collectively set goals. For example, a Native American woman may be able to use her role as a member of the community and a designated leader to work on the primary level with her community to bring about change (Barrios and Eagan 2002). A Latina or Japanese American organizer, who could provide important technical assistance or research skills but would not work on this primary level, would take a very different role in relation to the community. Although we emphasize the necessity of participation by community members in primary roles, the important roles that can be played by nonmembers of the community on the secondary and tertiary levels should not be underestimated (Yoshihama and Carr 2003; Hyde 2004; Abu-Lughod 2002; Barrios and Eagan 2002).

Education, Participation, and Capacity Building

What does this analysis suggest about community organizing with women of color? Using an empowerment framework that stresses the core concepts of education, participation, and capacity building, we can develop sensitive and effective methods for community practice (Gutiérrez and Lewis 1999). Many of the methods described here are equally relevant to organizers and community members, and the processes of education, participation, and capacity building should take place within the organizer as well as with community members (see chapter 8). These reciprocal process methods can be summarized as follows:

EDUCATION
1. Learn about, understand, and participate in the women's ethnic community.
2. Recognize and build upon ways in which women of color have worked effectively within their own communities; build upon existing structures.
3. Serve as a facilitator, and view the situation through the lens or vision of women of color.

PARTICIPATION
4. Use the process of praxis, or action based on critical reflection (Freire 1973) to understand the historical, political, and social context of the organizing effort.
5. Begin with the formation of small groups.

6. Recognize and embrace the conflict that characterizes cross-cultural work.

CAPACITY BUILDING

7. Involve women of color in leadership roles.
8. Understand and support the need that women of color may have for their own separate programs and organizations.

Education

Educational efforts toward community organizing and change need to be grounded in the ways in which women of color share similarities and differences with European American women and men of color. Community organizers have often recognized the impact of powerlessness on women of color from the perspective of institutional racism. Frequently overlooked in this process, however, is the role of gender inequity in influencing the life chances of women of color. The field has often ignored the history of community participation by women of color. When women of color are viewed solely as members of their racial or ethnic group and gender is not taken into account, community organizers may alienate women of color and reinforce ways in which sexism, both in the larger society and within ethnic minority communities, is a form of oppression (Collins 2000; Abu-Lughod 2002; Harris-Perry 2011).

As suggested in earlier chapters, an important first step in effective community organizing involves defining community. The fact that women of color can be members of multiple communities and hold multiple identities based on race, gender, geography, and other factors presents both a challenge and an opportunity for organizers. From an organizing perspective, however, the central issue for organizing will often define the community. For example, if the issue is toxic waste dumping in a community, then the neighborhood or city may be an appropriate level for work. If the issue is sterilization abuse and reproductive rights, then gender may be the focus. Awareness of these memberships in multiple communities can be helpful when an organizer is building coalitions or alliances between different groups.

An organizer who is from a different racial, ethnic, or class background from that of the women she works with must recognize how her life experience has colored her perceptions and how her status has affected her power relative to the political structure. Her beliefs and perceptions should not dominate the organizing effort. She must work toward serving as a facilitator and view the situation through the "lens" or "vision" of women of color. In part, this requires allowing this vision to alter the way the organizer views her own work and sharing that new information with others hoping to organize and work within communities of color (Gutiérrez et al., in press; Lewis 2009; Zetzer 2005).

When organizing with low-income women in a housing project, one of the authors (Lewis) initially attempted to separate individual from community concerns. She believed at first that group members would work on individual problem resolution for eight weeks and then, having established a pattern of interaction within the group, would be able to work cooperatively on analysis and resolution of community concerns. It became clear within the first two meetings that the group could not separate and sequentially work with individual and community concerns. As one participant put it, "My individual problems are the community's problems." The flexibility to alter the design based on the realities of the community allowed the group to continue working toward resolution of its identified goals, not those of the facilitator/researcher. This example illustrates the importance of understanding the community's lens on reality and the process of praxis, or action based on critical reflection, to unravel and address the salient historical, social, and political forces at work. In the preceding example, had the outside organizer insisted on separating the individual from the community problem, she would have alienated and probably lost committed community activists for whom this separation was an artificial and inappropriate one. By respecting the community's vision of the intimate interdependence of these levels, however, she was able to facilitate a process through which participants proceeded to make change on both the individual and community levels (Lewis 2009).

Organizers should also use the process of praxis to understand and address the historical, political, and social contexts of the organizing effort. This means that the organizing process as well as the outcome will inform both the organized community and "community" of the organizer. As organizers and community groups analyze the process and outcome of organizing efforts, the outcome of a tactic often emerges as less important than what the community and organizer learn about the nature of the problem being addressed. In this way, community issues are often redefined.

The involvement of women of color in the battered women's movement clearly illustrates this principle. When many feminist shelters observed that they were unsuccessful in reaching women of color, they defined the problem as that of inadequate outreach. When this outreach was unsuccessful, women of color in some localities provided feedback to many shelter programs that their approach was alienating and foreign to communities of color. They often identified the lack of women of color in administrative or permanent staff positions as one way in which the program indicated a lack of commitment to their community. Programs that have been most successful with women of color have been those that addressed their own racism, classism, and ethnocentrism in the development of alternative programs (Zetzer 2005; Wilson et al. 2010).

Participation

Participating in the women's ethnic community is an important step for educating the organizer and building bridges for future work. This participation can result in an analysis of societal institutions, including the one represented by the organizer, and how they might ultimately benefit or hurt the community. Churches, community centers, schools, and social clubs can be avenues for reaching women of color and effecting change within the community. Knowledge can also be gained about specific communities of color through reading and participation in community events. When an organizer is not an ongoing member of the community of women with whom she will be working, developing an understanding of the community's cultural context is vital (Abram et al. 2005; Few 2007).

In an effort to become involved in the community, one organizer participated in activities sponsored by the local community center. She worked for several months in enrichment programming for the children of the community before proceeding to work with the women. During this time, she became aware of community members' patterns of interaction, their relationships with agencies in the city, and other potential issues in the community. Community members and group participants had the opportunity to meet and talk with the community worker and to watch her interact with their children. Many of the initial participants in subsequent organizing efforts later mentioned that their decision to participate in the work was directly related to their approval of the facilitator's work with their children and the nature of her presence in the community.

Effective organizing often begins with the formation of small groups. The small group provides the ideal environment for exploring the social and political aspects of "personal" problems and for developing strategies for work toward social change (Abu-Lughod 2002; Gutiérrez et al. 2005; Lewis and Gutiérrez 2003). It can also be a forum for identifying common goals among diverse groups of women.

The small-group or house meeting strategy has been the primary way in which women of color have been organizing movements to improve conditions in ghettos and barrios and global communities (Dolphyne et al. 2001). This strategy involves organizing small groups of individuals to work on specific problems and later coordinating these small groups so that they can work in coalition with others on joint issues. Many grassroots movements for women of color around the world emerged from initially informal discussion groups. The building of these alliances to develop community efforts can be particularly challenging when they involve more than one ethnic or other group. This is particularly true because the United States remains a highly segregated society in which many people experience little meaningful interaction with those outside their own race, class, ethnic group, or sexual orientation (Harris-Perry 2011). Effective organizing across diverse groups requires breaking down societal boundaries to build alliances (Gutiérrez et al., in press; P. Jones 2007; Prigoff 2000; Hyde 2004). Furthermore, it necessitates recognizing and embracing the conflict that characterizes cross-cultural work. Conflicts will inevitably arise both within those organizations that have been successful in reaching a diverse group and between the organization and a larger community that may be threatened by the absence of expected boundaries. In some respects, the emergence of conflict is an indication that meaningful cross-cultural work is taking place. However, the sources and resolution of conflict will affect the outcomes of the organizing effort. The extent to which the organizer anticipates conflict related to group interaction, the effects of internalized oppression, wider political strategies to hinder or destroy the community change effort, and similar factors will often determine whether organizing efforts are successful (P. Jones 2007).

Conflict includes the discomfort many organizers feel when they find themselves the sole person from a different ethnic or class background in a group of women of color or when they attempt to participate for the first time in a community event that has previously been attended solely by persons from the community. It is important for organizers to recognize that they will be "tested" by community members to determine whether they, as others who came before, are present only to "take." Giving on the community's terms, as illustrated in the earlier example of the author's work with children, is one example of the testing process experienced by someone attempting to enter the community.

It is our experience that European American organizers are often less comfortable than women of color with the conflict engendered by the development of a multicultural organization. Conflicts are a part of our everyday lives. They reflect choices about fact, value, and strategy alternatives that we face intra- or interpersonally (Lewis 2009; Morelli and Spencer 2000). Too often, women have been socialized into conflict-avoidance behaviors. These behaviors only temporarily delay conflicts, which will resurface when issues are not addressed directly. Addressing a conflict has often been misconstrued as synonymous with confrontation, another conflict-resolution strategy. They are, however, quite different. Confrontation often means the minimization of or attack on a party with which there is conflict. This minimization, either at the personal or political levels, can easily be perceived as a threat, which inevitably leads to an escalation of the conflict rather than a dialogue about its nature (Few et al. 2003).

Addressing conflict directly means employing interpersonal skills such as engagement, active listening, and consensus building. It means viewing the situation through various lenses in the presence of all who are involved in the conflict and then managing to reach some consensus about how to proceed. The process of reaching this consensus often involves being open about our differing conflict styles and managing to hear the content, rather than just the affect, of the messages being presented (Chávez et al. 2008). To do so also requires taking a strengths-based approach—in this case, acknowledging the capacity or strengths in the conflict style of the group—on the part of those who have been privy to only one way of handling conflicts. In this way, conflict-avoidance techniques may be valued for their ability to offset the attack, whereas confrontation approaches may be valued for their ability to focus immediate attention on the conflict (Stevens 2002).

Conflict management that results in genuine dialogue and analysis of the basis of difference will have a direct effect on the outcome of an organizing effort. For example, only after European Americans involved women of color in their organizations did many European American women encounter a different view of gender roles and how they translate into different strategies and goals. Once women of color were included in such organizations, work around sexual assault had to recognize and deal with the fears of many European American women concerning men of color. In one organization, it was only after the group began a campaign confronting the "myth of the black rapist" that women of color within the organization and in the larger community came to believe that the organization represented their needs.

Dealing with such conflict is difficult but valuable. If we are to work toward a more equitable society, this vision must be integral to the work of our organizations. We must know ourselves and be open to knowing others. Dealing with community backlash and conflict also requires taking risks to speak out in support of our vision. The inability to resolve these conflicts has resulted in the death of some organizations and has minimized our ability to work in coalition.

Capacity Building

Contemporary organizing by women of color has often taken a grassroots approach based upon existing networks of family, friends, or informal and formal ethnic community institutions. In this way, individual, family, and community interests are viewed as compatible and integrated with one another. Many African American women, Latinas, and other women of color describe themselves as motivated to engage in activism because of their commitment to their communities and ethnic group (Collins 2000; Dolphyne et al. 2001). Women also have often been active in the mutual aid societies within ethnic communities, such as the Hui among the Chinese, the Ko among the Japanese, and the tribal councils among Native Americans. Each of these organizations has served as a vehicle for assisting individual ethnic group members, families, and entire communities through the establishment of business loans, funerals, and community programs.

Organizers must recognize and build upon these networks and the myriad ways in which women of color have worked effectively within their own communities. Outside organizers, regardless of their own race or ethnicity, need to work with community leaders and learn from them the most effective ways of working in particular communities. Working with existing leaders may involve organizers in different types of activities from those in which they may usually engage. For example, to provide survival services, existing community leaders may be active in church-related activities or with municipal agencies (Gutiérrez et al. 2005). Organizers can learn from these women ways that they have found to survive and leverage political power.

Organizers also need to recognize how women of color have been involved in advocating for women's rights since the beginning of the feminist movement. For example, many of the first shelters for battered women were founded by women of color responding to the needs in their communities (Taylor 2005; Lewis and Gutiérrez 2003; Rosado and Baretto 2002; Segal and Martinez 2007). Recognition of the contributions of women of color to feminist causes can help to break down some of the barriers and difficulties that exist in this work.

As suggested earlier, however, community organizing with women of color may involve a broader perspective from the one initially envisioned by the organizer. This broader perspective would recognize the many ways in which race, gender, class, and ethnicity are intertwined. Consequently, it would underscore the impossibility of separating the needs of women from those of their families and communities (Segal and Martinez 2007). The role of women in the civil rights movements of the 1950s and 1960s certainly illustrates the importance of gender to mobilization efforts. The successful Montgomery, Alabama, bus boycott, for example, is usually credited to African American male ministers who were in public leadership positions. However, the impetus for the boycott was a group of African American women who impressed on the ministers that the cause was just and that they would launch the boycott themselves if the ministers did not take a public stance. The women raised the consciousness of the ministers and in this way contributed significantly to social action. However, they were willing to work behind the scenes, rather than spearheading the boycott themselves, because they thought it was imperative that African American men's leadership be supported. This delicate interaction of race, ethnicity, class, and gender must be in the forefront of the organizer's praxis perspective.

All too often, organizing with women of color has taken the unidirectional "outreach approach," in which communities of color are targets of change rather than active participants and collaborators. When this former approach is used, women of color often resist organizing efforts and, in some cases, undermine them (Stevens 2002; Barrios and Eagan 2002). It is crucial, therefore, to involve women of color in leadership roles from the onset. Predominantly European American organizations wishing to collaborate with women of color will need to incorporate women of color as leaders and active participants before taking on this kind of work. Such collaboration may require redefining the kind of work the organization does, as well as looking critically at its members' attitudes toward institutions such as the church and the family. The history of attempts at collaboration suggests that cross-cultural work requires identifying how racism may exclude women of color from leadership roles (Gutiérrez and Lewis 1999). Successful collaboration will require that European American organizers change their interactions with women of color and be capable of sharing power and control of their programs. This type of organizational work embraces the tenet of feminist organizing that "diversity is strength."

Issues of perceived or actual social class differences must be taken into account, even when the organizer is from the same ethnic or gender background as the community in which she is working. As noted earlier, the definition of community may be psychological as well as geographic. Those entering, or reentering, communities need to be cognizant that their economic or educational backgrounds may be perceived as making them somehow different from other community members. They must anticipate suspicion or backlash as a possible consequence. As in other conflict situations, a process of dialogue and action can be used to work through this problem, such that the organizer can then participate in the community on the latter's own terms. Perhaps one of the highest compliments paid to one of the authors was in a community meeting in which she was introduced to others as "not an educated fool."

One method for building effective coalitions is the incorporation of informal "debriefing" groups for community workers. These groups would include all members of the community and would provide opportunities for input and clarification of the organizing process. Those in key leadership positions would model their ongoing praxis experiences by being open about the choices made in the organizing effort and the assumptions upon which these choices rested. Debriefing sessions would allow for community members who are not an integral part of the organizing effort to share additional strategies and to evaluate the impact of the design on the community to date. Some groups have used the house meeting strategy to provide debriefing opportunities, whereas others have relied upon formal written materials such as community newsletters to keep community members informed. Consistent ongoing debriefing efforts need to be built into the organizing design and expanded as needed.

Within the realm of organizing, there is room for multiethnic organizations and cross-ethnic coalitions, but also for organizations developed by and for women of color. In the latter regard, organizers need to understand and support the need that women of color may have for their own separate programs and organizations. For women of color, a separate group or organization in which we can explore who we are in relation to the communities in which we live can often provide the basis for creating a vision for future work. A separate organization is one means for building on strengths and nurturing capacity within a community. In work with women of color in an educational setting, the formation of a women of color caucus had a positive impact on the ability of a women's studies program to hire more faculty of color and to develop courses that were more racially and ethnically inclusive. Although the formation was initially viewed by some as divisive, all participants in the program ultimately recognized that the caucus was a critical element in the empowerment of women of color and their capacity to work for positive change for all.

Summary

This chapter has used a framework of education, participation, and capacity building to explore empowering strategies and approaches for community organizing with women of color. In part on the basis of the pioneering work of Rivera and Erlich (1998), we have argued that different roles are appropriate for an organizer, depending upon her relationship to the community (e.g., whether she is a member, a nonmember with a similar racial or ethnic background, or a person of a different racial or ethnic group).

Regardless of the role played, however, several principles are critical in effective organizing with women of color. These include being an active learner and facilitator who can view a given situation through the "lenses" of women of color, recognizing and embracing the conflict that characterizes cross-cultural work, involving women of color in leadership roles, and in other ways contributing to the building of community capacity. Both feminist perspectives and cultural perspectives on organizing in communities of color offer valuable lessons for organizers who cross race, ethnic, gender, class, and other lines in their organizing efforts.

ACKNOWLEDGMENTS

This chapter was updated and reprinted from L. M. Guriérrez and E. A. Lewis, "Community Organizing with Women of Color," *Journal of Community Practice* 1, no. 2 (1994): 22–44. Published by Taylor and Francis, Ltd., hppt://www.inoformaworld .com. Reprinted with permission of the publishers.

REFERENCES

Abram, F. Y., J. A. Slosar, and R. Walls. 2005. "Reverse Mission: A Model for International Social Work Education and Transformative Intra-national Practice." *International Social Work* 48, no. 2:161–176.

Abu-Lughod, L. 2002. "Do Muslim Women Really Need Saving? Anthropological Reflections on Cultural Relativism and Its Others." *American Anthropologist* 104, no. 3:783–790.

Alinsky, S. D. 1972. *Rules for Radicals.* New York: Random House.

Bradshaw, C., S. Soifer, and L. Gutierrez. 1994. "Toward a Hybrid Model for Effective Organizing in Communities of Color." *Journal of Community Practice* 1, no. 1:25–41.

Barrios, P., and M. Eagan. 2002. "Living in a Bicultural World and Finding the Way Home: Native Women's Stories." *Affilia* 17, no. 2:206–228.

Chávez, V., B. Duran, Q. E. Baker, M. M. Avila, and N. Wallerstein. 2008. "The Dance of Race and Privilege in Community-Based Participatory Research." In *Community-Based Participatory Research for Health: From Process to Outcomes*, edited by M. Minkler and N. Wallerstein, 91–103. 2nd ed. San Francisco: Jossey-Bass.

Chávez, V., M. Minkler, N. Wallerstein, and M. S. Spencer. 2010. "Community Organizing for Health and Social Justice." In *Prevention Is Primary: Strategies for Community Well-Being*, edited by L. Cohen, V. Chávez, and S. Chehimi, 87–112. 2nd ed. San Francisco: Jossey-Bass.

Collins, P. 2000. *Black Feminist Thought: Knowledge, Consciousness, and the Politics of Empowerment.* 2nd ed. New York: Routledge.

Dolphyne, F. A., E. Ofei-Aboagye, and D. A. Akuffo, eds. 2001. *Experiences in Capacity-Building for Ghanaian Women.* Accra, Ghana: Asempa, Christian Council of Ghana.

Few, A. L. 2007. "Integrating Black Consciousness and Critical Race Feminism into Family Studies Research." Family Issues 28, no. 4:452–473.

Few, A. L, D. P. Stephens, and M. Rouse-Arnett. 2003. "Sister-to-Sister Talk: Transcending Boundaries and Challenges in Qualitative Research with Black Women." *Family Relations* 52, no. 3:205–215.

Freire, P. 1973. *Pedagogy of the Oppressed.* New York: Seabury Press.

Guadelupe, K. L. and D. Lum, eds. 2005. *Multidimensional Contextual Practice: Diversity and Transcendence.* Belmont, Calif.: Brooks/Cole.

Gutiérrez, L., A. Dessel, E. Lewis, and M. Spencer. In press. "Promoting Multicultural Communication and Collaboration: Dialogue, Mediation, Consensus Building, and

Intergroup Empowerment." In Weil, M. O., ed. *Handbook of Community Practice*. 2nd ed. New York: Sage.

Gutiérrez, L., and E. Lewis. 1999. *Empowering Women of Color*. New York: Columbia University Press.

Gutiérrez, L., E. Lewis, L. Wernick, B. A. Nagda, N. Shore. 2005. "Multicultural Community Practice Strategies and Intergroup Empowerment." In *Handbook of Community Practice*, edited by M. Weil, L. Gutiérrez, M. Reisch, R. Cnaan, D. Gamble, and B. Mulroy, 341–359. Thousand Oaks, Calif.: Sage.

Harris-Perry, M. 2011. *Sister Citizen: Shame, Stereotypes, and the Black Woman in America*. New Haven, Conn.: Yale University Press.

Hyde, C. A. 2004. "Gendered Perceptions of Community Needs and Concerns: An Exploratory Analysis." *Journal of Human Behavior in the Social Environment* 8, no. 4:45–65.

———. 2008. "Feminist Social Work Practice." In *Encyclopedia of Social Work*, edited by T. Mizrahi and L. Davis, 216–221. 20th ed. New York: Oxford University Press.

Jones, P. 2007. *Aftershock: Confronting Trauma in a Violent World; A Guide for Activists and Their Allies*. New York: Lantern Books.

Jones, R. G. 2010. "Putting Privilege into Practice through 'Intersectional Reflexivity': Ruminations, Interventions, and Possibilities." *Reflections: Narratives of Professional Helping* 10, no. 1:122–125

Lewis, E., L. Gutiérrez, and I. Sakamoto. 2001. "Women of Color: Sources of Resilience and Vulnerability." In *Handbook of Social Work Practice with Vulnerable and Resilient Populations*, edited by A. Gitterman, 820–840. 2nd ed. New York: Columbia University Press.

Lewis, E. A. 2009. "Group- versus Individual-Based Intersectionality and Praxis in Feminist and Womynist Research Foundations." In *Handbook of Feminist Family Studies*, edited by S. A. Lloyd, A. L. Few, and K. R. Allen, 304–315. Los Angeles: Sage.

Lewis, E. A., and L. M. Gutiérrez. 2003. "Intersections of Gender, Race and Ethnicity in Group Work." In *Gender and Groupwork*, edited by A. Mullender and M. B. Cohen, 132–143. London: Routledge.

McGoldrick, M., and K. Hardy, eds. 2008. *Re-visioning Family Therapy: Race, Culture, and Gender in Clinical Practice*. New York: Guilford.

Midgley, J. 2007. "Global Inequality, Power, and the Unipolar World." *International Social Work* 50, no. 5:613–626.

Morelli, P. T., and M. S. Spencer. 2000. "Use and Support of Multicultural and Antiracist Education: Research-Informed Interdisciplinary Social Work Practice." *Social Work* 45, no. 2:167–175.

Prigoff, A. 2000. *Economics for Social Workers: Social Outcomes of Economic Globalization with Strategies for Community Action*. Belmont, Calif.: Thomson Learning.

Reed, B. G., P. A. Newman, Z. Suarez, and E. A. Lewis. In press. "Interpersonal Practice beyond Diversity and Towards Social Justice: The Importance of Critical Consciousness." In *Social Work Practice*, edited by B. Seabury and C. Garvin. 2nd ed. New York: Sage.

Rivera, F., and J. Erlich. 1998. *Community Organizing in a Diverse Society*. 3rd ed. Boston: Allyn and Bacon.

Rosado, R. Q., and E. Barreto. 2002. "An Integral Model of Well-Being and Its Implications for the Helping Professions." In *Latino/Hispanic Liaisons and Visions for Human Behavior in the Social Environment*, edited by José Torres and Felix Rivera, 57–84. Binghamton, N.Y.: Haworth Social Work Practice Press.

Segal, M. T., and T. A. Martinez. 2007. *Intersections of Gender, Race, and Class*. Los Angeles: Roxbury.

Spencer, M., E. Lewis, and L. Gutiérrez. 2000. "Multicultural Perspectives on Direct Practice in Social Work." In *Handbook of Direct Practice in Social Work: Future Directions*, edited by P. Allen-Meares and C. Garvin, 131–149. New York: NASW Press.

Stall, S., and R. Stoecker. 2008. "Community Organizing or Organizing Community? Gender and the Crafts of Empowerment." In *The Community Development Reader*, edited by J. DeFilippis and S. Saegert, 241–248. New York, Routledge.

Stevens, J. W. 2002. *Smart and Sassy: The Strengths of Inner-City Black Girls.* New York: Oxford.

Taylor, D. 2005. "American Environmentalism: The Role of Race, Class, and Gender in Shaping Activism, 1820–1995." In *Environmental Sociology: From Analysis to Action*, edited by L. King, and D. McCarthy, 87–106. Oxford, U.K.: Rowman and Littlefield.

Wilson, R. J., F. Y. Abram, and J. L. Anderson. 2010. "Exploring a Feminist-Based Empowerment Model of Community Building." *Qualitative Social Work* 9, no. 4:519–535.

Yoshihama, M., and E. S. Carr. 2003. "Community Participation Reconsidered: Feminist Participatory Action Research with Hmong Women." *Journal of Community Practice* 10, no. 3:85–103.

Zetzer, H. A. 2010. "White Out: Privilege and Its Problems." In *Explorations in Diversity: Examining Privilege and Oppression in a Multicultural Society*, edited by S. Anderson and V. A. Middleton, 11–24. 2nd ed. Florence, Ky.: Cengage Learning.

13

African American Barbershops and Beauty Salons

An Innovative Approach to Reducing Health Disparities through Community Building and Health Education

LAURA LINNAN
STEPHEN THOMAS
HEATHER D'ANGELO
YVONNE OWENS FERGUSON

A goal of Healthy People 2020 (U.S. Department of Health and Human Services [USDHHS] 2011), the nation's road map to achieving health equity, is the elimination of health disparities. Yet despite decades of gains in the overall health status for the general population, racial and ethnic health disparities persist (USDHHS 2011). Racial and ethnic health disparities exist across a broad spectrum of health outcomes and behavioral risk factors, and African Americans carry a greater proportion of the burden of health disparities than do other racial and ethnic groups. Compared with whites, African Americans have higher rates of overall mortality, obesity, cancer, diabetes, heart disease, stroke, and HIV and have the highest rates of infant mortality among all racial and ethnic groups (Flegal et al. 2010; National Center for Health Statistics 2010).

To make progress toward eliminating racial and ethnic health disparities, communities must be engaged in exploring the context of existing health disparities, formulating solutions, and ultimately making the decisions that affect their health. Community building and community organizing are strategies that lie at the heart of addressing racial health disparities. Interventions that address "hot-button issues" identified by community members are critical when attempting to understand and affect the complex interplay of behavioral, environmental, and policy-driven factors that shape health disparities. Building community capacity by engaging with the community at each step of the process is essential for sustainability (Giachello et al. 2003; Wallerstein and Duran 2010). The involvement of community members as equals in decision-making processes can help build relationships based on trust that promote the type of changes that are the foundation of a serious effort to affect health disparities (Wallerstein and Duran 2010).

Applying community organizing strategies to address health disparities is important for all populations, but particularly perhaps for African Americans, given that traditional interventions have largely failed to reduce health disparities in this population (Adderley-Kelly and Green 2005). The National Cancer Institute (2006) and the Institute of Medicine (2008) both have emphasized the importance of empowerment and working collaboratively with communities in the development of culturally appropriate, evidence-based interventions to address health disparities. Similarly, there is growing consensus at the National Institutes of Health that accelerating efforts to eliminate racial and ethnic health disparities will require innovative community-based interventions and building trust with respected community partners in priority populations, such as African Americans who reside in high-risk urban neighborhoods.

A promising approach in such work is to begin in community settings that are not clinical or academic in nature, but rather shared social spaces. Every ethnic group has safe zones; community-empowered centers where people can gather, share cultural secrets, connect with their ethnicity's historical narrative and engage in writing new chapters of that story. The African American church is one example of this approach that has been documented in the literature (Campbell et al. 2007). However, the urgency of persistent and often growing health disparities demands that we go further in finding new partners and more effective interventions to close the health disparity gap. This is the context within which partnerships with black barbershops and beauty salons have gained credibility. While the practice of working with barbershops and salons is not new, recent community-based participatory research in these settings has ushered in creative new efforts to transform barbershops and salons into reliable venues for interventions that are both scientifically sound and culturally relevant, while also fostering enhanced community building. From the perspective of culturally relevant science, for example, Victor and colleagues (2010) conducted one of the first randomized clinical trials in black barbershops focused on control of hypertension among African American men. The authors concluded that "the effect of blood pressure screening on [hypertension] control among black male barbershop patrons was improved when barbers were enabled to become health educators, monitor BP, and promote physician follow-up" (Victor et al. 2010). Clearly more research is needed if this approach is to be disseminated and scaled for large urban populations. In the African American community, however, beauty salons and barbershops have a legacy of community building and community organizing and have the potential to be places where community members and academics can come together to address health disparities in the community.

This chapter will review the important social, political, and economic history of U.S.-based African American beauty salons and barbershops, and provide two examples of how community building and -organizing principles have been used to conduct community-engaged research designed to address health disparities among African Americans living in the inner-city neighborhoods of Pittsburgh, Pennsylvania, and the mixed urban/rural communities of central North Carolina.

Beauty Salons and Barbershops in Contemporary and Historical Perspective

Beauty salons and barbershops are found in almost every town in the United States, and almost seven hundred thousand barbers and cosmetologists were employed in 2008. Almost half are self-employed and many own their own salon or barbershop (Bureau of Labor Statistics 2010). There are approximately 85,500 barbershops and 474,400 beauty salons in the United States, including both self-employed businesses and those that have employees on the payroll (U.S. Census Bureau 2002).

With their rich history and prominent role in the lives of African Americans, beauty salons and barbershops have served as settings for community building and community organizing beginning in the 1800s and continuing today (Bristol 2009; Harris-Lacewell 2004; Willet 2000). Originally a place where black barbers provided shaves, haircuts, and wigs to such notables as Thomas Jefferson and Benjamin Franklin, barbershops evolved and adapted to the racial climate and policies of the United States. Throughout history, barbering was one of the few professions that provided African American men with economic mobility and stability (Bristol 2009).

Although their history does not date as far back as that of barbershops, hairdressing, and owning a beauty salon, provided one of a limited number of avenues for African American women to become entrepreneurs at a time when the majority of African Americans were marginalized with limited access to economic opportunities (Byrd and Tharps 2001; Peiss 1998; Willet 2000). In fact, Annie Turnbo Malone and Madam C. J. Walker, both pioneers in the hair care and beauty industry, are documented as being the wealthiest African American women during the early 1900s, with the latter becoming the first African American millionaire (Bundles 1990; Byrd and Tharps 2001; Willet 2000). Historically, improving the overall health and well-being of African Americans has been an integral part of the community organizing and community building functions of African American–owned barbershops and beauty salons (Bristol 2009; Bundles 1990; Peiss 1998; Willet 2000). As early as the 1830s, some African American barbershops became centers for abolitionists, soliciting customers to sign antislavery petitions and carrying abolitionist publications (Bristol 2009). Barbershops also served as part of the Underground Railroad (Bristol 2009). During the civil rights movement, the African American beauty salon was used as a meeting place for activities, because, unlike the church and other prominent African American institutions, it was a less visible institution within the community (Willet 2000).

Serving as a natural setting for information sharing is one of the critical attributes of the African American barbershop and beauty salon that historically made them optimal sites for organizing and building communities (Bristol 2009; Willet 2000), as well as addressing health disparities (Linnan et al. 2005; Luque et al. 2010).

Another critical attribute of the African American barbershop and beauty salon is the unique relationship between the barber or stylist and his or her customers (Bristol 2009; Harris-Lacewell 2004; Hart et al. 2008). Often, customers establish long-term, friendly, trusted relationships with their preferred barber or stylist (Bristol 2009; Willet 2000). The high number of repeat contacts between the customer and barber or stylist form the type of "weak ties" that are thought to fill important gaps in social support, by extending beyond close family bonds that might be geographically displaced and yet are accessible to everyone within a "limited physical and temporal context" (Adelman et al. 1987; Granovetter 1973). From conversations about politics and the economy, to health and personal relationships, barbers and stylists have routinely served as a sounding board for their customers (Bristol 2009); and are excellent examples of "natural helpers" (Eng et al. 2009) who have been mobilized to promote health within the African American community (see for example Wilson et al. 2008; Hess et al. 2007; Johnson et al. 2010; Luque et al. 2010).

In addition to barbershops and beauty salons providing a safe haven for addressing social justice issues (Bristol 2009; Harris-Lacewell 2004) whose barbers and stylists serve as natural helpers (Bristol 2009), shop and salon owners tend to be deeply concerned about the health and well-being of their communities (Bristol 2009; Linnan et al. 2002; Hart et al. 2008). Engagement with these owners as gatekeepers has been essential for implementing health-promotion activities that address health disparities in the African American community (Linnan et al. 2002; Luque et al. 2010; Releford et al. 2010) while building community.

What follows are two detailed descriptions of barbershop and beauty salon interventions in two separate locations, Pittsburgh, Pennsylvania, and central North Carolina. Working in collaboration with informal networks of barbershops and salons to disseminate health information in these communities became one viable means of working to reduce health disparities while further building on these establishments' sense of community. However, we are mindful of the caution of Musa and colleagues (2009) who emphasize that these same informal networks in the black community are also potential means for the spread of rumors, concerns, or conspiracy theories, which may reduce health care service utilization. Thus, efforts to monitor the quality and accuracy of the information provided, addressing myths and misconceptions about health risk and the causes of health problems, as well as taking time to build trust and authentic relationships with barbershop/salon owners and stylists/barbers and their customers, were hallmarks of these efforts.

Overview of Beauty Salon and Barbershop Interventions

It is beyond the scope of this chapter to review the robust and growing literature on beauty salons and barbershops as both intervention settings and places to recruit participants into a wide range of health disparities research studies, but the reader is referred to Linnan and colleagues (under review) for a systematic review of this work. Briefly, barbershop and salon interventions have addressed a variety of health problems, including cancer, hypertension, diabetes, kidney disease, stroke, and cardiovascular disease and health behaviors such as diet, physical activity, and smoking. In these studies, the level and type of stylist/barber involvement, as well as level/type of community collaboration varied, but typically included the development and use of culturally relevant educational materials in barbershop- or salon-based settings (Linnan et al., under review; Luque et al. 2010) and education of barbers and stylists in the health area of interest. An urban beauty salon intervention that randomized salons serving predominantly African American and Afro-Caribbean women to receive breast health messages from trained stylists or to serve as controls also included the use of a community advisory board consisting of community leaders, salon owners, breast cancer survivors, and health care advocates in designing the training curriculum (Wilson et al. 2008). As illustrated in more detail below, when such an approach is used, actively engaging a range of relevant community members as partners in the research from the onset, the goodness-of-fit of such work with principles of community building and organizing may best be realized.

Predominant themes in the literature on community-academic partnerships to address health issues through beauty salons and barbershops included that (1) barbers and stylists felt it important to them personally that they help their clients by sharing health information with them, (2) many already talk to their clients about health, (3) customers are interested in receiving health information from their stylists or barbers, and (4) male customers showed a willingness to obtain not only education but also medical services such as prostate cancer screening tests, blood pressure and blood glucose measurements, physical measurements, and fitness assessments in the barbershop (Linnan et al. 2010).

Although beauty salons and barbershops are promising settings for health interventions, there are challenges to creating successful interventions in these settings to address health disparities. With a few exceptions, such as the BEAUTY project described below, the majority of such interventions are "community placed" rather than community based. That is, even when community partnerships are formed, the issues addressed by interventions have largely been selected by researchers rather than by the community itself. Using the setting to deliver health education messages or provide screenings may provide short-term health benefits to the community. But employing community building and community organizing principles to help ensure that the community itself is deeply involved in deciding which messages should be delivered takes this a step further and may increase trust and the likelihood of program sustainability, while building community capacity and improving sense of community.

Our review of the literature revealed little about the ways in which community building and organizing approaches were used in studies to date. We therefore turn now to two different approaches to working with beauty salons and barbershops and the ways in which these settings and owners/stylists/barbers were mobilized to address health disparities, as well as challenges faced in the process.

Health Advocates In-Reach and Research: Mobilizing Black Barbershops to Promote Health and Prevent Disease

In 2001, the Department of Health and Human Services (DHHS) launched a national public awareness campaign designed to address racial and ethnic health disparities by encouraging African Americans to establish a medical home. Although many African American communities hosted Take a Loved One to the Doctor Day, however, one of the authors (Dr. Stephen Thomas) and his colleagues at the Research Center of Excellence on Minority Health Disparities in the University of Pittsburgh's Graduate School of Public Health (hereafter the Pittsburgh Research Center), realized there was a major a problem with the campaign. Far too many people in Pittsburgh's black neighborhoods had no doctor, no medical home. Recognizing that the elimination of health disparities required the full array of health professionals and not simply physicians and, further, that a public health approach tailored to the local community context was needed, Dr. Thomas and his team launched Take a Health Professional to the People Day. They partnered with a network of black barbershops and salons in Pittsburgh, as the venue for public health education, clinical screenings, and assessments.

In this approach, teams of health professionals would come to the people in the trusted venue of local barbershops and salons. This innovative twist on the DHHS campaign evolved over time from three barbershops and ten health professionals in 2001 to ten barbershops/salons and over two hundred health professionals screening approximately seven hundred people in one day at the height of the program in 2008 and ultimately became a year-round community-engaged research program, Health Advocates In-Reach and Research (HAIR). The concept of using barbershops and salons to deliver health services to African Americans captured the imagination of local and national media, resulting in a segment on National Public Radio's *Morning Edition* (Jones 2002), and extensive news coverage on the day of the event.

Building Trust and Training the Barbers

Early in the process it became clear that the barbers and stylists were the linchpin for any success. The barbershops/salons were businesses first, and anything that would disrupt their ability to serve their clientele would be inappropriate. Barbers were well aware of the health problems plaguing the community and they wanted to make a meaningful contribution to a solution. However, there were natural tensions between university researchers and the cultural milieu of black barbershops. To find common ground and establish trust, a full-time staff member engaged barbers using principles of community-based participatory research, which share with community building and organizing a focus on community as a unit of identity, an accent on community strengths, and a commitment to local capacity building and sustainability (Israel et al. 2005). Methods included conducting structured interviews with barbers, carrying out participant observations, and using anthropological field methods to construct a typology of the organization and structure of black barbershops in Pittsburgh. For example, barbershops were classified into three types: owner-operator, independent barbers renting chairs, and absentee landlord. Findings also suggested that those barbershops where the owner was also an active barber were more likely to fully embrace the incorporation of health education and delivery of medical services in their shops.

Theater was used as an innovative approach to gain barbers' trust. A local playwright transformed field notes and observations into a script for a one-act play, *A Healthy Day in the Neighborhood*, that conveyed the full range of human emotion and cultural context of the barbershop where the public health education would take place. Barbers had a chance to "see" themselves on stage as actors played the role of barbers as lay health advocates. For many of the barbers it was an "aha moment"—they got it. The play decreased cultural barriers between barbers and researchers and laid a foundation of mutual respect upon which to build the public health education programs.

Barbers were trained as lay health advocates through a formal program that included becoming certified in cardiopulmonary resuscitation (CPR); in this way they could be legitimately called "lifesavers." In 2008, 700 blood pressure screens, 150 depression screens, and smaller numbers of echocardiograms and prostate exams were conducted throughout the HAIR barbershop network. All clinical screenings were conducted by physicians, nurses, dentists, and other health professionals. Working with their community collaborators, Thomas and his colleagues decided at the inception of HAIR that people needed access to medical care providers and the role of the barbers was to reinforce relevant health promotion and disease prevention messages while at the same time making their shops welcoming to health care professionals.

Gilbert (2010), describes the urban context that anchored the HAIR network barbers and their customers in an extensive interorganizational network consisting of the Pittsburgh Research Center, the Kingsley Association (a community-based service organization), the National Broadcasting Company (NBC) affiliate WPXI-TV and other media partners and the Robert Wood Johnson Foundation and local foundations. Together they established and promoted the Healthy Black Family Project, a community-based intervention designed to provide health promotion and disease prevention services at no cost for people at risk for type 2 diabetes and hypertension identified in the barbershops (Thomas and Quinn 2008; Ford et al. 2009). This constellation of assets contributed to a notion of the community as a "unit of solution" (Eng et al. 1985) whereby capacity for community development was concentrated on promoting health and preventing disease. With the humble barbershop being featured on television news as a neighborhood setting, not for the far too commonly depicted crime scenes, but rather a place where hundreds of physicians, dentist, pharmacists, nurses, and other public health professionals came to listen, learn, and serve the African American community. The burdens of race and history crushing the people living in these communities was lifted, if only for a day, and their stories were heard and elevated beyond the confines of their daily suffering. Public awareness was raised about chronic disease being related not only to individual lifestyle behaviors or access to medical care but also to degradation of the neighborhood environment, racial segregation, and poverty where African Americans lived, worked, played, and worshiped. These broader social determinants of health became new targets for intervention.

Engaging Academic Health Science Professionals in Community Outreach

Over time, the ten barbershops in the HAIR network became a stable infrastructure for conducting ongoing public health education year round. The university dedicated a full-time staff member with responsibility for weekly visits to the shops and service as a liaison to clinical investigators interested in using the HAIR infrastructure for recruitment of participants to other health disparities clinical trials research. Additionally, the stability made it possible to build relationships across selected schools of health sciences that also had a commitment to address health disparities but lacked a coordinated mechanism to engage the community. For example, the HAIR barbershops served as venues to train pharmacy students in communication skills, train dentistry students in oral examinations, serve as a clinical rotation for nursing students, and recruit eligible individuals into clinical trial research through the Asthma Research Center and Department of Psychiatry in the School of Medicine. For the barbers, the addition of health care providers added value to their service delivery and commitment to improving the community. They witnessed firsthand the burdens of chronic disease on their customers, their family members, and themselves and appreciated being able to serve as key venues in these new efforts that ideally would contribute to the health of their communities.

The Mayo Clinic's Center for Translational Science Activities (CTSA) established a formal course with the Pittsburgh Research Center that included a one-week rotation known as urban immersion (Mayo Clinic 2007) to take place in the city. Physician scientists from the CTSA would be integrated with teams of health professionals who worked in the barbershops. The aim was to build their "cultural confidence" and conduct simulations of advanced screening techniques (Thomas et al. 2011). For example, in 2008, a Mayo physician demonstrated the use of a laptop echocardiogram on thirteen participants in one of the participating barbershops (Huskins et al. 2008), benefiting customers with diagnosed or suspected heart problems while further demonstrating the viability of the barbershop as an important venue for using sophisticated diagnostic methods designed to improve health care access.

Lessons

The HAIR project transformed a network of trusted barbershops and beauty salons into portals for dissemination of health promotion and disease prevention information and delivery of clinical services. Along the way, however, significant challenges were encountered. These included the intensive time and staff effort needed to establish trusting relations with selected barbershops and salons, and the need to overcome the significant amount of distrust toward the university and medical establishment built up over the years. For example, although several of the HAIR barbershops were located less than one mile from the academic health center, these neighborhoods had significant burdens of preventable chronic disease. This contradiction was not lost on the barbers, who had concluded that their health, and the lives of the people they served, were of less importance than those of white people who lived farther away.

Once trust was established with the barbers and they were willing to host health professionals in their shops, the academic partners also did not fully appreciate the time and effort needed to prepare health professionals (90 percent of whom were white) for the cultural environment they were about to enter. The HAIR barbershops were located in high-crime neighborhoods and the often clear apprehension felt by health care professionals entering the community was observed by the barbers, often creating tension. In time a mandatory orientation was instituted for health professionals, which proved highly successful, although it was another demand on staff time and the budget.

Other obstacles emerged when the success of the program generated even more demand for expansion across the city and into neighboring counties, beyond the capacity of the university to respond to. This led to dashed expectations and exposed the vulnerability of innovative initiatives like HAIR, funded only by federal grants and foundations, and unable to be sustained beyond the life cycle of a grant. Although community building and community-engaged research make a commitment to long-term involvement and sustainability (Israel et al. 2005), such challenges are not uncommon in practice, particularly in difficult economic times.

Despite such challenges, the gratifying opportunities and outcomes of this work made it well worth the effort. Examples of the benefits include the following:

1. Establishment of the HAIR barbershop network galvanized the academic health center to incorporate community outreach into formal training programs, internships, clinical rotations, and coursework for academic

credit. This legitimized the community as an important venue for turning out culturally sensitive practitioners, adding value to the teaching, research, and service mission of the university.

2. The HAIR barbershop network provided a venue for "proof of concept" sophisticated clinical assessments. As noted above, the use by cardiologists of a laptop echocardiogram in the barbershop to determine the feasibility and acceptability of this diagnostic tool for African Americans proved a major success (Huskins et al. 2008) and, in the process, brought access to this high-tech assessment tool to community members who otherwise would likely have gone without.

3. Over the years, as establishment of the HAIR barbershop network matured, the Comprehensive Cancer Center conducted quarterly prostate cancer-screening services though these venues on a routine basis (Browne 2007) and the Cancer Center established a seven-hundred-thousand-dollar fund to cover costs associated with case finding for individuals with no insurance. In Big Tom's Full-Service Barbershop, a white female nurse conducted rectal digital exams and PSA blood draws. The barbershop in turn received a mini-grant, used to renovate space to meet state guidelines for privacy. This development was evidence of significant institutional commitment made possible by creating the infrastructure for ongoing community engagement.

As community-engaged research moves "from the margins to the mainstream" (Horowitz et al. 2009) so too will innovative partnerships with natural leaders and the cultural spaces they occupy, such as black barbershops and salons. Passage of the Patient Protection Act of 2010 (see chapter 21) creates new opportunities for sustainable funding mechanisms focused on supporting culturally relevant interventions like the HAIR barbershop network, and will hopefully translate into more such interventions, "with" communities rather than "on" communities, in the years ahead.

The North Carolina BEAUTY and Health Project: Preventing Cancer in African American Beauty Salons

The North Carolina Bringing Education and Understanding to You (BEAUTY) and Health Project (hereafter the BEAUTY Project) is an eleven-year-old, ongoing partnership between researchers at University of North Carolina, Chapel Hill, and beauty salon owners, licensed stylists, and their customers, with an aim of reducing health disparities among African American women. In 2000, one of the authors (Dr. Laura Linnan) and an interdisciplinary team of researchers from the university's Gillings School of Global Public Health convened an advisory board that consisted of a group of salon owners, stylists, directors of local beauty schools, and product distributors to ask them the question, "What do you think of the idea of promoting health in beauty salons?" A community-based participatory research approach (CBPR) (Israel et al. 1998; Minkler and Wallerstein 2008) was used, both to help answer this question and subsequently to work collaboratively with salon owners and their customers to build a series of participatory research projects. Over the past decade, this initial effort has blossomed to include work with over eighty beauty salons and more than eighteen hundred of their customers. Although not a focus of this chapter, we also expanded efforts in 2004, based on the urging of our advisory board, to adapt and use the model in more than forty barbershops with over one thousand of their customers. Ongoing, funded CBPR continues in both beauty salons and barbershops at this writing, with efforts expanded to new populations (Latina salons), new methods (online continuing education courses for licensed stylists), and new health issues (occupational health and safety, prostate/colorectal cancer, and weight loss/weight gain prevention).

Background on the BEAUTY Project: Building Relationships and Trust

In 2000, the BEAUTY advisory board members decided to meet monthly to discuss and plan the project. Consistent with the community organizing principle of "starting where the people are" (Nyswander 1956) and to understand whether the idea of promoting health in the salons was even viable, board members emphasized that the cooperation of licensed stylists was needed, and recommended that they be polled to determine whether they would be interested in participating in a salon-based project. Advisory board members reviewed the survey instrument, assisted in the administration of the survey to all fifty-eight stylists in one North Carolina county, helped the research team interpret the survey results, and actively shared key findings with salons and stylists in the county (for detailed findings, see Linnan et al. 2001). Briefly, findings revealed that (1) stylists routinely talked with their customers during visits, including talking about health; (2) stylists were interested in attending training in how to deliver health messages in the salon; and (3) stylists were most comfortable and willing to talk with their customers about exercise, healthy eating, and healthy weight. Since these behaviors are preventable risk factors for many chronic diseases and were the most comfortable for stylists to talk about, they were selected as the first issues to be addressed. The survey results were also used to develop the initial stylist training workshop, which was the preferred method for receiving training, as reported by cosmetologists.

While stylists were clearly supportive of the idea of promoting health, the CBPR team embarked on a second formative study to observe "how things worked" in the salon so as to create the most culturally and contextually appropriate intervention. Using a standardized protocol, an observational study in ten salons (five African American and five white salons) was conducted to assess which health topics were talked about most, which were not discussed, who initiated the conversations, how much time was spent in the salon, what health myths or misconceptions were raised, and so forth. The CBPR partnership then drew on this information to create an intervention that was appropriate for the salon and effective for initiating conversation between the stylist and the customer about health. Once again, the advisory board's review of initial findings provided important insights and guidance. For example, when we shared our data, advisory board members pointed out that health talk was initiated equally by customers and stylists, so we decided that our intervention focus must include mirror stickers with the slogan "Ask Me about the BEAUTY Project" as customers sat in the chair to prompt discussion with her stylist, as well as training for the stylist on how to start the conversation during a typical visit. Observational findings confirmed that (1) health topics were discussed in approximately one in five conversations; (2) diet, exercise, and stress were among the most commonly discussed health topics; (3) there were few differences in the topics discussed in African American versus white salons, but African American women spent more time in the salons, on average, than did white customers (Solomon et al. 2004). These results were extremely helpful in gaining an understanding of what type of intervention might be culturally and contextually appropriate, what methods might be useful, and how to begin with health topics of greatest interest to the customer that matched the comfort level of the stylist. For example, it was important to focus our initial intervention efforts on diet, exercise, and stress versus some other topics such as tobacco or health screenings. If stylists were not comfortable with the topic, or customers were not ready to discuss it, we would set up unnecessary barriers to intervention success at the outset. Thus, we started with topics and methods that were the best "fit" for the salon environment, the stylists and the customers.

Focus group discussions also were conducted with salon customers to discover their thoughts about health, beauty, and the possibility of promoting health in the salons (Kim et al. 2007). These revealed that women were very interested in receiving health information in the salons and that at different ages, women had different thoughts about beauty and health. Using this formative research the partnership developed an intervention that included a training workshop for stylists, as well as materials for the salons (educational display) and print materials for customers, all packaged in a campaign format. The stylist training workshop agenda focused on dispelling myths and misconceptions about health and cancer prevention, sharing the "good news" about cancer prevention with specific messages about physical activity and healthy eating. Particular attention was focused on specific public health recommendations regarding diet and physical activity. The messages were introduced at the stylist training workshop through discussion, with staff demonstrations of how to weave messages into a typical visit with a customer. Stylists then tried out via role playing how best to deliver the messages during a typical customer appointment. The educational displays and print materials were interactive and encouraged customers to ask stylists questions about key health messages.

The BEAUTY CBPR partnership recruited two salons to participate in a pilot test of the intervention materials and campaign developed. Results of this eight-week pilot study revealed that stylists were enthusiastic partners in the training work-shops and reported a willingness to deliver the targeted health information in conversations with their customers. In addition, customers reported an increase in self-efficacy and actual behavioral changes in diet and physical activity, with these changes significantly more likely among customers who had more contact with their stylists (Linnan et al. 2005). Changes were evident both at immediate postintervention and as part of a twelve-month follow-up. The results provided encouraging support for a larger effectiveness trial, funded in forty African American beauty salons by the American Cancer Society (Linnan et al. 2007) as well as several barbershop-based intervention studies funded by the National Cancer Institute and the Centers for Disease Control and Prevention.

Lessons Learned

With a foundation of community organizing and CBPR principles, such as starting where the people are, engaging natural helpers (Eng et al. 2009), and in other ways building on community strengths, the North Carolina BEAUTY and Health Project has evolved based on an ongoing collaboration with advisory board mem-bers. Active participation of residents, stylists, and other advisory board members made it possible for the BEAUTY CBPR team to get a high (85 percent) response rate to the initial survey of stylists, to help identify salons to participate in a series of formative research studies, and to create a recruitment video and then success-fully recruit salons into both the initial pilot study and larger effectiveness trial. The BEAUTY advisory board members were crucial in developing strategies to recruit salons and cosmetologists, developing key messages, and designing a culturally appropriate cosmetologist training workshop.

The BEAUTY advisory board members and the participating cosmetologists/ owners provided assistance with the interpretation of the preliminary results, with the advisory board also helping the academic researchers in pursuing con-tinued funding for a wide range of additional studies. Indeed, without the advisory board members' inside knowledge of the beauty industry and of the local commu-nity and a high level of motivation to improve the health of their customers, the BEAUTY Project and subsequent salon and barbershop-based studies would not have been possible.

There are a number of important challenges when working with beauty salon owners and stylists. First, stylists/owners are busy people. There is not a lot of time to add new tasks or training opportunities into their day. Some owners are present in the salons daily, others less often. Stylists may be permanent, full-time employees, rent space in a salon and work full or part time, or have other arrangements with owners. When in the salon, they are seeing as many customers as possible. Thus, finding ways to help them integrate brief messages into their typical conversations is essential. Second, and related to the first, is the need to be mindful of not asking too much of the stylists, as in their attending trainings, starting conversations, offering advice, and so on. We learned along the way that as part of their professional training, stylists are typically taught to be great listeners but not necessarily to initiate conversations with their customers. As a result, our training and intervention materials have to take that reality into account by encouraging customers to initiate conversations and by providing materials (mirror stickers, displays in the salon) as cues for customers to ask questions. Third, salons are not like other settings (e.g., worksites, schools, or churches) where individuals come on a particular day or time for a specific duration. In salons, most women schedule an appointment, but others just walk in when services are required. The amount of time spent depends on the hair care services being provided. Nearly 20 percent of women in this study visited the salons weekly, and up to 80 percent returned at least once every eight weeks. Thus, initial campaigns were designed to change messages about every eight to ten weeks, with the knowledge that these would reach women and yet not bore customers who came more often. During this collaboration, the academic researchers also learned about the best ways to enhance the business of the salon via local newspaper coverage and other media exposure. In subsequent studies that included randomized trials, training workshops were offered, in the "comparison" salons, on tax preparation and marketing strategies that would enhance these small businesses.

Despite the challenges, there are many advantages to working with community partners in designing and intervening in historically deeply valued community settings. These include the prevalence of salons in most communities, the "natural helper" role of stylists, and the fact that salons are places where social connections occur regularly and where many women spend considerable time. With the added benefit of a community building and CBPR approach to work in partnership with owners, stylists, and their customers, we have witnessed and have contributed to the growing literature on how to best address disparities in health within these important public health settings.

Summary

This chapter presented two examples of interventions based in beauty salons and barbershops, interventions guided by community organizing and community building principles and by community-based participatory research approaches in Pennsylvania and North Carolina, respectively. Given the unique historical, political, economic, and social realities of beauty salons and barbershops in the African American community particularly, there are a number of excellent opportunities for employing community organizing approaches to mobilizing these settings to promote health. Recognizing and building on the role of beauty salons and barbershops as places of strength, safety, rich cultural heritage, and social connections, these two examples contribute to the growing evidence in support of working collaboratively with beauty salon/barbershop owners and stylists/barbers and their customers to address disparities in health.

REFERENCES

Adderley-Kelly, B., and P. M. Green. 2005. "Strategies for Successful Conduct of Research with Low-Income African American Populations." *Nursing Outlook* 53, no. 3:147–152. doi:10.1016/j.outlook.2005.03.004.

Adelman, M. B., M. R. Parks, and T. L. Albrecht. 1987. "Beyond Close Relationships: Support in Weak Ties." In *Communicating Social Support*, edited by T. Albrecht and M. Adelman, 126–147. Newbury Park, Calif.: Sage.

Bristol, D. W. 2009. *Knights of the Razor: Black Barbers in Slavery and Freedom.* Baltimore: Johns Hopkins University Press.

Browne, M. C. 2006. "Program: Take a Health Professional to the People: A Community Outreach Strategy for Mobilizing African American Barber Shops and Beauty Salons as Health Promotion Sites." *Health Education and Behavior* 33, no. 4:428–429.

———. 2007. "Program: 'Full Service': Talking about Fighting Prostate Cancer—in the Barber Shop!" *Health Education and Behavior* 34, no. 4:557–558. doi:10.1177/1090198107305336.

Bundles, A. P. 1990. *Madam C. J. Walker.* New York: Chelsea House.

Bureau of Labor Statistics, U.S. Department of Labor. 2010. "Occupational Outlook Handbook, 2010–11 Edition: Barbers, Cosmetologists, and Other Personal Appearance Workers." http://www.bls.gov.libproxy.lib.unc.edu/oco/ocos332.htm.

Byrd, A. D., and L. L. Tharps. 2001. *Hair Story: Untangling the Roots of Black Hair in America.* New York: St. Martin's Press.

Campbell, M. K., M. A. Hudson, K. Resnicow, N. Blakeney, A. Paxton, and M. Baskin. 2007. "Church-Based Health Promotion Interventions: Evidence and Lessons Learned." *Public Health* 28, no. 1:213.

Eng, E., J. Hatch, and A. Callan. 1985. "Institutionalizing Social Support through the Church and into the Community." *Health Education and Behavior* 12, no. 1:81–92.

Eng, E., S. Rhodes, and E. A. Parker. 2009. "Natural Helper Models to Enhance a Community's Health and Competence." In *Emerging Theories in Health Promotion Practice and Research*, edited by R. J. DiClemente, R. A. Crosby, and M. C. Kegler, 303–330. 2nd ed. San Francisco: Jossey-Bass.

Flegal, K. M., M. D. Carroll, C. L. Ogden, and L. R. Curtin. 2010. "Prevalence and Trends in Obesity among U.S. Adults, 1999–2008. *JAMA: The Journal of the American Medical Association* 303, no. 3:235–241. doi:10.1001/jama.2009.2014.

Ford, A. F., K. Reddick, M. C. Browne, A. Robins, S. B. Thomas, and S. Crouse Quinn. 2009. "Beyond the Cathedral: Building Trust to Engage the African American Community in Health Promotion and Disease Prevention." *Health Promotion Practice* 10 no. 4: 485–489.

Giachello, A. L., J. O. Arrom, M. Davis, J. V. Sayad, D. Ramirez, C. Nandi, and Chicago Southeast Diabetes Community Action Coalition. 2003. "Reducing Diabetes Health Disparities through Community-Based Participatory Action Research: The Chicago Southeast Diabetes Community Action Coalition." *Public Health Reports* 118, no. 4:309–323.

Gilbert, K. L., S. C. Quinn, et al. 2011. "The Urban Context: A Place to Eliminate Health Disparities and Build Organizational Capacity." *Journal of Prevention and Intervention in the Community* 39, no. 1:77–92.

Granovetter, M. S. 1973. "The Strength of Weak Ties." *American Journal of Sociology* 78, no. 6:1360–1380.

Harris-Lacewell, M. V. 2004. *Barbershops, Bibles, and BET: Everyday Talk and Black Political Thought.* Princeton, N.J.: Princeton University Press.

Hart, A., Jr., S. M. Underwood, W. R. Smith, D. J. Bowen, B. M. Rivers, R. A. Jones, and J. C. Allen. 2008. "Recruiting African-American Barbershops for Prostate Cancer Education." *Journal of the National Medical Association* 100, no. 9:1012–1020.

Hess, P. L., J. S. Reingold, J. Jones, M. A. Fellman, P. Knowles, J. E. Ravenell, and R. G. Victor. 2007. "Barbershops as Hypertension Detection, Referral, and Follow-Up Centers for Black Men." *Hypertension* 49, no. 5:1040–1046. doi:10.1161/HYPERTENSIONAHA.106.080432.

Horowitz, C. R., M. Robinson, et al. 2009. "Community-Based Participatory Research from the Margin to the Mainstream: Are Researchers Prepared?" *Circulation* 119, no. 19:2633–2642.

Huskins, C., B. Thomas, F. Ford, C. Browne, E. L. Greene, G. Robins, and E. Gabriel. 2008. "Using Innovative Community Engagement Strategies to Enhance the Education and Training of Scholars in Minority Health and Health Disparities Research." Poster Presentation at the Science of Health Disparities Research, NIH, National Institute on Minority Health and Health Disparities, Gaylord National Resort and Convention Center, National Harbor, Md., December 16–18.

Institute of Medicine. 2008. *Challenges and Successes in Reducing Health Disparities: Workshop Summary.* Washington, D.C.: National Academies Press.

Israel, B. A., et al. 2005. *Methods in Community-Based Participatory Research for Health.* San Franciso: Jossey-Bass.

Israel, B. A., A. J. Schulz, E. A. Parker, and A. B. Becker. 1998. "Review of Community-Based Research: Assessing Partnership Approaches to Improve Public Health." *Annual Review of Public Health* 19:173–202. doi:10.1146/annurev.publhealth.19.1.173.

Johnson, L. T., P. A. Ralston, and E. Jones. 2010. "Beauty Salon Health Intervention Increases Fruit and Vegetable Consumption in African-American Women." *Journal of the American Dietetic Association* 110, no. 6:941–945. doi:10.1016/j.jada.2010.03.012.

Jones, R. 2002. "Program Enlists Barbershops in Health Cause." http://www.npr.org.libproxy. lib.unc.edu/templates/story/story.php?storyId=838158.

Kim, K., L. Linnan, N. Kulik, V. Carlisle, A. Enga, M. Bentley. 2007. "Linking Beauty and Health among African American Women: Using Focus Group Results to Build Culturally and Contextually Appropriate Interventions." *Journal of Social and Behavioral Health Sciences* 1, no 1:41–59.

Linnan, L., H. D'Angelo, and C. Harrington. Under review. "Promoting Health in Beauty Salons and Barbershops: A Systematic Review of the Literature."

Linnan, L., Y. Ferguson, Y. Wasilewski, A. M. Lee, J. Yang, F. Solomon, and M. Katz. 2005. "Using Community-Based Participatory Research Methods to Reach Women with Health Messages: Results from the North Carolina BEAUTY and Health Pilot Project." *Health Promotion Practice* 6, no. 2:164–173.

Linnan, L., J. Rose, V. Carlisle, K. Evenson, E. G. Hooten, A. Mangum, A. Ammerman, et al. 2007. "The North Carolina BEAUTY and Health Project: Overview and Baseline Results." *Community Psychologist* 40, no 2:61–66.

Linnan, L. A., K. M. Emmons, and D. B. Abrams. 2002. "Beauty and the Beast: Results of the Rhode Island Smokefree Shop Initiative." *American Journal of Public Health* 92, no. 1:27–28.

Linnan, L. A., A. E. Kim, Y. Wasilewski, A. M. Lee, J. Yang, and F. Solomon. 2001. "Working with Licensed Cosmetologists to Promote Health: Results from the North Carolina BEAUTY and Health Pilot Study." *Preventive Medicine* 33, no. 6:606–612.

Linnan, L. A., P. L. Reiter, C. Duffy, D. Hales, D. S. Ward, and A. J. Viera. 2010. "Assessing and Promoting Physical Activity in African American Barbershops: Results of the FITStop Pilot Study." *American Journal of Men's Health* 5, no 1:38–46.

Luque, J. S., B. M. Rivers, M. Kambon, R. Brookins, B. L. Green, and C. D. Meade. 2010. "Barbers against Prostate Cancer: A Feasibility Study for Training Barbers to Deliver Prostate Cancer Education in an Urban African American Community." *Journal of Cancer Education: The Official Journal of the American Association for Cancer Education* 25, no. 1:96–100.

Mayo Clinic CTSA Education Resources. 2007. "Urban Immersion: Taking Healthcare to the People: Mayo Clinic, Univ. of Pittsburgh Collaborate to Reach Patients Where They Live and Work." October 10. http://ctsa.mayo.edu/news/healthcare.html.

Minkler, M., and N. Wallerstein. 2008. Community-Based Participatory Research for Health: From Process to Outcomes. 2nd ed. San Francisco: Jossey-Bass.

Musa, D., R. Schulz, R. Harris, M. Silverman, and S. B. Thomas. 2009. "Trust in the Health Care System and the Use of Preventive Health Services by Older Black and White Adults." *American Journal of Public Health* 99, no. 7:1293.

National Cancer Institute. 2006. *The NCI Strategic Plan for Leading the Nation to Eliminate the Suffering and Death Due to Cancer.* Bethesda, Md.: National Institutes of Health.

National Center for Health Statistics. 2010. *Health, United States, 2009: With Special Feature on Medical Technology.* Hyattsville, Md.: US Department of Health and Human Services.

Nyswander, D. 1956. "Education for Health: Some Principles and Their Application." *Health Education Monographs* 14:65–70.

Peiss, K. 1998. *Hope in a Jar: The Making of America's Beauty Culture.* New York: Metropolitan Books.

Releford, B. J., S. K. Frencher, Jr., A. K. Yancey, and K. Norris. 2010. "Cardiovascular Disease Control through Barbershops: Design of a Nationwide Outreach Program." *Journal of the National Medical Association* 102, no. 4:336–345.

Solomon, F. M., L. A. Linnan, Y. Wasilewski, A. M. Lee, M. L. Katz, and J. Yang. 2004. "Observational Study in Ten Beauty Salons: Results Informing Development of the North Carolina BEAUTY and Health Project." *Health Education and Behavior* 31, no. 6:790–807.

Thomas, S. B., and S. C., Quinn. 2008. "Poverty and elimination of urban health disparities: challenge and opportunity." *Ann. N. Y. Acad. Sci.* 1136:111–25.

Thomas, S. B., S. C. Quinn, J. Butler, C. S. Fryer, and M. A. Garza. 2011. "Toward a Fourth Generation of Disparities Research to Achieve Health Equity." *Annual Review of Public Health* 32, no. 1:399–416.

U.S. Census Bureau. 2002. "Economic Census 2002." http://www.census.gov.libproxy.lib.unc.edu/econ/census02/.

U.S. Department of Health and Human Services (USDHHS). 2011. "Healthy People 2020." www.healthypeople.gov.

Victor, R. G., J. E. Ravenell, A. Freeman, D. Leonard, D. G. Bhat, M. Shafiq, and K. Bibbins-Domingo. 2010. "Effectiveness of a Barber-Based Intervention for Improving Hypertension Control in Black Men: The BARBER-1 Study; A Cluster Randomized Trial." *Archives of Internal Medicine*, October 25. doi:10.1001/archinternmed.2010.

Wallerstein, N., and Duran, B. 2010. "Community-Based Participatory Research Contributions to Intervention Research: The Intersection of Science and Practice to Improve Health Equity." Supplement, *American Journal of Public Health* 100, no. 1:S40–6.

Wallerstein, N. B., and B. Duran. 2006. "Using Community-Based Participatory Research to Address Health Disparities." *Health Promotion Practice* 7, no. 3:312–323.

Willet, J. A. 2000. *Permanent Waves: The Making of the American Beauty Shop.* New York: New York University Press.

Wilson, T. E., M. Fraser-White, J. Feldman, P. Homel, S. Wright, G. King, and R. Browne. 2008. "Hair Salon Stylists as Breast Cancer Prevention Lay Health Advisors for African American and Afro-Caribbean Women." *Journal of Health Care for the Poor and Underserved* 19, no. 1:216–226.

14

Popular Education, Participatory Research, and Community Organizing with Immigrant Restaurant Workers in San Francisco's Chinatown

A Case Study

CHARLOTTE CHANG
ALICIA L. SALVATORE
PAM TAU LEE
SHAW SAN LIU
MEREDITH MINKLER

Popular education has been used across diverse settings, cultures, and populations and has been a major influence on the development of social movements and social change processes worldwide. Although most strongly linked with participatory research whose "Southern tradition" was deeply rooted in the approach developed by adult education scholar and practitioner Paulo Freire (1982; Beder 1996; Wallerstein and Duran 2008), popular education also has played a major role in Freirian and other approaches to community organizing (Horton 1998; Su 2009; see chapter 4). Indeed, such consummate community organizers as Martin Luther King Jr. and Fred Ross received early training at the Highlander Center, in Appalachian Tennessee, whose use of popular education and literacy as a vehicle for civic participation and community organizing dates back to the center's inception in 1932 (Horton 1998). As discussed in chapter 4, popular education focuses on the lived experience of the learners themselves and is defined as "a community education effort aimed at empowering adults through cooperative study and action, directed toward achieving a more just and equitable society (Arnold et al. 1995; Hurst 1995)" (Richard 2004, 47).

In this chapter we review the shared roots and influences of popular education, participatory research, and community organizing. We then present a case example from San Francisco's Chinatown that illustrates how popular education techniques were applied in investigating the working conditions and health of immigrant restaurant workers and collaboratively advocating for sustainable improvements for workers. We describe how this approach helped to integrally weave together broader goals common to both community organizing and participatory research such as leadership development, empowerment, social justice through action, and improvements in worker health and well-being. We conclude by discussing lessons learned from the partnership about how popular education, participatory research, and community organizing can be mutually reinforcing in the struggle for social justice and health equity for marginalized populations.

Popular Education

As suggested above, popular education "serves the interests of the popular classes (exploited sectors of society), [and] involves them in critically analyzing their social situation and in organizing to act collectively to change the oppressive conditions of their lives" (Arnold et al. 1995, 5). Inherent to popular education is an emphasis on the perspective of the learner as well as larger educational and social change goals (Beder 1996). Beder (1996) identifies three key components of popular education approaches: praxis, collective and participatory orientation, and action. Briefly, *praxis* is action based on critical reflection (Freire 1973) and involves an iterative process that permeates decision making throughout a popular education endeavor (Beder 1996). The *collective and participatory orientation* of popular education underscores its focus on group process and the "owning" of that process, as well as the information uncovered by the members themselves. It further recognizes the need for the generation of group, rather than individual, solutions and for a sustainable infrastructure for "collective social action," including community capacity building and the development and nurturing of new leaders (Beder 1996; Su 2009). Finally, the *action* component of popular education is reflected in the fact that this approach "is always rooted in struggles for democratic social change" and in the belief that "ordinary people can make that change" (Richard 2004, 48).

Participatory Research

When communities find they require data to support their organizing needs and efforts to improve their health and welfare, participatory research can provide an important and promising alternative to traditional outside expert–driven research paradigms. Participatory research has been defined as "systematic investigation with the collaboration of those affected by the issue being studied for purposes of education and taking action or effecting social change" (George et al. 1996, 7). Popular education and similar approaches from participatory research's Southern tradition not only question traditional conceptualizations of the nature and production of knowledge but also emphasize the need for knowledge generation to be both democratic and emancipatory in its processes and outcomes (Wallerstein and Duran 2008). Among the central principles of this approach are that participatory research should be co-learning and mutually beneficial, involve an empowering process that contributes to community capacity, and balance research and action (Israel et al. 2008).

While community organizing and participatory research have many similar goals, such as participatory and empowering processes and social change, those engaged in community organizing and participatory research may also have differing, if consistent and aligned, aims. For example, unlike traditional community organizing, participatory research often involves academic or other professionally trained researchers as key partners. Additionally, while action is central to community organizing, participatory research occurs along a spectrum, with a high degree of community participation and a strong focus on social change action at one end and less participation and a greater focus on knowledge generation and more pragmatic improvements to organizational functioning at the other (Wallerstein and Duran 2008). Although "balancing research and action" is a core participatory research principle (Israel et al. 2008), tensions between the knowledge generation aspect and the community action aspect of this approach commonly arise. Despite such challenges, real opportunities exist for merging participatory research and community organizing efforts. Popular education can be a powerful means for integrating these two paradigms and more effectively promoting their common community capacity building and empowerment goals.

Case Study: Popular Education, Participatory Research, and Community Organizing with Immigrant Restaurant Workers in San Francisco's Chinatown

A recent example of the successful integration of participatory research, community organizing, and popular education may be found in a participatory, action-oriented study of immigrant restaurant workers' working conditions and health, conducted in San Francisco's Chinatown, and the subsequent organizing campaign in which all authors participated. Combining critical analysis and consciousness-raising with action helped to improve the quality and salience of the research and the effectiveness of concomitant organizing efforts. This process also strengthened community capacity through the enhancement of restaurant worker leadership and the increased visibility of the Chinese Progressive Association, a community-based organization located in the heart of Chinatown, as a potent resource for change in the community and beyond.

The Community and Partnership

Chinatown is a vibrant, dynamic neighborhood in San Francisco. Home to over thirteen thousand residents and numerous local businesses, Chinatown is the cultural hub of the city's Chinese immigrant community. In the city's increasingly service-oriented economy, restaurants stand out as an important source of jobs, employing approximately one-third of Chinatown residents (U.S. Census Bureau 2000). Health and safety problems abound in restaurants and include traditional occupational health concerns such as cuts, burns, falls, and on-the-job stress (Chung et al. 2000; Restaurant Opportunities Center of New York 2005; Teran et al. 2002; Webster 2001). Health problems also encompass serious economic and other social vulnerabilities when employers do not pay the legal minimum wage and engage in "wage theft" by delaying or evading payment of wages earned, sometimes for periods as long as several months (Chung 2005; Teran et al. 2002).

The Chinese Progressive Association (CPA) had been organizing around such worker issues for over thirty years when it formed a partnership in 2007 with the University of California, Berkeley, School of Public Health and its Labor Occupational Health Program (LOHP); the San Francisco Department of Public Health; and the University of California, San Francisco, Division of Occupational and Environmental Medicine. The partnership soon expanded to include six current and former Chinese restaurant workers who provided on-the-ground community expertise to the research and were the focal point of CPA's efforts to develop leaders for its campaign to address the working conditions of Chinese immigrant workers.

Building on previous collaborations between various partners on separate efforts, the new partnership formed to carry out a participatory research study of working conditions and health among Chinatown restaurant workers. Ecological in nature, the study included focus groups with restaurant workers, a survey of working conditions and health among 433 Chinatown restaurant workers, observations of working conditions in 106 of the 108 neighborhood restaurants, and an evaluation of the partnership (Chang 2010; Gaydos et al. 2011; Minkler et al. 2010; Salvatore and Krause 2010).

Integrating Participatory Research and Community Organizing

As Kathleen M. Roe and Brick Lancaster (2005) have pointed out, "Research and practice are best understood as a partnership, learning from and informing each other" (129). Integrating participatory research and community organizing requires open communication, mutual consideration, and careful planning on the part of all collaborators. In the Chinatown project, many hours of partnership meetings—both formal and informal—were dedicated to discussing and reflecting upon the varying needs, strengths, and visions for community change of different partners, the goals of the partnership, and adaptations needed to better bridge the two. In this project, adoption by the full partnership of the community partner's (CPA's) need to recruit worker partners who could then become leaders for the organization's citywide organizing campaign made possible a more efficient use of time and resources and more cohesive connections between the research and organizing components of the worker partners' training.

Critical to the integration of the participatory research and organizing aspects of the project was the project director herself (Pam Tau Lee), a university partner at LOHP, longtime community organizer in Chinatown, and founding board member of CPA. A veteran of previous participatory research collaborations between labor organizations and academic researchers and an experienced popular educator, the project director served several critical roles. As an "insider" in both the community and the university and someone who could understand the differing needs and complementary goals of the research and organizing, she acted as a bridge between the different partners. She worked closely with CPA organizers (led by Shaw San Liu) to coordinate and conduct the many partnership meetings, worker trainings, research activities, organizing activities, and actions involved. Finally, she provided critical mentorship for CPA organizers throughout the research process. Although CPA had decades of experience organizing in the community, it had never before conducted research with academic and health department professionals. The mentorship provided by the project director was doubly important, as it enabled CPA organizers, in turn, to facilitate the worker partners' participation in the study.

Popular Education Approach

As suggested above, popular education permeated all stages of the Chinatown project. Two organizers at CPA and the project director developed an evolving, progressively more intensive curriculum for worker partners that drew heavily from popular education practices to address the dual needs of the research and the organizing.

Interactive, Participatory, and Learner-Centered Trainings

To introduce and prepare worker partners who had no prior experience conducting research, CPA organizers and the project director developed an initial eight-week training. Conducted at the CPA office in Chinatown, these trainings were designed to help worker partners view themselves as experts in restaurant work and realize their value to the research partnership and organizing efforts. Sessions aimed to deepen worker partners' reflections about the realities of Chinatown restaurant work, teach them about participatory research, and facilitate greater familiarity and comfort with CPA and the other project partners. Training activities focused on developing skills necessary for research, such as how to recruit workers and organizing (e.g., effective communication, public speaking, group facilitation, and the filing of work-related complaints). After the initial training and making a commitment to work with CPA on the project and campaign, worker partners continued to meet weekly or biweekly for additional training on workplace health and safety, workers' rights, survey design, interviewing, confidentiality, and informed consent, as well as to participate in CPA organizing activities. Interactive activities such as risk mapping (Brown 1995, 2008; Mujica

1992), neighborhood mapping, workshops on policymaking, power mapping (Ritas et al. 2008), and mock food inspections in a simulated kitchen were used in training sessions. Such exercises enhanced worker partners' participation, assisted them in drawing connections between their own lives and study and organizing goals, and elicited their knowledge and expertise.

One popular education activity used to trigger workers' reflections about their experiences and generate new knowledge began with the project director and CPA organizers displaying pictures of Chinese restaurant workers in various work-related situations. Responding to the prompt "What kind of questions would these workers have about their working conditions?" worker partners related stories that revealed several important issues. For example, one worker partner described a situation she had experienced at the restaurant where she worked. A fight had broken out and the boss did not call or allow any workers to call 911, fearing the negative impact that having police cars parked in front of the restaurant could have on his business. Another worker partner shared a story of a coworker who suffered a head injury after slipping on the floor. The coworkers who walked the injured worker to the hospital were yelled at by the boss for leaving work and the injured worker was fired upon her return to work. When asked for assistance with medical bills for the work-related injury, the boss told the injured worker that the incident was her own fault and the expenses were her sole responsibility.

These stories led not only to additional questions being added to the worker survey regarding workplace abuses, such as being yelled at and witnessing or experiencing violence, but also to training on how to handle emergency situations at work. A "Frequently Asked Questions" booklet was developed for workers with a corresponding curriculum for English as a second language classes. Among the questions addressed were "Can I call 911 when violence breaks out and a worker is injured?" "Is my employer supposed to provide me gloves when I wash dishes?" "Can workers seek medical help if they get hurt at work?" "Can my employer withhold money from my first paycheck?" and "When should I get my pay when I leave the company?"

Critical Reflection

Critical reflection was a central component of the worker trainings throughout all stages of the research and organizing. Following activities like those described above, the project director and CPA organizers engaged worker partners in facilitated reflections about the larger political and economic contexts of the specific issues they were discussing. For example, during a session about the value of engaging in research, the project director and CPA organizers shared examples of participatory research that had been conducted with Latina hotel room cleaners, Koreatown restaurant workers, and Chinese immigrant workers at a local computer chip factory. Worker partners then took part in a critical analysis of the status of immigrant workers in the restaurant industry and in the country in general. In discussing the root causes of workplace hazards and their health impacts, worker partners concluded that "it's important to use the law to protect people." As dialogue progressed, they linked the problems that immigrant workers face in Chinatown and similar neighborhoods to broader policies and globalization trends. The group raised concerns about polluting factories moving overseas, often to China, where the problems are shifted to other workers. In the words of one worker partner, "They transfer the problems over to China and then we complain about it [unfair labor practices]." She went on to ask "What responsibility does the U.S. have when the companies move to China?"

The project director and CPA organizers additionally used research ethics training (required for all federally funded research involving human subjects) to raise workers' consciousness about the human rights and social justice abuses that made such a formal review process important. When human rights abuses such as those committed by Nazi forces in World War II in the name of science were discussed, worker partners reflected on their own historical trauma. "Japan did the same to China," noted one worker partner when discussing the atrocities committed by the Japanese army in his homeland during World War II. The discussion went on to explore how participatory research can help protect the safety of study participants in part through the active engagement of workers as study partners and not simply research "subjects."

Worker partners also engaged in critical reflection during the six monthly data interpretation workshops that were held after the worker survey and restaurant observations had been completed. These workshops were conducted in Chinese by the project director and CPA organizers with additional support from university and health department partners, who wore simultaneous transitional equipment. The workshops employed hands-on learning to teach worker partners to speak "data language" and to facilitate interpretation of checklist and survey findings. Worker partners provided many insights into the data not originally apparent to other partners, explaining, for example, that the relatively high proportion of workers who reported receiving "sick leave" benefits (58 percent) most likely reflected the misconception that making up an unpaid sick day with an extra day of work was in fact "sick leave" (CPA 2010). They also suggested that the apparent underreporting of workplace abuses, such as being yelled at (reported by 42 percent), could be due to the fact that only workers for whom "yelling had made them cry" would have responded affirmatively to this question. Worker partners explained that they are constantly being yelled at by their supervisors.

During the data interpretation phase the project director and CPA organizers also engaged worker partners in reflections about their definitions of "a good life" and "a good job." Through group dialogue, workers came to the consensus that "a good life" for Chinese immigrants is one in which "good health means everything." "Harmonious families and doing one's best to provide," good academic achievement for children, and the absence of extramarital relationships were also key elements. Worker partners discussed how the shrinking numbers of manufacturing jobs in the United States and the increased reliance on the service sectors of the economy contributed to workers' vulnerability and increased the importance of good health. They noted that without good health, immigrant workers with few or no English skills and little or no formal education are unable to keep up with the physically demanding tasks of the low-wage service jobs available to them. When asked for a definition of "good health," worker partners dismissed problems, such as back pain, that they perceived to be minor problems, explaining that "health doesn't impact your [ability to] work. Unless you're in the hospital and you can't move."

Worker partners reflected that "a good job" should include "income enough for a stable life," "a reasonable work environment and working conditions, including a reasonable workload and respect on the job," "good benefits, including health care, paid vacation, and paid sick leave," and having "a job you like." They went on to note that the economic difficulties of their own lives did not afford them the luxury of obtaining the latter. As one worker explained, "Right now, if you're in a position of choosing between two jobs, one that you enjoy doing and one that you dislike, you choose the one that pays more, even if you hate it." Another added, "People just deal with reality. What you want and what's reality are different."

Included in these discussions was critical reflection on workers' immigration experiences. Comparing life in the United States with their lives back in China, worker partners recalled their own experiences and noted the numerous challenges facing immigrants coming to this country. Language was considered to be among the greatest barriers faced. Lack of English proficiency not only resulted in great difficulty finding jobs but also presented challenges in standing up for oneself when faced by discrimination. "Here in America," one worker noted, "it's hard for me to communicate with people. Even when I'm being treated badly, I'm not able to protect myself." Worker partners felt that learning English was especially difficult for immigrants in their late forties or older, and although most immigrants want to learn the language, family responsibilities and long work hours make it difficult to attend classes or study.

Action

Along with interactive, learner-centered activities and critical reflection, action was central popular education component in the worker partners' leadership development training. Even prior to reaching the "action phase" of the project (described below) action was incorporated in the worker partner trainings; as one CPA organizer remarked, "Experiencing the struggle and directly confronting power" was an indispensable step. She went on to note that because fear is common in early experiences in organizing, particularly among low-income, immigrant workers, some of whom may also be undocumented, "the action piece and stepping up to take risks and coming out the other end is essential."

Activities requiring worker partners to take action in the community were introduced incrementally. Early on, worker partners passed out fliers in Chinatown on topics such as wage and hour violations, a task that several found to be challenging because of its public nature. CPA's organizing campaigns around political elections and winning back wages for workers also offered ongoing opportunities for worker partners to gain experience in a wider range of activities and issues. In one instance, a poultry market in Chinatown owed thousands of dollars of back wages to its workers from minimum-wage violations and suspensions in payment of wages. Poultry market workers approached CPA and together with that organization pressured the market owner to pay the owed wages. Worker partners became involved in the campaign, joining the picket lines and attending planning sessions. In another case, a Chinatown restaurant employer owed ten months' back pay to workers. In support of their peers, worker partners participated in two public delegations and a series of meetings with the employer, who later began to pay back wages. With time, worker partners took on increasingly visible roles, sharing their personal experiences at public hearings on city budget cuts and participating in demonstrations for immigrant rights.

Throughout the worker partners' participation in actions, the project director and CPA organizers continued to facilitate praxis by providing opportunities for reflection to reinforce critical analysis and further consciousness-raising and learning. Discussions during and after the poultry market campaign revealed that the experience was particularly influential and inspiring to worker partners as an example of the possibilities of organizing and the attention CPA and the issue could receive in the local media. At the time, worker partners felt that Chinatown community members seemed "not as scared" as they had been before to voice complaints about unfair practices at work.

In these discussions, worker partners also considered the incentives for employers to withhold wages within the larger economic and political context. They noted that larger issues such as the high rent costs for business space, fierce competition, and a weak economy that prevented the raising of prices were encouraging the downward pressure on wages and abuse of workers in other ways. Such reflections, together with their experiences with action, were the foundation for subsequent recommendations for change and organizing demands made by CPA organizers and worker partners (discussed below).

Participatory Research: Translating Research to Action

Consistent with both participatory research principles and community organizing goals, the partnership recognized the importance of translating research into action.

Research findings corroborated most of the concerns expressed by the worker partners and CPA. Results from the survey of 433 restaurant workers indicated that wage theft and pay-related violations—the problems of greatest concern to workers—were widespread. Fifty percent of workers surveyed did not receive minimum wage, 17 percent were not paid on time, and 76 percent of workers who worked more than forty hours a week were not paid overtime wages. Approximately a third of workers indicated that their bosses took some portion of tips. Findings also revealed high proportions of respondents reporting accidents and injuries. About half (48 percent) of workers had been burned on the job in the previous twelve months, 40 percent had been cut or had cut themselves, and 17 percent had slipped or fallen (Salvatore and Krause 2010; CPA 2010).

The study's observations of working conditions in 106 restaurants supported worker-reported data. Checklist data indicated multiple preventable hazards, including an absence of anti-slip mats (52 percent), wet and greasy floors (62 percent), lack of posting of required labor laws (65 percent), and lack of fully stocked first aid kits (82 percent) (CPA 2010; Gaydos et al. 2011; Minkler et al. 2010; Minkler and Salvatore, in press).

In the dissemination and action phase of the participatory research project, the worker leadership development that had been fostered through popular education activities bolstered the organizing initiatives taken by CPA and its allies, as well as activities developed by the health department and university partners to translate findings into action.

CPA organizers and worker partners led these efforts with a range of policy and educational initiatives. A key step in translating the research into action was CPA's drafting and launch of a comprehensive report, *Check Please!*, summarizing findings of the participatory research and worker focus groups (CPA 2010). Reporting primarily on project findings, CPA also drew upon additional studies to illustrate that the working conditions in Chinatown reflected broader trends in the city and across the country for low-wage workers (Bernhardt et al. 2009; Mujeres Unidas y Activas 2007; Restaurant Opportunities Center of New York 2005). The recommendations for improving the conditions of low-wage workers made in this report advocated improvements for low-wage workers throughout the city and featured a "low-wage worker bill of rights," developed by the San Francisco Progressive Workers Alliance (PWA), a coalition founded by CPA and other local worker centers and organizations.

A significant moment of worker leadership was the large press conference held to launch CPA's report (CPA 2010). Worker partners had a prominent role in this public meeting, presenting research findings and recommended actions to the almost two hundred members of the community present, including four of the eleven members of the San Francisco Board of Supervisors and other local government officials. Several worker partners were interviewed and photographed by local and ethnic media reporters (see video of the launch event and associated press conferences at http://www.youtube.com/user/cpasf).

Following the launch event, a major milestone in the organizing and actions has been the joint work of CPA, worker partners, the PWA, and the board of supervisors in preparing the San Francisco Wage Theft Prevention Ordinance. CPA and the PWA introduced this novel legislation with a kick-off press event on the steps of city hall and with a public hearing in which worker partners and other members of the original study team participated. Provisions of the ordinance aim to improve efficiency in the processing and handling of workers' labor violation claims and holding employers accountable through a variety of means, including enhancing the city's ability to investigate and address problems, eliminating delays in citations, imposing penalties for failure to post the legal minimum wage, and requiring public notification when violations are found. The ordinance also called for better education for workers on their rights and information on investigations of their employers, and increased protection from employer retaliation. In introducing the legislation, Supervisor Eric Mar remarked, "I am proud to be introducing local legislation that is drawn from action-based research and bottom-up grassroots organizing that will help strengthen labor law enforcement in San Francisco and give workers a meaningful voice in stopping wage theft in our City" (Eric Mar, personal communication, May 12, 2011). The board of supervisors unanimously passed the ordinance and Mayor Ed Lee signed it into law four months after it was first introduced.

In addition to the development of the ordinance, CPA and PWA have called for a citywide task force to improve the interorganizational coordination of agencies responsible for enforcing labor laws and workers' rights, such as the Office of Labor Standards Enforcement (OLSE), the city attorney' office, and the Department of Public Health. Voluntary programs that could help to promote and create additional rewards for the "high-road" employers who comply with labor laws and maintain healthy and safe working conditions are also being explored. The need to recognize and reward "high-road" and "good" employers was stressed by CPA and worker partners, who emphasized that within and beyond Chinatown there are employers who want to do the right thing but must compete against those who ignore even basic labor standards. As stated in CPA's report, "Ultimately, the high road is the only road that can lead to a healthy Chinatown where workers have stable living wage jobs, local businesses compete fairly and grow, customer and public health are protected, and the community can thrive" (CPA 2010, 24). Finally, recognizing that worker protections are also needed outside Chinatown, CPA and community partners have stressed a citywide approach that brings together the voices of low-wage worker communities across industries, ethnicities, age, genders, and sexual orientations.

CPA and worker partners have scaled up educational activities for immigrant workers. Popular education sessions, which began early in the project with worker partners, have increased in number and scope to reflect study findings and include a wider number of participants. Ongoing efforts include worker teas, held monthly at CPA. Worker partners play a central role in planning these activities, defining issues and topics to be discussed, facilitating education sessions, and conducting outreach with community members.

Other members of the participatory research partnership are also leading efforts to translate study findings into sustainable improvements for restaurant workers. As a result of the significant lack of labor law postings documented in this research, and the results of a subsequent study to examine compliance with labor law postings in restaurants within and beyond Chinatown, the San Francisco Department of Public Health (SFDPH) now requires proof of workers' compensation insurance coverage for all new and change-of-business health permits. The health department is also taking steps to assess and improve citywide compliance with these policies. These efforts included sending formal letters to regulatory bodies such as the OLSE to inform them of the participatory research study findings and set up meetings about improving enforcement of these laws. Currently, OLSE and the SFDPH are exploring mechanisms to improve violator identification and enforcement (Gaydos et al. 2011). Additionally, LOHP and the health department have obtained new funding to explore feasible ways to involve food safety inspectors, who are trained public health professionals and have a regular presence in restaurants, in the promotion of workers' health.

Personal Transformation and Organizational Growth

Although community organizing and participatory research guided by popular education are heavily focused on engaging participants in taking action and changing their reality, an equally strong emphasis on personal and collective transformation underscores the importance of documenting changes on these levels as well. In the Chinatown project, worker partners reported overcoming fears of engaging with new people and "talking to strangers," experience speaking in public, a greater sense of "courage" and confidence, and a deepened analysis of and perspective on social issues. In Freire's (1973) words, the changes worker partners noted in themselves were part of developing a *critical consciousness* and a belief in their ability to transform their world.

Evidence of the worker partners' transformation emerged at the project midpoint, when they began to feel comfortable discussing their own "leadership potential," a dramatic change from the beginning of the project, when they shied away from use of the word *leader*. As the project continued, further shifts were observed, with worker partners moving from simply "wanting to help other workers" to owning issues and solutions themselves through the public sharing of their own stories and experiences working in restaurants and living in the community.

Worker partners directly attributed their changes to the experiences they had with CPA and the project. One described her growth in the following way: "[My leadership skills] increased a lot. After CPA and being a coordinator [worker leader at CPA] really increased it. It's like yesterday at the hearing, I went and spoke. In the beginning, I was really scared. If I had never been to CPA before, I would have been more afraid. Yesterday I wasn't afraid at all."

Similarly, another worker leader reported that the trainings, activities, and experiences with CPA and the project had changed her thinking, noting, "[Previously,] I didn't dare to fight for anything. When I was working, [the boss] said,

'Work,' and I would work. Later, when my old boss asked me to go back, I would tell him I wanted minimum wage, I did not want to be owed wages."

Several worker partners also mentioned that because of their participation at CPA and in the project, friends and family now viewed them as "people who help new immigrants and restaurant workers." One worker partner explained that because she volunteers at CPA, her husband recommended her as a resource to an acquaintance who was owed back wages at work. Another worker partner counseled an out-of-work friend to go to CPA if she needed help with housing or employment. Worker partners have gone on to educate and inspire their children and spouses about the movement, with some of these family members in turn beginning to participate in and support community activities.

Currently, worker partners are an integral part of CPA's Worker Committee, which serves as the leadership core for the organization. They have continued to take on increasingly higher profile roles and have been largely responsible for activities that foster community and build CPA's membership base among Chinese immigrants in the city. These worker partners now frequently speak at public events, such as demonstrations on anti–wage theft and immigration; serve as emcees for CPA's Lunar New Year celebration program and other fund-raising and awareness-raising events; and represent the organization at educational exchanges with other workers and community groups in San Francisco and nationally, such as the U.S. Social Forum. Recently, thirty youth and adult grassroots members of CPA and staff, including some worker partners, traveled to the San Diego–Mexico border region to learn from and build community with area workers, organizations, and activists working on immigration, housing, and environmental justice issues. Worker partners' and CPA's goals have continued to expand beyond Chinatown, as exemplified in the stated goal of the U.S.-Mexico Border Exchange Trip, to "challenge mainstream notions of immigration, to deepen our analysis about the root causes of globalization and immigration, as well as to inspire us to continue building with all communities" (CPA 2011a). Throughout this process of transformation and reflecting popular education's collective and participatory orientation, the formation of a group identity to provide mutual support in worker partners' leadership development has been an important part of the experience. One CPA organizer explained the importance of leadership development's occurring "people to people—not just organizer to leader, but leader to leader. Getting people to challenge each other and support each other and push each other to grow as part of a group process." On the whole, worker partners have perceived a very positive environment and the development of friendships over the course of their participation. One worker partner likened the other worker partners to being "just like family." Another described the benefits of co-learning in the group, remarking that time spent in the company of the other worker partners was good because "sometimes they are bolder than I am and I can learn some skills from them."

At the organizational level, CPA organizers mentioned a number of areas of increased capacity that resulted from their involvement in the participatory research project. For example, the research grant allowed them to obtain resources to develop community leaders in a more proactive and prospective way than prior, more reactive efforts dictated by the tight time pressures of earlier campaigns. In particular, the outreach and recruitment efforts of the worker partners, as well as the research findings and subsequent CPA report and launch, raised CPA's profile and brought greater visibility to workers' rights in Chinatown, and in the larger Chinese immigrant community in San Francisco. Immediately following the survey data collection, one worker organizer observed that people in the community were increasingly able to connect real workers with CPA's name, something that drew people to the organization: "In the past they only read the papers and saw on TV what activities were happening and saw CPA. But now when they [worker partners] go to do outreach and talk to people, it leads other people to know us. . . . [When people come into CPA], I ask them why, how did they come to know this place? She says, I saw it on the flier! Those people passing out the flier told me."

Finally, the data generated in the study also has helped CPA to more effectively generate additional resources through grant writing to support their mission to "educate, organize, and empower the low-income and working-class immigrant Chinese community in San Francisco to build collective power with other oppressed communities to demand better living and working conditions and justice for all people" (CPA 2011b).

Lessons Learned

The integration of popular education, participatory research, and community organizing can be a potent means of studying and addressing collective health and social problems. These approaches can complement and strengthen each other by improving the relevance and quality of research, helping in more effectively working toward shared goals of empowerment and capacity building, and resulting in a stronger foundation for promoting action for change.

Benefits to Participatory Research

Popular education and community organizing orientations provide many benefits for the research process. Involving members of the community most affected by the health issue being studied can increase the relevance of the research and improve instruments, participant recruitment, data collection, and interpretation of findings (Israel et al. 1998; Cargo and Mercer 2008; Minkler and Wallerstein 2008a). In the Chinatown study, worker partners expanded the focus of the investigation to include a careful look at wage theft as a major health issue and helped develop research instruments that were culturally and linguistically appropriate. Worker partners' lay knowledge and experiences also were key to identifying and addressing such ethical concerns as fear of employer retaliation and essential in improving the relevance and cultural sensitivity of both survey items and the restaurant-level occupational checklist (Gaydos et al. 2011; Minkler et al. 2010).

Additionally, the high-level community participation helped to ensure that the research findings were both communicated back to the community and used as the basis of action to address issues of concern (Cargo and Mercer 2008; Green et al. 2001; Green and Mercer 2001; Israel et al. 1998; Minkler and Wallerstein 2008a, 2008b).

Empowerment and Community Capacity

Empowerment and capacity building at both the individual and organizational levels are central goals of both action-oriented participatory research and community organizing (Israel et al. 1998; Minkler and Wallerstein 2008b; Wing et al. 2008). The use of a popular education approach combining critical reflection and action enhanced the development of a core group of worker leaders in the Chinese immigrant worker community, furthered the expansion of CPA's community and worker networks, and resulted in a higher profile for the organization and its causes. This process also greatly facilitated translation of the research findings into action, as with the launch and dissemination of the community report on the research, the creation of legislation to prevent wage theft, and the development of coalitions and alliances with other worker and community groups facing similar issues across the city, country, and international borders.

On an individual level in participatory research and in community organizing informed by popular education, community partners should themselves see changes in their capacity and power. The dramatic changes often described by worker partners in the Chinatown project, who went from eschewing the title of *leader* to testifying before the board of supervisors, participating in rallies, telling their own stories in the media, and actively working for change for and with other low-wage workers, was a critical outcome of this project.

Yet the co-learning critical to participatory research and popular education further suggests the importance of ensuring that outside researcher partners also are growing through their collaboration in the work. Both university and health department partners in the Chinatown project commented on how much their work with CPA and the worker partners had increased their own understanding of problems, such as wage theft, and the immense benefits that community partners, with their expert knowledge of their community, brought to the research and its action outcomes. As Bernard (2002) reminds us, "For Freirians in occupational health concerned with generating an assertive, critically thinking, united workforce . . . we need to unleash the full power of popular education and not limit ourselves to promoting the form without the critical—including self-critical—content" (7).

At the organizational level, enhanced capacity and strength should be a key outcome of such work. In the Chinatown project, the integral role that the worker partners who were hired and trained through the study now play as a Worker Committee leadership core for the CPA, and the organization's enhanced visibility and increased resource base, provide important examples of such growth and change.

Conclusion

The case study from San Francisco's Chinatown discussed in this chapter illustrates how integrating participatory research and community organizing efforts can support the distinct yet complementary ends of each while also furthering shared goals of community empowerment, capacity building, and social change. Popular education, one of the major philosophical traditions shaping the development of participatory research and an important approach to organizing in and of itself, can help to weave together the common threads of these two related but distinct paradigms. Popular education can enable participatory research partnerships to better study and address community-identified problems through community organizing and related social action. At the same time, it can provide community organizers with the philosophical grounding, skills, and resources needed to promote true, member-led action based on critical reflection, while using data gathered collaboratively that reflect lay and professional ways of knowing.

The Chinatown case study demonstrates the fluid boundaries that exist between popular education, community organizing, and participatory research as well as the potential of such fluidity for achieving change on multiple levels (Richard 2004). From these efforts come additional ripple effects as the individuals who participate in the process come to internalize the struggles and take ownership over the conceptualization of community issues and their solutions and begin to influence their families, friends, colleagues, and community. Discussions of the "good life" and "good jobs" initiated in worker trainings laid the foundation for recommendations for policy change and for building the base of support and leadership in the community, which, in turn, led to stronger linkages and alliances with diverse workers and communities across the city and the world.

From individual workers' feeling a new sense of power and empowerment, to their organizational home being increasingly recognized as a strong worker voice within and well beyond its Chinatown roots, to new proposed anti–wage theft legislation and the health department's using the data collected to help pressure for real changes in restaurant working conditions, the project helped lay the foundation for improving the health and lives of Chinese immigrant workers in the community and low-wage workers across the city. The project incorporated the critical expert knowledge of immigrant workers and facilitated their ability to work in genuine partnership with academic researchers in gaining new knowledge for change. This all occurred through a process that was itself empowering, helping to pave the way for more transformative change in the years ahead and demonstrating that knowledge is indeed power in community organizing (Alinsky 1971; Sen 2003). Reflecting on her experience, one worker partner summed this up well: "When I first got involved in this survey project, I thought it was impossible to change anything in Chinatown. But now that we have done so much work in the community and helped other workers recover wages, I see that change is possible. We can improve things. We must!"

ACKNOWLEDGMENTS

Funding for this work was provided by the National Institute of Occupational Safety and Health, the California Endowment, and the Occupational Health Internship Program. We are also deeply grateful to our project partners, Alex T. Tom, Alvaro Morales, Fei Yi Chen, Niklas Krause, Megan Gaydos, Robin Baker and Rajiv Bhatia, the CPA worker leaders, Hu Li Nong, Gan Lin, Li Li Shuang, Rong Wen Lan, Michelle Xiong, Zhu Bing Shu, and Li Zhen He, and community surveyors who were critical to the project's success. Sincere thanks also are extended to the many Chinatown restaurant workers who took part in this study and its subsequent action component. Finally, we are very grateful to the Progressive Workers Alliance, Young Workers United, the Data Center, and other organizational allies, as well as the San Francisco Department of Public Health, the Board of Supervisors, and the Mayor for their help in translating this work into action.

REFERENCES

Alinsky, S.D. 1971. *Rules for Radicals: A Pragmatic Primer for Realistic Radicals.* New York: Vintage Books.

Arnold, R., D. Bamdt, and B. Burke. 1995. *A New Weave: Popular Education in Canada and Central America.* Toronto: CUSO Development Education and Ontario Institute for Studies in Education, Adult Education Department.

Beder, H. 1996. "Popular Education: An Appropriate Educational Strategy for Community-Based Organizations." *New Directions for Adult and Continuing Education* 70:73–83.

Bernard, E. 2002. "Popular Education with a Cause." In *Teaching for Change: Popular Education and the Labor Movement,* edited by L. Delp, M. Outman-Kramer, S. J. Schurman, and K. Wong, 6–8. Los Angeles: UCLA Center for Labor Research and Education.

Bernhardt, A., R. Milkman, N. Theodore, D. Heckathorn, M. Auer, J. DeFilippis, A. L. Gonzalez, U. Narro, and J. Perelshteyn. 2009. *Broken Laws, Unprotected Workers: Violations of Employment and Labor Laws in America's Cities.* New York: National Employment Law Project.

Brown, M. P. 1995. "Worker Risk Mapping: An Education-for-Action Approach." *New Solutions* 5:22–30.

———. 2008. "Risk Mapping as a Tool for Community-Based Participatory Research and Organizing." In *Community-Based Participatory Research for Health: From Process to Outcomes,* edited by M. Minkler and N. Wallerstein, 453–457. San Francisco: Jossey-Bass.

Cargo, M., and S. L. Mercer. 2008. "The Value and Challenges of Participatory Research: Strengthening Its Practice." *Annual Review of Public Health* 29, no. 1: 325–350.

Chang, C. 2010. "Evaluation and Adaptations of a Community-Based Participatory Research Partnership in San Francisco's Chinatown." Ph.D. diss., University of California, Berkeley.

Chinese Progressive Association (CPA). 2010. *Check, Please! Health and Working Conditions in San Francisco Chinatown.* San Francisco: Chinese Progressive Association.

———. 2011a. "HAPI Hour: Border Trip Send off and Fundraiser." http://cpasf.org/content/hapi-hour-border-trip-send-and-fundraiser.

———. 2011b. "Mission." http://cpasf.org/node/5.

Chung, A. 2005. "'Politics without the Politics': The Evolving Political Cultures of Ethnic Non-profits in Koreatown, Los Angeles." *Journal of Ethnic and Migration Studies* 31, no. 5:911.

Chung, A., K. M. Shin, N. Garcia, J. H. Lee, and R. Vargas. 2000. "Workers Empowered: A Survey of Working Conditions in the Koreatown Restaurant Industry." http://kiwa .org/e/homefr.htm.

Freire, P. 1973. *Education for Critical Consciousness*. New York: Seabury Press.

——. 1982. "Creating Alternative Research Methods: Learning It by Doing It." In *Creating Knowledge: A Monopoly? Participatory Research in Development*, edited by B. L. Hall, A. Gilette, and R. Tandon. New Delhi: Society for Participatory Research in Asia.

Gaydos, M., R. Bhatia, A. Morales, P. T. Lee, C. Chang, A. Salvatore, et al. 2011. "Promoting Health Equity and Safety in San Francisco's Chinatown Restaurants: Findings and Lessons Learned from a Pilot Observational Survey." Supplement, *Public Health Reports* 126, no. 3: 62–69.

George, M. A., L. W. Green, and M. Daniel. 1996. "Evolution and Implications of P.A.R. for Public Health." *Health Promotion and Education* 3, no. 4:6–10.

Green, L. W., M. Daniel, and L. Novick. 2001. "Partnerships and Coalitions for Community-Based Research." Supplement, *Public Health Reports* 116, no. 1: 20–30.

Green, L. W., and S. L. Mercer. 2001. "Can Public Health Researchers and Agencies Reconcile the Push from Funding Bodies and the Pull From Communities?" *American Journal of Public Health* 91, no. 12:1926–1929.

Horton, M. 1998. *The Long Haul*. New York: Teachers College Press.

Hurst, J. 1995. "Popular Education." *Educator* 19:2–7.

Israel, B. A., A. J. Schulz, E. A. Parker, and A. B. Becker. 1998. "Review of Community-Based Research: Assessing Partnership Approaches to Improve Public Health." *Annual Review of Public Health* 19:173–202.

Israel, B. A., A. J. Schulz, E. A. Parker, A. B. Becker, A. J. Allen, and J. R. Guzman. 2008. "Critical Issues in Developing and Following Community-Based Participatory Research Principles." In *Community-Based Participatory Research for Health: From Process to Outcomes*, edited by M. Minkler and N. Wallerstein, 47–62. 2nd ed. San Francisco: Jossey-Bass.

Minkler, M., P. T. Lee, A. Tom, C. Chang, A. Morales, S. S. Liu, et al. 2010. "Using Community-Based Participatory Research to Design and Initiate a Study on Immigrant Worker Health and Safety in San Francisco's Chinatown Restaurants." *American Journal of Industrial Medicine* 53, no. 4:361–371.

Minkler, M., and A. Salvatore. In press. "Participatory Approaches for Study Design and Analysis in Dissemination and Implementation Research." In *Dissemination and Implementation Research in Health: Translating Science to Practice*, edited by R. Bronson, G. Coldditz, and E. Proctor. New York: Oxford University Press.

Minkler, M., and N. Wallerstein, eds. 2008a. *Community-Based Participatory Research for Health: From Process to Outcomes*. 2nd ed. San Francisco: Jossey-Bass.

——. 2008b. "Introduction to CBPR: New Issues and Emphases." In *Community-Based Participatory Research for Health: From Process to Outcomes*, edited by M. Minkler and N. Wallerstein, 5–24. San Francisco: Jossey-Bass.

Mujeres Unidas y Activas. 2007. *Behind Closed Doors: Working Conditions of California Household Workers*. San Francisco: Mujeres Unidas y Activas.

Mujica, J. 1992. "Coloring the Hazards: Risk Maps Research and Education to Fight Health Hazards." *American Journal of Industrial Medicine* 2, no. 5:767–770.

Restaurant Opportunities Center of New York. 2005. *Behind the Kitchen Door: Pervasive Inequality in New York City's Thriving Restaurant Industry*. New York: New York City Restaurant Industry Coalition.

Richard, A. M. 2004. "Learning to Change: A Case Study of Popular Education among Immigrant Women." Ph.D. diss., University of California, Berkeley.

Ritas, C., M. Minkler, A. Ni, and H. A. Halpin. 2008. "Using CBPR to Promote Policy Change: Exercises and Online Resources." In *Community-Based Participatory Research for Health: From Process to Outcomes*, edited by M. Minkler and N. Wallerstein, 459–463. San Francisco: Jossey-Bass.

Roe, K. M., and B. Lancaster. 2005. "Mind the Gap! Insights from the First Five Years of the Circle of Research and Practice." *Health Promotion Practice* 6, no. 2:129–133.

Salvatore, A. L., and N. Krause. 2010. "Health and Working Conditions of Restaurant Workers in San Francisco's Chinatown: Report of Preliminary Findings." Unpublished report, University of California, Berkeley.

Sen, R. 2003. *Stir It Up: Lessons in Community Organizing and Advocacy.* San Francisco: Jossey-Bass.

Su, C. 2009. *Streetwise for Book Smarts: Grassroots Organizing and Education Reform in the Bronx.* Ithaca, N.Y.: Cornell University Press.

Teran, S., R. Baker, and J. Sum. 2002. *Improving Health and Safety Conditions for California's Immigrant Workers* (report). Berkeley: Labor and Occupational Health Program, University of California, Berkeley.

U.S. Census Bureau. 2000. "Summary File 3: P49; Sex by Industry for the Employed Civilian Population over 16+ Years." http://factfinder.census.gov/.

Wallerstein, N., and B. Duran. 2008. "The Theoretical, Historical, and Practice Roots of CBPR." In *Community-Based Participatory Research for Health: From Process to Outcomes,* edited by M. Minkler and N. B. Wallerstein, 25–46. San Francisco: Jossey-Bass.

Webster, T. 2001. "Occupational Hazards in Eating and Drinking Places." *Compensation and Working Conditions* (Summer): 27–33. http://www.bls.gov/opub/cwc/archive/summmer2001.

Wing, S., R. A. Horton, N. Muhammad, G. R. Grant, M. Tajik, and K. Thu. 2008. "Integrating Epidemiology, Education, and Organizing for Environmental Justice: Community Health Effects of Industrial Hog Operations." *American Journal of Public Health* 98, no. 8: 1390–1397.

PART SIX

Using the Arts and the Internet as Tools for Community Organizing and Community Building

The past two decades have seen the application of many innovative new tools and approaches that have enriched community building and organizing; some of these, such as user-friendly approaches to neighborhood indicator development and digital technologies for community mapping, are discussed in earlier chapters and in the appendix. In this part, we focus in more detail on two such approaches that have particular potency for enhancing community building and organizing and reaching new and expanded populations with our work.

The Internet, and particularly the advent of the more interactive "Web 2.0" (O'Reilly 2005; Daniels 2011), with social media such as Facebook, have profoundly transformed many aspects of our lives, and also the ways in which we define and build communities and engage in organizing for health, welfare, and social change (Kanter and Fine 2010; Kaplan and Haenlein 2010). In chapter 15, Nickie Bazell Satariano and Amanda Wong provide a wide-ranging look at Internet support for community assessment, advocacy, and organizing and the special role of social media, such as Facebook and YouTube, in supporting and facilitating such work. They offer a wealth of short examples to illustrate the points being made, as well as a more detailed case study of how one organization, Collaborating Agencies Responding to Disasters (CARD), was able to greatly increase its impact and reach through embracing early on, and then continually expanding, its Internet presence and active engagement online. This chapter also provides a hypothetical case study of an organization whose mission is the prevention and early treatment of hepatitis B in Asians and Pacific Islanders who have disproportionately high rates of this condition. This hypothetical case also helps us visualize how our own organizations or causes, which are not yet taking full advantage of the Internet in their work, may benefit from including a diversified online strategy as part of their broader operations.

A number of Internet tools of particular use to organizers and community builders are highlighted in this chapter. They include the Community Tool Box (http://ctb.ku.edu) and Smart Chart 3.0 (http://smartchart.org), which demonstrate how the Internet provides access to a plethora of tools for help in growing new communities, advocating for your cause, and providing important sustainability resources. But as Bazell Satariano and Wong are careful to note, "netroots" organizing cannot and should not replace the interpersonal "real world" connections and community work that remain the heart and soul of effective community building and organizing practice. Sounding a theme that is repeated in chapter 22, they argue that online organizing and community building must be part of a larger strategy, without which their utility is severely limited. Finally, they note other challenges in this work, including the shrinking but still not insignificant digital divide that continues to limit online access in many communities.

If the Internet represents one of our most recent tools for advocacy and community building and organizing, using the arts as a vehicle for such works remains among the oldest. Yet texts on community organizing tend largely to overlook the potential—and the impressive track record—of the arts for building community and promoting social change. In chapter 16, Marian McDonald, Caricia Catalani, and Meredith Minkler examine the arts, including some new media art forms, as a vehicle for social change, their import in social movements nationally and internationally, and the theoretical bases for using the arts to stimulate community organizing and community building. When used by and with communities, the arts are seen as promoting organizing for health and welfare through a wide variety of often interrelated means, including getting people involved, facilitating assessment, promoting healing and community building, and offering culturally sensitive approaches to addressing health disparities. Using case studies, including the NAMES Project AIDS Memorial Quilt; a Latino youth arts project in Greater New Orleans (McDonald et al. 2006–2007); and the Clothesline Project, which promotes awareness of violence against women and children, McDonald and her colleagues vividly illustrate the power of art in community building and organizing. The chapter then turns to photovoice and videovoice—processes through which groups are given still cameras or video cameras and trained to use them to capture and reflect on strengths and concerns in their lives and communities, and as a basis for critical dialogue and subsequent action (Wang 1999; Catalani et al. 2012). Of particular interest in this chapter is the use of these techniques for reaching policymakers.

Although dozens of photovoice projects appear in the literature and have illustrated the potential of this approach with such groups as youth, rural women, the homeless, and people with particular health problems or conditions (see Catalani and Minkler 2010; www.photovoice.org), the newer videovoice technique has only recently begun to get traction. This chapter therefore focuses in more detail on a recent use of videovoice to build community, assess community assets and concerns, and advocate for social change in the Lower Ninth Ward in New Orleans two years after the devastation of Hurricane Katrina and its bitter aftermath. The chapter concludes by arguing that in the face of the often substantial challenges to organizing that communities and their professional partners confront today, the particular strengths of the arts as effective organizing tools should not be overlooked.

REFERENCES

Catalani, C., L. Campbell, S. Herbst, B. Springgate, B. Butler, and M. Minkler. 2012. "Videovoice: Community Assessment in Post-Katrina New Orleans." *Health Promotion Practice* 13, no. 1:18–28.

Catalani, C., and M. Minkler. 2010. "Photovoice: A Review of the Literature in Health and Public Health." *Health Education and Behavior* 37, no. 3:424–451.

Daniels, J., 2011. "Case Study: Web 2.0; Health Care Policy and Community Health Activism." In *Policy and Politics for Nurses and Other Advocates*, edited by D. M. Nickitas, D. J. Middaugh, and N. Aries, 277–285. Boston: Jones and Bartlett.

Kanter, B., and A. Fine. 2010. *The Networked Nonprofit: Connecting with Social Media to Drive Change*. San Francisco: Jossey-Bass.

Kaplan, A. M., and M. Haenlein. 2010. "Users of the World, Unite! The Challenges and Opportunities of Social Media." *Business Horizons* 53, no. 1:59–68.

McDonald, M., G. Antunez, and M. Gottemoeller. 2006–2007. "Using the Arts and Literature in Health Education." *International Quarterly of Community Health Education* 27, no. 3:265–278. Reprinted in the Silver Anniversary Series.

O'Reilly, T. 2005. "What Is Web 2.0: Design Patterns and Business Models for the Next Generation of Software." http:www.oreillynet.com/pub/a/oreilly/tim/news/2005/09/30/what-is-web-2.0.html?page=1.

Wang, C. C. 1999. "Photovoice: A Participatory Action Research Strategy Applied to Women's Health. *Journal of Women's Health* 8, no. 2:185–192.

15

Creating an Online Strategy to
Enhance Effective Community
Building and Organizing

NICKIE BAZELL SATARIANO
AMANDA WONG

Online interactions are such a pervasive part of our society that 92 percent of two-year-olds in the United States have a digital footprint, such as photos posted on the web, and one out of eight married couples in 2009 met via social media (Magid 2010; Qualman 2011). As of 2011, the social networking site Facebook had over 500 million registered users (Facebook 2011). If Facebook were a country, it would be the third most populous in the world after China and India (Grossman 2010).

Today's Internet landscape is infinitely dynamic. Aside from having access to an unlimited database of information, Internet users now continually edit, contribute, share, and discuss information. *Web 2.0*, the name given to this range of interactive and collaborative communication styles (O'Reilly 2005), "is not a new form of technology but rather a new way that everyday people" and tech developers use the Internet for participatory purposes (Daniels 2011, 278; Kaplan and Haenlein 2010). Much of this is made possible by social media. We define *social media* as a set of digital tools such as blogs, collaborative documents, photos, videos, and social networking sites that allow us to forge and nurture relationships with unprecedented ease and frequency (Kanter and Fine 2010; Kaplan and Haenlein 2010). These tools are inexpensive, easy to use, and represent a way of communicating that is here to stay. Social media is no teenage fad—in fact, the fastest-growing demographic on Facebook is women fifty-five and older (Lin 2010). Social media are effectively being used to engage thousands of people in a variety of issues to create social change.

Internet organizing was a key strategy in Barack Obama's 2008 presidential campaign, allowing him to involve millions of people he had never met in campaigning for him with a single click of a button (Carr 2008) and raising an unprecedented amount of money via online donations. Experts argue that his campaign's strategic use of social media tapped into formerly politically inactive populations by engaging key stakeholders in each community, and was the single biggest factor in winning him the race (Smith and Rainie 2008). The incoming Obama administration then used Web 2.0 and social media to engage thousands of Americans, in under a week's time, in reading about health care reform ideas and offering their own reactions and suggestions (Daniels 2011).

Recently, the whole world watched as social media played a critical role in ousting Egyptian president Hosni Mubarak in 2011. Facebook groups such as We Are All Khaled Said (named for a young man who was beaten to death by Egyptian security forces) grew from twenty thousand to four hundred thousand followers within weeks. Similarly, Twitter hashtags (the "#" symbol followed by a keyword Twitter users add to their posts to enter a conversation) such as #jan25—referring to the first day of the revolution—generated dozens of tweets (or Twitter posts) every minute just days after it was introduced. Such social media helped bring tens of thousands of protesters into the streets (Lister and Smith 2011). Organizers and protesters used cell phones to upload videos and photos to social media sites, giving their families and international allies real-time updates. When Internet access was shut down, they were able to record voicemails that were automatically transcribed into tweets ("Egypt Crisis" 2011). The successful role of social media in the Egyptian uprisings catalyzed similar organizing efforts by youth and their older allies in Jordan, Tunisia, Bahrain, Libya, Yemen, and other countries to gain civil rights and topple dictators through a domino effect during the "Arab Spring" of 2011 (Slackman 2011).

As this book goes to press, the similarly important role of Internet-supported organizing propelled the Occupy Wall Street movement, with supporters mobilizing around forthcoming demonstrations via Facebook and Twitter posts and providing real-time visual descriptions with photos and video streams taken on the ground by protesters or supporters.

With the demonstrated success of Internet organizing, the question facing community organizers today is not whether they *should* use social media for community building and advocacy, but *when* and *how* they should. Unfortunately, many groups have succumbed to the lure of easy-to-create Facebook pages and Twitter accounts without taking the time to think about "how to establish a consistent, sustainable, and easily recognizable presence that integrates and enhances both online and real-world activities" (Turner 2002, 55). Without an online strategy, these organizations are doing the digital equivalent of shouting at cars on the freeway—being ineffective. In this chapter we will discuss the potential for using the Internet for community organizing and will outline the steps for creating an online strategy. We will illustrate this through using both actual cases and a hypothetical example involving the use of the Internet to address hepatitis B and its high prevalence in Asian and Pacific Islander communities. We will also provide tips and warnings about the most popular social media tools, emphasizing that social media is an outlet that should be used by organizers who are directed by time-tested community organizing principles. Finally, we will showcase a nonprofit—Collaborating Agencies Responding to Disasters (CARD)—that has successfully incorporated an online strategy for education and community organizing.

Understanding Social Media

Why is social media so useful for community organizing? Beth Kanter and Allison Fine (2010) sum it up with the equation "social media powers social networks for social change" (9). Social media is a tool through which existing social networks communicate with each other in new and exciting ways. Consistent with the messages of Saul Alinsky (1971) and Paulo Freire (1973), who showed us that activism is most successful when organizers listen to and engage existing communities, social media offers new venues for such engagement. Gaining the support of key members of a community can in turn help move members of those individuals' social networks into action, because individuals become involved in collective action through their personal connections (Della Porta and Diani 2006). Internet organizers are still targeting social networks through individuals; they're just doing it through a different medium.

Community organizing principles such as listening to and assessing the community (see chapters 9 and 11), developing a long-term action strategy (Alinsky 1971), "starting where the people are" (Nyswander 1956), building community capacity and social capital (Chávez et al. 2010), and using social network mapping to assess and promote community identity (Amsden and Van Wynsberghe 2005) still apply in online organizing. What social media adds to community organizing, however, is an increased chance that people from different social networks will find your cause and join without being constrained by geography, time, or disability (Rheingold 2002). Online networks are larger, more diverse, and more "searchable." Key individuals are much easier to find and engage with than before. Ideas and issues spread faster through online social networks. Curious people can participate as vigorously as they want. The offline tactics of traditional organizing are still the key components of your toolbox; social media is merely a way to enhance, reinforce, and amplify them.

A key point to remember is that although social media powers social networks, it is not the only way you should maintain connections to your partners, target audience, and supporters. Nothing can substitute for face-to-face interactions and relationship building; social media aids in finding the right people to connect with, then helps keep the relationships fresh. Social media itself is not your social network. Barack Obama's 2008 presidential campaign again provides a good case in point. Thousands of Obama's online supporters had never been politically active. They joined his campaign's online social network because of friends, traditional media messages, and talking to activists (Rainie et al. 2011). His campaign's online organizing efforts simply enhanced, not replaced, their grassroots efforts on the ground where supporters pounded the pavement by standing on street corners, knocking on doors, and holding community events and fund-raisers around the country. The Obama campaign's online efforts helped to raise funds and brought people from outside the campaign to connect with people on the ground.

As Kanter and Fine (2010) suggest, social media tools for community organizers can be grouped into three categories:

1. Conversation starters like blogs (short for *weblogs*), news feeds, YouTube, and Twitter
2. Collaboration tools such as Wiki and Google Apps
3. Social network builders like Facebook, LinkedIn, Ning, and Twitter

(For a visual listing of current social media tools organized by purpose, visit http://theconversationprism.com). All these tools can be used, to varying effect, to accomplish common organizing activities such as community assessment, community and coalition building, political activism, fund-raising, and sustainability. However, you must first create an online strategy that will dictate how, why, and which tools to use.

Creating an Online Strategy for Community Organizing

Developing an effective online presence can help further the mission of most organizing groups or agencies. For example, volunteers are critical to most organizing efforts, and Americans who use the Internet and social media are more likely to volunteer than those who do not (Rainie et al. 2011). Giving your organization a social media presence is simply part of "going to where the people are" (see chapter 3). Unfortunately, it is not an easy task. As Sonja Herbert (2005) notes, moving your group solely from a static website to engaging your target audience through more versatile Web 2.0 tools requires the "rules of grocery shopping: never go in without a list, resist buying what you already have, and avoid flashy products with little value" (332). Before launching any online initiative, it's important to know what you want to accomplish and then match the appropriate tools to achieve those goals by creating a strategy (Kanter and Fine 2010; Spitfire Strategies 2011; Ukura 2009).

The willingness to devote organizational resources toward Internet use in daily activities is the first step in overcoming what McNutt (2008) calls the "organizational digital divide." Often organizations or community groups hire a consultant, find a tech-savvy person to design their website, or find a young person to create their Facebook page, expecting dramatic results from a few hours of work. But successfully organizing through Internet engagement requires building a dedicated internal team, from the executive director to the line staff, that understands the strategy and purpose of doing this. A recent study by ZeroDivide found that nonprofits that successfully leveraged technology for social change were most successful if the leadership integrated the Internet into its strategic plan, tailored messages via chosen web tools for specific audiences, and found ways to track and analyze all outgoing messages (Lee 2011).

We now walk through the steps to devising your strategy: identifying objectives, assessing your audience and environment, identifying your message, and evaluating your online activities.

Identifying Objectives

The first step is identifying what you want to accomplish with an Internet presence. Do you want to disseminate information about a specific topic or issues? Do you want to draw traffic to your website so followers access your new publications and resources? Promote an event or recruit volunteers for an event? Solicit donations? Encourage readers to take some action or advocacy step? Or lure journalists for media coverage? Most important, though, how does this support your long-term mission? Like successful community organizing, Internet organizing is not a stand-alone event; activities should build on each other to move toward a larger goal (see chapters 11 and 22).

To practice devising a strategy, let's assume you are a nonprofit whose overall goal is to reduce the incidence of hepatitis B among Asians and Pacific Islanders (API), who have much higher rates of infection and subsequent liver cancer than that of the general U.S. population (Chao et al. 2009). In the United States, API make up 4.5 percent of the population yet account for up to 70 percent of the country's 0.8–1.4 million people with hepatitis B (Centers for Disease Control and Prevention 2009). Because of the asymptomatic nature of the disease, the Institute of Medicine (2010) estimates that more than half those infected are unaware of their infection status, creating problems for surveillance and disease management. In addition, the social and cultural stigma of the disease contributes to low rates of screening for infection and liver cancer (Chao et al. 2009; Tran 2009; Institute of Medicine 2010). To raise awareness of disease management and prevention of hepatitis B in API communities, the two biggest roadblocks to fighting the disease are identifying those with chronic infection and overcoming the social stigma against them (Institute of Medicine 2010). Your nonprofit's objectives for using the Internet to accomplish your goal of reducing the incidence of hepatitis B in API populations in the United States are the following:

1. Facilitate online conversations that identify social issues contributing to the high rates of infection
2. Provide clear, easily accessible information about testing, prevention, and treatment to those with hepatitis B and their close contacts
3. Identify and partner with relevant community-based organizations to reach out to their constituents with the information above

Note that raising awareness of the issue is not an objective but an overarching goal. You should eventually be able to rewrite the preceding objectives out using George Doran's (1981) SMART (Specific, Measurable, Attainable, Relevant, Timely) criteria, but you will need to gather some more contextual information first.

Assessing Your Audience and Your Environment

Once you choose your objectives, define your audience by identifying and defining the groups that will help you to reach these objectives. Your ultimate targets are the key decision makers, policymakers, and "influencers" who can help you achieve your larger goal. But there may be several intermediate layers of target audiences. For example, you may not have direct access to the policymakers you hope to influence, and who are your ultimate targets. But mobilizing your online supporters for a media-worthy event may well generate the attention you need to reach policymakers. The people who you hope to attract to your event are your immediate targets. All your targets should be identified in detail. For example:

- How old are they?
- What do they use the Internet for?
- What social media tools are they currently using, and how often do they use them?
- Who are the key decision makers you want to influence, and who do they listen to?

In order to answer many of these questions, you will need to assess your target audience by doing the online equivalent of listening to their conversations. As discussed in chapter 9, core principles of community assessment apply here: you must first listen to the general perceptions and beliefs of your target audience.

Listening to conversations online requires a fair amount of time. For starters, search for keywords on the Internet related to your topic of interest and divert them to a central reading place as they pop up, using feed readers—services that troll the web for keywords and topics you define and aggregate them in one place for you to read—such as Google Reader, Delicious, Digg, or Reddit. Use these services to answer questions such as the following:

- What is being said about your health or other topic?
- What are other groups doing to make change?
- What are the most up-to-date health or other relevant statistics?
- What seems to be working?
- What are your partners and opponents doing?

To assess your target audience, go to the sites they are using and read what they are reading. Your youth audience may be reading and posting to Facebook many times a day, whereas your political office-holder targets may be tweeting their vote on a measure. And if your targets are congregating in certain online locales, what are they talking about in relation to your goals/issues/partners/competitors? If they are on Twitter, what messages are they reposting—or, in Twitter-speak, "retweeting"?

Primary research can be conducted via surveys, focus groups, or interviews by asking your current supporters how often they engage through social media tools and if they would be willing to engage with your social media tools around specific issues. For a sample template of an online survey that can be adapted and sent out through an online survey site such as Survey Monkey, see "A Sample Audience Survey," in Idealware's *The Nonprofit Social Media Decision Guide* (Idealware 2010a). This tool will help you to assess how often—or if ever—your targets use social media tools. The *Decision Guide* also gauges the likelihood that your targets will follow your causes via various social media tools. While you are likely to gather some useful information from primary research, direct observations will tell you the most about what your audience is actually doing. If your targets are congregating in certain online locales, what are they talking about in relation to your goals/issues/partners/competitors? What are your opponents saying about you, and what are they specifically saying that causes the most reaction or following?

Although listening takes time, its payoffs can be enormous. In January 2010, an unidentified individual or group started a viral web campaign asking women to post their bra color on their Facebook status for breast cancer awareness. Spokespersons for the Susan G. Komen Foundation were dumbfounded by this outpouring of support and, after announcing they had not started this campaign, asked supporters to visit their website and Facebook page. As a result, the numbers of "likes" on their page increased from 135 to 135,000 in less than a day, with an accompanying increase in donations (Schulte 2010). Constant listening and assessing allowed this group to take early action that resulted in tangible results.

When describing your target audience, be as specific as possible. To avoid a common mistake, remember that "the 'general public' is never a target audience" (Spitfire Strategies 2011). In other words, if you are talking to everyone, you have failed to target anyone.

In our hypothetical hepatitis B example, your nonprofit polls its current volunteers and finds that many of them are college-aged students who not only show up at many of your awareness events but bring their friends as well. Some of them have even started clubs at their campus to address the issue. They are more likely to use Facebook than Twitter to communicate with their friends. Many of them access the Internet, including visiting Facebook, Yelp, and other networking sites, through their phones.

You also learn that your staff members and colleagues at similar organizations use social media to connect with their friends and supporters. They are more likely to use Twitter than Facebook, have mobile Internet access, and use feed readers that follow the keywords *hepatitis*, *Asian*, and *liver cancer*. Your volunteers who are personally affected by this disease are likely to have family members who use social media, ranging from teenagers to seniors, and use Facebook and photo sites like Flickr and Picasa to keep in touch with these family members.

You also search for Twitter hashtags like #hepatitis and #hbv and find that most searches reveal posts by the Centers for Disease Control and Prevention's (CDC's) Division of Viral Hepatitis, by a nonprofit organization like yours, and by a few unaffiliated individuals who post very frequently and whom everyone else seems to be following.

Based on these preliminary results, your objectives can now be rewritten as the following:

1. To facilitate online conversations on Facebook with college-aged students that identify issues contributing to the high rates of infection, and give them tools to talk about these issues with their family members
2. To provide clear, easily accessible information about testing, prevention, and treatment to those with hepatitis B and their close contacts through your website and Twitter posts
3. To use Twitter to identify and partner with relevant community-based organizations to reach out to their constituents with the information above
4. To maintain ongoing contact with these organizations

These objectives are much more specific, but we still need to know exactly what to write on Facebook and Twitter.

Identifying Your Message

Before you implement your online strategy, you need strong, clear, direct messages targeted toward your audience. This should be part of your existing communications strategy (Dorfman 2010). Postal mail and meeting with influencers in person are still a critical part of your communications strategy that can be supported by, but not replace, your Internet activities (for more details on framing messages, see chapter 22, on media advocacy). Just as you will target different audiences for different goals, you will create tailored messages specific to your audiences. Messages directed toward volunteers may aim to inspire participation in a campaign, whereas messages directed toward policymakers may focus on demanding responsibility and accountability.

As before, crafting this message requires listening to your audience, knowing where they converse, and seeing what is most likely to elicit a positive response. What kinds of messages were most likely to be retweeted? What kinds of action steps were people most likely to take part in? What are people most interested in hearing about?

For example, in the process of "listening" to what people are saying about your topic, you read a comment on a blog post about a *New York Times* article on the hepatitis B health disparity among Asian Americans. The writer comments, "This seems to be making a big deal out of a small issue. Everyone I know has already been vaccinated." Another person asks, "What is it about Asians?" If someone has not already responded to these comments, it would be worthwhile to politely respond to clear up any misunderstanding about the issue. More important, what these comments show you is that you need to answer the questions of "why Asians and hepatitis B?" and "what's wrong with the current system?" in most messages you craft.

Evaluating Your Impact and Your Strategy

Once you have created your online strategy, it is essential to pick the right metrics to match your strategy so you know if your methods are working. The good news is that most online activity can be measured. You just have to know how to set up your indicators and other measurement tools to enable you to gather the information that you need. You want to know who your audience is, who accesses your Facebook page and follows your tweets, and who takes action on your website. You want to know which individuals are engaged, and how they engage with your online content. The deeper the relationships that you have built with your audience, the more your efforts will pay off.

There are many resources to help you measure your impact. For instance, you can use Google Analytics to measure your reader growth, counting the number of subscribers versus visitors. It will also report to you whether those who accessed your page did so directly from a URL or if they were directed there from certain other sites and which pages they spent the most time on. You can use HootSuite to measure your reader engagement, that is, how much readers are interacting with you and your content and sharing the content with others on Twitter, Facebook, LinkedIn, and others. Most social media tools will have built in metrics. You can also use social media dashboards such as Socialbrite to update, monitor, manage, and maintain several communication outlets at once.

But there is a difference between measuring your social media activity and measuring the actual impact on your issue. Increasing your Facebook page likes may give you a larger member base through which you can increase the number of attendees at a given event. However, the number of people who sign petitions at your event doesn't necessarily correlate well with the number of invitations your organization sent out to its supports via Facebook or Twitter.

To gauge the effectiveness of your social media activity in promoting offline action, consider polling your donors, event attendees, and volunteers about how they heard about your organization or cause. Did they hear about you through a friend? And if so, did this friend tell them in person or via a Facebook status update, a tweet, an e-mail, or a link on the friend's blog? Easy-to-use online survey tools such as SurveyMonkey, Zoomerang, and Google Forms provide a free or low-cost method of tracking such information.

If you have answered most of the questions in the preceding sections and have a clear, specific picture of whom to talk to, why you are talking to them, and how to talk to them, then you have successfully outlined an online strategy. For a more detailed step-by-step walk-through, however, you may want to use a tool such as Smart Chart 3.0 (http://smartchart.org), an interactive worksheet for creating an online communications strategy. Another indispensable online resource is the Community Tool Box (http://ctb.ku.edu), which contains a multitude of case studies; worksheets; and forums on community organizing topics such as devising an action plan, conducting a community assessment, advocating for change, and sustaining the initiative (for more information, see Fawcett et al. 2003).

Engaging Your Audience Using Social Media

Just as community organizing theories inform your online strategy, engaging your audience through social media requires etiquette, or in this context, netiquette. Part of building your network involves recognizing and rewarding people for passing your message on to their networks. This can take the form of retweets, sharing their links on your sites if appropriate, or mentioning their event or cause in your blog. You can also send a personal thank you note with a link to your website. You may not need something from them in the immediate future, but your follow-ups are an investment in relationships that may someday be fruitful.

As in offline conversations, Tweets and Facebook posts are continuous streams. You must consistently insert your presence into the stream in the form of contributions or comments on other items in the stream. Such posts may also help you direct the conversation in a way you want it to go. In the previous example about misleading comments to a hepatitis B news article, your nonprofit would want to publicly reply that most Asians with hepatitis B are infected early in life and show no physical symptoms and so may already be infected by the time routine vaccinations take place (Chang et al. 2009). Then you might direct readers to your website or your Facebook page for more information or encourage them to attend your next educational event.

Remember that your online strategy should not be composed purely of social media tools. In our hepatitis B nonprofit example, after gaining the attention of our target audience through Facebook and Twitter communities, we want to direct its members to an online resource—namely, a website or electronic educational literature. Websites, e-mail lists, and searchable online databases are components of your online strategy that are just as important as your social media tools.

While there are many free and low-cost tools available on the Internet to help you get out your message or to help viewers to take an action, all tools are not created equal—they meet different needs and require different amounts of staff time and financial resources. Social media may be inexpensive, but its effective use requires time and dedication. In box 15.1, we summarize possible uses of several of the currently most popular Internet tools.

BOX 15.1.

Popular Internet Tools and Their Effective Use

Facebook

By far the most popular social networking site in the world, Facebook offers a large selection of features to keep your supporters engaged and potential supporters informed. Unlike many organizational websites, Facebook is not meant to be static. With Facebook, you can create an organizational profile; post updates, photos, videos, links, and polls; and collect donations. A poll of 460 social media–using nonprofits found that Facebook was most useful to them as a way to receive feedback on their activities, to start discussions, and to drive traffic to their website (Idealware 2010a). The more dynamic your Facebook page, group, or event page is, the more successful you will be in gaining and maintaining connections. On average, successful organizations spend two and a half hours a week on Facebook (Idealware 2010b).

In the hypothetical case of your hepatitis B nonprofit, creating a Facebook page would engage new audiences from among the college demographic by illustrating your activities with pictures and videos that can jump-start conversations. Linked events and calls to action, such as asking people to change their photo to an event poster, posting on an opponent's wall, signing a petition, or attending an event can make your page a good one-stop shop for participation while also driving offline participation. Offline gatherings are also an opportune time to ask your supporters to "like" your Facebook page so your updates will become part of their "feed," or the stream of updates they see when they log into the social network.

A restriction with Facebook is that you don't have access to users' personal contact information. This is why it is important to direct your supporters from Facebook to your group's website to provide their background and contact information. Also, as people show up at an event advertised on Facebook, ask them to sign in and share their contact info.

Twitter

Twitter is an example of a microblogging site. The popular 140-character limit ensures that messages are to the point and can be read quickly. It's also a very popular tool for quickly posting links to news articles or other media. The speedy nature of the service means that Twitter posts, or tweets, are numerous and can drown out your message in the stream. Your organization can use social media managers like HootSuite or TweetDeck to preschedule tweets and keep track of who has retweeted you, mentioned you, private messaged you, and visited your Twitter page. You can also use lists and "hashtag" (the symbol # followed by your keyword) searches to listen in on what people are saying about your cause. Note that Facebook has a microblogging feature, also known as status updates, that can be linked to your Twitter account to update both simultaneously.

Although Twitter had over 105 million users as of April 2010, it is used by an older and more specific population than Facebook (Yarow, 2010). Surveys show that most Twitter users in the United States are twenty-five and older, implying that many are working professionals (Idealware 2010b; Smith 2010). It follows that nonprofits found Twitter to be most useful for connecting with similar organizations, drawing media mentions, asking questions, and coordinating real-time events (Idealware 2010a). However, be careful about patting yourself on the back when you see an increase in your Twitter followers—the previous study also found that only a small percentage of those who read tweets actually take action or otherwise engage. Twitter is most useful as a listening and professional networking tool.

Blogs

A blog consists of static content updated fairly frequently by the organization, often by a single writer. Blogs include personal messages, personal expertise, and personal experiences. This combination of personality and information is what can differentiate it from a website. While blogs can be useful in generating thoughtful conversation, they are very time intensive. Many nonprofits polled by Idealware admitted that blogs were not vastly successful in engaging many supporters unless the blogger was a skilled writer and demonstrated a unique, specific expertise in a topic (Idealware 2010a).

Visual Media–Sharing Sites

These are often the most viewed and most successful types of conversation starters. A 2011 survey found that 28 percent of adult Internet users visited video-sharing sites such as YouTube daily (Pew 2011). Online visual media are also easy to measure, since these sites automatically track the number of views. They are useful as places to upload your organization's media files, but can also be used to engage audiences through video votes, photo contests, and event invitations.

YouTube: This is the largest video-sharing site currently in use. Many nonprofits use YouTube to illustrate their work or educate their audience. It is important to test out various types of videos to see what your audience likes— short and sweet, informative and sentimental, and so on. Be sure to embed your videos on your other social media sites such as Facebook pages, your website, and Twitter. Those, and not video channels, are the main drivers of views. All of your community organization's social media channels should be linked. Also be sure to include your organization's website and social media information in the video description. If you think your video may be controversial, be sure to monitor and respond to the comments section quickly to prevent it from turning into a hate fest, or even disable comments altogether. While there are plenty of YouTube videos with blistering comment exchanges, you want to be able to control the conversation, which requires your frequent intervention.

SlideShare: This is a popular site for sharing PowerPoint presentations. Organizations can create profiles and upload all relevant presentations. This is a great way to share information between colleagues and potential partners.

Flickr: This is a popular photo-sharing site that allows commenting and easy integration with other social media sites. Its simplicity and ease of embedding has propelled Flickr to the top of photo-sharing sites. Be sure to tag your photos and albums appropriately, to increase "searchability."

Online Advocacy and Activism

The countless communities and social networks we maintain via the Internet have been increasingly used for online advocacy and activism. Using Internet tools in this way can not only build community but also give its members a purpose that can result in efforts to promote policy change. Hick and McNutt (2002) propose a framework that categorizes online activism on a quadrant spectrum of conflict-based versus consensus-based approaches and technology-dependent versus technology-enhanced techniques. For example, an issue that requires a change in the power structure and supporters in an offline context will most likely use a conflict-based, technology-enhanced approach. Knowing your audience, key stakeholders, and technology capacity will dictate the type of approach you choose. Similarly, Vegh (2003) defines three types of Internet mobilization: calling for offline action (such as attending a rally), calling for an offline action that may be more effective online (such as e-mailing a policymaker), and calling for online action that is only possible online (such as Facebook messaging and e-mail campaigns).

You may use rallies, meetings, or other offline activities to incorporate people into your online activities, either by signing up for an e-mail list, "liking" your organization's Facebook page, or following a Twitter feed. Similarly, your organization may use Facebook groups and e-mail action alerts for increasing attendance at events and asking supporters to write to their policymakers. These action alerts can also be used for flash campaigns such as the viral bra-color example. Finally, Twitter posts are useful for coordinating rallies and events in real time, since they are easily connected to smart phones and texts.

The ease of mass action via the Internet is seductive. Yet, as Packer (2003) notes in describing the success of MoveOn.org, one of the world's most successful advocacy organizations, in-person street presence remains the most powerful culmination of Internet advocacy. Again, the Internet enhances advocacy but is not, in and of itself, the most effective agent of change.

Closing the Digital Divide

As we have emphasized, the Internet is simply a tool for organizing. The online strategy that guides your online activities should be informed by your bigger, and mostly offline, organizing plan that builds on the tenets of community organizing. Some of the underserved communities we hope to reach may not be using the Internet at all, or they may not have regular access to the Internet. As discussed in chapter 16, the "digital divide" or gap between those who have access to the Internet and those who do not, is created by factors such as technology access, generational gaps, literacy, geographic location, mental and physical disabilities, and traditional socioeconomic barriers that marginalize communities (Herbert 2005; Jansen 2010). Although 93 percent of teens and 80 percent of all adults in the United States use the Internet, recent studies show that high income and being able bodied are the strongest predictors of Internet access and usage, and that there is a racial disparity in Internet access (Jansen 2010; Madden 2010; Fox 2011).

Fortunately, there are many efforts to bridge the digital divide. In 2005, the White House released a report recognizing the widening digital divide and outlined steps to tackle the problem. Subsequent pilot programs showed that we can successfully bridge this gap by providing computers and training to key households in underserved communities (Kreps 2005). Organizations such as the Digital Divide Network (www.digitaldivide.net), ZeroDivide (http://zerodivide .org), and the Community Technology Centers Network (www.ctcnet.org) provide an overview of the movements to bridge the divide, give searchable geographic locations of local technology resources and programs, and even test websites for disability access (www.techsoup.org).

We also should be mindful of the utility of cell phones as an alternative way to reach an audience. By 2010, over 300 million Americans had access to cell phones, and the number of people who own mobile phones and use them to access the Internet is increasing almost equally across racial and ethnic groups. This growth is especially large among youth and people of color (Rainie et al. 2011). Programs like Speak to Tweet, a service developed by Google for Egypt that automatically translates recorded voicemails into Tweets, further help close the divide ("Egypt Crisis" 2011).

But whether through a computer or a cell phone, Internet access is not enough to drive action and engagement. Over a decade ago, Norris (2001) pointed to the existence of a "democratic divide" among those already online, between those who were willing and knew how to use the Internet for civil (or health) engagement, and those who did not, and this gap remains substantial. This is loosely translated to what many Internet users term the "1 percent rule"—that for every 100 people online, 89 read content, 10 comment on it, and just 1 person actually created the content (Arthur 2006). A big part of our effectiveness in online organizing will involve overcoming not only the traditional digital divide, but also the 1 percent rule, and moving more Internet users from passively reading material or hosting static websites to working on- and offline to help bring about change. We end with a brief case study of a disaster preparedness organization that illustrates this point.

Collaborating Agencies Responding to Disasters: A Case Study

Collaborating Agencies Responding to Disasters, or CARD (http://www.cardcanhelp .org), is a good example of an organization that has successfully transitioned into using social media to further its mission. CARD was created by local nonprofit agencies after the 1989 Loma Prieta earthquake in California—before the Internet became popular—to fill a long-existing gap and provide emergency preparedness and disaster response resources designed specifically for nonprofits. For a decade, their grassroots community organizing efforts around disaster issues were handled through landline phones, paper newsletters, and in-person meetings. Then in 2000, CARD's new executive director, Ana-Marie Jones, recognized the value of embracing new technologies and online opportunities. She started by outfitting the office with a new computer network as well as shifting outreach strategies from paper mailers and fax blasts to e-mails, a website, and eventually social media.

It wasn't easy to make this shift inside an organization whose primary constituents often didn't have current technology. Early on, Jones encouraged staff members to use the Internet and social media tools in their personal lives, so that they could learn the value of these tools for building personal networks. She helped convince their collaborating partners that social media was essential to nonprofits by citing trends, gathering success stories, and illustrating how much easier it was to post agency information on Facebook or Twitter than on a traditional static website or in paper newsletters. She also shared stories of people who had donated to a cause because a friend had made a request on Facebook.

With buy-in from staff and partners, CARD mapped out an online strategy. To connect with its target market, it searched for nonprofits on various social media sites, including Facebook, Twitter, and LinkedIn. Since many of CARD's nonprofit agencies and emergency management partners didn't use Twitter, the group copied and pasted its Tweets and sent them out through e-mail. CARD also displayed incoming Tweets at conferences so that participants could experience Twitter in real time and see what people were saying about its presentations. Making social media accessible for people who were not yet users lured many participants into trying it out. Years of working with nonprofits on a hard-to-sell topic like disaster preparedness taught CARD what its audience needed: empowerment through trainings that specifically addressed nonprofit needs and concerns, as well as socialized, simplified, and institutionalized activities that were critical to both everyday preparedness and disaster resilience.

Through "listening" on Twitter, CARD learned how (and how not) to spread its message. For example, a federal agency posted multiple items where the only difference in the subject line was the last word (*hurricane, fire, floods, terrorism,* etc.) When CARD retweeted, it looked to some people as though they had received the same message multiple times. CARD learned not to retweet certain messages without first making changes.

Despite CARD's having a strategy, it was difficult to avoid common mistakes. At first, the group kept each social media tool separate, which was more time consuming. Then it autolinked many of its social media tools, which required using greater care when choosing messages. Eventually, however, it developed a specific use for each tool and embraced HootSuite as its management system. CARD uses LinkedIn to connect with its colleagues and partners in the nonprofit sector, emergency management, and philanthropy. Status updates keep the group's stakeholders informed about CARD's activities and its commitment to fear-free emergency preparedness. It uses Facebook for everyday updates, posting classes and opportunities, thanking and highlighting the efforts of the agencies CARD serves, and sharing information important to its partners. It uses Twitter for fast information retrieval, keeping current on emerging trends, and sharing resources and links to its website and other social media tools.

Aside from using social media tools to keep longtime clients engaged and to reach out to new clients, CARD also used social media to stay abreast of funder activities. Promoting its funders' events to its followers maintained a good and informative working relationship with its sources of financial support. CARD, in short, provides a clear example of how an organization can use the Internet and social media to greatly increase its effectiveness in reaching its target audiences and strengthen its partnerships—in this case, with potentially lifesaving results.

Conclusion

This chapter introduces a framework through which grassroots and nonprofit organizations can benefit from "harnessing the power of the Internet" (Herbert 2005, 331) by engaging the public and work partners. But while using the Internet can be essential to furthering your cause, remember to stick to your community organizing principles. Your online efforts are not effective without your offline efforts, where in-person communications and engagement with your target audience are essential to moving toward your mission and meeting your objectives. The key to Barack Obama's 2008 presidential campaign was not only getting thousands of people to donate small sums of money via the web but also turning millions of voters out to the polls on Election Day.

Just as your community organizing activities may change, so will the online tools that are available. New social media tools are introduced every day, and remaining static in your online strategy and implementation will only result in static support and results. Just as you need to remain agile in responding to opponents and the changing political landscape, it is essential to be flexible in consistently evaluating and adapting your online strategy to best meet the needs of your supporters and your mission.

ACKNOWLEDGMENTS

We are extremely grateful to Dan Cohen, Sonja Herbert, Ana-Marie Jones, Beth Kanter, Tina Lee, Diana Ngo, and Adam Satariano for lending their expertise to this chapter. We also thank the Asian Liver Center at Stanford University, for its wonderful work in online education and organizing with the API population, and to CARD for allowing us to share a snapshot of its excellent work.

REFERENCES

Alinsky, S. D. 1971. *Rules For Radicals: A Practical Primer For Realistic Radicals.* New York: Random House.

Amsden, J., and R. VanWynsberghe. 2005. "Community Mapping as a Research Tool with Youth." *Action Research* 3, no. 4:357–81.

Arthur, C. 2006. "What Is the 1 Percent Rule?" *Guardian*, July 20.

Carr, D. 2008. "How Obama Tapped into Social Networks' Power." *New York Times*, November 9.

Centers for Disease Control and Prevention (CDC). 2009. "Notice to Readers: National Hepatitis B Initiative for Asian Americans/Native Hawaiian and Other Pacific Islanders." *Morbidity and Mortality Weekly Report* 58, no. 18:503.

Chang, E. T., E. Sue, J. Zola, and S. K. So. 2009. "3 For Life: A Model Pilot Program to Prevent Hepatitis B Virus Infection and Liver Cancer in Asian and Pacific Islander Americans." *American Journal of Health Promotion* 23, no. 3:176–181.

Chao, S. D., E. T. Chang, and S. K. So. 2009. "Eliminating the Threat of Chronic Hepatitis B in the Asian and Pacific Islander Community: A Call To Action." *Asian Pacific Journal of Cancer Prevention* 10, no. 3:497–512.

Chávez, V. M., N. Minkler, N. Wallerstein, and M. Spencer. 2010. "Community Organizing for Health and Social Justice." In *Prevention Is Primary: Strategies for Community Well-Being*, edited by V. Chávez, L. Cohen, and S. Chehimi, 87–112. 2nd ed. San Francisco: Jossey-Bass.

Daniels, J., 2011. "Case Study: Web 2.0, Health Care Policy, and Community Health Activism." In *Policy and Politics for Nurses and Other Advocates*, edited by D. M. Nickitas, D. J. Middaugh, and N. Aries, 277–285. Boston: Jones and Bartlett.

Della Porta, D., and M. Diani. 2006. *Social Movements: An Introduction.* Malden, Mass.: Blackwell.

Doran, G. T. 1981. "There's a S.M.A.R.T. Way to Write Management's Goals and Objectives." *Management Review* 70 no. 11:35–36.

Dorfman, L. 2010. "Using Media Advocacy to Influence Policy." In *Prevention Is Primary: Strategies for Community Well-Being*, edited by V. Chavez, L. Cohen, and S. Chehimi, 157–180. 2nd ed. San Francisco: Jossey-Bass.

"Egypt Crisis: Google Launches 'Speak To Tweet' Service." 2011. *Telegraph*, February 1. http://www.telegraph.co.uk/news/worldnews/africaandindianocean/egypt/8295219/Egypt-crisis-Google-launches-speak-to-tweet-service.html.

Facebook. 2011. "Statistics." http://www.facebook.com/press/info.php?statistics.

Fawcett, S., J. Schultz, V. Carson, V. Renault, and V. Francisco. 2003. "Using Internet-Based Tools to Build Capacity for Community-Based Participatory Research and Other Efforts to Promote Health and Development." *In Community-Based Participatory Research for Health: From Process to Outcomes*, edited by M. Minkler and N. Wallerstein, 155–78. San Francisco: Jossey-Bass.

Fox, S. 2011. *Americans Living with Disability and Their Technology Profile.* Washington, D.C.: Pew Internet and American Life Project.

Freire, P. 1973. *Education for Critical Consciousness.* New York: Seabury Press.

Grossman, L. 2010. "Person of the Year 2010: Mark Zuckerberg." *Time*, December 15.

Herbert, S. 2005. "Harnessing the Power of the Internet for Advocacy and Organizing." In *Community Organizing and Community Building for Health*, edited by M. Minkler, 331–345. 2nd ed. New Brunswick, N.J.: Rutgers University Press.

Hick, S., and J. G. McNutt. 2002. *Advocacy, Activism, and the Internet: Community Organization and Social Policy.* Chicago: Lyceum Books.

Idealware. 2010a. *The Nonprofit Social Media Decision Guide.* Portland, Maine: Idealware.

———. 2010b. *Using Social Media to Meet Nonprofit Goals: The Results of a Survey*. Portland, Maine: Idealware.

Institute of Medicine. 2010. *Hepatitis and Liver Cancer: A National Strategy for Prevention and Control of Hepatitis B and C*. Washington, D.C.: National Academies Press.

Jansen, J. 2010. *Use of the Internet in Higher-Income Households*. Washington, D.C.: Pew Internet and American Life Project.

Kanter, B., and A. Fine. 2010. *The Networked Nonprofit: Connecting with Social Media to Drive Change*. San Francisco: Jossey-Bass.

Kaplan, A. M., and M. Haenlein. 2010. "Users of the World, Unite! The Challenges and Opportunities of Social Media." *Business Horizons* 53, no. 1:59–68.

Kreps, G. L. 2005. "Disseminating Relevant Health Information to Underserved Audiences: Implications of the Digital Divide Pilot Projects." Supplement, *Journal of the Medical Library Association* 93, no. 4:S68.

Lee, T. 2011. *Mobilizing Communities in a Connected Age: A Portfolio Assessment of Advocacy Organizations*. San Francisco: ZeroDivide.

Lin, E. 2010. "SFN Report: Women 55 and Older Fastest-Growing Facebook Demographic." *SFNBlog.com* (blog). http://www.sfnblog.com/industry_trends/2010/04/sfn_report_women_55_and_older_fastest-gr.php.

Lister, T., and E. Smith. 2011. "Social Media @ the Front Line in Egypt." CNN, January 27 http://articles.cnn.com/2011-01-27/world/egypt.protests.social.media_1_social-media-twitter-entry-muslim-brotherhood?_s=PM:WORLD.

Magid, L. 2010. "Study: 92 percent of U.S. 2-Year-Olds Have Online Record." http://news.cnet.com/8301-19518_3-20018728-238.html?tag=cnetRiver.

Madden, M. 2010. *Four or More: The New Demographic*. Washington, D.C.: Pew Internet and American Life Project.

McNutt, J. 2008. "Advocacy Organizations and the Organizational Digital Divide." *Currents: New Scholarship in the Human Services* 7, no. 2:1–13.

Norris, P. 2001. *Digital Divide: Civic Engagement, Information Poverty, and the Internet Worldwide*. Cambridge, U.K.: Cambridge University Press.

Nyswander, D. 1956. "Education for Health: Some Principles and Their Application." *California Health* 14 (November): 65–70.

O'Reilly, T. 2005. "What Is Web 2.0?: Design Patterns and Business Models for the Next Generation of Software." http:www.oreillynet.com/pub/a/oreilly/tim/news/2005/09/30/what-is-web-2.0.html?page=1.

Packer, G. 2003. "Smart-Mobbing the War." *New York Times*, March 9, sec. 6, 46.

Pew Internet and the American Life Project. 2011. "Online Activities, Daily." http://www.pewinternet.org/Trend-Data/Online-Activities-Daily.aspx.

Qualman, E. 2011. *Socialnomics: How Social Media Transforms the Way We Live and Do Business*. Hoboken: John Wiley and Sons.

Rainie, L., K. Purcell, and A. Smith. 2011. *The Social Side of the Internet: Technology Use Has Become Deeply Embedded in Group Life and Is Affecting the Way Civic and Social Groups Behave and the Way They Impact Their Communities*. Washington, D.C.: Pew Internet and American Life Project.

Rheingold, H. 2002. *Smart Mobs: The Next Social Revolution*. Cambridge, Mass.: Perseus.

Schulte, B. 2010. "Breast Cancer Awareness Goes Viral On Facebook . . . with Bra Color Updates." *Washington Post*, January 9.

Slackman, M. 2011. "Bullets Stall Youthful Push for Arab Spring." *New York Times*, March 17.

Smith, A., and L. Rainie. 2008. *The Internet and the 2008 Election*. Washington, D.C.: Pew Internet and American Life Project.

Spitfire Strategies. 2011. "Smart Chart 3.0: An Interactive Tool to Help Nonprofits Make Smart Communications Choices." http://smartchart.org.

Tran, T. T. 2009. "Understanding Cultural Barriers in Hepatitis B Virus Infection." Supplement, *Cleveland Clinic Journal of Medicine* 76, no. 3:S10.

Turner, R. 2002. "Public Policy, Technology, and the Nonprofit Sector: Notes from the Field." In *Activism, Advocacy, and the Internet*, edited by S. Hick and J. McNutt, 43–57. Chicago: Lyceum.

Vegh, S. 2003. "Classifying Forms of Online Activism: The Case of Cyberprotests against the World Bank." In *Cyberactivism: Online Activism in Theory and Practice*, edited by M. McCaughey and M. Ayers, 71–95. New York: Routledge.

Ukura, K. 2009. "Web Advice from COMM-ORG: The Online Conference on Community Organizing." COMM-ORG. http://comm-org.wisc.edu/co/node/18.

Yarow, J. 2010. "Twitter CEO Ev Williams' Keynote From Chirp." Business Insider. http://www.businessinsider.com/live-twitter-ceo-ev-williams-keynote-from-chirp-2010–4.

16

Using the Arts and New Media in Community Organizing and Community Building

An Overview and Case Study from Post-Katrina New Orleans

MARIAN MCDONALD

CARICIA CATALANI

MEREDITH MINKLER

Community organizing allows people who share a particular geographic space or identity to find shared issues and goals, as well as the resources they can use collectively to achieve those goals (see chapter 1). This definition is intentionally broad, as the processes, efforts, communities, and goals that constitute organizing techniques are diverse.

The arts, including literature, music, video, painting, photography, and other forms of artistic expression, are powerful tools for community organizing in health and related areas (McDonald et al. 2006–2007; Chávez et al. 2004; Catalani and Minkler 2010). They can draw attention to an issue, offer catharsis for a community after a crisis, pull communities together to create art, and communicate across cultural and language barriers. As Vivian Chávez and her colleagues (2004) note, "The cultural diversity, personal sensitivity, and passion that characterize some of the arts resonate with some key principles and commitments of health promotion" (396), including the fostering of high-level community participation and building on community and individuals' strengths.

In this chapter, the authors draw on diverse examples to illustrate how the arts have served as vehicles for change, to highlight their legacy in social movements nationally and globally, and to point out the theoretical basis of their use in community organizing and community building. Brief examples describe how the arts have been used to foster community organizing for health; this is followed by a discussion of two increasingly popular visual methodologies—*photovoice* and *videovoice*—which enable individuals to get behind still cameras and video cameras, respectively, to "research issues of concern, communicate their knowledge, and advocate for change" (Catalani et al. 2012, 3; C. C. Wang et al. 2004; C. C. Wang and Burris 1997). A videovoice case study in post–Hurricane Katrina New Orleans then is used to explore how a community-academic-filmmaker partnership used this approach for studying and engaging in policy-focused change and to describe its ripple effects (Catalani et al. 2012).

Community Organizing for Change and the Arts as a Vehicle

Communities interested in organizing for change decide on the strategies to use by looking critically at who their target is (e.g., who has the ability to make the desired change?), identifying the resources available to them, and deciding on the best way to effect the changes they seek (see chapters 9 and 11). In each of the case studies explored in this chapter, community groups chose the arts as the vehicle for accomplishing their goals.

The Arts as Vehicle for Social Change

Artistic expression is universal to human culture and has historically tapped into the most deeply felt ways of understanding and interpreting the world. The act of creating increases feelings of well-being and can help facilitate feelings of belonging. Furthermore, the creation of some form of art is not dependent on language or literacy level, but can be undertaken by anyone with the will and desire to do so. The power of art for community organizing, then, lies in the power of the arts to communicate a message and elicit an emotional response, as well as in the creation of art itself.

The arts and literature have always played a role in the processes of community organizing and of social change, though they are typically seen as incidental or secondary. Poet and activist Audre Lorde (1984) challenged this view in her classic essay on the importance of poetry in people's lives, especially the lives of women: "For women . . . poetry is not a luxury. It is a vital necessity of our existence. It forms the quality of the light within which we predicate our hopes and dreams toward survival and change, first made into language, then into idea, then into more tangible action" (37).

Lorde sees poetry, and other forms of creativity and expression, as necessary precursors to action. Her view has been shared by many artists, educators, and advocates throughout history and across the globe. These figures include African American jazz singer Billie Holiday, whose insistence upon singing a song about Southern lynchings shocked audiences; Chilean songwriter Victor Jara, who courageously sang against the murderers of the 1973 coup d'état; and Maya Lin, the Chinese American architect whose design of the Vietnam War Memorial helped to create the conditions for national healing (www.thewall-usa.com).

Legacy of the Arts in Social Movements
in the United States and Beyond

Within the United States, the arts have played an important role in social movements. Woody Guthrie's melodic tributes to the working people ("This Land is Your Land") and his biting criticisms of injustice ("Deportees") won him audiences in the strife-torn 1940s and an enduring place in U.S. culture (Cray 2004; Guthrie 1958). Legendary African American actor and singer Paul Robeson resisted bigotry and repression with his masterful performances in the 1950s, helping set the stage for the civil rights movement. The forceful refrain of the gospel-turned-civil-rights song "We Shall Overcome" became an anthem of the fight against segregation and for civil rights and later was embraced by the labor, peace, and women's movements.

Although this book focuses on the United States, the nation's increasing diversity, combined with the lessons to be learned from organizing successes in other countries, make it important to look beyond our borders. In countries where democratic forces have challenged domination and foreign interference, the battle for control over cultural expression has been key. In Nicaragua, the victory over dictator Anastasio Somoza helped put in place new and popular forms of expression, from a grassroots literacy campaign to a new song movement and the flourishing of murals and poetry workshops (Cardenal 1982; Randall 1991). With the change of government in 1990 and a determined "rollback" of Sandinista influence, one of the first tactics of Managua's conservative mayor Arnoldo Alemán was to paint over some of the city's most impressive pro-Sandinista murals. More recently, new technology has facilitated artistic expression and citizen media in the Middle East and North Africa, as videos and photographs recorded by protesters' mobile phones and shared through sites like YouTube, Flickr, and Facebook have allowed a powerful inside look at repression that is usually largely closed off to the outside world (Preston and Stelter 2011).

The arts have historically been deeply rooted in change processes, providing a rich tradition for those involved in health-related change. It is against this backdrop that the use of the arts in organizing around health can be understood.

Theoretical Bases for Using the Arts
in Community Organizing for Health

To be effective, community organizing for health needs to begin with a people's reality. Central to that reality is culture, including people's collective past and hopes for the future. As Amilcar Cabral (1979), an African leader who fought for the independence of Guinea-Bissau, noted, "Culture is the dynamic synthesis, at the level of individual or community consciousness, of the material and spiritual historical reality of a society or a human group, of the relations existing between [people] and nature as well as among social classes or sectors. Cultural manifestations are the various forms in which this synthesis is expressed, individually, or collectively, at each stage in the evolution of the society or group" (210).

The international women's movement also has demonstrated, through a wide array of literary and other art forms, the indispensable role of culture in the development of consciousness and identity (McIntyre and Lykes 2004; Randall 1991; hooks 1994). Specifically, the concept of the development of *the voice* has been advanced as a key element of the process of transforming women's lives (Randall 1991; McIntyre and Lykes 2004).

The creation of a voice to break the silence is a central idea in the work of the late Brazilian scholar of adult education Paulo Freire, whose writings have transformed the world's views of education and popular culture (Freire 1970, 1990a, 1990b; Su 2009; see also chapter 4). Of particular concern to Freire was "education for critical consciousness" through which people who have been alienated from their culture are encouraged to identify, examine, and act on the root causes of their oppression. This Freirian notion of "conscientization" always involves group, rather than merely individual, transformation, or "consciousness-raising." Initially developed as a literacy method for Brazilian peasants, Freire's approach involved "teaching people to read, which teaching them to read the political and social situation in which they lived" so that they could help transform it (Carroll and Minkler 2000, 23). The use of pictures and other visual symbols to capture the themes generated in this process is central to the methodology (see chapter 4 and appendix 9).

Freire's (1970, 1990a, 1990b) concept of empowerment, rooted in critical consciousness and developed through practice, has been applied in education, public health, social welfare, and community organizing projects throughout the Americas and around the globe (Laver et al. 2005–2006; Horton and Freire 1990; Su 2009; Wallerstein 2006; see also chapter 4).

The theoretical and practical legacy of feminism also provides numerous conceptual bases for using the arts in community health organizing. Feminism's tenets of the personal as political, the importance of relationships and process, and the embracing of diversity all encourage creative and collective expression (McIntyre and Lykes 2004).

More recently, participatory new-media theories have offered a framework for understanding the impacts of an increasingly interconnected and digital world on social inequities, with particular implications on using the arts in community organizing. Participatory new media theorists argue that enhanced access to digital tools (computers, mobile devices, audio/photo/video recording tools, etc.) and the Internet result in a radical democratization in the production and communication of arts, knowledge, and culture (Benkler 2006; Rheingold 2008; Jenkins 2003). The digital divide—the gap between those with access to digital and information technology and those without—presents potential for further disparity between global haves and have-nots (Lorence and Park 2008; Fox and Livingston 2007). Recent research indicates that this gap is shrinking. As of 2010, fully 82 percent of English-speaking Latinos and 71 percent of African Americans as compared with 80 percent of whites used the Internet, more people of color than whites accessed the Internet through their mobile phones, and laptop ownership was about even across these groups (Smith 2010). For monolingual Spanish-speaking Latinos, the rates lagged significantly (Fox 2010; Livingston 2010).

Whether in the virtual or physical world, the arts also promote health through the development and expansion of social support. With the exception of more collaborative arts such as film, music, and theater, the arts are often solitary activities in the creation stage. However, the act of sharing the arts through community events, online social-networking and media-sharing sites, or person-to-person exchanges can be profoundly social and collective. By creating common reference points through culture, communities begin to break down isolation, share their common experiences, and build collective vision. This community building process is often a critical precursor to community organizing (see chapters 4 and 5).

The Arts in Urban Life

The arts play a particularly important role in urban health organizing, because of the very nature of cities. The physical environment of cities—sidewalks, buildings, subways, and parks—provides unique public places that serve as sites where people can express themselves. Additionally, the population density of cities brings people into frequent contact, creating endless opportunities for common experiences and communication. For many people living in the city, popular culture is their only possible exposure to art forms.

A number of forms of art and literature have been used in cities to give voice to communities. These include community murals, guerilla theater, poetry slams, dance brigades, participatory video, hip-hop music, and graffiti (Boal 1979; Brown 2010; Chávez et al. 2004; E. L. Wang 2010). The forms used are as diverse as communities themselves.

A reality of most major urban areas today is their diversity of culture, language, and ethnicity. The arts can give voice to the heterogeneity of urban populations, breaking down barriers in the process. Ethnic, racial, and linguistic diversity exists in urban areas, alongside diversity of age, gender, economic status, and sexual orientation and identity. When organizing for urban community health, health professionals and activists need to address diversity directly, rather than ignore or downplay it (Cutting and Themba-Nixon 2006). The arts can be effectively used to express and respect diversity, in a process that can weave unity among the community's different threads.

The Arts in the Practice of Community Organizing for Health

Health education leader Dorothy Nyswander's (1956) admonition to "start where the people are" suggests that organizers need to familiarize themselves with a people's cultural expressions as a part of working with the community. As Freire asks, "How is it possible for us to work in a community without feeling the spirit of the culture that has been there for many years, without trying to understand the soul of the culture?" (Horton and Freire 1990, 131).

In the community, the arts can promote organizing for health in the following ways, often simultaneously:

1. *To get people involved.* The use of art forms and activities involves people who might otherwise be disinterested or intimidated by more explicitly health-oriented or community organizing activities. Simply put, the arts make getting involved fun. For example, rap and dance contests have increasingly been used in the San Francisco Bay Area and elsewhere to involve both straight and LGBTQQ (lesbian, gay, bisexual, transgender, queer, and questioning) youth in building awareness of HIV/AIDS and STIs (sexually transmitted diseases) (Brown 2010).

2. *To find out about a community.* The arts can be a valuable strategy for conducting community needs assessments and mapping community assets (Kretzman and McKnight 1993; Catalani and Minkler 2010; see also chapter 9). Poetry and arts workshops, offered to the community at low or no cost, can provide valuable insights into the community, its leaders, and its history. Initiated in Greater New Orleans in 1996, the Discubriendo El Arte (Summer Arts Discovery) program illustrates the use of the arts for community assessment, while also building community in a low-resource, predominantly monolingual Latino housing project (McDonald et al. 2006–2007). Discubriendo El Arte was the first stage of a community health–organizing plan developed by the Latino Health Outreach Project, a multicultural and bilingual collaboration of students and faculty at Tulane's School of Public Health and Tropical Medicine. At the invitation of local Latino community activists, door-to-door and other outreach was conducted, followed by collective community assessment and asset mapping. Extensive data were gathered and arts activities designed around the themes of community, family, and school, to elicit the children's perceptions of their community. Through arts workshops, the group was able to establish rapport with both children and their mothers and laid the basis for a series of *charlas* (talks) over the following months.

The process of carrying out Discubriendo El Arte allowed the Tulane team to make a number of useful observations concerning language preferences, family unity, gender roles, and recurrent themes, which in turn helped in the planning of future community health–organizing, which continued for several years and helped this community use its voice and be heard.

3. *To increase awareness and relay health education messages.* The arts are powerful messengers. Because they tap into people's feelings, they have the potential to shape consciousness. Furthermore, visual and oral representations are easy to grasp, regardless of literacy level, and positive messages can be developed and promoted in popular culture (Stuckey 2010). An example is a song that gained airtime in Spanish-speaking communities throughout the Americas in the 1990s.

Ponte el Sombrero (Put on your hat) encourages condom use in a playful, non-threatening way.

Bringing health messages though such mediums has sometimes been referred to as "edutainment" or "enter-education," whereby education and entertainment are combined (Zeedyk and Wallace 2003). In this approach, the message is relayed through an already established medium of popular (and commercial) culture, such as a television show, film, or song. Examples are the portrayals of community struggles with drugs and violence on HBO's *The Wire*, an HIV-positive member of the cast on MTV's *Real World*, or story lines about diabetes on the Spanish-language soap opera *Amarte así*. While potentially very effective, this approach to relaying a message can be challenging for community organizers for a number of reasons. First, communities typically don't have access to screenwriters, songwriters, and producers and hence have little control over the messages portrayed or solutions proposed; they also have no access to the arts industry's distribution systems. Although newer approaches such as media advocacy (see chapter 22) and participatory media production (see videovoice example below) are helping communities become far more savvy in gaining access to and using the media to help give visibility to their concerns and issues, access remains a significant barrier. Second, edutainment overwhelmingly relies on commercial culture, in which the recipient of the message is by design a detached listener or observer, as opposed to an active agent. Because these vehicles are external to community, they can sometimes encourage a passive, consumer approach, as opposed to empowerment, as discussed below.

4. *To attract attention to an issue.* A cultural manifestation of an issue will often catch people's attention, changing their perceptions. The Clothesline Project, begun in 1990 by women in Massachusetts to promote awareness of violence against women, provides a classic example. The project urges victims and survivors of violence against women to create a T-shirt that expresses their feelings. A white T-shirt is used in memory of a murdered woman, a blue T-shirt for survivors of childhood sexual abuse, yellow for a battered woman, and so on. When a series of these T-shirts are made, they are displayed in a public place on a clothesline, a graphic and moving statement about the realities so many women and children face, and a powerful way of "airing society's dirty laundry" (Hippe 2000). The project, which today includes some thirty thousand to fifty thousand shirts in many countries, took a simple, accessible medium and transformed it into a powerful voice against the pervasive problems of child sexual abuse, intimate partner violence, and violence against women (personal communication from Carol Tozelotoze, March 13, 2011; see also http://www.clotheslineproject.org/).

5. *To promote community building.* Through its emphasis on high-level participation and building and strengthening relationships, the community building framework allows for unfettered forms of community expression, to which the arts and literature are particularly well suited. Cultural forms of expression rooted in the community help not only to give voice to concerns but also to

establish the collective life, whether through celebration, ritual, or mourning. Such community expressions can be powerful tools in achieving organizing goals, particularly in communities of color, where oppression has often entailed the belittling or outright suppression of traditional cultural forms of expression (Duran and Duran 1995; Tuhiwai Smith 2008). The Names Project/AIDS Memorial Quilt (http:// www.aidsquilt.org/quiltfacts.htm), highlighted below, is among the most potent examples of community building through the arts with often marginalized groups.

6. *To promote healing.* The restorative and healing powers of the arts have long been acknowledged (Stuckey 2010). The creative process is restorative and transformative, often helping to heal the one who undertakes it (Longman 1994). At the same time, the fruits of the creative process offer insights to others with similar experiences and help to promote their healing though an interactive process.

The Vietnam War Memorial in Washington, D.C., provides a powerful example. The simple, stark wall where the names of the dead are etched has become a mecca for millions who need to reflect on, cry about, or exorcise the war. It has served to promote the healing, understanding, and forgiveness so elusive to the country in the years following the war (Randall 1991; www.thewall-usa.com).

In working with war-traumatized Guatemalan children, McIntyre and Lykes (2004; Lykes 1997) found that drama, body movements, and play elicited opinions from children who had been silenced and terrorized by the violence of war. The opportunity to voice their fear, sadness, and anger through characters allowed them to express themselves and respond openly to the researcher's questions. Lykes hypothesized that without the drama, the children would have been too afraid to express their experiences and true feelings, and their need for psychological and social support would have been harder to ascertain.

7. *To promote culturally competent health organizing efforts and address health disparities.* One of the major challenges facing community organizing for health is effectively addressing widespread health disparities based on race, ethnicity, gender, language, age, disabilities, geography, and sexual orientation. Racial and ethnic health disparities are widespread and require multiple urgent responses (U.S. Department of Health and Human Services 2011). Health disparities can be addressed in part by promoting cultural and linguistic competence in health promotion and health delivery, both arenas of importance for community health organizing (Betancourt et al. 2003).

Cultural competence is defined broadly by the federal Office of Minority Health as a set of skills that allows individuals or institutions to increase their appreciation of cultural differences and to act sensitively, appropriately, and respectfully toward different cultures (http://minorityhealth.hhs.gov/templates/browse.aspx?lvl=2&lvlID=11).

The arts are a natural and extremely effective vehicle for promoting cultural competence, because people create in the forms and language that are most deeply rooted in their culture, experience, values, and history. The arts provide for an intimate and immediate expression of what is culturally appropriate and meaningful for communities—and, by extension, for community organizing.

8. *To empower.* Perhaps the most important aspect of using the arts in community organizing for health is the ways that the creative process can empower individuals and communities. When a person or community becomes involved in a creative process it can be exhilarating. When one *becomes* the video maker, the poet, or the muralist, and is transformed through that process, change can take place both in the messenger and the audience (Boal 1979; Catalani et al. 2012). Perhaps the best-known example of this process, and indeed of all the preceding roles of the arts in organizing, is the Names Project's AIDS Memorial Quilt. Begun in San Francisco in 1987 by gay activist Cleve Jones and others to commemorate those who had died of AIDS, the Names Project attracted tens of thousands of others and grew from a memorial into a method for activism. The quilt's October 1996 display in Washington, D.C., constituted both the largest AIDS event and the largest community art event in history, with panels representing contributors from over forty nations. By November 2011, the quilt had over ninety thousand panels. The project's stated goals—to "provide a creative means for remembrance and healing," to graphically depict "the enormity of the AIDS epidemic," to increase public awareness and HIV/AIDS prevention, and to raise funds for community-based AIDS service organizations—well capture the multiple roles and contributions of this historic effort http://www.aidsquilt.org/Newsite/index.htm).

The community-organization method employed in the Quilt project reflects the feminist precept that the personal is political and was also a grassroots organizing effort with people, often from marginalized groups excluded from the mainstream of organized power, coming together to meet their needs (Miller 2009).

Photovoice and Videovoice

As illustrated above, a wide range of artistic approaches have been used in community organizing and community building for health, often in the process engaging groups and populations for whom more traditional health education approaches have held little appeal. We turn now to two increasingly popular approaches—photovoice and videovoice—and end with a powerful case study of the latter that provides a bridge to the future as new media technologies play an ever greater role in our professional fields and in the world.

Photovoice was described in a seminal paper (C. C. Wang and Burris 1997) as having three goals: "(1) to enable people to record and reflect their community's strengths and concerns, (2) to promote critical dialogue and knowledge about important issues through large- and small-group discussion of photographs, and (3) to reach policymakers" (369). First used with rural women in Yunnan, China (C. C. Wang et al. 1996), the method involves providing people with cameras and asking them to photograph their everyday reality or an issue of shared concern, typically including pictures of both assets and problems or challenges. They then engage in critical reflective dialogue about the pictures and their contexts, often using as an aid the mnemonic SHOWED (Shaffer 1983): What do you *See* here? What's really *Happening* here? How does this relate to *Our* lives? *Why* does this problem, concern, or strength *Exist*? What can we *Do* about it?

Photovoice has been widely used in to study and address a diversity of public health and social justice concerns, ranging from infectious disease epidemics (Mamary et al. 2007) and chronic health problems (Oliffe and Bottorff 2007) to homelessness (C. C. Wang et al. 2000), political violence (McIntyre and Lykes 2004), and discrimination (Graziano 2004). Similarly, the method has been implemented with age groups ranging from preadolescents (Wilson et al. 2007) to seniors (Baker and Wang 2006) and with underserved communities in the United States, Asia, Africa, Latin America, and Europe (Allotey et al. 2003; Catalani and Minkler 2010; www.photovoice.com).

The capacity of photovoice to reach—and touch—policymakers is illustrated in the Flint photovoice project in Michigan (C. C. Wang et al. 2004). Catalyzed by leaders of a neighborhood violence prevention coalition, the Flint project began by recruiting local facilitators and professional photographers, who participated in a "train-the-trainers" session. They were introduced to the photovoice concept and method; discussed cameras, ethics, and power; and took part in a guided photo shoot. Four groups, totaling over forty youth, community leaders and activists, and policymakers, took part. Project organizers recruited policymakers at the project's outset to help build the political will that would be needed to later implement photovoice participants' policy and program recommendations (C. C. Wang et al. 2004).

The policymakers' experiential participation as photographers offered several advantages, as they took it upon themselves to provide venues, such as legislative breakfasts, city hall, government agencies, and news programs, at which to present all participants' efforts. The local health department director's involvement in the project thus resulted in his introducing the photovoice method as part of an ongoing gonorrhea control initiative whose goal was to tap the insights of consumers and providers. Finally, the policymakers' participation set the stage for interactions in which participants, representing widely disparate age, socioeconomic status, neighborhoods, and social power, were able to communicate and collaborate across such differences. The long-term relationships established among diverse participants was seen by project coordinators and community members as one of the most powerful outcomes of this project (C. C. Wang et al. 2004).

A review of the photovoice literature by Catalani and Minkler (2010) found that photovoice projects, particularly those that more equitably engage community partners, commonly result in several outcomes associated with policy change, including enhanced community involvement in action and advocacy, enriched public health research, and individual empowerment.

As noted above, the videovoice method builds on and complements photovoice, as well as participatory media and participatory video, as this has been developed and used by Chávez et al. (2004) and others (Benkler 2006; Chandra and Batada 2006; Freudenthaal et al. 2006). *Videovoice* is defined as "a research and advocacy approach through which people, who are usually the consumers of mainstream media, get behind video cameras to research issues of concern, communicate their knowledge, and advocate for change" (Catalani et al. 2012, 20).

Like photovoice, videovoice is action oriented and facilitates the use of media as "an advocacy tool to reach policy makers, health planners, community leaders, and other people who can be mobilized to make change" (C. C. Wang and Pies 2004, 96). Unlike photovoice, however, videovoice is able to capture movement, audio, and sequential narrative and, during the dissemination stage, to be shared in theaters, living rooms, classrooms, and websites such as YouTube.com (Catalani et al. 2012). We turn now to a videovoice project that illustrates the utility and potency of this powerful new method for community building and organizing.

The New Orleans Videovoice Project: Community Building, Assessment, and Capacity Building in Post-Katrina New Orleans

When Hurricane Katrina hit and the levees broke in New Orleans in August 2005, the historic flooding, coupled with a tragically slow and bungled government response effort, left fifteen hundred dead and resulted in the loss of 200,000 homes, 850 schools, 18,700 businesses, and some 220,000 jobs (Louisiana Recovery Authority 2006). These losses were disproportionately endured by low-income African American and other marginalized communities, and millions fled to other parts of the country and beyond its borders (Drury et al. 2008)

The New Orleans videovoice project was conceived and implemented two years after the hurricane and its bitter aftermath by a partnership of academic researchers, independent filmmakers, and community members from the Central City neighborhood. The project began during the development of the city's master plan for rebuilding, a time when community partners sought to influence the local agenda, discourse, and action.

Initiated by REACH NOLA, a New Orleans community-academic partnership, the New Orleans videovoice project was guided by community-based participatory research (CBPR) principles emphasizing collaboration and equitable participation by all partners during all stages of the research process (Israel et al. 2005). As a part of this process, the partnership collaboratively designed the video production plan, timeline, and budget and developed two project goals: (1) to use film to engage a broad array of community members, including core partners, neighborhood residents, and local decision makers, in dialogue around community needs and assets and (2) to mobilize and act on identified public health and related community needs and assets. Community partners agreed that video was the appropriate medium for capturing New Orleans's unique culture, particularly music, dance, and storytelling. In addition, community partners pointed out that enhancing participants' video production skills could better prepare them to find quality jobs in New Orleans, particularly given the city's burgeoning, government-subsidized film industry.

The project's leadership committee recruited additional community partners through fliers; announcements at local social service, arts, and faith-based organizations; and word of mouth. The ten community partners selected for participation were primarily African American men, but they represented considerable diversity in age (twenty-eight to seventy-eight years old), income, and education. Each community partner was told that he or she would receive a stipend of two hundred dollars for his or her participation, in addition to a video camera and several copies of the final film production at the project's conclusion and access to all project footage and data (Catalani et al. 2012).

The videovoice method included several stages taking place throughout a twenty-week period. A key initial stage involved conducting co-trainings in video production, community research, and media ethics. An initial weeklong training and orientation was followed by eighteen weeks in which systematic data collection, transcribing, interpretation, and editing of footage took place as part of an iterative process in which all partners participated and continued to learn from each other as they co-created the film (Catalani et al. 2012). As partners collected video footage about community needs and assets through neighbor interviews and everyday neighborhood sites, sounds, and events, they met weekly to discuss what had been captured using the aforementioned SHOWED technique (Shaffer 1983). During an iterative process of data collection and discussion, partners identified three major themes: healthy housing, economic development, and education. With the help of filmmaker partners, community partners learned Final Cut Pro editing software and led the film-editing process with the mentorship of filmmaker partners.

The final film, *In Harmony*, was a twenty-two-minute exploration of community assets and needs rooted in the city's history, current neighborhood conditions, and future hopes from the perspective of the people who call it home (Catalani et al. 2009). Partners strategically shared the film with community members and local policy- and decision makers through online and offline screenings. Approximately two hundred people attended two community premiere celebrations in popular local venues and participated in follow-up action-oriented discussions. The nature of these lively and moving events was captured in the words of those who spoke, including an elderly African American woman who remarked that this was the first time in her life she had been engaged in an open and frank discussion of race and racism in the presence of white people. Postscreening written evaluations revealed that the vast majority (83 percent) agreed very strongly that the film brought up issues that they cared about. Most respondents (80 percent) indicated that they were interested in joining with others to take action on the issues raised and most (69 percent) reported that they would be interested in participating in the next videovoice filmmaking project, with many signing up on the spot for further involvement.

The final films were shared online through YouTube (www.youtube.com/VideoVoiceCollective) in November 2008 and, within two months, had received over forty-four hundred views from across the North America, Europe, South America, Asia, Northern Africa, and the Middle East. Finally, the film and extras were made into a DVD and strategically distributed to over one thousand people.

Project evaluation revealed a range of outcomes, from individual empowerment to community capacity building. The participatory evaluation of the project indicated a high level of equitable engagement between community, academic, and filmmaker partners. All partners reported enhanced sense of control, noting that they felt more in command of the issues that mattered most to them after participating in the videovoice project. Additionally, all partners reported that they were more engaged in community action and had more confidence in their ability to carry out community projects, particularly video production projects. In keeping with the desire to transfer skills to the community, four local partners went on to gain employment that used their newfound video skills, and several continued to initiate new projects without the aid of outside filmmakers or researchers. One of these individuals, a former teacher, became the director of a new organization: the New Orleans Videovoices Project. With the help of additional grant funds, she has led four additional videovoice projects with several New Orleans communities.

Project outcomes extended far beyond the partners themselves. As noted above, many of the two hundred community members at the initial screenings expressed their interest in becoming involved, and several of these went on to become partners in future videovoice projects as a part of the New Orleans Videovoices Project. These included a video in collaboration with youth returning to the Tremé neighborhood and a video in collaboration with a community clinic in the historic African American neighborhood of Algiers.

The New Orleans videovoice project, in sum, built local capacity to produce media and work collaboratively on social justice projects while enhancing understanding of local concerns through a rich and innovative community assessment.

Conclusion

The arts have been a catalyst for change and growth in wide-ranging circumstances, providing a rich legacy for health organizers and promoters to draw on in their community organizing and community building efforts. As Vivian Chávez and her colleagues (2004) suggest with respect to participatory video, such an approach "has the potential to open communication and promote dialogue. Its images, sounds and music can motivate and inspire," while bringing in new partners who can share additional skills, which in turn may help attract the interest of audiences including funders, government agencies, health workers, youth, and community coalitions (401). Given the many challenges that will confront community health organizing in the coming decades, new ways to awaken and empower ourselves and our communities are needed. The arts can be among our most effective tools.

ACKNOWLEDGMENTS

The authors gratefully acknowledge Giovanni Antunez and Megan Gottemoeller, who coauthored a related earlier paper with the first author, and Patricia Wakimoto and Peter Solomon for helpful suggestions and assistance with editing. Portions of this article were adapted from M. McDonald, G. Antunez, and M. Gottemoeller, "Using the Arts and Literature in Health Education," *International Quarterly of Community Health Education* 27, no. 3 (2006–2007): 265–278. Used with permission of Baywood Publishing Company, Inc.

REFERENCES

Allotey, P., D. Reidpath, A. Kouame, and R. Cummins. 2003. "The DALY, Context, and the Determinants of the Severity of Disease: An Exploratory Comparison of Paraplegia in Australia and Cameroon." *Social Science and Medicine* 57, no. 5:949–958.

Baker, T. A., and C. C. Wang. 2006. "Photovoice: Use of a Participatory Action Research Method to Explore the Chronic Pain Experience in Older Adults." *Qualitative Health Research* 16, no. 10:1405–1413.

Benkler, Y. 2006. *The Wealth of Networks: How Social Production Transforms Markets and Freedom.* New Haven, Conn: Yale University Press.

Betancourt, J., Green, A., and E. Carrillo. 2003. "Defining Cultural Competence: A Practical Framework for Addressing Racial/Ethnic Disparities in Health or Health Care." *Public Health Reports* 118 no. 4:293–302.

Boal, A. 1979. *Theater of the Oppressed.* New York: Urizen Books.

Brown, W. 2010. "Community-Based Youth Sexual Health Intervention in Oakland House/Ball Culture." YouTube. http://www.youtube.com/watch?v=7t6xOIpoZR8.

Cabral, A. 1979. "The Role of Culture in the Liberation Struggle." In *Communication and Class Struggle*, edited by A. Matterlart and S. Siegelaub. New York: International General.

Cardenal, E. 1982. "Defendiendo la cultura, el hombre, y el planeta." *Nicaragua* 3:149–152.

Carroll, J., and M. Minkler. 2000. "Freire's Message for Social Workers: Looking Back and Looking Ahead." *Journal of Community Practice* 8, no. 1:21–36.

Catalani, C., L. Campbell, S. Herbst, B. Springgate, B. Butler, and M. Minkler. 2012. "Videovoice: Community Assessment in Post-Katrina New Orleans." *Health Promotion Practice* 13, no. 1:18–28.

Catalani, C., and M. Minkler. 2010. "Photovoice: A Review of the Literature in Health and Public Health." *Health Education and Behavior* 37, 3:424–451.

Catalani, C., A. Veneziale, L. Campbell, S. Herbst, A. Wilson, C. McCullough, Barnes, J. Alexander, J. Sherman, M. Burton-Oatis, S. Alexander, S., B. Springgate, B. Butler, and M. Minkler. 2009. "In Harmony: Reflections, Thoughts, and Hopes of Central City, New Orleans." Community Engaged Scholarship for Health (CES4Health.info). notehttp://www.ces4health .info/find-products/view-product.aspx?code=5P3GZ4HT.

Chandra, A., and A. Batada. 2006. "Exploring Stress and Coping among Urban African American Adolescents: The Shifting the Lens Study." *Prevention of Chronic Diseases* 3, no. 2:A40.

Chávez, V., B. Israel, A. J., Allen, III, M. F. DeCarlo, R. Lichtenstein, A. Schulz, I. Bayer, et al. 2004. "A Bridge between Communities: Video-Making Using Principles of Community-Based Participatory Research." *Health Promotion Practice* 5, no. 4:395–403.

Cray, E. 2004. *Ramblin' Man: The Life and Times of Woody Guthrie.* New York: W. W. Norton.

Cutting, H., and M. Themba-Nixon. 2006. *Talking the Walk: A Communications Guide for Social Justice.* Oakland, Calif.: AK Press.

Drury, S., M. S. Scheeringa, and C. H. Zeahan. 2008. "The Traumatic Impact of Hurricane Katrina on Children in New Orleans." *Child Adolescent Psychiatric Clinics of North America* 17, no. 3:685–702

Duran, E., and B. Duran. 1995. *Native American Postcolonial Psychology.* Albany: State University of New York Press.

Fox, S. 2010. "Latinos Online." Pew Internet and American Life Project. http://www.pewinternet.org/Commentary/2010/September/Latinos-Online-2010.aspx.

Fox, S., and G. Livingston. 2007. "Latinos Online: Hispanics with Lower Levels of Education and English Proficiency Remain Largely Disconnected from the Internet." Pew Internet and American Life Project. http://www.pewinternet.org/Reports/2007/Latinos-Online.aspx.

Freire, P. 1970. "Cultural Action and Conscientization." *Harvard Educational Review* 40, no. 3:39–68.

———. 1990a. *Education for Critical Consciousness.* New York: Continuum.

———. 1990b. *Pedagogy of the Oppressed.* New York: Continuum.

Graziano, K. J. 2004. "Oppression and Resiliency in a Post-Apartheid South Africa: Unheard Voices of Black Gay Men and Lesbians." *Cultural Diversity and Ethnic Minority Psychology* 10, no. 3:302–316.

Guthrie, W. 1958. *California to the New York Islands.* New York: Guthrie Children's Trust Fund.

Hippe, P. C. 2000. "Clothing Their Resistance in Hegemonic Dress: The Clothesline Project's Response to Violence Against Women." *Clothing and Textiles Research Journal* 18, no. 3:163–177.

hooks, b. 1994. *Outlaw Culture: Resisting Representations.* New York: Routledge.

Horton, M., and P. Freire. 1990. *We Make the Road by Walking: Conversations on Education and Social Change.* Philadelphia: Temple University Press.

Israel, B., E. Eng, A. Schultz, and E. Parker. 2005. "Introduction to Methods in Community-Based Participatory Research for Health." In *Methods in Community-Based Participatory Research for Health*, edited by B. Israel, E. Eng, A. Schultz, and E. Parker, 3–26. San Francisco: Jossey-Bass.

Jenkins, H., D. Thorburn, and B. Seawell. 2003. *Democracy and New Media.* Cambridge, Mass.: MIT Press.

Kretzmann, J., and J. McKnight. 1993. *Building Communities from the Inside Out: A Path toward Finding and Mobilizing a Community's Assets.* Chicago: ACTA.

Laver, S.M.L., B. Van Der Borne, and G. Kok. 2005–2006. "Using Theory to Design an Intervention for HIV/AIDS Prevention in Farm Workers in Rural Zimbabwe." *International Quarterly of Community Health Education* 25, no. 1/2:135–48

Livingston, G. 2010. "The Latino Digital Divide: The Native Born versus the Foreign Born." Pew Hispanic Center. http://pewhispanic.org/files/reports/123.pdf.

Longman, R. 1994. "Creating Art: Your RX for Health." *American Artist* 58:68–73.

Lorde, A. 1984. *Sister Outsider.* Freedom, Calif.: Crossing Press.

Lorence, D., and H. Park. 2008. "Group Disparities and Health Information: A Study of Online Access for the Underserved." *Health Informatics Journal* 14, no. 1:29–38.

Louisiana Recovery Authority. 2006. *Quarterly Report: February–May.* Baton Rouge: Louisiana Recovery Authority, State of Louisiana. http://lra.louisiana.gov/assets/docs/searchable/Quarterly%20Reports/Feb2006Qtreport.pdf.

Lykes, M. B. 1997. "Activist Participatory Research Among Maya of Guatemala: Constructing Meanings from Situated Knowledge." *Journal of Social Issues* 53, no. 4:725–746.

Mamary, E., J. Mccright and K. Roe. 2007. "Our Lives: An Examination of Sexual Health Issues Using Photovoice by Non-gay-identified American Men Who Have Sex with Men." *Culture, Health and Sexuality* 9, no. 4:359.

McDonald, M., G. Antunez, and M. Gottemoeller. 2006–2007. "Using the Arts and Literature in Health Education." *International Quarterly of Community Health Education* 27, no. 3: 265–278. Reprinted in the Silver Anniversary Series.

McIntyre, A., and M. B. Lykes. 2004. "Weaving Words and Pictures in/through Participatory Action Research." In *Traveling Companions: Feminism, Teaching, and Action Research*, edited by M. B. Miller, P. Maguire, and A. McIntyre, 57–77. Westport, Conn.: Praeger.

Miller, M. 2009. *A Community Organizer's Tale: People and Power in San Francisco.* Berkeley: Calif.: Heyday Books.

Oliffe, J. L., and J. L. Bottorff. 2007. "Further Than the Eye Can See? Photo Elicitation and Research with Men." *Qualitative Health Research* 17, no. 6:850–858.

Preston, J., and B. Stelter. 2011. "Cellphones Become the World's Eyes and Ears on Protests." *New York Times*, February 18. http://www.nytimes.com/2011/02/19/world/middleeast/19video.html?partner=rss&emc=rss.

Randall, M. 1991. *Walking to the Edge: Essays of Resistance.* Boston: South End Press.

Rheingold, H. 2008. *Using Participatory Media and Public Voice to Encourage Civic Engagement: Civic Life Online; Learning How Digital Media Can Engage Youth.* John D. and Catherine T. MacArthur Foundation Series on Digital Media and Learning, 97–118. Cambridge: Massachusetts Institute of Technology.

Shaffer, R. 1983. *Beyond the Dispensary.* Nairobi, Kenya: Amref.

Smith, A. 2010. *Technology Trends among People of Color.* Washington, D.C.: Pew Internet and American Life Project.

Stuckey, H. L. 2010. "The Connection between Art, Healing, and Public Health: A Review of Current Literature." *American Journal of Public Health* 100, no. 2:254–263.

Su, C. 2009. *Streetwise for Book Smarts: Grassroots Organizing and Education Reform in the Bronx.* Ithaca, N.Y.: Cornell University Press.

Tuhiwai Smith, L. 2008. *Decolonializing Methodologies: Research and Indigenous People.* London: Zed Books.

U.S. Department of Health and Human Services. 2011. "Healthy People 2020." www.healthypeople.gov.

Wallerstein, N. 2006. "The Effectiveness of Empowerment Strategies to Improve Health." Health Evidence Network, World Health Organization, Copenhagen. http://www.euro.who.int/HEN/Syntheses/empowerment/20060119_10.

Wang, C., M. A. Burris, Y. P. Xiang. 1996. "Chinese Village Women as Visual Anthropologists: A Participatory Approach to Reaching Policymakers." *Social Science and Medicine* 42:1391–1400.

Wang, C. C., and M. A. Burris. 1997. "Photovoice: Concept, Methodology, and Use for Participatory Needs Assessment." *Health Education and Behavior* 24:369–387.

Wang, C. C., J. L. Cash, and L. S. Powers. 2000. "Who Knows the Streets as Well as the Homeless? Promoting Personal and Community Action Through Photovoice." *Health Promotion Practice* 1:1, 81–89.

Wang, C. C., S. Morrel-Samuels, and P. M. Hutchison. 2004. "Flint Photovoice: Community Building among Youths, Adults, and Policymakers." *American Journal of Public Health* 94, no. 6:911–913.

Wang, C. C., and C. A. Pies. 2004. "Family, Maternal, and Child Health through Photovoice." *Maternal and Child Health Journal* 8, no. 2:95–102.

Wang, E. L. 2010. "The Beat of Boyle Street: Empowering Aboriginal Youth through Music Making." *New Directions for Youth Development* 125:61–70.

Wilson, N., S. Dasho, A. C. Martin, N. Wallerstein, C. C. Wang, and M. Minkler. 2007. "Engaging Young Adolescents in Social Action through Photovoice: The Youth Empowerment Strategies (YES!) Project." *Journal of Early Adolescence* 27, no. 2:241–261.

Zeedyk, M. S., and L. Wallace. 2003. "Tackling Children's Road Safety through Edutainment: An Evaluation of Effectiveness." *Health Education Research* 18, no. 4:493–505.

PART SEVEN

Building, Maintaining, and Evaluating Effective Coalitions and Community Organizing Efforts

Former surgeon general Joycelyn Elders used to say that to the skeptic, a partnership was an unnatural act between nonconsenting adults. And indeed, many of us have seen partnerships (or more formal coalitions) fall apart when they have come together primarily because of a stipulation of funding and do not represent any genuine shared concern with working collaboratively to help bring about change. Even when the commitment is there, moreover, the challenges to coalitions are many. As public health leader Lawrence W. Green (2000) points out, for example, "Most organizations will resist giving up resources, credit, visibility and autonomy." Further, "not everyone insists on being the coordinator, but nobody wishes to be the coordinatee" (64–65).

Although the challenges to coalitions and related partnerships are indeed numerous, as this part makes clear, done well, and particularly when grounded in a strong theory base, coalitions and other partnerships can not only function effectively but also make a real impact in terms of community and policy change on both the short- and longer-term levels (Wallerstein et al. 2002; Wolff 2010).

We begin in chapter 17 with Fran Butterfoss and Michele Kegler's widely used coalition for community action theory (CCAT). Building on Feighery and Rogers (1990), they define coalitions as "formal, long-term collaborations that are composed of diverse organizations, factions, or constituencies who agree to work together to achieve a common goal." They stress in particular the action orientation of community coalitions and the importance of a guiding theory that is not simply an academic exercise but rather aimed at improving how coalitions work in practice.

After introducing the multiple theories that contributed to CCAT, Butterfoss and Kegler discuss the benefits and costs of coalitions and then lay out a set of constructs and "practice-proven propositions" for understanding coalition development, maintenance, and effective functioning. The various stages of coalitions, and the tasks associated with each, are described, with attention to such key issues as coalition context, leadership and staffing, and so forth. Finally, the authors come full circle to stress the need for careful documentation of both short-term successes and longer-term impacts, once again, toward the end of improving practice.

Many of the propositions and challenges laid out in chapter 17 are illustrated within a real-world context in the chapter that follows. In chapter 18, Adam Becker and his colleagues present a case study of coalition building and community organizing to address the problem of childhood obesity in the largely Puerto Rican Humboldt Park area of Chicago. Often referred to as one of the most serious and difficult public health issues of our time, the childhood obesity epidemic (one in five children is now clinically obese) is particularly problematic in low-income communities of color, where a host of environmental and other factors conspire against healthy eating and physical activity (Ogden et al. 2010; Bell and Lee 2011).

Yet such neighborhoods are also replete with strengths, including, in Humboldt Park, a determined community member who translated her personal need for exercise into the Muévete walking club, which then expanded to include other activities. Indeed, a strength of this coalition, which also posed challenges, was its conscious decision to have an organic, local approach to planning and (evolving) intervention development, rather than a more formal initial assessment process. Although chapter 18 does indeed illustrate a number of the propositions laid out in Butterfoss and Kegler's CCAT, it challenges others, providing some of the additional "real world" testing that can in turn help guide further theory refinement.

Finally, Becker and his colleagues beautifully illustrate the importance of a true ecological approach to addressing complex health and social problems. Through its Producemobile, the Muévete walking club, a farmers' market, rooftop gardens at local schools, and such policies as allocating new park land for urban agriculture, the

Humboldt coalition's many activities helped create sustainable change on multiple levels.

Although not without difficulties—some coalition partners, for example, dropped out because of the primacy of the focus on the Puerto Rican community—this case study well illustrates the power of a strong, if informal, coalition. Indeed, substantial reductions in childhood obesity rates over the six years of the coalition's work, at a time when obesity rates in boys were continuing to climb nationally (Ogden et al. 2010)—stand as an important testament to the effectiveness of the Humboldt coalition's community building and organizing on multiple levels.

A persistent challenge in community organizing and coalition-building work has involved the difficulty of evaluating such efforts—and doing so in a way that doesn't in the process mitigate community empowerment and other core principles of community building and organizing initiatives. The distrust of evaluation in many low-income communities of color, moreover, only adds to these difficulties. Indeed, health education leader Kathleen M. Roe is fond of quoting African American and Native American commentators who define evaluation as "victimization" and "intellectual theft," respectively (Roe et al. 2005). She cites in particular the powerful words of Candace Fleming (1992), who notes that among Native Americans, evaluation means the loss of funding, programs, and autonomy; the loss of wonderfully talented and committed people; diminished respect in the eyes of the community and the culture; and missed opportunities to help shape one's own future.

Fortunately, the past two decades have seen the development of a growing body of methods and tools for evaluating community organizing, coalitions, and community-based initiatives in ways that can empower, rather than disempower, the involved communities and program staff. In particular, the advent of participatory or empowerment evaluation has caught the imagination of many and is increasingly being used, either on its own or in conjunction with more traditional evaluation methods, to help engage community members and project staff as integral members of the evaluation team. In the final chapter of this part, Chris Coombe in chapter 19 provides a comprehensive introduction to the theory and practice of participatory evaluation, defined by Steve Fawcett and his colleagues (2003) as a systematic and collaborative approach in which those taking part in a project or effort are involved in understanding and evaluating it. Coombe describes the roots of participatory research in multiple traditions, among them action research, popular education, feminist research, and community-based participatory research. She further distinguishes between the "pragmatic stream" in participatory research, most concerned with program improvement, and the "transformative stream," emphasizing equity and social change (Cousins and Whitmore 1998).

Drawing on the work of various theorists and practitioners, the chapter then offers a useful eight-step process for participatory evaluation, emphasizing its goodness-of-fit with principles of community organizing and capacity building. The challenges of this approach are discussed, and its utility underscored, particularly given the often messy and complex contexts and realities that community building and organizing entail (Roe et al. 2005).

REFERENCES

Bell, J., and M. M. Lee. 2011. *Why Place and Race Matter: Impacting Health through a Focus on Race and Place*. Oakland, Calif.: PolicyLink.

Cousins, B. J., and E. Whitmore. 1998. "Framing Participatory Evaluation." In *New Directions for Evaluation*, no. 80:5–23.

Fawcett, S. B., R. I. Boothroyd, J. A. Schultz, V. T. Francisco, V. Carson, and R. Bremby. 2003. "Building Capacity for Participatory Evaluation within Community Initiatives." *Journal of Prevention and Intervention in the Community* 26, no. 2: 21–36.

Feighery, E., and T. Rogers. 1990. *Building and Maintaining Effective Coalitions*. Palo Alto, Calif.: Health Promotion Resource Center, Stanford Center for Research in Disease Prevention.

Fleming, C. M. 1992. "American Indians and Alaska Natives: Changing Societies Past and Present." In *Cultural Competence for Evaluators: A Guide for Alcohol and Other Drug Abuse Prevention Practitioners Working with Ethnic/Racial Communities*, edited by M. I. Orlandi, 147–71. Rockville, Md.: U.S. Department of Health and Human Services.

Green, L. 2000. "Caveats on Coalitions: In Praise of Partnerships." *Health Promotion Practice* 1, no. 1:64–5.

Ogden, C. L., M. D. Carroll, L. R. Curtin, M. M. Lamb, and K. M. Flegal. 2010. "Prevalence of High Body Mass Index in US Children and Adolescents, 2007–2008." *Journal of the American Medical Association* 303 (January 20). http://jama.ama-assn.org/content/303/3/242.full .pdf.

Roe, K. M., K. Roe, C. Goette Carpenter, and C. Bernstein Sibley. 2005. "Community Building through Empowering Evaluation: A Case Study of Community Planning for HIV Prevention." In *Community Organizing and Community Building for Health*, edited by M. Minkler, 386–402. 2nd ed. New Brunswick, N.J.: Rutgers University Press.

Wallerstein, N., M. Polascek, and K. Maltrud. 2002. "Participatory Evaluation Model for Coalitions: The Development of Systems Indicators." *Health Promotion Practice* 3, no. 3:361–373.

Wolff, T. 2010. *The Power of Collaborative Solutions: Six Principles and Effective Tools for Building Healthy Communities*. San Francisco: Jossey-Bass.

17

A Coalition Model for
Community Action

FRANCES D. BUTTERFOSS
MICHELLE C. KEGLER

The development of community coalitions has escalated rapidly over the past thirty years. Thousands of coalitions anchored by government or community-based organizations have been created to support community-based, health-related activities across the United States. For example, coalitions of health-related agencies, schools, and community-based action groups have formed to prevent tobacco use and promote healthy weight and physical activity among youth. Advocates for environmental issues, such as asthma and lead contamination, have rallied to highlight their issue or promote favorable policy and legislation. Civic and faith-based groups have developed coalitions to ensure adequate housing for the elderly and health insurance for low-income populations. Coalitions develop when different sectors of the community, state, or nation join together to create opportunities that will benefit all their partners in achieving mutual goals. The best of these coalitions have been vehicles to bring people together, expand available resources, focus on a problem of community concern, and achieve results better than those that any single group or agency could have achieved alone.

Coalitions, however, are not a panacea. Although they are usually built from unselfish motives to improve communities, coalitions still may experience difficulties that are common to many types of organizations, as well as some that are unique to collaborative efforts (Dowling et al. 2000; Wolff 2010). With the initiation of a coalition, frustrations can arise. Promised resources may not be made available, conflicting interests may prevent the coalition from having its desired effect in the community, and recognition for accomplishments may be slow in coming. Because it involves a long-term investment of time and resources, a coalition should not be built if a simpler, less complex structure will get the job done or if the community does not embrace this approach.

Coalitions are now commonplace in community-based efforts to improve health. Clearly, communities are committed to the *practice* of building coalitions.

However, it is equally important to forge and refine a comprehensive *theory* of community coalitions. The community coalition action theory, complete with constructs and propositions, has been developed to increase our understanding of how community coalitions work in practice (Butterfoss and Kegler 2009). Before this model is presented in detail here, its underpinnings will be highlighted, beginning with the rationale for collaboration.

Collaboration

Collaboration begins when a perceived need exists and two or more organizations anticipate deriving a benefit that depends on mutual action (Gray 2000). Collaboration is "a mutually beneficial and well-defined relationship entered into by two or more organizations to achieve common goals" (Mattesich et al. 2001, 7). These organizations often enter into a formal, sustained commitment to mutual relationships/goals; jointly developed structures; shared responsibility; mutual authority/accountability; and shared resources/rewards.

Collaboration represents the highest level of working relationships that organizations can experience. Collaboration changes the way organizations work together—it moves them from competing to building consensus; from working alone to including others from diverse cultures, fields, and settings; from thinking mostly about activities, services, and programs to looking for complex, integrated strategies; and from focusing on short-term accomplishments to broad policy, systems, and environmental changes (Butterfoss 2007).

Despite their rewards, effective collaborations must acknowledge and respect each organization's self-interest (i.e., structure, agenda, values, and culture), relationships, linkages, and how power is shared and distributed (Gray 2000). Three types of working relationships build on each other and may lead to collaboration: networking, cooperation, and coordination. These relationships exist across a continuum in which (1) linkages become more intense and are influenced by common goals, tasks, rules, and resources; (2) purposes become more complex as information sharing gives way to joint problem solving; (3) agreements become more formal, with operating procedures and policies; and (4) relationships take more time to develop and involve greater risks and rewards (Himmelman 2001).

Coalitions: Effective Vehicles for Collaboration

Coalitions are formal, long-term collaborations that are composed of diverse organizations, factions, or constituencies that agree to work together to achieve a common goal (Feighery and Rogers 1990). A coalition is action oriented and focuses on reducing or preventing a community problem by analyzing the issue, identifying and implementing solutions, and creating social change (Butterfoss et al. 1993; Butterfoss and Kegler 2002). The best coalitions bring people together, expand resources, focus on issues of community concern, and achieve better results than any single group could achieve alone (Butterfoss and Kegler 2002). Technically, partnerships assume a more businesslike arrangement and may involve as few as two partners, but the terms *coalitions* and *partnerships* are used interchangeably. Coalition members may be individuals, organizations, or groups. However, if a coalition is composed solely of individuals, then it should be classified as an organization or network. Membership size may vary, but a coalition usually involves both professional and grassroots organizations.

Coalitions are one of the most effective strategies for achieving community change. Through advocacy and education, coalitions are critical for mobilizing communities to develop and implement effective strategies and policies for the following reasons (CDC 2008):

1. Coalitions are versatile—they have been used effectively in all states; in thousands of cities, towns, and counties across the United States; and in many other countries.
2. Science supports coalitions as an effective approach for changing social norms and policies that lead to decreased morbidity and mortality (Crowley et al. 2000; National Cancer Institute 2005; Roussos and Fawcett 2000).
3. While the financial investment in coalitions is relatively low, they effectively leverage resources (e.g., members' services, time, and expertise) that enhance public health outcomes.
4. Coalitions enhance the stability of public health programs by building political/public support, securing/maintaining funding, and advocating for policy change.

Types of Coalitions

Coalitions may be categorized by their patterns of formation, functions, or structures that accommodate these functions. However, most are typed according to membership or geographic focus. Three types of coalitions are based on *membership* (Feighery and Rogers 1990):

- *Grassroots coalitions* are organized by advocates in times of crisis to pressure policymakers to act on an issue. They can be controversial, but effective, in reaching their goals and often disband when the crisis ends, such as when a group of residents pressures county officials to pass a smoke-free public places ordinance.
- *Professional coalitions* are formed by professional organizations or agencies to increase their power and influence, such as when health professionals pressure their state licensing board to establish more group homes for mental health patients. Although funding is provided to address community issues, the strategies usually come from professionals or institutions; local residents are secondary players (Wolff 2010).

- *Community coalitions* of professional and grassroots members are formed to influence more long-term health and welfare practices for their community, such as obesity prevention coalitions (see chapter 18). Community ownership is higher in these groups, but external funding is often required to provide needed resources.

Coalitions may also be classified by their *geography*—they may focus on community, regional, state, national, or international levels. *Community coalitions* operate in neighborhoods, towns, cities, or counties and usually serve a defined location that is recognized by local residents as representing and serving them (Clarke et al. 2006). Its members reflect the diversity and wisdom of that community, at both grassroots and "grasstops" (professional) levels (Butterfoss et al. 1993). These members have direct experience with the social/health problem of interest and are actively engaged in decision making and problem solving.

State coalitions develop to facilitate communication and develop strategies over larger geographic areas. Effective state coalitions immediately forge relationships with community coalitions or do so when they recognize the need to disseminate information and strategies widely. Likewise, community coalitions mobilize to form state coalitions when they realize the benefits of more widespread commitment and support for their issue, for example, statewide health care access (see chapter 21). Both approaches work well—the key is to link local and state concerns and resources. Many community coalitions are funded through state-level public health initiatives that have statewide coalitions.

Benefits of Community Coalitions

Coalitions and other collaborative efforts in public health offer many direct and indirect benefits (Butterfoss 2007), such as the following:

- Serving as effective and efficient vehicles for exchanging knowledge and ideas
- Demonstrating and developing community buy-in or concern for issues
- Establishing greater credibility, trust, and communication among community agencies and sectors
- Mobilizing diverse populations, talents, resources, and strategies
- Sharing costs and associated risks
- Leveraging resources to minimize duplication of efforts and services
- Negotiating potential conflict by sharing power
- Reducing the social acceptability of health risk behaviors
- Advocating for policy change by enlisting political and constituent support
- Developing synergy that allows organizations to adopt new issues without having sole responsibility for them

When real community involvement exists, coalitions address community health concerns while empowering or developing capacity in those communities.

Coalition membership may lead to increased community participation and leadership, skills, resources, social/ interorganizational networks, sense of community, community power, and successful community problem solving (Kegler et al. 2007).

The overarching benefits that coalitions provide are improved trust and communication among agencies and organizations, as evidenced by increased networking; information sharing; and access to ideas, materials, and resources. This may help coalitions to more effectively engage their priority populations. In turn, community members are more likely to support and use public programs/services when they have input into setting priorities and tailoring programs/services to local needs and services. Open and transparent communication that is facilitated through community coalitions also may increase public awareness of relevant policy/legislative issues and provide better evaluation of the impact of coalition strategies (Jackson and Maddy 2001).

Coalitions are best suited to assessing community assets and needs, enacting strategic/action planning, conducting social marketing campaigns, implementing policy and environmental change strategies, educating community members and policymakers, providing technical assistance or training, garnering financial and in-kind resources, and enhancing community buy-in and involvement. Coalitions should focus on promising or evidence-based strategies that are more likely to be effective and less on one-on-one education and costly programs or services that compete with those offered by their members.

Although coalitions are used in health promotion and disease prevention efforts of every kind, the most effective coalition examples exist in tobacco control and prevention's nearly forty-year history of educating communities about the negative health effects of tobacco use and secondhand smoke exposure and advocating for evidence-based policy strategies. This has led to decreased tobacco consumption, prevention of initiating tobacco use, and decreased tobacco-related disease and mortality. Tobacco control coalitions have (National Cancer Institute 2005) effected the following:

- Advocated for increased tobacco excise taxes at state and local levels
- Reduced and eliminated tobacco product advertising and promotion
- Established countermarketing campaigns to disseminate anti-tobacco media messages promoting the adoption of healthy behaviors and to provide information on health risks
- Decreased social acceptability of tobacco by educating diverse groups (e.g., faith based, low income, youth) to further relay messages and create social norm change
- Expanded smoke-free environments in work/public places and taken action in preemption states
- Limited availability of and access to tobacco products, particularly to persons under eighteen years old

To summarize, coalitions are excellent vehicles for consensus building and active involvement of diverse organizations and constituencies in addressing community problems. They enable communities to build capacity and to intervene using a social-ecological approach. By involving community members, coalitions help to ensure that interventions meet the needs of the community and are culturally sensitive. Community participation through coalitions also facilitates ownership, which, in turn, is thought to increase the chances of successful institutionalization into the community (Butterfoss 2007). These advantages of community coalition approaches are widely accepted by government agencies and foundations, and, as a result, the majority of prevention initiatives over the past two decades have required the formation of community coalitions as a condition of funding. The next section describes the theory, constructs, and assumptions developed to further our understanding of community coalitions.

Community Coalition Action Theory

Although clear theoretical underpinnings have always existed for community coalitions, until the past decade, the practice of coalition building outpaced the development of coalition theory. Once viewed as atheoretical with an insufficient conceptual and empirical base, the literature now is rich with case studies, evaluation/research findings, and conceptual frameworks to explain coalition functioning and how they are instrumental in creating community change. The community coalition action theory (CCAT) attempts to synthesize and provide an overarching framework for what is known about coalitions both empirically and from years of collective experiences (Butterfoss and Kegler 2009). The theoretical underpinnings of CCAT, which is articulated in "practice-proven propositions," stem from prior work in community development, participation and empowerment, interorganizational relationships, and social capital (Butterfoss and Kegler 2002).

The field of community development and related work in citizen participation articulates the underlying philosophy for community-driven approaches— that people deserve a voice in designing changes that affect or take place in their communities, that communities have the capacity to address their own problems, and that resident involvement and ownership in community change leads to greater sustainability (see chapter 1). Individual, organizational, and community empowerment are essential to participatory approaches, such as coalition-based initiatives, that build community capacity for change (Chávez et al. 2010; Wendel et al. 2009; see chapters 1 and 3).

Coalition theory also draws from interorganizational relations research to explain why organizations enter collaborative relationships (e.g., to acquire resources and reduce uncertainty), the stages of collaboration, and how benefits must outweigh costs to ensure continued participation (Butterfoss et al. 2008). Social capital, described as the trust, networks, and norms of reciprocity that enable people to effectively work together, includes two operational levels (Putnam 2000; Kawachi et al. 2008; Kreuter and Lezin 2002). CCAT recognizes both implicitly: *bonding social capital* creates group cohesion and a sense of belonging, which may result from a coalition's positive organizational climate. *Bridging social capital* refers to factors that facilitate the linking of organizations within a community, as well as connections to resources external to the community (Kreuter and Lezin 2002).

CCAT has been described in detail elsewhere (Butterfoss and Kegler 2002, 2009); the definitions of constructs are listed in Table 17.1 and propositions of constructs in Table 17.2. According to the model illustrated in Figure 17.1, coalitions progress through stages from formation to institutionalization, with frequent loops back to earlier stages as new issues arise or as planning cycles are repeated (propositions 1 and 2). Researchers have presented various series of stages and specific tasks that should be accomplished for each (Butterfoss and Kegler 2009); however, we suggest three stages: formation, maintenance, and institutionalization. To illustrate the overlapping nature of tasks that must be achieved during maintenance and implementation, they have been combined and represented in Figure 17.1 as *maintenance*. Contextual factors of the community, such as the sociopolitical climate, norms, geography, and history that surround collaborative efforts, affect each stage (proposition 3).

In the *formation stage*, a convener or lead agency with given strengths and linkages to the community brings together core organizations that recruit an

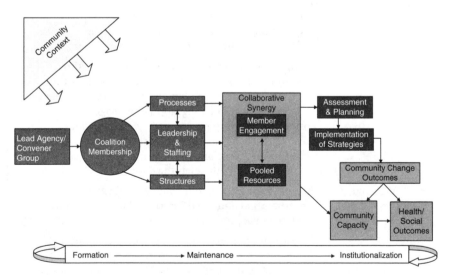

FIGURE 17.1 Community Coalition Action Theory (CCAT). From F. D. Butterfoss, "Toward a Comprehensive Understanding of Community Coalitions: Moving from Practice to Theory," in *Emerging Theories in Health Promotion Practice and Research*, edited by R. DiClemente, L. Crosby, and M. C. Kegler, 236–276, 2nd ed. (San Francisco: Jossey-Bass, 2009).

TABLE 17.1.

Constructs and Definitions, Community Coalition Action Theory

Construct	Definition
Stages of development	The specific stages or phases that a coalition progresses through from formation to implementation to maintenance to institutionalization. Coalitions may recycle through stages more than once or as new members are recruited, plans are renewed, or new issues are added.
Community context	The specific factors in the community that may enhance or inhibit coalition function and influence how the coalition moves through its stages of development. These factors include history of collaboration, politics, social capital, trust between community sectors and organizations, geography, and community readiness.
Lead agency/ convener group	The organization that responds to an opportunity, threat, or mandate by agreeing to convene the coalition; provides technical assistance or financial or material support; lends its credibility and reputation to the coalition; and provides valuable networks/ contacts.
Coalition membership	The core group of people who represent diverse interest groups, agencies, organizations, and institutions and are committed to resolving a health or social issue by becoming coalition members.
Processes	The means by which business is conducted in the coalition setting by developing clear processes that facilitate staff and member communication, problem solving, decision making, conflict management, orientation, training, planning, evaluation, and resource allocation. These processes help create a positive organizational climate in which the benefits of participation outweigh the costs.
Leadership and staffing	The volunteer leaders and paid staff with the interpersonal and organizational skills to facilitate the collaborative process and improve coalition functioning.
Structures	The formalized organizational arrangement, rules, roles, and procedures that are developed in a coalition to maximize its effectiveness. These include vision and mission statements, goals and objectives, an organizational chart, steering committee and work groups, job descriptions, meeting schedules, and communication channels.

(continued)

TABLE 17.1. Constructs and Definitions, Community
Coalition Action Theory (*continued*)

Construct	Definition
Pooled member and external resources	The resources that are contributed or elicited as in-kind contributions, grants, donations, fund-raisers, or dues from member organizations or external sources that ensure effective coalition assessment, planning, and implementation of strategies.
Member engagement	The satisfaction, commitment, and participation of members in the work of the coalition.
Collaborative synergy	The mechanism through which coalitions gain a collaborative advantage through engagement of diverse members and pooling of member, community, and external resources.
Assessment and planning	The comprehensive assessment and planning activities that make successful implementation of effective strategies more likely.
Implementation of strategies	The strategic actions that a coalition implements across multiple ecological levels that make changes in community policies, practices, and environments more likely.
Community change outcomes	The measurable changes in community policies, practices, and environments that may increase community capacity and improve health or social outcomes.
Health/social outcomes	The measurable changes in health status and social conditions of a community that are the ultimate indicators of coalition effectiveness.
Community capacity	The characteristics of communities that affect their ability to identify, mobilize, and address social and public health problems. Participation in a coalition may enhance these characteristics, which include citizen participation and leadership, resources, skills, social and interorganizational networks, sense of community, and power.

From F. D. Butterfoss, "Toward a Comprehensive Understanding of Community Coalitions: Moving from Practice to Theory," in *Emerging Theories in Health Promotion Practice and Research*, edited by R. DiClemente, L. Crosby, and M. C. Kegler, 236–276, 2nd ed. (San Francisco: Jossey-Bass, 2009). Reprinted with permission.

TABLE 17.2.

Constructs and Related Propositions, Community Coalition Action Theory

Construct		Proposition
Stages of development	1.	Coalitions develop in specific stages and recycle through these stages as new members are recruited, plans are renewed, and/or new issues are added.
	2.	At each stage, specific factors enhance coalition function and progression to the next stage.
Community context	3.	Coalitions are heavily influenced by contextual factors in the community throughout all stages of development.
Lead agency/ convener group	4.	Coalitions form when a lead agency/convener responds to an opportunity, threat, or mandate.
	5.	Coalition formation is more likely when the lead agency/convener provides technical assistance, financial or material support, credibility, and valuable networks/contacts.
	6.	Coalition formation is likely to be more successful when the lead agency/convener enlists community gatekeepers to help develop credibility and trust with others in the community.
Coalition membership	7.	Coalition formation usually begins by recruiting a core group of people who are committed to resolving the health or social issue.
	8.	More effective coalitions result when the core group expands to include a broad constituency of participants who represent diverse interest groups and organizations.
Processes	9.	Open and frequent communication among staff and members helps make collaborative synergy more likely through member engagement and pooling of resources.
	10.	Shared and formalized decision making helps make collaborative synergy more likely through member engagement and pooling of resources.
	11.	Conflict management helps make collaborative synergy more likely through member engagement and pooling of resources.
Leadership and staffing	12.	Strong leadership from a team of staff and members improves coalition functioning and makes collaborative synergy more likely through member engagement and pooling of resources.

(continued)

TABLE 17.2. Constructs and Related Propositions, Community
Coalition Action Theory (*continued*)

Construct		Proposition
		Paid staff make collaborative synergy more likely through member engagement and pooling of resources.
Structures	13.	Formalized rules, roles, structures, and procedures improve collaborative functioning and make collaborative synergy more likely through member engagement and pooling of resources.
Member engagement	14.	Satisfied and committed members will participate more fully in the work of the coalition.
Pooled member and external resources	15.	The synergistic pooling of member and external resources prompts comprehensive assessment, planning, and implementation of strategies.
Assessment and planning	16.	Successful implementation of effective strategies is more likely when comprehensive assessment and planning occur.
Implementation of strategies	17.	Coalitions are more likely to create change in community policies, practices, and environments when they direct interventions at multiple levels.
Community change outcomes	18.	Coalitions that are able to change community environments, policies, and practices are more likely to increase capacity and improve health/social outcomes.
Health/social outcomes	19.	The ultimate indicator of coalition effectiveness is the improvement in health and social outcomes.
Community capacity	20.	By participating in successful coalitions, community members/organizations develop capacity and build social capital that can be applied to other health and social issues.

From F. D. Butterfoss, "Toward a Comprehensive Understanding of Community Coalitions: Moving from Practice to Theory," in *Emerging Theories in Health Promotion Practice and Research*, edited by R. DiClemente, L. Crosby, and M. C. Kegler, 236–276, 2nd ed. (San Francisco: Jossey-Bass, 2009). Reprinted with permission.

initial group of community partners to initiate a coalition effort focusing on a health or social issue of concern (propositions 4–8). The coalition identifies key leaders and staff, who then develop structures (for example, committees and rules) and operating procedures (processes) that promote coalition effectiveness. Structural and process elements in the coalition (propositions 9–14) can help to ensure a positive organizational climate, an engaged coalition membership, and the pooling of member and external resources. This stage also requires balancing benefits associated with membership to ensure they outweigh any costs of participation.

The *maintenance stage* involves sustaining member involvement and creating collaborative synergy (proposition 15). Success in this stage also depends on the mobilization and pooling of member and external resources (proposition 16). The coalition relies on resources from members and external sources to design creative and comprehensive strategies or to identify and adapt evidence-based interventions that are appropriate for the local context and have the greatest chance of leading to the desired health or social outcomes. Acquisition of resources, combined with engaged coalition members and a comprehensive and multilevel planning and implementation process, lead to changes in community policies, practices, and environments (propositions 17 and 18).

The maintenance stage also includes implementation of multilevel strategies of sufficient duration and intensity to have an effect. If these strategies are effective, shorter-term outcomes occur, such as changes in individual knowledge, beliefs, self-efficacy, and behavior, as well as transitional changes in community systems, policies, practices, and environments (proposition 19). These intermediate changes should lead to long-term outcomes, such as reductions in morbidity and mortality or substantive progress toward other social goals (proposition 20).

Finally, in the *institutionalization stage*, successful strategies lead to outcomes. If resources have been adequately mobilized and strategies effectively address an ongoing need, coalition strategies may become institutionalized as part of a long-term coalition or may be adopted by other community organizations. The coalition itself may or may not be institutionalized in a community. Both maintenance and institutionalization stages have the potential to increase community capacity to solve problems. Progress in ameliorating one community problem can potentially increase the capacity of local organizations to apply these skills and resources to address additional issues that resonate with the community (proposition 21). The rest of this chapter will describe these stages in more detail to highlight their common issues and challenges.

Coalition Formation

Coalitions typically form when a lead agency or convener group responds to an opportunity, such as new funding; a threat, such as the closing of a rural hospital; or a mandate from higher levels of administration, such as state or federal government for local agencies or regional or national headquarters for other types of organizations. Community-based organizations, health departments or other local government units, or educational institutions or local hospitals may serve as conveners, depending on the particular project and its required financial accountability systems. The lead agency initiates coalition formation by recruiting a core group of community leaders and providing initial support for the coalition.

Some community groups may not have 501c(3) status and, therefore, have difficulties accepting grant funds, which often support coalition formation. One model that has worked in some smaller communities is for a regional organization to serve as the fiscal sponsor, while another more local organization takes responsibility for coalition building and strategic aspects of an initiative.

Research on coalitions suggests that coalitions often evolve from other, preexisting coalitions and networks (Butterfoss et al. 2006), which may accelerate their development. On the other hand, new initiatives can inherit past agendas, old ways of thinking, and grievances and conflicts that may limit coalition effectiveness (Kadushin et al. 2005). Composition of the core group affects its ability to engage a broad spectrum of the community (Kegler et al. 2010). Communities are often divided, sometimes by social class or race/ethnicity; values and ideology; or features of the geography, such as waterways that congest bridges, tunnels, and roads. According to CCAT, the core group must recruit those committed to the prioritized issue and a broad constituency of diverse groups and organizations, including community gatekeepers. This pooling of diverse views, perspectives, and resources is the hallmark of a coalition approach and enables them to address problems in ways that a single agency could not achieve on its own. Effective coalitions are deliberate in recruiting diverse members with specific expertise, constituencies, perspectives, backgrounds, and sectors.

Another important task in the formation stage of coalition development is the selection of staff and leadership. Effective coalition leadership requires a collection of qualities and skills that are typically not found in one individual, but rather in a team of committed leaders. Coalitions are labor intensive in terms of cultivating and maintaining relationships and ensuring smooth and efficient group processes. Insufficient or poor leadership can lead to coalition failure through endless meetings with no real substance or infrequent meetings with no progress between meetings. Empirical research on coalitions shows a consistent relationship between leader competence and member satisfaction. Research also demonstrates relationships between staff competence and member satisfaction, member benefits, participation, action plan quality, resource mobilization, implementation of planned activities, and perceived accomplishments (Kegler et al. 2005; Florin et al. 2000).

Coalition leaders and staff organize the structures through which coalitions accomplish their work and are responsible for coalition processes, such as communication and decision making that keep members satisfied and committed to coalition efforts. Practically speaking, coalitions accomplish much of their day-to-day work in small groups. Therefore, managing group processes, such as decision making, communication, and conflict management, is critical (Kegler et al. 2005; Butterfoss et al. 2006; Florin et al. 2000).

CCAT asserts that more formal coalitions are better able to engage members, pool resources, and assess and plan well. Formalization is the degree to which rules, roles, and procedures are precisely defined. Examples of formal structures include committees, written memoranda of understanding, bylaws, policy and procedures manuals; clearly defined roles; mission statements, goals, and objectives; and regular reorientation to the mission, goals, roles, and procedures of collaboration (Butterfoss 2007). Formal structures often result in the routinization or persistent implementation of the partnership's operations. The more routinized operations become, the more likely it is that they will be sustained. Some coalitions, especially those with a high proportion of grassroots residents, may resist formalization, viewing it as inconsistent with local culture. The external trappings of formalization may not be essential (e.g., bylaws or Robert's Rules of Order), but the underlying advantages of clarity of mission, continuity between meetings, and transparent processes usually are essential to success.

Coalition Maintenance and Implementation

Following coalition formation, coalitions must plan, select, and implement actions to address their priority issues. At this point in a coalition's life cycle, members have been recruited, structures and processes are in place, and, ideally, members are enthused about their upcoming collaborative work. Members are the lifeblood of a coalition—they set its vision, course, and outcomes and represent the authentic voices of the community. Capable coalition members are sought after, recruited, trained, and valued. Member engagement is best defined as the process by which members are empowered and develop a sense of belonging to the coalition (Butterfoss and Kegler 2009). Positive engagement is evidenced by commitment to the mission and goals of the coalition, high levels of participation both in and outside of coalition meetings and activities, and satisfaction with the work of the coalition (Butterfoss and Kegler 2009). Engaging members over time is more likely when the benefits of membership outweigh the costs and when members experience a positive coalition environment (Butterfoss 2007).

To foster member engagement, coalitions should review their roster annually and ask for letters of commitment. However, members often participate in coalitions with varying levels of intensity—they may be core members who assume leadership roles or those who seek networking opportunities. Members rarely stay active throughout the coalition's life and may experience burnout if they do. Having different categories of membership provides flexibility that allows members to move into/out of activities depending on competing loyalties or demands from home or work. Categories of members for community coalitions include the following (Butterfoss 2007):

- *Active members*—involved in the work of the coalition, attend most meetings/events, serve on work groups, assume leadership roles, recruit members, and help fund-raise.
- *Less active members*—lend their name and credibility to coalition efforts, publicly promote its work, and provide valuable connections to key organizations or populations, even if they only attend occasional coalition meetings or

events. These members include community leaders, administrators, school officials, politicians, and religious leaders.

- *Inactive members*—networkers or those who want to stay informed and receive mailings, but rarely attend meetings. They may be asked to do specific tasks or become active later.
- *Shared members*—more than one individual is selected by their organization to alternately attend meetings and share responsibilities. The downside of this arrangement is that valuable time is spent in "catching members up" and they often are unprepared to make decisions.

Coalition maintenance also entails the ongoing pooling of resources and mobilization of talents and diverse approaches to problem solving. When human and material resources are relatively scarce, collaboration is a necessary and logical strategy for addressing community problems, such as health disparities. Disparities and inequities in health have multiple causes and consequences that require complex solutions from multiple disciplines and organizations. In some communities, health and human services organizations are limited in addressing such issues because of fragmented services and unequal access to resources. By sharing their human and material resources, finances, and time, coalitions provide a multifaceted approach that can reverse the declining trend in civic engagement and reengage organizations to address local problems (Wolff 2010).

Members are a coalition's greatest asset—they bring energy, knowledge, skills, expertise, perspectives, connections, and tangible resources to the table. The power to combine the perspectives, resources, and skills of a group of individuals and organizations has been termed *synergy* (Lasker et al. 2001). This pooling of resources ensures more effective assessment, planning, and implementation of comprehensive strategies that give coalitions unique advantages over less collaborative problem solving approaches (Lasker et al. 2001). Both internal and external partners can provide meeting facilities, mailing lists, referrals, loans or donations, equipment, supplies, and cosponsorship of events (Braithwaite et al. 2000).

Effective coalitions have leaders who promote productive interactions among diverse members and who make good use of their participants' in-kind resources, financial resources, and time (Lasker et al. 2001). High levels of synergy that result from collaborative administration and management enhance the ability of coalitions to obtain sufficient nonfinancial resources from their participants (e.g., skills, information, connections, and endorsements). In short, the synergy that is created from collaborative work results in greater accomplishments than each group working on its own could ever achieve (Lasker et al. 2001).

Coalitions achieve their goals by pooling resources, combined with assessing a situation and selecting actions that target the most critical determinants of a particular problem. Once a coalition is formed and has its structures and processes in place, one of its first priorities is often to conduct a community assessment. Community assessment is the process of understanding a community in terms of its strengths, needs, constituencies, history and politics, leadership structure, and related factors that affect community problem solving (Bartholomew et al. 2006; see also chapter 9). Assessment also involves identifying a priority health issue or social issue, determining whom it affects disproportionately, and assessing its behavioral and environmental determinants. According to CCAT, coalitions that conduct comprehensive community assessments are better positioned to select and implement strategies that will make a difference.

Successful implementation depends on numerous factors, such as sufficient resources, completion of tasks on schedule, fidelity to the planned strategies, and supportive organizational and community environments. Assuming the strategies link logically to planned outcomes, the likelihood of achieving these outcomes depends on the extent to which the strategies are implemented and reach the priority populations. Adaptations of interventions that have been previously evaluated (evidence based) or are commonly accepted as best practices increase the likelihood that interventions will result in community change and, ultimately, desired health and social outcomes.

Most researchers and practitioners agree that effective health promotion efforts require change at multiple levels, including environmental and policy change. Using best practices or evidence-based interventions should minimize the tendency of coalitions to focus on building community awareness. A focus on quick wins may help to maintain member interest, but is unlikely to lead to more valued outcomes and may explain why some coalition-based efforts are not able to achieve systems or health outcomes change (Kreuter et al. 2000).

Community context affects the coalition planning and implementation process in a variety of ways (Kegler et al., in press). For example, geography can shape assessment methods, community history and valuing of collaboration can facilitate sharing of resources, and historical divides can affect who participates in coalition activities.

Institutionalization: Planning for Sustainability

Most communities currently face a tough environment with limited and shorter funding cycles, increased competition for resources, and economic downturns. Sustainability often is misunderstood as involving only sustained funding, since when the funding ends, so does the commitment. However, sustainability does not depend on one strategy, policy, or approach, but instead requires developing community understanding and leadership to embed new solutions in institutions— literally, *institution*alizing polices and organizational practices within community norms. With this understanding of sustainability, even if funding and efforts diminish, health has been embedded and lasting change remains (CDC 2011).

Despite their critical role in promoting health and preventing disease, many coalitions are unable to sustain their efforts long enough to change policies, systems, and environments. In order to create and build momentum to maintain community-wide change, coalitions must fulfill their missions and be effectively managed and governed. Sustainable coalitions (1) develop strong, experienced leaders; (2) have broad, deep organizational and community ties; (3) coordinate efforts; (4) implement evidence-based interventions; and (5) allow adequate time for sustainability planning (Feinberg et al. 2008; Nelson et al. 2007). Sustainability planning should begin early and continue throughout the life of the coalition. A sustained coalition will be more likely to attract varied funding sources and establish credibility among its constituency and policymakers (CDC 2008).

Besides developing coalitions and partnerships, sustainability involves initiating a groundswell of community strategies that create change at the local level and assembling a wide range of disciplines to work with communities to improve their health. Sustainability can be considered from short- and long-term perspectives (CDC 2011). *Short-term sustainability* deals with tasks that must be done to keep a strategy in place long enough to achieve its objectives. It means having buy-in and support from key decision makers and community volunteers; having sufficient leadership and funding, as well as clear communications; and putting procedures in place to monitor results and modify strategies that are not working. *Long-term sustainability* is more proactive and future oriented. It means (1) having a long-term plan for assuring the viability of an organization or a community-led initiative that manages several policy, systems, and environmental change strategies; (2) developing a diverse funding portfolio, collaborative leaders, and marketing/branding strategies; and (3) ensuring that the community, its organizations, and strategies are ready to respond to changes in the environment.

Future of Coalition Approaches

With the advent of evidence-based medicine and outcomes-based interventions, coalitions have been criticized as not meeting expectations for success (Green 2000; Hallfors et al. 2003). Given the tremendous infusion of resources, both monetary and in donated volunteer time, some feel that this criticism is well deserved. In truth, the overall evidence for positive coalition outcomes is modest. Traditional scientific methodology may not be adequate to capture the outcomes of these complex collaborative organizations (Berkowitz 2001; Gabriel 2000; Merzel and D'Affliti 2003).

Future research efforts should focus on what coalitions contribute to community-based strategies above and beyond more traditional approaches (Lasker et al. 2001; Berkowitz 2001; Butterfoss et al. 2001). For example, do coalitions develop more innovative strategies due to the pooling of expertise and resources? Do they reach previously untapped community assets? Are they better able to implement certain interventions, such as policy or media advocacy efforts, than are traditional public health and social service agencies? What are the long-term benefits and unintended positive outcomes for communities?

Community coalitions, like other community-level initiatives, are challenged to document intermediate and long-term outcomes and attribute resulting changes to the initiative (Florin et al. 2000; Gabriel 2000). Through strengthening the theoretical base and developing a model of action for community coalitions, this area of scientific inquiry will be advanced. Researchers and evaluators with access to large numbers of coalitions are challenged to use the CCAT model to field-test our assumptions and advance the understanding of which coalition characteristics and interactions are most likely to fuel goal attainment. Practitioners, the frontline coalition pioneers, will determine whether this model is useful to increase local support and capacity for further coalition development.

ACKNOWLEDGEMENTS

Portions of this chapter were adapted from F. D. Butterfoss and M. C. Kegler, "The Coalition Action Model," in *Emerging Theories in Health Promotion Practice and Research*, 2nd ed., edited by R. DiClementi, R. A. Crosby, and M. C. Kegler, 237–276 (San Francisco: Jossey-Bass). Reprinted with permission of John Wiley and Sons.

REFERENCES

Bartholomew, L., G. Parcel, G. Kok, and N. Gottlieb. 2006. *Planning Health Promotion Programs: An Intervention Mapping Approach*. 2nd ed. Jossey-Bass: San Francisco.

Berkowitz, B. 2001. "Studying the Outcomes of Community-Based Coalitions." *American Journal of Community Psychology* 29, no. 2:213–28.

Braithwaite, R., S. Taylor, and J. Austin. 2000. *Building Health Coalitions in the Black Community*. Thousand Oaks: Sage.

Butterfoss, F., S. Cashman, P. Foster-Fishman, and M. Kegler. 2001. "Roundtable Discussion of Berkowitz's Paper." *American Journal of Community Psychology* 29, no. 2:229–40.

Butterfoss, F., R. Goodman, and A. Wandersman. 1993. "Community Coalitions for Prevention and Health Promotion." *Health Education Research* 8, no. 3:315–30.

Butterfoss, F., M. Kegler, and V. Francisco. 2008. "Mobilizing Organizations for Health Promotion: Theories of Organizational Change." In *Health Behavior and Health Education: Theory, Research, and Practice*, edited by K. Glanz, B. Rimer, and V. Viswanath, 335–61. 4th ed. San Francisco: Jossey-Bass.

Butterfoss, F. D. 2007. *Coalitions and Partnerships for Community Health*. San Francisco: Jossey-Bass.

Butterfoss, F. D., L. A. Gilmore, J. W. Krieger, L. L. LaChance, M. Lara, J. R. Meurer, E. A. Nichols, C. E. Orians, J. W. Peterson, S. W. Rose, et al. 2006. "From Formation to Action: How Allies Against Asthma Coalitions Are Getting the Job Done." Supplement, *Health Promotion Practice* 7, no 2:34–43.

Butterfoss, F. D., and M. C. Kegler. 2002. "Toward a Comprehensive Understanding of Community Coalitions: Moving from Practice to Theory." In *Emerging Theories in Health Promotion Practice and Research*, edited by R. DiClemente, L. Crosby, and M. C. Kegler, 157–93. San Francisco: Jossey-Bass.

———. 2009. "Community Coalition Action Theory." In *Emerging Theories in Health Promotion Practice and Research*, edited by R. DiClemente, L. Crosby, and M. C. Kegler, 236–276. 2nd ed. San Francisco: Jossey-Bass.

Butterfoss, F. D., L. L. LaChance, and C. E. Orians. 2006. "Building Allies Coalitions: Why Formation Matters." Supplement, *Health Promotion Practice* 7, no 2:23–33.

Centers for Disease Control and Prevention (CDC). 2008. *Best Practices Users Guide: Coalitions—State and Community Interventions*. St. Louis, Mich.: U.S. Department of Health and Human Services, National Center for Chronic Disease Prevention and Health Promotion, Office on Smoking and Health. http://www.cdc.gov/tobacco/stateandcommunity/bp_user_guide/pdfs/user_guide.pdf.

———. 2011. *A Sustainability Planning Guide for Healthy Communities*. Division of Adult and Community Health, Healthy Communities Program. http://www.cdc.gov/healthy communitiesprogram/pdf/sustainability_guide.pdf.

Chávez, V, M. N. Minkler, N. Wallerstein, and M. Spencer. 2010. "Community Organizing for Health and Social Justice." In *Prevention Is Primary: Strategies for Community Well-Being*, edited by V. Chávez, L. Cohen, and S. Chehimi, 87–112. 2nd ed. San Francisco: Jossey-Bass.

Clarke, N. M., L. J. Doctor, A. R. Friedman, L. L. Lachance, C. R. Houle, X. Geng, and J. A. Grisso. 2006. "Community Coalitions to Control Chronic Disease: Allies Against Asthma as a Model and Case Study." Supplement, *Health Promotion Practice* 7, no. 2:14–22.

Crowley, K. M., P. Yu, and S. J. Kaftarian. 2000. "Prevention Actions and Activities Make a Difference: A Structural Equation Model of Coalition Building." *Evaluation and Program Planning* 23, no. 3:381–88.

Dowling, J., H. J. O'Donnell, and Wellington Consulting Group. 2000. *A Development Manual for Asthma Coalitions*. Northbrook, Ill.: CHEST Foundation and American College of Chest Physicians.

Feighery, E., and T. Rogers. 1990. *Building and Maintaining Effective Coalitions*. Palo Alto, Calif.: Health Promotion Resource Center, Stanford Center for Research in Disease Prevention.

Feinberg, M. E., D. E. Bontempo, and M. T. Greenberg. 2008. "Predictors and Level of Sustainability of Community Prevention Coalitions." *American Journal of Preventive Medicine* 34, no. 6:495–501.

Florin, P., R. Mitchell, J. Stevenson, and I. Klein. 2000. "Predicting Intermediate Outcomes for Prevention Coalitions: A Developmental Perspective." *Evaluation and Program Planning* 23:341–46.

Gabriel, R. 2000. "Methodological Challenges in Evaluating Community Partnerships and Coalitions: Still Crazy after All These Years." *Journal of Community Psychology* 28, no. 3:339–52.

Gray, B. 2000. "Assessing Inter-organizational Collaboration: Multiple Conceptions and Multiple Methods." In *Cooperative Strategy: Economic, Business, and Organizational Issues*, edited by D. Faulkner and M. de Rond. 243–260. New York: Oxford University Press.

Green, L. 2000. "Caveats on Coalitions: In Praise of Partnerships." *Health Promotion Practice* 1, no. 1:64–5.

Hallfors, D., H. Cho, D. Livert, and C. Kadushin. 2002. "'Fighting Back' against Substance Abuse: Are Community Coalitions Winning?" *American Journal of Preventive Medicine* 23, no. 4:237–45.

Himmelman, A. 2001. "On Coalitions and the Transformation of Power Relations: Collaborative Betterment and Collaborative Empowerment." *American Journal of Community Psychology* 29, no. 2:277–84.

Jackson, D., and W. Maddy. 2001. "Introduction to Coalitions." Ohio State University Fact Sheet CDFS-1. Columbus, Ohio: Ohio Center for Action on Coalitions. http://ohioline.osu.edu/bc-fact/0001.html.

Kadushin, C., M. Lindholm, D. Ryan, A. Brodsky, and L. Saxe. 2005. "Why It Is So Difficult to Form Effective Community Coalitions." *City and Community* 4, no. 3:255–75.

Kawachi, I., S. V. Subramanian, and D. Kim. 2008. *Social Capital and Health*. New York: Springer Science and Business Media.

Kegler, M., B. Norton, and B. Aronson. 2007. "Skill Improvement among Coalition Members in the California Healthy Cities and Communities Program." *Health Education Research* 22, no. 3:450–57.

Kegler, M., J. Rigler, and S. Honeycutt. 2010. "How Does Community Context Influence Coalitions in the Formation Stage? A Multiple Case Study Based on the Community Coalition Action Theory." *BMC Public Health* 10:90.

———. In press. "The Role of Community Context in Planning and Implementing Community-Based Health Promotion Projects." *Evaluation and Program Planning.*

Kegler, M., C. Williams, C. Cassell, J. Santelli, S. Kegler, S. Montgomery, et al. 2005. "Mobilizing Communities for Teen Pregnancy Prevention: Associations between Coalition Characteristics and Perceived Accomplishments." Supplement, *Journal of Adolescent Health* 37, no. 3:31–41.

Kreuter, M., and N. Lezin. 2002. "Social Capital Theory: Implications for Community-Based Health Promotion." In *Emerging Theories in Health Promotion Practice and Research*, edited by R. DiClemente, L. Crosby, and M. C. Kegler, 228–54. San Francisco: Jossey-Bass.

Kreuter, M., N. Lezin, and L. Young. 2000. "Evaluating Community-Based Collaborative Mechanisms: Implications for Practitioners." *Health Promotion Practice* I no. I:49–63.

Lasker, R., E. Weiss, and R. Miller. 2001. "Partnership Synergy: A Practical Framework for Studying and Strengthening the Collaborative Advantage." *Millbank Quarterly* 79, no. 2:179–205.

Mattesich, P., M. Murray-Close, and B. Monsey. 2001. *Collaboration: What Makes It Work; A Review of the Research Literature on Factors Influencing Successful Collaboration.* 2nd ed. St. Paul, Minn.: Amherst H. Wilder Foundation.

Merzel, C., and J. D'Affliti. 2003. "Reconsidering Community-Based Health Promotion: Promise, Performance, and Potential." *American Journal of Public Health* 93, no. 4:557–74.

National Cancer Institute. 2005. "ASSIST: Shaping the Future of Tobacco Prevention and Control." Tobacco Control Monograph no. 16. Bethesda, Md.: U.S. Department of Health and Human Services, National Institutes of Health, National Cancer Institute.

Nelson, D. E., J. H. Reynolds, D. A. Luke, N. B. Mueller, M. H. Eischen, J. Jordan, R. B. Lancaster, S. E. Marcus, and D. Vallone. 2007. "Successfully Maintaining Program Funding during Trying Times: Lessons Learned from Tobacco Control Programs in Five States." *Journal of Public Health Management and Practice* 13, no. 6:612–20.

Putnam, R. 2000. *Bowling Alone: The Collapse and Revival of American Community.* New York: Simon and Schuster.

Roussos, S., and S. Fawcett. 2000. "A Review of Collaborative Partnerships as a Strategy for Improving Community Health." *Annual Review of Public Health* 21:369–402.

Wendel, M., J. Burdine, K. McLeroy, A. Alaniz, B. Norton, and M. Felix. 2009. "Community Capacity: Theory and Application." In *Emerging Theories in Health Promotion Practice and Research*, edited by R. DiClemente, L. Crosby, and M. C. Kegler, 277–302. 2nd ed. San Francisco: Jossey-Bass.

Wolff, T. 2010. *The Power of Collaborative Solutions: Six Principles and Effective Tools for Building Healthy Communities.* San Francisco: Jossey-Bass.

18

Community Organizing for Obesity Prevention in Humboldt Park, Chicago

The Challenges and Successes of Coalition Building across Two Organizing Traditions

ADAM B. BECKER

KATHERINE KAUFER CHRISTOFFEL

JOSÉ E. LÓPEZ

JOSÉ LUIS RODRÍGUEZ

As described in chapter 17, community coalitions are particularly useful in confronting complex public health problems that require intervention at multiple levels of social organization (e.g., family, community, institution). Childhood obesity is arguably one of the most complex public health problems of our time—and one of the most critical. Some predict that because of obesity and its sequelae, the current generation of children will be the first with a shorter life expectancy than that of the generation before it (Olshansky et al. 2005).

At its core, obesity is the result of a caloric imbalance—consuming more calories through diet than the number of calories expended through physical activity. While on the surface, this imbalance may seem to be an individual-level problem that can be solved by supporting individuals to eat less and exercise more, further examination finds risk factors across multiple levels: family, institutions, communities, and society at large. Because the problem is so complex, a coalition-based approach is ideally suited to addressing it. Very few, if any, organizations have the capacity and expertise to identify and address factors at all these levels. Some organizations may specialize in assisting individuals through health education, nutrition, and activity programming. Others may focus on environmental change to increase access to healthy food and safe opportunities for physical activity in communities. Still others may have expertise in advocacy and public policy to address, for example, food and transportation systems across municipalities or at the state or federal levels. A coalition can combine and coordinate the resources and efforts of individual organizations with expertise across these spheres of influence such that obesity is addressed at multiple levels.

In addition to the complexity of obesity, significant disparities in obesity prevalence exist among communities (Freedman 2011). Communities of color and low-income communities experience higher rates than those of white or economically advantaged communities. Coalitions that originate in or focus on these hardest-hit communities are an essential element of efforts to reduce disparities. However, obesity is not the only public health problem faced by low-income communities of color in the United States.

To assess the utility of coalitions in addressing childhood obesity, a number of questions need to be answered. What are the opportunities and challenges for forming a community-based coalition to focus on a single public health problem in a community that is focused on a broader range of health and social issues? What processes are most helpful when public health–focused organizations come together with community-focused organizations to tackle such issues? What are the limitations of such processes? And how can these relationships and the efforts that emerge from them be sustained over time—especially when resources are limited?

This chapter explores some of these issues through the experience of Community Organizing for Obesity Prevention in Humboldt Park (CO-OP HP), in Chicago. CO-OP HP is a multisector coalition of diverse organizations focused on the health and well-being of the predominantly Puerto Rican sections of the Humboldt Park and West Town neighborhoods (referred to hereafter as Humboldt Park) in the city. After a brief description of the problem and the history and primary activities of CO-OP HP, we turn to the primary questions posed above. We discuss these questions with an analysis of CO-OP HP's experiences through an application of the community coalition action theory, described in chapter 17.

The Public Health Scope of Childhood Obesity

Childhood obesity rates in the United States have increased dramatically over the past four decades, from about 5 percent of children ages two to nineteen years old in the early 1970s to 14–18 percent in the early 2000s (Lavizzo-Mourey and Robert Wood Johnson Foundation 2009). While there is evidence that these rates have begun leveling off at approximately 17 percent for all children, this represents almost one in five children already obese, and rates among boys in the highest percentiles of body mass index appear to remain on the rise (Ogden et al. 2010).

This situation predicts a large and ongoing burden of ill health for these children throughout their lives, and for society as well. Childhood obesity, caused by overnutrition, inactivity, or both, results in myriad health problems. Overweight and obese children are significantly more likely to become overweight or obese adults (Biro and Wein 2010; Centers for Disease Control 2011; Whitaker et al. 1997; Serdula et al. 1993). Research has linked obesity to diabetes, coronary artery disease, cerebral vascular disease, hypertension, liver disease, arthritis, many of the most prevalent cancers, asthma, depression, and sleep disorders. And while many of these diseases and conditions may not be manifested until adulthood, a growing number of obesity-related health problems have begun to emerge in childhood (Freedman et al. 2007). These include type 2 diabetes (which is no longer called *adult-onset diabetes*, since it is increasingly seen in youth), hypertension, premature puberty, fatty liver disease, anxiety, depression, and orthopedic and dermatologic conditions. Physical and emotional health problems are not the only results of obesity. In childhood, obesity has been linked to underperforming in school (Caird et al. 2011). In addition, the high rates of adult obesity in our country result in higher health care costs (E. A. Finkelstein et al. 2009) and lower worker productivity (E. A. Finkelstein et al. 2010) and renders more young people physically unfit for the military than ever in U.S. history (Mission Readiness 2010), framed by some as a problem for national security.

The Social Ecology of Childhood Obesity

The causes of obesity are as diverse as the outcomes, and a social-ecological analysis therefore is helpful (Becker et al. 2008; Davison and Birch 2001). The concept of *social ecology* frames public health problems and health-related behavior within multiple levels of social organization (McLeroy et al. 1988; Sallis et al. 2008). With respect to obesity, *individual* factors related to nutrition and physical activity behaviors include knowledge about healthy lifestyles, attitudes towards diet and exercise, beliefs about the importance of maintaining a healthy body weight, and issues related to taste and preferences for food and activity. Children are embedded in *family* contexts and do not have sole control over their own diet and activity, so family-level factors also must be considered. These include family income and other financial resources; norms related to food and activity; meal preparation and organization practices in the home; the work patterns of parents and caregivers; and conditions of the home environment as they relate to sleep, stress, and other factors. Children and families interact daily with public and private *institutions* (e.g., schools, churches, workplaces, child care) that often serve food and may or may not provide sufficient opportunities for physical activity.

Community environments are also a critical determinant of diet and physical activity. Many low-income communities of color have poor access to healthy food. Foods that are low in nutrients and high in calories are often cheaper and more available in such communities. Facilities for physical activity may be unaffordable or nonexistent for members of communities that experience health disparities. Further, crime and traffic may limit residents' ability to be physically active on streets and sidewalks or in community parks. *Society* at large helps to set norms about appropriate behavior for corporations and governments, which in turn create products, provide services, and set policies that shape the context of obesity—for better and for worse (Nestle 2007).

Because of this broad array of factors that contribute to obesity, and because many of these factors result from social issues that are beyond the control of individuals and families, a coalition approach within the context of community organizing is necessary.

Establishing the Coalition

CO-OP HP emerged in response to the results of a multicommunity study of health and health disparities in Chicago. The study, conducted by the Sinai Urban Health Institute (SUHI) beginning in 2002 (Shah and Whitman 2010), found that diabetes and childhood obesity rates were significantly higher in Humboldt Park than in other Chicago neighborhoods. A local philanthropic organization, the Otho S. A. Sprague Memorial Institute (Sprague), approached the lead author of the Sinai study and leaders of the Consortium to Lower Obesity in Chicago Children (CLOCC; a citywide coalition initiated with funding from Sprague), expressing interest in supporting a collaborative effort to address the obesity problem in Humboldt Park. Together, they approached leaders of the Puerto Rican Cultural Center (PRCC) to serve as a local convener and begin forming a coalition in Humboldt Park to find ways to foster healthy lifestyles that could lower obesity levels. PRCC was well suited for this task because of its long-standing history of community organizing, with a focus on the health and well-being of the Puerto Rican community in Humboldt Park.

CO-OP HP is in many respects a classic coalition as described in chapter 17. Coalition leaders sought to develop a structured arrangement for collaboration among a diverse set of organizations, most located within the Humboldt Park community. CO-OP HP was formed to address the singular public health problem of obesity and its diverse contributing and protective factors. Early CO-OP HP activities were focused on problem analysis, data gathering, intervention planning and implementation, and both individual behavior and community change.

But in many other regards, CO-OP HP is not a typical public health coalition. Coalition membership was never formalized and to this day is evolving. Some groups joined because of an interest in obesity prevention, others because of interests as diverse as economic development, protecting the community from the effects of gentrification, or broader health disparities and social justice issues. While CO-OP HP was focused on action, partners did not use the traditional public health approach to intervention development and evaluation. Instead, it linked to existing programs in the city and created local strategies that evolved as partners responded to successes and challenges and a growing understanding of the barriers to healthy eating and physical activity in the community. Strategies also evolved as resources became available or disappeared, as community needs shifted, and as new opportunities emerged.

Coalition Activities

In response to the SUHI community study and several subsequent CO-OP HP–led data-collection efforts, the coalition's leadership agreed to pilot or bring to Humboldt Park a variety of intervention approaches that would ultimately increase healthy eating and physical activity in the community and strengthen health-related resources to support healthy lifestyles. To address low levels of fruit and vegetable consumption, local leaders identified both nutrition education and access to fresh produce as priorities. Working with CLOCC staff, CO-OP HP identified opportunities to educate Humboldt Park residents and organizations about CLOCC's healthy-lifestyle message, *5-4-3-2-1 Go!* (Evans et al. 2011; Stahl et al. 2010; for details about the message, see http://www.clocc.net/partners/54321Go/index.html).

To address food access, coalition partners and staff identified three existing Chicago-area resources that they could make more available to the community. A local farmers' market was developing in Humboldt Park but struggling to gain a foothold. Coalition leadership and staff worked with the market's originating partners to relocate the market and to assist with its management. CO-OP HP staff also partnered with a citywide organization to bring its community-supported agriculture program, or CSA, called Market Basket, to community residents in Humboldt Park. In this program, consumers ordered bags of produce weekly; these were then delivered to the PRCC for local pickup. A third food intervention CO-OP HP identified was Producemobile. In this program, the Greater Chicago Food Depository (http://www.chicagosfoodbank.org), a member of the national Feeding America network, sends a truck full of produce to high-need community settings for free distribution. Local organizations arrange the distribution site, manage the often long lines of consumers, get the produce off the truck and into bags, and clean up the location after delivery is complete.

The coalition also initiated a number of approaches related primarily to increasing physical activity for community members. A cornerstone of CO-OP HP's physical-activity work was the Muévete intervention. Muévete's founder was a thirty-year-old local resident who was told by her physician that she was obese and needed to lose weight to get her elevated cholesterol and borderline hypertension under control or face a lifetime of medication. She started Muévete as a walking club around Humboldt Park and it later evolved into an aerobic dance program, using Latin and other culturally relevant music to inspire the growing number of women (and some of their children) who participated in the program. Finally, and because a physical-activity goal of the coalition was to increase the numbers of community members who cycled regularly, organized bike rides began, among them a tour of outdoor murals depicting Puerto Rican history and culture. Over time, the bike tours expanded to include the market and local gardens. As interest in cycling grew, other partner organizations joined in. One original CO-OP HP partner, Bickerdike Redevelopment Corporation, developed Bickerbikes, a bicycle safety and repair program for youth. Youth from that program have become avid champions of cycling, organizing bike trips around the city and integrating bicycles into cultural parades and food distribution programs.

Some of these early coalition strategies are still operating in Humboldt Park, while others have evolved and taken on lives of their own. Originally, for example, CO-OP HP staff ran their own produce distribution program based on Market Basket, La Cosecha (the harvest). The farmers' market has evolved into a community market and serves as an opportunity for farmers, local gardeners, and local business to sell healthy food and beverages. Muévete has expanded over the years to include two additional park-based programs, several new community- and school-based programs, and a variety of appearances and special sessions at community events all over Chicago. The program is now a featured strategy of a new National Institutes of Health–funded diabetes prevention program in the community. The Bickerbikes program paved the way for West Town Bikes (http://westtownbikes.org/), a nonprofit organization whose mission is to promote bicycling; educate youth, with a focus on underserved populations; and foster and serve Humboldt Park's growing bicycling community. The evolution and sustainability of these programs will be discussed in more depth as an example of the impact of the CO-OP HP coalition on outcomes related to community capacity.

A Critical Analysis of the Coalition

An analysis of the experience of CO-OP HP through elements of the community coalition action theory (CCAT) can help in exploring the opportunities and challenges the coalition faced in addressing three concerns that confront most coalitions: identifying a singular shared focus among diverse organizations, often with multiple goals themselves; developing effective and appropriate interventions that are locally driven and sustainable; and maintaining relationships and strategies long enough to achieve desired health, social, and community capacity outcomes. In the following paragraphs, we use the theory to examine CO-OP HP's efforts to address these three concerns, sometimes explicitly and strategically, and sometimes implicitly. First, we examine the combined CCAT constructs of stages of development, lead agency or convening group, and coalition membership and how these influenced the development of a shared singular focus. Next, we address the assessment, planning, and implementation of strategies and how these processes contributed to and challenged the coalition's successes. Finally, we address sustainability of CO-OP HP relationships and strategies as it relates to the three most important outcomes of CO-OP HP, all among the original purposes of the coalition: community change outcomes, health and social outcomes, and community capacity. We conclude with lessons learned that may provide guidance to other community-based, public health–focused coalitions.

Creating Singular Focus: Stages of Development, Convening Group, and Membership

A number of organizational and coalition theories describe stages of development and how groups cycle and recycle through these stages as new members are recruited, plans are made and renewed, and new focus issues are taken on (Butterfoss 2009; see chapter 17; Johnson and Johnson 2008). At each stage, specific factors enhance group function and progression to the next stage. CCAT describes three primary stages: formation, maintenance, and institutionalization. In the formation stage, a convening organization brings together a number of "core organizations" to recruit an initial set of coalition members or partners. Members work together to identify key roles for coalition leadership and functioning, develop structures and processes for decision making and action, and promote the goals of the coalition.

CO-OP HP was initiated by four primary organizations with specific roles and areas of expertise. Sprague funded the coalition and remained an active partner for several years—attending regular meetings and providing ongoing guidance and supplemental support to the primary partners. PRCC was the local "anchor" organization. It hired and housed staff, hosted meetings, led publicity and intervention marketing strategies, and recruited other organizations in the Humboldt Park community to join the coalition. The Sinai Urban Health Institute was the original fiscal and managing agent of the coalition and provided direction in ongoing community data collection as the coalition worked to solidify a unifying focus and agree upon a set of strategies. CLOCC provided content expertise in obesity prevention and worked to ensure that its resources and partners would connect to and support the local coalition.

Another set of partners joined during this formation stage. Bickerdike (http://www.bickerdike.org/) was the first to join the founding partners. Bickerdike's mission is focused on community redevelopment for the benefit of and control by the lower- and moderate-income residents of its geographic area. As the anchor organization for another community-based organizing strategy, Bickerdike was developing and implementing a "quality-of-life plan" through a participatory planning process. The plan included goals for improving the health of residents, making Bickerdike, as the steward of that plan, a likely partner in the CO-OP HP endeavor. The second group to join was Centro Sin Fronteras, a local grassroots organization in the Mexican American community, with a track record of mobilizing thousands of constituents at a time for support of varied initiatives. A third member was Association House, established in 1899, with a continued mission to offer services to economically disadvantaged individuals and families in Humboldt Park. Association House currently carries out its mission through providing human services, child welfare activities, behavioral health services, and a continuing-education center. Several other diverse organizations and individuals, including a local hospital, the local park district branch, and the leadership of a local public health clinic, were invited to join as well.

There are a number of aspects of the coalition's formation that are of particular note with regard to CCAT constructs and propositions related to the likelihood of success. First, there were multiple lead organizations. Each had slightly different primary missions, with overlap around obesity prevention. A coalition in its own right, CLOCC was solely focused on childhood obesity prevention. In contrast, the Sinai Urban Health Institute concentrated on a variety of public health concerns in the community, largely from a social epidemiological perspective and a desire to understand health disparities and develop effective approaches to addressing them. PRCC was focused broadly on health and social issues in the Puerto Rican population within Humboldt Park, emphasizing cultural vibrancy and peoples' livelihoods. It also paid particular attention to protecting the community from the pressures of gentrification and the negative effects of political and economic marginalization. Centro sin Fronteras and Association House were invited to join in order to broaden the coalition's focus to include all the primary racial and ethnic groups represented in Humboldt Park.

The original composition of the coalition had specific impacts on its evolution over the years and on its current membership. The collaboration between the three lead organizations—PRCC, CLOCC, and the Sinai Urban Health Institute— succeeded in part because of the synergy among their primary missions, and the ability of all to pursue their primary missions within the context of CO-OP HP.

The primary missions of other participating organizations were not as clearly linked to childhood obesity prevention in the Puerto Rican community, the intersection among these three primary missions. For example, Centro sin Fronteras was focused primarily on the political and economic rights of Mexican immigrants. The local hospital and public health clinic were focused on their health care and treatment missions. Bickerdike was focused on housing and community economic development in the broader racially and ethnically diverse Humboldt Park community. As CO-OP HP evolved, those whose primary missions were not at the intersection of disparities in obesity among Puerto Rican children found it more challenging to stay committed. With PRCC serving as the convening partner and anchor organization, commitment to the Puerto Rican community became a primary feature of the coalition, and some early members, who did not share that focus, transitioned out. Expanding the mission and purview of CO-OP HP to other segments of the community or to broader health and health disparities issues may have helped more original members to stay involved but early attempts proved to be difficult and, had they been successful, might have led eventually to a lack of focus and difficulties related to sustainability.

Developing Community-Relevant Sustainable Interventions: The Benefits and Challenges of Assessment and Planning

A second proposition of CCAT—and of public health in general—is that successful implementation of effective strategies is more likely when comprehensive assessment and planning occur. Public health organizations, like those in social work and related fields, often put time and resources into careful assessment of community needs (and increasingly also of community assets), study the feasibility of specific approaches, and engage in rational planning before developing interventions. Community organization and community building approaches, however, frequently need to maintain flexibility and remain open to unanticipated challenges and opportunities that come along. Further, well-planned and well-delivered interventions require funding for staff that will plan, implement, and assess the strategies. Perhaps most important, this "comprehensive rational public health planning" model (Issel 2009) is often foreign to the way indigenous community-driven strategies evolve. CO-OP HP didn't have the financial resources needed to hire staff with expertise in both community organizing and obesity-related interventions that could plan and implement strategies combining both organizing and public health approaches. For this reason, CO-OP HP frequently chose not to play the role of an intervention implementer, and often instead served as a liaison between the Humboldt Park community and existing interventions and programs available from citywide organizations. In the latter role, it provided coordination and ensured participation.

The selection of strategies was based only in part on formal community needs assessments. Early data gathered by the coalition indicated that community members were not eating the recommended daily amounts of fresh produce, and the food distributions programs were selected because of this need. However, CO-OP HP partners did not formally assess interest among residents in the various types of distribution that were eventually developed or coordinated. Because funds were limited, CO-OP HP staff scanned Chicago organizations and programs looking for partners who had resources to bring healthy food into Humboldt Park and offered to play the role of local coordinator. The coalition relied on partner organizations' staff to develop and coordinate a variety of physical-activity programs. Some strategies were developed locally (Muévete, cycling programs), but these too were based only on the gaps in healthful behavior identified through data collection, not on information about what area residents preferred. This approach to assessment was both effective and challenging. Decisions about which behaviors to focus on were consistent with the findings of data collection, but the selection of specific approaches might have been better informed by more thorough feasibility assessments, funds permitting, and more community engagement in the selection process.

The coalition's approach to intervention planning was also related to its capacity and values. Because many of the interventions were run by external partners, CO-OP HP staff and leaders could not expect to play a directive role in their planning. However, even the locally developed strategies did not use a formal planning process. A goal of CO-OP HP, which undergirds the decision not to engage in formal planning, was that the strategies developed had to be sustainable. All the member organizations understood that efforts initiated with substantial funding at the outset are the most vulnerable when funding cannot be sustained. Therefore, coalition strategies emerged from local interest and commitments and many of the local organizational members, PRCC chief among them, contributed significant in-kind resources to initiate and guide them. Local strategies were created by people who wanted them for themselves as well as for their fellow community members. This local approach to strategy development did not involve formal planning in the public health sense of the term, but was necessary to ensure that local commitment and engagement would remain high.

The benefits of developing and running programs without formal assessment and planning were that CO-OP HP didn't need to raise funds or hire staff with these sets of expertise. All available resources could be dedicated directly to the programs themselves. The coalition did not require a large team of full-time staff to run programs and didn't need substantial management infrastructure to train or oversee staff coordinating or running programs.

There were also downsides to this lack of formal assessment and planning, however. Community participation was not constant for any of the programs. While the Producemobile did not make decisions to deliver produce based upon the number of participants, Market Basket did require a steady minimum of orders. Because Market Basket was developed outside Humboldt Park, CO-OP HP staff struggled to influence the types of produce included in bags to be more culturally appropriate for the Puerto Rican community. Eventually, challenges became such that the relationship between CO-OP HP and the organization running Market Basket dissolved and coalition staff developed its own version, La Cosecha. But even under the management of CO-OP HP staff, La Cosecha struggled to maintain participation. Eventually CO-OP HP staff decided to discontinue the program.

A formal community assessment might have uncovered a lack of interest among residents in buying produce without the power to select what would be in their delivery or a preference to buy produce where they bought their other groceries. Muévete, especially in its early days, had fluctuating participation and this was, at times, frustrating to its founder and director. Formal community assessment and program planning might have led to the development of interventions that not only addressed the greatest needs for supporting behavior change but were also delivered from the outset in the ways that were most acceptable to residents.

A second challenge of the lack of formal assessment and planning was that evaluation was difficult. While all programs tracked participation, the impact of the programs on sustained behavior change or change in health outcomes was difficult to measure. Because programs were not formally planned, it was difficult to develop formal evaluation plans that would link to specific elements of interventions. Not having predetermined steps and tactics meant not being able to develop in advance process evaluation tools or approaches to assessing the effectiveness of any particular tactics. Nonetheless, in some cases evaluations were designed retrospectively in order to learn lessons for program improvement.

As discussed in CCAT, this lack of formal assessment and intervention planning might be seen as a critical error on the part of the coalition. Challenges resulted, to be sure. However, the informal and organic nature of program development in the coalition adhered to an important value that the partners shared. Partners believed (and continue to maintain) that programs needed to develop out of the passion and commitment of the convening partner (PRCC) and CO-OP HP staff and volunteers. They believe that formally planned programs with solid funding streams attached would eventually die out if the money or the public health–trained and oriented partners had to disengage. Because of these beliefs, the essential elements of the coalition's interventions—those that would have been a part of the strategies regardless of where they were located, *and* the unique elements that evolved, and those that were shaped by the people and places involved—were critical to their success. The intervention strategies that have continued have done so because they have adapted to evolving community conditions and resident interests, the economic resources of participants, the fluctuating commitment of external partners, and the inconsistent availability of funding.

Over time, it has become clear that the coalition interventions that continue (often in evolved states) endure because they serve multiple functions. This would have been difficult, if not impossible, to accomplish if formal public health assessment and planning had been used in intervention development. For example, the local farmers' market has continued because it responded to local conditions by changing lead and managing partners, changing locations, expanding to include local artisans, and allowing local businesses to sell packaged foods. Had the market been more formally planned, with specific elements to address only healthy food access, such adaptations likely would have been unimaginable or resisted by program planners. Healthy food access is now one purpose of the market, along with others that allowed the effort to grow into something sustainable: developing and sustaining local businesses and creating a self-reliant cycle of supply and demand. For these reasons the market continues even as it struggles at times to bring in a sufficient number of farmers and gardeners.

Multilevel Approaches: Building toward Sustainable Outcomes

A third proposition of CCAT is that coalitions are more likely to create long-lasting change in community policies, practices, and environments when they direct interventions at multiple levels. This proposition is upheld by the experience of the coalition. Many of the intervention strategies of CO-OP HP were initially focused on individual behavior change. Public education and programs that fit more into a "service delivery" mode of intervention than one of environmental change were the most common among early CO-OP HP strategies. Produce delivery and physical-activity programs didn't set out to change environment or policy. However, as program staff and partners experienced challenges in keeping these programs going, coalition leadership began to focus on *institutional* policy change.

For example, Producemobile, Muévete, and eventually the farmers' market and newly developing urban agriculture projects have come to be housed at the local Chicago Park District site in Humboldt Park. Pressures on the park district staff to bring in program registration fees periodically resulted in pressure on CO-OP HP to allow the park to charge for participation in Muévete. Space needs became problematic from time to time as fee-generating programs became higher priority. Discussions with park district leadership at higher levels frequently were needed in the early years until institutional support for coalition programs could be garnered at higher levels within the citywide agency. While park district staff were always willing to compromise, this institutional support for CO-OP HP only emerged over time and required flexibility, patience, and an interest in open communication on the part of all parties.

More recently, coalition staff has been working with a high school affiliated with PRCC to develop a network of rooftop greenhouses run by students. Like all enduring CO-OP HP–connected strategies, this one serves multiple purposes. Students are learning a trade (gardening), they are learning about Puerto Rican culture (by growing plants that provide key ingredients for traditional dishes), and they are developing business experience (selling what they grow through local markets and an emerging cooperative store). To get the greenhouse established, PRCC and other coalition staff had to learn about local zoning and code restrictions and negotiate with government agency personnel to acquire permits and zoning allowances to build the greenhouses. Partly in response to this, city agencies are now considering new zoning and regulatory opportunities to support local and urban agriculture initiatives.

The coalition has also recently developed a number of approaches to environmental change—many of them evolving from the earlier experiences of, and challenges with, the more individually focused interventions. Buen Provecho is a strategy to engage local restaurants and other food retailers to sell healthier food. This approach continues to evolve as CO-OP HP staff and partners develop a greater understanding of the needs and interests of community residents related to produce consumption and shopping preferences. Staff learned how challenging it is to improve healthy food consumption through programs run outside traditional retail settings. Turning to local businesses and encouraging and supporting them to diversify their menus and merchandise became a central strategy of the coalition to create more sustainable change in the food environment that is integrated into the business models of local entrepreneurs.

Physical-activity programs also helped CO-OP HP staff to see firsthand some of the challenges in walking, biking, and other forms of physical activity in the neighborhood. Staff have begun working with partner organizations and local government and elected officials to introduce traffic-calming strategies in and around the local park. As coalition strategies have diversified and begun to focus on change at multiple levels (individual, community, societal), partner organizations have had increasing success in raising funds to keep these activities going in Humboldt Park.

The final propositions of CCAT address the issue of outcomes: community change outcomes, health and social outcomes, and capacity among coalition partners. CO-OP HP members set out to accomplish goals in all three outcome areas, but these accomplishments have come only gradually, and efforts towards achievement are ongoing. Yet there are real changes, both already visible and on the horizon.

More local stores are selling produce and more restaurants are promoting their produce-centered menu items. The park will soon have more designated walking and traffic-calming infrastructure. One rooftop greenhouse is up and running and others are planned. An acre of land in the park has been committed for the creation of an urban agriculture project that will grow produce that can be sold in the community. A cooperative store is under development that will serve as another outlet for selling produce grown within the community. This system of strategies fulfills both the public health mission of the coalition to increase produce consumption and the social and cultural mission of connecting people back to the production of the food they eat.

Signs of health outcome improvement are beginning to emerge as well. In 2010 CLOCC conducted a second wave of the community survey that was originally conducted when CO-OP HP was established. And although the two waves differed in some ways, weighted analysis indicated that rates of obesity among Puerto Rican children have decreased significantly during the six years of the coalition's existence. Rates among Puerto Rican adults and among children of other races and ethnicities have not decreased, suggesting that the CO-OP HP strategies, which are largely focused on Puerto Rican residents and on children, are making a difference.

Finally, the coalition and partner organization staff have markedly increased capacity as a result of the CO-OP HP experience. The Muévete leader now runs multiple programs, has helped to start programs in three other Chicago communities, and has recently been fully funded under a National Institutes of Health–funded diabetes prevention study in Humboldt Park. While maintaining headquarters and a workspace in Chicago's West Town neighborhood, West Town Bikes has become a citywide service provider for youth programs in Chicago. And in a shining example of how the coalition initiatives become sustainable entities, the leaders of West Town Bikes, in collaboration with CO-OP HP and PRCC staff, developed a for-profit business called Ciclo Urbano. This full-service community bicycle shop supports the Humboldt Park and West Town neighborhoods. The shop focuses on affordable and reliable transportation, offering bicycle sales, service, new and used bike parts, and accessories. All sales from the shop support West Town Bikes' larger mission of providing bicycle education to Chicago youth.

Staff members of the coalition's lead organization (PRCC) and member organization CLOCC have become adept at working on environmental and policy change. CLOCC is helping to develop CO-OP HP approaches in other Chicago communities. PRCC staff is engaging in public health strategies focused on issues other than obesity, giving credence to the CCAT proposition that increased capacity developed through coalition engagement can eventually be transferred to other communities and other public health issues.

Lessons for Coalitions Addressing Public Health Concerns

Coalition staff and partner organizations have learned a number of lessons through the CO-OP HP experience that support many of the propositions put forward in CCAT:

1. Coalitions can be developed to address multiple issues and leaders can have multiple agendas. However, membership may be more challenging to sustain if not all members share the same agendas. A single-issue coalition may be better able to recruit members who stay involved if all have a shared mission. Organizational membership in a multi-issue coalition may need to be structured more flexibly and leaders may need to be prepared for greater fluctuation and inconsistency of membership.

2. Public health approaches to needs and asset assessment and intervention planning are not always comfortable to or perceived as important by members of non–public health organizations. Interventions that evolve locally and organically with informal and flexible plans may be easier to sustain, because they can adapt to changing circumstances. However, these may also be harder to evaluate. Interventions that are not based on formal needs assessment may need to be highly flexible, in order to evolve to meet needs, and the community assets, that are understood only as the program unfolds.

3. Coalitions that form with a stronger focus on individual-level factors and take a more service-delivery and program-oriented approach can evolve to develop a focus on the more "upstream" environmental and policy change approaches of successful community coalitions. However, this focus may evolve more easily among coalitions whose leadership is focused on multilevel factors and structural change in work they do outside of the coalition. In addition, they may be more likely to evolve in this way if they are attentive to the barriers they encounter in attempting to meet individual community member needs through the more individually focused strategies they start out with.

4. Desired outcomes (in community environment, health, and capacity) can be achieved by coalitions, even if they do not have sustained membership, follow public health assessment and planning approaches, or focus on "upstream" factors from the outset. However, this may require that such coalitions develop strategies that serve multiple functions, adapt to changing conditions, and include processes that enable members to base decisions on their evolving understanding of the needs and assets of the community. Attention to barriers and challenges, self-reflection, and open communications among partners with differing philosophical and political views may be essential to the eventual development of more environmental and policy change goals.

Conclusion

CCAT is a useful guide for analyzing public health coalitions. The experience of our coalition—CO-OP HP—supports many of the propositions of the theory, which also helps to explain some challenging aspects of this coalition. At the same time, the CO-OP HP experience challenges some CCAT premises, by illustrating factors that can contribute to the success of community coalitions that vary from the template described by the theory. In this way, COOP-HP may help guide the further development of CCAT, to help it match a broader range of real-world coalition activities. Of equal importance, however, the case study presented in this chapter demonstrates how a multisector coalition of diverse organizations can make a real difference in the health and well-being of children by supporting and promoting change on the individual through the broad, socioenvironmental levels.

ACKNOWLEDGMENTS

The authors and other staff and leadership of Community Organizing for Obesity Prevention in Humboldt Park (CO-OP HP) would like to acknowledge the following organizations that have provided financial support: the Otho S. A. Sprague Memorial Institute; Kraft Foods; the Chicago Tribune Charities; the Michael and Susan Dell Foundation; the Chicago Community Trust; Local Initiatives Support Corporation, Chicago; and the Administration for Children and Families of the Department of Health and Human Services. The authors would also like to thank the staff and partners of the Puerto Rican Cultural Center, who have volunteered for and participated in CO-OP HP events and programs. Special thanks go to Matt Longjohn, MD, MPH, founding executive director of the Consortium to Lower Obesity in Chicago Children, and Miguel Morales, the first CO-OP HP manager, who contributed significantly to the development of the coalition. This chapter is dedicated to the children and families of the Greater Humboldt Park community. Their strength and resilience in the face of challenging community conditions is a constant inspiration.

REFERENCES

Becker, A. B., M. Longjohn, and K. K. Christoffel. 2008. "Taking on Obesity in a Big City: Consortium to Lower Obesity in Chicago Children (CLOCC)." *Progress in Pediatric Cardiology* 25:199–206.

Biro, F. M., and M. Wien. 2010. "Childhood Obesity and Adult Morbidities." Supplement, *American Journal of Clinical Nutrition* 91, no. 5:1499S–1505S.

Butterfoss, F. 2009. "Community Coalition Action Theory." In *Emerging Theories in Health Promotion Practice and Research*, edited by R. DiClemente, L. Crosby, and M. C. Kegler, 236–76. 2nd ed. San Francisco: Jossey-Bass.

Caird, J., J. Kavanagh, K. Oliver, S. Oliver, A. O'Mara, C. Stansfield, and J. Thomas. 2011. *Childhood Obesity and Educational Attainment: A Systematic Review.* London: EPPI-Centre, Social Science Research Unit, Institute of Education, University of London.

Centers for Disease Control and Prevention. 2011. "Overweight and Obesity: Consequences."
     http://www.cdc.gov/NCCDPHP/DNPA/obesity/childhood/consequences.htm.

Davison, K. K., and L. L. Birch. 2001. "Childhood Overweight: A Contextual Model and
     Recommendations for Future Research." *Obesity Review* 2, no. 3:159–71.

Evans, W. D., K. K. Christoffel, J. Necheles, A. B. Becker, and J. Snider. 2011. "Outcomes of the
     5-4-3-2-1 Go! Childhood Obesity Prevention Trial." *American Journal of Health Behavior* 35,
     no. 2:189–198.

Finkelstein, E. A., M. DiBonaventura, S. M. Burgess, and B. C. Hale. 2010. "The Costs of
     Obesity in the Workplace." *Journal of Occupational and Environmental Medicine* 52,
     no. 10:971–976.

Finkelstein, E. A., J. G. Trogdon, J. W. Cohen, and W. Dietz. 2009. "Annual Medical Spending
     Attributable to Obesity: Payer- and Service-Specific Estimates." *Health Affairs* 28,
     no. 5:822–831.

Freedman, D. S. 2011. "Obesity—United States, 1988–2008" (CDC Health Disparities and
     Inequalities Report). Supplement, *Morbidity and Mortality Weekly Report* 60 (January 14):
     73–77.

Freedman, D. S., Z. Mei, S. R. Srinivasan, G. S. Berenson, and W. H. Dietz. 2007. "Cardiovascu-
     lar Risk Factors and Excess Adiposity among Overweight Children and Adolescents:
     The Bogalusa Heart Study." *Journal of Pediatrics* 150, no. 1:12–17. http://www.jpeds.com/
     article/S0022-3476(06)00817-1/abstract.

Issel, M. L. 2009. *Health Program Planning and Evaluation: A Practical, Systematic Approach for
     Community Health.* Sudbury, Mass.: Jones and Bartlett.

Johnson, D. W., and F. P. Johnson. 2008. *Joining Together: Group Theory and Group Skills.* 10th ed.
     Old Tappan, N.J.: Pearson.

McLeroy, K. R., D. Bibeau, A. Steckler, and K. Glanz. 1988. "An Ecological Perspective on Health
     Promotion Programs." *Health Education and Behavior* 15:351–377.

Mission: Readiness. 2010. "Too Fat to Fight: Retired Military Leaders Want Junk Food out of
     America's Schools." http://cdn.missionreadiness.org/MR_Too_Fat_to_Fight-1.pdf.

Nestle, M. 2007. *Food Politics: How the Food Industry Influences Nutrition and Health.*
     Berkeley and Los Angeles: University of California Press.

Ogden, C. L., M. D. Carroll, L. R. Curtin, M. M. Lamb, and K. M. Flegal. 2010. "Prevalence of High
     Body Mass Index in US Children and Adolescents, 2007–2008." *Journal of the American
     Medical Association* 303 (January 20). http://jama.ama-assn.org/content/303/3/242
     .full.pdf.

Olshansky, J. S., D. J. Passaro, R. C. Hershow, J. Layden, B. A. Carnes, J. Brody, L. Hayflick,
     R. N. Butler, D. B. Allison, and D. S. Ludwig. 2005. "A Potential Decline in Life Expectancy
     in the United States in the 21st Century." *New England Journal of Medicine* 352 (March):
     1138–1145.

Lavizzo-Mourey, R., and Robert Wood Johnson Foundation. 2009. *The Road to Reform:
     President's Message from the 2008 Annual Report.* 2009. Princeton, N.J.: Robert Wood
     Johnson Foundation.

Sallis, J. F., N. Owen, and E. B. Fisher. 2008. "Ecological Models of Health Behavior." In *Health
     Behavior and Health Education: Theory, Research, and Practice,* edited by K. Glanz,
     B. K. Rimer, and K. Viswanath, 465–486. 4th ed. San Francisco: Jossey-Bass.

Serdula, M. K., D. Ivery, R. J. Coates, D. S. Freedman, D. F. Williamson, and T. Byers. 1993. "Do
     Obese Children Become Obese Adults? A Review of the Literature." *Preventive Medicine*
     22:167–177.

Shah, A. M., and S. Whitman. 2010. "Sinai's Improving Community Health Survey: Methodology
     and Key Findings." In *Urban Health: Combating Disparities with Local Data,* edited by
     S. Whitman, A. M. Shah, and M. R. Benjamins, 37–68. New York: Oxford University Press.

Stahl, C. E, J. W. Necheles, J. H. Mayefky, L. K. Wright, and K. M. Rankin. 2010. "*5-4-3-2-1 Go!* Coordinating Pediatric Resident Education and Community Health Promotion to Address the Obesity Epidemic in Children and Youth." *Clinical Pediatrics* 50, no. 3:215–24.

Whitaker, R. C., J. A. Wright, M. S. Pepe, K. D. Seidel, and W. H. Dietz. 1997. "Predicting Obesity in Young Adulthood from Childhood and Parental Obesity." *New England Journal of Medicine* 337 (September 25): 869–873.

19

Participatory Approaches to Evaluating Community Organizing and Coalition Building

CHRIS M. COOMBE

Evaluation is one of the most challenging and promising issues in community organizing and community building for health and welfare. In recent years, funders and government decision makers have increasingly focused on evidence-based practice, accountability, and measurable outcomes to prove program success. However, community organizing and community building efforts emphasize empowerment, collaboration, participation, community competence, and equity as essential to achieving the long-term aim of changing the conditions that contribute to health and well-being (Chávez et al. 2010). While communities see such capacity building as an important outcome, its impact on health can be elusive to evaluate, and the focus on measuring narrow health indicators may not capture longer-term effects on community health and equity (Wallerstein et al. 2011).

The result has been a tension in which community practitioners often feel that evaluation is imposed upon them in an externally driven process that does not consider the unique resources, capacity, or context of their community, and they fear that evaluation will result in loss of funding because of perceived lack of success by decision makers (Judd et al. 2001). Further, many organizations lack the skills, knowledge, and resources needed to conduct standard "objective" outcome evaluation. Faced with insufficient resources to address complex and intransigent health and social problems, community practitioners are often reluctant to spend scarce funds on an external evaluator to assess the value and worth of their work in a process they perceive to be proving rather than improving (Margerison 1987).

Over the past several decades, these challenges, combined with the expansion of comprehensive community initiatives, coalitions, and community-based participatory research (CBPR), have led to the development and widespread acceptance of participatory and collaborative methods and approaches to evaluation (Connell et al. 1995; Fetterman and Wandersman 2005; Scarinci et al. 2009; Springett and Wallerstein 2008; Sufian et al. 2011; Wallerstein 2002, 2007).

Central among them is participatory evaluation, a partnership approach to evaluation that engages those who have a stake in the project, program, or initiative in all aspects of evaluation design and implementation. Findings are applied as they emerge to solve problems and adjust course. Most important for community organizing and community building, participatory evaluation also departs from conventional evaluation by rethinking who owns and controls the process of creating, interpreting, and applying knowledge and to what end. In the emancipatory stream of participatory evaluation, both the process and products of evaluation are used to transform power relations and to promote social action and change (Cousins and Whitmore 1998).

This chapter examines how participatory approaches to evaluation can be used not only for assessing the merit and effectiveness of community organizing, but also for building organizational and community capacity for social change. First, some limitations of conventional evaluation are discussed to establish the rationale for a more participatory approach. Next, the theoretical foundation of participatory approaches to evaluation is described, including its roots in participatory research traditions from several disciplines. Drawing upon recent work in participatory evaluation, a practical framework then is suggested for incorporating this approach at each step of the evaluation process. The final sections discuss some of the benefits as well as challenges of this approach.

Limitations of Conventional Evaluation: Rationale for a Participatory Approach

Participatory approaches to evaluation arose in response to the limitations of conventional program evaluation, in particular the questions of what is knowledge, who creates it, how, and to what end. The traditional and still-dominant approach to evaluating community health promotion programs is rooted in the positivist paradigm of the medical and natural sciences, which views knowledge as an objective reality that can be discovered by impartial observers. Using the scientific method and experimental design, unbiased external evaluators test hypotheses by measuring the impact of a program on specified outcomes, using statistical-analysis techniques designed to show change and causal relationships. While this is a powerful research model, there are some important limitations to its usefulness in evaluating community organizing and community building endeavors.

First, community initiatives and community organizing involve complex systems change that requires intervention at multiple levels, making it difficult to determine causal relationships. Community efforts are dynamic and continually evolving to respond to rapidly changing environments. As a result, strategies, targets, and indicators are likely to change throughout the project, making evaluation unpredictable. Further, funder requirements to focus on predetermined quantifiable measures of success may shift priorities to more short-term and easily measured individual behaviors or risk factors rather than empowerment, capacity building, and systems change. Judging program success by narrowly focused indicators views health problems as caused by individuals, rather than by broader social determinants of health that are complex, interrelated, and difficult to link to individual health outcomes. In addition, examining only if a program works does not address the questions of how, for whom, and under what circumstances, thus limiting the usefulness of the evaluation.

Second, positivist notions of objectivity and expert knowledge determine not only what types of evidence are valuable but also who controls the development of knowledge. In conventional evaluation, the external expert evaluator determines what is to be studied, what methods are used, and what conclusions may be drawn from the findings. Those directly involved in the program are considered biased, and, while they may be consulted, it is the evaluator as impartial observer who is regarded to have the expertise, insight, knowledge, and objectivity for interpreting the meaning of the data.

However, much researcher-centered investigation has been flawed by theory rooted in the perceptions, biases, and agendas of the external observer. For example, the outside evaluator may be asking the wrong questions or misinterpreting the results, resulting in an evaluation that may miss the mark or be invalid. A constructivist research paradigm is based on the notion that objectivity may be gained not through detachment from the setting but through deep involvement in and reflection about the setting. As Whyte (1991) suggests, "Science is not achieved by distancing oneself from the world; as generations of scientists know, the greatest conceptual and methodological challenge comes from engagement with the world" (21).

A further limitation of a research approach that relies on the separate and hierarchical relationship between evaluator and community is that it fosters dependence and reinforces power imbalances. Program participants are in effect dependent on the outside agent for interpretation of the reality of their experience. Decision making as well as knowledge and skills needed for conducting evaluation remain with the evaluator and external to the organization's own process of planning and development. This is counter to the fundamental principles and strategies of community organizing and community building to promote health, which are empowerment, ownership, and community control of its own endeavors and destinies, as stated in the Ottawa Charter for Health Promotion (WHO 1986).

A final limitation is that evaluation results may not be applied or as useful as they might be, thus missing an important aim of evaluation. Stoecker (2005) refers to the externally driven evaluation as the "comprehensive final exam" model of evaluation (202), in which evaluation threatens to expose weaknesses and failures once the project is completed. However, evaluators often have information and insights that could inform program implementation and build organizational capacity throughout the intervention, but are constrained by role expectations or lack of training in these areas. In addition, reflection and analysis are conducted as activities separate from organizational planning and action, rather than as necessary, sequential steps in an integrated, collaborative decision-making process. Finally, because action planning is distinct from evaluation, which is perceived as external to the organization, programs and strategies may be less effective, because they are not based on all the available data.

Participatory evaluation was developed to address some of the limitations of using conventional evaluation to assess community initiatives and organizing. Community and other stakeholder engagement in the evaluation process is now widely accepted and indeed expected by many practitioners, evaluators, and funders of community health promotion efforts (Springett and Wallerstein 2008). Participatory and traditional approaches to evaluation are not mutually exclusive, and elements of both can provide a more complete assessment. Evaluation has the potential to build a dynamic community of transformative learning, thereby contributing to the empowerment and capacity of disenfranchised communities to bring about change (Fetterman et al. 1996). In the words of the turn-of-the century social reformer Jane Addams (1907), "We slowly learn that life consists of processes as well as results, and that failure may come quite as easily from ignoring the adequacy of one's method as from selfish or ignoble aims" (http://womenshistory.about.com/od/quotes/a/jane_addams.htm).

What Is Participatory Evaluation?

As suggested above, participatory evaluation (of which empowerment evaluation is a prominent form) is a collaborative approach to evaluation in which those who are involved in the work contribute to understanding it and improving it (Fawcett et al. 2003). It is the systematic assessment of the value and progress of an effort by those who have a vested interest in it (the stakeholders), in a cyclical process of investigation, education, and action (Cousins and Whitmore 1998).

Participatory evaluation is not new. It arose from a number of research traditions aimed at legitimizing community members' experiential knowledge, acknowledging the role of values in research, empowering community members, democratizing research inquiry, enhancing the relevance of evaluation data for communities, and applying knowledge for bringing about social change. These research and social change traditions include action research (Lewin 1946), popular education (Freire 1970), grounded theory (Glaser and Strauss 1967; Strauss and Corbin 1990), naturalistic inquiry (Lincoln and Guba 1985), feminist research (Maguire 1987; Frisby et al. 2009), and a wide range of participatory and CBPR (community-based participatory research) traditions (Brown 1992; Cargo and Mercer 2008; Corburn 2005; Fals-Borda and Rahman 1991; Israel et al. 1998; Minkler and Wallerstein 2008).

Participatory approaches to assessing community health and social welfare programs, including empowerment evaluation (Fetterman et al. 1996; Fetterman and Wandersman 2005) and theory-based evaluation (Weiss 1995), gained momentum during the late 1980s and have been applied in varying degrees to a wide range of health promotion programs, coalitions and CBPR partnerships (Lachance et al. 2006; Israel, Lantz, et al. 2005; Scarinci et al. 2009), community initiatives (Fawcett et al. 2003), policy change capacity building (Israel et al. 2010), and to a lesser extent, community organizing and mobilization (Watson-Thompson et al. 2008). Cousins and Whitmore (1998) suggest that participatory evaluation has emerged in two main streams distinguished primarily by function. The *pragmatic stream* emphasizes program improvement as the principle aim of participatory approaches. The *transformative or emancipatory stream* is based on an explicit ideological commitment to reallocating power and promoting social change. While these streams are not mutually exclusive, the latter is most consistent with community organizing and community building for health and is the focus of this chapter.

A set of guiding principles forms the basis for transformative participatory evaluation (Cousins and Whitmore 1998):

- Participation and ownership by the community
- Collaborative, co-learning process in which all participants are equitably engaged in and responsible for the evaluation
- Application of findings to promote action and change on multiple levels
- Transformation of power relationships by empowering and building capacity of local community and changing systems

In a spirit of collaborative inquiry and action, community members and outside evaluators work hand in hand on a more equal footing than in traditional evaluation (Fetterman and Wandersman 2005). Local participants are at the center of defining the agenda, determining what issues are investigated and what questions are asked, and gathering and making meaning of data. As members of the community, local investigators often have experiences and contextualized knowledge that can help shape the inquiry and interpret results (Corburn 2005). External evaluators are resources, allies, coaches, facilitators, and advocates, building the capacity of local participants to perform credible evaluation. As results emerge, evaluators actively support community planning, organizational development, and action to improve the current organizing effort and work toward broader social change (Fetterman and Wandersman 2005; Cousins and Whitmore 1998; Springett and Wallerstein 2008; Fawcett et al. 2003). Professional and academic partners further can apply their expertise and connections to help translate findings into policy or funding opportunities. Optimally, both local and external participants are transformed in the process—skills and understanding are deepened, the balance of power shifts, and stronger ties, energy, and commitment are generated.

Like other forms of CBPR, participatory evaluation links knowing and doing through a cyclical process of investigation, education, and action. Insights are applied to the program or organizing effort to improve effectiveness. Scarce resources can be targeted or redirected to strategies that work best. More information is then gathered on the results of the actions. This process of critical reflection becomes self-generating and builds the capacity of communities for future problem solving, planning, action, and assessment. In this way, both the process and findings of participatory evaluation build community competence.

A Framework for Using Participatory Evaluation

As suggested above, participatory evaluation is not a specific methodology, but an approach to evaluation based on a set of key principles that guide evaluation design, process, and methods (Burke 1998; Fetterman and Wandersman 2005). The evaluation process itself is intended to transform participants and empower communities as co-creators of knowledge, while results are translated into actions, systems, and policies at multiple levels (Wallerstein 2007).

As with any evaluation, determining whether, how, and to what degree to use participatory evaluation depends on the history of collaboration among partners, skills and resources available, the evaluation question, and the mission of the coalition or community organizing effort. How "participatory" a particular evaluation is can vary along a continuum on key dimensions. For example, the level and type of participation by different stakeholders may differ at various stages in the evaluation; however, decision making remains a joint responsibility throughout the process, as community control and ownership are defining elements of transformative participatory evaluation.

Participatory evaluation has become more widely adopted in community initiatives and coalitions, resulting in a number of well-documented measures, indicators, and methods (Fawcett et al. 2003; Lachance et al. 2006; Lempa et al. 2008). In addition, a number of frameworks have been developed that lay out key steps in participatory evaluation for community initiatives and coalitions (Fawcett et al. 1996; Maltrud et al. 1997; Zukoski and Luluquisen 2002; Springett and Wallerstein 2008; Stoecker 2005). The following eight-step process of participatory evaluation draws from key elements of several frameworks (Fetterman et al. 1996; Fetterman and Wandersman 2005; Patton 1997; Springett and Wallerstein 2008), focusing primarily on aspects that differ from conventional evaluation.

Step 1: Jointly Identify the Purpose of the Evaluation and Commit to a Participatory Approach

Those groups and organizations with a vested interest in the organizing effort determine the parameters of the evaluation, including what will be evaluated and the extent and type of participation by stakeholders. Important considerations are the project's stage of development; whether there is a history of collaboration in the community; past experience with evaluation and participatory research; resources available for evaluation, including time, people, money, and skills; and resources needed, such as training and outside expertise. Participants establish a set of guiding principles to facilitate the process (Israel et al. 1998; Roe et al. 2005; Wallerstein 2002).

Step 2: Build an Evaluation Team

Collaborative partnerships require adequate time to establish and maintain relationships, build trust, and develop the means to understand differences and resolve conflicts. Laying the proper groundwork is critical to success and there are three key tasks at this stage. First, formally identify who will be involved, the level and nature of participation expected, and what personal and institutional resources each partner brings to the table. Acknowledge existing power relationships and distribution of resources, and establish guiding principles and operating norms that foster equitable participation within the team.

Second, identify roles of participants, providing multiple mechanisms for participation and recognizing that participation may change at different stages of the evaluation, as well as in response to changing conditions in organizations and in the community. As described earlier, the roles of evaluator and community member differ significantly from those in traditional evaluation, and co-learning and capacity building are integral to the process. Plan early in the evaluation to address specific needs of all partners for training and knowledge. For example, external evaluators and funders must gain a deep understanding of the community, the historical and current context, and the program (Wandersman et al. 2003). Community members may need knowledge of standards and methods in evaluation research.

Third, participants should engage their broader constituencies early on in order to build trust and ownership of the evaluation process, inspire confidence and vision, address concerns, and build a "culture" of transformative evaluation and learning.

Step 3: Clearly Articulate the Organizing Effort's Goals and Objectives and Identify Indicators of Change and Progress

Community projects are often implemented before assumptions, goals, and targets are clearly identified. In transformative participatory evaluation, the community decides what is to be evaluated and how. At this step, professional evaluators facilitate discussion to make explicit the community's implicit theory underlying the effort (Weiss 1995). Objectives and evaluation criteria emerge from answering such questions as the following:

- What results would we like to see?
- How would we know if we achieved them?
- What level of change is desirable or acceptable?
- How will we know if we are making progress?
- What changes (intermediate outcomes) could serve as benchmarks or early markers of movement toward our goals?

- How will we assess our process and our performance?
- How will we take into account the effects of environmental conditions outside our control?

Community organizing and community building efforts aim for change at multiple levels that may be difficult to specify or that may emerge during the process. Include indicators of healthier environments, systems, or policies, rather than focusing solely on individual behavior change or long-term health outcomes typical of models of health education program planning. Consider measures of collaboration (Pearson et al. 2011; Sandoval et al. 2011; Granner et al. 2004), empowerment and community control (Israel et al. 1994; appendix 10), and community competence or capacity (Eng and Parker 1994; Aspen Institute 1996; Goodman et al. 1999; Smith 2008), consistent with the underlying premises of community organizing. Wallerstein and her colleagues developed a useful three-level framework for identifying process, people/population, and system indicators (Wallerstein 2002). Logic models linking actions to outcomes have gained increasing acceptance as a tool for program planning and evaluation and may be useful for community organizing (Milstein and Chapel 2002). Finally, there is a substantial body of practice on developing community-level indicators (Jackson et al. 2003; NeighborWorks America 2007; see chapters 9 and 10).

Step 4: Select, Develop, and Test Methods for Tracking Progress and Documenting Change

The participatory evaluation team develops monitoring and evaluation systems that are realistic and make the best use of community resources while ensuring that results are valid and methods are free enough from bias to be credible to interested audiences. Identify both quantitative and qualitative data-collection methods that are appropriate to the community and the issue, build community competence through training and data sharing, expand or make use of technology, and are potentially sustainable. Take advantage of existing resources such as data collection by other projects that overlap with your initiative or program. For example, a number of funder-driven comprehensive initiatives, such as the Food and Fitness Initiative of the W. K. Kellogg Foundation, have monitoring, documentation, and data-collection systems that may be relevant and available (see box 19.1).

There has been a rapid growth in creative participatory assessment and research techniques in the past decade that are published and available on the web, at such sites as the Community Tool Box (http://ctb.ke.edu), and in print (Scarincia et al. 2009). A sample of these is available in box 19.1.

Step 5: Collect Data and Track Progress

Participatory evaluation involves community members, to the extent feasible, in documenting the organizing effort and its effects. If needed, train selected evaluation team and other community members in data-collection methods such as interviewing, conducting focus groups, or mapping communities (see chapters 9, 10 and 14). Systems for recording activities and events as they unfold should be developed closely with those who will be using them. Consolidating efforts and information with partner organizations and others doing similar research, such as adding questions to an existing survey, can maximize resources, strengthen links between projects, and build ongoing community capacity to collect and use data (Zukowski and Luluquisen 2002; see chapter 14). Use of technology, such as Internet-based resources and handheld computers for recording data in the field (Gravlee et al. 2006) can expand the community's ability to "create" and use knowledge (see chapter 15 and appendix 6). The Community Tool Box Online Documentation System (http://ctb.ku.edu/en/services/ods.aspx), for example, is a publicly available web-based tool for recording data on community initiatives (Fawcett and Schultz 2008; http://ctb.ku.edu/en/services/ods.aspx; see box 19.1).

Step 6: Analyze and Interpret Data Collectively

Making sense of the data is a collaborative effort that combines technical expertise, experiential knowledge, and deep understanding of the community. Organize and integrate different types of data into a common body of information that participants can work with and discuss. Build consensus on findings and incorporate preliminary implications and recommendations with the results to set the stage for moving from knowledge to action. View results in the larger context, examining environmental factors that are beyond the control of the initiative or organizing project. Frame findings in terms of community strengths rather than deficits (see chapters 9 and 10).

Step 7: Communicate Results to Relevant Audiences

Unlike more conventional approaches, participatory evaluation communicates findings to key stakeholders as information emerges rather than waiting for a final product. Using evaluation data, engage participants and the community at large in reflection, interpretation of meaning, and problem solving to improve the project or take advantage of new opportunities. Share achievements as they occur to energize the community and build trust and commitment to the project. Support can be garnered from prospective funders, new constituencies, and neighboring communities.

Teamwork and mutual learning are critical. Professional evaluators share expertise in compiling and presenting data in both written and visual form, while community evaluation team members contribute expertise in communicating with diverse constituencies in understandable and meaningful ways. Use creative media, such as video, theater, art, poster, websites, and social media for sharing results to get the word out more effectively than reports and presentations alone. For example, as discussed in chapter 16, photovoice, a participatory method of research developed by Wang and Burris (1994) that combines photography with

action in a Freireian dialogue approach, has been used to evaluate and disseminate a range of community development programs, including a culture camp for
Anishinaabe youth to address childhood obesity and diabetes (Harris et al. 2008;
see also Catalani and Minkler 2010).

Data can be presented in terms of strengths and resilience rather than
deficits. For example, in the Harlem Birth Project, Mullings and Wali (2001)
presented data on percentage employed rather than percentage unemployed.
Convey project outcomes to interested parties outside the community as well,
thereby contributing to other empowerment efforts, building networks beyond
the local level, and setting the agenda for future research and action. Professional
evaluators take a more active role in helping communities effect social change by
using their expertise and connections in academic, funding, and policy arenas.

Step 8: Translate Findings into Actions, Systems, or Policies

Evaluation findings must be acted upon to be useful to the community. In this
step the group determines how to use the lessons learned to strengthen or
expand organizing efforts, institutionalize changes, and plan future actions.
Valuable information about how the process worked in relation to outcomes may
lead the project to redefine objectives, adjust strategies, redirect scarce resources,
or modify methods.

External evaluators use organizational development, facilitation, and training
skills to help the project strengthen its leadership and structure, integrate evaluation into ongoing operations, and seek out new funding resources. Participatory
evaluation is a process of learning, creating knowledge, and building relationships
that is an important outcome in and of itself (Roe et al. 2005).

In recent years there has been considerable attention paid to evaluating
partnership and capacity building as both process and outcomes of community
initiatives and coalitions. A number of frameworks, methods, and tools for
conducting participatory evaluation are described in the literature, and as noted
earlier, many are publicly available and can be accessed online. In addition,
there is a substantial body of research and practice on CBPR (community-based
participatory research) that is relevant to conducting participatory evaluation
(Cargo and Mercer 2008; Israel, Eng, et al. 2005; Minkler and Wallerstein 2008).
However, there are few published accounts of evaluation of community organizing
per se, in part because community organizing is often one component of a larger
intervention and may not be evaluated and reported separately. One notable
exception involves a youth community mobilization effort in a low-income,
predominantly African American, inner-city neighborhood in Kansas City to
create conditions that prevent youth violence. Working together, community
members and outside experts from the Work Group for Community Health and
Development at the University of Kansas engaged in a strategic planning and
implementation process that included establishment of the Ivanhoe Neighborhood Council Youth Project (INCYP). With assistance from the work group, the

BOX 19.1.

Sample Resources for Evaluating
Community Organizing and
Related Work

Resources for Evaluating Community Organizing. Alliance for Social Justice. Includes tools and strategies for evaluating organizing and advocacy work, including core components and measures of community organizing. http://www .afj.org/for-nonprofits-foundations/reco/.

Evaluating Community Programs and Initiatives. KU Work Group for Community Health and Development. 2010. Chapters 36–39. From the Community Tool Box: http://ctb.ku.edu/en/tablecontents/chapter_1036.aspx.

Grassroots action and learning for social change: Evaluating community organizing. Center for Evaluation Innovation. A framework that includes sample benchmarks and data collection methods for the core components of community organizing (Foster and Louie 2010).

Participatory PB Evaluation in Toronto. A report of a two-year participatory evaluation of a participatory budgeting process of the Toronto Housing Authority (Participatory Budget Project 2011). http://www.watsonblogs.org/participatory budgeting/torontope.html.

Movement Building Indicators. Asian Communities for Reproductive Justice. Includes a framework, indicators, and worksheets to assess leadership development, policy advocacy, communications, and relationship building (Nakae et al. 2009). http://reproductivejustice.org/movement-building-indicators.

Community Organizing Evaluation Project. The French American Charitable Trust. An evaluation framework to make it easier for community organizing groups to measure impact and make important decisions about organization growth while also elevating the importance of community organizing in the funding community. Three reports describe the evaluation project (FACT 2004). http://www.factservices.org/evaluation.html.

W. K. Kellogg Foundation Evaluation Handbook. A framework for thinking about evaluation as a relevant and useful program tool. (W. K. Kellogg Foundation 1998) http://www.wkkf.org/knowledge-center/resources/2010/ W-K-Kellogg-Foundation-Evaluation-Handbook.aspx.

Point K Practical Tools for Planning, Evaluation, and Action. The Innovation Network. Free resources that aim to help nonprofits and funders transform evaluation for social change (The Innovation Network 2011). http://www .innonet.org/ index.php?section_id=4&content_id=16.

Resource Library: Evaluation. Center for Collaborative Planning. A collection of resources on Asset-Based Community Development (ABCD), advocacy, community building, strategic planning, and other relevant topics. http://www .connectccp.org/resources/library.shtml#N_5_.

INCYP developed, carried out, and evaluated a project that included leadership development, neighborhood mobilization, and evaluation of community change (Watson-Thompson 2008).

While the aforementioned resources for evaluating coalitions, community initiatives, and CBPR are highly relevant, community organizing and community building entail particular attention to evaluating collective power, equity, systems change, and policy advocacy. Frameworks, indicators, and measures are developing rapidly in these areas. A number of resources are available on the Internet through organizations or consulting groups that specialize in community organizing and empowerment, and several are listed in box 19.1.

Benefits of Participatory Approaches to Evaluation

In addition to the benefits described earlier, participatory evaluation has the potential to advance the field of evaluation and increase its effectiveness. First, it can help overcome resistance to and suspicion of evaluation, demystify the process, and institutionalize evaluation methods within communities (Cousins and Whitmore 1998; Springett and Wallerstein 2008). When the community shares ownership of goals, process, and skills, evaluation becomes an integral part of organizing for change. Being responsible for evaluation can also push an organization to examine its assumptions and make implicit theory explicit, thus contributing to the development of local theory.

Second, participatory evaluation can enhance the integration of qualitative and quantitative methods (Fawcett et al. 1996). Such complex interventions as community organizing efforts and broad-based health initiatives involve multiple factors. Integration of qualitative information with quantitative data on accomplishments can increase understanding of which factors contribute to the functioning of the initiative or organizing effort and in what ways.

Third, such evaluation can adapt, evolve, and invent evaluation methods, indicators, and instruments. Community participation in evaluation can be a rich source of innovation in the development of methods, such as writing or telling stories (Janzen et al. 2010). For example, collaborative programs often lead to unanticipated outcomes that were not specified in the design of the program and evaluation and can be difficult to identify. A participatory qualitative data-collection process for capturing such outcomes is the most significant change (MSC) technique (Davies and Dart 2005), a process similar to the dialogue process in photovoice (Wang and Burris 1994; see chapter 16). MSC involves use of stories to identify program impacts through a systematic process of searching for significant changes and deliberating on their value. Stakeholders write stories of what they see as significant change, and dialogue with others to select those of most importance.

Fourth, participatory evaluation can enhance the ability of communities to do systematic data collection (Hollister and Hill 1995; Wallerstein 2007). Participatory evaluation can provide an incentive for local organizations to maintain their records in relatively common formats so that records data can be pulled together to create a community database. Community members of the evaluation team can gather new data of their own to give clout and credibility to advocacy efforts, using methods ranging from mapping conditions of the physical environment to conducting photovoice or related projects (see chapters 14 and 16).

Fifth, participatory evaluation can creatively link community investigators and outside evaluators in a mutual learning partnership (Fawcett et al. 1996; Roe et al. 2005). Training, facilitation, and technical assistance enable community stakeholders to understand and apply evaluation methods within the field's standards for validity and rigor. The experiential wisdom of community leadership can ensure that evaluation questions are important, data-collection methods realistic and culturally sensitive, and findings relevant and applicable within the local cultural context. Evaluators can help ensure that community voices are heard by policymakers and other audiences. Funders and institutional partici- pants can gain deeper understanding of the critical role of the macrolevel context in the success of community efforts, influencing allocation of resources.

Challenges of Using Participatory Evaluation

There are a number of philosophical and practical challenges to the evolving practice of participatory evaluation (Springett and Wallerstein 2008). First, as noted earlier, participatory evaluation frameworks may conflict with traditional assumptions about objectivity and distance. Charges of bias, conflict of interest, and misuse of data or findings can undermine the credibility of the evaluation, thereby lessening its clout. This may be particularly critical in policy and funding arenas. While the purpose of any evaluation is improvement, evaluation has never been neutral, and participatory evaluation simply makes explicit the importance of community self-determination and the goal of equity.

Participatory evaluation must meet the field's standards for propriety and accuracy, as well as utility and feasibility (Joint Committee on Educational Evalua- tion 1994). Evaluators can increase accuracy and propriety by exploring ways to minimize participant bias and including multiple methods, measures, and data sources in the evaluation design. Qualitative researchers have developed a num- ber of strategies for addressing concerns of validity and reliability (see Brown 1995; Lincoln and Guba 1985: Curry et al. 2009). In addition, Judd and colleagues (2001) developed a typology of standards for evaluating community-based programs that combines elements of both traditional and transformational approaches united in a salutogenic or health-and-well-being orientation.

Because of the paradigm shift involved, participatory evaluation can be challenging for traditional evaluators. As a process of codiscovery (Mayer 1996), it models the learning process and is quite fluid. Investigators must continually sample a changing environment and evaluate situations by degrees rather than as absolutes. Like grounded theory in qualitative methods (Glaser and Strauss 1967;

Strauss and Corbin 1990), the logic and hypotheses are often drawn directly from the data.

A second key challenge in participatory evaluation is that both professional evaluators and community members of the evaluation team must develop new skills and understanding in order for genuine empowerment to occur. Outside evaluators must develop or hone their skills in being able to work hands on with community investigators in areas such as organizational development, program planning, implementation, grant writing, and advocacy. Community evaluators may need training in evaluation methods in order to ensure rigor. Group-process skills such as team building, collaborative problem solving, negotiation, conflict resolution, and consensus building may not be part of the everyday repertoire of many community members or evaluators and must be learned. As Paul Light (2002) of the Brookings Institution has said, "We've got a bunch of evaluators who do program evaluation; we've got a very small number of evaluators who do capacity-building evaluation" (10–11).

As outsiders, professional evaluators must be particularly cognizant of the history of the community, structural practices of racial and economic injustice, the local ethnic and political culture, and the aims of the project. They must be able to openly address power and resource differences; understand empowerment and collaboration as outcomes as well as processes; talk with, not down to, the community; and commit themselves to eliminating inequity. Above all, diverse players must operate under principles of ongoing mutual learning, collaboration, and respect.

A third challenge of participatory evaluation is that it takes a great deal of time, effort, and personal commitment, which both evaluators and community members may find difficult to provide (Sufian et al. 2011). They may feel that the process is diverting precious resources away from their "real work," whether it involves the evaluation or the community organizing. Ironically, what may seem like an opportunity for capacity building to enthusiastic researchers may seem like yet another "unfunded mandate" to participants, placing too much responsibility on the community for fixing "its" problem (Fetterman 1996; Israel et al. 1998; Israel, Lantz, et al. 2005). Evaluation must be feasible and practical, balancing the interests of both professional evaluators and community members.

A fourth challenge is that the greatest strength of this emerging approach is also one of its greatest hurdles—being responsive to rapid and unexpected shifts in program design and operation. To be effective, community organizing and community-based health initiatives must be flexible, developmental, and responsive to changing local needs and conditions (Brown 1995; see chapters 7 and 11). This requires continual collection, description, reflection, and feedback of information about a group, organization, or community in all its complexity (and, not uncommonly, all its chaos). Besides being time consuming, such a process conflicts with conventional notions of scientific rigor in evaluation, which preclude continual tampering with the intervention (Wallerstein et al. 2011).

A final challenge posed by participatory evaluation relates to indicators and measurement. As noted above, community organizing, community building, and comprehensive community initiatives typically address complex problems with multiple causes affecting different constituencies in interrelated ways. Participation, collaboration, empowerment, and community competence and capacity remain challenging to conceptualize and measure, though there is now a substantial body of work in this area (Israel et al. 1994; Eng and Parker 1994; Parker et al. 2001; Connell et al. 1995; Smith 2008; Wallerstein 2002, 2007). Assessing the impacts of these concepts and constructs on policy and systems change is particularly difficult, in part because such changes often take place over a long time period. Further, as discussed in chapter 20, contextual factors, and the fact that numerous actors typically play a role in hitting the "policy levers" that can bring about change, make it extremely difficult to tease out the impact of a *particular* organizing effort or community-based initiative, let alone the role of constructs like *empowerment*. Yet here too, the application of new or refined approaches, such as multimethod case study analysis that includes a participatory evaluation component, may help develop a better understanding of the potential contribution of an organizing effort to a larger policy or systems-level change (Minkler 2010; Yin 2003).

Conclusion

Participatory evaluation can be a powerful tool for coalitions, community organizing efforts, and community-based initiatives that have empowerment, capacity building, and social change as goals. The evaluation process itself can strengthen participation and ownership, build community competence, and reveal important outcomes that might be overlooked in conventional evaluations.

Participatory evaluation pays attention to the real voices of real people, demystifying and democratizing the process of developing knowledge. Working as a team, evaluators and community members learn from each other and increase their abilities to have an impact on conditions affecting the community. Participatory evaluation has the potential for transformation.

Finally, participatory evaluation is both an art and a science, requiring changes in philosophy and practice by professional evaluators, community investigators and practitioners, and funders. It requires new skills, new relationships, and a fair amount of faith. Given the enormity of the problems facing impoverished and disenfranchised communities, it is an investment we need to make. Participatory evaluation can make an important contribution to building healthy, competent, and self-determined communities.

REFERENCES

Addams, J. 1907. *Social Ethics*. Cambridge, Mass.: Belknap Press.
Aspen Institute. 1996. *Measuring Community Capacity Building: A Workbook in Progress for Rural Communities*. Aspen, Colo.: Aspen Institute Rural Economic Policy Program.

Brown, P. 1992. "Popular Epidemiology and Toxic Waste Contamination: Lay and Professional Ways of Knowing." *Journal of Health and Social Behavior* 33, no. 3:267–281.

———. 1995. "The Role of the Evaluator in Comprehensive Community Initiatives." In *New Approaches to Evaluating Community Initiatives: Concepts, Methods, and Contexts*, edited by J. P. Connell, A. C. Kubisch, L. B. Schorr, and C. J. Weiss, 201–25. Washington, D.C.: Aspen Institute.

Burke, B. 1998. "Evaluating for a Change: Reflections on Participatory Methodology." *New Directions for Evaluation* 80, no. 1:43–55.

Cargo, M., and S. L. Mercer. 2008. "The Value and Challenges of Participatory Research: Strengthening Its Practice." *Annual Review of Public Health* 2, no. 9:325–350.

Catalani, C., and M. Minkler. 2010. "Photovoice: A Review of the Literature in Health and Public Health." *Health Education and Behavior* 37, no. 3:424–451.

Center for Collaborative Planning. N.d. "Resource Library: Evaluation." http://www.connectccp.org/resources/library.shtml#N 5.

Chávez, V. M., N. Minkler, N. Wallerstein, and M. Spencer. 2010. "Community Organizing for Health and Social Justice." In *Prevention Is Primary: Strategies for Community Well-Being*, edited by L. Cohen, C. Chávez, and S. Chehimi, 87 112. 2nd cd. San Francisco: Jossey-Bass.

Connell, J. P., A. C. Kubisch, L. B. Schorr, and C. H. Weiss, eds. 1995. *New Approaches to Evaluating Community Initiatives*. Vol. 1, *Concepts, Methods, and Contexts*. Washington, D.C.: Aspen Institute.

Corburn, J. 2005. *Street Science: Community Knowledge and Environmental Health Justice*. Cambridge, Mass.: MIT Press.

Cousins, J. B., and E. Whitmore. 1998. "Framing Participatory Evaluation." In *Understanding and Practicing Participatory Evaluation*, edited by E. Whitmore, 5–24. San Francisco: Jossey-Bass.

Curry, L. A., I. M. Nembhard, and E. H. Bradley. 2009. "Qualitative and Mixed Methods Provide Unique Contributions to Outcomes Research." *Circulation* 119:1442–1452.

Davies, R., and J. Dart. 2005. "The 'Most Significant Change' (MSC) Technique: A Guide to Its Use." http://mande.co.uk/docs/MSCGuide.pdf.

Eng, E., and E. Parker. 1994. "Measuring Community Competence in the Mississippi Delta." *Health Education Quarterly* 21, no. 2:199–220.

Fals-Borda, O., and M. A. Rahman, eds. 1991. *Action and Knowledge: Breaking the Monopoly with Participatory Action Research*. New York: Apex Press.

Fawcett, S. B., R. I. Boothroyd, J. A. Schultz, V. T. Francisco, V. Carson, and R. Bremby. 2003. "Building Capacity for Participatory Evaluation within Community Initiatives." *Journal of Prevention and Intervention in the Community* 26 no. 2:21–36.

Fawcett, S. B., A. Paine-Andrews, V. T. Francisco, J. A. Schultz, K. P. Richter, R. K. Lewis, K. J. Harris, E. L. Williams, J. Y. Berkley, C. M. Lopez, et al. 1996. "Empowering Community Health Initiatives through Evaluation." In *Empowerment Evaluation: Knowledge and Tools for Self-Assessment and Accountability*, edited by D. M. Fetterman, S. J. Kaftarian, and A. Wandersman. Thousand Oaks, Calif.: Sage.

Fawcett, S. B., and J. A. Schultz. 2008. "Supporting Participatory Evaluation Using the Community Tool Box Online Documentation System." In *Community-Based Participatory Research for Health: From Process to Outcomes*, edited by M. Minkler and N. Wallerstein, 419–24. 2nd ed. San Francisco: Jossey-Bass.

Fetterman, D. M. 1996. "Empowerment Evaluation: An Introduction to Theory and Practice." In *Empowerment Evaluation: Knowledge and Tools for Self-Assessment and Accountability*, edited by D. M. Fetterman, S. J. Kaftarian, and A. Wandersman, 3–46. Thousand Oaks, Calif.: Sage.

Fetterman, D. M., S. J. Kaftarian, and A. Wandersman, eds. 1996. *Empowerment Evaluation: Knowledge and Tools for Self-Assessment and Accountability*. Thousand Oaks, Calif.: Sage.

Fetterman, D. M., and A. Wandersman. 2005. *Empowerment Evaluation: Principles in Practice.* Thousand Oaks, Calif.: Sage.

Foster, C. C., and J. Louie. 2010. *Grassroots Action and Learning for Social Change: Evaluating Community Organizing.* Center for Evaluation Innovation. http://www.innonet.org/client_docs/File/center_pubs/evaluating_community_organizing.pdf.

Freire, P. 1970. *Pedagogy of the Oppressed.* New York: Seabury Press.

Frisby, W., P. Maguire, and C. Reid. 2009. "The F Word Has Everything to Do with It: How Feminist Theories Inform Action Research." *Action Research* 7, no. 1:13–29.

Glaser, B. G., and A. L. Strauss. 1967. *The Discovery of Grounded Theory: Strategies for Qualitative Research.* Chicago: Aldine.

Goodman, R. M, M. Speers, K. McLeroy, S. Fawcett, M. Kegler, E. Parker., S. R. Smith, et al. 1999. "Identifying and Defining the Dimensions of Community Capacity to Provide a Basis for Measurement." *Health Education and Behavior* 25, no. 3:258–278.

Granner, M. L., and P. A. Sharpe. 2004. "Evaluating Community Coalition Characteristics and Functioning: A Summary of Measurement Tools." *Health Education Research* 19, no. 5:514–532.

Gravlee, C. C., S. Zenk, S. Woods, Z. Rowe, and A. J. Schulz. 2006. "Handheld Computers for Systematic Observation of the Social and Physical Environment: The Neighborhood Observational Checklist." *Field Methods* 18, no. 4:328–397.

Harris, L., L. Fain. T. Hoaglund, and Youth Research Team. 2008. "Addressing Diabetes and Childhood Obesity in the American Indian Community by Promoting Culture and Traditional Foods: A Photovoice Project." Minnesota Department of Health. http://www.health.state.mn.us/ommh/conferences/disparity08/sessionc7.pdf.

Hollister, R. G., and J. Hill. 1995. "Problems in the Evaluation of Communitywide Initiatives." In *New Approaches to Evaluating Community Initiatives: Concepts, Methods, and Contexts*, edited by J. P. Connell, A. C. Kubisch, L. B. Schorr, and C. H. Weiss. Washington, D.C.: Aspen Institute.

Israel, B. A., B. Checkoway, A. J. Schulz, and M. Zimmerman. 1994. "Health Education and Community Empowerment: Conceptualizing and Measuring Perceptions of Individual, Organizational, and Community Control." *Health Education Quarterly* 21, no. 2:149–170.

Israel, B. A., C. M. Coombe, R. R. Cheezum, A. J. Schulz, R. McGranaghan, et al. 2010. "Community-Based Participatory Research: A Capacity Building Approach for Policy Advocacy Aimed at Eliminating Health Disparities." *American Journal of Public Health* 100, no. 11:2094–2102.

Israel, B. A., E. Eng, A. J. Schulz, and E. Parker, eds. 2005. *Methods in Community-Based Participatory Research for Health.* San Francisco: Jossey-Bass.

Israel, B. A., P. M. Lantz, R. J. McGranaghan, D. L. Kerr, and J. Ricardo-Guzmsan. 2005. "Documentation and Evaluation of Community-Based Participatory Research Partnerships: The Use of In-Depth Interviews and Closed-Ended Questionnaires." In *Methods in Community-Based Participatory Research for Health*, edited by B. A. Israel, E. Eng, A. J. Schulz, and E. Parker, 255–277. San Francisco: Jossey-Bass.

Israel, B. A., A. Schulz, E. Parker, and A. Becker. 1998. "Review of Community-Based Research: Assessing Partnership Approaches to Improve Public Health." *Annual Review of Public Health* 19:173–202.

Jackson, S. F., S. Cleverly, B. Poland, D. Burman, R. Edwards, and A. Robertson. 2003. "Working with Toronto Neighbourhoods toward Developing Indicators of Community Capacity." *Health Promotion International* 18, no. 4:339–350.

Janzen, R., S. M. Pancer, G. Nelson, C. Loomis, and J. Hasford. 2010. "Evaluating Community Participation as Prevention: Life Narratives of Youth." *Journal of Community Psychology* 38, no. 8:992–1006.

Joint Committee on Educational Evaluation. 1994. *The Program Evaluation Standards: How to Assess Evaluations of Educational Programs*. Thousand Oaks, Calif.: Sage.

Judd, J., C. J. Frankish, and G. Moulton. 2001. "Setting Standards in the Evaluation of Community-Based Health Promotion Programmes—a Unifying Approach." *Health Promotion International* 16, no. 4:367–380.

Lachance, L. L., C. R. Houle, E. F. Cassidy, E. Bourcier, J. H. Cohn, C. E. Orians, K. Coughey, X. Geng, C. L. M. Joseph, M. D. Lyde, et al. 2006. "Collaborative Design and Implementation of a Multisite Community Coalition Evaluation." Supplement, *Health Promotion Practice* 7:44S.

Lempa, M., R. M. Goodman, J. Rice, and A. B. Becker. 2008. "Development of Scales Measuring the Capacity of Community-Based Initiatives." *Health Education and Behavior* 35, no. 3:298–315.

Lewin, K. 1946. "Action Research and Minority Problems." *Journal of Social Issues* 2:34–46.

Light, P. 2002. "A Conversation with Paul Light." *Evaluation Exchange* (Harvard Family Research Project) 8, no. 2:10–11.

Lincoln, Y., and E. Guba. 1985. *Naturalistic Inquiry*. Beverly Hills, Calif.: Sage.

Maguire, P. 1987. *Doing Participatory Research: A Feminist Approach*. Amherst: Center for International Education, University of Massachusetts.

Maltrud, K., M. Polacsek, and N. Wallerstein. 1997. *Participatory Evaluation Workbook for Community Initiatives*. Albuquerque: Master's Program in Public Health Education, University of New Mexico.

Margerison, C. J. 1987. "Integrating Action Research and Action Learning in Organization Development." *Organization Development Journal* (Winter): 89–91.

Mayer, S. E. 1996. "Building Community Capacity with Evaluation Activities That Empower." In *Empowerment Evaluation: Knowledge and Tools for Self-Assessment and Accountability*, edited by D. M. Fetterman, S. J. Kaftarian, and A. Wandersman, 323–378. Thousand Oaks, Calif.: Sage.

Milstein, B., and T. Chapel. 2002. "Developing a Logic Model or Theory of Change." Community Tool Box. http://ctb.ke.edu.

Minkler, M. 2010. "Linking Science and Policy through Community-Based Participatory Research to Eliminate Health Disparities." Supplement, *American Journal of Public Health* 100, no. 1:S81–S87.

Minkler, M., and N. Wallerstein, eds. 2008. *Community-Based Participatory Research: From Processes to Outcomes*. 2nd ed. San Francisco: Jossey-Bass.

Mullings, L., and A. Wali. 2001. *Stress and Resilience: The Social Context of Reproduction in Central Harlem*. New York: Kluwer Academic.

Nakae, M., M. Cowman, and E. Shen. 2009. "Movement Building Indicators." Momentum Series, vol. 6. Asian Communities for Reproductive Justice. http://reproductivejustice.org/assets/docs/ACRJ-MS6-Movement-Building-Indicators.pdf.

NeighborWorks America. 2007. "Success Measures Outcome Indicators." Neighborhood Reinvestment Corporation. http://www.nw.org/network/ps/successmeasures/documents/indictors_with_discriptons.pdf.

Parker, E. A., R. L. Lichtenstein, A. J. Schulz, B. A. Israel, M. A. Schork, K. J. Steinman, and S. A. James. 2001. "Disentangling Measures of Individual Perceptions of Community Social Dynamics: Results of a Community Survey." *Health Education and Behavior* 28, no. 4:462–486.

Participatory Budgeting Project. 2011. "Participatory PB Evaluation in Toronto." Watsonblogs project, hosted by the Watson Institute for International Studies at Brown University. http://www.watsonblogs.org/participatorybudgeting/torontope.html.

Patton, M. Q. 1997. *Utilization-Focused Evaluation: The New Century Text*. 3rd ed. Thousand Oaks, Calif.: Sage.

Pearson, C., B. Duran, D. Martin, J. Lucero, J. Sandoval, et al. 2011. "CBPR Variable Matrix: Research for Improved Health in Academic/Community Partnerships." *NARCH V— Research for Change: Cross-Site Multi-cultural Community-Based Participatory Research.* http://hsc.unm.edu/SOM/fcm/cpr/cbprmodel/Variables/CBPR-InteractiveModel/ CBPRVariables-Matrix/.

Roe, K. M., K. Roe, C. Goette Carpenter, and C. Bernstein Sibley. 2005. "Community Building through Empowering Evaluation: A Case Study of Community Planning for HIV Prevention." In *Community Organizing and Community Building for Health,* edited by M. Minkler, 386–402. 2nd ed. New Brunswick, N.J.: Rutgers University Press.

Sandoval, J. J., M. Lucero, L. Oetzel, M. Avila, M. Belone, et al. 2011. "Process and Outcome Constructs for Evaluating Community-Based Participatory Research Projects: A Matrix of Existing Measures and Measurement Tools." Unpublished manuscript.

Scarincia, I. C., R. E. Johnson, C. Hardy, J. Marrone, and E. E. Partridge. 2009. "Planning and Implementation of a Participatory Evaluation Strategy: A Viable Approach in the Evaluation of Community-Based Participatory Research Programs Addressing Cancer Disparities." *Evaluation and Program Planning* 32, no. 3:221–228.

Smith, N. 2008. "Measuring Community Capacity: State of the Field Review and Recommendations for Future Research." Health Policy Research Program, *Health Canada.*

Springett, J., and N. Wallerstein. 2008. "Issues in Participatory Evaluation." In *Community-Based Participatory Research for Health,* edited by M. Minkler and N. Wallerstein, 199–215. 2nd ed. San Francisco: Jossey-Bass.

Stoecker, R. 2005. *Research Methods for Community Change: A Project-Based Approach.* Thousand Oaks, Calif.: Sage.

Strauss, A. L., and J. Corbin. 1990. *Basics of Qualitative Research: Grounded Theory Procedures and Techniques.* Newbury Park, Calif.: Sage.

Sufian, M., J. A. Grunbaum, T. H. Akintobi, A. Dozier, M. Eder, S. Jones, S. Mullan, et al. 2011. "Program Evaluation and Evaluating Community Engagement." In *Principles of Community Engagement,* by Clinical and Translational Science Awards Consortium Community Engagement Key Function Committee Task Force on Principles of Community Engagement. 2nd ed. NIH Publication No. 11-7782. Washington D.C.: National Institutes of Health.

Wallerstein, N. 2002. "Participatory Evaluation Model for Coalitions: The Development of Systems Indicators." *Health Promotion Practice* 3, no. 3:361–373.

———. 2007. "Making Traces: Evidence for Practice and Evaluation." In *Critical Public Health: A Reader,* edited by J. Greene and R. Labonte, 80–91. London, Routledge.

Wallerstein, N., I. H. Yen, and S. L. Syme. 2011. "Integration of Social Epidemiology and Community-Engaged Interventions to Improve Health Equity." *American Journal of Public Health* 101, no. 5:822–830.

Wandersman, A., D. C. Keener, J. Snell-Johns, R. L. Miller, P. Flahspohler, M. Livet-Dye, J. Mendez, T. Behrens, B. Bolson, and L. V. Robinson. 2003. "Empowerment Evaluation: Principles and Action." In *Participatory Community Research: Theories and Methods in Action,* edited by L. A. Jason, C. B. Keys, Y. Suarez-Balcazar, R. R. Taylor, M. Davis, J. Durlack, and D. Isenberg, 139–156. Washington, D.C.: American Psychological Association.

Wang, C., and M. A. Burris. 1994. "Empowerment through Photo Novella: Portraits of Participation." *Health Education and Behavior* 21, no. 2:171–186.

Watson-Thompson, J., S. B. Fawcett, and J. A. Schultz. 2008. "A Framework for Community Mobilization to Promote Healthy Youth Development." Supplement, *American Journal of Preventive Medicine* 34, no. 3:S72–S81.

Weiss, C. H. 1995. "Nothing as Practical as Good Theory: Exploring Theory-Based Evaluation in Comprehensive Community Initiatives." In *Concepts, Methods, and Contexts,* edited by

J. P. Connell, A. C. Kubisch, L. B. Schorr, and C. H. Weiss, 65–92. Washington, D.C.: Aspen Institute.

Whyte, W. F., ed. 1991. *Participatory Action Research*. Newbury Park, Calif.: Sage.

W. K. Kellogg Foundation. 1998. *W. K. Kellogg Foundation Evaluation Handbook*. Battle Creek, Mich: W. K. Kellogg Foundation. http://www.wkkf.org/knowledge-center/resources/ 2010/ W-K-Kellogg-Foundation-Evaluation-Handbook.aspx.

——. N.d. "Food and Fitness Initiative." http://www.foodandcommunity.org/What-We-Do/ overview/increase-access-to-good-food-and-physical-activity.aspx.

World Health Organization (WHO). 1986. *Ottawa Charter for Health Promotion*. Copenhagen: WHO Europe. http://www.who.int/hpr/NPH/docs/ottawa_charter_hp.pdf.

Yin, R. 2003. *Case Study Research: Design and Methods*. 3rd ed. Thousands Oaks, Calif.: Sage.

Zukoski, A., and M. Luluquisen. 2002. "Participatory Evaluation: What Is It? Why Do It? What Are the Challenges?" In *Community-Based Public Health Policy and Practice* 5:1–6.

PART EIGHT

Influencing Policy through Community Organizing and Media Advocacy

With its emphasis on community mobilization to bring about change, influencing the policy process would seem a logical area of concern for community organizers in fields such as health education and social welfare and for the communities with which they are engaged. Yet community residents often regard policy as abstract and confusing, and as Toby Citrin (2000) has pointed out, many professionals shy away from policy advocacy as well, deeming it too time consuming and risky. As a result, valuable opportunities for potentially influencing the lives of large numbers of people may be lost.

In the final part of this volume, we turn our attention to the increasingly appreciated role that community organizing can play in helping to promote changes in policy or the broader policy environment. In chapter 20, Angela Glover Blackwell and her colleagues offer a brief introduction to the policymaking process, highlighting several popular models (e.g., Longest 2006) and the key steps or stages in the process that transcend specific models and approaches. Building on the work of Makani Themba-Nixon (1999) and her colleagues (Themba-Nixon et al. 2008) and others, they then elaborate on each of these steps with attention to the particular roles that community organizers and their allies can play at different stages in the process.

The bulk of the chapter then is devoted to two case studies, each of which demonstrates the powerful role that community organizing can play in advocating for policy enactment, change, and implementation. In the first, we learn how a community-and-academic partnership in Harlem, New York, used a combination of participatory research and community organizing and advocacy to address the problem of inadequate policy and programmatic support to ensure the successful reintegration of drug users leaving jail and prisons (Lee et al. 2006). The partnership's use of multimethod data collection; its reframing of substance abuse and inmate reentry as public health, and not simply criminal justice issues; and its bringing together of a broad citywide coalition to press for policy and systems change are discussed. We learn about the not insignificant challenges posed along the way (including the defunding of this work well before it had resulted in policy outcomes), but also about the partnership's commitment to the effort even without outside funding. The partnership's substantial contributions to several key policy changes—such as the reinstatement of Medicaid coverage (and hence access to drug treatment and vital medications) immediately upon release—are described and provide a wonderful testament to the role of community organizing and advocacy, along with powerful data, in helping bring about policy-level change.

In the second case study, we learn of the efforts of the nationally recognized faith-based organization ISAIAH and its partners in the area of social equity in public transit policy in Minneapolis, Minnesota. The Stops for Us campaign used principles of community organizing and advocacy to successfully fight to reinstate three light rail stops in a part of the city whose residents were disproportionately low-income people of color and people with disabilities. The case study then describes how ISAIAH then worked with PolicyLink and other partners on a broader campaign, Healthy Corridor for All, to ensure continued movement in the direction of healthy and just policy choices and increased community engagement in decision-making processes. Their conducting of a community-driven health impact assessment both helped identify community concerns and health and equity impacts of the pending transit development in the Central Corridor neighborhoods, but also increased the capacity of local community groups for exploring the relationship between health and land use and for taking part in land use and transit-oriented development policymaking. This case study, in sum, is a perfect example of the need to consider both distributive and procedural justice in policymaking, with the latter involving genuine and ongoing community engagement in policymaking (Minkler 2010). The chapter concludes by calling for the application of community building principles to policy design (see appendix 1), so that our policies themselves will be grounded in and reflect a commitment to high-level community participation and civic engagement.

In earlier parts of this book, we have seen the applicability of a variety of techniques and approaches to influencing policy, key among them online activism (chapter 15) and photovoice and videovoice (chapter 16). The final chapter of this volume, describes and vividly demonstrates another tool with tremendous potential for community organizing into the twenty-first century: media advocacy. Written by Lori Dorfman and Priscilla Gonzalez of one of the nation's premier media advocacy organizations, the Berkeley Media Studies Group, chapter 22 views media advocacy as rooted in the broader area of community advocacy. Drawing on the earlier work of Lawrence Wallack and his colleagues (1999), it defines *media advocacy* as the "strategic use of mass media" to advance a policy goal or initiative. Whereas traditional media approaches try to fill the "knowledge gap," we learn in this chapter how media advocacy is concerned instead with filling the "power gap" by highlighting alternative definitions of problems and policy-level approaches to their solution (Wallack et al. 1999). Its strategies are seen to include working with community groups to harness the power of the media for changing the environment in which a problem occurs. To do this, advocates and concerned community members are encouraged to begin with an *overall strategy* (what do we want to change and how?) to a *media strategy* (knowing when and where the use of the media, including social media, could make the biggest impact) to only then worrying about an *access strategy* (such as getting a journalist's attention). With riveting examples, among them a local health department's campaign to expose and successfully fight a "responsible choices" partnership between Coca Cola and the American Academy of Family Physicians, the authors illustrate how such planning can make a difference in exposing and changing harmful practices in promoting healthy public and private policy.

The critical role of framing is stressed, as advocates eschew what Iyengar (1991) calls "episodic" stories (focused on individuals absent of context) to instead provide thematic stories offering background and context that evoke the need for policy or other environmental change.

Media advocacy is increasingly being used by a plethora of groups and communities to transform the ways in which their issues and concerns are portrayed and handled by the mass media. By using a wide-angle lens to shift our gaze from the personal to the social, and from individual behavior to the broader policy and environmental contexts that heavily shape individual behavior, media advocacy represents a tool with immense and well-demonstrated potential for community organizing and social change.

REFERENCES

Citrin, T. 2000. "Policy Issues in a Community-Based Approach." In *Community-Based Public Health: A Partnership Model*, edited by T. A. Bruce and S. U. McKane, 83–90. Washington, D.C.: American Public Health Association.

Iyengar, S. 1991. *Is Anyone Responsible?* Chicago: University of Chicago Press.

Lee, J., D. Vlahov, and N. Freudenberg. 2006. "Primary Care and Health Insurance among Women Released from New York City Jails." *Journal of Health Care for the Poor and Underserved* 17, no. 1:200–217.

Longest, B. B. 2006. *Health Policymaking in the United States*. 3rd ed. Chicago: Health Administration Press.

Minkler, M. 2010. "Linking Science and Policy through Community-Based Participatory Research to Eliminate Health Disparities." Supplement, *American Journal of Public Health* 100, no. 1:S81–S87.

Themba-Nixon, M. 1999. *Making Policy, Making Change: How Communities Are Taking Law into Their Own Hands*. San Francisco: Jossey-Bass.

Themba-Nixon, M. N., M. Minkler, and N. Freudenberg. 2008. "The Role of CBPR in Policy Advocacy." In *Community-Based Participatory Research: From Process to Outcomes*, edited by M. Minkler and N. Wallerstein, 307–322. San Francisco: Jossey-Bass.

Wallack L., K. Woodruff, L. Dorfman, and I. Diaz. 1999. *News for a Change: An Advocates' Guide to Working with the Media*. Thousand Oaks, Calif.: Sage.

20

Using Community Organizing and Community Building to Influence Public Policy

ANGELA GLOVER BLACKWELL

MILDRED THOMPSON

NICHOLAS FREUDENBERG

JEANNE AYERS

DORAN SCHRANTZ

MEREDITH MINKLER

In public health, urban and regional planning, social work, and related fields, a hallmark of community organizing and community building lies in their commitment to action and social change. Although such action may take many forms, community builders and organizers increasingly are turning to policy approaches as among the most potent for affecting the health and well-being of communities.

The rationale for an emphasis on policy in the health field is well documented. The dramatic declines in U.S. mortality rates over the past century have been attributed in large part to environmental and policy-related changes in sanitation, water supply, and food quality (McGinnis and Foege 1993; House et al. 2008). More recently, community organizing and the subsequent development of social movements in areas such as women's rights, HIV/AIDS prevention, disability rights, and environmental and climate justice have played a crucial role in changing policies on the local through the national levels (Brown et al. 2012). Successful efforts in many parts of the country to ban smoking in public places, curb the sale of handguns, and promote healthier food environments, as well as the enactment of legislation (albeit inadequate) to clean up toxic waste, are among the many policy-related victories that took root in local community organizing and community building efforts. Finally, on a global level, the healthy cities/healthy communities movement has, since its inception, focused on broad policy-level changes as a means of helping communities realize their visions of a healthy place in which to live, work, and play (Corburn 2009; O'Neill and Simard 2006; see chapter 9).

For many community residents, however, "public policy has become unfamiliar and irrelevant, complicated, inaccessible and confusing" (Blackwell and Colmenar

2000, 162). And even those who *do* believe in the importance of public policy often feel ineffectual in their ability to influence major decisions affecting their lives. In a similar way, professionals in health, social work, and related fields who work on the community level sometimes have been reluctant to focus on policy-related activity, which they perceive as taking place primarily "out there" on the state and national levels—levels seen as being far removed from their day-to-day community organizing efforts (Minkler and Freudenberg 2010). Confusion over the extent to which nonprofit organizations can engage in policy advocacy without jeopardizing their funding also have been cause for concern, though as Homan (2011) and others have noted, this fear is often exaggerated and not in line with actual federal or foundation grantee guidelines (see chapter 7).

Despite the challenges faced, health professionals and their community partners, as well as policymakers themselves, increasingly are recognizing community organizing and community building as critical strategies for helping to effect healthy public policy. Indeed, if community building principles are taken seriously, policymaking itself may become a process of community building, with community members engaged at every step, from framing the issues to interpreting the data, discussing the options, and working for the adoption of the policy change they wish to see.

We begin this chapter by offering a conceptual framework for understanding policy and policy advocacy from a community organizing and community building perspective, including a look at the key steps involved in this process. We then offer two examples demonstrating some of the many ways in which local community organizing and community-based partnership efforts have worked to influence the policymaking process. We conclude by broadening our gaze to suggest how the application of community building and community organizing principles should be an integral part of policy design.

Conceptual Framework

For the purposes of this chapter, policies are defined as the laws and regulations, including both formal and informal rules, "by which opportunities are framed—what is allowed, encouraged, discouraged, or prohibited" (Bell and Standish 2005, 339). As Bell and Standish go on to note, "Policies also determine the shape, size and character of communities," including, for example, neighborhood density and population composition, and whether businesses (including polluting industries) can move in (339).

As Milio (1998) has pointed out, "The intent [of policy] is to achieve a more acceptable state of affairs and, from a public health perspective, a more health-promoting society" (15). From the perspective of health equity, policies should be designed that "[provide] all people with fair opportunities to attain their full health potential to the extent possible" (Braveman 2006, 167), in large part by working to eliminate unfair or unjust conditions resulting in health disparities (see also Giles and Liburd 2010; Bell and Lee 2011).

Many models of the policymaking process have relevance for those engaged in community organizing and community building. Among the most influential is a model developed by political scientist John Kingdon (2003) that posits that in order to get the attention of policymakers, we need to address three processes: convincing decision makers that a problem exists; proposing feasible, politically attractive proposals to solve the problem; and negotiating the politics that influence whether a proposal succeeds in the political arena. The first stage, moving a policy issue onto the political agenda, is often the starting point for community organizing, and Kingdon's model has been used to help examine community-based agenda setting on issues such as teen access to birth control (Brindis et al. 2009), food security (Brechwich Vásquez et al. 2007), and asthma prevention through environmental policy change (Minkler et al. 2010).

Theorists also stress the importance of a "window of opportunity" for policy that opens when there is a favorable coming together of problems, potential solutions, and political circumstances, often accompanied by community or public engagement (Kingdon 2003). Identifying opening "policy windows" and being able to jump through them are important skills for community organizers. Monitoring developments in all three processes (getting your problem on the agenda, proposing a feasible solution, and getting to passage and implementation) is also a critical task for organizers and their allies, who can be ready to move in any of the three arenas as needed (Minkler and Freudenberg 2010).

Health policy researcher Beauford B. B. Longest Jr. (2006) describes the policy process as highly political, reflecting a mix of influences on both public and individual interests and rarely proceeding on the basis of rational or empirical decision making. Core components of his model suggest that it is also "distinctly cyclical," with a circular flow of interactions and influences between the various stages, and that it involves "an open system" in which "the process interacts with and is affected by events and circumstances in its external environment." The three distinct but interconnected phases in this model are the following:

- *Policy formulation*, encompassing activities involved in setting the policy agenda and later in the actual development of legislation
- *Policy implementation*, involving all those activities connected with rule making to guide the actual implementing and operationalizing of a policy
- *Policy modification*, including the revisiting and possible alteration of all previous decisions and compromises made during the policymaking process

As Longest's model suggests, the formal enactment of legislation serves as a bridge between the policy formulation process and the subsequent implementation phase. The policy modification phase then comes into play as a feedback loop through which minor tweaking of the legislation—or a major revisiting of the agenda-setting process—may take place. Both the political nature of policymaking and the dynamic nature of the external environment in which policymaking occurs underscore the likelihood of policy modification—and in extreme cases, even repeal—during this phase of the process.

Finally, both these and other popular models of the policymaking process (Milio 1998; Bardach 2000) suggest the existence of a series of steps or stages through which such processes typically progress, albeit with many feedback loops and circuitous detours along the way. Drawing on these various models, and on the work of organizer Makani Themba-Nixon (1999, 2010), we summarize these stages and corresponding roles for organizers and advocates along the way:

- *Problem identification and refinement.* Policymakers and advocates identify problems or issues to be addressed in future legislation. Advocates and community organizers may "test the waters" at this stage, working with community members and conducting research to identify a shared problem or vision and to discover the true extent of support (or opposition) it may entail. As Themba-Nixon (2010) points out, "A good organizer carefully dissects how key constituents will perceive their self interests as they relate to the proposed policy" (147).
- *Setting an agenda and creating awareness.* In policy terms, as Kingdon (2003) notes, the agenda is the list of issue areas to which policymakers are paying attention. Town hall meetings, public and policy awareness campaigns, media advocacy, and other means (e.g., testifying at hearing) all may be critical in both creating wider community awareness and getting on the policy agenda.
- *Setting policy objectives.* Clear objectives for the policy are identified based on the problem-reframing process. A SWOT analysis may be conducted at this stage to help community members lay out the *strengths* and *weaknesses* internal to their case and the *opportunities* and *threats* in the larger environment (Barry 1997; see also appendix 7).
- *Designing alternative courses of action and weighing their consequences.* In this "marketplace stage" competing interests are offered and compromises discussed. Advocates, organizers, and community members assess the likelihood of winning on their initial proposal and discuss alternatives if these seem necessary. Having a clear "pocketbook angle" (Staples 2004; see chapter 11) may also be critical at this stage to be able to show that the advocates' proposed solution is ideally cost saving, or at minimum cost neutral or worthy of the price tag attached.
- *Victory and defense.* Although not typically listed in policy process models, community celebrations of victories and attaining media exposure for these wins is an important part of the process from a community organizing and community building perspective. Concurrent with this stage, however, legal and other challenges must be anticipated and prepared for (Themba 1999; Temba-Nixon 2010).

- *Assigning implementation responsibility.* Decision makers identify the agency or unit with responsibility (and ideally the resources) for implementation; community groups work to ensure that enforcement takes place and that oversight mechanisms are in place.
- *Evaluation.* Many methods are employed for assessing policy impact and outcomes, such as stakeholder interviews, case studies, and tracking of media coverage, as well as more tailored advocacy evaluation methods, including policymaker ratings and the Bellwether methodology, through which a sample of influential and knowledgeable people in the public or private sectors are interviewed concerning a range of current policy issues (Coffman 2002; Coffman and Reed 2009). From a community organizing and community building perspective, participatory or empowerment evaluation (Wallerstein et al. 2002; Fetterman and Wandersman 2005) ideally is employed throughout the process to enable community members to play an active role in the evaluation procedure (see chapter 19).

As suggested above, and despite the linear listing of stages in policy process models like that described here, this process is in reality a dynamic and frequently convoluted one. The often substantial role of private interest groups and political considerations also should not be underestimated, as captured in the saying popularized by Otto van Bismarck over a century ago, that "laws are like sausages. You should never watch them being made." Yet despite the messiness, involvement in the policymaking process has never been more vital for those concerned with community building and improving the public's health. We turn now to two brief case studies illustrating successful efforts by diverse grassroots groups, community-based organizations, and coalitions, often aided by professionals in public health and related fields, to create and shape healthy public policy.

Influencing Policy through Community Organizing and Community Building: Case Examples

Changing Policies to Foster Reintegration of Inmates Leaving Jail in New York City

In New York City, where nearly one hundred thousand inmates are released from prison or jail annually, many return to jail or prison within a year, making their release, not one way, but a "round trip." (Freudenberg et al. 2005). The communities of Central and East Harlem, whose returning inmates often are incarcerated for crimes related to poverty, violence, substance abuse, and mental illness, have been particularly affected by this confluence of problems (Freudenberg 2001; Freudenberg et al. 2005; Van Olphen et al. 2003; Freudenberg et al. 2010).

The intersection of reentry issues with substance abuse, the longtime focus of the Center for Urban Epidemiologic Studies (CUES) in New York, led its Policy Work Group to identify reintegration of drug users who have served time in jail and prison as a priority concern. CUES included as partners community residents and representatives of advocacy organizations, the New York City Department of Health and Mental Hygiene, and academics from Hunter College and the New York Academy of Medicine. An active Community Advisory Board also worked with CUES throughout the process. Together, the diverse membership of the Policy Work Group recast the problem of inmate reentry in a public health framework. They noted, for example, that high proportions of returning inmates had substance abuse and other mental health problems, and frequently conditions such as HIV/AIDS, tuberculosis, and hepatitis C as well. They further defined the problem in terms of such barriers to reintegration as the fact that 90 percent of returning inmates had not completed high school and many were impoverished, homeless, and unemployed (Freudenberg 2001; Freudenberg et al. 2005, 2010; Van Olphen et al. 2003).

As noted above, critical to translating a community issue into an actionable policy agenda is "doing your homework," and finding out the extent of the problem and its ramifications. The Policy Work Group undertook a wide range of fact-finding methods, including secondary data analysis regarding substance abuse and incarceration, focus groups with former inmates, survey research with providers, public opinion polling, and policy analysis. Together, this research helped uncover eleven different policies that appeared to work against successful community reintegration. For example, the policy of terminating, rather then temporarily suspending, Medicaid coverage for inmates while they were incarcerated often precluded their getting timely access to substance abuse counseling and treatment on their release, contributing, for many, to the "round trip" nature of their incarceration (Freudenberg et al. 2005; Van Olphen et al. 2003).

To increase awareness of the problem among community members and policymakers, the Policy Work Group shared its findings through community forums and facilitated discussions that in turn helped further hone their policy objectives and targets. Consistent with Themba's (1999; Themba-Nixon 2010) reminder to begin by identifying the individuals or institutions with the power to address the community's demands and help ameliorate the problem, CUES, its Community Advisory Board, and its Policy Work Group identified and targeted those government entities with the power to make the relevant policy changes they sought— among them New York's Department of Correction, the city council, the mayor, and the state legislature. Further, and in keeping with Staples' (2004; chapter 11) reminder to address the "pocketbook angle" in desired policy changes, the Policy Work Group advocated for and got an Independent Budget Office study of the annual costs of reincarceration, using the results to further push for policy change. A key finding of this analysis—that having Medicaid in the year after release significantly reduced reincarceration rates by two-thirds (Lee et al. 2006) packed substantial "political punch" (chapter 9) demonstrating cost savings to the city and state and helping strengthen the case for policy change.

CUES and its Policy Work Group also played a key role in helping bring together a broader citywide coalition, the Community Reintegration Network, which also pushed for action from the New York City Council and the mayor. Their policy reports, among them *Coming Home from Jail: An Action Plan to Improve NYC Reentry Policies and Programs* (Hunter College and Community Reintegration Network 2003) were widely distributed to city officials and other stakeholders and included both the human and fiscal costs of current policies and alternative approaches. Throughout this process, moreover, community members affected by the problem—substance abusers who were former inmates—continued to play a key role. In the words of one such participant: "All the work done in the Policy Group has been informed by the action people who have come out of the prisons and jails. I think that has kind of grounded our work and also gives strength to the work we do. Because it isn't just us thinking about it from the policy point of view, but actually from the affected folks that are saying 'these are the problems we are facing.'"

CUES and its Policy Work Group's leadership and organization, together with the effective advocacy of the Community Reintegration Network, contributed to a number of important changes in programs, practices and policies. Among these were the Department of Correction's agreement, in 2004, to release most inmates during daylight hours rather than in the middle of the night, and city legislation that same year mandating discharge planning and relevant social services for all inmates prior to release. The latter policy was expanded the following year to include help finding housing and employment. The Community Reintegration Network and other institutions also worked to create new or expanded programs for reentering inmates, including job training, follow-up services, and health care. Finally, and of perhaps greatest importance, the Policy Work Group and its allies were described by policymakers and others as having played a key role in getting the New York State legislature to pass a bill in 2007 reinstating Medicaid coverage to inmates upon their release, replacing the previous policy that had permanently revoked benefits upon incarceration.

Considerable caution must be used, of course, in attempting to document such potential contributions (Sterman 2006; Minkler et al. 2008). As Guthrie and her colleagues (2006) have noted, "Most policy work involves multiple players 'hitting' numerous leverage points. In this complex system, it is difficult to sort out the distinct effect of any individual player or any single activity" (9). Our interviews with policymakers and other key stakeholders, as well as documents review and other data sources, however (Minkler et al. 2008), indicated that the Policy Work Group and its allies had made a substantial contribution to these critical policy- and systems-level changes, in the process improving the prospects for successful community reintegration for this large and vulnerable population. Moreover, by these actions, the Policy Work Group and its supporters contributed to making improved jail reentry an important policy goal of the New York City mayor, ensuring continued attention to the issue and a mobilized advocacy community that could continue to monitor city performance in this area.

Organizing for Transit and Transit-Oriented Development:
The Central Corridor Light Rail and ISAIAH, St. Paul, Minnesota

In June 2006, the Metropolitan Council, the planning agency for Minnesota's Twin
Cities region, approved a plan to construct a light rail transit (LRT) line linking the
downtowns of St. Paul and Minneapolis, referred to as the Central Corridor (CC).
Data from the American Community Survey suggest that the CC encompasses
some of the most economically and racially diverse areas of St. Paul, with large
populations of African Americans and of Hmong and other Asian Americans.
Residents living along the CC have lower educational attainment levels, lower
incomes (Malekafzali and Bergstrom 2011), and higher rates of infant mortality
and asthma hospitalizations than those of their Twin Cities counterparts
(Minnesota Department of Health 2010).

In addition to the present-day challenges faced by the CC communities, there
are historic wounds related to transportation planning. The construction of the
interstate highway I-94 in the early 1960s forcibly displaced thousands of African
Americans from the vibrant Rondo neighborhood, the heart of St Paul's largest
black community at the time (Sanders 1992). Consequently, many community
members questioned whether the new $957 million in public investment slated
for the Central Corridor Light Rail Transit (CCLRT) would again displace existing
residents and dismantle communities or if instead it could leverage much-needed
opportunity. High-capacity community organizing and power building, particularly among those most affected by the new light rail, would be critical to ensuring
that local residents benefited from the significant projected public and private
investments.

Creating healthy communities and health equity requires the negotiation
and alignment of the interests of the public and private sectors and community
organizations. This is apparent in the case of the CC LRT line, where many organizations have played important roles. While the focus of this case study is ISAIAH,
a faith-based community organizing group of approximately ninety congregations
(http://www.isaiah-mn.org), other key community organizations are also briefly
highlighted.

As ISAIAH's clergy, congregation members, leaders, staff organizers, and allies
learned about the project, they urged the organization to become involved.
ISAIAH's member congregations had a record of effectively advocating for civil
rights, opportunity housing, public transit, job creation, equity in education,
health care, and other policies at local, regional, and state levels. Through their
work on the CC, the congregations came to see such changes as, in Corburn's
(2009) words, necessary conditions for healthy lives and healthy communities.
Congregations were also motivated by the opportunity to address long-standing
patterns of structural racism and racial and health inequities.

ISAIAH was part of the Transit Partners Coalition, which, after five years,
won state funding for the CCLRT in 2008. Coalition members were optimistic that
LRT construction could help stimulate the local economy and provide access to

grocery stores, parks, jobs, and schools for the residents of the low-income neighborhoods along the line. However, once state funding was secured, the Met Council (the Twin Cities' federally designated Metropolitan Planning Organization), which was responsible for planning the system, removed three critical stops from the line. Planners cited cost considerations and federal criteria for matching funds, including the cost-effectiveness index, which evaluated transit projects based on the number of riders, distance traveled, and speed of transit. Using these criteria, which had been established in the administration or President George W. Bush, the planners removed the stops in the Rondo and Frogtown neighborhoods. These neighborhoods have large populations of transit-dependent people, low-income residents, people of color, immigrants, and people with disabilities (Metropolitan Council 2009).

The removal of the three stops provided a powerful and specific new issue around which to mobilize, and led to the formation of the Stops for Us coalition, created to fight for the missing stations. In addition to ISAIAH, key coalition members included the Preserve and Benefit Historic Rondo Committee, the Alliance for Metropolitan Stability, and the neighborhood organizing groups Community Stabilization Project and Aurora St. Anthony Neighborhood Association. These groups brought a wide range of additional equity advocates and partners together to organize power and influence key decision makers. The Stops for Us coalition thus came to include neighborhood associations, a bus riders organization, housing advocates, and faith-based institutions, including the District 7 Planning Council, Jewish Community Action, Just Equity, MICAH (the Metropolitan Interfaith Council on Affordable Housing), and Got Voice? Got Power!

To help create awareness, ISAIAH worked with the twenty congregations most heavily affected by the CCLRT build-out and formed the multiracial St. Paul Pastors Collaborative. The collaborative connected issues of transit access to health by constructing intentional conversations in its members' congregations whereby pastors would invite members to help lead the organizing efforts. Those leaders and organizers then raised the issue of transportation investments and racial and health equity across the organization in small congregation meetings and large public meetings ranging from ten to thirty-five hundred people. Structured conversations using a range of tools, including the award-winning documentary *Unnatural Causes: Is Inequality Making Us Sick?*, were helpful in building awareness of racial and health equity across the organization. ISAIAH organizers and leaders then connected these ISAIAH faith communities to the broader community movement. The Stops for Us coalition partners then began a multifaceted policy advocacy campaign. They organized public meetings with hundreds of people of faith, attended planning commission hearings along with other community stakeholders, and met with the mayor of St. Paul, the Ramsey County commissioners, and relevant congressional representatives. Achieving the goal of reinstating the three stops required that decision makers at all levels of government work in concert with one another. To get these diverse decision makers and community stakeholders aligned, the Stops for Us coalition convened a table of community members and public officials from the local through the federal levels. The coalition also engaged officials in regular meetings with representatives from the community to develop a strong and unified voice that could shift the political will at all levels, and particularly with the primary decision-making target, the Federal Transit Administration (FTA). ISAIAH leaders met with the FTA administrator in Washington, D.C., and with the chair of the House Transportation and Infrastructure Committee, a veteran Minnesota congressman. Health and community impacts were placed at the center of these discussions, with health identified as being at least as important as "efficiency." These efforts, together with the ongoing work of the coalition, paid off: When the FTA director announced the end of the cost effectiveness index, he came to Minnesota for his press conference, and pointed to the restored stops on the CC light rail line as an example of effective policymaking that reflected the transit priorities of the new Obama administration. In further recognition of the importance of its organizing work, the Stops for Us coalition received an award from the U.S. Environmental Protection Agency in 2010 for national achievements in environmental justice.

To ensure that policymakers did not derail healthy and just policy choices again in the CC, and to create more equitable decision-making processes, ISAIAH focused its efforts on the next set of policy decisions and created the Healthy Corridor for All campaign. The focus of this new undertaking was to conduct a community-driven health impact assessment (HIA) to identify community concerns and health and equity impacts of the pending development around the CC transit line. The HIA would also serve as a process to build the capacity of local groups, in particular those representing low-income people and communities of color, to identify the relationship between health and land use and to participate in land use and transit-oriented development policymaking. ISAIAH recognized that to ensure health and racial equity in the CC development decisions, it would be crucial to organize and sustain a coalition equipped to influence a wide array of policy decisions and committed to doing so. The HIA served as a key tool in this organizing effort by bringing public health and policy research into the organizing and decision-making process. ISAIAH and its partner TakeAction Minnesota Hmong Organizing Program, or TAM HOP, oversaw the community organizing dimension of the project while PolicyLink, a national organization focused on health and regional equity, led the research and provided technical support.[1] The HIA was led by a diverse, twenty-two-member community steering committee, made up of representatives of the housing, labor, faith, and business communities. The steering committee focused the HIA on three primary goal areas: a healthy economy, affordable housing, and access to transportation. The committee created awareness by generating political conversations about these issues in the policy-making arena. The HIA was designed to inform and influence the decisions of two key policymaker targets—the St. Paul Planning Commission and City Council—about the zoning of properties around the transit stations and in the surrounding neighborhoods. Preliminary findings from the HIA, released in March 2011, indicated potential threats to small businesses on the CC and the significant likelihood of involuntary displacement of low-income residents of color in the absence of attention to affordable housing preservation and development. Policy proposals emerging directly from the HIA were aimed at zoning that would protect the stability of affordable housing and small businesses and guide transit-related investment in ways that would serve existing residents and spur equitable development. As of this writing, partners and steering committee members are refining a set of recommendations and a "policy library" to guide decision makers and to provide a basis for continued organizing. (For more information on the Healthy Corridor for All effort and the HIA findings and policy recommendations, see http://www.isaiah-mn.org/Issues/HIACommunityMeeting030511.htm).

The Next Step: Grounding Public Policy in Community Organizing and Community Building

As this chapter has attempted to demonstrate, community organizing and community building strategies have been used effectively by grassroots groups and coalitions, and by health professionals and academic and other partners working with local communities, to help put into place a wide array of healthy public policies. As illustrated in the two case studies, we also are seeing increasing efforts to break down the silos such that decision-making bodies in areas such as criminal justice and transportation consider the health and social justice impacts of their programs, practices, and policies. California's new Health in All Policies, or HiAP, initiative, through which diverse state agencies and departments are strongly recommended to consider the health impacts of their policies (Rudolph et al. 2010) is a particularly encouraging example in this regard, and also one responsive to community input and engagement. The increased accent on regional efforts to address health and social equity is also important to achieving change on a far broader scale than traditional community organizing often has envisioned (Pastor et al. 2009). These efforts are critical. And the increasing interest among both communities, faith-based and other local and regional organizations, and their professional allies in working to address inequities through policy change offers an important counter to the weakening of some forms of civic engagement that also is a part of our social landscape (Putman 2000, 2001).

As suggested earlier, however, for community building and community organizing to reach their full potential in a democratic society, policymaking must itself be transformed such that local community residents are involved at every stage of the process. In Themba-Nixon's (2010) words, "The best kind of policy initiative engages the community that shares the problem and insures that the initiative is part of the solution" (138). Further, as Blackwell and Colmenar (2002) suggest, "Approaching policy in this way could bring isolated and fragmented movements for change to scale, moving results from years of experimentation and innovation into policies" (163). Community building principles (see appendix 1) similarly should be applied to policy design, so that the policies enacted themselves encourage and ideally mandate high-level community involvement in devising solutions to complex health and social problems. Such an approach not only holds the promise of improving policy but may have tangible payoffs for health and well-being as well. As Burris and colleagues (2007) have noted, "Participation in governance is at once a function and a catalyst of people's empowerment" (154) and contribute to what Marmot (2006) describes as a pathway "linking autonomy and social engagement to health" (2088).

Conclusion

Although efforts to influence policy are time consuming and fraught with difficulties, they represent critical avenues for improving the public's health, and therefore should be considered an important part of the community organizer and community builder's tool kit. By intentionally focusing on the policy level, professionals and community residents can help translate community concerns into concrete action and influence decision making through the democratization of knowledge and access.

At the same time, as suggested in the examples above, community involvement in the policymaking process can enhance community capacity building and contribute to a more engaged populace. To promote such community involvement, however, the very nature of our policies should be reconsidered such that community building becomes a central consideration in how policies are shaped and what they look like. It is only through such reorientation that the oft-repeated phrases *civic engagement*, *empowered communities*, and indeed, *community building* itself can reach their full potential.

ACKNOWLEDGMENTS

The authors offer our deep thanks to Makani Themba-Nixon for her major contributions to our thinking and collaboration on related earlier work. We also are very grateful to colleagues at ISAIAH and to Victor Rubin and Shireen Malekafzali at PolicyLink for their contributions to, and help in documenting, the Minnesota case study. Finally, we are grateful to the Center for Urban Epidemiologic Studies' Policy Work Group and its many partners for sharing their inspiring example of policy change to support community reintegration of incarcerated persons in New York City.

NOTE

1. The Health Impact Project of the Pew Charitable Trusts and the Robert Wood Johnson Foundation, along with the Center for Prevention of Blue Cross/Blue Shield of Minnesota, provided funding for the HIA discussed in this chapter.

REFERENCES

Bardach, E. 2000. *A Practical Guide for Policy Analysis: The Eightfold Path to More Effective Problem Solving.* New York: Chatham House of Seven Bridges Press.

Barry, B. W. 1997. *Strategic Workbook for Nonprofit Organizations.* St. Paul, Minn.: Wilder Foundation.

Bell, J., and M. M. Lee. 2011. *Why Place and Race Matter: Impacting Health through a Focus on Race and Place.* Oakland, Calif.: PolicyLink.

Bell, J., and M. Standish. 2005. "Communities and Health Policy: A Pathway for Change." *Health Affairs* 24, no. 2:339–342.

Blackwell, A. G., and R. Colmenar. 2000. "Community Building: From Local Wisdom to Public Policy." *Public Health Reports* 115:161–166.

Braveman, P. 2006. "Health Disparities and Health Equality: Concepts and Measurement." *Annual Review of Public Health* 57:167–194.

Brechwich Vásquez, V., D. Lanza, S. Hennessey-Lavery, S. Facente, H. A. Halpin, and M. Minkler. 2007. "Addressing Food Security through Public Policy Action in a Community-Based Participatory Research Partnership." *Health Promotion Practice* 8:342–349.

Brindis, C. D., S. P. Geierstanger, and A. Faxio. 2009. "The Role of Policy Advocacy in Assuring Comprehensive Family Life Education in California." *Health Education and Behavior* 36:1095–1108.

Brown, P., R. Morello-Frosch, and S. Zavestoski. 2012. *Contested Illnesses: Citizens, Science, and Health Social Movements.* Berkeley and Los Angeles: University of California Press.

Burris, S., Hancock, T., Lin, V. and Herzog, A. 2007. Emerging Strategies for Healthy Urban Governance. Supplement, *Journal of Urban Health* 84, no. 1:154–163.

Coffman, J. 2002. *Public Communication Campaign Evaluation: An Environmental Scan of Challenges, Criticisms, Practice, and Opportunities.* Cambridge, Mass.: Harvard Family Research Project.

Coffman, J., and Reed, E. 2009. "Unique Methods in Advocacy Evaluation." Los Angeles: The California Endowment. http://www.calendow.org/uploadedFiles/Evaluation/Coffman%20Reed%20Unique%20Methods%20(paper).pdf.

Corburn, J. 2009. *Toward the Healthy City: People, Places, and the Politics of Urban Planning.* Cambridge, Mass.: MIT Press.

Fetterman, D., and A. Wandersman. 2005. *Empowerment Evaluation: Principles in Practice.* New York: Guilford Press.

Freudenberg, N. 2001. "Jails, Prisons, and the Health of Urban Populations: Review of the Impacts of the Correctional System on Community Health." *Journal of Urban Health* 78:214–235.

Freudenberg N., M. Ramaswamy, J. Daniels, M. Crum, D. C. Ompad, and D. Vlahov. 2010. "Reducing Drug Use, Human Immunodeficiency Virus Risk, and Recidivism among Young Men Leaving Jail: Evaluation of the REAL MEN Re-entry Program." *Journal of Adolescent Health* 47, no. 5:448–55.

Freudenberg, N., M. A. Rogers, C. Ritas, and M. Nerney. 2005. "Community Reintegration Network Policy Report—Coming Back to Harlem from Jail or Prison: One-Way or Round-Trip." In *Methods in Community-Based Participatory Research for Health*, edited by B. A. Israel, E. Eng, A. J. Schulz, and E. A. Parker, 453–458. San Francisco: Jossey-Bass.

Giles, W. H., and L. C. Liburd. 2010. "Advancing Health Equity and Social Justice." In *Prevention Is Primary: Strategies for Community Well-Being*, edited by L. Cohen, V. Chávez, and S. Chehimi, 34–53. 2nd ed. San Francisco: Jossey-Bass.

Guthrie, K., J. Louise, and C. C. Foster. 2006. *The Challenge of Assessing Policy and Advocacy Activities: Moving from Theory to Practice.* Los Angeles: California Endowment.

Homan, M. S. 2011. *Promoting Community Change: Making It Happen in the Real World.* 5th ed. Pacific Grove, Calif.: Brooks/Cole.

House, J., R. F. Schoeni, G. A. Kaplan, and H. Pollack. 2008. "The Health Effects of Social and Economic Policy: The Promise and Challenge for Research and Policy." In *Making Americans Healthier: Social and Economic Policy as Health Policy*, edited by R. Schoeni, J. House, G. Kaplan, and H. Pollack, 3–26. New York: Russell Sage.

Hunter College and Community Reintegration Network. 2003. *Coming Home from Jail: An Action Plan to Improve NYC Reentry Policies and Programs*. New York: Hunter College and Community Reintegration Network.

Kingdon, J. 2003. *Agendas, Alternatives, and Public Policies*. 2nd ed. New York: Longman Press.

Lee, J., D. Vlahov, N. Freudenberg. 2006. "Primary Care and Health Insurance among Women Released from New York City Jails." *Journal of Health Care for the Poor and Underserved* 17, no. 1:200–17.

Longest, B. 2006. *Health Policymaking in the United States*. 3rd ed. Chicago: Health Administration Press.

Malekafzali, S., and D. Bergstrom. 2011. *Healthy Corridor for All: A Community Participatory Health Impact Assessment on Transit Oriented Development in Saint Paul, Minnesota*. St. Paul, Minn., and Oakland, Calif.: PolicyLink, ISAIAH, TakeAction Minnesota.

Marmot, M. 2006. "Health in an Unequal World." *Lancet* 368, no. 9552:2081–2094.

McGinnis, J. M., and Foege, W. 1993. "Actual Causes of Death in the United States: Dying." *Journal of the American Medical Association* 270, no. 18: 2207–2212.

Metropolitan Council. 2009. *Central Corridor Final Environmental Impact Statement*. Minneapolis, Minn.: Metropolitan Council. http://www.metrocouncil.org/transportation/ccorridor/FEISJuly2009.htm.

Minnesota Department of Health. 2010. "Healthy Communities Count! Core Counts." Minnesota Department of Health, Healthy Communities Count! http://www.health.state.mn.us/divs/eh/hazardous/lightrail/corecounts.html.

Milio, N. 1998. "Priorities and Strategies for Promoting Community-Based Prevention Policies." *Journal of Public Health Management Practice* 4, no. 3:14–28.

Minkler M., V. Breckwich Vásquez, C. Chang, J. Miller, V. Rubin, A. G. Blackwell, M. Thompson, R. Flournoy, and J. Bell. 2008. *Promoting Healthy Public Policy through Community-Based Participatory Research: Ten Case Studies*. Oakland, Calif.: PolicyLink.

Minkler, M., and N. Freudenberg. 2010. "From Community-Based Participatory Research to Policy Change." In *Handbook for Engaged Scholarship: Contemporary Landscapes, Future Directions*, edited by H. E. Fitzgerald, C. Burack, and C. and S. Seifer, vol. 2, 275–294. East Lansing: Michigan State University.

Minkler, M., A. P. Garcia, J. Williams, T. LoPresti, and J. Lilly. 2010. "Sí, Se Puede: Using Participatory Research to Promote Environmental Justice in a Latino Community in San Diego, CA." *Journal of Urban Health* 87, no. 5:796–812.

O'Neill, M., and P. Simard. 2006. "Choosing Indicators to Evaluate Healthy Cities Projects: A Political Task?" *Health Promotion International* 21, no. 2:145–152.

Pastor, M., C. Brenner, and M. Matsuoka. 2009. *This Could Be the Start of Something Big: How Social Movements for Regional Equity Are Reshaping Metropolitan America*. Syracuse, N.Y.: Cornell University

Putnam, R. D. 2000. *Bowling Alone: The Collapse and Revival of American Community*. New York: Simon and Schuster.

———. 2001. "Social Capital: Measurement and Consequences." *Canadian Journal of Policy Research* 2 (Spring): 41–51.

Rudolph, L., A. Sisson, J. Caplan, L. Dillon, K. Ben-Moshe, M. Mohammadi, S. Sattelmeyer, and M. Walker. 2010. "Health in All Policies Task Force Report to the Strategic Growth Council." Health in All Policies (HiAP). http://www.cdph.ca.gov/programs/CCDPHP/Documents/HiAP_Final_Report_12%203%2010.pdf.

Sanders, M. 1992. "Before There Was Interstate 94 . . . There Was Rondo." In *Voices: A Collection of Writings and Stories for a Diverse Community*, edited by M. Clark. St. Paul, Minnesota: St. Paul Department of Planning and Economic Development. http://www.mnhs.org/library/tips/history_topics/112rondo.html.

Staples, L. 2004. *Roots to Power.* 2nd ed. New York: Praeger.

Sterman, J. D. 2006. "Learning from Evidence in a Complex World." *American Journal of Public Health* 96:505–514.

Themba, M. 1999. *Making Policy, Making Change: How Communities Are Taking Law into Their Own Hands.* Oakland, Calif.: Chardon Press.

Themba-Nixon, M. 2010. "The Power of Local Communities to Foster Policy." In *Prevention Is Primary: Strategies for Community Well-Being*, edited by L. Cohen, V. Chávez, and S. Chehimi, 137–156. 2nd ed. San Francisco: Jossey-Bass.

Van Olphen, J., N. Freudenberg, A. G. Galea, S. Palermo, and C. Ritas. 2003. "Advocating Policies to Promote Community Reintegration of Drug Users Leaving Jail: A Case Study of First Steps in a Policy Change Campaign Guided by Community-Based Participatory Research." In *Community-Based Participatory Research*, edited by M. Minkler and N. Wallerstein, 371–389. 1st ed. San Francisco: Jossey-Bass.

Wallerstein, N., M. Polascek, and K. Maltrud. 2002. "Participatory Evaluation Model for Coalitions: A Systems Indicator Approach from New Mexico." *Journal of Health Promotion Practice* 3, no. 3:361–373.

21

Organizing for Health Care Reform

National and State-Level Efforts and Perspectives

JACQUIE ANDERSON

MICHAEL MILLER

ANDREW MCGUIRE

This chapter begins with an overview of how constituencies were built and mobilized and how "systems of advocacy" developed that helped make possible the passage of the Patient Protection and Affordable Care Act of 2010, despite an increasingly hostile political environment and widespread disinformation campaign. Lessons learned from state-level health care reform efforts, as well as from the failed national health care reform initiative under President Bill Clinton, will then be discussed. The impact on movement building of key setbacks along the way (e.g., loss of the public option critical to many more liberal supporters, and efforts of a well-orchestrated opposition movement to decrease public support during the crucial summer months before the final vote) also will be highlighted. The chapter then will examine an effort to establish "Medicare for All," or single payer coverage, in the state of California and its organizing- and coalition-building strategies.[1]

On March 23, 2010, President Barack Obama made history when he signed the Patient Protection and Affordable Care Act (ACA) into law. The ACA holds the promise of providing affordable access to health care for more than 30 million Americans who now lack coverage and of improving coverage for tens of millions more. The ACA also has the potential to promote greater racial and economic equity, since the majority of the Americans who will be receiving coverage will be low-income families and communities of color (Henry J. Kaiser Family Foundation 2010). Key among its provisions were increased coverage through an expansion of Medicaid and by providing premium subsidies to low- and middle-income people (in the form of income-based tax credits) available through new, regulated insurance marketplaces, called exchanges, that were expected to reach about two-thirds of the uninsured population in the United States. The ACA also included a major overhaul of health insurance law, prohibiting carriers from imposing preexisting-condition exclusions, setting arbitrary dollar caps on coverage, or charging differential rates based on health status. The reformed health law further would require carriers to offer coverage to all comers, offer at least a minimum-benefit package, and spend at least a minimum percentage of premium dollars on paying for the health care of their subscribers. The ACA purported to control costs while offering quality improvements. It further made significant new investments in public health, by requiring new private health insurance plans to fully cover the costs of a number of recommended preventive services. This means patients pay no deductibles or copayments or otherwise share costs of these services such as mammograms and colonoscopies. In addition, the law also requires coverage for a new annual wellness visit under Medicare and eliminates cost sharing for recommended preventive services covered by that federal program. The ACA also imposes a responsibility on most individuals and many employers to contribute to the cost of coverage. It thus required that all Americans carry a minimum-level insurance by 2014.

Equally significant, however, is what the ACA does not contain. Efforts to expand coverage for all based on Medicare were never able to gain serious political traction in Congress and the question of how coverage for immigrants would be addressed quickly became a lightning rod during the debate (with certain immigrants excluded from coverage altogether). Elements of the original proposal that had broad popular backing but were opposed by various health care industry groups, such as creating a public insurance plan (the "public option") to compete with private insurers, fell by the wayside during the debate (Halpin 2010, 1120).

Compromises on components of the bill separate from the public option attracted less public attention but are perhaps equally important. Some have already contributed to the difficult implementation period that followed immediately upon passage—such as the four-year delay in the main expansion of coverage and the failure to provide sufficient federal financial assistance to state governments during the transition period to full ACA implementation. The impact of others—such as inadequate subsidies for some low-wage workers—may not be apparent until after the law goes into effect. Indeed, the Center for Medicare and Medicaid Services (Foster 2009; Truffer et. al. 2010) has estimated that in 2019, when health care reform is fully implemented, there will still be over 20 million uninsured Americans, and the cost of care will still be rising faster than inflation.

Notwithstanding these limitations, passage of the ACA was widely heralded as representing the greatest victory in a one-hundred-year struggle for universal health insurance in United States and the greatest expansion of the social welfare state since the 1960s. The idea of health insurance for all was first advanced in the United States by Theodore Roosevelt during his unsuccessful bid for reelection as president as an independent candidate in 1912 and was advanced periodically and unsuccessfully by both Democratic and Republican presidents over the ensuing years. There were, of course, some partial victories, most notably the creation of Medicare and Medicaid in 1965 to cover older adults and certain low-income families. Medicare in particular was critical, in covering the oldest and sickest

Americans with guaranteed health insurance through a government-financed and -run health system (Bhattacharya and Lakdawalla 2006; Satiani 2009). Passage of the State Children's Health Insurance Program (SCHIP), in 1997, which extended insurance coverage to children from families with too much income to qualify for Medicaid but too little to afford private insurance) was also a critical step forward (Brady and Kellser 2010). But the idea of a national health insurance program for Americans of all ages remained an elusive goal.

The ultimate passage of the ACA could never have been achieved without the active engagement of hundreds of local, state, and national consumer organizations and thousands of grassroots activists. Consumer advocates played a critical role in efforts leading up to the passage of the ACA. Indeed, while there were many factors that contributed to its passage, it would not have been possible to achieve the consumer-focused law as written without the decades-long work of advocates at the local, state, and national levels. Passage and implementation of incremental national, state, and local health care reforms paved the way for the comprehensive national reform law that was enacted in 2010. National, state, and local consumer groups skilled in public education; policy analysis; community organizing; and administrative, legislative, and legal advocacy engaged community members most affected by the law and worked to make sure that the concerns and priorities of families and individuals were protected throughout the polarized and divisive debates that occurred (Antos et al. 2010).

Organizing a Grassroots Movement: A Key Challenge

Historically, there has been a disconnect between those organizing for health care reform and health care reform's most logical constituent—the uninsured. This disconnect has led to an ongoing difficulty in building a popular movement on behalf of national health reform.

Unlike other social movements (e.g., the civil rights or women's movement), the uninsured have not formed mass-based organizations to effect political change. While the proportion of the population which is uninsured has grown from 12.9 percent in 1987 to 16.7 percent in 2009 (Carmen et al. 2009), this has not translated into political power. Key challenges in engaging the uninsured have been (1) the fleeting nature of being uninsured, with many families moving on and off insurance, depending on their changing employment situation; (2) the more pressing economic issues facing the uninsured (e.g., food, shelter, and employment); (3) for those uninsured who are sick, the often overwhelming task of managing their own health care and financial challenges; and (4) the general lack of interest of many of the uninsured in electoral politics—they are less likely to vote so their interests are less likely to be considered in conversations about health care reform. As a result of this lack of cohesion among the uninsured, different organizing and mobilizing strategies had to be developed to create an effective popular voice for reform.

This voice was built gradually over time. As discussed below, advocates used the experience, insights, and information they had gained in prior decades both in state-based campaigns and from the resounding failure of the 1993–1994 Clinton health care reform initiative, to craft their strategies for the ACA campaign. Starting in the 1980s, in response to the first wave of policy "devolution" to state government initiated by the administration of President Ronald Reagan, a network of state-based health care advocacy organizations began to emerge, many seeded with funding from the Villers Foundation (Community Catalyst 2009). Key among these groups were Health Care for All Massachusetts, Campaign for Better Health Care, Tennessee Health Care Campaign, and the Oregon Health Action Campaign. These organizations interacted with, and overlapped with, networks of multi-issue consumer organizations, such as Citizen Action and the U.S. Public Interest Research Group. They were influenced too by the social change movements of the 1960s and the community organizing strategies of Saul Alinsky (1972; Miller 2009; Sen 2003: see chapters 4 and 11).

Systems of Advocacy

The advocacy organizations that engaged in the campaign for the ACA were drawing on the successes and failures of two and a half decades of experience at the state and federal level. This experience helped organizations understand what capacities they would need to bring to the table to be successful. Recognizing the need to mobilize the voice of the uninsured but also to transcend the limits of what could be achieved in focusing only on this constituency, state-based organizations developed "systems of advocacy" to marshal and deploy the capacities needed to run a successful campaign. These systems of advocacy involve networks of organizations brought together around six major capacities, each representing a different and complementary collection of related skills, abilities, and resources (Community Catalyst 2006). These capacities include the following (Grantmakers in Health 2010):

Policy analysis and advocacy: the ability to compile, analyze, and synthesize policy and to develop policy options and conduct legislative and administrative advocacy.

Broad-based coalitions and strategic alliances: the ability to bring together large numbers of different organizations and stakeholders in coordinated campaigns to achieve common policy goals.

Grassroots organizing and mobilizing: the ability to engage people at the local level and to put a human face on the need for better health care access.

Communication: the ability to communicate persuasively and use the media and other communications strategies to build public and political support and counter opposition arguments.

Strategic campaign development: the ability to plan and coordinate advocacy campaigns, including anticipating impending opportunities
and threats and synchronizing advocacy responses in a timely manner, and the ability to adapt advocacy tactics to evolving political
dynamics.

Fund-raising: the ability to generate resources from diverse sources to
build organizational infrastructure, maintain core functions, and
implement campaigns.

Prequels to the ACA Campaign

For more than two decades, as health reform policymaking shifted from the
federal government to the states, consumer advocates in a number of states
used those opportunities to push to expand health coverage and improve care.
Typically these efforts focused on Medicaid, the Children's Health Insurance
Program (CHIP) and private insurance reform. It was through these state-level
campaigns that organizations developed the skills, relationships, and strategic
insights that undergirded the mobilization in support of the ACA.

State advocates developed systems of advocacy that helped to engage
consumer, key organizational, and other interested stakeholders in advocating
for the passage of the national health care reform law. This advocacy at the state
level was critical: state advocacy organizations and systems of advocacy served as
a credible source of information and trusted local community voices. Throughout
the country, core members of these systems include grassroots organizations,
state health advocacy organizations, legal services groups, fiscal analysis groups,
organizations of color, and disease-specific groups. Contradicting Alinsky's (1972)
early admonition to focus on individual self-interest, these systems worked,
because organizations moved beyond their own self-interest on particular issues
and towards a shared vision of health care reform based on their common
long-term interest (Miller 2009; Wolff 2010).

Another critical experience on which the campaign for the ACA was built
involved learning from the failure of the effort to adopt a national health plan
under the Clinton administration. A detailed review of the history and strategic
lessons from the Clinton era is beyond the scope of this chapter, and may be found
elsewhere (Brady and Kellser 2010; Oberlander 2007; Skocpol 1995, 1997; Starr
1995). But several key lessons from that effort are worthy of mention. Key among
these was that it is a mistake to "let the perfect be the enemy of the good." Many
Clinton-era health care reform advocates focused on getting the perfect, as
opposed to the best possible, bill and offered at best only tepid backing of the
Clinton plan, while most of the major industry stakeholder groups opposed it and
undermined public support for reform. The $20 million "Harry and Louise" adver-
tisement campaign mounted by the opposition, in which an "average American
couple" discussed their fears about losing their doctor and other (untrue) aspects

of the Clinton plan was particularly successful in spreading misinformation and stoking fears among millions of Americans through sixty-second television spots (Daniels et al. 2012). The failure of the Clinton forces to successfully counter this ad campaign was a fatal mistake. Still another problem, however, involved what many perceived as the lack of interest shown by Hillary Clinton and fellow reform effort leader Ira Magaziner in harnessing the grassroots support that did exist for health care reform, while coming up with an extremely complicated plan that few could understand. Although in a Washington environment dominated by special interests, grassroots support was still unlikely to overcome the united opposition of insurers, providers, and employers, much more effective use could have been made of the grassroots support that was available, particularly early on in the campaign. Still another important lesson from the failed Clinton health care reform effort involved the need for better coordination among advocacy organizations. During the Clinton debate, there were few mechanisms—formal or informal—to foster coordination and collaboration among advocacy groups.

While the Clinton campaign highlighted some of the weaknesses of the health reform advocacy community, a number of state-level campaigns offered guideposts for success. We turn now to one of these, the 2006 campaign to create near-universal coverage in Massachusetts.

The Massachusetts Experience

Although most state reform efforts were incremental in nature, occasionally there have been efforts at more comprehensive reform, with Illinois, Vermont, Hawaii, and California providing important examples. Although the campaign for single payer health care reform currently under way in California is discussed in detail below, among most successful of these state efforts to date, and the one that was in many ways a direct prequel to the ACA campaign, occurred in Massachusetts in 2006 (Wielawski 2007; Long and Gruber 2010). Massachusetts became the first state in the country to achieve near-universal access to affordable health care (Zhu et al. 2010).

The Massachusetts experience provided two different types of lessons later made use of by organizers in support of the ACA. The first was in what reform might look like, and the second involved how it could be achieved. Many aspects of the ACA were modeled after the Massachusetts law's key provisions—expanded Medicaid eligibility, new subsidized coverage options for people with low and moderate incomes, new insurance exchanges through which individuals and small businesses can purchase health coverage, and new individual and employer requirements. By 2011, Massachusetts has achieved nearly universal coverage (about 98 percent of residents had health insurance in 2010, including practically all [99.8 percent] of the states' children). Although Massachusetts has far fewer undocumented immigrants than do states like California, the law still was credited with greatly improving access to needed care. In addition, health reform continues to earn broad support from policymakers, advocates, providers, health plans, foundations, and community members (Raymond 2011; Jacobs and Scokpol 2010).

The law, of course, did not solve all the problems of the Massachusetts health care system. In particular, high costs remain a persistent problem for both third-party payers and consumers. In addition, Massachusetts faced a lack of primary care providers prior to the passage of health reform and that continues to be a challenge. Further, a number of operational shortcomings have led to coverage gaps even for people eligible to receive financial assistance in affording insurance. Finally, while significant progress has been made in reducing racial and ethnic disparities in rates of health insurance, disparities in health status remain a major concern (Blumberg et al. 2007). Despite these limitations, however, consumer advocates trying to pass national reform looked to Massachusetts for an example of a health care system that achieved nearly universal coverage, had broad support, and provided a clear rallying cry and beacon of what was possible. The success of Massachusetts was important in persuading advocates to accept provisions, such as the individual-responsibility requirement in the ACA, without which the overall effort might be rejected.

As noted above, however, the Massachusetts legislation was also instructive because of *how* it was enacted. The pivotal role played by consumer advocates and the strong system of advocacy that existed in the state ensured that the consumer voice—with the exception of those supporting single payer—was a key part of the process of passing the state's health care reform legislation. Consistent with community organizing and coalition-building theory (Alinsky 1972; Miller 2009; Wolff 2010; Butterfoss 2009; see chapters 4, 11, and 17), consumer advocates in Massachusetts effectively brought the voices of the uninsured into the debate. But they also broadened the base of popular support for reform, particularly through building an alliance with the Greater Boston Interfaith Organization (GBIO) (MassAct! 2005).

GBIO is a broad-based, multi-issue organization that works to coalesce, train, and organize the communities of Greater Boston across all religious, racial, ethnic, class, and neighborhood lines for the public good (Barber and Miller 2007). This organization included people from among the most to some of the least affluent communities across the Greater Boston area. Members worked together to demonstrate that access to health insurance is an issue that crosses economic, ideological, and racial lines. Their strong message emphasized the moral impera-tive for health care justice and helped to ground the work of the advocates in the lives of real people (Chirba-Martin et al. 2008).

Advocates in Massachusetts organized Affordable Care Today (ACT), a statewide coalition staffed by Massachusetts's leading consumer health advocacy organization, Health Care for All (Raymond 2011; Health Care for all Massachusetts 2006). Health Care for All was the locus of activity pulling together a system of advocacy that involved consumers, community and religious organizations, business, labor unions, community health centers and physicians, hospitals, and health plans. The ACT structure made it possible to coordinate the advocacy capacities of the various members in service of the common goal. Consistent with coalition theory (Butterfoss 2009; see chapter 17), different organizations in the system brought different skills and resources to bear, including communications expertise, legal policy research and analysis, grassroots organizing, and financial resources. The effectiveness of the system was due to the strong organizational relationships and connections that were built and strengthened through past collaborative work and the systems and structures that were put into place to ensure that there was a process for reaching agreement on a host of different issues (Community Catalyst 2006). The substantive policy issues, organizational strategies, and stakeholder relationships in Massachusetts thus all helped inform the campaign for the ACA.

National Health Reform: Putting It All Together

As noted above, the passage of national health care reform in 2010 built upon and applied the lessons of state-based reform efforts and of the failure of the Clinton-era reform effort. Moreover, the systems of advocacy described above were evident among national advocacy organizations as well. National organizations with specialized skills, such as policy analysis and research, legal analysis, communications, organizing, and mobilizing frequently mirrored the systems of advocacy that existed in the states. There was a clear understanding that passing the health care reform bill in a dynamic and ever changing political and economic environment was going to require complementary and diverse skills and knowledge that existed among national organizations. Key national advocacy organizations, including the Center on Budget and Policy Priorities, Community Catalyst, Families USA, the Georgetown Center for Children and Families, and Health Care for America Now, worked with state advocates to pass national reform. Other advocacy organizations that also played key roles were the faith-based PICO National Network, the U.S. Public Interest Research Group, the American Cancer Society/Cancer Action Network, AARP, and Consumers Union. Within this constellation of national organization, some of which had state affiliates and some of which did not, there existed all the capacities necessary for the systems of advocacy that would be essential for passage. In addition, like the ACT coalition in Massachusetts, new coordinating mechanisms developed among national consumer advocacy organizations. The largest and most formal such mechanism was Health Care for America Now (HCAN), created in 2008 as a national grassroots campaign dedicated to building a national movement to win, implement, and improve comprehensive health care reform. HCAN's key strategy involved helping mobilize people in their communities to lobby their U.S. senators and representatives in Congress to win quality, affordable health care. Core members of HCAN included two large national unions—Service Employees International

Union (SEIU) and the American Federation of State, County and Municipal Employees (AFSCME)—which provided substantial financial support, as well as grassroots groups such as USAction, ACORN (Association of Community Organizations for Reform Now), and the Center for Community Change. But HCAN was not the only venue for advocacy group collaboration. National organizations participated in a shifting set of informal coalitions based on the overriding issue of health care reform and the changing capacities and needs of the campaign. Although the national effort was less unified than the campaign in Massachusetts, with multiple constellations of national and state advocacy organizations, there was a shared objective, coupled with a sense of urgency and commitment, that compensated for this lack of organizational tidiness. Many advocates were keenly aware of the failure of the 1994 Clinton plan (many had been actively involved in that effort) and were paying heed to Jonathan Oberlander's (2007) cautionary note: "The window for enacting a comprehensive plan for health care reform never stays open for long, so failure comes at a high price—namely, the loss of political will to do anything meaningful about the uninsured for some time to come" (1679).

The success of engaging consumers in the national health care reform debate in order to secure passage of the ACA was based on three main premises. The first was engaging the uninsured to protect their own interests and tell their own story. Although there was never really a mass-based organization of the uninsured, there was a consistent effort to bring the voices of the uninsured, those with preexisting conditions, and others disadvantaged by the current system into the public debate via testimony, organized community events, and stories in the media. As discussed in chapter 9, the importance of giving human form and voice to statistics, in this case about the uninsured or those who faced financial ruin as a result of catastrophic illness and associated health care costs cannot be underemphasized (see also Barber et al. 2007). Advocates adapted nationally developed messages in support of health care reform for their particular state and local political environment; they responded quickly to local attacks on the law. They identified and engaged individuals who benefited from early reforms and communicated these stories to the public to support pro-reform activity.

A second key premise for success involved engaging other interested stakeholders (unions, faith institutions, multi-issue grassroots community organization groups) who may have constituents affected by problems in the health care system but who were also motivated by a values proposition—that is, as organizations and individuals, they were motivated not only by self-interest but equally or perhaps more so by a conviction that the current health care arrangements in the United States were unjust. As Wolff (2010) and other organizers and coalition builders note, such inclusion of groups motivated by values and concerns beyond simple self-interest can be a major plus in building momentum around an issue or concern.

Third, expanding the definition of health reform, in an effort to appeal to the general public and diffuse people's fear of change, was an important strategy.

This was done by focusing more attention on various insurance industry behaviors such as rate increases, denial of coverage to those with preexisting conditions, and experience rating in order to make health reform relevant to a generally more affluent and politically engaged constituency. Less public attention was devoted to the goal of expanding coverage to the tens of millions who could not afford it.

The lessons learned and strategies developed by advocates were repeatedly tested during the difficult campaign for ACA passage, perhaps most severely by the summer congressional recess in August 2009, during which opponents of reform circulated wild accusations about "death panels" (which ostensibly would determine who was "worthy of care") and later when the public option was dropped from the legislation to secure enough votes in the Senate for final passage (Halpin and Harbage 2010). The public option had been based on a concept originally known as CHOICE and developed by health care leaders meeting in California in 2001–2002 (Halpin 2003). Envisioned as part of the state's Health Care Options Program initiative, CHOICE "built on a model of managed competition," but added a new "public option" to broaden the array of choices available to consumers. Developed as "a policy compromise between a single payer system and managed competition among private plans" (Halpin and Harbage 2010, 1118), the public option was later built into the federal plan in a similar manner. As Halpin and Harbage note, however, "What progressives saw as the benefits of a public option, conservatives saw as its flaws" (1117).

The public debate over this important but controversial element of the original plan was accompanied by substantial community organizing on both sides. In spring 2009, for example, a host of organizations, under the leadership of former Vermont governor Howard Dean and AFL-CIO (American Federation of Labor–Congress of Industrial Organizations) president Donald Trumka, called the public option a "line in the sand" and got more than four hundred thousand members of MoveOn.org and other groups to sign a petition to this effect and also urged them to contact their individual congressional representatives (Halpin 2010; MoveOn.org 2009).

Consistent with community organizing principles stressing the need to broaden the power base for a desired change (Alinsky 1972; Staples 2004; see chapters 4 and 11), initial framing of the legislation as *consumer protection for the insured* rather than as a *coverage expansion for the uninsured* was meant to build as broad a base of public support as possible. But opposition attacks, aimed primarily at older adults, who often saw themselves as having little to gain directly from either coverage expansion or insurance reform, undermined public support for the bill. At this point, the ability of advocacy organizations to mobilize the voices of people harmed by the current system as well as a wide base of supporters—including the powerful older-Americans' organization AARP proved critical. Although public opinion remained (and remains) divided, enough support was preserved to allow legislative progress to continue.

While the "death panel" debate was primarily a test of the mobilizing and communications strategies honed by advocates after the Clinton effort, the jettisoning of the public option tested ACA supporters' ability to adhere to their commitment not to "let the perfect be the enemy of the good." This was particularly difficult, since for many, the public option already represented a compromise from the Medicare for All position. Indeed for some backers, the removal of the public option proved a bridge too far and they withdrew their support for the ACA. However, most of the coalition that backed the legislation stuck with it and helped thread the legislative needle for final enactment.

Although passage of the ACA represents a historic milestone in the struggle for health care for all, the efforts to reform the financing of the U.S. health care system along the lines of universal social insurance continue (and indeed may be aided by the passage of the ACA if early progress in this direction in Vermont is carried to a successful conclusion). It is to the lessons of one such effort, Medicare for All and the California OneCare Campaign, that we turn below.

Medicare for All at the State Level

In my view, the fight for universal and comprehensive health care is the civil rights battle of our time. Like the other great struggles in our history that have made us a more democratic and just society, victory will require a strong and united grassroots movement that is prepared to take on the very powerful and wealthy special interests that benefit from this failing health care system.

—U.S. Senator Bernie Sanders (Independent, Vermont)

From Prohibition in Kansas in 1881 to Wyoming's becoming the first state in the union to grant women the right to vote in 1890, the history of the United States is replete with examples of legislative victories at the state level that eventually were adopted nationally. Not surprisingly in this context, advocates for a wide range of causes routinely begin their campaigns at the state (or local) level. This section of the chapter will focus on efforts to pass a Medicare for All type of health care reform in California. Health care reform activists work on the assumption that success in California will inexorably lead to a national single payer health care system.

To place the California effort in context, in May 2011, the state of Vermont enacted a law that, when fully implemented, will establish a single payer health care system (Hsiao 2011). Over a dozen other states have pending legislation that, if enacted, would mandate versions of a single payer system. In California, there have been attempts since 1918 to enact legislation to mandate a single payer health care system. A review and analysis of the current Medicare for All campaign will illuminate the central role of community organizing and coalition building in transforming health care reform from a novel idea to a burgeoning grassroots movement. Although there are unique political issues specific to California, core components of this campaign are necessary ingredients for other policy-focused organizing and movement building. Before describing the details of the campaign, it is useful to place the California reform effort in an historical context.

A Brief History of Health Care Reform in California

The first effort to provide universal health insurance to Californians was in the form of a failed statewide ballot initiative in 1918. Incredibly, the next effort for such coverage was a short-lived campaign in 1935 sponsored by the California Medical Association (CMA). Opponents within the CMA quashed the plan. In 1944, Governor Earl Warren introduced his plan for a state-run health insurance system and was met with virulent opposition from the CMA, the state Chamber of Commerce, the *Los Angeles Times* and a savvy political consulting firm. Warren's plan failed to get a vote in the Assembly or Senate, and his amended version, introduced two more times, met with similar results (Mitchell 2002).

Forty-six years later, the CMA's Proposition 166, which would have created "a doctor-controlled employer mandate plan," was resoundingly defeated by over two-thirds of voters. (Danelski et al. 1995). Finally, a grassroots effort successfully placed Proposition 186 on the 1994 statewide ballot, an initiative that would have established a single payer system in California. This effort began after the defeat of the Clinton health reform initiative and was supported by a broad coalition of organizations, including the California Physicians' Alliance, Health Access, Neighbor to Neighbor, the California Nurses Association, SEIU, the Consumers Union, the League of Women Voters of California, and AARP California, to name but a few. Although thousands of volunteers were recruited to work on the campaign, the proponents could raise only about $2 million to conduct their campaign and purchase TV and radio ad time. With the opposition spending at least $10 million on a statewide media campaign featuring negative ads, Proposition 186 was crushed at the polls with a 73 percent vote in opposition.

The State Strategy Group and the Campaign for Single Payer

The genesis of the current single payer campaign can be traced to the failed Proposition 186. Shortly after the vote in 1994, Health Care for All–California (HCA) was established with the sole mission of bringing single payer health reform to California. HCA was created as a chapter-based organization with a sole focus on grassroots organizing. In the fall of 2002, HCA began convening monthly meetings in Sacramento with many organizations to establish a single payer coalition. The goal of the newly created coalition was to support a single payer bill in the 2003 legislative session. After interviewing a range of legislators as possible authors for the bill, former senator Sheila Kuehl was chosen, and her bill, SB 921, was modeled after a publicly vetted proposal that had been drafted by an HCA board member.

In the spring of 2003, after a massive lobbying campaign, SB 921 passed the Senate. The following year, after the grassroots campaign had lobbied and secured twenty Assembly coauthors and signed up over five hundred statewide and local organizations as endorsers, the Assembly health committee also passed the bill. But the legislation still failed to get to the floor of the Assembly.

California is one of three legislatures that require a two-thirds vote of both houses in order to enact a tax or funding bill. Passage of the finance portion of a single payer bill will require either a two-thirds vote of both houses or will be enacted by placing the finance bill on the statewide ballot for approval by majority vote. This affords advocates two strategies to pursue: either work to elect single payer–supporting legislators until two-thirds of both houses support and vote for single payer, or place the finance portion of the single payer plan on the ballot. Currently, advocates are pursuing the "two-thirds" option, although there are discussions about a possible initiative campaign if a robust grassroots movement for single payer matures.

As Minkler (2010) and others (Staples 2004; see chapter 20) point out, a critical part of policy-focused organizing and advocacy is "doing your homework" and gathering the hard data that can help make the case for change. The HCA hired a prominent research consulting firm, the Lewin Group, to conduct an economic study of SB 921. The Lewin Group's findings showed that if SB 921 took effect in 2006, there would be a first-year savings of $8 billion in health care spending in California and a cumulative savings of over $335 billion over the next decade. These figures proved invaluable for advocates during the next legislative session. Although many legislators supported the "idea" of a single payer system, many were deeply concerned that if all California residents were guaranteed coverage, with no copayments or deductibles as called for in SB 921, greatly increased state spending on health care would result.

Coalition Expansion

Sen (2003), Staples (2004), and other social action organizers and movement builders emphasize that a major part of successful organizing and movement building is substantially broadening your base (see chapter 11). In early 2006, representatives of HCA and the California School Employees Association (CSEA) met and agreed to form a new, informal organization called the State Strategy Group (SSG). Members of HCA agreed to recruit nonprofit member organizations to the SSG while members of CSEA worked to recruit other unions, including the powerful California Nurses Association and the California Teachers Association. Consistent with community organizing principles reminding us to meet on members' own turf and to foster buy-in and ownership, the first meeting of the SSG took place at the state headquarters of CSEA. There, the SSG was clearly defined as an informal coalition with a two-pronged mission: getting support of single payer legislation and supporting the expansion and nurturing of the grassroots movement in favor of the legislation. The SSG member organizations agreed to meet at least monthly by conference call and in person as needed. By sharing information, coordinating strategic planning, and executing agreed-upon plans, the SSG served as the nerve center for the statewide campaign. The executive director of HCA was chosen as the chairperson of the SSG and staff were hired to transform the SSG into a formal campaign committee that would conduct electoral campaigns and, if necessary, an initiative campaign.

The SSG and its twenty-seven-member organizations have conducted an array of activities, some independently and others jointly. For example, beginning in August 2006, HCA launched the OneCareNow 365-City Campaign—a campaign that was both simple and unprecedented in California. An "event" in support of single payer was conducted in a different city of California every day for a year, with the choice of cities determined by population size. The first event was held in Morro Bay, with a population of approximately ten thousand. Each day thereafter, the next-most-populated city held an event, until, one year later, there was a massive event in Los Angeles, California's largest city (www.californiaonecare .org).

Many SSG partners helped conduct the 365-City campaign; among them were the League of Women Voters, the California Alliance for Retired Americans, CSEA, the California Nurses Association, the California Teachers Association, Progressive Democrats of America, and the Progressive Caucus of the Democratic Party. The types of events were determined by local organizers and ranged from informational forums, to street theater, to "freeway blogging" (activists holding signs on freeway overpasses during rush hour), to protest marches, and so on. The last event, in front of the Los Angeles City Hall, was the largest rally in support of single payer in California history and featured Senator Sheila Kuehl, state insurance commissioner John Garamendi, comedian Lily Tomlin, U.S. representative Dennis Kucinich, labor leader and activist Dolores Huerta, and numerous community and grassroots leaders.

OneCareNow also produced over ninety 30-second video ads and "aired" them sequentially over a one-year period beginning March 2010, with ads appearing daily on YouTube, select SSG-member websites, and single payer websites in other states, as well as in more traditional radio and TV spots. The "talent" for the 365 ads came from celebrities (such as comedian Paula Poundstone and actor Elliot Gould); individuals who told their stories of being harmed by the existing "nonsystem" of health care; and supportive politicians, business owners, religious leaders, and community members up and down the state. All the ads have a distinct campaign "look" so that viewers can connect one ad to the next and see them all as a part of one campaign for single payer.

Social action organizers from Saul Alinsky (1972) onward have stressed the importance of taking advantage of relevant anniversaries, current events, and so forth by linking your cause to these critical moments. The SSG demonstrated this principle when it took advantage of the release of Michael Moore's controversial and widely viewed documentary film *Sicko*, about the failed U.S. health care system. At each theater in California that exhibited *Sicko*, SSG coalition members set up tables and passed out information, recruiting a total of over forty thousand new supporters to the campaign. Moviegoers in some areas were also asked to host house parties, at which neighbors could come together to talk more about both their own experiences with the health care system and the California single payer bill as an important step toward real change.

As Bazell Satariano and Wong note in chapter 15, despite many new online and other strategies for social change, the key to effective organizing remains communicating with and engaging community members in more personal ways. For half a dozen years, students in nursing, medicine, public health, and allied health professions have led a rally and lobby day in support of single payer at the state capitol. Members of the SSG attend the rallies, hire buses to bring supporters, provide funds for printing materials, videotape the rally, and post on YouTube. And after each rally, the students and SSG members also walk the halls of the capitol to visit and lobby legislators.

Reaching out to one's professional and other peers also is critical to success. Each organizational member of the SSG has therefore worked in a coordinated fashion to activate its members to call, write letters and e-mail their legislators, and compose and send letters to editors of their local newspapers. SSG's organizational members similarly have sent action alert "blasts" to their members or database of supporters and, during elections, have recruited and trained volunteers in get-out-the-vote campaigns on behalf of candidates who are single payer supporters.

Finally, and because of the importance to organizing and movement building of feeling part of something bigger (Staples 2004), the SSG held a State Strategic Summit in Los Angeles in 2008, which was attended by over three hundred single payer activists from all over California. Among the results of the strategic planning conducted at the summit, an effort called the Healthy Majority Campaign was launched to elect two-thirds majorities of single payer supporters in the Assembly and Senate—a "healthy" supermajority. As of June 2011, the campaign was two votes shy of a two-thirds majority in both houses. After achieving a two-thirds majority of Democrats in both houses, the campaign will shift to conducting primary campaigns against Democrats that do not support single payer with the goal of getting all Democrats to vote for single payer legislation.

As a result of the constellation of grassroots activities coordinated by the SSG, support for single payer grew throughout the state and among legislators. Thus, after significant expansion of the campaign effort, SB 840 (formerly SB 921) passed both houses of the legislature in two consecutive legislative sessions but fell to Governor Arnold Schwarzenegger's vetoes. However, the funding portion of the legislation, which requires a two-thirds vote, was removed from the bill. SB 840 was the first single payer universal health care plan in U.S. history to be passed in a state legislature and brought to a governor's desk.

Marrying Grassroots and Netroots: A Ringside View of the California OneCare Campaign

As illustrated above, numerous organizations are working to pass single payer in California and the SSG serves as the coordinating body for these organizational efforts. An in-depth description of one of the member organizations, California OneCare (OneCare), is now provided to illustrate in greater detail community organizing at the grassroots level, through both on- and offline activism.

Shortly after the highly successful 365-City Campaign, the executive director of HCA proposed to the board, and got approval for, the launching of OneCare as a new nonprofit organization. HCA would continue with its mission of chapter development while OneCare would fuse its grassroots and netroots organizing efforts, further develop and expand its collaborative relationship with the entertainment industry, continue to produce educational and documentary videos for activists, and produce and distribute public service announcements for radio and TV.

The OneCare grassroots campaign is designed to recruit and educate supporters for single payer reform. Additionally, the online, or netroots, component of the campaign is dedicated to the recruitment and establishment of OneCare Teams. Composed of three or more activists who are trained using web-based tools, the OneCare Teams are mini-campaign organizations. Team members have the choice of being an "online" activist or engaging in community-based trainings and activities with fellow team members. To date, the distinction between online and grassroots activism frequently becomes blurred when a team member decides to shift from one role to the other. The campaign encourages team members to engage in a way that fits their personal circumstances and needs. Consistent with the literature stressing the importance of combining on- and offline strategies for activism and policy change (Daniels 2011; see chapter 15), the OneCare campaign is committed to promoting the connection and synergy of netroots and grassroots activists for single payer. This will dramatically expand the reach and power of the mass movement for single payer in California.

The OneCare campaign staff work closely with the health policy bloggers and diarists on the most popular blog sites; for example, *Daily Kos*, *Digby*, and *Firedoglake*, as well as the *Huffington Post*. The *Daily Kos* diarists have formed a California single payer interest group that communicates regularly online. In addition, two board members of California OneCare have presented the details of the campaign at two annual conferences of Netroots Nation. Forging a working relationship with the progressive blogosphere significantly expands the reach of the campaign to millions who read the blogs. After blogging colleagues reach people online, the campaign has created a way for the newly interested online activists to become engaged with the campaign.

Typically, people get involved because of their personal experiences with health care and an ability to personally identify with the issues at hand. After being directed to the OneCare website by bloggers, people can and do view numerous videos that have been produced by the OneCare filmmakers. Using the idea that everyone will need adequate health care, and highlighting personal experiences with the failures of the current "nonsystem" of care, the OneCare campaign video, *California OneCare: Full Care, for All, for Less,* creates a conduit through which viewers can increase their commitment to and engagement with the new plan. The fourteen-minute video engages activists by establishing identification with those who have direct experiences with the failures of current health care and then explaining the available alternatives. It is the goal of the website and online activities to guide Internet users on a path of discovery regarding single payer in an effort to get people involved in the campaign at three different levels.

At the first level of involvement and learning, users decide for themselves whether and how they wish to be involved, which creates stronger convictions and supporters. By offering as much current information to new users as possible in the form of articles, essays, links, videos, and online discussion groups, OneCare enhances users' ability to learn as much as they can about the issue, making it possible for them to make informed decisions about where they stand on an issue. The OneCare website features current, categorized news stories that can be subscribed to by RSS or e-mail, thus allowing users to have the information come to them. These news items appear on the front page of the website in descending chronological order to create a full archive that can be explored at the users' leisure. Combined with a video archive linked through YouTube and social bookmarking links as a part of every page and article, users can also easily share the articles they find interesting (or infuriating) in other public and private forums as points of discussion.

At the second level of involvement, once a user has formed an opinion, opportunities are created through which he or she can connect to others with similar issue interests. The new site is fully integrated with social networking sites, including Facebook, LinkedIn and Twitter. Additionally, OneCare has a dedicated Facebook page that allows for more tightly focused discussion forums and media sharing. This multifaceted approach to social networking gives users the most options for how they may connect and to what extent they want to participate, reinforcing the personal nature of this issue. Further, educating users who actively consume materials from the learning portions of OneCare's web presence allows people to have more productive discussions and to make smart choices in helping to connect with newer users.

At the last level, people are asked to get directly involved as a OneCare Team member. Once people have made up their minds and feel supported through the other strategic portions of the site, it will become easier to make a commitment to things like signing a petition, donating money, attending rallies, participating in flash mobs, and engaging in other real-world actions.

Of course, many users that will never make it to this last level. But OneCare is aware that even those who never make it past level 1 or 2, and may never attend a rally, might still tell their friends, who in turn might become more involved. This power of collaboration is central to the growth and power of any contemporary grassroots campaign, since it establishes user ownership of the issue (Staples 2004; see chapters 11 and 15).

By combining a top-down information portal that originates content from the campaign with the bottom-up methods of social networking to tie the wide variety of supporters and future users together, OneCare has created a more controlled, open-source movement that focuses on educating people about single payer and, of course, about the importance of voting.

The long-term goal of the campaign is to establish at least one OneCare Team per ZIP Code in California—approximately sixteen hundred OneCare Teams. The campaign teams become a political force when all the teams within a given Assembly or Senate district are organized by a paid, full-time organizer who is accountable to OneCare. The organizer is responsible for the educational activity and political activism within the electoral district as well as the recruitment of new volunteers.

The responsibility of a volunteer campaign team leader is to assemble at least one team of three people who will make at least one community presentation each month and then to stay in touch with the groups that form as a result of the presentation. Organizing faith-based communities is the primary objective during the beginning phase of the campaign. Communities of faith are more apt to see the lack of health care as a moral issue that has been shown to be a powerful force in the single payer movement. The people who are identified as leaders on this issue in their faith community have a natural constituent group for ongoing education on this issue and their associations make it more likely that interest will be sustained throughout the beginning phase of the campaign. The purpose is to motivate and sustain interest of the volunteer base for the eventual political activity of the next phase of the campaign. Among the tasks to accomplish this, the OneCare campaign tasks ahead range from recruiting and training team members to engaging team members in electoral campaigns in key Assembly and Senate races.

It is beyond the scope of this chapter to provide details about other aspects of the OneCare campaign, including, for example, its recruitment and engagement of over sixty Hollywood actors and comedians to appear in ads and publicly support the netroots and grassroots dimensions of the work. Interested readers are referred to the organization's website (www.californiaonecare.org) for more information about this ambitious state-level effort and its activities and outcomes.

A Final Note on Medicare for All

Passage of single payer legislation at the state level mimics the political route for the enactment of single payer in Canada. Canadian Medicare (providing health care coverage for people of all ages) was first instituted in Saskatchewan province before it was adapted in the other provinces. Likewise, California activists are committed to solving the health care crisis for the nation by eliminating the for-profit, market approach to providing insurance. The State Strategy Group is hopeful that its multipronged approach and genuine community engagement on multiple levels will succeed where decades of prior efforts have not. The Affordable Care Act is a partial step towards a single payer system. And, in the opinion of this author (McGuire) and growing numbers of analysts, advocates, policymakers, and everyday folks around the country, a single payer system is the only way that all residents of the United States can receive the health care they deserve. In this chapter, we have presented two different accounts of and perspectives on community organizing and movement building for improving health care access through, respectively, the historic Affordable Care Act and the groundbreaking state-level Medicare for All campaign in California. Although differing in a number of respects, both these landmark efforts illustrate the importance of grassroots organizing and coalition building as part of a multipronged campaign to improve health care coverage in the only industrialized nation in the world that has yet to provide universal health care access to its citizens.

NOTE

1. Medicare for All is referred to as *single payer* throughout the chapter.

REFERENCES

Alinsky, S. D. 1972. Rules for Radicals: A Practical Primer for Realistic Radicals. New York: Random House.

Antos, J., J. Bertko, M. Chernew, D. Culter, F. de Brantes, D. Goldman, B. Kocher, M. McClellan, E. McGlynn, M. Pauly, et al. 2010. "Bending the Curve through Health Reform Implementation." *American Journal of Managed Care* 16, no. 11:804–812.

Barber, C., and M. Miller. 2007. Affordable Health Care for All: What Does Affordable Really Mean? Boston: Community Catalyst.

Bhattacharya, J., and D. Lakdawalla. 2006. "Does Medicare Benefit the Poor?" *Journal of Public Economics* 90, no. 2:277–292.

Blumberg, L. J., J. Holahan, J. Hadley, and K. Nordahl. 2007. Setting a Standard of Affordability for Health Insurance Coverage. *Health Aff (Millbank)*, no. 26:w463–w473.

Butterfoss, F. 2009. "The Community Coalition Action Theory." In *Emerging Theories in Health Promotion Practice and Research: Strategies for Improving Public Health*, edited by R. J. DiClemente, R. A. Crosby, and M. C. Kegler, 157–193. 2nd ed. San Francisco: Jossey-Bass.

Brady, D. W., and D. P. Kessler. 2010. "Why Is Health Reform So Difficult?" Journal of Health Politics, Policy and Law 35, no. 2:161–175.

Carmen, D., B. D. Proctor, and J. C. Smith. 2010. "Health Insurance Historical Tables." In *Income, Poverty, and Health Insurance Coverage in the United States: 2009.* Washington, D.C.: U.S. Census Bureau.

Chirba-Martin, M. A., and A. Torres. 2008. "Universal Health Care in Massachusetts: Setting the Standard for National Reform." *Fordham Urban Law Journal* 35, no. 3:409–446.

Community Catalyst. 2006. "Consumer Health Advocacy: A View from 16 States." Boston: Community Catalyst.

———. 2009. "Funding Makes a Difference: The Role of Philanthropy in Massachusetts's Journey to Health Care Reform." Boston: Community Catalyst.

Danelski, A. E., D. E. Altman, J. Eldred, M. James, and D. Rowland. 1995. *The California Single-Payer Debate: The Defeat of Proposition 186*. Menlo Park, Calif.: Kaiser Family Foundation.

Daniels, J., 2011. "Case Study: Web 2.0; Health Care Policy and Community Health Activism." In *Policy and Politics for Nurses and Other Advocates*, edited by D. M. Nickitas, D. J. Middaugh, and N. Aries, 277–285. Boston: Jones and Bartlett.

Daniels, J., B. Glickstein, and D. J. Mason. 2012. "Using the Power of the Media to Influence Health Policy and Politics." In *Policy and Politics in Nursing and Health Care*, edited by D. J. Mason, J. K. Leavitt, and M. W. Chaffee, 88–104. 6th ed. New York: Elsevier.

Foster, R. S. 2009. *Estimated Financial Effects of the "America's Affordable Health Choices Act of 2009 (H.R. 3200)," as Reported by the Ways and Means Committee*. Baltimore: Centers for Medicare and Medicaid Services.

Grantmakers in Health. 2010. *Building Capacity for Health Advocacy at the State and Local Level*. Washington, D.C.: Grantmakers in Health. http://www.gih.org/usr_doc/Building_Capacity_for_Health_Advocacy_at_the_State_and_Local_Level .pdf

Greater Boston Interfaith Organization. N.d. "Health Care: The Fight for Quality, Affordable Health Care for All." http://www.gbio.org/.

Halpin, H. A. 2003. "Getting to a Single Payer System Using Market Forces: The CHOICE Program." In *Covering America: Real Remedies for the Uninsured*. Vol. 3. Washington, D.C.: Economic and Social Research Institute.

Halpin, H. A., and P. Harbage. 2010. "The Origins and Demise of the Public Option." *Health Affairs* 26, no. 6:1117–24.

Health Care for All Massachusetts. 2006. *2006 Annual Report*. Boston: Health Care for All. http://www.hcfama.org/_data/global/resources/live/HCFA%20Annual%20Report%202020 06.pdf.

Henry J. Kaiser Foundation. 2010. "Health Reform and Communities of Color: Implications for Racial and Ethnic Health Disparities." Menlo Park, Calif.: Kaiser Family Foundation.

Hsiao, W. C. 2011. "State-Based, Single Payer Health Care: A Solution for the United States?" *New England Journal of Medicine*, 364, no. 13:1188–1190.

Jacobs, L. R., and T. Scokpol. 2010. *Health Care Reform and American Politics: What Everyone Needs to Know*. New York: Oxford University Press.

Long, P., and J. Gruber. 2010. "Projecting the Impact of the Affordable Care Act on California." *Health Affairs* 30, no. 1:63–70.

MassAct! 2005. "Health Care Advocates Collect Over 38,000 Signatures for Health Reform Ballot Proposal in Ten Days." October 4. http://www.massact.com/documents/20051004 PRMassACT.pdf.

Miller, M. 2009. *A Community Organizer's Tale: People and Power in San Francisco*. Berkeley: Calif.: Heyday Books.

Minkler, M. 2010. "Linking Science and Policy through Community-Based Participatory Research to Eliminate Health Disparities." Supplement, *American Journal of Public Health* 100, no. 1:S81–S87.

Mitchell, D.J.B. 2002. "Impeding Earl Warren: California's Health Insurance Plan That Wasn't and What Might Have Been." *Journal of Health Politics, Policy and Law* 27, no. 6:30.

MoveOn.org. 2009. "Stand with Dr. Dean Petition." http://pol.moveon.org/standwithdrdean/.

Oberlander, J. 2007. "Learning from Failure in Health Care Reform." *New England Journal of Medicine*, no. 367:1677–1679.

Raymond, A. G. 2011. *Lessons from the Implementation of Massachusetts Health Reform*. Boston: Blue Cross Blue Shield Foundation of Massachusetts.

Satiani, B. 2009. "A Medicare Primer." *Journal of Vascular Surgery* 50, no. 2:453–460.

Sen, R. 2003. *Stir It Up: Lessons in Community Organizing and Advocacy*. San Francisco: Jossey-Bass.

Skocpol, T. 1995. "The Rise and Resounding Demise of the Clinton Plan." *Health Affairs* 14, no. 1:66–85.

———. 1997. *Boomerang: Health Care Reform and the Turn against Government*. New York: Norton.

Staples, L. 2004. *Roots to Power: A Manual for Grassroots Organizing*. 2nd ed. New York: Praeger.

Starr, P. 1995 "What Happened to Health Care Reform?" *American Prospect*, 20:20–31.

Truffer, C. J., S. Keehan, S. Smith, J. Cylus, A. Sisko, J. A. Poisal, J. Lizonitz, and M. K. Clemens. 2010. "Health Spending Projections through 2019: The Recession's Impact Continues." *Health Affairs* 29, no. 3. doi:10.1377/hlthaff.2009.1074.

Wielawski, I. M. 2007. *Forging Consensus: The Path to Health Reform in Massachusetts*. Boston: Blue Cross Blue Shield of Massachusetts Foundation. http://bluecrossfoundation.

Wolff, T. 2010. *The Power of Collaborative Solutions: Six Principles and Effective Tools for Building Healthy Communities*. San Francisco: Jossey-Bass.

Zhu, J., P. Brawarsky, S. Lipsitz, H. Huskamp, and J. S. Haas. 2010. "Massachusetts Health Reform and Disparities in Coverage, Access, and Health Status." *Journal of General Internal Medicine* 25, no. 12:1356–1362.

22

Media Advocacy

A Strategy for Helping Communities Change Policy

LORI DORFMAN

PRISCILLA GONZALEZ

The primary tool available to communities for influencing social conditions and creating healthy environments is policy. Policies define the structures and set the rules by which we live (see chapter 20). If public health practitioners and community organizers are going to improve social conditions and physical environments in lasting and meaningful ways, they must be involved in policy development and policy advocacy. And being successful in policy advocacy means paying attention to the news.

The reach of the media is intoxicating. In our society, the news media largely determine what issues we collectively think about, how we think about them, and what kinds of alternatives are considered viable. The public and policymakers do not consider issues seriously unless they are visible, and they are not visible unless the media have brought them to light.

Nonprofit organizations, health departments, and community activists often are unhappy with how their issues are presented in the news. Media advocacy addresses this problem. It is an approach to health communication that differs significantly from traditional mass communication approaches (Wallack et al. 1999). Despite the media's enormous reach and potential as a tool for change, public health professionals rarely use mass media to its full advantage. Rather, they tend to use it in its least effective capacity: to convey personal health information to consumers. By contrast, media advocacy harnesses the power of the news to mobilize advocates and apply pressure for policy change. Media advocacy helps people understand the importance and reach of news coverage, the need to participate actively in shaping such coverage, and the methods for doing so effectively.

First Comes Strategy

Media advocacy relies on four layers of strategy. The first is the overall strategy, which includes the policy goal and what it will take to enact it. Based on that, advocates develop their media strategy and their message strategy—what they want to say, who will say it, and to whom. After the first three layers of strategy are in place, advocates can determine the best way to attract the attention of journalists and other media contacts—the access strategy.

Develop an Overall Strategy

Getting media attention should never be an advocate's first consideration. Before talking to reporters or even determining what to say, public health advocates must know what they want to change in concrete terms, the more specific the better (Dorfman et al. 2005; Themba 1999). Further, advocates need to know how to create the change, for example, through legislation, a vote, administrative petition, or some other process (Wallack 1999; Wallack et al. 1993; Chapman 2001).

The overall strategy will determine how to approach the problem, and thus also how to approach the media. Media advocates use these questions to develop their overall strategy:

1. What is the problem or issue? How the problem is defined will determine the solution.
2. What is a solution or ameliorative policy? Solutions are usually incremental, since it is impossible to be comprehensive and strategic at the same time, and for most groups, resources are too limited to be comprehensive.
3. Who has the power to make the necessary change? When the goal is the policy, the target is not the person with the problem. Instead, the target is the person or body that can enact the policy (e.g., legislature, city council, business, school board, principal, mayor, building manager, CEO).
4. Who must be mobilized to apply the necessary pressure? Who cares about this issue, and whom will the target listen to? These are the secondary targets. The "general public" is not specific enough to be a target audience; media advocacy is not about raising awareness among the general public, but about sparking action among particular power holders.
5. What do the targets need to hear? What they need to hear, and from whom they need to hear it, are the two key questions that form the foundation for a message strategy (Dorfman et al. 2005).

The evolution of tobacco control illustrates how the answers to these questions will shape the strategy. In the 1950s and 1960s, the problem was defined as smoking, so the solution was to warn smokers about the danger and help them quit; that usually led to noncontroversial education programs but could include policies like instituting reimbursement for cessation programs in health insur-ance. The target was the smoker, and education campaigns would aim to reach them directly or indirectly through their families or employers. In this scenario, the targets need to hear that they could well get a debilitating illness and die early, or perhaps they need to hear that cessation works, though it takes time. Later, health educators learned that if young people were the target of the campaign, the message should be about more proximate detriments of smoking such as bad breath or yellowing teeth. All of these answers assume a problem definition that holds the individual responsible for smoking.

Eventually, tobacco control advocates learned that greater success would come from understanding the problem at a population level and instituting primary prevention. From this perspective, the problem is defined not as smoking but as tobacco and the industries that promotes it. The solutions are policies that reshape the environment such as excise taxes, advertising restrictions, or clean indoor air ordinances. The immediate target is not the smoker but the policy-maker, and those who can put public pressure on policymakers. The messages explain how the policy will save lives, save money, and create a healthier society. As discussed in chapter 7, in California, a multilevel anti-tobacco effort, paid for through a new cigarette tax, put its greatest emphasis on changing state and local policies on tobacco. The program, which continues today, is widely credited with a reduction in the state's smoking rate of more than three times the national average over a ten-year period (California Tobacco Control Program 2010).

Those concerned about obesity are now developing a similar problem defini-tion and menu of policy options, including improving school foods, menu label-ing, financing for supermarkets in underserved areas, making it easier for schools and communities to share playgrounds, and taxing sugary beverages (Dorfman et al. 2005; Mercer et al. 2003). For example, the California Center for Public Health Advocacy (CCPHA) has played a critical role in shaping the debate around soda taxes as a policy solution to address obesity. In a 2009 report, *Bubbling Over: Soda Consumption and Its Link to Obesity in California*, CCPHA and the University of California, Los Angeles, Center for Health Policy Research presented strong evi-dence linking soda to the obesity epidemic (Babey et al. 2009). While the authors acknowledged that individuals have a responsibility, their recommendations focused more on creating policies to improve environments, such as marketing restrictions in schools and taxes on sugary beverages whose revenues could fund obesity prevention in California. A day after the release of the report, the *San Francisco Chronicle* announced in a front-page story that then–San Francisco mayor Gavin Newsom was considering "a fee on soft drinks" (Knight 2009). While the fee did not gain immediate political traction, it fueled a national discussion about sugary beverages. CCPHA's specific definition of the problem—that soda consumption contributes to obesity—supported its mayor's policy recommenda-tions, such as introducing taxes on sugary drinks (Knight 2009).

Develop a Media Strategy

Traditional mass communication strategies focus on delivering a message, so people can make better decisions. They assume that what's missing is informa-tion, as in the example above of tobacco control in its earliest days. The idea then was to use mass media to alert smokers to the health dangers of cigarettes. But policy and environmental change require a different approach to mass communication, one that helps people act as citizens to change policy decisions. Media advocacy's strategic use of mass media in combination with community organizing to advance healthy public policies is that strategy (Wallack et al. 1993). Instead of conceptualizing the audience as consumers of information, media advocates think of them as participants in democracy (Chapman and Lupton 1994). Media advocacy seeks to raise the volume of voices for social change and shape the sound, so that it resonates with the social justice values that are the basis of public health (Beauchamp 1976; Wallack and Lawrence 2005).

Media advocacy differs in many ways from traditional public health campaigns. It is most marked by an emphasis on the following:

1. Linking public health and social problems to inequities in social arrangements rather than to flaws in the individual
2. Changing public policy rather than personal health behavior
3. Focusing primarily on reaching opinion leaders and policymakers rather than those who have the problem (the traditional audience of public health communication campaigns)
4. Working with groups to increase participation and amplify their voices rather than providing health behavior change messages

5. Having a primary goal of reducing the power gap rather than just filling the information gap (Dorfman and Wallack 2012).

Focus on the News

Media advocacy focuses on the news because decades of communications research shows that the news sets the agenda for the public, for policymakers, and for other media (Dearing and Rogers 1996; Leskovec et al. 2009; Pew Research Center 2010). Policymakers see news as a barometer of public concerns. The media accord legitimacy and credibility to the issues they cover. In reflecting the issues of the day, the news media select what people and policymakers discuss. And, by setting the public agenda, the media also determine what is not being discussed. This is one way that the news media shape public debate, by narrowing the topics under discussion. Media advocates aim to get their issues covered by the news media at key moments in the policy process (as determined by their overall strategy).

Developing a media strategy means first deciding when the media spotlight would make a difference. When might media attention have a direct impact on the policymaking process (e.g., during the budget negotiations or before an important school board vote)? After you know when, you must decide where the media attention should appear. Which outlets would reach the target audience? To reach a state legislator, advocates might want coverage in the newspaper at the capitol and in the news outlets in the legislator's home district. For a business executive, an advocate might seek coverage in the trade press or on the business pages in the newspapers near the company headquarters. To do this well, and get the responses from reporters when they pitch stories, media advocates monitor the media and develop relationships with reporters and bloggers. Monitoring the media is crucial because it helps advocates identify which reporters are interested in their issue and whether the reporting is covering all the aspects they think are important. Finally, media advocates decide whether to create news, piggyback on breaking news, write op-eds, post blogs, submit letters, request editorials, or purchase advertising. These decisions will link directly to the access strategy.

Use Social Media

Media advocates also use social media, such as Facebook, YouTube, and blogs, to reach specific audiences and to gain access to the mainstream media (see chapter 15). Media advocates at the health department in Contra Costa County, California, did this in October 2009, to shame the American Academy of Family Physicians after the organization partnered with the Coca-Cola Company to develop "educational materials to teach consumers how to make the right choices and incorporate the products they love into a balanced diet and a healthy lifestyle" (American Academy of Family Physicians 2009). The physicians were outraged that their professional organization, dedicated to protecting children's health, would partner with a major purveyor of sugar in the midst of a national obesity crisis. In the public health department's press release, the director of Contra Costa Health Services, Dr. William Walker, explained, "This is ridiculous. Having the soda industry create materials about making the right choices is like having the fox guard the hen house. This is reminiscent of when the tobacco industry enlisted doctors to endorse cigarette brands as 'mild'" (Contra Costa Health Services 2009).

To protest the partnership, clinicians in the county came together to publicly resign their membership from the American Academy of Family Physicians (AAFP). In a strategic move, the health department organized a press conference that coincided with a California Senate hearing discussing a soda tax, a policy that public health advocates hoped would raise revenues for prevention and reduce soda consumption. The health department saw this bold statement as an opportunity to spark national discussion and pressure the AAFP to withdraw from the partnership. But the night before the news conference, a crisis on the San Francisco Bay Bridge—a major commuter artery—captured the media's attention. Only one reporter attended the county's news conference on the AAFP controversy.

Undaunted, the public health department used social media to get the story out. The communications staff created a short but compelling video showing Contra Costa Health Services director and county health officer Walker and twenty other doctors in front of the regional medical center as Dr. Walker tore up his AAFP membership card. Dr. Walker expressed his and his colleagues' outrage, saying, "I am appalled and ashamed of the partnership between Coca-Cola and the American Academy of Family Physicians. . . . How can any organization that claims to promote public health join forces with a company that promotes products that sicken our children?" (Contra Costa Health Services 2009).

The health department posted the video along with another newsworthy component: a photograph in which doctors in their white coats and stethoscopes—a powerful visual that symbolizes physicians and their credibility and validity as authentic voices for health—expressed their disapproval of the Coke-AAFP partnership by giving a collective thumbs-down. To help the story go viral, the health department uploaded to its website the video, photo, and links to the news story written by the local reporter; posted links to these on the health department's Facebook page; and used the department's Twitter account to alert media contacts. They then e-mailed the story to their networks throughout the county, which in turn forwarded it through their own social networks to hundreds of contacts around the nation.

The strategic use of social media helped spark a national discussion about partnerships between health organizations and food and beverage corporations whose products and marketing contribute to obesity. The story spread quickly, prompting e-mails and comments that the health department posted on its website. News outlets like the *Kansas City Business Journal*, the *Chicago Tribune*, KQED radio, and CBS news used the local story and online content to inform their news coverage and further spread the story in print, on the radio, and on television.

Best of all, the widespread attention pressured the AAFP to respond. The California chapter of the AAFP formally declared its opposition to the AAFP-Coke partnership. Despite the initial response from only one newspaper, the health department "expanded the national dialogue on sweetened beverages and health, educated the Bay Area public, and supported a California legislative strategy [to tax soda]" (Brunner et al. 2011).

Develop a Message Strategy

A message has three components: a problem statement, a solution, and a values statement. It answers the questions, What's wrong? Why does it matter? and, What should be done? These questions should look familiar, because, once again, the message will be derived from the overall strategy. There might be several correct answers to these questions, so media advocates must be strategic and choose the answers that link to the current status of the overall strategy. Advocates must be able to articulate why this problem and solution matter, which values support their goal, and what will happen if nothing is done.

Whatever message advocates develop is going to be heard in a messy, loud media context that is dominated by well-financed campaigns from corporations, some with "anti-health" goals. Public health can rarely compete in this message environment; we simply do not have the resources in most cases. The marketing campaign for a single candy bar, for example, can outspend the entire national 5-a-Day campaign encouraging families to eat more fruits and vegetables (Consumers Union and California Pan-Ethnic Health Network 2005). Therefore, we need to be strategic not just in the overall strategy but also in how the issue is characterized or framed.

Frame for Access and Frame for Content

Framing for media advocates includes what to emphasize to gain the attention of reporters (i.e., framing for access), which may not be what you emphasize once you have their attention (i.e., framing for content). For example, in injury control the dominant frame is that injuries are inevitable, accidental, and thus probably unavoidable. Framing for content means you shape the story to emphasize that injuries are predictable and thus can be prevented (at a population level, if not for any given individual). Framing for content is challenging because media advocates often bump up against larger societal frames that can contradict a public health perspective (see section on framing challenges below). But first, to gain access to reporters so you can make your points about injury and connect them to your policy solution, you will have to identify what is newsworthy about the story *now*. That means creating news, one of the general tactics in an access strategy.

Develop an Access Strategy

To get a reporter's attention, or frame for access, media advocates pay attention to those tenets of newsworthiness that grab journalists' attention: controversy, irony, a local angle, anniversaries and milestones, breakthroughs, populations of interest, and injustice (Wallack et al. 1999). Then they create news using story elements that make it easy for reporters to tell the story. These may include compelling visuals and symbols, concise media bites, and social math that uses comparisons or analogies to make large numbers meaningful (e.g., comparing the number of tobacco-related deaths each week to the number who die in jetliner crashes—or number of fast food outlets to grocery stores in poor communities). For example, advocates can make their point about the excessive amount of sugar children drink in soda without uttering a single number when they let people know that drinking one twenty-ounce Coke, which is now marketed and sold as a single serving, has more sugar than six Krispy Kreme donuts.

Create News

One common way to create news is to release a report. In CCPHA's example, the organization used the report *Bubbling Over*, about social consumption and obesity, as a way to create news about the harmful health consequences of soda and prompt discussion about policy solutions. CCPHA also prepared brief documents and tool kits that reporters and advocates could use in either writing stories or talking to the media. These included news releases; Spanish-language materials; a media kit; contacts for spokespersons familiar with the study; fact sheets; and a list of policy recommendations that highlighted the environment and role of organizations, cities, and policymakers, not just individuals. In doing something about sugary beverages, CCPHA's media bites included social math to illustrate the massive quantity of sugar adolescents were consuming, "39 pounds of sugar each year in soda and other sugar-sweetened beverages" (CCPHA 2009).

The resulting media coverage was dramatic. Prominent news coverage appeared in, among other periodicals, the *New York Times*, *Sacramento Bee*, *San Francisco Chronicle*, *Los Angeles Times*, and *Fresno Bee*, with many featuring front-page coverage. CCPHA also prepared a video that television outlets, such as ABC, used to talk about the study and policy recommendations. Finally, CCPHA used its e-mail network to disseminate the report to public health professionals and other allies.

Localize the Story

Because CCPHA provided fact sheets that broke down the data by county, local news reporters could make the information relevant to the audience of their papers. The fact sheets gave them clear specifics about the story for their region, which meant they were more likely to do the story in the first place—and had more to say about it.

Then Comes Framing

How should public health advocates answer challenging arguments from opponents? Tobacco companies say they sell a legal product. Alcohol companies insist that most people drink responsibly and the companies shouldn't be blamed if some people abuse their products. Junk food purveyors say that it is parents' responsibility to control what children eat. Car companies say that the key to greater safety on the road is changes in driver behavior (Dorfman et al. 2005).

These are tough arguments to counter. After all, each one is truthful—if incomplete. But each industry argument has a common feature: each frames the debate in terms of a single, widely held, important American value: personal responsibility. The trouble is, when public health battles are framed solely in terms of personal responsibility, audiences can't see how the settings and circumstances surrounding individuals contribute to their health status. Public health advocates need to "reframe" the message so the landscape around individuals comes into view. When public health advocates make the landscape visible, they bolster their arguments for public health solutions.

Regardless of how well public health advocates make their case, if the change is significant, it will be contested. Inevitably, environmental changes are more controversial than changes in personal behavior, because they generally require a shift in resources or responsibility. How the message is framed can either strengthen support for public health policy or reinforce the opposition.

Typical News Frames Are More Often Portraits Than Landscapes

Most news is framed around newsworthy events or actions from individuals. Shanto Iyengar's (1991) seminal research showed that nearly 80 percent of television news is episodic, focused narrowly on incidents, events, or people. Other research has upheld that finding in studies of television (Chavez and Dorfman

1996; Dorfman et al. 1997) and print news (Woodruff et al. 2003; McManus and Dorfman 2005, 2002).

In a series of experiments, Iyengar found that when people watch news stories that lack context—what he called *episodic stories*—viewers focus on the individuals. Without any other information, they tend to attribute responsibility for the problem and its solution to the people portrayed in the story—in other words, they blame the victim. After watching episodic news stories, viewers are more likely to distance themselves from the "victims" portrayed, look to them to work harder to solve their own problem or accept the consequences of their behavior, and gain no insight into the social and political circumstances that contribute to the individual problem (Iyengar 1991). To counter this dominant episodic news frame, advocates must help reporters do a better job describing the landscape surrounding individuals and events so the context of public health problems becomes visible. Iyengar called these stories *thematic*.

Thematic stories may engage viewers with a personal story, but they also give them more: background, consequences, and other information that provide context. Iyengar found that viewers who see thematic stories understand that responsibility is shared between individuals and their institutions, and are more likely to recognize that government or other institutions have a role to play in solving the problem.

A simple way to distinguish story types is to think of the difference between a portrait and a landscape. In a news story framed as a portrait, audiences may learn a great deal about an individual or an event, with great drama and emotion. But it is hard to see what surrounds that individual or what brought him or her to that moment in time. A landscape story pulls back the lens to take a broader view. It may include people and events, but connects them to the larger social and economic forces. News stories framed in such a manner are more likely to evoke solutions that don't focus exclusively on individuals, but also address the policies, institutions, and conditions that surround and affect them (Dorfman et al. 2005; Dorfman and Wallack 2012).

The key value that is affected by portrait and landscape frames is *responsibility*. News stories focused on people or events evoke feelings of personal responsibility in audiences. Landscape stories evoke shared responsibility between individuals and institutions. Advocates should strive to make stories about the landscape as vivid and interesting as those about the portrait. This is not easy to do, but crucial. The framing challenge for public health educators and other social change professionals is to create landscape stories that are as compelling as portrait narratives and invoke their core values.

There are economic imperatives in the media business that compel reporters to pursue portraits rather than landscapes. Corporate concentration has forced news outlets to abandon public interest goals to pursue profit in the form of larger audiences. Stories framed as portraits serve that purpose better than those framed as landscapes because they are easier stories to tell and presumably attract a larger audience. And landscape stories are harder to tell.

TABLE 22.1.

Reframing Tobacco

Tobacco	A problem of corporate behavior and government regulation, rather than just the behavior of the smoker
Responsibility	Belongs to the tobacco industry and those who regulate it
Solution	Policies on availability and youth access (e.g., vending machines), excise taxes, secondhand smoke, and marketing
Appeal	Policies save money; protect lives; prevent initiation among youth; promote health; and burden industry, rather than victims
Story elements	Story elements show, rather than tell, whether the news story is for TV, print, or the web, including images, media bites, social math, and symbols that evoke values (e.g., fairness, health, freedom)

But while it is more difficult to tell a compelling landscape story, it can be done, especially when public health advocates provide the story elements that make reporters' job easier. As noted above, tobacco is a terrific example of reframing. First it was thought of as a personal problem of smokers who were addicted. Then it was reframed to be understood as a problem of corporate behavior and government regulation, rather than just the behavior of the smoker. Once advocates emphasized that perspective, and used their role as sources to help journalists tell a new story, the issue was understood differently (table 22.1).

Make Values Visible

Cognitive linguist George Lakoff describes three conceptual levels for framing messages in the context of public health and other social or political issues (Lakoff, personal communication, June 2004). Level 1 is the expression of overarching values like fairness, responsibility, equality, and equity—the core values that motivate media advocates to change the world. Level 2 is the general issue being addressed, like housing, the environment, schools, or health. Level 3 is about the nitty-gritty of those issues, including the policy detail or strategy and tactics for achieving change.

Messages can be generated from any level, but level 1 is most important, since it is at level 1 that people connect in the deepest way. According to Lakoff, people's support or rejection of an issue will be largely determined by whether they can identify and connect with the level 1 value. Values are motivators, and messages for policy change should reinforce and activate values. Messages, therefore, should articulate level 1 values and not get mired in level 3 minutiae. Public health advocates must know the level 3 details—what needs changing and how the change will occur—but those details needn't be prominent in the message. In fact, if level 3 details crowd out level 1 values, Lakoff contends, the message will be less effective.

Advocates' tendency is to argue the fallacy of their opponent's level 1 frame; they often want to counter their opponents' message point by point. Cognitive linguists and other communications scholars suggest that advocates should resist this impulse because such arguments will only reinforce the existing frame. Thus, media advocates will have the strategic advantage when they set the level 1 frame themselves, not when they respond to an opponent's frame.

Different level 2 issues can share the same level 1 values. In fact, using level 2 categories can be a useful device in reframing an issue, as when violence is cast as a public health issue, or physical activity is seen as an education issue. Below are sample messages from the two issues we've been using as examples, tobacco and soda, that share the same level 1 value, in this case fairness and equity. The policies used here are examples—at any given time, the specifics of the policy may change, depending on the overall strategy. When it does, the values statement may remain consistent, or it too may change.

For soda, with a level 3 policy goal of limiting its accessibility, the message might be: *We want children to grow up in wholesome environments that foster health. It is not fair that everywhere they turn in this neighborhood sugary drinks are cheap and easy to find, but free drinking water is nowhere to be found. Every family should have the opportunity to raise its children in a healthy environment. That's why we're asking the parks district to repair drinking fountains and provide cold drinking water where children play.*

For tobacco, with a level 3 policy goal of enacting clean indoor air laws across all sectors of the city, the message might be: *While we have achieved great progress in reducing smoking, there are still large populations, primarily in low-income communities of color, that are regularly exposed to toxic secondhand smoke. It is not fair that some of our cities' workers are protected and others are not. We should enact uniform clean indoor ordinances to protect workers in all workplaces, including restaurants and bars.*

For both messages, the level 1 value was fairness and equity, while the level 2 topic was different.

Evaluation

The ultimate outcome measure for media advocacy is whether or not the desired policy passed. However, disentangling media advocacy's contribution to the policy process from the effects of community organizing or policy advocacy—or other events or secular trends—is challenging, especially because policies can take years, sometimes decades, to enact and implement (Stead et al. 2002; Schooler et al. 1996; Sterman 2006). Most evidence for media advocacy's success comes from tobacco (Niederdeppe et al. 2007) and alcohol (Harwood et al. 2005; Holder and Treno 1997; Stewart and Casswell 1993) policy campaigns, likely because media advocacy was developed first in those fields. Many evaluations are qualitative case studies that describe the process of conducting media advocacy (Jernigan and Wright 1996; Seevak 1997; Dean 2006), although some researchers are experimenting to verify basic concepts underlying media advocacy in experiments (Major 2009). Complicating matters, measuring media effects is difficult in and of itself (Coffman 2002). Dorfman and colleagues (2002) provide a framework for evaluators who want to assess media advocacy in relation to other sorts of health communications. As media advocates expand their practice, we should start to see evaluations of media advocacy practiced in a variety of public health and social policy arenas.

Conclusion

Media advocacy is in service to community organizing and policy advocacy; it does not stand on its own. That is why one cannot have a media strategy without an overall strategy. Advocates must know what they want, why they want it, and how they are going to get it, all before going to the media. In this way, media advocacy can amplify and accelerate policy advocacy.

Media advocacy is one of the few public health interventions that focuses upstream to change the environment in which people make health decisions. Public health matters are too important to be left to strategies that are at the mercy of media producers who have other priorities. That is one reason why, in public health, we cannot depend on public service advertising, for example.

The focus on policy is critical because usually, although not always, it is the mechanism with which we can improve health environments—and therefore also health outcomes—for the broadest population. It is also where we can improve health environments for those populations that suffer most from premature death, preventable illness, and injury. Media advocacy can accelerate and amplify that policy work so we can arrive faster at our goals for safe, healthful environments for everyone.

ACKNOWLEDGMENTS

Adapted from L. Dorfman, "Using Media Advocacy to Influence Policy," in *Community Health Education Methods: A Practical Guide*, edited by R. J. Bensley and J. Brookins-Fisher, 361–386, 3rd ed. (Sudbury, Mass.: Jones and Bartlett, 2009). With permission of the publisher.

REFERENCES

American Academy of Family Physicians. 2009. "American Academy of Family Physicians Launches Consumer Alliance with First Partner: The Coca-Cola Company." October 6. http://www.aafp.org/online/en/home/media/releases/newsreleases-statements-2009/consumeralliance-cocacola.html.

Babey, S. H., J. Malia, Y. Hongjian, and H. Goldstein. 2009. *Bubbling Over: Soda Consumption and Its Link to Obesity in California.* Los Angles: UCLA Center for Health Policy Research.

Beauchamp, D. E. 1976. "Public Health as Social Justice." *Inquiry* 13, no. 1:3–14.

Brunner, W., K. Fowlie, and J. Freestone. 2011. *Using Media to Advance Public Health Agendas*. Martinez, Calif.: Contra Costa Health Services. http://cchealth.org/groups/health_services/pdf/media_paper.pdf.

California Center for Public Health Advocacy (CCPHA). 2009. "New Research Shows Direct Link Between Soda and Obesity." http://www.publichealthadvocacy.org/_PDFs/Bubbling_Pressrelease.pdf.

California Tobacco Control Program, California Department of Public Health. 2010. "Two Decades of the California Tobacco Control Program: California Tobacco Survey, 1990–2008." http://www.cdph.ca.gov/.

Chapman, S. 2001. "Advocacy in Public Health: Roles and Challenges." *International Journal of Epidemiology* 30:1226–1232.

Chapman, S., and D. Lupton. 1994. *The Fight for Pubic Health: Principles and Practices of Media Advocacy*. London: British Medical Journal.

Chávez, V., and L. Dorfman. 1996. "Spanish Language Television News Portrayals of Youth and Violence in California." *International Quarterly of Community Health Education* 16, no. 2:121–138.

Coffman, J. 2002. *Public Communication Campaign Evaluation: An Environmental Scan of Challenges, Criticisms, Practice, and Opportunities*. Cambridge, Mass.: Harvard Family Research Project.

Consumers Union and California Pan-Ethnic Health Network. 2005. "Out of Balance: Marketing of Soda, Candy, Snacks, and Fast Foods Drowns Out Healthful Messages." http://www.consumersunion.org/pdf/OutofBalance.pdf.

Contra Costa Health Services. 2009. "Dr. Walker Resigns Membership in American Academy of Family Physicians to Protest Its Partnership with Coca-Cola." http://cchealth.org/groups/health_services/aafp_protest.php.

Dean, R. 2006. *Issue 16: Moving from Head to Heart; Using Media Advocacy to Talk about Affordable Housing*. Berkeley, Calif.: Berkeley Media Studies Group. http://bmsg.org/pub-issues.php.

Dearing, J. W., and E. M. Rogers. 1996. *Agenda-Setting*. Thousand Oaks, Calif.: Sage.

Dorfman, L., J. Ervice, and K. Woodruff. 2002. *Voices for Change: A Taxonomy of Public Communications Campaigns and Their Evaluation Challenges*. Berkeley, Calif.: Berkeley Media Studies Group. http://www.bmsg.org/pdfs/Taxonomy_Evaluation.pdf.

Dorfman, L., and L. Wallack. 2012. "Putting Policy into Health Communication: The Role of Media Advocacy." In *Public Communication Campaigns*, edited by D. E. Rice and C. K. Atkin. 4th ed. Newbury Park, Calif.: Sage.

Dorfman, L., L. Wallack, and K. Woodruff. 2005. "More Than a Message: Framing Public Health Advocacy to Change Corporate Practices." *Health Education and Behavior* 32, no. 4:320–336.

Dorfman, L., P. Wilbur, E. O. Lingas, K. Woodruff, and L. Wallack. 2005. *Accelerating Policy on Nutrition: Lessons from Tobacco, Alcohol, Firearms, and Traffic Safety*. http://www.bmsg.org/proj-food-obesity.php.

Dorfman, L., K. Woodruff, V. Chavez, and L. Wallack. 1997. "Youth and Violence on Local Television News in California." *American Journal of Public Health* 87, no. 8:1311–1316.

Harwood, E. M., J. C. Witson, D. P. Fan, and A. C. Wagenaar. 2005. "Media Advocacy and Underage Drinking Policies: A Study of Louisiana News Media from 1994 through 2003." *Health Promotion Practice* 6, no. 3:246–257.

Holder, H. D., and A. J. Treno. 1997. "Media Advocacy in Community Prevention: News as a Means to Advance Policy Change." *Addiction* 92:189–200.

Iyengar, S. 1991. *Is Anyone Responsible?* Chicago: University of Chicago Press.

Jernigan, D. H., and P. A. Wright. 1996. "Media Advocacy: Lessons from Community Experiences." *Journal of Public Health Policy* 17, no. 3:306–330.

Knight, H. 2009. "S.F. Looks at Fee on Soft Drinks." *San Francisco Chronicle*, September 18, A1.

Leskovec, J., L. Backstrom, and J. Kleinberg. 2009. "Meme-Tracking and the Dynamics of the News Cycle." In *Proceedings of the 15th ACM SIGKDD International Conference on Knowledge Discovery and Data Mining (KDD '09)*, 497–506. New York: ACM.

Major, L. H. 2009. "Break It to Me Harshly: The Effects of Intersecting News Frames in Lung Cancer and Obesity Coverage." *Journal of Health Communication* 14:174–188.

McManus, J., and L. Dorfman. 2002. "Youth Violence Stories Focus on Events, Not Causes." *Newspaper Research Journal* 23, no. 4:6–12.

———. 2005. "Functional Truth or Sexist Distortion? Assessing a Feminist Critique of Intimate Violence Reporting." *Journalism* 6, no. 1:43–65.

Mercer, S. L., L. W. Green, A. C. Rosenthal, C. G. Husten, L. K. Khan, and W. H. Dietz. 2003. "Possible Lessons from the Tobacco Experience for Obesity Control." *American Journal of Clinical Nutrition* 77, no. 4:1073S–1082S.

Niederdeppe, J., M. C. Farrelly, and D. Wenter. 2007. "Media Advocacy, Tobacco Control Policy Change, and Teen Smoking in Florida." *Tobacco Control* 16:47–52.

Pew Research Center. 2010. *New Media, Old Media: How Blogs and Social Media Agendas Relate and Differ from the Traditional Press*. Washington, D.C.: Pew Research Center.

Schooler, C. S., S. Sundar, and J. Flora. 1996. "Effects of the Stanford Five-City Project Media Advocacy Program." *Health Education and Behavior* 23:346–364.

Seevak, A. 1997. *Issue 3: Oakland Shows the Way*. Berkeley, Calif.: Berkeley Media Studies Group. http://bmsg.org/pub-issues.php.

Stead, M., H. Gerard, and E. Douglas. 2002. "The Challenge of Evaluating Complex Interventions: A Framework for Evaluating Media Advocacy." *Health Education Research* 17, no. 3:351–364.

Sterman, J. D. 2006. "Learning from Evidence in a Complex World." *American Journal of Public Health* 96, no. 3:505–514.

Stewart, L., and S. Casswell. 1993. "Media Advocacy for Alcohol Policy Support: Results from the New Zealand Community Action Project." *Health Promotion International* 8, no. 3:167–175.

Themba, M. 1999. *Making Policy Making Change: How Communities Are Taking the Law into Their Own Hands*. Berkeley, Calif.: Chardon Press.

Wallack, L. 1999. "The California Violence Prevention Initiative: Advancing Policy to Ban Saturday Night Specials." *Health Education and Behavior* 26, no. 6:841–857.

Wallack, L., L. Dorfman, D. Jernigan, and M. Themba. 1993. *Media Advocacy and Public Health: Power for Prevention*. Newbury Park, Calif.: Sage.

Wallack, L., and R. Lawrence. 2005. "Talking about Public Health: Developing America's 'Second Language.'" *American Journal of Public Health* 95, no. 4:567–570.

Wallack L., K. Woodruff, L. Dorfman, and I. Diaz. 1999. *News for a Change: An Advocates' Guide to Working with the Media*. Thousand Oaks, Calif.: Sage.

Woodruff, K., L. Dorfman, V. Berends, and P. Agron. 2003. "Coverage of Childhood Nutrition Policies in California Newspapers." *Journal of Public Health Policy* 24, no. 2:150–158.

Appendixes

APPENDIX 1

Principles of Community Building

A Policy Perspective

ANGELA GLOVER BLACKWELL

RAYMOND A. COLMENAR

Editor's note: As illustrated in this volume, the term *community building* is used in a variety of ways—for example, as communities' efforts to increase a sense of identity and cohesion or as an orientation to practice that puts community at the center of the discussion (see chapter 5). Yet *community building* also increasingly is used in reference to more macro- and multilevel efforts, often within poor neighborhoods, to build social capital and address poverty, racism, health and social equity, and related issues through partnership and policy approaches. The following list of community building principles reflects this broad orientation.

Community building may be defined as "continuous, self renewing efforts by residents and professionals to engage in collective action, aimed at problem solving and enrichment, that creates new or strengthened social networks, new capacities for group action and support, and new standards and expectations for the life of the community" (Blackwell 1999, ii). Central to community building are developing a strategic vision and building the capacity to solve not only the problem at hand but also new ones as they rise.

From a policy perspective, community building means policies that reinvest in communities, are sensitive to the particularities of place, build and sustain social capital, promote community participation, and strengthen families and neighborhoods. These are the basic tenets of community building:

- Strengthen communities holistically. In other words, support all aspects of community living, including economic opportunity, affordable housing, safety and security, youth development, transportation and utility industries, health care, early childhood, and education, rather than target bits and pieces of the community puzzle.

Reprinted from A. G. Blackwell and R. A. Colmenar, "Community Building: From Local Wisdom to Public Policy," *Public Health Reports* 115, nos. 2 and 3 (2000): 161–66, by permission of Oxford University Press.

- Build local capacity for problem solving and build relationships between communities and resource institutions. Community organizing is at the heart of community building. Policies should encourage organizational development and make linkages and partnerships between community organizations and other institutions. They should recognize the value of community assets, strengthen these, and invest in building more.
- Foster community participation in policy development and implementation. This can be done through community planning, alternative governance structures, and new financing methods that allow local authorities and even neighborhoods to have a say in the deployment of resources.
- Deal explicitly with issues of "race" and ethnicity and their role in creating social and economic deprivation. The face of poverty remains disproportionately African American and Latina(o). Community building efforts seek to level the playing field and create equitable outcomes for all groups.
- Break down the isolation of poor communities. Community improvement should be viewed in the context of the broader region. Neighborhoods must be linked to the larger context of regional development.
- Tailor programs to local conditions. The most effective solutions to local problems come from within the community itself, and steps must be taken to engage the community in local problem solving.
- Build accountability mechanisms so that efforts are tied to community standards. This enables communities to maintain improvements and monitor the progress they are making toward achieving a better quality of life.

REFERENCES

Blackwell, A. G. 1999. Foreword to *Stories of Renewal: Community Building and the Future of Urban America*, by J. Walsh. New York: Rockefeller Foundation.

Appendix 2

Action-Oriented Community
Diagnosis Procedure

EUGENIA ENG
LYNN BLANCHARD

Editor's note: Eugenia Eng and Lynn Blanchard developed the tool in this appendix over several years. Its emphasis on assessing and contributing to community competence rather than merely identifying needs amply illustrates chapter 9's perspective on community assessment. Additionally, the broad range of assessment techniques incorporated in this procedure underscores the utility of triangulation (the use of multiple methods) to provide the richest possible database for analysis.

I. Specify the target population and determine its component parts using social and demographic characteristics that may identify commonalities among groups of people.
   A. Race or ethnicity
   B. Religion
   C. Income level
   D. Occupation
   E. Age

II. Review secondary data sources, and identify possible subpopulations of interest and geographic locations.
   A. County and townships
   B. Faith-based organizations, schools, and fire districts
   C. Towns
   D. Agency service delivery areas
   E. Industries and other major employers
   F. Transportation arteries and services
   G. Health and other vital statistics

III. Conduct windshield tours of targeted areas, and note daily living conditions, resources, and evidence of problems.
  A. Housing types and conditions
  B. Recreational and commercial facilities
  C. Private and public sector services
  D. Social and civic activities
  E. Identifiable neighborhoods or residential clusters
  F. Conditions of roads and distances people must travel
  G. Maintenance of buildings, grounds, and yards

IV. Contact and interview local agency providers serving targeted areas.
  A. What are the communities most in need, and why?
  B. Which communities have histories of meeting their own needs, and how?
  C. What services are being provided by agencies or other organized groups? Which are utilized, and which are underutilized?
  D. What, in their opinion, are the major problems still facing communities they serve?
  E. Where do they recommend finding additional information to document needs?
    — Referrals to other service providers
    — Referrals to leaders of community organizations
    — Referrals to informed members of communities

V. Select a community and contact and interview community informants most frequently cited in provider interviews.
  A. What is the name their community is most commonly known as?
  B. Describe a time when there was a problem in their community that they tried to resolve.
    — How was the need determined?
    — How did the community members organize themselves?
    — Who were the influential people involved?
  C. In their opinion, what are the present needs in their community?
  D. Who would have to be involved to get things done in their community?
  E. What outside services or resources do people in their community know and use to meet their needs?
  F. What other people like themselves who know about their community do they recommend being contacted?
  G. Would they be interested in attending a meeting to find out the results from these interviews? And what do they suggest as times and places to hold such a meeting?

VI. Tabulate the results from the secondary data, the provider interviews, and the community informant interviews, and analyze the degree of convergence among the needs identified.
  A. Determine the extent of agreement/disagreement across the three lists of needs on how each identified need is defined.

B. Determine the extent of agreement/disagreement across the three lists of needs on the priority accorded to each identified need.

VII. Present the findings in meetings with community informants interviewed and other influential community members frequently cited by the providers and community informants.

A. Assess the validity of the definitions for each need, and redefine them, if necessary, according to how they are manifested in this community.

B. Determine a priority listing of needs according to interest in undertaking a solution.

C. Select a need with high priority, and determine questions that need to be answered, such as:

— Who suffers from this problem?

— When is this problem most prevalent?

— How severe are the short- and long-term consequences from this problem?

— What are the possible causes of this problem?

— What is the range of solutions for reducing or controlling this problem?

— What are the available resources and additional resources required for each possible solution?

D. Plan the next steps for finding answers to the questions.

APPENDIX 3

Challenging Ourselves

Critical Self-Reflection on Power and Privilege

CHERYL A. HYDE

One of the more common, and mistaken, assumptions that community practitioners make is thinking that because they are "fighting the good fight," they do not need to address issues regarding their own power and privilege. Yet engaging in practice under the banner of social justice (or any other "right reason") does not result in an automatic community of shared interests. Nor does it inoculate against the dividends that one might accrue because of race, class, gender, sexual orientation, or other aspect of an individual's cultural identity. Because so much of community practice is relational (see chapter 5), I suggest that it is essential for practitioners to undertake in some rigorous self-exploration as part of their broader anti-oppression work. In this appendix, I offer one approach to such critical reflection that I have used in teaching and training efforts.

Like many individuals who engage in anti-oppression teaching and practice, I ground much of my thinking in Peggy McIntosh's (1989) classic essay, "White Privilege: Unpacking the Invisible Knapsack." By delineating the many ways in which white individuals benefit from usually unrecognized or unacknowledged everyday expectations, rituals, and processes (e.g., "I am never asked to speak for all the people of my racial group" [11]), McIntosh connects the personal with broader structures that promote or protect racism and then issues a call to action: "A 'white' skin in the United States opens many doors for whites whether or not we approve of the way dominance has been conferred on us. Individual acts can palliate, but cannot end, these problems. To redesign social systems we need first to acknowledge their colossal unseen dimensions. The silences and denials surrounding privilege are the key political tool here" (12).

Part of the power of McIntosh's essay is that the reader needs to contend with the cumulative impact that seemingly minor activities can have on the perpetuation of racism. In demanding that whites dissect their racial privilege, and then take steps to challenge it, she provided a foundation for much of the anti-oppression work that followed. Comparable examinations can happen for other privileges based on class, gender, sexual orientation, and so forth; indeed, there are many, many examples in the literature (for varying approaches see Adams 1997; Connell 2005; Gerschick 1993; Goodman 2001; hooks 2000; Tappan 2006; Wallerstein 1999).

While McIntosh's contribution to antiracism work cannot be underestimated, her approach does, I think, fall short in four important ways. First, it does not distinguish between how we see our own privilege and how others might perceive or experience our identity. McIntosh is focused on the former, yet those with whom we interact also bring to the encounters an awareness (or not) of privilege as beneficiaries or as those denied such benefits. Second, she is focused on race and racism, which is understandable, but incomplete. Race is not the only attribute that shapes how we negotiate the world. Third, because of this primary focus on race, McIntosh does not capture how different cultural attributes interact and differentially shape privilege. For example, a white middle-class woman and a white working-class woman both hold racial privilege, yet the manifestation of that privilege will present differently because of class. And fourth, even though McIntosh notes that "unseen dimensions" support societal structures, she nonetheless neglects the broad, systemic impact of labor market, educational, residential, and other forms of institutionalized racism (Jones 2000). Fundamentally, hers is an intrapersonal framework for addressing racism; certainly critical but not sufficient. Grappling with these points, while still employing the essential insights of McIntosh, became the catalyst for the approach that I use.

One Approach to Critical Self-Reflection

Before outlining my approach to a *critical self-reflection* for community practitioners, I want to emphasize, first, that this is a framework that I have found useful as a learner, teacher, trainer, and practitioner. It is not, however, the only model out there and it is well worth the effort to find a process that both works well and authentically challenges you as a community practitioner. Second, two assessments have been constructed for this appendix (see tables A3.1 and A3.2), but are adapted from tools that others and I have developed (Axner, n.d.; Burghardt 2011; Katz 1978; McIntosh 1989). These tools work best when the individual pushes him- or herself to honestly complete them and then when a group debriefing can support further exploration and exchange of ideas.

Step 1: Our Complex Cultural Selves

The first step in this process is to understand the basics of one's culture and the impact on identity. Here, I am referring to the values, attitudes, beliefs, practices, and rituals that shape who we are and how we act, all of which flow from the various groups of which we are members. The primary cultural dimensions that I focus on are race, gender, citizenship status (in the United States), sexual orientation, class, religion, and physical/mental ability. There may be other dimensions that are important to an understanding of the cultural self (e.g., region of the country or level of education), but I find that these are the significant ones and serve as important springboards to self-awareness.

So turn to the Cultural Identity Inventory (table A3.1) and consider the first three columns: "cultural dimensions," "manifestations, and "interactions." For each dimension, indicate *what you are* (note any conflicting messages or challenges

TABLE A3.1.

Cultural Identity Inventory

Cultural Dimension	Manifestations	Interactions	Domination/ Subordination	Vantage Points
Indicate for each (note any conflict concerning this identifier)	What values, actions, or messages are associated with the dimension?	Does the effect of this dimension interact with any other dimension? How so?	If dominant—what privileges do you have? How have you responded? If subordinate—what have you been denied? How have you responded?	How do you understand this aspect of yourself? How do you think or experience the way others see you?
Gender				
Race				
Class				
Sexual orientation				
Citizenship				
Religion				
Physical/mental ability				
Other?				

Review and reflect on your inventory. Consider these questions:
1. What are your overall reactions to this information (any affirmations, surprises, points of confusion)?
2. Does any dimension stand out as particularly important to your overall cultural identity and why?
3. What have you learned about yourself? What next steps in this process do you see yourself taking?

to this self-identification) and whether there are any important values, messages, or actions associated with that dimension. For example, if you are a lesbian, did you receive messages of acceptance or condemnation? Or if you are a male, were you told that certain emotions, or displays of emotion, were not manly (i.e., unacceptable)? As you start this inventory, you may be able to see how different affiliations influence one another; for example, how messages about being female are shaped by one's religion. You should note these connections as they became apparent. What should begin to become apparent is that we are more than just one or two cultural attributes. The foundation of our cultural selves is the complex whole that is generated from these dimensions.

It also is important to understand that the level of influence exerted by these dimensions on one's cultural self may not be the same, and may vary over time. You may even want to note if a particular dimension is exerting a relatively strong (or weak) effect on you, and why. If we imagine these dimensions arrayed in a pie chart, some wedges will be larger than others; and sometime in the future, these wedges could be resized. This is one reason why it is unwise (and even foolish) to assume that you know a person's culture based on just one or two characteristics. What is important to you may not be as significant to another, because that individual is perhaps more concerned with, or influenced by, a different cultural dimension. There is fluidity to the components of one's identity, depending on specific challenges of a given time and place, as well as negotiating daily life.

Step 2: Privilege and Power

Within each of these dimensions there is a dominant and a subordinate group (see table A3.1, column 4). A dominant group is one that *as a group* has access to economic, social, political, and civic privileges. This access is temporal and systemic, and the privileges may be consciously sought or unconsciously acquired. The point is not whether each individual in a given group always (and knowingly) enjoys privilege or even wants it (or asked for it). It is about the *societal group*, which, through its collective activity, turns that privilege over time into societal power. So in twenty-first-century America, the privileged groups include men, whites, the middle/upper classes, heterosexuals, citizens, the able-bodied, and Christians. Continuing with the Cultural Identity Inventory, indicate whether you are a member of the dominant or subordinate group for each cultural dimension in column 4.

Individuals who find themselves mostly or exclusively in dominant-status groups are not bad or evil. Rather, by virtue of these group memberships, they have benefited from various societal "perks," whether they asked for them or not. But once such privilege is revealed, these individuals have an obligation to question, challenge, and otherwise act in good faith to work toward the dismantling of a system that generates such disproportionate rewards based on group membership. And the key here is taking action; wallowing in guilt or engaging in excessive handwringing does nothing to contribute to anti-oppression work (indeed, such responses just further underscore one's privileges).

Conversely, the individuals who find themselves mostly or exclusively in subordinate-status groups do not have license to claim victimhood and then withdraw from any constructive action. The tasks for those with less privilege is to understand the injuries, hidden or explicit, that group subordination may have caused (for an excellent analysis of this, see Sennett and Cobb's (1972) classic work, *The Hidden Injuries of Class*). How, for example, has one addressed internalized oppression? Individuals from subordinate-status groups also need to take action against oppressive structure and processes, though their paths to, and strategies for, that action will likely differ from the work that dominant-group individuals undertake.

For most of us, however, it isn't a matter of being in either all-dominant or all-subordinate groups. Instead, our cultural identities are composed of a mix. So we might have access to racial or gender privilege, yet be in subordinate groups for religion and sexual orientation. To further complicate this understanding, as noted above, not all dimensions have equal "weight" on our overall identity. We should not, however, let this complexity become an excuse for not owning the privilege that we may have. Yes, I may need to contend with a disability or gender discrimination, yet I also need to be mindful that as a white, professional person, I benefit from race and class privilege. Moreover, these societal dividends provide me with some resources with which to address or cope with subordination that results from membership in other groups. It is essential that we push ourselves to understand the implications of this complexity.

Step 3: Understanding Different Vantage Points

A final factor that I consider in this particular approach to understanding cultural identity focuses on how we see ourselves versus how others perceive us. While it is tempting to think that we have primary or sole control over the making of our cultural identity, we do not. When we interact with, or are simply in the presence of, others, our cultural identity is being shaped by that individual's ideas, beliefs, attitudes, experiences, and so forth. This may not always be fair, but in relationship building, we are always negotiating the perceptions and reactions of others and hopefully in the process can address any misperceptions.

Referring again to the Cultural Identity Inventory, column 5, push yourself to consider your subjective (self-)understanding of each cultural dimension and then the understandings of others. If you are white, how do you view this and how do you experience others viewing that? If you have a disability that is not readily apparent, how do you understand this and how might others (if at all)? The point of this aspect of the inventory is to understand that how you move through life does not necessary correspond with how others see that journey. What you think might be central to your identity may not even register with someone else. Conversely, what you minimize (such as racial privilege) may be of central import to others. Making the genuine effort to understand how others experience you is critical to relationship building and essential if you want to deconstruct and challenge your own societal privileges.

Step 4: Synthesis and Next Steps

Now comes the difficult work—digesting and then acting on what you have uncovered by virtue of doing this inventory. Consider these three questions: (1) What are your overall reactions to this inventory? (2) Does any dimension stand out as particularly important to your overall cultural identity and why? and (3) What have you learned about yourself and what next steps in this process do you see yourself taking? In other words, the inventory, in itself, does not constitute anti-oppression work. It is the precursor to anti-oppression actions. If you have pushed yourself to be honest and reflective thus far, then you have laid a foundation for considering what you need to do. Perhaps education is needed—if so, how will you go about getting it? Maybe an important relationship needs to be repaired—how might you take the steps to make amends? Or perhaps the inventory revealed that some skills, such as assertiveness training, are needed—where will you obtain this? Did you become aware of new potential problems or challenges for other groups, and if so, how might you respond?

It is tempting, and perhaps even human nature, to try to minimize the inventory messages that we don't want to know. It is not easy to think of oneself as "privileged," particularly if we don't ask for it or believe we use that privilege to our advantage. Often, we become more focused on those parts of our identity associated with subordinate-group membership and then don't see the privilege we might have. We also run the risk of becoming paralyzed by building an identity of victimization. Self-awareness, flexibility, empathy, and openness are essential; but perhaps most important is understanding that anti-oppression work takes time (Burghardt 2011; hooks 2003). Be patient with yourself and others as more authentic relationships are built.

Connecting to Community Practice

Community practitioners would be wise to take a page from the training manual of most clinical social workers, therapists, and counselors who are trained to be cognizant in the "use of self." *Use of self* may be defined as the knowledge and skill sets employed by the practitioner in such a way that he or she becomes an instrument to facilitate change (Heydt and Sherman 2005). Within the parameters of the therapeutic relationship, the practitioner is able to model and reflect transformative possibilities for the client. Yet this approach is not without its dangers, and considerable self-awareness is necessary if the practitioner wishes to minimize unnecessarily complicated or messy relationships with clients. As part of this training, these practitioners learn to recognize and address the emotions generated in the therapeutic relationship; identify what client/actions might "push buttons"; negotiate expectations of the client, including the maintenance of "appropriate" boundaries; and work through resistance and reluctance. The cultural selves of both practitioner and client significantly affect these dynamics, as cultural variations in seeking help, dealing with authority and power, and building relationships come into play (Heydt and Sherman 2005; Reupert 2006). Thus, the *use of self* is actually the *use of the cultural self.*

How does this translate to community practice? The strategic use of self is concerned with relationship building that encourages constructive change, which in many respects is the core of community practice. In order to be an effective community organizer or other practitioner who can build the relationships necessary for increasing community capacity, that individual needs to understand how his or her cultural identity affects facilitating and sustaining relationships. The

---

TABLE A3.2.

Assessment: Connecting Cultural Identity to Community Practice

Cultural Dimension	As strength/asset to my community practice	As challenge/concern to my community practice	What do I need to continue my development?
Gender			
Race			
Class			
Sexual orientation			
Citizenship			
Religion			
Physical/ mental ability			
Other?			

Note the ways in which the different components of your cultural identity have influenced you as a community practitioner. Specifically, record how that attribute has (1) given you strengths/assets and (2) provided challenges/concerns.

A. Indicate what you need to continue your development (i.e., how can you build upon your strengths or address concerns).

B. How does this assessment inform your cognizance of "use of self"?

Adapted from M. Axner, *Diversity and Community Strengths* (Lawrence, Kan.: Work Group for Community Health and Development, University of Kansas, 2011), Community Tool Box, http://ctb.ku.edu/en/tablecontents/sub_section_tools_1170.aspx. Used with permission from the Work Group for Community Health and Development, University of Kansas.

assumption is that if one does not acknowledge or address the affect of privilege, then one risks poisoning this critical aspect of practice. Moreover, the ability to build authentic connections rests on how well one understands oneself. Many practitioners want to move quickly to finding commonalities, but the realities of oppression—including the personal side—need to be addressed first (Burghardt 2011). Time, patience, and humility are essential ingredients in this process.

Building on the insights from the Cultural Identity Inventory, one needs to turn to making connections between that awareness and community practice. For this, another assessment is suggested (see table A3.2). Adapted from Axner's (n.d.) exercise, the goal is to identify how one's cultural identity helps and hinders one's community practice abilities and then extend these findings by determining what one needs to continue with his or her development. This information is then linked to an emerging use of self. By systematically engaging in this self-assessment, one will not only understand how cultural attributes of the practitioner become part of practice (for better or worse), but also begin to think strategically about how to maximize the assets and minimize the concerns.

Some Concluding Thoughts

Community practitioners typically are concerned with, and adept at analyzing, the power structures and processes that affect their constituencies. In this appendix, I have challenged practitioners to look at a more personal aspect of power—the privileges derived from membership in dominant-status groups. I have argued that one's cultural identity largely is determined by these memberships and I have highlighted the need for reflecting on the multiple and often intersecting identities we hold (woman, Latina, middle class, etc.). With a more comprehensive understanding of our cultural identities, including the ways in which the various dimensions can change and be challenged over time, we are better situated to build authentic relationships with constituents and community members. In more fully understanding how we benefit from oppressive systems, we are more likely to find the tools to dismantle the attendant structures and processes. This is a critical aspect of "fighting the good fight" and takes time, self-patience, and an openness to continued learning. In doing so, we forge better bonds with our partners and allies and, ultimately, create better communities for us all.

REFERENCES

Adams, M. 1997. "Pedagogical Frameworks for Social Justice Education." In *Teaching for Diversity and Social Justice: A Sourcebook*, edited by M. Adams, L. A. Bell and P. Griffin, 30–43. New York: Routledge.

Axner, M. n.d. "Diversity and Community Strengths." *Community Toolbox*. http://ctb.ku .edu/en/tablecontents/sub_section_tools_1170.aspx.

Burghardt, S. 2011. "Why Can't We All Just Get Along? Building Effective Coalitions While Resolving the Not-So-Hidden Realities of Race, Gender, Sexuality, and Class." *Macro Practice in Social Work for the 21st Century*, 176–214. Thousand Oaks, Calif.: Sage.

Connell, R. W. 2005. *Masculinities*. 2nd ed. Berkeley and Los Angeles: University of California Press.

Gerschick, T. 1993. "Should and Can a White, Heterosexual, Middle-Class Man Teach Students about Social Inequality and Oppression?" In *Multicultural Teaching in the University*, edited by D. Schoem, L. Frankel, X. Zuniga and E. Lewis, 200–207. Westport, Conn.: Praeger.

Goodman, D. J. 2001. *Promoting Diversity and Social Justice: Educating People from Privileged Groups*. Thousand Oaks, Calif.: Sage.

Heydt, M. J., and N. E. Sherman. 2005. "Conscious Use of Self: Tuning the Instrument of Social Work Practice with Cultural Competence." *Journal of Baccalaureate Social Work* 10, no. 2:25–40.

hooks, b. 2000a. *Feminist Theory: From Margin to Center*. 2nd ed. Boston: South End Press.

———. 2000b. *Where We Stand: Class Matters*. New York: Routledge.

———. 2003. *Teaching Community: A Pedagogy of Hope*. New York: Routledge.

Jones, C. P. 2000. "Levels of Racism: A Theoretic Framework and a Gardener's Tale." *American Journal of Public Health* 8:1212–1215.

Katz, J. 1978. *White Awareness*. Norman: University of Oklahoma Press.

McIntosh, P. 1989. "White Privilege: Unpacking the Invisible Knapsack." *Peace and Freedom*, January/February, 10–12.

Reupert, A. 2007. "Social Worker's Use of Self." *Clinical Social Work Journal* 35:107–116.

Sennett, R., and J. Cobb. 1972. *The Hidden Injuries of Class*. New York: W. W. Norton.

Tappan, M. B. 2006. "Reframing Internalized Oppression and Internalized Domination: From the Psychological to the Sociocultural." *Teachers College Record* 108, no. 10:2115–2144.

Wallerstein, N. 1999. "Power between Evaluator and Community: Research Relationships within New Mexico's Healthier Communities." *Social Science and Medicine* 49:39–53.

APPENDIX 4

A Ladder of Community Participation in Public Health

MARY ANNE MORGAN

JENNIFER LIFSHAY

The Ladder of Community Participation illustrates a range of approaches that can be used to engage diverse communities around traditional and emerging public health issues. The Ladder provides a conceptual framework to help public health leaders plan and evaluate community engagement efforts. It can be used to stimulate internal dialogue and frame discussions with community partners about how to work effectively to accomplish shared public health goals. Contra Costa Health Services developed the Ladder based on more than ten years of experience with engaging the local community in a range of public health issues. It also builds on earlier work in the field (e.g., Arnstein 1969; Chess et al. 1995). More information about the Ladder of Community Participation and its application is available in the article "Community Engagement in Public Health," which can be found at http://cchealth.org/groups/public_health/pdf/community_engagement_in_ph.pdf.

Community Leads	Community members initiate and direct the effort	• Community organizes and advocates for government response
Power Sharing	Community members and local health department (LHD) define and solve problems together	• Partnerships and collaborations • Meetings called jointly by government, community • Funding of community groups to implement projects • Community oversight and monitoring of activities
Bridging	Community members are conduits of information and input to and from local health departments	• *Promotoras* • Patient navigators
Comprehensive Consultation and Influence	LHD asks community members for substantive ongoing input	• Advisory boards, task forces, etc. • Ongoing dialogue processes
Limited Input/Consult	LHD asks community members for specific, periodic input	• Focus groups • Client surveys, questionnaires • Town hall meetings, public hearings • Photovoice
Inform and Educate	Health department provides education to the community	• Media campaigns, press releases • Health education classes • Brochures, newsletters
Health Department Leads	LHD initiates and directs the community to act	• Public health outbreak investigations • Legal and enforcement actions • Emergency response (earthquakes, toxic spills)

FIGURE A4.1   A Ladder of Community Participation in Public Health

REFERENCES

Arnstein, S. R. 1969 "A Ladder of Citizen Participation." *Journal of American Institute of Planners* 35, no. 4:216–224.

Chess, C., B. J. Hance, and P. M. Sandman. 1995. "Ladder of Citizen Participation." In *Improving Dialogue with Communities: A Short Guide For Government Risk Communication*. State of New Jersey—Department of Environmental Protection, Division of Science and Research and Environmental Communication Research Program, New Jersey Agricultural Experiment Station, Cook College, Rutgers University.

APPENDIX 5

Coalition Member Assessment

TOM WOLFF

For each item, please circle the number that best shows your agreement with the statement about that aspect of the coalition.

VISION: PLANNING, IMPLEMENTATION, PROGRESS

1 = Strongly agree   5 = Strongly disagree

1. The coalition has a clear vision and mission.	1 2 3 4 5
2. There is consistent follow-through on coalition activities.	1 2 3 4 5
3. The coalition uses activities that are effective in helping reach its goals.	1 2 3 4 5
4. The coalition has developed targeted action planning for community and systems change.	1 2 3 4 5
5. The coalition effectively reconciles differences among members.	1 2 3 4 5
6. The coalition engages in collaborative problem solving of jointly shared problems, resulting in innovative solutions.	1 2 3 4 5
7. The coalition expands available resources by having partners bring resources to the table or identify others with resources.	1 2 3 4 5

LEADERSHIP AND MEMBERSHIP

1 = Strongly agree   5 = Strongly disagree

8. The coalition develops and supports leadership.	1 2 3 4 5
9. There are opportunities for coalition members to take leadership roles, and members are willing to take them.	1 2 3 4 5

Adapted from *The Power of Collaborative Solutions: Six Principles and Effective Tools for Building Healthy Communities* (San Francisco: Jossey-Bass, 2010). Reprinted with permission of John Wiley and Sons Inc. and the author.

10. Leadership responsibilities are shared in the coalition.	1 2 3 4 5
11. The coalition creates greater ownership by partners in joint ventures and projects.	1 2 3 4 5
12. The coalition has broad and appropriate membership for the issue it is addressing.	1 2 3 4 5
13. The coalition membership is diverse.	1 2 3 4 5
14. Members display commitment and they take on tasks.	1 2 3 4 5

STRUCTURE

1 = Strongly agree   5 = Strongly disagree

15. The coalition has regular meeting cycles that members can expect.	1 2 3 4 5
16. The coalition has active workgroups and committees.	1 2 3 4 5
17. Members get agendas for the meetings prior to the meeting and minutes afterward.	1 2 3 4 5
18. The work of the meeting, as outlined in the agenda, gets accomplished.	1 2 3 4 5
19. The coalition has a viable organization structure that functions competently.	1 2 3 4 5

COMMUNICATION

1 = Strongly agree   5 = Strongly disagree

20. Communication among members of the coalition is effective.	1 2 3 4 5
21. Communication between the coalition and the broader community related to its chosen issues is effective.	1 2 3 4 5
22. Coalition members are listened to and heard.	1 2 3 4 5

ACTIVITIES

1 = Strongly agree   5 = Strongly disagree

23. Information gets exchanged at coalition meetings.	1 2 3 4 5
24. The coalition develops new materials and new programs.	1 2 3 4 5
25. The coalition advocates for change.	1 2 3 4 5
26. New and more perspectives are shared on issues.	1 2 3 4 5
27. Outcomes are more comprehensive than those achieved without a coalition.	1 2 3 4 5

Outcomes

Open-Ended Question

28. What changes occurred because of the coalition that otherwise would not have occurred?

1 = Strongly agree   5 = Strongly disagree

29. The coalition has been able to achieve its goals and create concrete outcomes.	1 2 3 4 5
30. The coalition is serving as a catalyst for positive change related to the issues it has chosen to work on.	1 2 3 4 5
31. The coalition creates community changes as seen in changes in programs, policies, and practices that enhance people's lives.	1 2 3 4 5
32. The coalition has effected changes in programs, policies, and practices in many sectors and systems in the community related to the issues it has chosen to work on.	1 2 3 4 5
Definitions Programs can be new or modified interventions, new protocols, and new products, such as educational materials, marketing or branding materials, and new presentations. Policies can include facility or agency policies, state policies, federal policies, or institutional or agency policies. For practice changes, consider changes at facilities as well as other institutions and organizations; changes by various practitioners (including physicians, nursing or social work staff members, and facility administrators); changes by government; or changes by individuals affected by the issue.	

Open-Ended Question

33. What specific changes in programs, policies, and practices have you seen that were created by the work of this coalition?

1 = Strongly agree   5 = Strongly disagree

34. The outcomes created are the ones that matter.	1 2 3 4 5
35. After each activity or project, the leadership of the committee or task force evaluates how it went in order to learn from experience.	1 2 3 4 5

RELATIONSHIPS

1 = Strongly agree   5 = Strongly disagree

36. Old or existing partnerships have been enhanced as a result of the coalition.	1 2 3 4 5
37. New relationships have been built with new partners as a result of the coalition.	1 2 3 4 5
38. Members of the community related to the issue now know more about each other's resources as a result of the coalition.	1 2 3 4 5

SYSTEMS OUTCOMES

1 = Strongly agree   5 = Strongly disagree

39. As a result of the coalition's formation, systems changes have happened, including changes in relationships in the larger community that works on the issues the coalition has identified and in the capacity of the coalition to address emerging issues.	1 2 3 4 5
40. We have seen positive changes in the community that works on our issue(s) as a result of the coalition: partners are more collaborative and more cooperative.	1 2 3 4 5
41. The coalition helped the people in the community gain access to more resources both within and outside the coalition in order to reach their goals.	1 2 3 4 5

BENEFITS FROM PARTICIPATION

1 = Strongly agree   5 = Strongly disagree

42. The community and its residents are better off today because of this coalition.	1 2 3 4 5

43. I have benefited from participation in the coalition through

    a. Building relationships with other coalition members

    b. Exchanging information with others—networking

    c. Working with others on issues of importance

    d. Being part of a process that brings about meaningful change

44. My agency has benefited from its participation in the coalition through

    a. Modified programs

    b. Developing new programs

    c. Gaining access to new or more resources

    d. Creating solutions collaboratively with other coalition partners

OVERALL RATING

OPEN-ENDED QUESTIONS

45. What changes happened in your own organization as a result of the coalition that would not otherwise have occurred?

46. What happened that surprised you that you did not plan for as an outcome?

47. As a result of the coalition work, what are the three most significant things you have learned?

APPENDIX 6

Community Mapping and Digital Technology

Tools for Organizers

JOSH KIRSCHENBAUM

JASON CORBURN

Countless questions about socioeconomic conditions, health, development opportunities, and neighborhood change can be answered by community mapping. Mapping is the visual representation of data by geography or location, linking information to place to support social and economic change on a community level. Mapping is a powerful tool for two reasons: (1) it makes patterns based on place much easier to identify and analyze and (2) it provides a visual way of communicating those patterns to a broad audience, quickly and dramatically, which can help residents organize as they "see" their place in a new way. The central value of a map is that it helps tell a story about what is happening in our communities. These stories can help bring people into organizing efforts, deepen local understanding of complex issues linking place and health, and support decision making and consensus building by translating place-based knowledge into program design, policy development, organizing, and advocacy. As activists increasingly use web-based mapping platforms and link these to social media and handheld devices, digital maps of places hold the potential to transform community organizing for health equity. But they may also place new demands on activists to be tech savvy and possibly overreliant on technology to address the social and political change they seek (Corburn 2005).

Community Mapping: A Visual Narrative

Community mapping is a vibrant way of telling a neighborhood's story. It can highlight the rich array of community assets, display the concentration of childhood asthma, analyze the relationship between income and location of services, or document vacant lots and buildings.

The products of community mapping can take several forms. *Context maps* represent one or a few variables by a broad unit of geography (for example, income level by census tract). *Display maps* are more complex, illustrating single or multiple variables by smaller units of geography (such as the condition of individual properties at the parcel level). *Analytical maps* are the most complex, layering and analyzing multiple variables by various levels of geography. An analytical map might combine income at the census tract level and condition of individual properties at the parcel level and highlight how the two variables relate to each other.

Community maps can be hand drawn or computer generated. Some complex computer-generated maps are also interactive, using Internet technologies that allow participants to analyze data and create other maps based on the locations and kinds of data that interest them. Increasingly, community practitioners are using computer software such as geographic information systems (GIS) for creating maps and analyzing data. As defined by the U.S. Geological Survey (2003), GIS are "computer system(s) capable of assembling, storing, manipulating, and displaying geographically referenced information—data identified according to location." GIS are not just tools for making maps or visually displaying data; they are used for analyzing many layers of data, allowing users to see information over time. The term *GIS* usually refers to the type of software used, while *geographic information science (GISc)* is the term used to describe the development, analysis, use, users, and often public application and display of GIS (Mark 2000).

More recently, web-based platforms have allowed community organizers to create maps without investing in expensive software or requiring intensive technical training. Web-based maps can also be shared more widely and easily than can GIS-generated maps; often all that is required is an Internet or cell phone connection. One of the most widely used and free web-based mapping tools is Google's My Maps (maps.google.com). Using the My Maps feature in Google Maps, organizers and community residents can mark assets and liabilities in their community, share this information easily on the web with others, and allow a number of users to edit or "ground truth" this information over time. This program, unlike more difficult-to-use GIS software, allows users to easily add descriptive text into the map, embed photos and videos, and link a series of community maps to an aerial or satellite image of the earth's surface, called Google Earth (www.google.com/earth/index.html).

How to Use Community Mapping

Community mapping involves five broad steps, some of which can be implemented simultaneously. The process begins and ends with local communities, and each step builds on the information obtained in a previous step.

Step 1: Identify Community Issues and Build a Community Mapping Collaborative

All community mapping efforts start with community-based organizations (CBOs) and residents and their in-depth understanding of community conditions, assets, and problems. Community knowledge is used to identify issues and problems; set benchmarks, goals, and outcomes; locate opportunities for revitalization; frame data-gathering efforts; determine the appropriate types of geography and maps; and use maps for community building purposes. By designing and leading the mapping process, community residents and organizations are better positioned to ensure that the maps offer community benefits and accurately reflect community needs. Community leadership also promotes community values in the mapping process and better equips community groups to use the resulting maps for advocacy and organizing purposes.

Step 2: Determine the Appropriate Geography

Selecting the appropriate geographies is one of the first decisions in the mapping process. Community mapping projects can use a range of geographic units for mapping, ranging from individual parcels to census tracts to entire neighborhoods. Most initiatives will include several different geographies, from parcels or census tracts to cities and counties, which can allow for a range of data inputs and comparisons across space. The smaller the geography, the more detailed the data, but it may be more time intensive to acquire. One benefit of online mapping tools is that they are not limited by questions of scale; activists can input their own data and display at various scales. Decisions about appropriate scale should be driven by research hypotheses, organizing goals, and models of social change.

Step 3: Collect Data

Community mapping initiatives are only as strong as the data on which the maps are built. Maps that are most useful in a community context will likely consist of information from many sources while also reflecting community members' lived experiences. There are four major data types used in community mapping projects: public statistics, commercial data, administrative data, and survey data.

PUBLIC STATISTICS. Census data are the primary source of public data for community mapping. They can be categorized into five major groups: demographics, socioeconomic characteristics, housing, business and the economy, and transportation. The American Fact Finder (http://factfinder.Census.gov/servlet/BasicFactservlet) is particularly useful for creating thematic maps and setting the geographic area and the specific census characteristics to be mapped.

ADMINISTRATIVE DATA. Administrative data collected by state and local government agencies (such as tax assessors, police departments, city agencies, zoning offices, and school districts) are key inputs for community mapping projects. These data are usually available for small levels of geography (smaller than census tracts) and often for parcel-level mapping. Public health data collected by cities and states is increasingly including geographic information that allows for spatial analysis and mapping.

COMMERCIAL DATA. Data are available for sale from companies such as DataQuick and Dun and Bradstreet and from real estate brokers and others seeking current data about available properties often use them. This information is expensive, however, so only a few community mapping efforts use this resource.

ORIGINAL DATA: SURVEYS. Many community mapping and GIS projects augment public and administrative data with information that community organizations collect themselves. Such original data collection is the basis of many asset-mapping programs in which community groups and residents map local assets and resources. Data may be collected about assets such as social networks, health, recreation facilities, volunteer opportunities, trees and green spaces, murals, and community gathering sites. They can be gathered by volunteers, including youth, students, and residents. For original data collection to be most useful, data collectors must know why they are collecting the information and how it will be used. Community-gathered information for mapping is increasingly done using widely available technology, such as cell phones. For example, a nonprofit group called Ushahadi has developed free software with which community residents can send information via text message, e-mail, Twitter, and web forms to a website that maps this information on a public website (www.ushahidi.com).

Step 4: Create Maps Using GIS and Other Technologies

Some mapping projects require a significant technology investment, such as GIS. There are five components of GIS:

HARDWARE. Hardware is the physical computer on which GIS operates. GIS software runs on a wide range of hardware types, from centralized computer servers to desktop computers. You do not have to buy a special kind of computer to run GIS. Because GIS requires a very large amount of memory, however, it is often a good idea to dedicate a computer to the project.

SOFTWARE. GIS software provides the functions and tools needed to store, analyze, and display geographic information. (For a comprehensive review of GIS software packages, see http://www.geoplan.ufl.edu/software.html.)

DATA. Data are the most important ingredients of GIS projects. GIS transforms tabular databases into layered geographic information or maps.

PEOPLE. GIS technology is of limited value without the involvement of people who have the capacity to manage it and develop plans for applying it to real-world problems.

METHODS. A successful GIS project operates according to a well-designed working collaborative and implementation plan.

As noted, mapping community data requires not only investments in hardware and software but also staff support. For most community groups, developing the in-house technological capacity is too expensive. Therefore, many community organizations develop partnerships with technology or mapping intermediaries, such as universities, to maintain GIS technology.

Because community mapping projects often use computers and the Internet, low-income and low-wealth communities may need to strengthen their technology infrastructure Even though community groups are not expected to build and maintain GIS applications, they must have the technological capacity to be informed partners and users of these systems. However, building organizational and community capacity to use technology may have secondary benefits, such as job skills and other educational opportunities.

Web-based mapping technologies can often complement or in some cases take the place of GIS-generated maps. The Google maps applications mentioned above allow community activists to create professional-looking maps without the expense or learning required of GIS. These free web-based programs may allow organizers to leapfrog the entry barriers facing the use of GIS. However, few of these mapping applications include GIS-like detailed spatial analyses that accompany mapping.

Step 5: Use Maps to Promote Community Building, Organizing, and Neighborhood Revitalization

The ultimate purpose of community mapping is to improve programs, policy advocacy, and research. Effective community groups will use GIS outputs and maps as a foundation for campaigns to promote community building and equitable development. In this step of the mapping process, community organizations transform data and spatial analysis into action. Web-based mapping applications offer easy, low-cost mapping opportunities for community organizations that are reluctant or unable to invest in more intensive technologies, such as GIS. As handheld devices and mobile computing power have become increasingly available to community organizations, mapping has become a regular part of campaigns to promote more healthy and equitable communities. Yet, like any other technology, these are just tools; are never deterministic; and will increasingly demand that community organizations be not just consumers, but developers and producers of the next generation of mapping technologies to ensure that they serve community, not just corporate, interests.

REFERENCES

Corburn, J. 2005. *Street Science: Community Knowledge and Environmental Health Justice.* Cambridge, Mass.: MIT Press.

Mark, D. M. 2000. "Geographic Information Science: Critical Issues in an Emerging Cross-Disciplinary Research Domain." *Journal of the Urban and Regional Information Systems Association* 12, no. 1:45–54.

U.S. Geological Survey. 2003. "Geographic Information Systems." http://erg.usgs.gov/isb/pubs/gis_poster/.

Appendix 7

Using Force Field and "SWOT" Analysis as Strategic Tools in Community Organizing

MEREDITH MINKLER

CHRIS COOMBE

More than sixty years ago, German social psychologist Kurt Lewin (1947) developed what he termed "force field analysis" as a way of understanding social situations and promoting change. Half a century later, a related tool, "SWOT analysis," is being widely applied by health and social service professionals and community groups alike to examine the "strengths, weaknesses, opportunities, and threats" that exist relative to their organizations as a technique for strategic planning (Barry 1997). Although neither of these tools was designed with community organizers in mind, both have been used effectively in community organizing practice and are summarized briefly here.

Force Field Analysis

Lewin (1947) argued that social situations exist in a state of "quasi-stationary social equilibria" caused by driving and resisting forces that work in opposition to one another. When the forces are weighted most heavily on the driving side, change is likely to take place. When the resisting or restraining forces are most powerful, however, no change is likely. Strengthening existing driving forces, or adding new ones, helps increase the likelihood of change, as does removing or weakening resisting forces. Of the two, however, the latter is most likely to enable change to occur that is of a more sustained or lasting nature.

Force field analysis has been used to help think through the challenges facing a local HIV/AIDS prevention and organizing project at a difficult time in its history (Wohlfeiler 1997); to help nutritionists and their community partners plan their fight against food vending machines in school cafeterias; to promote adolescents' involvement in their own health care (MacDuffie and DePoy 2004); and to assist health department staff as they assess the forces working for and against community involvement in getting a local antismoking ordinance (Ellis et al. 1995).

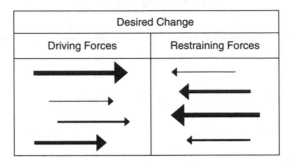

FIGURE A7.1 Sample Model for Conducting a Force Field Analysis. Label each arrow. Thickness of arrow indicates relative strength of each force. Alternatively, numbers may be used, with 1 indicating weakest and 5 the strongest forces.

To conduct a force field analysis as part of a community organizing effort, draw a diagram as in figure A7.1 and follow these simple steps:

1. On a large chalkboard, whiteboard, or large piece of butcher block paper or easel pad, write the change being sought in the middle of the page, atop a line running down the paper or board. On one side of the line, have group members list those factors or forces working for the change they want to see. These forces might include, for example, buy-in from the president of the board or other key players, likely positive media attention as a result of the change, and so on.
2. On the other side, list those forces likely to work against a change (e.g., fiscal costs, opposition of a key coalition or other community group, labor-intensive nature of enacting the change).
3. Beneath each force listed draw an arrow whose thickness is used to illustrate the relative strength of that factor. Group members may, if preferred, use numbers from 1 to 5 to indicate the relative strength of the force under consideration.
4. Brainstorm first about which resisting forces can most easily be removed or weakened and how this might occur, having a note taker keep track of the ideas generated. Remove or change the thickness of the arrows (or change the number assigned to denote weakened strength) to indicate which forces can be weakened or removed through the various tactics discussed.
5. Repeat this process for the driving forces, in this case looking at which forces can be strengthened and what new driving forces might be added to increase the chances of success in achieving the desired change.
6. Decide on "next steps": which strategies will you use in what order, and who will be responsible for follow up on each of the action steps involved?

SWOT Analysis

Although SWOT analysis is most often used in the field of business as part of corporate strategic planning, it has become a common planning approach within community organizations and health departments and can be a powerful tool for developing organizing strategies (Barry 1997). Also called *environmental scanning* or *situation analysis*, SWOT is a process by which participants assess where they are by identifying strengths and weaknesses internal to their organizations and opportunities and threats in the external environment that will influence the effectiveness of potential organizing efforts. The group then develops strategies that maximize strengths and take advantage of opportunities while overcoming weaknesses and avoiding threats. Although there are a number of ways of conducting a SWOT analysis, one that works well in a community setting proceeds in the following steps:

1. Place four large sheets of paper on the wall or a tabletop, with the papers labeled, respectively, "Strengths," "Weaknesses," "Opportunities," and "Threats."

2. Explain to the group that *Strengths* and *Weaknesses* refer to factors *internal* to their organization or agency, and thus ideally within their control; *Opportunities* and *Threats* refer to forces in the *external* environment, such as a budget cut or a new and community-friendly mayor or city council, that may have an impact on the organizing issue at hand.

3. Give each participant a set of several blank stick-on notes or other small adhesive papers in each of four colors, using a different color for each of the four categories. Have each participant think of important SWOT factors and write each on individual small colored papers, for example, a Strength on yellow, a Weakness on blue, and so forth.

4. Have team members place the colored papers they have filled out on the appropriate large sheets of paper (S, W, O, or T).

5. As a group, look for common themes in each area and cluster items together by moving the colored papers around as needed. Add any new factors that come up and identify urgent or high priority issues.

6. Stepping back, look across all four areas to identify the strategic or critical issues that emerge from the discussion. A critical issue is typically a challenge, dynamic tension, or conflict around which change needs to occur. For example, your environmental justice organization has just received a grant for neighborhood organizing (Strength), a new toxic waste incinerator is being proposed for a high-asthma neighborhood (Threat), and a key planning commission official has been exposed for accepting bribes from the industry backing the incinerator (Opportunity).

7. Look for a "fit" between different forces and your core issue. Prioritize strategic issues by importance and timing, decide what area to focus on, and brainstorm possible scenarios.

Several variations on the SWOT analysis exist, including approaches for creating strategic action plans to prioritize issues by available resources, appropriate timelines, and barriers to reaching goals (VeneKlasen and Miller 2002). A variant

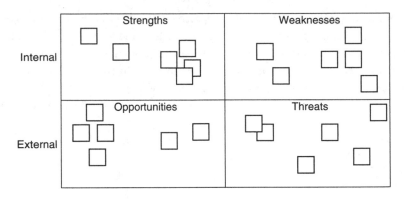

FIGURE A7.2 A Simple "SWOT" Analysis Schema. Small squares represent a stick-on note or other small adhesive paper, color-coded by whether the idea listed on each represents an S, W, O, or T. These later may be clustered to indicate overlapping or related issues.

of the SWOT analysis created specifically with advocates and organizers in mind was developed by the Berkeley Media Studies Group (BMSG) for use in developing "a coordinated strategy toward policy goals" (BMSG 1995, 1). Called the ACTION framework for strategic planning, this approach involves group brainstorming around factors that can advance or serve as obstacles to the group's policy goals, the new information or intelligence needed (which might include polls, media monitoring, etc.), and the most important "next steps" to be taken to advance the overall policy goal. The acronym ACTION is used by BMSG to capture the following elements:

Assets and strengths

Challenges, barriers, or liabilities

Threats (external)

Information needs

Opportunities

Next steps

Whether using force field analysis, the SWOT tool, or variations such as ACTION, approaches to environmental or strategic analysis like these lay the foundation for generating potential organizing and policy advocacy strategies and provide criteria for making informed planning decisions.

REFERENCES

Barry, B. W. 1997. *Strategic Planning Workbook for Nonprofit Organizations.* St. Paul, Minn.: Amherst H. Wilder Foundation.
Berkeley Media Studies Group (BMSG). 1995. *ACTION Framework for Strategic Planning.* Berkeley, Calif.: Berkeley Media Studies Group.

Ellis, G., D. F. Reed, and H. Scheider. 1995. "Mobilizing a Low-Income African-American Community around Tobacco Control: A Force Field Analysis." *Health Education Quarterly* 22, no. 4:443–457.

Lewin, K. 1947. "Quasi-stationary Social Equilibria and the Problem of Social Change." In *Readings in Social Psychology*, edited by T. M. Newcomb and E. L. Hartley. New York: Holt, Rinehart and Winston.

MacDuffie, H., and E. DePoy. 2004. "Force Field Analysis: A Model for Promoting Adolescents' Involvement in Their Own Health Care." *Health Promotion Practice* 5:306.

VeneKlasen, L., and V. Miller. 2002. *A New Weave of Power, People, and Politics*. Oklahoma City, Okla.: World Neighbors.

Wohlfeiler, D. 1997. "Community Organizing and Community Building among Gay and Bisexual Men: The Stop AIDS Project." In *Community Organizing and Community Building for Health*, edited by M. Minkler, 230–243. New Brunswick, N.J.: Rutgers University Press.

Appendix 8

A Checklist for Action

MARK S. HOMAN

The following checklist will become so routine that these questions will frame your perspective of any setting for action. Your need to answer these questions will guide everything you do, and your ability to answer them will powerfully increase the likelihood of your success.

- From whom do we want to get a response?
- What responses do we want to get?
- What action or series of actions has the best chance of producing that response?
- Are the members of our organization able and willing to take these actions?
- How do the actions we decide to take lead to the needed development of our organization?
- How do our actions produce immediate gains in a way that helps us achieve our long-term goals?
- Is everything we are doing relevant to the outcomes we want to produce?
- How will we assess the effectiveness of our chosen approach to help refine the next steps we should take?
- What are we doing to keep this interesting?

Reprinted from M. S. Homan, *Promoting Community Change: Making It Happen in the Real World*, 5th ed. (Pacific Grove, Calif.: Brooks/Cole, 2011), 381. Reprinted with permission of the publisher.

APPENDIX 9

Criteria for Creating Triggers or Codes for Freirian Organizing

NINA WALLERSTEIN

Editor's note: As described in chapters 3 and 4, Brazilian scholar of adult education Paulo Freire's "education for critical consciousness" has become an important approach in community organizing both nationally and internationally, particularly with low-income and less-educated groups. One of the steps in the Freirian approach, as in other popular education methods, involves the development of triggers or codes, which are discussion catalysts based on themes that emerge in group discussion and are re-presented back to the group to facilitate deeper dialogue about root causes, other consequences of the issue or problem, and action plans to bring about change. In this appendix, Freirian scholar and educator Nina Wallerstein presents her own tips for the selection and development of codes or triggers that can facilitate this process in either classroom or community situations.

To help facilitate groups in developing triggers or codes, the following steps may be helpful.

1. Identify the issue that you want to address. This issue should be a problem that people can relate to on an emotional and social level. It should be an issue that will trigger full participation in the discussion. In choosing an issue, think about the following criteria:
   a. It should be familiar to your class or community participants and should represent a problem that people care about and want to solve.
   b. It should include both a personal and a sociocultural dimension, so that discussion can lead to both personal and social actions to change the situation.

Reprinted by permission of the author.

   c. It should not present an overwhelming problem, but should enable participants during the discussion to strategize short- or long-term actions for change.
2. Identify the physical form that will best portray this issue: a sociodrama, written role play, song, slide or series of slides, video segment, or picture. Good visual triggers contain people so that discussion participants can imagine what the people in the picture might be feeling. Juxtaposition of images also works to present the multiple sides of an issue.
3. Role plays or sociodramas can be easily developed with the following steps:
   a. Brainstorm a list of possible feelings or reactions to the issue.
   b. Decide on each character who will represent the different feelings or reactions. (It is best to have a minimum of three characters with three points of view. With two characters, the problem can become too polarized for people to identify solutions.)
   c. Create the scripts for each character. This script can be either written out verbatim or sketched out as an outline.
   d. Remember not to write a solution into the script, but only present the problem. The action strategies should come out of the group discussion following the role play or sociodrama.

Keep it short. Each role play or sociodrama should last no more than five or ten minutes.

Appendix 10

Scale for Measuring Perceptions of Control at the Individual, Organizational, Neighborhood, and beyond-the-Neighborhood Levels

BARBARA A. ISRAEL
AMY J. SCHULZ
EDITH A. PARKER
ADAM B. BECKER

Note from Barbara Israel: My colleagues at the University of Michigan and I initially developed the Perceived Control Scale with respondents from Detroit, Michigan, who are primarily of African American or European American descent (Israel et al. 1994; Schulz et al. 1995). The Revised Perceived Control Scale presented here is a revision of this earlier scale and has been tested with African American women living on the east side of Detroit as part of a longitudinal, community-based, participatory research project known as the Eastside Village Health Worker Partnership (Becket et al. 2002, 2005; Schulz et al. 1998; Schulz et al. 2003).

The scale assesses individual perceptions of control or influence at four levels of analysis—individual, organizational, neighborhood, and beyond the neighborhood. In accordance with our conceptualization of empowerment across all four levels, the intent of the items at the individual level is to assess perceptions of individual influence over decisions that affect the individual's life in general. At the organizational and neighborhood levels, the intent is to assess both perceptions of individual influence within an organizational and neighborhood context and the perceived influence of the organization and neighborhood. Items measuring perceived control beyond the neighborhood level are intended to assess the perceptions of influence of the neighborhood in broader areas, such as the city, state, and national levels (Becker et al. 2002, 2005). Questions measuring perceived control at the organizational level pertain to the organization that respondents identify as being most important to them.

The scale provides a partial measure of empowerment, examining individual perceptions of control or influence at multiple levels. It does not, however, measure the development of conscientization, or critical consciousness (see chapters 2 and 12), nor does it assess the broader social, political, economic, and cultural contexts that affect empowerment. The scale is further limited in that it does not measure actual control or obtain a collective assessment, at the organizational, neighborhood, or beyond-the-neighborhood levels of perceived or actual control. For these reasons, we strongly suggest that this survey instrument be used in combination with qualitative approaches such as focus groups, community observations, and in-depth semistructured interviews. Finally, concepts of neighborhood, community, control, and empowerment may differ across cultures and regions, and these differences should be taken into account when the scale is adapted to other areas or population groups.

Despite these limitations, the perceived control indices presented here have considerable potential use for health educators and other social change professionals engaged in empowerment interventions. See Israel and colleagues (1994) and Becker and colleagues (2002) for a more detailed look at the instrument's conceptual grounding and development, its strengths and limitations, and its applications in the field.

Revised Perceived Control Scale Items:
Multiple Levels of Empowerment Indices

For the first nine items, the interviewer asked the participants, "For each of the following, please tell me whether you agree strongly, agree somewhat, disagree somewhat, or disagree strongly."

1. I can influence decisions that affect my life.
2. I am satisfied with the amount of influence I have over decisions that affect my life.
3. I can influence decisions that affect my neighborhood.
4. I am satisfied with the amount of influence I have over decisions that affect my neighborhood.
5. By working together with others in my neighborhood, I can influence decisions that affect my neighborhood.
6. My neighborhood has influence over things that affect my life.
7. By working together, people in my neighborhood can influence decisions that affect the neighborhood.
8. People in this neighborhood have connections to people who can influence what happens outside the neighborhood.
9. People in my neighborhood work together to influence decisions at the city, state, or national level.

Participants were asked a number of general questions about organizational membership. For the last five items of the Revised Perceived Control Scale, the interviewer asked the participants, "Thinking about the organization that you identified as most important to you, would you say that you agree strongly, agree somewhat, disagree somewhat, or disagree strongly with the following statements?"

10. I can influence the decisions that this organization makes.
11. This organization has influence over decisions that affect my life.
12. This organization is effective in achieving its goals.
13. This organization can influence decisions that affect the neighborhood or community.
14. I am satisfied with the amount of influence I have over decisions that this organization makes.

Indices

- Perceived control at the individual level includes items 1 and 2 above (alpha = .61).
- Perceived control at the organizational level includes items 10 through 14 above (alpha = .67).
- Perceived control at the neighborhood level includes items 3 through 7 above (alpha = .77).
- Perceived control beyond the neighborhood level includes items 8 and 9 above (alpha = .64).
- Perceived control at multiple levels includes all fourteen items above (alpha = .77).

(The alpha coefficients presented here were generated from the longitudinal survey questionnaire administered as part of the Eastside Village Health Worker Partnership [Becker et al. 2002]).

REFERENCES

Becker, A. B., B. A. Israel, A. J. Schulz, E. A. Parker, and L. Klem. 2002. "Predictors of Perceived Control among African American Women in Detroit: Exploring Empowerment as a Multi-level Construct." *Health Education and Behavior* 29, no. 6:699–715.
———. 2005. "Stress, Empowerment, and Urban Health: Health Effects of Perceived Control at Multiple Levels Among African American Women in Detroit, Michigan." *Journal of Urban Health* 82, no. 1:122–141.
Israel, B. A., B. N. Checkoway, A. J. Schulz, and M. A. Zimmerman. 1994. "Health Education and Community Empowerment: Conceptualizing and Measuring Perceptions of Individual, Organizational, and Community Control." *Health Education Quarterly* 21, no. 2:149–170.
Schulz, A. J., B. A. Israel, E. A. Parker, M. Lockett, Y. Hill, and R. Wills. 2003. "Engaging Women in Community-Based Participatory Research for Health: The East Side Village Health Worker Partnership." In *Community-Based Participatory Research for Health*, edited by M. Minkler and N. Wallerstein, 293–315. San Francisco: Jossey-Bass.
Schulz, A. J., B. A. Israel, M. A. Zimmerman, and B. N. Checkoway. 1995. "Empowerment as a Multi-level Construct: Perceived Control at the Individual, Organizational, and Community Levels." *Health Education Research* 10, no. 3:309–327.
Schulz, A. J., E. A. Parker, B. A. Israel, A. B. Becker, B. J. Maciak, and R. Hollis. 1998. "Conducting a Participatory Community-Based Survey: Collecting and Interpreting Data for a Community Health Intervention on Detroit's East Side." *Journal of Public Health Management and Practice* 4, no. 2:10–24.

APPENDIX 11

Policy Bingo

MARY M. LEE
REBECCA FLOURNOY
JUDITH BELL
VICTOR RUBIN

An important step for new policy advocates is to understand the terms commonly used in the policy process. "Policy bingo" is a fun way to become familiar with some of those terms. (This version is based on land use bingo, a similar game developed by Catalina Garzon and others at the Pacific Institute [www.pacinstitute.org].) There are many additional resources that can be helpful. A comprehensive set of tools can be found in PolicyLink's *Advocating for Policy Change* (http://www.policylink.org/site/c.lkIXLbMNJrE/b.5153189/k.47F4/Advocating_For_Change.htm). The reader also is directed to the PolicyLink report *Advocating for Equitable Development*, (http://www.policylink.org/atf/cf/%7B97C6D565-BB43–406D-A6D5-ECA3BBF35AF0%7D/AdvocatingForED_final.pdf). For more information about specific policy issues, please visit the PolicyLink website (www.policylink.org).

Instructions

Create policy bingo cards by creating grids with four categories times four categories, and randomly insert terms from the "Terms and Definitions" list. Make sure you do not have any term listed more than once per card. See the sample cards. Ideally you will have as many different cards as you have participants in the game.

1. Prepare copies of your policy bingo cards and handouts of the "Terms and Definitions" list. Bring poker chips, coins, or other materials for participants to be able to mark items as they will be called out during the game.
2. On the day of the event, distribute (1) one bingo card, (2) one "Terms and Definitions" list, and (3) a stack of sixteen poker chips or coins to each participant.

3. Explain to participants that you will be reading definitions, and they can put a poker chip/coin on the term that corresponds with the definition read when it appears on their card. They can use the "Terms and Definitions" sheet to match the definition you read with the terms on their cards. Once anyone gets 4 across, 4 down, or 4 diagonally in a row they should shout, "Policy bingo!" This person wins the game, provided he or she got the definitions right! This will be confirmed through step 6 below.

4. To start the game, take the "Terms and Definitions" list and randomly select definitions to read. You can check each definition as you read it, to make sure you read each definition only once.

5. After playing the game, have the winner read out his or her answer match-ups (terms with definitions) and engage participants in deciding whether that matching was correct. If people disagree with the match, use this as an opportunity to engage in more discussion of the term in question, and ensure that the full group ends up with a clear understanding of each term and definition. The winner is declared only once this group process has taken place to ensure that the matches are correct. This stage in the process should also be used to ask for questions or observations about these terms and participants' familiarity with them. Are there other meanings for any of the terms? Common misunderstandings?

6. If using the game with teachers, college students, or professionals in community-based organizations or government agencies, engage in a discussion about their comfort level in using this tool with other groups. Are there populations with which it might work particularly well? Less well? What modifications might they offer in helping tailor the game to a particular audience?

Policy Bingo: Terms and Definitions

Advocacy: Engaging in efforts to design, change, or defeat policies.

Public policy: System of laws, regulatory measures, and priorities that guide government and administrative agencies.

Ballot initiative: A process that allows the public to vote on the adoption of new laws. Requires specific number of signatures by voters to get on ballot and to be passed.

Legislature: Decision-making bodies—usually elected—with the power to make, change, or repeal the laws of the nation or the state.

Legislation: Law crafted by a legislative body.

Ordinance: A policy, typically a statute or regulation, enacted at the local level.

Municipal: Related to a town or city and its local government.

Regulation: A rule or order issued by an agency or executive body, dealing with a specific program; has the force and effect of a law.

Commission: A group generally appointed by elected officials to act on their behalf.

Statute: A law enacted by a legislature and expressed in a formal document.

Lobbying: Attempt to influence legislators or other public officials to vote for or against a specific piece of legislation or to take or not to take specific official action.

Hearing: Session where testimony is given by experts, members of the public, or both.

Town hall: A gathering open to the public where elected officials and other public figures and community residents are invited to attend to share their views about current events and topics of interest to the community.

Coalition: A group of organizations working together for a common goal.

Community organizing: The process of bringing people together to work on issues of common interest, so that they can shape decisions and policies that will affect them. Typically designed to empower community residents and to increase their influence with key decision makers.

Litigation: Process of using the court system to resolve a legal dispute.

Grass roots: Origins in the community, particularly at the local level. These efforts are typically generated naturally from among residents rather than being imposed by traditional sources of power.

Amendment: A proposal that would change a specific bill or other measure by either adding or deleting language, or both.

Appropriation: Legislation that provides the money to support government agencies or programs.

Moratorium: A legally authorized, temporary suspension or postponement of activity; typically for a stated period during which the particular activity is not allowed or a change in policy is not allowed to take effect.

POLICY BINGO			
Ballot Initiatives	Legislature	Coalition	Legislation
Lobbying	Litigation	Grass Roots	Regulation
Appropriation	Municipal	Advocacy	Public Policy
Commission	Town Hall	Hearing	Amendment

POLICY BINGO			
Ordinance	Municipal	Legislation	Community Organizing
Legislature	Regulation	Town Hall	Grass Roots
Coalition	Public Policy	Appropriation	Ballot Initiatives
Hearing	Amendment	Statute	Litigation

POLICY BINGO			
Legislation	Advocacy	Community Organizing	Coalition
Town Hall	Hearing	Appropriation	Ordinance
Lobbying	Grass Roots	Legislature	Statute
Ballot Initiatives	Commission	Amendment	Litigation

ABOUT THE CONTRIBUTORS

JACQUIE ANDERSON is director of state consumer health advocacy at the Community Catalyst, where she provides state-level health policy, community organizing, and community education to consumer health advocacy and community organizations across the country. Her key areas of interest are organizational development and community organizing. Jacquie oversees Consumer Voices for Coverage for Community Catalyst and the Robert Wood Johnson Foundation and also oversees Southern Health Partners, Community Catalyst's work in eleven southeastern states. She has more than fifteen years of experience working with community organizations on issues related to social justice and holds bachelor's degrees from the University of Manitoba and the University of Windsor and a master's degree from the University of Toronto.

JEANNE AYERS, RN, MPH, currently serves as assistant commissioner for the Minnesota Department of Health. Her prior positions include director of nursing and preventive services at the University of Minnesota Boynton Health Service and executive director of the Center for Public Health Education and Outreach at the School of Public Health, University of Minnesota. Ayers was chief architect of ISAIAH's health equity and healthy communities work and launched and directed the Healthy Heartland Initiative, a partnership of community organizations in five Midwestern states dedicated to building organizing capacity for health and racial equity. Ayers, who holds an MPH from the University of Minnesota, received the university's 2010 Josie R. Johnson Human Rights and Social Justice Award for her work on health and racial equity.

NICKIE BAZELL SATARIANO is an HIV/AIDS activist who has worked at the local, national, and international levels to help reduce health inequities. She is the HIV program manager for the health justice organization, the Asian and Pacific Islander American Health Forum, in San Francisco. Bazell Satariano received her MPH in health and social behavior from the University of California, Berkeley, School of Public Health.

ADAM B. BECKER, PhD, MPH, is executive director of the Consortium to Lower Obesity in Chicago Children (CLOCC), a nationally recognized organization with a coordinated, multisector and multilevel approach to preventing childhood obesity housed at Children's Memorial Hospital in Chicago. CLOCC's broad-based network of over three thousand individuals representing over twelve hundred organizations has been identified as a leading community model by the Institute of Medicine, the American Medical Association, and the Centers for Disease Control and Prevention. Dr. Becker has helped develop and provide technical assistance to local and statewide coalitions addressing obesity, youth violence, HIV/AIDS, chronic disease, tobacco control, and public health system capacity building.

JUDITH BELL is president of PolicyLink and has been there since its founding in 1990. Under her central leadership, PolicyLink has developed into a national voice for access and opportunity for all people—particularly low-income people and communities of color. Bell oversees efforts to develop and advocate for an array of equitable policies, including those focused on improving health and infrastructure. Bell helped create the Promise Neighborhoods Institute at PolicyLink, and also led PolicyLink's push for a national Healthy Food Financing Initiative to improve access to healthy foods in underserved communities. She continues to engage in efforts to change policy at the national, state, and local levels and is also a regular speaker, trainer, and media voice on these issues.

ANGELA GLOVER BLACKWELL is founder and CEO of PolicyLink. Under her leadership, PolicyLink has become a leading voice in the movement to use public policy to improve access and opportunity for all low-income people and communities of color, particularly in the areas of health, housing, transportation, education, and infrastructure. Prior to founding PolicyLink, Blackwell served as senior vice president at the Rockefeller Foundation, where she oversaw the foundation's domestic and cultural divisions. A lawyer by training, she gained national recognition as founder of the Oakland, California, Urban Strategies Council, where she pioneered new approaches to neighborhood revitalization. As a leading voice in the movement for equity in the United States, Blackwell is a frequent commentator for some of the nation's top news organizations, including the *Washington Post*, *Salon*, and the *Huffington Post*, and has appeared regularly on such shows as public radio's *Marketplace*, *The Tavis Smiley Show*, *Nightline*, and PBS's *Now*.

LYNN BLANCHARD, PhD, MPH, is director of the Carolina Center for Public Service at the University of North Carolina at Chapel Hill and also holds an appointment as clinical associate professor in health behavior and health education at the University of North Carolina School of Public Health. Her interests center on public service and how people work together to address issues of shared concern. Blanchard has developed and worked with a wide array of community programs, including those focused on visioning and priority setting, health improvement (including children with special needs, HIV/AIDS, community water fluoridation, walking clubs, and community service exchange systems). She is a certified trainer in True Colors, an interactive workshop around communication and work style preference.

FRANCES D. BUTTERFOSS, PhD, is a health educator and president of Coalitions Work, a consulting group that helps communities develop and sustain health promotion/disease prevention coalitions. She is an adjunct professor at Eastern Virginia Medical School and Old Dominion University in Norfolk, Virginia.

CARICIA CATALANI, DrPH, MPH, is a researcher, advocate, and teacher whose work focuses on information technology and mobile communication tools for global health research and action. With a special emphasis on community-based participatory research and participatory design, Dr. Catalani is most interested in investigating how community engagement improves partnerships, programs, and impacts. She has 18 years of experience working on community health projects and research with underserved populations, including victims of disaster, the urban poor, sex workers, and people living with HIV/AIDS in the United States, South Asia, West Africa, Latin America, and the Caribbean.

CHARLOTTE CHANG, DrPH, is a postdoctoral scholar at the Labor Occupational Health Program at the University of California, Berkeley. Her dissertation research at the UC Berkeley School of Public Health focused on the evaluation of a partici- patory research partnership in San Francisco's Chinatown. Chang's interests are in immigrant and worker health, participatory research, and translational research.

KATHERINE KAUFER CHRISTOFFEL, MD, MPH, is a professor of pediatrics and preventive medicine at the Feinberg School of Medicine, Northwestern University Medical School, and is an attending pediatrician at Children's Memorial Hospital in Chicago. She has done research and advocacy work on varied topics, always at the border between clinical medicine and public health. Christoffel has worked in primary care practice, injury prevention (particularly pedestrian and firearm injuries), and obesity. At Children's Memorial Hospital and Research Center in Chicago, Dr. Christoffel serves as the director for the Center for Obesity Management and Prevention and Medical Director for the Consortium to Lower Obesity in Chicago Children.

RAYMOND A. COLMENAR is a senior program officer for the California Endowment, one of the largest health foundations in the United States. Previously, he was associate director of PolicyLink, where he led projects in California focused on state-level fiscal reform, school construction policy, and equitable public infra- structure investment. His other previous professional positions include senior research associate at the Rockefeller Foundation, executive director of the South of Market Problem Solving Council, and policy analyst for the City and County of San Francisco. He is chair of the board of directors of Filipinos for Affirmative Action and was a Rockefeller Foundation Next Generation Leadership Fellow. Colmenar holds a bachelor's degree from the University of California, San Diego, and a master's of public policy from the University of California, Berkeley.

CHRIS M. COOMBE, PhD, MPH, is an assistant research scientist in the Department of Health Behavior and Health Education at the University of Michigan School of Public Health. For more than twenty-five years she has been developing, implementing, and evaluating community-based interventions and collaborations using a participatory approach. Dr. Coombe trains academics and community members in policy advocacy, community-based participatory research, and health disparities research and has extensive experience in mobilizing and engaging diverse partners for policy and systems change. Her research interests focus on the impact of urban environments (particularly economic, racial, residential, and land use patterns) on health and health inequities. Coombe received her doctorate from the University of Michigan and a master's in public health from the University of California, Berkeley.

JASON CORBURN is an associate professor of city and regional planning and a member of the Global Metropolitan Studies Initiative at the University of California, Berkeley. He also codirects the joint master of city planning and master of public health degree program at UC Berkeley. His research focuses on the links between environmental health and social justice in cities, notions of expertise in science-based policymaking, and the role of local knowledge in addressing environmental and public health problems. Corburn is currently working with the city of Richmond, California, a local health department, and several nonprofits to help implement "healthy city planning" projects and develop healthy city indicators, all aimed at reducing health inequities. He is also working with local organizations in the South Bronx, New York, to stop the siting of a jail in the community and to generate development alternatives that promote human health, job creation, and environmental quality.

HEATHER D'ANGELO is a doctoral candidate in health behavior at the University of North Carolina at Chapel Hill. She received her MHS from the Johns Hopkins Bloomberg School of Public Health. Her current research focuses on neighborhood disparities in healthy food access and availability. Heather's interests include health disparities, participatory research, and food and nutrition policy.

LORI DORFMAN, DrPH, directs the Berkeley Media Studies Group, a project of the Public Health Institute. BMSG studies the media for how they portray public health issues and then applies those lessons to media advocacy training and strategic consultation for grassroots and leadership groups so they can become stronger voices in policy debate. Dorfman received her MPH and DrPH from the University of California, Berkeley.

GALEN ELLIS has worked with nonprofits, advocacy organizations, public agencies, and foundations for over twenty-five years to develop collaborative planning and evaluation approaches. Her primary interest lies in increasing individual and organizational capacity to improve community health and quality of life. Ellis has presented nationally on community building, multicultural collaboration, and policy advocacy and has authored numerous publications that tie health education and planning theory to grounded practice.

EUGENIA ENG, DrPH, MPH, is a professor of health behavior and health education at the University of North Carolina, Chapel Hill. She focuses on the integration of community development and health education interventions in the rural United States and developing countries. Her current research projects apply community-based research principles to the design and evaluation of lay health advisor interventions and looks at the influence of sociocultural factors on sexually transmitted diseases and early detection of breast cancer. Dr. Eng directs the Community Health Scholars postdoctoral program at UNC. She teaches community organization; cross-cultural aspects of health education practices; community diagnosis; and health issues relevant to women, ethnic minorities, and developing nations.

YVONNE OWENS FERGUSON, PhD., MPH, is a public health consultant in Haymarket, Virginia, and was a Kellogg health scholar in the community track from 2008 to 2010 at the University of North Carolina Gillings School of Global Public Health, Chapel Hill. She works to achieve health equity for underserved communities, both domestically and internationally, by translating public health research into policy and practice.

REBECCA FLOURNOY is associate director for PolicyLink and leads research, policy analysis, capacity-building, and advocacy efforts to improve community environments in ways that support good health. Her work focuses on ensuring equitable access to high-quality and affordable healthy food, as well as healthy school and housing environments, clean air, appealing and safe opportunities for physical activity, and other components of healthy communities. Flournoy has played a key role in advancing a national Healthy Food Financing Initiative and related efforts in California. She has over fifteen years of experience in public health and holds an MPH from the University of Michigan. Before joining PolicyLink, Flournoy was a researcher at the Kaiser Family Foundation, collaborating on survey projects with reporters at the *Washington Post* and National Public Radio.

NICHOLAS FREUDENBERG is Distinguished Professor of Public Health at the City University of New York School of Public Health at Hunter College, where he directs the CUNY doctoral program in public health. He has worked to develop; implement; and evaluate program, advocacy, and policy interventions to improve conditions and reentry practices in New York City jails for more than twenty years.

PRISCILLA GONZALEZ, MPH, is a research associate at the Berkeley Media Studies Group. She completed her master's in public health degree at the University of California, Berkeley, and her bachelor of arts in human biology at

Stanford University. Deeply committed to eliminating health inequities in under-served communities, she focuses on action-oriented research and its translation. Specific projects include documenting and investigating food marketing directed at children and communities of color, the personal responsibility rhetoric of tobacco as it compares with that of obesity, and investigating the online marketing of sugary beverages to youth. Prior to joining BSMG, Priscilla worked on various community-based participatory research projects in areas such as farmworker health, environmental justice, and home care worker health.

LORRAINE M. GUTIÉRREZ is a professor of social work and psychology at the University of Michigan. Her research is focused on empowerment theory and practice, the experiences of women of color, and multicultural organizational and community change strategies. She coordinates the Detroit Initiative in Psychology, a program of scholarship, teaching, and service, with community-based organiza-tions in Detroit. Her work includes qualitative, quantitative, and community-based research.

TREVOR HANCOCK is a public health physician and professor and senior scholar at the School of Public Health and Social Policy, University of Victoria in British Columbia. Much of his work in the past twenty-five years has been in the area of healthy cities and communities, an approach he helped to pioneer. In the early 1980s, he assisted in designing the first community health survey and health status report for the city of Toronto. As an adviser to the World Health Organization in Europe, he helped organize the first technical workshop on healthy city indicators in Barcelona in 1987 and has maintained his interest in the subject ever since. In 1999, he coauthored with Ronald Labonte and Rick Edwards a major review for Health Canada of population health indicators at the community level.

MARK S. HOMAN, MSW, LCSW, recently retired from the social services faculty at Pima Community College. He has also taught and lectured in graduate and undergraduate programs at numerous colleges and universities in the United States and abroad. For more than thirty years he has been active in community organization and development work, and he often serves as consultant to public and private groups working to strengthen communities. Homan is the author of two widely used books, *Promoting Community Change: Making It Happen in the Real World* (5th ed., Brookes/Cole, 2011) and *Rules of the Game: Lessons from the Field of Community Change* (Brookes/Cole, 1999).

CHERYL A. HYDE, MSW, PhD is associate professor at Temple University, School of Social Work. She also serves as coordinator for the Community and Policy Practice Concentration and is assistant director for education, training, and community outreach for the Center for Intervention Practice and Research. Her primary areas of scholarship and teaching are organizational and community capacity building, multicultural education, feminist praxis, social movements and collective action, and socioeconomic class issues. She is a past president of the Association for Community Organization and Social Administration, former editor of the *Journal of Progressive Human Services*, and a member of several social science and social work editorial boards and has practice experience in feminist, labor, and anti-oppression movements.

BARBARA A. ISRAEL, DrPH, MPH, is a professor in the Department of Health Behavior and Health Education at the University of Michigan School of Public Health and is deputy editor of the journal *Health Education and Behavior*. She received her doctorate in public health from the University of North Carolina at Chapel Hill. Dr. Israel has published widely in the areas of community-based participatory research, community empowerment, evaluation, stress and health, and social networks. She has extensive experience conducting community-based participatory research in collaboration with partners in diverse ethnic communities.

MICHELLE C. KEGLER, DrPH, MPH, is an associate professor in the Department of Behavioral Sciences and Health Education at the Rollins School of Public Health. Dr. Kegler came to Emory in 1999 and has served as the director of graduate studies for BSHE since 2008. Formerly, she was a part of the founding leadership of the Emory Prevention Research Center, serving as deputy director for its first five years and as co-leader of the Center's Research and Evaluation cores. Dr. Kegler is a recognized expert in community-based participatory research (CBPR) with over twenty-five years' experience designing, implementing and evaluating community-based health promotion programs. She has an established track record in CBPR, environmental influences on health, tobacco control, evaluation, and community collaboration.

JOSH KIRSCHENBAUM is vice president for strategic direction at PolicyLink. He is one of the original PolicyLink staff members, has led community building and technology projects, and now brings a wealth of organizational knowledge to build diverse alliances and implement strategic initiatives. Prior to joining PolicyLink, Kirschenbaum was the director of special projects at the University of California, Berkeley, Institute of Urban and Regional Development, where he managed a defense-conversion research program and fostered partnerships between the university and the City of Oakland to strengthen and revitalize low-income neighborhoods. He holds a BA from Brown University and an MS in city and regional planning from the University of California, Berkeley.

JOHN P. KRETZMANN is codirector of the Asset-Based Community Development Institute at Northwestern University's Institute for Policy Research. A former community developer and organizer, he writes on community building themes and is coauthor of *Building Communities from the Inside Out: A Path toward Finding* *and Mobilizing a Community's Assets* (ACTA, 1997), one of the field's most cited works.

RONALD LABONTE holds a Canada Research Chair in Globalization and Health Equity at the Institute of Population Health, and is professor in the Faculty of Medicine, University of Ottawa. His work focuses on the health equity impacts of contemporary globalization, on which he has published extensively. From 2005 until 2008 he chaired the Globalization Knowledge Network for the World Health Organization's Commission on the Social Determinants of Health, some of the work from which is published in the book *Globalization and Health: Pathways, Evidence, and Policy* (Routledge, 2009). Prior to his globalization work, Labonte spent twenty-five years engaged in community-level health promotion practice.

MARY M. LEE is an associate director at PolicyLink. She is a member of the organization's health team, providing research, technical assistance, and training to public and private agencies collaborating to build healthy communities. She has coauthored reports and journal articles on access to healthy food, the built environment, and the impact of place and race on health. A graduate of Boalt Hall School of Law, University of California, Berkeley, Lee is a practicing attorney with over twenty-five years of experience working on civil rights, land use, and economic development strategies to revitalize neighborhoods and enhance public participation in the policy arena. She has been an adjunct professor of law and teaches public policy and civil rights courses. Lee also served on boards of several community organizations, as a transportation commissioner for the City of Los Angeles, as a consultant to the commission to reform the Los Angeles City Charter, and currently as a member of the Los Angeles Food Policy Council.

PAM TAU LEE was project director on staff at the Labor Occupational Health Program at the University of California, Berkeley, School of Public Health. She was a founding member of the Chinese Progressive Association and the Asian Pacific Environmental Network. Lee is a practitioner of popular education and community-based participatory research who has made major contributions to improving working conditions of immigrants and women. She has worked extensively with unions, worker centers, and joint labor-management commit-tees, as well as community-based organizations. She currently teaches part time at the Community College of San Francisco in the Labor and Community Studies Department.

EDITH A. LEWIS, MSW, PhD, LMSW, is an associate professor of social work at the University of Michigan. Her primary research interests include methods used by women of color to offset personal, familial, community, and professional role strain. She has taught in the areas of ethnoconsciousness, community and social systems methods, global and feminist practice, and family and group theories and practice.

JENNIFER LIFSHAY leads community health assessment, planning, and evaluation projects for Contra Costa Health Services' Public Health Department. Prior to her work with CCHS she did strategic planning and monitoring and evaluation work with several Bay Area youth development organizations. She holds an MPH in behavioral sciences from the University of California, Berkeley, and an MBA from Columbia University.

LAURA LINNAN, ScD, is a professor in the Department of Health Behavior and Health Education at the University of North Carolina Gillings School of Global Public Health, Chapel Hill. She is also a member of the Lineberger Comprehensive Cancer Center and is director of the Carolina Collaborative for Research on Work and Health. Linnan received her doctorate in health and social behavior from Harvard University. She has extensive experience planning, implementing, and evaluating multilevel community-based interventions focused on a wide range of chronic disease outcomes among individuals and groups that suffer health disparities. Linnan's special areas of expertise include interventions in worksites, beauty salons and barbershops, and designing innovative ways of using mixed methods to evaluate key processes and outcomes associated with community-based participatory research.

SHAW SAN LIU is the lead organizer for the Tenants and Workers Center of the Chinese Progressive Association. She leads the work of the organization in the areas of low-wage worker/tenant organizing, grassroots leadership development, alliance building, and advocacy. CPA recently published a report on the health and working conditions of Chinatown restaurant workers and cofounded the San Francisco Progressive Workers Alliance. In May 2011 CPA launched the Campaign to End Wage Theft to protect the rights of all working people.

JOSÉ E. LÓPEZ is executive director of the Juan Antonio Corretjer Puerto Rican Cultural Center in Chicago and professor of history at Columbia College, the University of Illinois, and Northeastern Illinois University. For more than thirty-five years the PRCC has served as a catalyst for addressing some of the most important issues and historical events of the Puerto Rican diaspora and Latino communities in Chicago. As a professor, López has taught many of Chicago's most prominent Latino leaders, and for the past thirty years, he has been a leading figure in the struggle for Puerto Rican human rights in the construction of a Latino agenda in the United States and throughout the Americas.

MARTY MARTINSON, DrPH, is a faculty member at San Francisco State University in the Department of Health Education and also teaches critical gerontology at the University of California, Berkeley, School of Public Health. She is consultant and former project director of the California Senior Leaders Program, which facilitates recognition, support, and advocacy efforts for community builders and activists who are sixty years of age and older. Martinson received her master's in social justice education from the University of Massachusetts, Amherst, and her master's and doctorate in public health at the University of California, Berkeley. Her research is primarily focused on critical perspectives in aging and health.

MARIAN MCDONALD is associate director for minority and women's health for the National Center for Infectious Diseases at the Centers for Disease Control and Prevention in Atlanta. Active in minority health and women's health for three decades, she was formerly a health education professor at Tulane University's School of Public Health and Tropical Medicine, where she taught courses on community organization and race, gender, and ethnicity in health promotion. A poet and lifelong cultural worker, she has published her poetry in numerous publications in the Americas.

ANDREW MCGUIRE is the executive director of California OneCare, and formerly was executive director of the Trauma Foundation at San Francisco General Hospital for thirty-six years. He served as the first director of Action Against Burns in Boston and was a founding board member of Mothers Against Drunk Drivers (MADD). An activist and filmmaker (*Here's Looking at You, Kid* and *Heroic Measures*), he has directed public health grassroots campaigns since 1974 and has received Kellogg and MacArthur Fellowships for his achievements, as well as an Emmy Award for Heroic Measures.

JOHN L. MCKNIGHT is founding director (emeritus) of the community studies program at the Institute for Policy Research at Northwestern University, where he is an emeritus professor in both the School of Speech and the School of Education and Social Policy. He has worked with communities across the United States and Canada and is author of *The Careless Society: Community and Its Counterfeits* (Basic Books, 1995) and coauthor of the widely cited workbook *Building Communities from the Inside Out: A Path toward Finding and Mobilizing a Community's Assets* (ACTA, 1997).

MICHAEL MILLER is policy director of Community Catalyst, where he focuses on providing policy and strategy support to state-based consumer health advocacy groups. Over the course of his career, Miller has developed expertise in areas such as Medicaid, the State Children's Health Insurance Program (SCHIP), and Medicare, developing state-level options to expand coverage for the uninsured, long-term care financing and delivery, and managed care reform. Prior to joining Community Catalyst, Miller was the policy director for Health Care for All. He also worked for the City of Boston Elderly Commission as a policy analyst and for the Alzheimer's Association of eastern Massachusetts as director of the Community Partnership Project. Miller holds a bachelor's degree from Brown University and a master's degree in public policy from Tufts University.

MEREDITH MINKLER, DrPH, MPH, is professor and former director of health and social behavior at the School of Public Health, University of California,

Berkeley, where she was founding director of the UC Center on Aging. She has over thirty years' experience teaching, conducting research, and working with under-served communities on community-identified issues through community build-ing, community organizing, and community-based participatory research (CBPR). Her current research and service includes documenting the impacts of CBPR on healthy public policy, an ecological CBPR and organizing project on immigrant worker health and safety in Chinatown restaurants, a social action and empower-ment project with rural Latino youth, and a healthy-aging and community building project for and with older activists in California. Dr. Minkler is coauthor or editor of eight books and over 130 peer-reviewed publications, including the book *Community-Based Participatory Research for Health: From Process to Outcomes* (with Nina Wallerstein; 2nd ed., Jossey-Bass, 2008).

MARY ANNE MORGAN, MPH, has over thirty years of experience working with local health departments, community-based organizations, health advocates, and community leaders to address critical public health issues. She has provided technical assistance, training, and program development to regional public health associations and statewide initiatives in areas that include community engagement strategies, chronic disease prevention, elder abuse, community violence prevention, and social and environmental justice.

BARACK OBAMA is the forty-fourth president of the United States. He previously served as United States senator for Illinois. For three years, Obama was the director of the Developing Communities Project, an institutionally based community organ-ization on Chicago's far south side. He has also been a consultant and instructor for the Gamaliel Foundation, an organizing institute working throughout the Midwest. After graduating from Harvard Law School, Obama taught constitutional law at the University of Chicago Law School for twelve years. During this time he also directed the Illinois Project Vote, which registered 150,000 African Americans in the state. In 1996 Obama was elected to the Illinois Senate. While a state senator Obama was able to gain support for ethics reform and health care laws. Obama was reelected twice and held the position until he was elected as one of Illinois's two U.S. sena-tors in 2004. He resigned in 2008 to become president of the United States.

EDITH A. PARKER, DrPH, is a professor and head of the Department of Community and Behavioral Health in the University of Iowa College of Public Health. Previously she was associate dean for academic affairs at the University of Michigan School of Public Health and associate professor of health behavior and health education. Her research focuses on the development, implementation, and evaluation of community-based participatory interventions to improve health status and reduce health disparities. Her research includes studies focused on women's and children's health, childhood asthma, environmental justice, and environmental risk communication. She has directed studies funded by the National Institutes of Health and the Centers for Disease Control and Prevention.

CHERI PIES, MSW, DrPH, is on the faculty of the University of California, Berkeley, School of Public Health, where she is a lecturer in the Maternal and Child Health Program and the Doctor of Public Health Program. She was previously the director of the Family, Maternal, and Child Health Programs for Contra Costa Health Services. Her professional work and interests include implementing a life course perspective in maternal and child health practice, education and training, community capacity building, development of longitudinal data systems for planning and evaluation, photovoice, women's health and reproductive issues, women and HIV, and parenting support for nontraditional families.

JOSÉ LUIS RODRÍGUEZ, is the program director for CO-OP HP (Community Organizing for Obesity Prevention in Humboldt Park). He is a community activist and has been involved with the community building work of the Puerto Rican Cultural Center–Juan Antonio Corretjer for approximately thirty years. Rodríguez is a member of the board of directors of the Division Street Business Development Association and West Town Bikes/Ciclo Urbano. He is an advisory member to Youth Empowering Strategies Nutrition/Fitness Program at Roberto Clemente High School and a Steering Committee member of the Greater Humboldt Park Community of Wellness. He is interested in community building work that empowers community residents and businesses to address the myriad socio-economic problems that affect his community and take ownership in finding solutions to resolve them.

VICTOR RUBIN is vice president for research and leads knowledge-building, evaluation, and qualitative and quantitative analysis activities to build a strong research base for PolicyLink. Recently he has been particularly deeply involved in analyses of equity issues in infrastructure, and in strategies to address health disparities through improvements to the built environment. Rubin previously directed the U.S. Department of Housing and Urban Development's Office of University Partnerships and served as a director of the University-Oakland Metropolitan Forum, a partnership based at the University of California, Berkeley, where he was also an adjunct associate professor of city and regional planning. Rubin holds a BA in public affairs from the University of Chicago and an MCP and PhD in city and regional planning from UC Berkeley.

ALICIA L. SALVATORE, DrPH, MPH, is a postdoctoral fellow at the Stanford Prevention Research Center at the Stanford School of Medicine. For fifteen years, she has worked collaboratively with communities, health care providers, and other stakeholders to research and promote community health in the United States and internationally. Her recent research focuses on the development and evaluation of ecological interventions to promote the health of low-wage and immigrant workers and to reduce environmental disparities facing urban and rural communities. Some of her current projects include youth-led research with high school students in the Salinas Valley, studies of refugee gardens and neighborhood food environments in Northern California, and a randomized-controlled evaluation of the government of India's rural, community-led total sanitation program.

DORAN SCHRANTZ is executive director of the faith-based community organizing group ISAIAH, in Minnesota. She has also been a professional organizer since 2000. She is the national trainer for the Gamaliel Foundation and has organized local and statewide issue campaigns in partnership with the Grassroots Policy Project. Schrantz has been a critical leader in organizing ISAIAH's Faith In Democracy worldview and values framework. She is a member of St. Matthew's Lutheran Church in St. Paul.

AMY J. SCHULZ is professor in the Department of Health Behavior and Heath Education and associate director for the Center for Research on Ethnicity, Culture and Health at the University of Michigan School of Public Health. She has had extensive experience working with and facilitating community-based participatory research partnerships to promote health equity, with a particular focus on the engagement of community partners in the development of research priorities; the design and evaluation of interventions; and the translation and dissemination of research findings in community, practice and policy venues.

LEE STAPLES is a clinical professor at Boston University School of Social Work, where he teaches community organizing and macro social work practice. He received his PhD in sociology and social work from Boston University. Since the late 1960s, he has been engaged in numerous social change efforts as organizer, supervisor, staff director, trainer, consultant, coach, and educator. His work has included organizing around welfare rights, housing, child care, mental health consumers, labor, neighborhood, and public health. Staples has done extensive training and consulting with nongovernment organizations in the Balkans and currently is involved in a variety of community organizing efforts, including immigrant rights, affordable housing, environmental justice, and the rights of patients with psychiatric conditions.

CELINA SU is associate professor in the Department of Political Sciences at Brooklyn College in New York. Her research interests lie in civil society and the cultural politics of education and health policy. Particular areas of expertise include participatory democracy and civic engagement, especially in local politics; politics of health and education policy; civil society, especially grassroots and social movement organizations; and mixed participatory methods using both quantitative and qualitative approaches with an emphasis on the latter in public policy research. Celina received her BA in both economics and English from Wesleyan University and her PhD in urban studies from Massachusetts Institute of Technology.

STEPHEN THOMAS, PhD, is professor of health services administration in the School of Public Health and director of the University of Maryland Center for Health Equity at the University of Maryland in College Park. One of the nation's leading scholars in the effort to eliminate racial and ethnic health disparities, Dr. Thomas has applied his expertise to address a variety of conditions from which minority groups generally face far poorer outcomes, including cardiovascular disease, diabetes, obesity, and HIV/AIDS. He is principal investigator of the Research Center of Excellence on Minority Health Disparities, funded by the National Institutes of Health–National Institute on Minority Health and Health Disparities. He is also principal investigator, with Dr. Sandra Quinn, of the NIH National Bioethics Research Infrastructure Initiative: Building Trust Between Minorities and Researchers funded in 2009.

MILDRED THOMPSON is senior director and director of the PolicyLink Center for Health and Place. As part of her work, she conducts research focused on understanding community factors that affect health disparities, and identifies practice and policy changes needed to improve individual, family, and community health. She has authored several reports and journal articles focused on reducing health disparities, increasing awareness about social determinants of health, and effective ways to influence policy change. Prior to joining PolicyLink, Thompson was director of Community Health Services for the Alameda County Public Health Department; director for Healthy Start, a federal infant mortality reduction program; and director of the San Antonio Neighborhood Health Center. She has degrees in nursing and psychology and an MS in social work from New York University. Thompson has also taught at Mills College and San Francisco State University and has worked as an organizational development consultant.

NINA WALLERSTEIN, DrPH, is professor in the Department of Family and Community Medicine and was founding director of the Master in Public Health Program at the University of New Mexico until 2007. She currently is director of the Center for Participatory Research and of the developing community engagement and research component of the Clinical Translational Science Center. Wallerstein received her DrPH at the School of Public Health, University of California, Berkeley. For over twenty-five years, she has been involved in empowerment/popular education and participatory research with youth, women, tribes, and community building efforts. She is the coeditor (with Meredith Minkler) of *Community-Based Participatory Research for Health* (2nd ed., Jossey-Bass, 2008); coauthor of *Problem-Posing at Work: Popular Educator's Guide* (rev. ed., Grassroots Press, 2004); and author of several health and adult education books and over one hundred articles and book chapters on participatory intervention research, adolescent health promotion, alcohol and addictions prevention research, empowerment theory, and popular health education.

CHERYL L. WALTER, PhD, is the lead evaluator for a federal grant to improve the special education system in California. Her doctorate in social welfare is from the University of California, Berkeley, where she also received her MSW and her MPH. She has served as a board member and development director of the Women's Cancer Resource Center in Berkeley and as clinical staff and then executive director of the Gay and Lesbian Resource Center in Santa Barbara, California.

SHERYL WALTON, MPH, is a community health educator specializing in supporting residents, community groups, and agencies seeking to work with and build on the assets and strengths of low-income, multicultural communities to improve health and quality of life. Walton is the principal consultant with Walton and Associates and project director of the Pangaea Global AIDS Foundation's Late Diagnosis Project in Oakland, California. She also is the nation's lead trainer for TimeBanksUSA. Other clients have included the Bay Area Black United Fund and several foundations and government agencies. For over seventeen years, Walton worked for three local health departments, developing, managing, and coordinating community-based participatory research place-based initiatives: Contra Costa's Healthy Neighborhoods Project, Berkeley's Community Action Teams, and Alameda County's City-County Neighborhood Initiative in the Sobrante Park neighborhood. Walton serves on several boards, including Oakland's Central City East Project Area Committee, TimeBanksUSA, and Berkeley's Black Infant Health Program. She received her BA from Mills College in human development and ethnic studies and her master's in public health from the University of California, Berkeley.

TOM WOLFF is a community psychology practitioner who is committed to issues of social justice and community. He is the founder of Tom Wolff and Associates and is a nationally recognized consultant on coalition building and community development, consulting with individuals, organizations, and communities across North America. His newest book is *The Power of Collaborative Solutions* (Jossey-Bass, 2010). Tom's clients include federal, state and local government agencies; foundations; hospitals; nonprofit organizations; professional associations; and grassroots groups.

AMANDA WONG, MPH, is the cofounder and chair of Team HBV Collegiate Chapters, an international network of college students dedicated to fighting the hepatitis B and liver cancer health disparity among Asians and Pacific Islanders. She specializes in building capacity through health education and prevention among underserved populations and has lectured and designed national training sessions to empower young leaders in community health outreach methods. She holds a master of public health degree from the University of California, Berkeley, in infectious diseases and vaccinology and is a second-year medical student.

INDEX